NAPOLEON AND THE

BIRTH

OF MODERN SPAIN

NAPOLEON

AND THE

BIRTH

OF

MODERN SPAIN

II

THE STRUGGLE, WITHOUT AND WITHIN

BY GABRIEL H. LOVETT

NEW YORK UNIVERSITY PRESS

1965

ABBREVIATIONS

AHN	Archivo Histórico Nacional
BAE	Biblioteca de Autores Españoles
BH	Bulletin Hispanique
BRAH	Boletín de la Real Academia de la Historia
CDF	Colección Documental del Fraile
RABM	Revista de Archivos, Bibliotecas y Museos
REP	Revista de Estudios Políticos
RH	Revue Hispanique
RQH	Revue des Questions Historiques

CONTENTS

THE STRUGGLE,
WITHOUT AND WITHIN

X

SPAIN IS SPLIT ASUNDER

[1]

THE Cortes of Cádiz enacted in the midst of a terrible war far-reaching reforms, which constituted in the eyes of the liberal majority the foundation of a brave new Spain. The decisive impulse to this work of innovation was of course provided by the war itself. Revolutions are often the consequence of wars, and the Cádiz revolution—for so it must be called—is a case in point. But while the revolutionary process can be brought to a head by war, its seeds have usually been planted a long time before the radical change occurs.

The age of eighteenth-century Enlightenment, which shot its rays of philosophic rationalism and political and religious iconoclasm at full strength through the rest of Europe, struck Spain only tangentially, but sufficiently to produce an intellectual minority adhering in varying degrees to the new doctrines. The glorification of reason as the most fundamental guide in the relationship between man and the universe and between man and society; the attack on tradition as an absolute value in assessing age-old institutions such as aristocracy and the Church; and the ferocious propaganda against these establishments carried out by Europe's foremost writers, found some, though relatively modest, echoes south of the Pyrenees.

In eighteenth-century Spain, tradition and religion were much too strong and inspired too much awe, respect, and love to come under massive attack. The institution of monarchy was never questioned —but then, even in the rest of prerevolutionary Europe, the attack of Enlightenment was not directed against the throne—and the broad mass of the people stood solidly behind its Church. True, the reformists around Charles III, who had absorbed much of the new spirit, did their utmost to change the face of Spain. Their efforts, however, were directed mostly at Spain's administrative, economic, and cultural problems and aimed to bring their country abreast of the other leading powers in Europe.

Aranda, Floridablanca, and Campomanes,[1] though greatly influenced by European Enlightenment, did not attempt to bring about fundamental changes in Spain's political and social fabric, but only to point to and contain the abuses perpetrated by the privileged classes. Unwilling to put into practice fully what they may have believed deep in their hearts, they gave most of their attention to reforms in Spain's administration and economy. Where they did carry further than in any other field the spirit of the age was in the relation between Church and State. Ardent regalists, firmly believing that all reforms must emanate from the throne and that no other power in the kingdom must be allowed to challenge the absolute authority of the monarch, they staunchly defended the Crown's supremacy in matters claimed by the Church to fall under its sole jurisdiction. The expulsion of the Jesuits was doubtless their boldest measure, but it was carried out in the name of regalism and with full approval of the king. Furthermore, whatever intimate thoughts Spanish statesmen may have harbored with respect to religion, they never openly challenged Catholic dogma.[2] King Charles III himself was a most devout Catholic.

In the second half of the eighteenth century, then, the prime movers of Spanish Enlightenment were above all the king and his ministers. Throughout the country the reforms with which they were trying to reshape Spain were strongly supported by a select minority. Members of the professions, of the rising middle class,

1. Statesman, jurist, and economist, Pedro Rodríguez de Campomanes (1723–1803) is one of the outstanding personalities of eighteenth-century Spain. As *fiscal* (crown solicitor) of the Council of Castile and later as president of this body, he did much to stimulate Spanish economy and to reform Spain's administrative machine. He wrote many treatises on a wide variety of subjects, and as a tribute to his intellectual stature the Academy of History elected him its president in 1764. A convinced regalist, he played an important role in the expulsion of the Jesuits in 1767.

2. An exception is furnished in the person of Count Aranda, who in 1765 became grand master of Spanish Freemasonry.

which was growing rich with the reinvigorated economy, even members of the clergy, mainly the so-called Jansenists,[3] were the elements among whom Enlightenment had stirred a responsive chord. Many of these forward-looking Spaniards belonged to the influential Economic Societies,[4] in whose activities at least part of the ideas held by them found a practical expression. A number of them were no doubt interested in changes of a more fundamental nature than those fostered by the government.

It must not be thought, however, that these men formed a compact group openly advocating a radical reformist program. This would have been impossible in the absolute monarchy of Charles III, with its strict limitations of freedom, with a weakened but still redoubtable Inquisition doing its utmost to prevent Spaniards from absorbing any subversive doctrines, and with a people on the whole still clinging to tradition. What was happening was that in various ways certain circles and certain individuals endeavored to "insure a return to the Golden Age through the virtue of Science, through the reform of minds and hearts."[5] Those who were too bold in the verbal or written expression of their opinions felt the heavy hand of censorship and persecution. Let us keep in mind that "the men who welcomed the Enlightenment were a minority of their own classes; they were perforce a much smaller proportion of all Spaniards."[6]

Yet, while placing Spanish Enlightenment in its proper perspective, the effect of contemporary European thought on Spain must not be underestimated. The Economic Societies, which endeavored to promote agriculture and handicraft through education for and practical help to the lower classes; the universities, which, at the impulse of the Crown, were modernizing their curricula and using new textbooks more in accordance with the spirit of the age; the periodical press, which disseminated this new spirit; and the literary societies and *tertulias*, which engaged in discussions on a wide range of subjects; all left an imprint which could not be eradicated.[7] It must also be kept in mind that those who most readily accepted the new

3. See Chapter I.
4. See Chapter I.
5. Sarrailh, *L'Espagne éclairée de la seconde moitié du 18ième siècle,* p. 711.
6. Herr, *The Eighteenth-Century Revolution in Spain,* pp. 198–99.
7. Cf. Herr, Chapter VI.

ideas were the intellectual elite of the nation and that radical changes in a nation's political and social structure are normally brought about precisely by the intelligentsia.

The written word was of paramount importance in this slow diffusion of the new ideas. Descartes, Leibniz, Locke, Montesquieu, Rousseau, Voltaire, and the *Encyclopédie* all found their way into Spain and were avidly read by the cultured few. In the second half of the eighteenth century French neoclassic literature was warmly received and used as a model by a group of Spanish literati who contributed to the *afrancesamiento* that was taking hold of important sectors of Spanish society.[8] But the Spanish reform-minded did not need to draw exclusively on foreign sources for inspiration. There were enough eighteenth-century Spaniards who had written or were writing in the new spirit. Superstition was attacked and reason and experience were given a decisive role in the writings of one of the most important of these, the Benedictine monk Benito Jerónimo Feijóo (1676–1764). Economic freedom was preached as early as 1732 in the *Miscelánea económico-política* of Zabala y Auñón, and later in the works of Campomanes and especially Jovellanos. Spanish historians delving in the nation's past opened the way for a search for better institutions. These the reform-minded now thought to have existed in the Middle Ages, when Spain was supposed to have enjoyed a measure of political freedom through the medieval Cortes. The relative representation the Spanish people had enjoyed before the Habsburg dynasty became entrenched in Spain acted more and more like a magnet on Spanish reformists and was to have a profound influence on the evolution of their political thinking.[9]

With the advent of the French Revolution the pulse of reformism quickened within the circle of Spanish progressives. Despite censorship the revolutionary thunder was heard in Spain, and notwithstanding their revulsion at the excesses committed in neighboring France in the name of liberty, equality, and fraternity, and notwithstanding the war against the French Republic, they welcomed in varying

8. This Frenchification, found in speech, dress, and manners as well as in literature, and due to some extent to the fact that Spain was ruled by a dynasty —the Bourbons—imported from France and adhering to a foreign policy based on the Franco-Spanish alliance, did not, however, necessarily go hand in hand with the reform movement.

9. Cf. Herr, Chapter xii.

degrees some of the basic principles underlying the great upheaval. Liberty, equality, tolerance in matters of religion struck a responsive echo, perhaps, only in the more radical elements of the reformist group, but "what was really happening was that the seductive principles voiced in France were stealthily stirring the progressives out of their belief that all improvement must come from above."[10] The dictatorship of Godoy and the corruption pervading the court of Charles IV naturally contributed to alienating a good portion of the intelligentsia from enlightened despotism.

Nevertheless, at the sight of the order and progress achieved in France under Bonaparte and impressed by the enlightened policies pursued by Godoy with respect to science, education, and letters, a number of the reform-minded remained faithful to the ideals of enlightened despotism. They chose to see the Napoleonic system as the perfect solution for Spain. Their former companions turned their back on Godoy, and without denying some of the principles of the French Revolution, rejected the Consular and Imperial experiment. They sought the cure for Spain's ills in the country's history, in "their study of the law of nature and nations, and their familiarity with the general theme of Montesquieu's writing."[11] Some of the former would join the *afrancesados* of Bayonne and the collaborators of Joseph's ephemeral rule, while from among the latter would come many of the liberals of the Cortes of Cádiz.

Strong opposition to these currents of reform throughout the eighteenth century and until the outbreak of the War of Independence in 1808 came from the massive forces of Spanish tradition, which were powerful enough to prevent any drastic modifications in Spanish society. By 1808, the aristocracy, though no longer a strong political factor, retained a commanding position through its huge landed wealth and its semifeudal privileges on a large portion of the land. The Church had been forced to contribute heavily to the war effort of Charles IV's government, and much of its property had been forcibly sold. But its imposing edifice was intact in spite of this financial effort and notwithstanding the inroads made in some of its ranks by the new ideas. As for the broad mass of the Spanish people, though they doubtless must have wished for an easing of the social

10. *Ibid.*, p. 375.
11. *Ibid.*, p. 440.

and economic burden under which they were suffering, king, father-land, and religion were ideals binding enough to exclude any thought of rebelling against the existing order of things.

In spite of their strength, the forces of tradition had been worried by the reformist tendencies they had seen growing in government and intellectual circles ever since the advent of Charles III in 1759. They had struck out at their enemies repeatedly and had achieved some notable successes. They had contributed to the fall in 1800 of Urquijo, who had come to grips with the papacy and the Inquisition, and the latter institution had been given a free hand by the throne to persecute the regalist and anti-Roman Jansenists. They had prevailed upon Charles IV soon afterward to have the illustrious Jovellanos arrested and sent off to prison in Mallorca.

However, in the last years of the reign of Charles IV, the ranks of the forward-looking minority had no doubt been swelled. The tensions at the corrupt Spanish court, the nationwide discontent with the regime of Godoy, the disastrous war against England at the side of Napoleonic France, could not fail to draw more cultured Spaniards into the camp of Enlightenment. By 1808, the ingredients of the scission between tradition and reform, which had been engendered during the reign of Charles III and had been considerably strengthened during the period of the French Revolution and the subsequent Franco-Spanish alliance, were there. But for the progress-minded minority to make a bold bid for political, social, and economic reform, thus openly challenging the party of tradition, an event of cataclysmic force must burst upon the Spanish scene.

The war against Napoleon was the explosion without which the liberal offensive and the open split would probably not have taken place, at least not for a long time. With the fall of the monarchy and the ineffectiveness of Spain's traditional institutions a vacuum was created in the spring and summer of 1808, which had perforce to be filled. At first, the slogan of the uprising was "King, Fatherland, and Religion," for the revolt was first and foremost the expression of a people's rage at seeing its freedom trampled. But since in the absence of Spain's legitimate monarch leadership had been thrown into the hands of new and revolutionary organs of government, the provincial juntas, and since the nation became aware of the inability of the old institutions to protect it against foreign aggression, a search soon began for new materials with which to strengthen Spain's political and social structure. For a while the search included all sectors of Spanish public opinion. Traditionalists and reformists alike, all felt that Spain stood at a crossroads, not only in terms of national freedom or oppression, but also in terms of stagnation or progress. The formation of the Supreme Junta, another revolutionary organ, was a further step away from the norms that had prevailed for centuries.

During the years 1808 and 1809, the war effort was uppermost in the minds of all patriotic Spaniards. But the future of the nation, too, was a subject engaging the attention of free Spain. Conservatives, reformists, aristocrats, churchmen, professionals, intellectuals, members of the commercial middle class, all were thinking of the best ways of remedying Spain's ills, of preventing it from falling again under the sway of a Godoy, of achieving a more rational administrative system. Traditionalists did not want a return to the rule by favorite, which had marked the reign of Charles IV and which incidentally had endangered the property of the privileged classes, especially that of the Church. But the defeats suffered in the war also shocked them into seeking new ways, and their interest in change was to a large extent prompted by their ardent desire to see the war brought to a victorious conclusion. They wanted change because change meant a more efficient conduct of the war.

The loyal reformists, not to be confused with the reform-minded who sought inspiration from Napoleonic France,[12] also desired speedy victory, but for them the future peace was as important as the present war. The events of 1808 had brought about a truly revolutionary situation, which gave them a unique opportunity to make an all-out bid for reform. They could easily justify in their own eyes as well as to the conservative elements the necessity of change in terms of the war effort, for reform would forcibly help the nation in its armed struggle. But in their hearts they knew that now was the time to strike a decisive blow for their political and social ideals.

The press, officially unfree but enjoying a de facto freedom, was the ideal channel through which they could disseminate these beliefs. On September 22, 1808, the *Semanario Patriótico*, which was directed by Manuel José Quintana, said:

12. See Chapter XIII.

If anyone had said at the beginning of last October that before a year had elapsed we would be free to write on government reforms, constitutional plans, scrutiny and limitation of power, and that hardly anything would be written in Spain that did not deal with these important matters, he would have been considered an addle-brained person who might have been jailed for the things he prophesied to others. Nevertheless, this is what is happening and posterity will perhaps not be surprised so much by the strange diversity of events which have brought us to where we are today, as by the ability and the boldness with which political principles are enunciated and examined in a nation whom, due to its long and continuous oppression, Europe thought entirely unfamiliar with such investigations and paralyzed by the most profound ignorance.[13]

After thus conveying to its readers the exhilaration that was gripping reformist circles in the face of the undreamed-of perspectives opening to them, the newspaper went on to state its position on the vital matter of organizing the nation politically in the absence of its legitimate monarch: "Only the nation can, through its representatives, reconstruct the executive power left in a disorganized state by the absence of the king. This is why it is necessary to call together at once a national assembly, whether it be called Cortes or whether it be given any other name. The Central and Supreme Junta can and must convoke this body and this is one of the first measures it must take."[14]

In the issue of Thursday, October 27, 1808, we read a significant piece on the French Revolution, despotism, and Napoleon, which may be considered illustrative of the thinking of the emerging liberals:

Because a frivolous, frenzied and inconsistent nation[15] has not been able to *turn its revolution to advantage;*[16] because it has had the misfortune of placing at the head of its government only inept or abominable leaders; because in short it has fallen prey to a despot, must others be condemned to suffer all the evils of a bad government and of tyranny . . . ? May the French Revolution remind us of the wrecks of ships that have run aground on shoals, wrecks that teach the seafarer to steer clear of the dangerous reefs *but do not* divert him from his route.[17]

13. *Apud* Argüelles, I, p. 117.
14. *Ibid.,* p. 118.
15. Read France.
16. Italics are Quintana's.
17. CDF, Vol. XVIII, pp. 149–50.

Spain's history as seen through reformist eyes was summarized in the following paragraph: "Our forefathers succumbed in the glorious struggle for their liberties and bequeathed onto us the monstrous arbitrariness which, reinforced by three centuries of suffering and usurpation and injustice, has brought us to the point where we have been enduring for twenty years the insolence of a Godoy, to see ourselves later on the verge of becoming the prey of a Bonaparte."[18]

The article ended with a vigorous denunciation of absolutism: " . . . the exercise of absolute power is unjust, because one will usurps the right to contradict all others. It is a tyranny and a usurpation, because it deprives men by force of essential rights . . . A government of this type is not a government: it is an abuse; it is war waged by one upon all others. In order to be an absolute sovereign one must be sovereignly wise, and to want to exercise with limited capacities an unlimited power is to endeavor insanely to rise above human nature."[19]

In the eyes of the new reformers the principal enemy of freedom was therefore absolutism, the absolutism that had destroyed Spain's medieval liberties and had finally produced the dictatorship of a Godoy. Quintana had thundered against this absolutism in some of the poems he had written during the reign of Charles IV, which saw the light only after the fall of the monarchy.[20] All the progressive elements in the country now took aim at the absolutist form of government and fired away at it in the impassioned writings that came out during the rule of the Suprema and that of the Regency, before the Cortes gathered on the Isla de León.

The central theme of this concerted attack on Spain's absolutist past was the restoration of medieval liberties, and this, of course, included the Cortes. The word acquired a magic force. It was the

18. Quintana, the author of the article, referred of course to the municipal liberties enjoyed by many towns in the Middle Ages, which were emasculated by the Habsburg dynasty, and to the unsuccessful revolt of the *comuneros* (1520–1521) against the central government. At the same time, a reference to the decadence of the once-important Cortes must also be read into this sentence.

19. *Ibid.*, pp. 150–51.

20. See Chapter XIV.

institution which would give Spain back the limited representative government it had once enjoyed; it was the panacea for all the ills Spain had suffered for centuries; it was the instrument which would enable the nation to win the longed-for victory over Napoleon. Besides, had not Fernando himself asked Spain to call together its representatives in his famous decree of May 5, 1808, before he surrendered to Bonaparte? The word Cortes can be found in the correspondence of the provincial juntas. It was on the lips of all patriotic Spaniards, and not only the reform-minded. For the reasons stated above most traditionalists also wanted the Cortes.[21] In October, 1808, Jovellanos had asked for the convocation, and in April, 1809, Calvo de Rozas presented the same demand to the Suprema in a written statement:

"The Spaniard must know now," said Calvo, "that he is not struggling so gloriously against the aggressor in order to place his independence, rescued at such a high price, once more at the mercy of a capricious Court or of an ambitious favorite, or entrust it to the personal qualities of a sovereign, which are unlikely not to change with age . . . Since the oppressor of our freedom has thought it advisable to add to the chains with which he is enslaving us the promise of a constitutional regime aimed at correcting the abuses from which we have suffered, let us face him with a system directed at the same goal, but let us undertake this with better faith and in the framework of legality.[22] Let us add this incentive to those which until now have been spurring the nation on . . . I feel that it is necessary to decide that reforms shall be introduced into all the branches of administration that require them and that these reforms will be incorporated into a Constitution, which, prepared with the greatest care, shall be presented to the duly represented nation as soon as circumstances allow it."[23]

Finally, as we have seen, the Suprema officially called for the meeting of Spain's representatives in the nation's traditional Cortes.

21. Cf. the project drawn up by the conservative Pérez Villamil in August, 1808 (Chapter VII, p. 300).

22. It is interesting to note at this point how the Constitution of Bayonne, enacted under pressure from Napoleon, exerted an undeniable influence on the thinking of reform-minded Spaniards in the patriotic camp. Without over-estimating this influence, we agree with Juretschke (Los afrancesados en la guerra de la independencia, chap. VIII) that the Constitution of Bayonne contributed to a certain extent to the enactment of the Cádiz reforms.

23. Apud Fernández Martín, Derecho parlamentario español, I, p. 437.

But this institution had lain in obscurity for such a long time[24] that there were practically as many opinions concerning the form and functions of the coming assembly as there were Spaniards. Some thought that the Cortes should limit itself strictly to the advisory role and subsidy voting, which part the Castillian assembly had played during the Middle Ages, and should give its full attention to the war effort.[25] Others were of the opinion that the Cortes should have full legislative power and write a constitutional text. There were those who said that Spain did not need a new constitution, since it had its own body of traditional laws enacted throughout its history and endowed with enough safeguards against despotism and corruption. All that was needed was the restoration of those laws guaranteeing a measure of national representation and preventing the establishment of a tyrannical form of government.[26] Still others pointed out that the form of the medieval Cortes, with their division into estates—nobility, clergy, towns—precluded any functioning of this institution in the Spain of the nineteenth century, and especially in a Spain fighting for its survival. Did it make any sense, they inquired, to think of restoring the archaic convocation by *brazos* (estates), when it had been essentially the lower classes who had given the signal of the revolt against the French usurpation and who now bore the brunt of

24. The Cortes of Castile, Aragón, Valencia, and Catalonia, meeting now as one body, were called together only six times in the course of the eighteenth century and were for all practical purposes devoted to purely dynastic business, such as taking the oath of loyalty to the king and the royal heir.

25. While in the opinions of many nineteenth- and twentieth-century historians, including Sánchez Albornoz (*España, un enigma histórico*, II, pp. 90–94) the Castilian Cortes on many occasions truly represented the interests of the people of Castile and often shared the legislative function with the king, a recent article on the question has claimed that the medieval Castilian Cortes was merely an advisory body called on to swear allegiance to the royal heir and to vote the subsidies requested by the king, with the right to petition but without any authority to limit the power of the monarch. (Pérez-Prendes y Muñoz de Arracó, "Cortes de Castilla y Cortes de Cádiz," *Revista de Estudios Políticos*, CXXVI, November–December, 1962, pp. 321–431). This was the type of assembly Fernando VII had in mind when he issued his decree of May 5, 1808 (see Chapter IV).

26. Jovellanos consistently took this position (see Chapter XIV). The word Constitution itself was used rather vaguely in those days. It could mean a written text containing the law of the land, but more often than not it would refer to the body of laws enacted throughout the country's history.

the fighting? Did it make any sense to keep representation of the third estate down to the thirty-seven towns that had had a vote at the last gathering of the Cortes in 1789 and not include important towns such as Cádiz, which had not been represented under the old system?

The answers requested by the Suprema in 1809, from 150 representative Spanish organisms and individuals, to its inquiry concerning the form and functions of the future Cortes, show this tremendous variety of opinions, which makes it difficult to determine exactly the strength of the reformist sector. The Bishop of Albarracín, writing from Valencia, wanted the old mode of representation (nobility, clergy, and towns) fully preserved. The Bishop of Barbastro, in a report surprising for the democratic tendencies it clearly manifested, declared himself in favor of the "legal known representation of the Monarchy in its former Cortes." He did not specifically mention *brazos*, however, and indicated that he had in mind a body made up of representatives chosen not along class lines but of those who had "the merits and qualifications demanded by law." Power would be divided among the Cortes, which would have full legislative attributions; the king, as the executive; and the judiciary, represented by the courts. The Cortes should write a constitution which should "determine the powers of those who are to govern and the rules they must follow to carry out their duties." But the bishop was not satisfied with political reform. He wanted to see the people freed from all the tributes and exactions to which they had been submitted too long. The tenth part of what the crop brought should be the sole tax paid by the peasant. Needless to say, the archaic seignorial rights must be abolished.[27]

The Bishop of Calahorra stated that only the Cortes, comprising the three estates, should have the faculty to enact laws. He considered that there had been entirely too many laws and decrees passed throughout Spanish history and he would like to see the famous *Siete Partidas*, written in the thirteenth century during the reign of Alphonso X, adopted as Spain's sole legal text.[28] The Bishop and

27. *Apud* Artola, *Los orígenes de la España contemporánea*, II, pp. 123–29.
28. *Ibid.*, pp. 129–37. The *Siete Partidas*, a codification of all extant laws, is not only a magnificent judicial compilation but also a first class literary

chapter of Córdoba asked for the revival of the Cortes in its original, medieval form. The king would enact the laws, but only after petition from the Cortes, while no tribute could be imposed without consent of the assembly.[29] The Bishop of Orihuela demanded above all love and respect for the Catholic religion on the part of king and kingdom. The king should be forced by law to call the Cortes every two years. The deputies, however, could only ask and petition, not truly legislate. The Bishop of Urgel was not afraid of monarchical despotism, for according to him the king would only rarely act as a tyrant. Only the king's ministers must be feared and prevented from using their power abusively. The Cortes would comprise two estates, the ecclesiastic and the secular, and would have full freedom of petition.[30]

The Audiencia of Galicia would have a law automatically promulgated by the king if it had been asked by three successive Cortes, meeting every three years.[31] The Cádiz municipal council suggested that the Spanish constitution be sought in the Visigothic Code, the *Fuero Juzgo*, and it would reestablish the old monarchy in which the kings were "supreme legislators, but their orders and decrees . . . had no force . . . except when they received the approval of the Cortes, which, composed of the three classes, represented the nation."[32] The Cortes would not limit itself to asking and begging, but would be empowered to take action to "contain the despotism of the kings, the licentiousness of their favorites and the arbitrariness of their ministers."[33] The city fathers of Granada suggested the adoption of the type of Cortes which protected Aragonese liberties in the Middle Ages.[34] The University of Mallorca advocated

---

monument. It established Castilian as the official language of the kingdom of Castile and León, and covering many aspects of Spanish medieval life, gives the reader invaluable information on medieval Spain.

29. *Ibid.*, pp. 150–64.
30. *Ibid.*, pp. 196–208.
31. *Ibid.*, pp. 249–54.
32. *Ibid.*, pp. 257–58.
33. *Ibid.*, p. 262.
34. The Aragonese Cortes consisted of representatives of the clergy, the higher nobility, the lower nobility, and the towns. The *justicia mayor*, a magistrate accountable solely to the estates for his conduct, took the oath of the new king with the words: "We who are each of us as good as you are and

the drafting of a new code of laws and sounded a warning note on the mood of the people: "The people know today, through long experience, that nothing can be achieved without them, and if, when they have given back to the nation power, liberty and authority at the cost of so many sacrifices, they see that all this has served merely to subject them to despotism, treating them with contempt and letting them live in sordidness, without giving them a share of the honor they have earned, it is to be feared that they will want to achieve unbridled freedom and equality, whereas they will have to be satisfied if they are granted a freedom and equality that are characteristic of civilized and organized nations."[35]

The Junta of Badajoz opposed the calling of the *brazos:* "Only to the people does Spain owe its freedom. Therefore the only justifiable representation is a popular representation. This does not mean that members of the clergy or the nobility cannot be chosen for the Cortes, but it does mean that these would merely be part and parcel of popular representation."[36] The Junta of Valencia wanted the Cortes to regain what it thought was at one time its full legislative power, without limiting its activities to mere petitioning.[37] The Junta of Mallorca, however, was in favor of retaining the original system.[38] The Junta of Trujillo demanded a new constitution.[39]

The historian Capmany took a traditionalist position. Though later usually siding with the liberals in the Cádiz Cortes, he always maintained a rather independent posture that makes it difficult to classify him along ideological lines. In his report to the Suprema he suggested the preservation of the three *brazos,* for a popular assembly would,

---

who together are stronger than you, have received you for our King and Lord on condition that you maintain our rights and privileges. If not, no."

35. Artola, ii, p. 289. The latter third of this translation is a rather free version of the original text, which would make little sense if translated more literally: . . . . *es de temer que descontento, no quiera adquirir la mal entendida libertad e igualdad, cuando si se le concede la que es característica de los pueblos civiles y bien organizados, es preciso se den todos por satisfechos.*

36. *Ibid.,* p. 294.

37. *Ibid.,* p. 300.

38. *Ibid.,* p. 307.

39. *Ibid.,* p. 321. The word *constitución* was used by this Junta in the sense of a new written text.

according to him, easily fall prey to a dictator. He also had some nice things to say of the oft-abused Spanish aristocracy: "Did not the aristocracy serve in the army? Did they not enlist under the banners raised by patriotism? Have many not sacrificed their lives on the battlefield . . . ? Have many others not chosen harsh captivity in the power of the enemy rather than bow their heads to the intrusive king?"[40]

On the whole, these answers do not provide the reader with a well-defined division between tradition and reform, since the great majority of those queried expressed a desire for changes. With respect to a desire for truly democratic reforms, this can only be found in a minority of the institutions and individuals who sent in their answers.

One of the most clear-cut positions in favor of a drastic political change was that taken by the Asturian economist Flórez Estrada, who in his constitutional project *Constitución para la nación española*, presented to the Suprema's Comisión de Cortes, rotundly affirmed: "The only acceptable law shall be that which is expressed and published by the nation itself represented in a sovereign body composed of delegates from all its provinces. The only acceptable sovereign shall be this body and it shall be a crime against the state to call the king sovereign and to say that sovereignty can reside anywhere but in this assembly."[41]

The anonymous author of the pamphlet *España y el español en presencia de sus cortes en 1810*, writing in Valencia, voiced a similar view. After stating that the Spanish people had suffered with docility the corruption of their own government but had revolted against the foreign aggressor, he declared that it was in the lower classes that pure patriotism was found. It was in the lower classes that treason had found absolutely no refuge. It was from here that had come forth those whom the French called *brigands* and who gave the enemy no peace.[42] "It is necessary to confess generously the truth," exclaimed

40. *Ibid.*, p. 453.

41. *Apud* Artola, I, p. 301.

42. *Op. cit.*, p. 15. *Brigands* or bandits was the name frequently given by the French to the Spanish guerrillas.

the anonymous author. "The lower classes were those who raised the banner of liberty *in the face of two simultaneous oppressions.*"[43] What, then, must be done? First of all the Cortes must be called, because "it is the last refuge of the people's hope."[44] If it were not called soon, passions would burst. The Cortes must have by its side a constitutional regency, which would inspire confidence in the people and would cause the defense of the nation to be carried on with greater energy. The main task of the Cortes was to write a constitution: "This soul of the state, backbone of national life, independence and essence; this shield of the sacred rights of the Nation and the citizen . . . writing the constitution is the principal duty of the Cortes for the salvation of Spain!" Moreover, this assembly should be in permanent session or should be represented by a permanent delegation when not in session.[45]

The constitution should be adapted to the needs of the Spanish character and the prevailing situation in Spain and should be capable of governing the nation if the king should disappear. This was entirely possible since the national assembly was the sole depositary of national sovereignty.[46] There would be one legislative body and three supreme councils dealing with the business of state of Spain and the Indies.[47] The press should be free, but an author should be answerable for his writings. In the case of statements offensive to religion or authority, or attacking a particular individual, the printers should give notice to a magistrate appointed for the purpose.[48]

The foregoing is a fairly coherent expression of what would be the liberal program in the Cortes of Cádiz: Sovereignty resided essentially in the nation represented in its Cortes. A new constitution must be drafted. The press must be freed from censorship. Spain's traditional religion should be respected. By suggesting that in the event of

43. *Ibid.* Italics in original text. The second oppression is, of course, the oppression of the Spanish people by their rulers. A statement which somewhat contradicts the earlier reference to the Spanish people's docility with respect to the corruption of their government.

44. *Ibid.,* p. 20.

45. *Ibid.,* pp. 31–32.

46. *Ibid.,* p. 42.

47. *Ibid.,* p. 44.

48. *Ibid.,* pp. 48–49.

the king's "disappearance" the constitution was fully capable of ruling in his stead, the author clearly showed the way to the emergence of a republic. Most of the Cádiz liberals would not be ready to go that far.

This reformist program has its more extreme conservative counterpart in the attitude of the few who were against calling the Cortes altogether, and in the more widely held opinion that the Cortes should deal exclusively with the war. It is difficult to pin down this ultraconservative posture in the answers to the Suprema's inquiry of 1809, and the clearest indications of what the ultramontane wing expected from the Cortes were really given after the Cortes had opened its sessions. In 1811, for instance, the author of *Aviso importante y urgente a la nación española. Juicio imparcial de sus cortes*[49] spelled out in La Coruña what he had looked forward to before the gathering of the assembly. In his view the deputies were supposed to: (1) Grant subsidies to carry on the war until final victory and to keep the peace in the unoccupied zones; (2) Appoint an executive made up of few men—the Regency could serve this purpose—who would be the depositary of full national sovereignty; (3) Retire to their homes once these two aims had been achieved, and gather again when the French had been ejected from Spain, to eliminate abuses and "establish a good system of government capable of remedying our ills, of making us happy and of protecting us from the danger of being once more the plaything of a minister and a favorite."[50]

On the eve of the opening of the Cortes, Quintana, writing in *El Observador* of September 21, 1810, apostrophized his countrymen in his ringing style, reminding them that their former Cortes were not suitable for the day's necessities, since their convocation, their gathering place, and the number of their members had often depended on the whim of the monarch; since they had been "without power to make laws, requesting what they should have been decreeing, reduced to a sterile manifestation of wishes for the public good, postponed, rebuffed, eternally frustrated by the monarchs . . . " No, the Spain of 1810 must erect a new edifice which would give

49. *Important and Urgent Notice to the Spanish Nation. An Impartial View of Its Cortes.*
50. CDF, CDLXIII, pp. 8–11.

Spaniards "the reward of the hard work and the sufferings to which inexorable fate is condemning [them] now."[51]

By the time, then, that the extraordinary Cortes opened on the Isle of León, the reform-minded knew what fundamental measures they expected from the national congress. They wanted the war effort to be carried on with the utmost energy. They also wanted reform of the political, social, and economic structure of the country. A new constitution was to safeguard the rights of the third estate,[52] provide for its permanent representation, and limit the powers of the king. They wanted legally-guaranteed freedom of the press, so that the new ideas could be freely disseminated throughout the land.

The peculiar geographical location of the first national Cortes, the atmosphere and the peculiar circumstances in which this momentous event took place doubtless favored the reformist sector. The permanent population of Cádiz was made up of a large portion of middle-class businessmen who through maritime trade had come into contact with other parts of the world and had absorbed eighteenth-century Enlightenment as much or more than the rest of intellectual and professional Spain. The lower classes of Cádiz naturally followed the lead of the bourgeoisie. Thus the liberals were always assured of a sympathetic local backing for whatever measures they proposed in the assembly. After the freedom of the press was proclaimed in the fall of 1810, this support became particularly articulate, and the phalanx of liberal newspapers provided a comforting chorus for the reformist leadership in the Cortes.

Equally important for the formation of a liberal majority in the Cortes was the great mass of refugees who constituted about half of the total population. Among those who had fled the mainland and had reached the sanctuary of the citadel were many men who came from the sectors most likely to advocate reform: writers, professionals, army officers, enlightened clergymen, government employees who had preferred exile to service under King Joseph. From among the refugees came the *suplentes* or substitute deputies who represented the occupied provinces and the colonies. The Spanish-American deputies, though often considered as forming a third

51. *El Observador*, No. 14, September 21, 1810, pp. 212–13, 221.
52. Meaning mainly the emerging Spanish middle class.

group because of the peculiar interests they represented, counted in their midst a strong contingent of men who would often vote for reform, partly because reform would in many respects benefit the inhabitants of Spain's overseas territories.

The circumstances in which the congress convened also afforded advantages to the progressive cause. Spain had just suffered a terrible blow. The French had overrun Andalucía, and at Cádiz free Spain had to stand or die. The deputies to the national Cortes, with the eyes of all Spain on them, were conscious of the crucial role they were to play. They were called upon to turn defeat into victory and to introduce into the worm-eaten political, social, and economic body of Spain changes recognized as indispensable by a majority of Spaniards, although the nature of the changes needed was conceived of in a variety of ways. They felt that by virtue of their election, but also because they now constituted the one big hope of fighting Spain, they had the duty and the right to take at least some drastic measures to defeat the invader and make certain that their country would never again fall prey to a favorite like Godoy or to a warlord like Napoleon. Deputies who normally would have taken a conservative stand were considerably influenced by these factors. Other members of the congress whose opinions oscillated between tradition and reform were no doubt affected by the reformist mood of the population of Cádiz and the propaganda barrage from the liberal press. Working in an atmosphere charged with the desire for change, many of these moderates were to swing to the more advanced point of view, at least at some crucial moments in the debates.

When the Cortes opened its sessions, out of slightly more than 100 deputies there were approximately 30 representatives who could be called conservatives, while the rest were reformists, ranging from moderates to radicals. But since all Spain thought that it was time for at least some change, it would be incorrect to presume that from the very beginning the Cortes split into two warring factions separated by a wide abyss. From the start there was, of course, a small group of radicals and a small group of ultraconservatives, but they constituted the extremist wings of their respective sectors. The majority of liberals were not fire-eating revolutionaries and the majority of conservatives were not black reactionaries. This picture is further complicated by the fact that a deputy could take quite a progressive stand on one issue and vote with the conservatives on another. True, the greater part of the liberal majority had a clear idea of the basic reforms it wanted, while the conservatives did not. But the liberals did not go into the Cortes with the complete revolutionary program which emerged after the assembly had functioned for more than three years. Only gradually, as reform after reform was passed by the congress, did the liberals emerge as the party fighting for a Spain radically different from the Spain envisioned by the conservatives.

[2]

In the Spanish Cortes of 1810, clergymen and lawyers constituted the backbone of the body of deputies. The solemn tone of the debates that rang through the theater of the Isla de León and through the church of San Felipe Neri, and the tendency to discuss various questions in terms of theology and civil and canon law, can no doubt be traced to this predominance of ecclesiastics and lawyers. A number of enlightened churchmen took the lead in the work of reform carried on by the assembly, and among these the most outstanding was Diego Muñoz Torrero.[53] Born in the province of Badajoz in 1761, he had been professor and rector of the University of Salamanca. In 1810, he was elected deputy for Extremadura. Muñoz Torrero was truly a gentleman and a scholar, a clergyman permeated with the humanitarianism of the eighteenth century, who gave his due to reason but without yielding an inch of his religious convictions. In him shone brightly the spirit of eighteenth-century Enlightenment in perfect harmony with traditional Spanish purity of faith. He was not a great orator, but his role in the Cortes, particularly in

53. Among the liberal ecclesiastics of the Cortes must be mentioned the Bishop of Mallorca, Bernardo Nadal y Crespi; Antonio José Ruiz de Padrón, deputy for the Canary Islands; Joaquín Lorenzo Villanueva, the author of the valuable *Mi viaje a las Cortes;* Juan Nicasio Gallego, the author of the famous poem *El dos de mayo;* the Extremadurans Manuel Luxán and Antonio Oliveros; and the Mexicans José Miguel Guridi Alcocer and José Miguel Gordoa y Barrios.

his rank of president of the constitutional commission, was of vital importance for the reformist cause.[54]

His was the first speech delivered in the assembly, and to his initiative is due the fundamental decree of September 24, which boldly stated that national sovereignty resided in the Cortes. Locke's *Treatises on Government* and Rousseau's *Contrat Social*, which contain the principles underlying the affirmation of national sovereignty, were known in Spain and no doubt influenced all Spanish reformists.[55] Muñoz Torrero, too, especially as a former rector of the University of Salamanca, was doubtless familiar with the ideas of the British philosopher and the author of the *Contrat Social*. But it was not only the works of Locke and Rousseau which accounted for the emphasis given by Muñoz Torrero and many others to the concept of national sovereignty. "The affirmation of national sovereignty derives essentially from the Spanish uprising."[56] "Bereft of its kings, handed over like a herd of cattle and treated as a rebel," says Toreno, "Spain had the obligation to . . . proclaim to the face of the world its right to constitute itself [as a nation] and to defend itself. The abdications of its sovereigns could not take this right away from her even if they had been made freely and voluntarily."[57]

Besides, the doctrine that the nation was the source of all authority was nothing new or foreign in Spanish history. Situations had arisen during the Middle Ages when the people themselves had decided on the succession to the throne. The famous *Compromiso de Caspe* of 1412, when representatives of Aragón, Catalonia, and Valencia gathered at Caspe to elect a monarch after King Martín of Aragón had died without offspring, is a case in point.

Muñoz Torrero's decree was approved, apparently, if we are to

---

54. He was persecuted, like so many other liberals, when Fernando returned from captivity in 1814. In jail until 1820, he returned to the national Cortes as deputy for Extremadura. Forced by the restoration of absolutism in 1823 to flee to Portugal, he was eventually arrested there for his liberal ideas and died in prison in 1829.

55. Cf. Rodríguez Aranda, "La recepción y el influjo de las ideas políticas de John Locke en España." *Revista de Estudios Políticos*, LXXVI (1945).

56. Sánchez Agesta, *Historia del constitucionalismo español*, p. 55.

57. *Op. cit.*, p. 289.

believe Toreno, after an interesting debate but with little opposition.[58] The importance of this decree cannot be overemphasized.
Here was the national congress of a nation that had lived under an
absolute monarchy for more than 300 years, proclaiming to the face
of the world that it and no other institution or person was the
embodiment of national sovereignty. It was a challenge to absolute
monarchy and to those who held absolutist ideas. While few among
the deputies disputed this claim of the Cortes, the decree came under
almost immediate attack from another member of the Church, the
venerable Don Pedro Quevedo y Quintano, bishop of Orense. The
Bishop was an ardent patriot, but ultraconservative in his views, and
the full meaning of Muñoz Torrero's decree was not lost on him. His
first reaction was to resign again from his post as regent and from
that of deputy for Extremadura, for which he had been elected, and
to ask for permission to return to his diocese. This was granted. But
the old gentleman went further. At the beginning of October he
published a paper attacking the first decree of the Cortes and reproaching his fellow regents for having meekly taken the oath of
loyalty to the assembly. Interestingly enough, some of the most
conservative deputies turned against the Bishop, while some reformists were of the opinion that Don Pedro Quevedo should not be
molested and should be allowed to return to Orense.

On October 18 it was decided that the Bishop would swear loyalty
to the sovereign nation as represented in its Cortes by a formula
demanded from all ecclesiastic, civil, and military personnel. The
Bishop offered more resistance, but finally, seeing that he did not
receive hoped-for support, he yielded and took the oath in the Cortes
on February 3, 1811.[59] This whole incident acquires importance only
in the light of events of subsequent years, for the Bishop could then

58. *Ibid.,* p. 288. Cf. also *Diario de las discusiones y actas de las Cortes* of
September 24, 1810. The *diario* for this day does not give a count of the votes
cast. The decree also provided among other things for the proclamation of
Fernando VII as Spain's sole and legitimate monarch, to whom the Cortes
swore their loyalty; the invalidity of the cession of the Crown; and the division of powers into legislative, executive, and judiciary. The Cortes declared
that it would exercise full legislative power.

59. Toreno, pp. 293–94. The Bishop had been ordered by the Cortes to
remain in Cádiz after publication of his paper (*ibid.,* p. 294).

point with pride to his attitude in 1810, when he was the first to raise the banner of absolutist legitimacy before the revolutionary Cortes.

The first confrontation of what later were to be two bitterly opposed groups came with the debate of freedom of the press, which opened on October 15. Freedom of the press had been one of the reforms on which the progressive minded had openly insisted ever since 1808. Particularly vocal in this demand had been Calvo de Rozas, defender of Zaragoza and member of the Suprema, who on September 12, 1809, in a paper to the Junta Central, stated his conviction that freedom of the press, i.e., the elimination of censorship previous to publication, was vital for the success of Spanish arms. Only if inept military leadership could be criticized would there be a drastic improvement in the military situation.[60] Alvaro Flórez Estrada, of whom Carlos Le Brun said that "it seemed that liberalism had been born with him,"[61] echoed this demand in an appeal from Cádiz to the Suprema at the end of 1809.[62] By the time the Cortes opened, it was a foregone conclusion that the reformists would make freedom of the press one of their first goals.

In the debate which, with some interruptions, lasted until early November, some of the speakers who had already attracted the attention of the Cortes and the public in September now gave a full measure of their oratorical talent. Agustín Argüelles and José Mexía, both reformists and both championing freedom of the press, dazzled their hearers with the brilliance of their oratory. Argüelles, born into the lower Asturian nobility, had studied law at the University of Oviedo and had served in the Supreme Junta's Cortes commission. He had been elected deputy for Asturias from among the Asturians residing in Cádiz. Of rather tall stature, with an expressive face, possessing a fine voice, extremely polite in his demeanor, he became the foremost orator of the Cortes. Though the development of his ideas was not always dominated by flawless logic and though he often spoke without the necessary preparation, his contemporaries usually felt they had lived through an unforgettable experience after listen-

---

60. AHN, Estado, Junta Central, *legajo* 22, *carpeta* D, No. 17.
61. *Retratos políticos de la revolución de España*, p. 66.
62. AHN, Estado, Junta Central, *legajo* 22, *carpeta* D, No. 22.

ing to one of his speeches. He possessed the gift of weaving words together into striking images, and the passion which animated him gave his words a feeling of utmost sincerity which never failed to make a deep impression on his listeners. More scholar than original thinker, he drew at least part of his ideological inspiration from the French Revolution and from the English political system. Perhaps no other figure among the deputies of the first Spanish national Cortes has been more identified with the momentous work of the assembly. Argüelles, called El Divino for his oratorical gifts, had a lion's share in pushing through the congress the laws that shaped modern Spain.

The discussion on freedom of the press was the first debate that acquainted the Cortes with the eloquence of the thirty-four-year-old deputy from Asturias.[63] Equating freedom of the press with progress, and censorship with decay, he declared that things might have been different in the previous twenty years if the nation had, through a free press, been aware of the degrading relationship between republican and Napoleonic France and monarchic Spain.[64]

Siding with Argüelles on this and on many other questions was the South American José Mexía. Born in Quito, in present-day Ecuador, Mexía was a highly educated man who had studied theology and medicine and held the position of professor of medicine at the University of Lima. On September 20, he had been elected in Cádiz to represent New Granada (modern Colombia and Ecuador). A more profound thinker than Argüelles and a magnificent speaker, Mexía would probably have been the greatest orator of the Cortes if he had paid more attention to the style of his discourses. Called the American Mirabeau by his friends, he supplemented his political activities with his work as editor of the liberal newspaper *La Abeja*, one of the most fighting reformist papers in Cádiz. Mexía did not live long enough to see the aftermath of the extraordinary Cortes. In 1813, yellow fever carried him off at the age of thirty-four.

---

63. Noteworthy is the youth of the liberal leaders in the Cortes.

64. Toreno, p. 300. Only in December, 1810, did stenographers begin to take down verbatim the speeches of the deputies. For the debates up to then we must rely on eyewitnesses such as Toreno, or on the summaries provided by the *Diario de las discusiones y actas de las Cortes*.

In his speech on freedom of the press Mexía recalled that before printing had been invented, people had been free to write and copy books without any special hindrance. While knowledge spread slowly, it was freer than in modern nations afflicted with censorship laws. If it came to choosing between freedom to express one's self in writing, without the benefit of printing, to printing without this freedom, he for one would choose the former: "A piece of bread eaten in freedom," exclaimed the young man from Quito, "is preferable to a royal feast with a sword hanging over one's head . . ."[65]

But it was Muñoz Torrero who in this crucial question made perhaps the greatest oratorical contribution to the cause of freedom of the press. During the session of October 17, the reformist clergyman pointed out that freedom of the press was an indispensable bulwark against despotism. If Spain had had freedom of the press, Fernando VII would not have been arrested in October, 1807 and his friends would not have been sent into exile.[66] If there had been no censorship, Godoy would not have climbed the steps to dictatorship. The advantages of having a free press clearly outweighed the disadvantages. "Freedom without a free press, though it may be the dream of a well-intentioned man, will always be a dream."[67]

The decisive day in this first great battle of the Cortes was October 19, when Article I of the decree on freedom of the press was approved by a vote of 68 to 33. This section stated that "all institutions and individuals of whatever class and status are free to write, print and publish their political ideas without the necessity of a license, examination or approval previous to publication . . ." On November 10, the full decree was promulgated. It contained twenty articles regulating printing and setting up a supreme censorship junta with residence near the government, as well as a junta for each provincial capital. These bodies would watch for abuses of the freedom to print and would report infractions to the authorities, so that violators would be prosecuted by the courts. But this newfound liberty of the written word applied only to political matters, for

65. *Ibid.*, p. 301.
66. See Chapter I.
67. *Diario de las discusiones y actas de las Cortes,* October 17, 1810, I, in CDF, LXII, p. 47; Toreno, p. 302.

writings dealing with religious topics remained subject to previous censorship of the Church.[68] This was disappointing to many reformists such as Mexía, who wanted total freedom to print. But it was only realistic for the liberals to accept this restriction. "The Inquisition had weighed down on the nation for three centuries," says Toreno, "and a step had been taken in the direction of tolerance, from the moment when censorship was torn out of the hands of that tribunal, and deposited in that of the bishops, among whom some were fanatical-minded but others were tolerant and scholarly."[69]

In March, 1811, a young man took his seat in the Cortes who was destined to be one of the great figures of the liberal movement and who in later years would occupy the highest posts in the Spanish government. Don José Queipo de Llano, Count Toreno, residing in Cádiz, was just under twenty-five years of age, but his unusual intellectual gifts, as well as the part he had played in the patriotic uprising, overcame the objections concerning his youth—the minimum age for deputies was twenty-five—and he was elected deputy for Asturias. Born in Oviedo in 1786, he was the prototype of the Spanish enlightened aristocrat of the turn of the century. His education had been excellent. In Madrid he had studied Latin, Greek, and humanities with some first-rate teachers, who had instilled in him the spirit of the age. A progressive clergyman had acquainted him with Rousseau's *Émile* and *Le Contrat social,* and these two works had only accentuated the reformist tendencies of his *Weltanschauung,* which were constantly nurtured by his intensive studies. Arriving in Oviedo after the *dos de mayo,* he had played an important role in the Asturian revolt, and together with Andrés Angel de la Vega he had gone to England to request British support for the uprising. In London, Toreno and his companion had been the toast of the town. Whenever they appeared in public they were greeted with the warmest show of affection. The first day they attended the opera in the loge of the Duke of Queensbury, the ovation to which they were treated was so great that the performance had to be suspended for

68. Specifically, of the bishops.

69. *Op. cit.,* p. 302; *Diario de las discusiones y actas de las Cortes,* October 19, 1810, I, in CDF, LXII, pp. 49–50; *Colección de los decretos,* I, in CDF, LXXVII, pp. 14–17; Belda and Labra, pp. 47–49.

almost an hour. In England Toreno met the great personalities of the day: Castlereagh; Wellesley; Holland, nephew of Charles Fox and one of the ministers in the Whig cabinet of 1806 and 1807; and Sheridan, the Irish playwright and politician. Back in Oviedo in December, he remained in the principality until September, 1809, when he went by sea to Andalucía. In June, 1810, he was entrusted by the deputies from the provinces with the task of petitioning the Regency for the prompt convocation of the Cortes, a demarche which made the regents aware of how strong was the popular desire for a quick gathering of the deputies.

Toreno was both a gentleman and a scholar.[70] Of a pleasant disposition, not as great an orator as his fellow Asturian, Argüelles, he was nevertheless a good speaker and his participation in the debates was always marked by his solid erudition. For more than two and a half months he sat in the Cortes without taking part in the debates. But once he began to have a share in the discussions he showed his mettle as a speaker, as a statesman, and as a scholar.[71]

Toreno's parliamentary debut coincided with another liberal attack on Spain's political and social fabric. This was the discussion of the abolition of the seignorial regime under which a large part of rural Spain was still living, and, it might be added, suffering. The liberals were determined to obtain the elimination of the rights of appointing judges on their land enjoyed by aristocratic and ecclesiastical landlords, as well as the onerous charges of feudal origin weighing on the peasants who lived on the lords' estates.[72] Actually, the jurisdictional power of the *señores* had been severely curtailed by the Crown under the Bourbon monarchy. Landlords could only appoint judges able to meet the requirements set by law, and the matters referred to their jurisdiction were in most instances civil cases. Still, the liberals, having laid down the principle that all sover-

70. His *Historia del levantamiento, guerra y revolución de España*, though containing quite a few factual errors, is still an indispensable work for any student of this period of Spanish history.

71. Cf. Pastor Díaz, *Galería de españoles célebres*, Vol. I.

72. Napoleon and Joseph had eliminated seignorial rights in French-occupied Spain, and the desire not to lag behind the reforms of the enemy probably was a factor, though not an important one, in the liberals' attack on this relic of feudalism.

eignty resided in the nation, were committed by their own logic to terminate a state of affairs under which private individuals exercised authority over huge areas of the land, no matter what circumstances had prompted Spanish kings to grant this authority in ages past. It was thus a matter of incorporating this private rule into the all-embracing dominion of the nation. As such it would be a political-administrative measure. On the other hand, by eliminating the various tributes—most of them in the form of money—which formed part of the *señorío* (seignorial domain) and which landlords could exact from the towns, villages, and individuals in their realm, the party of reform would strike a blow for social-economic freedom.

At the beginning of June the debate on the question of *señoríos* began in earnest. The fiery Manuel García Herreros, deputy for Soria and one of the radicals in the liberal camp, was the battering ram of the offensive against the seignorial regime. On June 1, García Herreros suggested that all jurisdictional *señoríos* as well as property sold or donated by the Crown revert to the nation. This last point brought into play the ticklish question of the possession of the land itself. Spain was not yet ready for a full-fledged agrarian reform. What the more radical liberals like García Herreros wanted was the reincorporation into the national patrimony of land alienated by Spanish kings out of pure caprice or because of financial pressure, and therefore, in reformist eyes, subject to reversion to the nation.[73] A few days later the deputy from Soria presented a concrete program for carrying out the reform. All purely jurisdictional *señoríos*, or land not belonging to the *señor* but over which he exercised jurisdictional rights, would be returned to the authority of the nation. Territorial *señoríos*, or land ownership accompanied by rights of feudal origin, including jurisdiction, and *señoríos solariegos*, or property over which the landlord exercised no jurisdiction but which entitled him to certain special rights vis-à-vis the tenants, would be reduced to the status of private property. All privileges and tributes of feudal origin would be eliminated. All property which

73. Land acquired during the reconquest of Spain from the Moors, or granted to individuals for specific meritorious service, did not fall in this category. Much alienation of land took place under the Habsburg kings, who were chronically beset by financial difficulties (Toreno, p. 356).

had been sold or ceded with the explicit or implicit proviso that it would revert to the Crown would be incorporated into the national patrimony and the owners compensated. To be assured of compensation or possession a *señor* would have to show the title to his land.[74]

Ultraconservatives strongly opposed the bill. The debate lasted into July. At one point García Herreros reminded the Cortes that his constituents, the *numantinos*,[75] had preferred to be devoured by fire rather than accept servitude. "I still conserve in my heart the heat of those flames," exclaimed García Herreros, "and it urges me to assure you that the Numantian people will recognize but one dominion, that of the nation."[76] And he pleaded passionately for social justice: "What benefit would the people derive from the feat of having chased the enemy beyond the Pyrenees if upon turning their faces to the fatherland they found a servitude more degrading than the one they had shaken off . . . ? Gentlemen, the day Your Majesty[77] passes the bill now under discussion, the Spanish people will recover their true liberty . . . That day will be greater than the *dos de mayo*, for if the people showed their true character in 1808, on this other day they will regain the right and dignity of free men."[78]

The liberal clergyman Joaquín Lorenzo Villanueva put the question to the assembly in the form of a syllogism: If the services rendered to the kings of Spain by a few noblemen freed the land from the Moors, the services rendered to the nation by the people have now freed the *señores* from the tyranny of the French. Therefore, if in the old days the noblemen were rewarded at the cost of people freed by them, let the people now be rewarded at the cost of the *señores*, "who without this help would have been slaves."[79]

Toreno, showing the influence of Locke and Rousseau, declared: "Men form society for the pursuit of happiness, not to forge their own fetters." "Nations are not herds which are given and taken

74. *Diario de las discusiones y actas de las Cortes*, VI, in CDF, LXVII, pp. 148, 182–83; Toreno, p. 357.

75. Soria stands close to the ruins of Numancia, which gained immortal fame through its stand against Rome.

76. *Diario de las discusiones y actas de las Cortes*, VI, in CDF, LXVII, p. 166.

77. Read "The Cortes."

78. *Ibid.*, p. 167.

79. *Ibid.*, p. 169.

according to the whims of their masters," he stated further. "Kings never had the right to use and never should have used people as if they were mere jewels."[80] When we consider that this statement was uttered by an aristocrat who owned several *señoríos* himself, the stand taken by Toreno is all the more admirable.

On June 5, the moderately conservative Ramón Lázaro Dou, representing Catalonia,[81] tried to show that the jurisdictional authority of the landlords was of little real import, since the *señorío* judges were required to act within the same legal framework as the royal magistrates. His fellow Catalan, Jaime Creus, later Bishop of Urgel, also supported the conservative thesis by pointing, with the authority of no less than a Montesquieu to back him up, to the desirability of maintaining a strong aristocracy as an indispensable intermediate power between king and people. In the session of June 11, he declared that in Catalonia both *señores* and peasants were against abolition, since the latter received substantial economic aid from their benevolent landlords.[82] Actually more than a defense of the seignorial regime *per se,* the speeches of the Catalan deputies were a reflection of the state of affairs in Catalonia, where *señoríos* were apparently far from unpopular with the rural masses.[83]

On June 6, Don Blas Ostolaza, substitute deputy for Peru and one of the leaders of the traditionalist group, rose to the defense of the *Ancien Régime*. In the historical novel *Cádiz,* Pérez Galdós describes him as "stout, with a ruddy and shiny face, a provocative look and a loud voice."[84] He was a priest—he had been the confessor of Charles IV and chaplain of Fernando VII—but shared none of the ideas of his ecclesiastical colleagues who had chosen eighteenth-century Enlightenment. An absolutist who could see nothing but harm in the reformist ideas advanced in the Cortes, he fought these tooth and nail

80. *Ibid.,* p. 208.

81. Lázaro Dou (1739–1832), an ecclesiastic, was rector of the University of Cervera. He was the first official president of the Cortes.

82. *Diario,* VI, in CDF, LXVII, pp. 188–93, 299.

83. Domínguez Ortíz, pp. 311–12. This lack of enthusiasm for the elimination of the *señoríos* was shared by the liberal-leaning Capmany, also representing Catalonia. Where the seignorial regime doubtless took on its harshest form was in Aragón.

84. *Op. cit.,* p. 97.

whenever he felt the occasion demanded it. After the return of Fernando in 1814, he was well rewarded for his staunch defense of altar and throne and became one of the key figures in the king's camarilla.[85] The arch-conservative scholar and critic Menéndez y Pelayo, who often displays a truly admirable objectivity in his treatment of this period, speaks of him as a man whose "conduct was not always exemplary."[86]

In the debate on the extinction of *señoríos* Ostolaza used the question under discussion as a springboard for an attack against the "pestilential influence" of French ways on Spain, which, he darkly hinted, must be behind this unsavory proposal to strip the *señores* of their rights. After all, Napoleon had issued a decree which bore great resemblance to the proposal now under consideration, the implication being that the liberals were secretly in sympathy with French revolutionary ideology while pretending to fight Napoleon. This was a line of attack which would be used again and again against the reformists, not only by their contemporaries but by conservative historians right down to our days. The strategy would pay off, for in the end it contributed powerfully to the liberals' fall. The only matter to be discussed in the Cortes, continued Ostolaza, was that of appropriating funds for the defense of the homeland. This was wherein lay the way to happiness for the Spanish people, and not in measures "which, deceitfully dubbed liberal, coincide with the revolutionary principles of Robespierre, the greatest enemy of the people . . ."[87]

Yet even this reactionary priest apparently realized that there are certain institutions which must disappear according to all sound logic. Admitting indirectly that the *señoríos* would have to be abolished provided there was proper indemnification, he concluded by saying that the question should not be acted upon until the money for indemnifying the *señores* was ready.[88]

Argüelles answered the conservative arguments with his usual

---

85. He later joined the Carlist cause and was shot after taking part in an insurrection in Valencia.

86. *Historia de los heterodoxos españoles*, VII, p. 55.

87. *Diario de las discusiones* . . . , June 6, 1811, VI, in CDF, LXVII, p. 195.

88. *Ibid.*

passion: "These seignorial rights could not possibly have been granted on legitimate grounds, because it would have been necessary to consult the people who were going to be affected by these grants. I do not conceive that the people could have consented to this infamous alienation . . ." Admitting that in spite of the seignorial regime some regions of the Peninsula such as Valencia and Murcia had prospered, the liberal orator from Asturias explained that this was due to the fertile nature of the soil of these areas as well as to the long sojourn in them of the Moors, skilled in agriculture and handicraft. "These rights," exclaimed El Divino, "oppress the people in the worst manner, aside from humiliating them and degrading them."[89]

Over the objections of the ultraconservatives the age-old institution was voted out of existence, and on August 6, 1811, the decree providing for abolition of *señoríos* was promulgated. All jurisdictional *señoríos* as well as all feudal privileges and tributes were eliminated, while territorial *señoríos* and *señoríos solariegos* simply became landed property. Seignorial landlords would have to produce their title to the land to prove that the property had been acquired in a manner precluding reversion to the nation. Finally, the nation would indemnify the *señores* for losses incurred in the abolition of the seignorial regime.[90]

89. *Diario de las discusiones* . . . , June 6, 1811, VI, in CDF, LXVII, p. 201.

90. *Colección de los decretos,* I, in CDF, LXXVII, pp. 193–96. Actual voting began on July 1, when Article I stipulating that all jurisdictional rights revert back to the nation was approved by 128 votes to 16 (*Diario de las discusiones* . . . , VI, in CDF, LXVII, p. 560). Most other provisions were approved by an equally overwhelming vote (*Diario de las discusiones* . . . , July 2, 4, 5, 1811, VI, in CDF, LXVIII, pp. 13–31). This lopsided decision is due in part to the fact that jurisdictional *señoríos* as well as privileges and tributes of feudal origin were obviously anachronistic in nature. Of more weight in the voting, however, was the prospect that landed property would remain essentially unchanged. As Artola points out, by transforming territorial *señoríos* and *señoríos solariegos* into private landed property, the liberals simply made tenants of the peasants living on the *señor*'s land and for all practical purposes assured the owner of continued payments of fees, the nature of which—feudal or otherwise—it was often difficult to determine and which now could be claimed by the *señor* to be payments for the use of his land (*op. cit.,* I, p. 469). At least in some parts of rural Spain some aspects of the *señorío* system itself must have subsisted for a long time after the victory of liberalism in the nineteenth century officially put an end to it. I have been told by the inhabitants of Navamorcuende, a *pueblo* set in the sierra fourteen miles north of

Shortly after the debate on seignorial rights the nobility again came under attack. This time it was in connection with a proposal by the war commission of the Cortes to the effect that military schools as well as the army and navy officer corps should be open to all Spaniards of "honorable families" without distinction of class. García Herreros, after declaring that neither the welfare of society nor the right of all its members to choose honorable careers permitted a continuation of the discrimination against the third estate in military academies, came back to the now popular theme of the lion's share assumed by the people in the national revolt against Napoleon:

What, gentlemen, would become of the Spanish nation if that revolution which we consider holy had been entrusted solely to the aristocracy? . . . When the nation was invaded and caught by surprise by those hordes of innumerable vandals, would the nobility have been able by itself to reconquer liberty? Was it not the people who with their awe-inspiring effort . . . tried to break the chains with which the tyrant endeavored to tie us to the chariot of his triumphs? . . . Some will say to me that noblemen have equally contributed to our cause and that they have rendered great services to the fatherland. I am glad of it. I do not doubt that the nobility has done its duty. But, gentlemen, how insufficient . . . would have been all the efforts and sacrifices if the salvation of the fatherland had depended exclusively on them!

García Herreros kept striking the iron of social equality while it was hot: "Gentlemen, the blood and the soul of the nobility is not different in any way from that of the plebeians . . . There are no slaves. Let all be free to pursue the career of honor and let these odious, unfair and impolitic distinctions be banished forever."[91]

The next day Ostolaza came to the defense of aristocracy. Nobility, according to Fernando's chaplain, was not an invention of tyranny, as French books would have the world believe. It was an expression of monarchical society. Like fatherhood, nobility was a

---

Talavera de la Reina, that up to the time of the Second Republic (1931), the owner of a certain property in the area had the right, backed up only by tradition, to receive 3 *fanegas* (about 4.80 bu.) of grain from every peasant in the *pueblo* who sowed more than 3 *fanegas* on his own plot. To this day (1964) the same property is the only one in the town entitled to receive its share of water during twenty-four consecutive hours per week.

91. *Diario de las discusiones* . . . , August 12, 1811, VII, in CDF, LXVIII, pp. 396–98.

divine institution, a sort of priesthood in social hierarchy, whose highest priests were the sovereigns themselves. Noblemen were the leaders and the models of the people. It was not fair to ascribe to the third estate the whole merit of the national uprising. What about Palafox, Infantado, Alburquerque, Daoiz and Velarde? And what military units had distinguished themselves more than the Spanish Guard and the Royal Bodyguards, which admitted only men of noble blood? Ostolaza concluded by asking that instead of integrating the aristocracy and the third estate in the same military academies, special colleges be set up for plebeians while the nobility maintained all its privileges in its own schools.[92]

Social equality won the day. On August 17, the Cortes decreed that all military and naval academies be opened to Spaniards with an honorable family background and that aristocratic origin henceforth cease to be a prerequisite for admission to the army and navy officer corps.[93]

92. *Ibid.,* pp. 402–403.
93. *Colección de los decretos,* I, in CFD, LXXVII, pp. 199–200.

XI

SPAIN IS SPLIT ASUNDER

(CONTINUED)

[1]

WHILE the discussions took place in the church of San Felipe Neri, the Constitutional Commission, elected the previous December, was hard at work on what would be the Cortes' crowning achievement, the new political Constitution of the Spanish monarchy. This commission comprised fifteen members, including ten Spaniards and five Spanish-Americans, nine lawyers and six clergymen. It was presided over by the liberal clergyman Muñoz Torrero. Its secretary, Evaristo Pérez de Castro, later played an important role in Spanish diplomacy and politics.[1] Liberals and conservatives were almost equally represented, but ultraconservative tendencies were served really only by Francisco Gutiérrez de la Huerta, a jurist from Burgos, and Juan Pablo Valiente, a member of the Council of the Indies, representing Sevilla, who refused to sign the constitutional project.[2] Others, like Alonso Cañedo, canon and vicar of Toledo and deputy for Oviedo, or Antonio Joaquín Pérez, a Mexican clergyman, held moderately conservative views. Among the liberals, besides Muñoz Torrero and

1. A moderate liberal, he was minister of justice in 1820 and became prime minister in 1838. While he was in office, the first Carlist War ended, in 1839.
2. Valiente was highly unpopular with the Cádiz population. On October 26, 1811, the spectators occupying the gallery of the Cortes rioted against the reactionary *sevillano*, forcing the military authorities to escort him away from the building and to transfer him to a warship anchored in the bay (Toreno, pp. 395–96).

Argüelles, sat José Espiga, a churchman representing the Junta Superior of Catalonia; Antonio Oliveros, a churchman from Extremadura; and Vicente Morales Duárez, a Peruvian jurist and professor, representing Lima, who was one of the leaders in the fight to grant Spanish-Americans political equality with Peninsular Spaniards.[3]

The Commission made its first report to the Cortes on August 18, 1811, and the debates began on August 25. According to Toreno, the constitutional debate, which with interruptions lasted five months, "was grave and solemn and . . . strengthening the authority of the Cortes, exalted the reputation of that body's members."[4] The liberals on the Constitutional Commission, who had apparently been successful in swaying their conservative colleagues on this organism on many vital points, were anxious to make it appear that the new Constitution was actually founded on traditional Spanish laws and customs. The preliminary discourse of the constitutional project, drawn up by Argüelles, stated explicitly that "the commission offers nothing in its project which is not set down in the most authentic and solemn manner in the different bodies of Spanish legislation."[5] This, however, did not mean that the reformists were ready to revive the old body of laws in its entirety. "When the commission said that its aim was to reestablish the old laws," Argüelles was to declare later, "it did not mean that the Congress could not deviate from them when it judged it advisable or necessary . . . It did know that the Nation, as a sovereign power, could destroy with one blow all the fundamental laws if the public interest had demanded it. But it also knew that the old Constitution[6] contained the fundamental principles of national well-being, and therefore the commission limited itself to reforming the principal defects it found in the old legislation."[7]

This was essentially what Jovellanos, who unfortunately was not

3. Comellas, "Las Cortes de Cádiz y La Constitución de 1812," *Revista de Estudios Políticos*, cxxvi (November–December, 1962), pp. 94–95; Belda and Labra, pp. 68–95.

4. *Op. cit.*, p. 384.

5. *Apud* Fernández Martín, *Derecho parlamentario español*, ii, p. 664.

6. The term must be understood here as meaning the body of Spanish traditional legislation.

7. Fernández Almagro, p. 86.

destined to see the Constitution enacted,[8] had always wanted. The one thing the great scholar tried to avoid was a break with Spain's past, for he foresaw tragic days for his country if the past were disregarded in any new legislation. If the old edifice was in need of repair, by all means repair it, he had suggested at the time of the Suprema, but do not tear it down. A similar position, though not quite as conservative, was taken by the great historian of Spanish law, Martínez Marina, who in his writings[9] suggested that from Spain's old "Constitution" and from Spain's medieval Cortes should be derived the guidelines for the country's modern legislators.[10] The reformists doubtless made an effort to combine tradition and progress, to preserve as much of the spirit of traditional law as possible, and to adapt it to the extraordinary circumstances in which they found themselves. In the proclamation with which the Cortes addressed the nation on August 28, 1812, we read: "The Holy Religion of your forefathers, the political laws of the former Kingdoms of Spain, her venerable uses and customs, everything has been brought together as a fundamental law in the political Constitution of the Monarchy."[11]

But the product brought forth by the labors of the Constitutional Commission, though preserving some links with Spain's past, was quite different in spirit and form from Spain's historical legislation. The influence of Locke, Rousseau, of eighteenth-century Enlightenment, and of the French Revolution only partly explains this development. Another factor was the difficulty of adapting the past to the needs of the present. Could the state of affairs that had prevailed in the Middle Ages have been restored and made to func-

8. He died in Asturias at the end of 1811. See Chapter XIV.

9. *Ensayo histórico-crítico sobre la antigua legislación y . . . principales cuerpos legales de los reinos de León y de Castilla* (1808), *Discurso sobre el origen de la monarquía y sobre la naturaleza del gobierno español* (1813), *Teoría de las Cortes* (1813), etc.

10. For Martínez Marina, too, "Constitution" meant the body of Spanish traditional legislation (cf. Maravall, "El pensamiento político en España a comienzos del siglo XIX: Martínez Marina," *Revista de Estudios Políticos,* LXXXI, pp. 29–82)

11. *El Español,* October 30, 1812, in CDF, CDXLV, pp. 437–38; Fernández Almagro, p. 85.

tion in the nineteenth century? Could the medieval Cortes, of which Martínez Marina spoke with such enthusiasm,[12] but which normally did not have, at least in Castile, full legislative power,[13] have been made operative when a worm-eaten monarchy had crumbled under the blows of a powerful conqueror, thereby releasing nationalistic forces of unheard-of violence and creating an entirely new state of affairs? What political freedom the Spanish kingdoms may have had during the Middle Ages lay buried under centuries of absolutism, and it is difficult to see how the national assemblies of 1810–1814 could have revived it in its original form. Perhaps the liberals should have made a more determined effort to salvage a more substantial part of traditional law. Perhaps they should have at least attempted to steer their course much more toward renovation than toward innovation.[14] But this would have required the presence and active participation in the commission's work of men of the stature of Jovellanos, who unfortunately could not serve his country in the Cortes.

"It was unfortunate," comments Menéndez y Pelayo, "that a century of absolutist glory . . . and another century of absolutist ineptitude, had made us lose all memory of our old political organization, and it was an illusion to think that in one day it was to rise from its tomb and that the same things were to be reborn with the same names, so that the Cortes of Cádiz might be somewhat similar to the old Cortes of Castile. How and whence was this to emerge? What education, aside from eighteenth-century education, had those leaders received? What social doctrine outside of the *Contrat Social* of Rousseau and Montesquieu's *Esprit des Lois* had they assimilated? . . . The dominating ideas in the new Congress had to be by virtue of an unavoidable historical law the ideas of the eighteenth century, which found there their final expression and were translated into laws."[15]

12. Cf. *Discurso sobre el origen de la monarquía y sobre la naturaleza del gobierno español.*

13. Cf. Pérez Prendes and Muñoz de Arracó, *op. cit.*

14. Cf. Suárez Verdeguer, *Conservadores, innovadores y renovadores en las postrimerías del Antiguo Régimen;* "Sobre las raíces de las reformas de las Cortes de Cádiz," *Revista de Estudios Políticos,* CXXVI, pp. 31–67.

15. *Historia de los heterodoxos españoles,* VII, p. 41. Menéndez y Pelayo does not mention Locke, whose thought also influenced the liberals (cf. Rodríguez Aranda, *op. cit.*).

In at least one area, however, the Cádiz legislators remained strongly faithful to the past. The preservation of religious unity was a cardinal point in the Constitution. Article 12,[16] which was approved without discussion, stated: "The Religion of the Spanish Nation is and shall perpetually be the Roman, Apostolic, Catholic faith, the only true faith. The Nation protects it through wise and just laws and forbids the practice of any other."[17] This may seem surprising in a document which in other aspects broke with Spanish absolutism.[18] But religion was such a vital factor in Spanish society and was so inextricably intertwined with Spain's historical development, that even those liberals who felt that this was a concession to obscurantism and intolerance were forced to give their approval to the article. Argüelles later recalled that "in the area of religion a grave error was committed, which gave rise to great ills but which was inevitable. Religious intolerance was consecrated anew and the worst part of it was that many who gave their approval to Article 12 with the most profound grief were aware of this fact."[19]

Toreno is undoubtedly right when he considers the failure of the liberals to oppose the article a wise move. It was just not possible to argue for religious tolerance at a time when the slogan *El Rey, la Patria y la Religión* had such an irresistible appeal over the face of the country. "With time," writes the Asturian liberal, "with the growth of enlightenment and with the birth of new interests, more moderate ideas in the matter of religion would have spread, and the Spaniards would then have permitted without raising any obstacles the establishment of Protestant temples next to Catholic altars, in the same manner as many of their ancestors had seen during centuries mosques and synagogues close to their churches."[20]

There can be no question but that the liberal majority was wise in not offending the Catholic Church at this juncture. At a time when

16. The Constitution comprised 10 *títulos* or titles, and 384 articles. It is the longest constitution in Spanish history.

17. Cf. *Constitución política de la Monarquía española*, CDF, DCCXLII, pp. 149–70.

18. Foreign liberals were dismayed by article 12 (Toreno, p. 385). It was one of the few articles to be unanimously approved.

19. *Examen histórico de la reforma constitucional*, I, p. 71.

20. *Op. cit.*, p. 385.

serious changes in Spain's political structure were coming under discussion, it would have been highly impolitic to antagonize such a powerful institution as the Church. For the time being it was enough to attack monarchical absolutism in all its aspects. The discussion of Article 3, which constituted a radical weakening of the position of the throne, cast a strong light on the basic ideological difference between liberals and conservatives. "Sovereignty," the article declared in its original form, "resides essentially in the Nation, and to the latter, consequently, belongs the right to establish its fundamental laws and to adopt the form of government best suited to its needs." This principle had already been accepted by the Cortes on September 24, but now the nation's right to give itself its basic laws was spelled out explicitly. Moreover, a new element had been introduced in the last part of the article: The nation considered itself entitled to choose for itself the most appropriate type of government. True, the capacity of the nation to establish its basic legislation implied its capacity to choose its form of government. But again, by emphasizing this possibility, the Constitutional Commission had seemingly extended the power of the nation. Developed to its logical conclusion, this doctrine would mean that Spain under certain circumstances might very well choose a republican form of government.

The debate on Article 3 did not last long in comparison with the discussion on the decree providing for the extinction of *señoríos*, but was pregnant with arguments pro and con and with contained passion. It was, from the political point of view, perhaps the most important provision in the whole constitutional project. On August 28, 1811, the conservative deputy for Valencia, Borrull, affirmed that only when the nation was bereft of all its sovereigns could it give itself the government it chose. This had been the case at the time of the Moorish invasion. But then the Christians who had sought refuge in the fastnesses of the Asturian mountains had adopted the monarchy, naming Pelayo as their king. Ever since, Spain had been a monarchy, and as long as there were heirs apparent, they were automatically entitled to the crown of their forbears. He also pointed to the contradiction between the solemn oath administered by the Cortes to the Regency, which underlined the preservation of the monarchical form of government, and the article under discussion, which gave the nation the right to choose the type of government it found most advisable. He furthermore disputed the assertion that the nation could by itself establish its legislative framework. It simply could not do so, since Spanish fundamental legislation had been extant for centuries. Furthermore, the King was a captive in enemy land, and in his absence no curtailment in his legislative power could be carried out.

The conservative deputy Morales Gallego did admit that sovereignty resided in the nation, but objected to the adverb "essentially." Opposed to the doctrine of the social contract, he put it to the assembly that societies were not formed by any pacts or agreements, but by the authority of patriarchs who exercised a decisive influence on their families and friends. Furthermore, in Spanish history the king had always had a large share in enacting the laws. Finally, how could the deputies swear allegiance to their sovereign Fernando — which they had done on September 24, 1810 — and now proclaim that sovereignty resided essentially in the nation?[21]

The Bishop of Calahorra, another traditionalist, recognized that in primitive times, before a determined form of government was established, the power to govern had resided in the community. But then, since some form of government is indispensable in any society, men chose specific political structures. Spain, since the times of the Goths, had been a monarchy, elective at first, hereditary after the twelfth century, in which the king, anointed and consecrated by the Church, exercised the supreme authority over his subjects. The Spanish people had transferred all sovereignty to the monarch, but the laws which he had sworn to uphold constituted a brake on his authority, as did the Cortes, without whose consent his decrees were invalid. This sovereignty which had once been alienated to the king could not be recovered by the nation.[22] The king is sovereign but must

21. *Diario de las discusiones y actas de las Cortes*, August 28, 1811, VIII, in CDF, LXIX, pp. 54–58.

22. The doctrine according to which the nation cannot regain the sovereignty it once delegated to its monarchs was not invented by the conservatives in the Cortes, but is found in Spanish political writing throughout the sixteenth and seventeenth centuries, in works like the *Idea de un príncipe político-cristiano representada en cien empresas* by Diego de Saavedra Fajardo (1584–1648).

observe the fundamental laws of the realm. Yes, the Bishop would agree to have the monarch fulfill the obligations which he had undertaken, and he saw no harm in some limitation on monarchical authority in the areas of justice, taxes, and administration. "In one word, let the Cortes gather frequently and let them deal energetically with the question of the observance of the Constitution. Let the king be told about the infractions the law has suffered, and the arbitrariness of the monarch will be subjected to a powerful brake, but let the king have the benefit of his sovereignty."[23]

On the liberal side, Toreno countered with arguments strongly flavored by the ideology of Rousseau. "What is the nation?" he asked rhetorically. "The union of all Spaniards of both hemispheres. And these men called Spaniards, why are they gathered in society? They are gathered like all men in other societies for their preservation and happiness. And how will they live securely and happily? By being masters of their fate, by maintaining always the right to establish whatever they consider useful to and advisable for the common good. And can they . . . yield or alienate this right? No, because they would give up their happiness, alienate their existence and change its form. This is something which is neither possible nor in their power to do." He ended his speech by reminding his listeners that the nation had proved that it was sovereign when it had refused to obey the orders of Napoleon and had "risen to resist oppression and give the world proof of the Spaniards' valor, constancy and love of independence."[24]

The next day, Juan Nicasio Gallego, the liberal priest representing Zamora, friend of Quintana and author of the famous poem *Dos de mayo*, took up the cudgels for the concept of national sovereignty. Again, the influence of Rousseau was strongly felt. "A nation is already a nation," declared Gallego, "before it establishes its constitutional laws and adopts a form of government." And what is the nation? An association of free men who have voluntarily formed a "moral body," which must be ruled by laws. These in turn derive from the will of the individuals making up the nation, and their sole function is the well-being and smooth working of society. With

23. *Diario de las discusiones y actas de las Cortes,* August 28, 1811, VIII, in CDF, LXIX, pp. 58–62.
24. *Ibid.,* pp. 64–67.

inexorable logic the clergyman-poet insisted that this nation, having freely contracted certain obligations toward itself, could annul these as soon as it saw that they prevented it from achieving happiness. And happiness, Gallego pointed out, was in the final analysis the only object for which they had been established. Therefore the nation could never alienate its essential sovereignty, for if it did, it would deprive itself of the means of promoting its happiness, and this would of course be an absurdity.

Faithful in many respects to the foundations of eighteenth-century philosophy, the deputy for Zamora and his colleagues made the concept of happiness and the pursuit of happiness an important ingredient of their political ideology. The individual must be given the broadest possible opportunity to develop his potentialities, for only thus would he be able to attain the basic aim of all human activities, happiness. And what applied to the individual also applied to society, which is formed by individuals. Any political structure erected by society must be designed to place this fundamental goal within easy reach of the individuals who have chosen to live together. Thus thought the liberals of the Cádiz Cortes, but thus had also thought the leaders of the North American Revolution.

"Gentlemen," sighed Gallego, "it is annoying to have to expound these truths which are the ABC of Public Law." But in case the deputies were still not convinced, well, here was a concrete example: The Cortes themselves, having gathered with the intention of fulfilling their obligations, had been forced to enact laws to rule themselves. These were agreed upon in the form of regulations governing procedures to be followed in the daily business of the assembly. And of course, whenever the congress felt that these rules were no longer meeting its requirements, it obviously had the right to change them. In the same manner, the nation, being entirely sovereign, was free to change its basic laws. "And finally," exclaimed Gallego, "with what power and what object are we enacting laws and discussing a constitution if the king may destroy it with a decree as soon as he arrives? All this is illegitimate and nil if the Nation is not essentially sovereign."[25] Alas, little did the good priest realize then how prophetic the first phrase was! His confidence in the power of a vote to establish this cherished sovereignty once and for all and to keep the king in

25. *Ibid.*, August 29, 1811, pp. 67–70.

check, which in the end proved to be completely unfounded, was of course the result of illusions shared unfortunately by most members of the liberal majority.

Another liberal, Colonel Francisco Fernández Golfín, representing Extremadura, who played a leading role in the Cortes of 1810–1814 as well as in the Constitutional period of 1820–1823,[26] placed more emphasis than his colleagues on the last part of Article 3, which stipulated that the nation was free to choose the most suitable form of government. He rejected the contention that this principle was already contained in the first part, which spoke of the nation's sovereignty and right to enact its fundamental legislation. The statement concerning the type of government to be chosen by the Spanish people was indispensable to provide for the moment when some changes in the relationship between king and nation were deemed essential.[27]

From the extreme left, back to the right with the Bishop of Calahorra, and then to the extreme right with Don Pedro Inguanzo y Rivero, representing Asturias, who later was to rise to the exalted position of archbishop of Toledo. The Asturian clergyman, whose erudition and logic compared favorably with the best the liberals had to offer, directed his fire first at the proposal that the Spanish people could henceforth choose the form of government that suited them best. If this doctrine was accepted, then the Cortes would become the prey of intrigues and internecine strife, which could force frequent changes in the Constitution and in the political structure that had been adopted. Furthermore, sovereignty was not an authority that could be exclusively applied to Spain. What effect would the sovereignty of the Spanish nation have on relations between Spain and other European nations? Would it be wise to adopt a theory that might provoke the resentment and aversion of other governments?[28]

26. He was minister of war during the second constitutional period. In 1831, after having joined the uprising led by Torrijos, he was captured with the latter and a number of other revolutionaries, and shot.

27. *Diario de las discusiones* . . . , August 29, 1811, VIII, in CDF, LXIX, pp. 74–75.

28. Very prophetic in a sense, for this is exactly what happened in 1823. After Spain had brought off a constitutional revolution, European absolutism intervened that year to restore the absolute power of Fernando VII.

Should Spain be the only nation in Europe to raise this revolutionary standard? Was the example of what happened to France during the Revolution not sufficiently repelling? Did history itself not show that the doctrine of popular sovereignty brought disaster to the people? Besides, who demanded this sovereignty with loud cries? Was it the peasants, the artisans, the lower classes, who after all constituted the majority of the people? No, the mass of the people only acted when driven by an impulse received from outside their ranks. Sometimes the people acted "like a pupil who is led by the hand, at other times like an enraged individual, if the fire of insurrection is lit. Even when they choose their representatives, they only do so because they are ordered to do so, and they normally do so without knowing what they do, nor what the object [of the elections] is." Inguanzo unfortunately understood better than his liberal opponents the mechanism which often governs popular elections, but he was forgetting that under certain circumstances the people are quite capable of rising spontaneously against unbearable oppression.

The idea of the social pact was very fine in theory, admitted Inguanzo, but could a nation revert to this initial state without a bloody revolution? It was a beautiful ideal, but it was impossible in practice. Moreover, there was no precedent whatever in the body of traditional Spanish law for the system of sovereignty now under discussion. True, Spanish monarchy had at one time been elective, but the right to elect any authority does not prove that the electors are in possession of that authority. If this were true, then the spiritual sovereignty of the pope resided in the college of cardinals, and before this it resided essentially in the clergy. "I repeat, gentlemen," declared the Asturian conservative toward the end of his discourse, "the Spanish people are docile and humble. They have blindly obeyed the great number of governments which have ruled in the course of this revolution.[29] They obey the Cortes with even greater pleasure, as an institution deriving from their will. They have no need to be shown the origin of the authority whence the decisions made by the government emanate. As a matter of fact, subjecting them to the scrutiny of their sovereignty might have an effect

29. Referring to the War of Independence.

opposite to the one sought, since . . . we might be left without any power to exercise anywhere."[30]

Unfortunately for the conservative cause the traditionalists could not marshal the oratorical and debating skill which their opponents could bring into battle at a moment's notice. Against one Inguanzo[31] and a few other men versed in debate, the liberals could always hurl their powerful team of Argüelles, Toreno, Muñoz Torrero, Villanueva, Gallego, García Herreros, and so on. Supporting one another ceaselessly, relieving one another at crucial moments, always ready to jump into the breach, they complemented each other brilliantly and to their superb teamwork as well as to the absence of similar activity and teamwork on the traditionalist side must be ascribed the many parliamentary successes the liberal cause won in the Cortes.[32]

In a masterful rebuttal of Inguanzo's arguments, Muñoz Torrero turned to the concrete situation of the struggle for independence. "Napoleon, supposing that all the rights of the nation belonged solely to the royal family, forced the latter to renounce them, and by virtue of this fact claims to have acquired a legitimate right to give us a constitution and to establish the government of Spain without considering the general will of the Nation." The real substance of Article 3 was therefore simply an affirmation of Spain's inalienable right not to recognize the government of Napoleon's brother, for it was exclusively up to the Spanish nation to determine its fundamental legislation and the form of its government. And as for this last point, there was really no problem. The Spanish nation had chosen in remote times the moderate monarchy as the system which best suited its needs, and since the nation now wanted to restore the state of affairs that had prevailed in the Middle Ages, when the king had shared legislative power with the Cortes, no deputy had the right to

30. *Ibid.*, pp. 77–83.

31. Actually, Inguanzo took only a small part in the debate on the constitutional project. Felipe Aner and Jaime Creus, both representing Catalonia, intervened most actively on the conservative side with forty-one and twenty-four speeches respectively (Comellas, "Las Cortes de Cádiz y la constitución de 1812," *Revista de Estudios Políticos,* cxxvi, p. 96).

32. A factor in liberal superiority during the debate on the constitutional project was the rule allowing members of the Constitutional Commission to take the floor without awaiting their turn (Comellas, *ibid.*).

oppose the national will and suggest that there be a change in the form of government. Skillfully Muñoz Torrero had played on the two themes with which the liberals hoped to gain the full support of a majority of all Spaniards: The principle of popular sovereignty was a powerful weapon in the struggle against the imposition of an unwanted ruler by a foreign aggressor, and the proposed Constitution, far from being a break with the past, continued the medieval tradition. There was, of course, much truth in the first of these assertions, but it was by no means the whole truth. Certainly, the idea of the supremacy of the nation contributed to harnessing the people's energies in their indomitable fight against Napoleon, but it could just as easily be turned against Spain's monarch. And the point was not lost on traditionalist Spain, no matter how hard the liberals tried to soft-pedal this aspect of the matter. As for the second of these *leitmotifs*, the link between the new instrument of government and Spain's medieval institutions was at best a tenuous one.

Finally it came to a vote. The first part of Article 3, dealing with national sovereignty and the legislative power of the nation, was approved by an overwhelming vote of 128 to 24. The last part, stating that the nation could adopt the form of government it saw fit, was eliminated from the Constitution by 87 votes against 63.[33] A comparison of both votes suggests that the great majority of representatives could calmly declare itself in favor of the principle of national sovereignty, since the qualms of the majority could be allayed—at least temporarily—with arguments pointing to the existence of a precedent for this doctrine in Spanish history and the affirmation of national sovereignty implicit in the uprising against Napoleon. The rejection of the last phrase, on the other hand, is more indicative of the true strength of advanced liberal thinking in the Cortes. Among the 87 voting for elimination, there were doubtless a number of deputies who considered that the phrase was merely redundant and not needed, since the statement to the effect that the nation had the right to legislate could be interpreted as implying that it could establish the political structure it considered most appropriate to its needs. But there must have been a substantial number of

33. *Diario de las discusiones y actas de las Cortes,* August 29, 1811, VIII, in CDF, LXIX, pp. 83–86.

representatives who felt that while the first part of the article did not constitute a danger for the monarchical form of the Spanish government,[34] the last words left the door open to changes in this basic political aspect of Spanish life. The 63 men who voted in favor of retaining the last part,[35] while not necessarily harboring republican sentiments, except perhaps in a small number of cases, constituted the really revolutionary element in the national assembly.

Few articles in the Constitution of 1812 are of more import for the understanding of modern Spanish history than Article 3, though debate on it was relatively short. Other articles were discussed over a longer period. This was the case of Articles 18 and 22, which by implication withheld full Spanish citizenship from inhabitants of the Spanish dominions who were free but of African origin, and granted them this right only if they met certain requirements in the area of morals and mores. It is surprising that the liberal majority, so imbued with high ethical principles, did not vote as one man to include persons of Negro origin in the citizenry.[36] Muñoz Torrero parried attacks on the Constitutional Commission's position by distinguishing between civil rights and political rights. Persons of African descent would automatically enjoy the former but not necessarily the latter.[37] It was the reactionary Ostolaza who on this point adopted an attitude more in accordance with enlightened thinking than that of many liberals. "I did not think," said Ostolaza, "that there would be so much difficulty in sanctioning ideas which are so eminently just and that . . . the protectors of exalted liberalism should be the ones most

34. Since the Cortes had made it clear on other occasions that it was determined to preserve the throne in the person of Fernando VII.

35. Which read: y de adoptar la forma de gobierno que más le convenga.

36. Nor did the Cortes decree the elimination of slavery. Article 5 defined the status of Spaniards—this status did not necessarily guarantee all the rights of full citizenship—as being enjoyed by (1) all free men born and residing in the dominions of Spain, as well as their children; (2) foreigners who had been granted naturalization by the Cortes; (3) those who without naturalization had been allowed by law to reside for ten years in any town of the realm; (4) freedmen, as soon as they were granted freedom in the Spanish territories. The last Hispanic stronghold of Negro slavery, Cuba, did not see the end of this institution until 1885.

37. Diario de las discusiones . . . , September 6, 1811, VIII, CDF, LXIX, pp. 204–205.

fiercely opposed to this measure . . . Read History and the chronicles and you will find men famous for their virtue and talents . . . who are descendants of slaves . . . Will you discriminate against them because they are African in origin?"[38]

When the long constitutional debate finally ended toward the end of January, 1812, the Cortes had approved an imposing document consisting of 10 chapters and 384 articles. The *Constitución doceañista*[39] as it was called, while preserving a few aspects of traditional Spanish political and social structure, constituted nonetheless a revolutionary step in Spain's historical development. It broke the absolutist line followed by Spain in preceding centuries and transformed the country into a constitutional, hereditary monarchy. It provided for a unicameral national assembly meeting yearly for a three-month session in the capital, whose deputies were to be elected by equal electoral districts of 70,000 souls, on the basis of residential manhood suffrage. The power to legislate would reside in the Cortes with the king (Art. 15), while the executive power would reside in the king[40] and the judicial in the judges. There were many restrictions on the monarch's authority: He could not impede the convocation of the Cortes; leave the kingdom without the assent of the Cortes (if he did, it would be understood that he had abdicated); abdicate without the consent of the Cortes; enter into an alliance or commercial treaty without this consent; marry without permission of the congress (if he did, it meant abdication, Art. 172). The Constitution created seven secretaries, for the departments of Foreign Affairs, Interior, Colonies, Grace and Justice, Finance, War, and Navy respectively (Art. 222), who would be responsible to the Cortes. All former Spanish councils were abolished. However, there was to be a Council of State composed of forty persons chosen by the Cortes (Art. 231). Personal security and property were guaranteed. All citizens were equal before the law, but a special judicial status was maintained in the case of military men and the clergy. Taxes were to be paid by all Spaniards in proportion to their capacity, and no

38. *Ibid.*, September 7, 1811, pp. 239–40.

39. *Doceañista* (from *año doce*), meaning "of the year '12" (1812).

40. The royal veto was automatically overridden if the Cortes upheld a law at the third successive session (Art. 149).

privileges were recognized in this field—a vital socioeconomic change in Spanish life (Art. 339). Finally, primary schools were to be established in all towns of the realm, in which children would be taught to read and write as well as the rudiments of arithmetic and religious catechism (Art. 366).

The Constitution brought into being a new unitarian nation, with no place for variations in law and authority on a geographical basis. It provided for uniform education and uniform political representation. It did away with the peculiar fusion of administrative and judicial powers that had characterized the institutions of the Spain of the *Ancien Régime*. It preserved the traditional and unique position the Catholic church had always enjoyed, but in place of a monarchy deriving its authority from God Himself it established a monarchy with a king whose once immense power had been drastically curtailed.

This Constitution was sooner or later bound to arouse considerable opposition, but since conservative deputies in the assembly had not really put up a systematic fight for their ideals, most of the articles had been passed by large majorities. Even Rafael de Vélez, the author of the ferocious antiliberal *Apología del altar y del trono*,[41] who was the first to draw a parallel between the *Constitución doceañista* and the French Constitution of 1791,[42] admitted that in Cádiz, at least, "hope was general and enthusiasm universal" at the time of the Constitution's proclamation.[43]

Bitter antagonism between the two factions in the Cortes developed only after the signing of the Constitution. But strong opposition to reformist legislation and to liberal thinking in the country had actually come earlier from some quarters outside the congress. Later, as the split within the Cortes became deeper, antiliberal attacks outside of the assembly grew apace. We have seen how the Bishop of Orense had refused to accept the principle of national sovereignty and had in the end only bowed to severe pressure from the congress.[44] After the promulgation of the Constitution a new and more

41. Published in Madrid in 1818.
42. *Op. cit.*, Vol. ii, pp. 173–96.
43. *Ibid.*, pp. 117–18.
44. See Chapter X.

bitter conflict arose between the assembly and the "slovenly and obstinate old man," as Alcalá Galiano, himself a liberal, described the Bishop.[45] A written declaration bearing his signature stated his willingness to swear loyalty to the Constitution and to have it observed in his diocese, but in view of a number of objectionable aspects he found in it, he reserved the right to demand at a later date revisions in the document. The Cortes, angered by this challenging attitude, declared the Bishop unworthy of the name of Spaniard, deprived him of all honors and income of civil origin, and issued orders for his immediate expulsion from Spain. This was made official by a decree promulgated on August 17. The Bishop went into exile to neighboring Portugal, and from there addressed a protest to the Regency dated September 20, 1812, in which he denied having refused obedience to the authority of the Cortes. He had sworn loyalty to the Constitution but had made public his dislike of its tenor. But was this such a crime? Not without logic Don Pedro de Quevedo y Quintano observed: "If the Bishop does not love the Constitution he loves his nation and since the Constitution has been accepted and established by it, and since it is a law of the state, and as long as it is, he will have it observed and will observe it himself . . . Can anyone ask more of him? What does it matter to the nation or to the Congress . . . whether the Bishop loves or fails to love the Constitution, as long as he bows to it and observes it faithfully?"[46]

This action against the Bishop of Orense as well as the previous struggle between him and the Cortes could not fail to cause conservatives throughout Spain to rally to the support of the old prelate. An example of this support is furnished by the pamphlet entitled *Important and Urgent Notice to the Spanish Nation. An Impartial View of Its Cortes*, which saw the light in La Coruña in 1811 and was

45. *Memorias*, I, p. 268.
46. *Diario de las discusiones y actas de las Cortes*, August 15, 1812, XIV, in CDF, LXXIV, pp. 387–403; *Representación del Obispo de Orense a la Regencia de España*, CDF, CDXLV, pp. 494–99. The punishment visited upon the Bishop of Orense derived from a proposition passed during the session of August 15 at the initiative of Argüelles, by a vote of 84 to 29, to the effect that whoever refused to swear unreserved loyalty to the Constitution would be deprived of the title of Spaniard and of his honors and income, and expelled from Spain within twenty-four hours.

reprinted in Madrid in 1815.[47] The author gave his unqualified support to the Bishop, whom he termed a "prelate as erudite as he is religious and possessed of a delicate conscience." At the same time he blasted the Cortes for stepping far beyond the limits that had been set for it. Instead of confining itself to providing weapons, money, and men for the war and appointing an executive body with sovereign power, made up of few men, the Cortes had arrogated supreme power to itself and had proceeded to change the social structure of Spain, to "take the dregs from the bottom of the glass and place them on top."[48] The reaction of the Cortes was to order the seizure of the pamphlet and its scrutiny by a special court which had been set up by the assembly to deal with activities and utterances of a subversive nature.[49]

This tribunal had been established after the furor aroused in the Cortes by the publication of a violent diatribe against the congress by the ex-regent Don Miguel de Lardizábal y Uribe. The pamphlet,[50] which had been printed in Alicante in September, 1811 and read in the Cortes on October 14, claimed that the assembly was dominated by a faction of alternate deputies and attacked the powers it had given itself and the measures that had been passed so far. It vehemently denied the validity of the doctrine of national sovereignty and declared that all supreme power resided in the king. The nation had no right to take back this authority it had once granted its sovereign.[51]

The special tribunal also looked into the case of the pamphlet by the dean of the Council of Castile, Don José Colón, *España vindicada en sus clases y autoridades de las falsas opiniones que se le atribuyen.*[52]

47. *Aviso importante y urgente a la nación española. Juicio imparcial de sus Cortes.* See Chapter X.

48. CDF, Vol. CDLXIII, p. 48.

49. Artola, I, p. 439.

50. *Manifiesto que presenta a la nación el consejero de Estado Don Miguel de Lardizábal y Uribe, uno de los cinco que compusieron el Supremo Consejo de Regencia de España e Indias sobre su conducta política en la noche del 24 de septiembre de 1810.*

51. Cf. *Colección de los decretos,* II, in CDF, LXXVIII, pp. 17–18; Toreno, pp. 393–95; Argüelles, I, pp. 99–100; Artola, I, pp. 435–37.

52. A rather free translation would be "Spain's Classes and Authorities Defended Against the Calumnies Hurled at Them."

The document, printed in Cádiz at about the same time as Lardizábal's *Manifiesto*, severely criticized the general work of the Cortes. The failure to include the traditional class division in the national representation and to limit the assembly's work to dealing with the war effort, and especially the administration of justice and of provincial government, came under scorching attack.[53]

In August, 1812, the special court condemned Lardizábal to exile while the other two pamphlets which had aroused the ire of the congress were simply referred to the magistrates of the towns where they had been published.[54] The high-handed action of the Cortes in dealing with outside antagonisms not through the means they themselves had established for such cases[55] but through the creation of a special court, which had handed down a sentence of exile against Lardizábal, and through immediate banishment, in the case of the Bishop of Orense, was found to arouse the bitter opposition of the conservatives and to deepen the division between *liberales* and *serviles*. But even men who otherwise shared much of the liberal ideology were repelled by the spectacle of the legislative body, which at least in some cases was shunning constitutional processes and was imposing its will in a manner somehow reminiscent of the despotism it had vowed to eliminate. Blanco-White, then residing in London, himself a partisan of reform though generally disapproving of the work of the Cortes, condemned in *El Español* the treatment accorded to Orense and Lardizábal. "Not even an assassin," he wrote in the issue of November 30, "caught flagrante delicto, should be sentenced in the manner with which the Cortes sentenced the Bishop of Orense; not even a traitor should be handed over to a special commission, as was the case with Lardizábal."[56]

Vocal, too, in condemning the work of the Cortes, was the conservative press in Cádiz. Among the traditionalist newspapers the most virulently antireformist was the *Censor General*. In its pages insults were hurled at liberal papers and attack after attack was published against the new ideas, the Cortes, and the Constitution.[57]

53. Toreno, p. 395; Argüelles, I, p. 108; Artola, I, pp. 438–39.

54. Artola, I, p. 440.

55. See Chapter X.

56. CDF, CDXLV, p. 485.

57. Solís, pp. 466–68.

The daily *Procurador General de la Nación y el Rey* was another paladin of king and altar.[58] In its issue of November 3, 1812, it published a thinly veiled attack on the liberals for "spreading new ideas and doctrines unknown to our forefathers," for "launching flanking attacks on the divine religion of our ancestors," and for "discrediting our magistrates." In a later number, speaking of the Constitution, it purported to praise what it considered the "true spirit" of the document, but expressed fears that the mass of the people would misunderstand the Constitution, misunderstand the concept of liberty, and interpret it as paving the way for revolt against legitimate laws and authority. This basic misinterpretation was constantly encouraged by the "innovators," who were telling the people that "kings are not patriarchs but tyrants of the Fatherland, that their authority is based exclusively on force backed up by superstition to keep the masses enslaved." The author of the article would have liked to see this liberal propaganda prevented from being printed, but since he was not in a position to do this he would limit himself to warning all Spaniards against this "seduction."[59]

There was a strange aspect to the publication of this conservative newspaper. The liberals were dismayed to discover that this same organ which continuously lambasted them was in fact financed by the Regency.[60] The five-man executive had from the beginning of its term in office been at best lukewarm in its attitude toward the Cortes. After Count La Bisbal resigned in the summer of 1812 and the reactionary Don Juan Pérez Villamil[61] took his place, friction between the executive and legislative bodies increased considerably. This finally led to the removal of the Regency in March, 1813, and to the appointment of a new, three-member executive.[62]

58. It began publication on October 1, 1812, and ended publication in Madrid in April, 1815 (Gómez Imaz, *Los periódicos durante la guerra de la independencia*, p. 238).

59. CDF, CXXVI, pp. 73–75, 282–86.

60. Solís, p. 495.

61. The man who had drawn up the proclamation of the mayors of Móstoles in May, 1808, and author in the same year of the *Carta sobre el modo de establecer el Consejo de Regencia del Reino con arreglo a nuestra constitución*. In this pamphlet he had shown an inclination for reform, but had become more and more conservative since then. See Chapter VII.

62. Cardinal Luis de Borbón, Don Pedro Agar, and Don Gabriel Císcar.

Opposition, finally, also came from the British Embassy in Cádiz. Ambassador Wellesley, in a secret letter written in September, 1812, attacked the liberals for their hostility to England, which he attributed to the influence of French ideas in their political education. Earlier his brother, the general, had written one of the deputies suggesting among other things the appointment of a regent of royal blood who would be granted all the powers reserved for the king, and the transformation of the Council of State into a chamber of landowners or grandees. What was wanted in British quarters was nothing less than a political structure modeled on the one ruling Great Britain at that very time.[63]

[2]

While debates in the Cortes in the period between the opening of the sessions in September, 1810, and the promulgation of the Constitution in March, 1812, gradually sharpened the division between liberals and conservatives, positions had not hardened to the point where it would be justified to speak of bitter antagonism. Reforms had usually been voted by wide majorities, which often, as in the case of the abolition of *señoríos*, had assumed overwhelming proportions. True, outside the Cortes, in free Spain, *señores* whose privileges had been eliminated, churchmen who did not like the decree of freedom of the press, conservative supporters of Orense and Lardizábal dismayed by the attitude of the Cortes toward these two men in 1811, were doubtless disgruntled by the time the Constitution was signed. But on the one hand, ultraconservative opposition in the Cortes was limited, by March, 1812, to at most 20-odd deputies, out of a potential vote of 50 conservatives. Lines were not at all clearly drawn between moderate conservatives and moderate liberals, and about 20 moderate conservatives had often voted for reforms—depending on the issue. On the other hand, dissent in the unoccupied zones, though strong in some quarters, had not yet truly crystallized into systematic opposition.

63. Artola, I, pp. 454–56.

Much of this changed after the signing of the Constitution, and for good reason. The liberals finally came into open collision with the most cohesive force of Spanish traditionalism, the Catholic Church, specifically over the issue of the Inquisition. Perhaps this could have been avoided with a little more caution on the part of the reformists. But the fact is that it did happen, and when it happened debates in the Cortes acquired an increasingly acrimonious tone and throughout free Spain dissension turned into bitter conflict. Moreover, the head-on clash between reform and Church brought many moderates into the traditionalist camp, thus greatly damaging the liberal cause. In the Cortes, liberals and a number of conservatives could still vote together on many matters not related to the Church, but on the fundamental issue of the Inquisition, which, even when not discussed, hovered over the assembly from April, 1812 on, the split would be decisive. When the matter finally came to a vote the liberal majority was considerably reduced and the true strength of liberalism and conservatism in the Cortes was revealed.[64]

Though the official struggle with the Church began after the proclamation of the Constitution, many preliminary skirmishes had been fought outside the congress ever since 1810. After the enactment of the decree ordering freedom of the press a number of liberal pamphlets and newspapers expressed openly anticlerical opinions. Conservative press and pamphlets blasted what they considered the heretical posture of their opponents, and beginning in July, 1811, demanded the reactivation of the Inquisition.[65] Liberals, on the other hand, clamored for its abolition.[66]

The Dominican preacher Francisco de Alvarado, writing from

---

64. See below.

65. The Suprema had appointed the Bishop of Orense inquisitor general. But only the pope could name inquisitors-general, whose names were presented to Rome by the kings of Spain, and communications with the Holy See had been interrupted. Furthermore, the previous inquisitor, Ramón José de Arce, who was collaborating with the French, was still alive, and though it was said he had resigned in 1808, it was not known whether the pope had accepted the resignation. For all these reasons, though the Council of the Inquisition had been reestablished by the Regency, the institution was in suspense (Toreno, p. 411).

66. *Ibid.*, p. 411; Menéndez y Pelayo, *Historia de los heterodoxos españoles,* VII, pp. 47–48; Solís, pp. 328–40.

Tavira, Portugal, under the pseudonym of El Filósofo Rancio (The Rancid Philosopher), fanned the raging polemic with his *Cartas críticas* to the deputy Francisco Rodríguez de la Bárcena. For Alvarado all evils stemmed from the French philosophers and from the Enlightenment, and Spain would not be happy until it enabled the Inquisition to "cleanse it of philosophers in the same manner as it had cleansed it of Jews."[67] In his letter of June 9, 1811, he defended the Inquisition's role, claiming that it had always been very slow in accepting denunciations, that its prisoners had been well treated and that few burnings had occurred.[68] A similar position was later taken by the Capuchin Fray Rafael de Vélez, the future bishop of Ceuta, in the treatise entitled *Preservativo contra la irreligión*[69] published in Madrid in 1813. Vélez thundered against eighteenth-century French philosophers and lumped them with Luther and Calvin as enemies of religion. The war was, according to him, essentially a war of "philosophy" against Spain and its sacred institutions. "Spaniards," he concluded, "neither France nor its philosophy will ever rule us."[70]

Liberal pamphlets and newspapers countered with their own flood of abuse the vituperations of their opponents. In Cádiz, newspapers like *El Conciso, El Duende, El Robespierre Español, La Abeja Española* hammered away at traditionalism and at the Church. Often their anticlericalism shocked even many liberals. This was the case of the opinions set down in *La Triple Alianza*, which was published on the Isla de León in February, 1811.[71] The impious tone of its second issue so horrified a good number of liberals in the Cortes that they agreed to have the matter referred to the Inquisition, in spite of the provisions of the decree on freedom of the press, stipulating that in matters of religion, censorship should be exercised by bishops. How-

67. *Op. cit.,* Vol. I, p. 37.

68. *Ibid.,* pp. 65–122.

69. The complete title is *Preservativo contra la irreligión o los planes de la filosofía contra la religión y el estado, realizados por la Francia para subyugar la Europa, seguidos por Napoleón en la conquista de España y dados a luz por algunos de nuestros sabios en perjuicio de nuestra patria.*

70. *Op. cit.,* p. 213.

71. The author was Don Manuel Alzáibar, an intimate friend of the deputy José Mexía. Alzáibar claimed that death was a necessary phenomenon of nature and attacked the doctrine of the immortality of the soul (Toreno, p. 411; Solís, p. 484; Menéndez y Pelayo, VII, p. 47).

ever, since the Inquisition had not been functioning since the beginning of the war, a commission of five was appointed to clear away obstacles to the reestablishment of the Holy Office.[72]

On April 22, 1812, the conservatives launched their great offensive to bring back the Inquisition in full force. The occasion was the scandal created in Cádiz by the publication of the *Diccionario crítico-burlesco*, whose author was the librarian of the Cortes, Bartolomé José Gallardo, a native of Extremadura, an arch-liberal and a great bibliographer. The *Diccionario*, in part a violent anticlerical satire which even liberals like Toreno condemned,[73] was the answer to a conservative attack on the reformists, entitled *Diccionario razonado, manual para inteligencia de ciertos escritores que por equivocación han nacido en España*,[74] which had been published toward the middle of 1811.[75] The *Diccionario crítico-burlesco* had come out on April 15, and a week later the author landed in jail after the Provincial Censorship Junta of Cádiz had condemned the tract as "atro-

72. Toreno, *ibid*. The commission was made up of the Bishop of Mallorca, Valiente, Gutiérrez de la Huerta, Pérez de la Puebla, and surprisingly, Muñoz Torrero. A majority of this body was favorable to the reactivation of the Inquisition, but because of rising sentiment in Cádiz against the age-old institution, the commission's report remained pigeonholed for many months (Toreno, p. 412).

73. *Ibid.*, p. 410. Although Toreno denies it (pp. 410–11), many liberal friends of Gallardo probably encouraged him to write it, but later became frightened by the violent reaction to its publication (cf. Jerónimo Gallardo y de Font, *Proceso de D. Bartolomé Gallardo y Blanco por su diccionario crítico-burlesco (1812–1813). Publicaciones del Congreso Histórico Internacional de la guerra de la independencia y su epoca (1807–1815)*, Vol. III, pp. 105–139).

74. "Itemized Dictionary, Manual for the Use of Certain Writers Who Were Born in Spain by Mistake."

75. It was attributed to the deputies Freire-Castrillón and Pastor Pérez. A sample of this pamphlet's style is provided by its definition of despotism: "Despotism: Any form of government which tries to limit the freedom to speak, write and act to their heart's content of certain privileged beings, sublime and strong spirits who were born to teach, direct and command despotically their fellow-men" (CDF, CXXXIII, p. 7). Or by the definition of liberty: "Liberty: In the philosophical sense it is the power of man to say, do, think and print and write freely to his heart's content without restraint or subjection to any law; to render to God the cult he wishes and in the manner he wants or does not want to render it; to have the right to be a Catholic, a Deist, an Atheist, a Moor, a Jew, without anyone stopping him" (*ibid.*, p. 13). These principles, which today are built into the institutions of the Western democracies, were of course anathema to Spanish traditionalists.

ciously subversive . . . and insulting to different Ministers of the Ecclesiastic Hierarchy and Religious orders."[76]

The attack of the *serviles* almost succeeded. The long-delayed report of the commission on the reestablishment of the Inquisition was read at the request of Don Francisco Riesco, inquisitor of the tribunal of Llerena, who received thunderous applause from antireformist spectators in the galleries. The commission's verdict was favorable to the reactivation of the Holy Office.[77] The liberals, realizing that a "triumph of the Inquisition would completely undermine the reforms that had been passed and foreshadow persecutions and the complete collapse of the reformist party,"[78] made desperate efforts to stave off defeat. They were saved by a motion by Nicasio Gallego to have the whole problem referred to the Constitutional Commission. This had been made possible by a decision of the Cortes in December, 1811, to the effect that any proposal dealing with matters covered by the Constitution could not come up for discussion on the floor without the Constitutional Commission having previously determined that it was not incompatible with any of the articles which had been approved.[79]

Thereafter, seeing their initial plan frustrated, the conservatives concentrated their fury on Gallardo. In the bitter and noisy session of July 21, in which the gallery lent its support to the liberals, Ostolaza demanded that the Supreme Censorship Junta take up the matter of the *Diccionario crítico-burlesco*. The clergyman Lera demanded that given the nature of the tract, ecclesiastic authorities be allowed to try the librarian. It had not been proved that the pamphlet opposed Catholic dogma, answered Toreno, implying that there was

76. Gallardo y Font, *op. cit.*, pp. 112–13. Gallardo was released from jail on July 16, 1812. In March, 1813, he was sentenced to pay the costs of the trial and on the twentieth of the month the ten copies of the work which had been seized were burned (*ibid.*, pp. 132–34). No other action was taken against the author, who no doubt owed this leniency to the protection of most liberals in the Cortes. An example of Gallardo's style: "*Fanaticism* [religious fanaticism, that is]: A psycho-moral disease, a cruel and almost desperate illness . . . It is a canine madness which sets the entrails on fire (*op. cit.*, i, p. 40). . . . *Friars:* There are good friars . . . But bad friars . . . have always been the plague of nations. They are filthy animals . . . liked by bigoted women" (*ibid.*, pp. 49–50).

77. Muñoz Torrero did not sign the report.

78. Toreno, p. 412.

79. *Ibid.* Gallego's motion was passed by a vote of 83 to 63.

no ground for ecclesiastical censure, and it was not necessary to "remind the Bishops of their obligations." Furthermore, since one junta had already censored the *Diccionario*, and the author had not appealed to the Supreme Censorship Junta, Ostolaza's motion to have the matter referred to the Supreme Censorship Junta should not be considered, as it would be contrary to the decree on freedom of the press. Golfín supported this argument and asked why the Cortes was to proceed only against Gallardo, while nothing was to be done about the *Diccionario razonado*.[80] Ostolaza then changed his own motion and, backing Lera, requested that the Regency hand the *Diccionario* over to episcopal censorship. Don José María Calatrava, another *extremeño*, a lawyer by profession and one of the outstanding figures of the liberal movement,[81] reminded the Cortes that according to the law of freedom of the press, if the accused did not appeal to the Supreme Censorship Junta, the matter must rest there. After his speech the question came up for a vote. A majority decided against deliberating on Ostolaza's motion—the liberals had carried the day.[82]

A final attack on Gallardo, launched on November 13 by the deputy and clergyman Simón López, who demanded the librarian be ousted from his post, was parried during the session of the twentieth when the liberal Zumalacárregui succeeded in having the assembly take an action similar to the one in July and vote—by a small majority of 64 to 40—that there were no grounds for discussing the conservative motion.[83]

---

80. Actually this *Diccionario* had also been condemned by the provincial junta in April, 1812, but Canon Ayala, who claimed to be the author, was not imprisoned (Gallardo y Font, p. 137).

81. After Fernando's return he was taken for imprisonment to Melilla, Spanish Morocco. President of the Cortes and minister of justice during the revolution of 1820–1823, he spent the absolutist decade of 1823–1833 in exile in Gibraltar, Lisbon, England, and France. Following Fernando's death in 1833, he returned to Spain and occupied the posts of premier in 1837 and president of the Supreme Court in 1840. He belonged to the radical wing of the liberal party.

82. *Diario de las discusiones y actas de las Cortes*, July 21, 1812, XIV, in CDF, LXXIV, pp. 213–26; Menéndez y Pelayo, pp. 55–56.

83. *Diario de las discusiones* . . . , November 13, 1812, XVI, in CDF, LXXVI, pp. 113 ff.; November 20, *ibid.*, pp. 167–71; *El Conciso*, November 21, 1812, No. 21, p. 4.

Not calculated to soften the attitude of the Church toward the liberals was the abolition of the generally disliked *Voto de Santiago*, a contribution levied on Spanish peasants to support the archbishopric, chapter, and hospital of Santiago, Galicia. By a vote of 85 to 26 the Cortes abolished the tribute on October 14.[84] This, added to earlier measures taken by the Cortes which tended to divert much income of the Church to the government,[85] only added fuel to the dispute between the clergy and the party of reform.

Meanwhile, the controversy on the Inquisition raged on. In June, the Cortes had received a petition from the eighty-six-year-old Bishop of Segovia for the reinstatement of the once feared tribunal, which, according to the Bishop, was desired not only by the clergy but by the whole Spanish people.[86] In December, six bishops[87] who had sought refuge on the island of Mallorca drew up a long pastoral letter in which the theme of the Inquisition came up again.[88] The tribunal must be restored, they argued, for it was the only effective means of limiting the abuses that had arisen out of the freedom of the press.[89] In this connection, the *Triple Alianza*[90] and the *Diccionario*

---

84. *Colección de los decretos*, III, CDF, LXXIX, p. 127. Out of the 150 normally voting deputies almost 40 did not vote on this question. Moderate conservatives in this group were reluctant to give their support to a tribute which was highly unpopular throughout Spain. On a crucial issue involving the Church or religion, they as well as a number of moderate reformists could be expected to vote with the hard core of conservatives. Cf. the vote on the abolition of the Inquisition, p. 478.

85. Of such nature were the order of April, 1811, to confiscate the gold and silver found in churches which was not necessary to the ritual, and the proposal (later approved) put forward by the ecclesiastic and finance commissions in August, 1811, to apply the income of charitable religious institutions to support of military hospitals (Menéndez y Pelayo, p. 84; Artola, I, p. 527).

86. *Representación que el Ilustrísimo Señor Obispo de Segovia ha hecho al Augusto Congreso de las Cortes, pidiendo el restablecimiento del Santo Tribunal de la Inquisición*, Cádiz, June 16, 1812, CDF, CXXIII, pp. 95–100.

87. The bishops of Lérida, Tortosa, Barcelona, Urgel, Teruel, and Pamplona.

88. *Instrucción pastoral de los ilustrísimos señores obispos de Lérida, Tortosa, Barcelona, Urgel, Teruel y Pamplona al clero y pueblo de sus diócesis*, published in Mallorca in 1813 and reprinted in Santiago in 1814.

89. *Op. cit.*, pp. 135–36.

90. See above.

crítico-burlesco came under vehement attack.[91] They also strongly emphasized the doctrine of the inviolability of the property of the Church as well as that of its ministers.[93] In the same month the Constitutional Commission read its report on the Inquisition. This report had been adopted by only a slight majority, but once it had reached the floor of the Cortes, it was the beginning of the end of the Holy Office. The Commission traced the history of the institution from its inception in southern France in the early thirteenth century, through its introduction into Castile in 1478, to the resistance it had aroused in Spain in the sixteenth and following centuries. The Inquisition was declared to be an institution that had been introduced into the realm against the wish of its inhabitants and which had never been authorized by the old Cortes. It was incompatible with the independence and sovereignty of the nation, with its Constitution, and with individual freedom. However, since the Constitution explicitly stated that it would protect the Catholic religion, it was suggested that the medieval practice of punishing heresy by special episcopal tribunals be revived. Once again, the liberals on the Commission had tried to link their doctrine with Spain's medieval past.[93]

In January, the full-fledged debate began.[94] There were many speeches pro and con, and the same brilliant speakers who had won their laurels in previous oratorical battles now had another opportunity to display their eloquence. On January 8, Ostolaza asked: "If some innocent persons suffered at the hands of the Inquisition, in what tribunal in world history has this not happened? Let men of good faith not confuse the excellence of an institution with the abuses inherent in human weakness . . . The procedure of the Inquisition has been attacked, torture has been mentioned, but are the gentlemen of the Commission unaware of the fact that a century ago

91. *Ibid.,* pp. 134–36, 187–88.

92. *Ibid.,* pp. 15–44, 73–128.

93. *Discusión del proyecto de decreto sobre el Tribunal de la Inquisición,* pp. 2–41; *Diario de las discusiones y actas de las Cortes,* December 9, 1812, XVI, CDF, LXXVI, pp. 306–307; Toreno, pp. 442–44.

94. The debate on the Inquisition is contained in a 694-page volume published in Cádiz in 1813 and entitled *Discusión del proyecto de decreto sobre el Tribunal de la Inquisición.*

the Inquisition abolished torture before any other tribunal did the same?[95] The Commission says that the Inquisition is opposed to progress and enlightenment . . . But when did letters and the arts flourish more than in the century following its establishment?"[96] Inguanzo, in a long discourse, made the point that the Commission's project was an usurpation of the power of the Church. Whether the Inquisition did or did not subsist was not as vital as whether the Catholic Church had the authority to "establish the means and laws it deems opportune to preserve the integrity and purity of religion among the faithful and guide them along the road of truth." He certainly did not recognize the right of the State to suppress an ecclesiastical institution, for this only the pope could accomplish.[97]

Speaking for the liberal side, Toreno declared that "The object of religion is to give men their eternal happiness, an aim which has nothing to do with civil laws . . . The Redeemer answered those who thought his reign was of this world: *Regnum meum non est de hoc mundo*[98] . . . Its weapons are preaching and persuasion . . . The Inquisition is incompatible with the Constitution. The very name Inquisition must be erased . . . When the Inquisition was born, the *fueros* of Aragón and Castile died."[99] More effective and convincing than the speeches of liberals like Argüelles, Toreno, and Mexía was the participation in the debate of the liberal ecclesiastics, the "Jansenists," as their conservative opponents called them, and especially of the churchman, scholar, and writer Lorenzo Villanueva, who himself had been a friend of five inquisitors general. Their general line of attack followed as a rule that taken by the regalists of the eighteenth century: The authority of the State was supreme and any defense of the Inquisition meant giving renewed

95. Perhaps on paper, but not in practice. Besides, as late as 1781 there was a hanging in Sevilla on orders of the Inquisition. As late as 1805 a priest, Miguel Salano, died in the dungeons of the Inquisition of Zaragoza, jailed for denying the existence of Purgatory and the primacy of the Pope, and for preaching against Church tithes (Menéndez y Pelayo, VI, pp. 478–82).

96. Ostolaza's speech of January 8 in *Discusión del proyecto de decreto sobre el Tribunal de la Inquisición*, pp. 86–108.

97. Ibid., pp. 90, 96–97, 125; Toreno, p. 444.

98. My kingdom is not of this world.

99. *Discusión*, pp. 219–20, 21, 26–27; Toreno, p. 444.

power to the Curia Romana, thus infringing upon the legitimate rights of temporal authority.[1]

In the meantime, agitation grew throughout the country in favor of the Inquisition. Petitions to maintain the Holy Office in its functions inundated the Cortes. They came from bishops, cathedral chapters, from the Junta of Galicia, and from a number of municipal authorities.[2] But in the Cortes, at least, the institution was doomed to defeat. The decisive vote came on January 22, 1813, when by a vote of 90 to 60 the Inquisition was toppled from its century-old pedestal.[3] The vote is quite significant. Though the liberals garnered a majority, their former majority was reduced by two-thirds, an indication that about 30 deputies who had often sided with the reformists on political, social, and economic questions had deserted their colleagues in this crucial battle and had voted on the conservative side. Moderates were willing to vote for a constitutional monarchy, for the abolition of *señorios*, for the integration of the third estate in military academies, for equality of rights for Creoles, for an improvement in the lot of the Indians, for the removal of all obstacles to the establishment of a liberal economy based on the principle of *laissez faire, laissez passer*,[4] for a system of taxation based on the principle of proportionality,[5] for the transformation of public land into private property,[6] and for other revolutionary political, social, and economic changes. But when it came to the preservation of what they considered the bulwark against religious subversion, they parted ways with their more advanced colleagues.

The final decree was published exactly one month later. It solemnly declared that the Roman Catholic religion would be pro-

1. Argüelles' speech in *Discusión*, pp. 127–43; Mexía, pp. 245–78; Villa-nueva, pp. 427–64.

2. Menéndez y Pelayo, pp. 76–77.

3. *Discusión*, p . 495.

4. In June, 1813, the Cortes eliminated the guild system as well as all obstacles to the circulation of products through Spain's various provinces.

5. In September, 1813, a new system of taxation was instituted which did away with the injustices of the past and placed a substantial share of the burden of taxation on the shoulders of the upper classes.

6. In January, 1813, a decree provided for the sale of common land to private individuals and for the distribution of small parcels of land to persons without property.

tected by laws in accordance with the Constitution, but that the Tribunal of the Inquisition was incompatible with the Constitution. Consequently, a law of the *Siete Partidas*, the famous legal codification compiled under Alfonso X in the thirteenth century, was revived, which left it up to the bishops and their vicars to try cases dealing with faith and to cooperate with secular judges, who in turn were empowered to impose on heretics the punishment established by law.[7]

The Cortes drew up a proclamation explaining to the nation the reasons that had moved it to take this momentous step,[8] and ordered that this document as well as the abolition decree be read on three consecutive Sundays in all churches of the realm. The reaction to this order can well be imagined. The Bishop of Santander threatened from Galicia to excommunicate anybody who read the decree. The Archbishop of Santiago fled his archbishopric rather than obey the order of the Cortes. The Bishop of Oviedo refused to receive the provincial governor who was to deliver the order to him. The ecclesiastical chapter of Cádiz disobeyed the Cortes and the decree was not read in the town's churches, a step which the Cortes suspected with reason to be supported by the Regency. The resulting conflict between the executive and the legislative led to the former's removal.[9] The new Regency took strong action. The vicar and another three clergymen were ousted from their positions, brought to trial, and eventually expelled from Cádiz.[10]

The papal nuncio, Don Pedro Gravina, became embroiled in the struggle. On March 5, he sent a representation to the Regency protesting against the abolition of the Inquisition, which he described as an insult to the primacy and rights of the Papacy, which had established the institution. At the same time he addressed a note to the Bishop of Jaén and to the ecclesiastical chapters of Málaga and Granada, exhorting them to join the Spanish clergy in opposing the decision of the Cortes. It was obvious that either the nuncio or the

---

7. *Colección de los decretos*, III, in CDF, LXXIX, pp. 199–201; *Discusión*, pp. 687–88. On the same day, another decree was published, ordering seizure of the Inquisition's property.

8. Cf. This proclamation in *Discusión*, pp. 689–94.

9. See above and Chapter IX.

10. Toreno, pp. 450–51, 453–54; Artola, I, p. 452.

Spanish government would have to give in, and since the new Regency and the Cortes still held the upper hand in Cádiz, the nuncio felt the wrath of his opponents. In July, 1813, he was expelled from Spain and betook himself to the southern Portuguese port of Tavira about thirteen miles west of the Spanish border.[11]

As unpopular with the Church as the abolition of the Inquisition was the decree rendered on February 18, 1813, on the reestablishment in free Spain of monasteries and convents damaged or destroyed by the war. It allowed the reunion of communities that had already received permission to this effect from the Regency, provided the establishments were not in ruins. But it severely restricted the number of religious communities by forbidding monks and nuns to beg for the money necessary for the rebuilding of damaged establishments; by prohibiting the maintenance or restoration of monasteries or convents with less than twelve professed members; by allowing only one community of a given order in a given town; and by forbidding the creation of new establishments and the admission to religious orders of new candidates until a final decision was taken in the matter of religious communities.[12] Although not as drastic as King Joseph's decree of 1809,[13] this edict would have greatly curtailed the activities of religious orders if it had been in effect long enough. Many monasteries and convents in territories once held by the French were uninhabitable after enemy evacuation, and monks and nuns would have been unable to turn to public charity. Fortunately for the clergy, liberal rule was not to last much longer than a year from the date of the decree's promulgation.

The liberals were now faced with the concentrated wrath of the Church, and, what was worse, with the wrath of at least a substantial part of the population which wanted to see its monks, friars, and nuns reinstated in their former establishments. It was tragic indeed that men who with few exceptions were good Catholics, without being fanatics in their beliefs,[14] should thus have incurred the enmity of the Church. Conservatives have maintained that the Cádiz liberals were

11. Toreno, pp. 450, 453, 454; Artola, I, pp. 452–53.
12. *Colección de los decretos*, III, in CDF, LXXIX, pp. 195–96; Toreno, pp. 445–48.
13. See Chapter XII.
14. A few liberal deputies were no doubt atheists or approached incredulity in matters of religion. A case in point is that of José Mexía.

at best lukewarm in their Catholicism and that behind their reforms there always lurked the influence of the Masonic lodges. These charges, though making very effective propaganda in the struggle to destroy the liberals' reputation, have very little basis in fact, if any. The orthodoxy of the majority of liberals cannot be questioned. Is it reasonable to apply the term irreligious to men who heard Mass before every session; who on October 26, 1810, at the suggestion of Villanueva, recited the hymn *Veni Creator* before proceeding with the election of the Regency;[15] who in June, 1812, declared Santa Teresa de Jesús, together with the apostle Santiago, patron saint of Spain;[16] who at the heading of the Constitution wrote the phrase: "In the name of the Omnipotent Lord Father, Son and Holy Ghost, Creator and Supreme Lawgiver of Society"; who without dissent approved Article 12 of the Constitution guaranteeing the Catholic religion maintenance of its unique status in Spain?[17] As for the question of Freemasonry, Solís has shown convincingly that though one, and perhaps two pro-French Masonic lodges functioned in Cádiz during the war, their influence on political events was practically nil, especially since they were closely watched by the government.[18]

As the battle of words raged on and as the conservative elements

15. Villanueva, *op. cit.*, pp. 19–20.

16. Toreno, p. 436.

17. If, as Argüelles indicates (see above), a number of liberals resented this, they did so not because they were anti-Catholic but because their Catholicism, though perfectly orthodox, had lost the fanaticism and intolerance normally found in traditionalist circles.

18. *Op. cit.*, pp. 316–27; Toreno, p. 408. It is possible that a Masonic lodge made its appearance in Madrid as early as 1727 (Menéndez y Pelayo, VI, p. 103). Méndez Bejarano claims there were ninety-seven lodges throughout Spain in the 1750s (*Historia política de los afrancesados*, p. 141). They are said to have continued their activities in spite of Fernando VI's decree of 1751 directed against this cult (Menéndez y Pelayo, VI, p. 103). During the War of Independence many were established in the occupied territories (*ibid.*, VII, pp. 29–36). As for free Spain, it is known that in 1813 there existed in Cádiz, besides the one or two pro-French lodges, a lodge of a distinctly liberal stamp. Aside from the fact that the deputy Mexía was one of its members it did not seem to have had any weight on developments in the Cortes. The actual connection between Freemasonry and liberalism was established after 1814, for the persecuted reformists clasped the outstretched hand of the equally persecuted Freemasons, and by the 1820s the influence of the latter in liberal circles was considerable (cf. Solís, pp. 325–27).

fostered throughout the country resistance to the work of the Cortes, elections for the ordinary Cortes of 1813 were held amidst clear indications that two irreconcilable Spains had emerged. These elections could now be held throughout the greater part of Spain with the progressive evacuation of the national territory by French troops, and their results were more favorable to the *serviles* than to the reformists.[19] In Cádiz the conservatives would have doubtless had a majority, but many conservative deputies remained on the main-land, refusing to go to Cádiz, partly because of dread of the yellow fever then raging in the port, but partly also because they feared they would not have in Cádiz the same freedom to give expression to their opinions as in the capital, and thus wanted to force the transfer of the government to Madrid. The liberals, on the other hand, fearing that their influence would wane in Madrid, delayed as much as possible the move to the capital. They were helped in this by the yellow fever epidemic, which made it imperative, because of the possibility of contagion, that the transfer of the congress await the abatement of the disease. While deputies of the extraordinary Cortes were forbid-den by decree to be candidates for the ordinary assembly, the Consti-tution authorized deputies of the *Cortes extraordinarias* to continue to represent the provinces on an interim basis until the newly elected representatives took their seats in the new assembly. Thus, with the failure of many of the recently elected deputies to come to their posts and also through the undeniable intellectual superiority of the liberal leaders over their conservative opponents, the liberals were able to maintain their majority in Cádiz and on the Isla de León.[20]

Meanwhile, and especially after the convening of the ordinary Cortes in October, 1813, tension between the two political parties in Spain increased to the point where members of both groups openly proclaimed the necessity of resorting to force to eliminate the oppo-

19. Even in the last months of the extraordinary Cortes conservative strength in the assembly had been growing as a number of deputies from newly liberated provinces had arrived in Cádiz. (Toreno, p. 482). The evac-uation of Spanish territories by French troops contributed, of course, to the growing tension between reformists and conservatives. As more and more Spaniards came into direct contact with the work of the Cortes, a substantial amount of them were bound to take sides, thus intensifying the struggle.

20. Toreno, p. 487.

sition. Conservative and liberal newspapers appealed to their followers to hold themselves in readiness for an armed showdown.[21] The
abyss could not be bridged any longer. There was now beginning the
long history of political struggle which has continued into the
twentieth century and has not yet been successfully resolved.

Conservative historians lay all the responsibility for Spain's unend-
ing civil war since the War of Independence at the door of the
reformists. The traditionalist Menéndez y Pelayo characterizes the
liberals as Utopians and dreamers, blind to the wishes of the people,
who preferred to "exalt the idol of their vague readings and chimeri-
cal meditations[22] to preserving the vestiges of the past and taking the
Nation's wish as their light and guide."[23] "More than the War of
Independence . . . it was the Cortes of 1812 which opened the door
to dissensions," writes present-day conservative Suárez Verdeguer.[24]

It is true that it was in Cádiz that the great split between liberals
and conservatives was initialed, but it would be unfair to place the
blame squarely on the shoulders of the liberals. Above all, what
happened in Cádiz should not obscure the vital role the War of
Independence as a whole played as a cause of the schism. The conflict itself was a most essential factor in the political developments of
wartime Spain, specifically in its effect at the very onset on Spain's
political structure, laying bare the weaknesses of this structure, as
well as in the peculiar manner in which it evolved.

The war gave a decisive twist to Spanish historical development.
The War of Independence was the eruption which unmasked all that
was rotten in the *Ancien Régime* and liberated elements that had
gathered strength in the second half of the eighteenth century and
especially after the French Revolution of 1789. Without the War of
Independence the ramshackle edifice of the *Ancien Régime* would in
all probability have continued to stand for some time. The factors
which within its own structure worked against its permanency, as
well as growing demands for changes from the enlightened middle

21. Artola, I, pp. 618–20.
22. Read "the Constitution."
23. *Op. cit.*, VII, p. 89.
24. "Génesis del liberalismo político español," *Historia de España, Arbor*,
1953, p. 529.

class and the intelligentsia, might have forced alterations, but these would have never had the scope of the reforms enacted in Cádiz and would not have aroused unyielding opposition. With the outbreak of the war, the forces within Spain which had absorbed a strong dose of eighteenth-century Enlightenment and had come under the influence of some of the principles of the French Revolution were set free. But they were set free not only because of the mere fact of the cataclysm engulfing all of Spain, but because the Old Regime and its institutions had shown themselves entirely incapable of resisting foreign aggression. If the Spanish monarchy had had the strength to fight back and provide leadership for the Spanish people, the centuries of absolutism, the weakness of Charles IV, and the dictatorship of Godoy would not have mattered in the final analysis. A king who would have remained in Spain and fought on even against impossible odds, surrounded by his idolizing subjects, would perhaps have been forced to make in the end certain concessions and to give his people a measure of political liberty, but at the same time he might very well have preserved a strong, unchallenged monarchical authority.

But Fernando did not fight. The war came with the king a captive, the institution of the monarchy swaying in the storm, and the nation thus deprived of effective leadership. Thoughtful Spaniards of all classes, not just reform-minded men, looked for causes of the disaster and found them in century-old absolutism, in outworn institutions, in mismanagement and abuse of power by ministers, among whom Godoy looked then like the epitome of corruption. Yes, absolutism could have better days, like the reign of Charles III, but it could not guarantee the nation against a Charles IV and a Godoy.

By the time the Cortes convened, most Spaniards were ready for a change. The liberal minority, representing essentially the ideals and interests of the rising middle class, wanted political, social, and economic changes that would bring forth a new state established on the principles of political and social freedom and justice, in which the bourgeoisie, supported by the intellectuals, would assume leadership. The rural masses—still the bulk of the population—doubtless hoped for an improvement in their social and economic condition. But these masses were too accustomed to subjection, too ignorant and therefore too inarticulate, and too loyal to the traditional pillars of Spanish society, the throne and the altar, to impose any reforms from below. Finally even the conservatives—mainly the bulk of the clergy, the aristocracy and the Old Regime's governing organisms and their bureaucracy—desired change. But though favorable to some kind of change, they had no clear idea of what they wanted. A return to a dimly perceived medieval era of municipal freedom and limited popular representation in the affairs of government, with some restrictions on the power of the king, ministers, and magistrates, but leaving most of the powers and privileges of throne, altar and nobility intact, would perhaps have been acceptable to them. But a number of concrete reforms that had to be enacted if Spain was to draw abreast of the great European nations were bound to meet with resistance.

The king, any king for that matter, not just the despicable Fernando VII, nurtured by centuries of absolutism, would resist any substantial limitation on his power and would certainly not welcome with open arms freedom of the press. The old bureaucracy must perforce look askance at any new government machinery which established a strict separation between administrative and judicial matters. The landed aristocracy and the men in its employ would not accept with equanimity the abolition of seignorial rights. The hostility of the Church could be expected to be aroused by any measure aiming at eliminating the Inquisition and at a drastic reduction in the number of religious communities. Thus there was a wide and powerful band of the Spanish social spectrum that was bound to put up resistance to any really meaningful reforms.

The vicissitudes of war, which had produced revolutionary organisms in the forms of juntas and had allowed reform-minded Spaniards to give expression to their opinions, finally placed power in the hands of a majority made up of reformist clergymen and professionals, many of whom were strongly imbued with the ideology of Enlightenment. If the war had not taken such an unfavorable turn in 1810 and if elections could have been held in many more areas than was actually possible, the liberals would probably not have been in a majority in the national assembly[25] and events would probably have

25. As shown in the elections of 1813, though this cannot be taken as conclusive proof. In 1810, no clear party division had appeared as yet and

taken another course. The inevitable change would then, perhaps, have come about through compromise—though the Spanish character does not lend itself easily to compromise on basic issues. As it was, Cádiz, the most reform-minded city in Spain, became the last fort of Spanish resistance. Thus, military defeat, inevitable in Andalucia because of superior French power and know-how, had propelled the liberals into a commanding position, for in Cádiz they were favored by Spain's inability to hold nationwide elections and by the necessity of electing alternate deputies, many of whom were favorable to reform.[26] In possession of a fairly clear program of reform and strongly supported by the reform-minded population, they saw their golden opportunity to forge a new Spain.

What, then, should they have done? Should they have limited themselves to evolving means for a successful prosecution of the war, as Fernando had indicated in his decree of May 5, 1808, before shamefully surrendering to Napoleon? But this would have been a betrayal of the wishes of the majority of the Spanish population, who wanted at least some kind of change. Should the liberals have lifted Spain's medieval institutions, such as the medieval Cortes, out of the dust piled on by centuries? The ultimate failure to incorporate more of Spain's past into the Constitution of 1812 was due not only to the undeniable influence of eighteenth-century rationalism and the French Revolution on the Cádiz lawmakers; it was also due to the difficulty of reviving in the nineteenth century institutions that even in the Middle Ages had not prevented civil strife and had not been able to prevent all power from ultimately slipping into the monarch's hands.

That most of the basic reforms enacted in Cádiz were bound to meet resistance from the king and the conservative sectors, no matter in what manner they were presented, is obvious. The limitations on the king's powers were in the end indispensable if a return to absolut-

---

the proportion of reformists to conservatives might just possibly have been maintained throughout the whole of Spain. In 1813, party lines were clearly drawn and moderates who might have voted for reformist deputies in 1810 and who were repelled by the program enacted in Cádiz in the intervening years voted conservative.

26. Among the substitutes were such outstanding liberals as Argüelles, Toreno, Mexía, Nicasio Gallego, Zorraquín, and Fernández Golfín.

ism was to be avoided, but the king was bound to resist them. The abolition of *señoríos* was an act of self-evident justice, but it offended the landowning aristocracy. As for freedom of the press, it was and is today inconceivable that a modern, constitutional monarchy could have truly free institutions, but not have this most important one. But freedom of the press in any shape or form, would have met the hostility of the conservatives. The Inquisition obviously had to be eliminated sooner or later if Spain was to have free institutions and join as an equal the nations of the West. Even in Spain, though much less virulent than in ages past, the Inquisition was an abominable anachronism. Naturally, any attempt at suppression of the Inquisition must perforce run head-on into violent clerical opposition.

As it was, the work of the Cortes seems on the whole of a rather moderate nature. The monarchical form of government was preserved. The landed aristocracy was not deprived of its landed property. Freedom of the press was limited to the political area. Religion was maintained in its privileged position, and instead of the Inquisition, special tribunals were set up to watch over the faith of every Spaniard. However, moderate as the revolution of 1810–1814 may seem to us, it must not be forgotten that, given the rhythm of the historical evolution of Spanish society, it was quite radical for the time.

Conservative historians from Menéndez y Pelayo[27] to Suárez Verdeguer[28] have charged that the liberals did not really represent the will of the broad mass of the Spanish people. From the political point of view this is probably true—even if it is not correct when considered in the light of the social and economic aspirations doubtless harbored by a majority of the rural masses. But given the circumstances under which the Cortes met, the liberals were isolated from occupied Spain, which for a long time included the greater portion of the national territory, and to a certain extent isolated also from the free zones. Yet it is in the nature of revolutions that they are normally carried out by an intellectual minority, which by virtue of its education and training thinks it has a more precise view of the

27. *Historia de los heterodoxos españoles,* Vol. VII.
28. "Génesis del liberalismo político español," *Historia de España, Arbor,* 1953, pp. 520–52.

nation's needs than the mass of the people. It must be kept in mind, however, that the liberals had the full support of the majority of the population of Cádiz—the seat of the national government—and that Cádiz did not have to be prodded into a reformist attitude, but on the contrary ardently wanted them to carry out domestic reforms.

The liberals were able to push through the Congress the reforms they considered indispensable for a successful prosecution of the war as well as for the building of a strong and prosperous Spain. They were sincere men, idealists, convinced that they had the answer for their nation's century-old plight. They did make endeavors to keep as much of Spain's past as possible. Perhaps they should have made a greater effort in this direction. Perhaps if they had followed the advice of Jovellanos and granted representation to the aristocracy and the clergy in a second chamber, the opposition might have been somewhat softer. Perhaps, too, if instead of attacking Church and throne at one and the same time, they had sought to limit the power of only one of these institutions, allying themselves with the other, they could have split the opposition. True, the Inquisition was an abominable institution and there had been too many monasteries and convents before the war. Yet it might have been wiser, especially in view of the fact that the Spanish popular masses were by no means unfavorably disposed toward the Holy Office and also since Article 12 of the Constitution exalted the Catholic religion, to let the Church enjoy full power, at least for the time being. Conversely, if they had decided to attack the power of the Church, they should perhaps have given full authority back to the king, with a number of guarantees against arbitrary power that a carefully studied revival of the more viable features of the medieval Cortes might have provided. All this, however, would have entailed more compromises than these men, who ardently desired a society erected on rational principles and on the ideals of liberty and equality, were ready to agree on.

Finally, the liberals might have been more circumspect in their handling of outspoken opposition. Their insistence that the Constitution be sworn to without reservations by everyone, thus attaching an absolute value to the constitutional oath, was unrealistic. Observance of a constitution cannot be guaranteed by an oath, as history has shown many times. Consequently, the punishment meted out to the

Bishop of Orense was perhaps too harsh, as even the reform-minded periodical *El Español* noted.[29] The treatment of Lardizábal and others who dared to attack the Cortes actually violated the law on freedom of the press, which had been promulgated by the assembly itself.

However, in spite of the undeniable errors committed by the liberals, in spite of their arrogance and intolerance of opposition, it would be grossly unfair to place the blame for Spain's great schism on their shoulders alone. For if they made mistakes, so did their opponents. The fact that no really coherent conservative program to solve Spain's political, social, and economic ills was presented during the war and that conservative sectors mistrusted any meaningful reform; the insistence of the Church that the Inquisition must be maintained at all costs; all this, too, contributed to the emergence of the civil strife which was to rend Spain thenceforward.

But no attempt at finding culprits in one or the other political camp can explain a historical process which the War of Independence and its accompanying defeats made largely inevitable. The fact remains that during the eighteenth century there came into existence an enlightened Spain, quantitatively very small but of considerable influence. This forward-looking minority was the father of nineteenth century liberalism. The latter went further in many respects than its progenitor, which had served enlightened despotism. Then came the War of Independence, the immediate cause of the great rift. Once the war had broken out and the old institutions had shown themselves incapable of organizing resistance, the reformists were bound to gain more and more influence. And once military defeat had driven the seat of Spain's government of national resistance to Cádiz, the conflict between traditionalist Spain and reformist Spain was bound to break out into the open. The War of Independence—the real culprit—had catapulted the reformists into a commanding position where they were forced to act. And act they could in only one direction, that of reform, a reform demanded by their own convictions, by the exigencies of the war and, most vociferously among all liberal-minded Spaniards, by the population of

29. See above.

Cádiz. In their endeavors to reform the Spanish political, social, and economic structure they were bound to clash in one way or another with the forces of tradition. It would have been difficult, if not impossible, to avoid this conflict, out of which arose modern Spain with its continuous struggle between Left and Right.

XII

A KING IN NAME

[1]

Whɪʟᴇ Spain's future was being decided in Cádiz, the greater part of the country was in the hands of the enemy. Between November and December, 1808, and the summer of 1812, French military suprem- acy could not be questioned, and at times it seemed that free Spain's continued existence was hanging by a thread. By early 1809, when Napoleon returned to Paris after his lightning Peninsular Campaign, it appeared that it was only a question of time before the whole Peninsula would fall under French rule.

At dawn on January 22, 1809, Madrid was awakened by the thunder of 100 rounds of cannon fire. It was not the sound of battle, for the fate of Madrid had been sealed at the end of the previous year. It was a sound presaging a long sojourn by Spain's new sovereign, Joseph Napoleon. Actually, Joseph was no newcomer. The *intruso* had briefly held sway in the capital the preceding July and had been forced to evacuate it by the glorious Spanish victory at Bailén.[1] He was back once more, to reign under the protection of the hated foreign bayonets. But the intrusive king was without question preferable to Napoleon himself. After the Emperor had reconquered much of Spain by military force alone, it was to be feared that he would claim his right of conquest, take over Spain, and rule it along purely military lines. It would have been a harsh regimen. In spite of a feeling of shame, then, of having to look forward to the restoration of an unwanted foreign king, *madrileños* could emit a sigh of relief.

1. See Chapters III and VII.

Between the two unavoidable evils Joseph was definitely the lesser one. Spanish authorities in Madrid were aware of this, and after the disaster of Uclés on January 13,[2] delegations had gone on a continuous pilgrimage to Joseph's latest residence at the country house of the Duchess of Alba on the outskirts of the city, requesting that he come to the capital.[3] After all, they argued, Napoleon himself had indicated that he would place his brother on the Spanish throne again, once the citizens of Madrid had publicly expressed their loyalty to his brother. Since this had taken place,[4] nothing stood in the way of Joseph's return.

Shortly after 9:00 A.M. on January 22, Joseph entered Madrid through Atocha Gate, the same gate through which the idolized Fernando VII had passed a year before. Napoleon's brother was on horseback, followed by a brilliant military staff. He rode up the Prado, turned left upon reaching Alcalá, followed the broad thoroughfare to the Puerta del Sol, then rode down Calle de las Carretas. The streets along the route of the royal cortege, specially decked out for the occasion, were lined with soldiers of the French garrison, but there were also a number of Spanish spectators. A few scattered bursts of applause rang out, but on the whole, faces showed neither enthusiasm nor hatred. Some expressed curiosity, others resignation, and others hope. The hope that the new king's rule might perhaps prove unwarranted some of the fears that had enveloped the capital since the grim December days. After passing through Calle de Atocha and Calle de Toledo, Joseph dismounted at the church of San Isidro. There he made a short speech: "The unity of our Holy Religion, the Independence of the Monarchy, the integrity of its territory and the freedom of its citizens are the conditions of the oath I took upon receiving my Crown. It will not be debased on my head."[5]

This declaration was followed by a Te Deum, after which the King rode through Calle de Toledo, Plaza Mayor, and Calle de la Almudena to the Royal Palace. Another 100 rounds announced his

2. See Chapter VIII.
3. Miot de Mélito, III, pp. 35–36. Since his arrival in the outskirts of Madrid at the beginning of December, Joseph had stayed mostly at the palace of El Pardo. He had also spent a short time in Aranjuez.
4. See Chapter VII.
5. Miot de Mélito, III, p. 37; AHN, Estado, *legajo* 3004.

entry into his residence. During the next few days Joseph tried hard to win the popularity of his subjects. He left the palace and visited a number of public establishments and hospitals, making a good impression with his friendliness and affable manners.[6] No matter how hostile Spaniards were to French rule, they could not help feeling momentarily disarmed in the presence of this charming man who looked so much like his brother, yet had so much softness in his expression and always had pleasant words for everybody.

Joseph Bonaparte, then forty-one years old, was the oldest son of the imperial family. He was probably, also, the one with the most regular facial features. Taller than Napoleon, he had a straight nose, a well-shaped mouth, and rather small but pleasant eyes, which seemed to peer at the world from behind a veil of melancholy. Mesonero Romanos, who saw him in London in 1833, many years after Joseph's ephemeral reign had ended, described him as a man whose deportment indicated great distinction and whose expressive Napoleonic face was quite different from what he had been led to believe in his childhood.[7]

In his tender years Mesonero Romanos had heard from his elders mostly disparaging comments about King Joseph. He had been told that *el intruso* was one-eyed, that he liked cards with a passion, and that he was a devotee of the bottle. Those Spaniards who did not meet the King personally believed these tales with a credulity that was the result both of their hatred of everything French and of the propaganda spread by the Spanish governments of national resistance. In caricatures disseminated throughout Spain by Spanish patriots, Joseph appeared as Pepe Botellas,[8] kneeling in a bottle, drunk as El rey de copas,[9] or sitting on a huge cucumber[10] and holding glasses and bottle, while a Negro slave offered him a leather *bota*[11] and a monkey held out a playing card showing the king of hearts.[12] This is the figure most Spaniards believed to be ruling from the

6. AHN, Estado, *legajo* 3004; Miot de Mélito, III, p. 38.
7. *Memorias de un setentón*, p. 80 n.
8. "Joe Bottles."
9. See Chapter VII.
10. In Spanish, *pepino*, an allusion to Pepe or Joe, the familiar version of the name Joseph.
11. Small leather wine bag.
12. Soldevila, *Historia de España*, VI, pp. 318–21.

Palacio de Oriente in Madrid. The intruder king was branded forever as Pepe Botellas.

Yet those Spaniards who met him soon realized that Napoleon's brother was none of these things. He certainly was not one-eyed.[13] Though pleasure-loving and a gourmet, he was no drunkard and no inveterate gambler. Patriotic propaganda might have struck closer to home if it had emphasized another foible common to men, his weakness for the opposite sex. Very popular with women, he neglected no opportunity to win the affections of an attractive woman through his undeniable personal charm and his privileged position. During his brief reign in Naples,[14] and especially in Spain, he made numerous conquests. His philandering was made considerably easier by the fact that during his five years in Spain his wife Julie, who resided in Paris or on their estate of Mortefontaine, never joined him. Julie was a fine woman and a devoted wife, who had given her husband two daughters, Zenaide and Charlotte, born in 1801 and 1802 respectively. But she was petite, with a poor figure, bulging eyes, a flat and stubby nose, and a generally sickly appearance. Even if she had accompanied Joseph, the latter would certainly not have remained faithful to her. His desire for freedom of action with respect to other women no doubt played an important role in his failure to have his family join him. But there were other reasons too. The continuing war in Spain, with the uncertainty as to the outcome, which so often weighed heavily on the intruder king's mind, and the vital importance of Julie as a messenger between Joseph and his imperial brother, a role she fulfilled faithfully throughout the war, were factors contributing to her long separation from her husband.

While at all times engaged in extramarital affairs, Joseph showed that he could still be a good husband and a good father, at least on the epistolary level. His correspondence with Julie reveals a great deal of affection for his wife and his children as well as solicitude for their health. In a letter of June 27, 1809, Julie wrote to her husband: "*Mon bon ami*,[15] I see in your letter of the 16th that you were worried

13. The legend of the *rey tuerto* (one-eyed king) probably arose because Joseph often used a monocle.
14. From 1806 to 1808.
15. Freely translated as "my dear."

about me . . . You must be reassured now, since I have written every day. My fever was very high, but fortunately it lasted only three days. Your children are fine. Adieu, *cher ami*, you know how much I love you."[16] "I hope your health improves," wrote Joseph to Julie on September 7, 1810.[17] Earlier in the same year, Joseph may have had pangs of conscience about his faraway family, for he wrote Napoleon on March 2: "Sire, I am writing to Julie to join me with my children. The weather is favorable. Shortly, it will be made unbearable through excessive heat."[18] But Julie and her daughters never came, and Joseph continued to find solace in the arms of beautiful Spanish women.

But there were other things in life outside affairs of state which Joseph found attractive. He liked literature and the arts. At the age of twenty-eight he had written a novel, and often, at intimate gatherings with his friends, he would recite lines from great French classic plays. He also liked uniforms and decorations, and was greatly preoccupied by questions of etiquette.[19] He was fond of riding and walking through the countryside, especially through the magnificent Casa de Campo, where, promenading along shady avenues or across inviting woodland, he could forget in the company of some courtiers and young women the problems of his government and of the war.[20]

Joseph was well educated but lacked his brother's phenomenal intelligence. Nonetheless he possessed a good amount of perspicacity and much common sense. He was also quite ambitious. Unfortunately his vanity often prevented him from placing a restraint upon his ambition in accordance with the realities surrounding him. Thinking himself a better ruler than his brother, he also stubbornly insisted on keeping the title of French Prince and the accompanying rights of succession to the French imperial throne in the event that Napoleon died without male children. This in spite of the fact that the Bayonne constitution stipulated that the Spanish Crown could

16. AHN, Estado, *legajo* 20, *carpeta* B, No. 5.
17. *Mémoires et correspondance politique et militaire du Roi Joseph*, VII, p. 330.
18. *Ibid.*, p. 265.
19. Geoffroy de Grandmaison, *L'Espagne et Napoléon*, Vol. II, p. 325; Villa-Urrutia, *El rey José Napoleón*, pp. 23–24.
20. Grandmaison, Vol. II, p. 342.

not be incorporated into the French realm. "Joseph is tempted to think," the Emperor is reputed to have commented on his brother's pretensions, "that I have usurped the succession to the king our father."[21]

Joseph was by nature indolent and vacillating and wanting in the decisiveness and determination that was such an integral part of Napoleon's character. Like all men who lack this quality, he was capable of great bursts of energy and assertiveness, but these did not last long and doubts and indecision would once more gain the upper hand. Underneath it all, though, the ambitious streak in him almost always maintained itself intact and gave him a certain basic confidence in himself and the role he was called on to play. He was generous and faithful to his friends, but too vulnerable to flattery. He could be hypocritical and at times quite capable of holding a grudge against someone he thought had not treated him fairly.[22]

What struck his contemporaries most was his kindness. Perhaps he was not at heart quite that soft, but made a show of much kindness to underline the difference between his brother's harshness and his own more agreeable nature. However, there was a basic gentleness in him that escaped none of those who came into close contact with him. General Hugo recalled how Joseph rode across the battlefield of Ocaña[23] through a hail of bullets and grapeshot, instructing French soldiers not to kill fleeing Spaniards. "My friends," the king was overheard saying, "spare the lives of these poor Spaniards. One day they will be your companions-in-arms."[24] On rare occasions this generosity toward the enemy could yield to a hardness that is surprising in a man like Joseph. After French troops atrociously sacked Bilbao in August, 1808, he wrote Napoleon: "Sire, the city of Bilbao has received a terrible lesson, but it will not be lost on the other towns of these northern provinces."[25] But this was unusual and may be explained by the shock of having been driven out of his new capital after a sojourn of only ten days. Typical of his goodheartedness was his solicitude for the starving population of Madrid during

---

21. *Ibid.*, p. 326; Villa-Urrutia, p. 21.
22. Villa-Urrutia, p. 23.
23. See Chapter VIII.
24. *Mémoires*, Vol. II, pp. 113–14.
25. *Mémoires et correspondance*, Vol. IV, p. 428.

the hunger of 1811–1812. The personal interest he took in the misfortune of the inhabitants, his visits to the poverty-stricken districts of the city, and his generous gifts of money to the underprivileged made even such a rabid Francophobe as Mesonero Romanos' father exclaim: "What a pity that this man's name is Bonaparte!"[26]

As early as Bayonne he had made a fine impression on the Spanish delegates, some of whom were later to change camps and follow the national resistance movement. His charm, his efforts from the first to express himself in the Spanish language—using many Italian words in the process, however—[27] his apparently sincere desire to please his future subjects, his reasonableness, his manifest wish to ingratiate himself with the Spanish Church, all made a most favorable impression. To many of the delegates this amiable, soft-spoken man, so reassuring after the trenchant manner of the Emperor, seemed to hold out the promise of a stronger, more orderly, rejuvenated Spain.[28] Indeed, Joseph did have the makings of a fairly good sovereign. It was his misfortune to have been destined for the Spain of 1808, where men of much greater talents would have failed had they been in his place.

Joseph Bonaparte was born in 1768 on the island of Corsica, like his brother Napoleon. He was the future emperor's favorite playmate and this mutual affection never really ceased, in spite of the strain that the Spanish episode placed on their friendship. After studying at Autun, France, he returned to Corsica in 1785, where he eventually obtained a modest position in the island's administrative service. Later we find him engaged in business in the great French port of Marseilles. There he married Julie Clary, daughter of one of the wealthy businessmen of the city and sister of the famous Désirée, with whom Napoleon became romantically involved. In 1796, he and Lucien Bonaparte became members of the French Republic's Council of the Five Hundred, and in 1797 he was appointed extraordinary envoy to Pope Pius VI. Helping Napoleon seize power in the coup d'état of 1799, he was in turn considerably helped by the latter's meteoric rise

26. *Op. cit.*, p. 88.
27. Joseph achieved only a mediocre knowledge of Spanish during his reign.
28. Grandmaison, Vol. 1, pp. 254–55.

to the Consulate and later to the Imperial throne. When Napoleon became emperor, Joseph was granted the title of French Prince, a more than nominal honor, for it meant that he would succeed Napoleon if the Emperor died without leaving a male heir. Then, in 1806, Joseph became king. It was only the kingdom of Naples, not the most glittering prize in Europe, yet a bona fide kingdom, over which he reigned until 1808. He was not a bad monarch and Naples did not fare badly during his reign. He took a sincere interest in the welfare of his subjects. He introduced reforms in the administration without resorting to draconian measures. He protected the arts and was generally liked.[29]

When he changed kingdoms he had every intention of being a good ruler. He would be a Spanish king first, Napoleon's brother second. He would preserve the integrity of the Spanish territory, and in spite of the role he had once played in the French Republic he would maintain the Catholic religion in its unique position. He would do his best to become a truly popular sovereign who brought peace and prosperity to his new subjects. With this fine resolve went in no small dose his usual ambition and vanity. Here he was, a native of a Mediterranean island, ruler of Spain and its vast overseas possessions, monarch of a land with a glorious tradition and a history that stretched back more than two thousand years.

At first he was tempted to keep the immensely long title of Spanish royalty which made mention of territories that had once belonged to the Spanish Crown, such as Italian Milan and French Burgundy.[30] Napoleon vetoed this and Joseph had to resign himself to be known merely as "Don Josef Napoleón, by the Grace of God and the Constitution of the State, King of Spain and the Indies."[31] But a title

29. *Mémoires et correspondance*, I, pp. 7–14; Villa-Urrutia, pp. 17–31.

30. Cf. the title of Charles IV: "Don Carlos, by the Grace of God, King of Castile, of León, of Aragón, of the Two Sicilies, of Jerusalem, of Navarra, of Granada, of Toledo, of Valencia, of Galicia, of Mallorca, of Menorca, of Sevilla, of Sardinia, of Córdoba, of Corsica, of Murcia, of Jaén, of the Algarve, of Algeciras, of Gibraltar, of the Canary Islands, of the East and West Indies, of the Spanish Main, Archduke of Austria, Duke of Burgundy, of Brabant, and Milan, Count of Habsburg, of Flanders, of Tyrol, and Barcelona, Lord of Vizcaya and Molina," etc. (Archivo del Real Palacio. *Papeles reservados de Fernando VII*, 104, f. 66).

31. Miot de Mélito, III, p. 7.

did not matter as much as the exalted position he occupied and the popularity he hoped to achieve. With an eye on this latter goal he filled the most important posts of his government with Spaniards who had accepted Joseph Bonaparte and were ready to cooperate with the new regime: Azanza, O'Farril, Urquijo, Cabarrús, Mazarredo, talented men whose careers would always be tainted by their betrayal of the national cause.

Joseph did his best to persuade Spaniards that his cause was their cause. In his proclamations, in his speeches, he hammered at the same theme: His reign signified the preservation of Spain's independence and the integrity of its territory. His presence would insure the stability of the monarchy and at the same time the introduction of reforms indispensable to its prosperity. Opposition to him was therefore contrary to the best interests of Spain.[32] On April 30, 1809, answering a series of speeches by a delegation which had brought the adhesion to the new king of a number of Spanish towns, Joseph stressed the great power which had been placed in his hands by Providence, the certainty of his triumph, and the futility of continued resistance on the part of the chiefs of the insurrection. The latter, he indicated, were only fighting to keep their odious privileges and were shedding the people's blood to keep them forever enslaved under the yoke of feudalism.[33]

To Napoleon, too, Joseph tried to make clear that he desired to be a king in fact and not in name and that Spain must therefore preserve its independence vis-à-vis France. In a letter written to his brother from Madrid on March 7, 1809, while assuring the Emperor of his unswerving friendship and his loyalty to him and to France, he expressed the opinion that an enslaved Spain would be no asset to France, far from it. "An enslaved Spain," he wrote, "would be an enemy as soon as the first occasion presented itself." "I want to acquire Spain for France and France for Spain," he continued, "but in order to achieve this the weaker one must be convinced that the stronger does not want to make a slave out of her." Spain would stop fighting if it could be persuaded that Joseph truly wanted a strong

32. Cf. for instance Joseph's proclamation of June 8, 1808, Chapter III, p. 128.

33. *Gaceta de Madrid*, May 1, 1809, AHN, Estado, *legajo* 2993.

and independent Spain. "All [Spaniards] would be France's best friends if they knew that though I am a French Prince I want and must govern Spain as a free and independent nation; if they saw the promises contained in the Constitution of Bayonne fulfilled . . . I know that the greatest happiness of a great people is their independence, as the greatest happiness of a man is a good conscience . . . If you do not agree, my shaky crown is at your disposal. God has taken away from me that of Naples. You may take back that of Spain."[34]

This offer to abdicate was not the first and was not to be the last. Joseph had been discouraged from the start by Spain's resistance to Napoleon's usurpation,[35] and this discouragement had only grown deeper with the defeat at Bailén and the evacuation of Madrid. He had toyed with the idea of giving up the Spanish Crown on the heels of these unfavorable developments.[36] Then, when Napoleon began his lightning compaign against the Spanish insurrection, he was hurt by the scant attention paid to him by his brother. Again, the thought of resigning presented itself to him, and his friend Count Miot de Mélito, to whom we owe an invaluable account of Joseph's reign contained in his own memoirs, urged him to follow this course. But Joseph did not resign then, and though he threatened to do so on a number of occasions in succeeding years, he did not relinquish his crown. In the end it was his ambition, his vanity, and his fear of displeasing Napoleon which kept him on the Spanish throne. Though beset with innumerable difficulties, faced with incomprehension on the part of his august brother, with hostility from the great majority of the Spanish population, and toward the end with a rapidly deteriorating military situation, he was loath to give up his kingdom. For to Joseph it was a kingdom, no matter how insecure it seemed. And then, who was he to fling to the feet of Europe's new Charlemagne the crown the latter had placed on his head? It would not be wise to antagonize Napoleon. Furthermore, as Miot de Mélito suggested, the desire not to show weakness by resigning was perhaps also a factor in his oft-renewed decision to stay in the royal palace of Madrid. Perhaps, too, "the wish not to jeopardize the future of the small

34. *Mémoires et correspondance*, vi, pp. 68–70.
35. See Chapter III.
36. See Chapter VII.

number of Spaniards who had joined him and whom he thought he could justify and protect better by persevering in his enterprise."[37]

Ceaselessly and often desperately he tried to convey to Napoleon his own view of his mission. To his wife, who often relayed her husband's messages to her brother-in-law, he wrote on July 16, 1810: "As for myself, I am resolved never to compromise with my duties. It must not be expected of me to govern Spain solely for the good of France. I owe much gratitude to France, which is my family. But never, not even in poverty, have I accustomed my soul to the idea of degrading itself for the sake of my family. In Spain I have duties which my conscience dictates to me. I shall not betray them."[38] Later in the same year, alluding to another one of his offers of abdication, he confided to Julie that he would be happier with her, with his children, and with a few friends than in his exalted position. The theme of his duty to the Spanish people came up again in this letter: "I can stay here only as long as I can make the Spanish nation happy, while serving the general policy of the Emperor. But any obstacle placed on the road that must be taken by a prince conscious of his duties makes my position here untenable."[39]

The temperamental outbursts of Joseph and his oft-repeated complaints about the situation in Spain, as well as his constant demands for men and money, could not fail to displease his authoritarian brother. Napoleon had resented Joseph's attitude from the first. After a disgruntled message from Joseph in the days when French troops were on the defensive behind the Ebro, Napoleon answered angrily from Paris on September 17, 1808: "My brother, I do not answer your letter, in which you show bad temper. It is a principle which I have been applying for a long time in my dealings with you."[40] The Emperor's relations with his brother did not improve with the victorious campaign against Spain in the fall of 1808. Joseph, his pride hurt by the disdainful manner in which Napoleon treated him, sulked in El Pardo, while Napoleon hurled his decrees of rejuvenation at Spain's *Ancien Régime*. Before the Emperor left

37. Miot de Mélito, III, p. 25.
38. *Mémoires et correspondance*, VII, p. 299.
39. *Ibid.*, pp. 330–31.
40. *Correspondance*, No. 14336.

Madrid in pursuit of the British army, he had a talk with Joseph and it seemed briefly that the two brothers might be able to patch up their differences. Joseph was granted the title of lieutenant general of the emperor, with direct command over the 30,000 troops in the Madrid area. Later, from Valladolid, Napoleon even invited Joseph to write to him candidly and in detailed fashion whenever he deemed it necessary.[41] Joseph wasted no time in doing so almost immediately, and Napoleon promptly showed that though he had asked for frankness he did not really appreciate it in the form the King displayed it. In a letter written a few days before returning to Madrid in January, 1809, Joseph, while speaking out against the humiliating attitude of French generals and soldiers toward the population of Madrid, found another object for his complaints in French ambassador La Forest. La Forest, he claimed, had been a supporter of Murat's schemes in relation to the Spanish throne and had never liked him. The ambassador did everything to reduce his authority and apparently wanted to treat him like a beaten enemy. No, he would never like Monsieur de La Forest.[42]

Joseph's hostility to La Forest, whom Miot de Mélito characterized as "a most obscure and verbose diplomat,"[43] though not entirely justified, was to some extent well founded. The ambassador, aware of the true state of things in Spain, considered Napoleon's brother primarily as a lieutenant of the Emperor and not as a sovereign in his own right. As the envoy of France he felt that his first duty was to Napoleon and he acted more as the plenipotentiary of a victorious nation to a defeated nation than as an ambassador to an equal power. He disliked what he considered Joseph's pro-Spanish sentiments and utterances and the role played by Spaniards at the King's court and in the King's cabinet. Relations between King and ambassador did not normally go beyond a coolly correct modus vivendi on a purely official level.[44]

To Joseph's grievances Napoleon replied with complaints of his

---

41. January 15, 1809, *Correspondance*, No. 14717.

42. *Mémoires et correspondance*, v, pp. 383–85.

43. *Op. cit.*, p. 165.

44. At the end of 1810 and the beginning of 1811, as La Forest, endeavoring to keep Joseph on the throne, spent many hours with the King, the atmosphere lost some of its chill. See below.

own. It was a mistake, he wrote on March 4, 1809, to send reinforcements to Zaragoza. It was wrong to form regiments with Spanish
prisoners.[45] It was unwise to offer deserters from Spain's armies of
national resistance the rank they held before changing sides. The
Emperor disapproved of Joseph's leniency toward members of the
old Council of Castile.[46] He found fault with the King's administration of Madrid, where it seemed that crime was rife. He laid at the
King's door the blame for the escape of Spanish prisoners. On April
2, 1809, he wrote bluntly: "My brother, the affairs of Spain are going
badly."[47] Joseph would answer in the same tone, indignantly rejecting criticism of his handling of the situation.[48] He would accuse his
brother of lack of confidence in him. He would offer his resignation.
His anger rising, Napoleon had declared to Count Roederer[49] in
February, 1809: "The King must be French. Spain must be French. It
is for France that I conquered Spain. I conquered it with [France's]
blood, with her arms, with her gold . . . " "I have only one passion,
one mistress: France," he continued. "I sleep with her." Joseph's
attitude toward Spain was wrong. "He wants to be loved by Spaniards," the Emperor said scornfully, "he wants to make them believe
he loves them. The love of kings is no nursemaid's affection."
He accused the King of being indolent. He, Napoleon, always
worked. He worked while he ate and while he was at the theater.
Even at night his responsibilities did not leave him, for he woke up
frequently to reflect about problems of state. If Joseph abandoned his
post and returned to Mortefontaine, he would have him arrested at
the border, he thundered. "Nothing will stop me. I do not need my
family. I do not have a family if it is not French!" In a slightly
lighter vein Napoleon then went on to mention Joseph's family: "I
shall shortly send him his wife. They will make children. She is in

45. Napoleon had himself suggested such a measure in a letter from
Valladolid on January 7, 1809 (*Mémoires et correspondance*, v, p. 317).

46. The King had secured the release of several members of the Council
who had been arrested on Napoleon's orders.

47. *Correspondance*, No. 14995.

48. Cf. especially his letter of March 7, 1809 (*Mémoires et correspondance*,
VI, pp. 68–71).

49. Roederer was shortly to be sent on a mission to Spain, at the end of
which he was to report to the Emperor on the situation in the Peninsula.

good health now. She is plump and fat. His wife's advice is sound. She will be useful to him."[50]

Napoleon finally became so displeased with his brother that he stopped writing him personally and had his orders and instructions to the King transmitted mostly through Marshal Berthier, the *major général de l'armée* (chief of staff). This was true for most of 1810. Only rarely did the *rey intruso* receive a letter from the Emperor during this period. One such missive was a short answer on January 14, 1810 to Joseph's best wishes for the New Year. It was not exactly filled with brotherly love. "My brother," it said, "I have your letter, which has been brought to me by your aide-de-camp Cassano. I thank you for what you say on the occasion of the New Year. The Duke of Dalmatia[51] must have the title of Chief of Staff of the Army of Spain. This was, I think, the title of Marshal Jourdan when I was in Spain."[52] Another one arrived in Madrid in April of the same year. Napoleon had dictated on the third of the month a highly official message informing the King of the Emperor's marriage to Archduchess Marie Louise of Austria. "I do not doubt," Napoleon had said, that [Your Majesty] shares the joy I feel as a result of an event which is of such importance for my imperial household and for the happiness of my peoples." The end of the letter was pure formality: "I am gladly taking advantage of this occasion to assure [Your Majesty] of the sentiments of perfect esteem and affectionate friendship with which I am *Monsieur mon frère, de votre Majesté, le bon frère Napoléon*."[53]

Joseph, deeply offended by his brother's silence and appalled by the state of his kingdom, would at times address the Emperor with the energy of desperation. "Sire," he wrote on August 25, 1810, "for the sake of your interest more than mine, whatever your will may be, make it known, *but do not allow* the continuation of the horrible

50. Vitrac, *Journal du comte P. L. Roederer*, pp. 239–56.
51. Marshal Soult.
52. *Correspondance*, No. 16138. Joseph's personal military adviser and one of the very few French military chiefs with whom he was on friendly terms, Marshal Jourdan had distinguished himself in the French Revolutionary wars and had a long and brilliant military career behind him.
53. AHN, Estado, *legajo* 3105. "Monsieur my brother, the good brother of Your Majesty, Napoleon."

anarchy which will devour this country as long as the central authority is ignored, as long as all the emotions of the Spanish nation are
trod upon, and as long as your brother is a king in name only and an
object of derision for some and of pity for others. If Your Majesty
believes that the same blood runs in my veins, you must realize that I
cannot bear such a situation much longer."[54]

But Joseph, though ambitious and vain, was not, as we have noted,
a single-minded nor a strong-willed person. At times he would
solemnly declare that France was his family and Spain his religion,
and he would rage against the Spanish policy of the Emperor and his
generals.[55] Yet he was basically incapable of taking a do-or-die stand
on what he thought were Spain's interests, if it meant a direct
collision with the interests of the Empire, or of abdicating the crown
in defiance of the Emperor's will. In a conversation held in February,
1811 with French ambassador La Forest, he bared his soul perhaps
more than on any other occasion. La Forest had been instructed by
Paris to convince Joseph to stay on in Madrid, and since the previous
December the envoy had used all his skill to bring the King around to
Napoleon's point of view. The two men had had many conversations
during this period, but this was perhaps the most important meeting.

Joseph began by assuring La Forest, i.e. Napoleon, that he was
completely at his brother's disposal and that his loyalty to Napoleon
must never be doubted. "I have seemed to stray from the road
[traced by the Emperor]," he said, "I have cried out, I have threatened. But this is only the result of the conduct which I have adopted
to gain the goodwill of Spaniards and of the difficulties I have
encountered. Actually, if I had been put to the test, it would have
been seen that I have too much common sense to take a single false
step."

This should not be interpreted as meaning that Joseph's Spanish
patriotism was nothing but a sham, a pose calculated to lure Spaniards into collaborating with France. He was sincere in his desire
to be a truly Spanish monarch. But he was just as truthful when

54. *Mémoires et correspondance*, VII, p. 321
55. Cf. for instance La Forest's dispatch of August 17, 1810, *Correspondance*, IV, p. 89.

he beat his chest and proclaimed his loyalty to Napoleon. Yes, he spoke two languages according as he addressed himself to Spain or to the Emperor. Each of these two languages was authentic, however. His seemingly contradictory attitude was due primarily to his basic softness, not to say weakness, which caused him to bend to the will of Napoleon and prevented him from adopting a truly clear-cut stand on the fundamental issues. In the same conversation with La Forest he stated unequivocally: "Thus, let it be clearly understood that in no case shall I leave except with the approval of the Emperor and with the certitude that I shall not disappoint my brother."[56]

A pathetic frankness can be detected in a dispatch attached to the foregoing communication of the French ambassador and written by Joseph for the benefit of Napoleon: "The fact is that I wish to please the Emperor who is also my brother. He had me recognized as king of Naples and king of Spain and guaranteed my political existence without my having requested it. I did not solicit the throne. I ascended it because he wanted me to do so. Does the Emperor wish today that I retire from office? I am quite ready to take this step, all the more so since the events of [the past] three years have given rise to a good many scruples and would stifle many regrets."[57]

[2]

The difficulties Joseph was having with Napoleon were partly responsible for the almost total lack of authority the King had over the French generals in Spain. These military leaders feared only the power of Napoleon, but since the Emperor was far removed from the areas where they held their commands, they behaved like monarchs in a conquered country. While paying Joseph the outward forms of respect, they ignored his orders and ruled their domains with an iron fist. Their attitude toward the population only compounded Joseph's problems, for it was impossible for him to gain the

56. La Forest, *Correspondance*, IV, p. 452.

57. *Ibid.*, p. 458. This very important conversation, as well as the written statement, in La Forest, *Correspondance*, IV, pp. 451–62

goodwill of his subjects if his generals behaved abominably. Their incredible exactions, their dishonesty, and their cruelty embittered the inhabitants permanently against French rule. Most of them lived like satraps, squeezing the last penny out of Spanish citizens living in the occupied zone and becoming rich in the process. General Keller-mann, who has been called a "pitiless extortioner,"[58] had all those denounced as rich arrested. He then entered into negotiations with their families and set the prisoners free against a substantial ransom, which he promptly pocketed. Not content with this kind of opera-tion he engaged in all sorts of shady dealings. At Valladolid he had either established or was tolerating an office where Spanish prisoners were sold for a high price to insurgent forces.[59] The behavior of the general was imitated practically by the whole army. Marshal Masséna wrote to Joseph in August, 1810 that "theft and brigandage were practiced to the last degree."[60]

Napoleon was not unaware of the dealings of his military chiefs in Spain. Time and again we find in his correspondence references to this seemingly insoluble problem. In a letter of September 17, 1810, to Berthier, he complained about the trafficking in prisoners that pre-vailed in Spain, and a month later he asked for some measures against dishonest officers.[61] On February 2, 1811, he instructed Berthier to forbid French generals in Spain to engage in real estate activities. "Their task," he added, "is to conquer and subjugate the country and not to make a financial profit."[62] "My cousin," he wrote Berthier on March 10, 1811, "I have just read the letter of the Duke of Istria[63] of February 20. He tells you that 50 men have done much harm in Spain and have forced me to send 100,000 more troops to the Peninsula. Let him name the guilty ones, so that I may have them punished."[64]

But only another visit to Spain by the Emperor could have stopped the generals. After the victorious conclusion of the Austrian war in

58. Gaffarel, *Règne de Joseph Bonaparte de 1810 à 1812. Les difficultés gouvernementales. Publicaeiones del Congreso Histórico Internacional de la guerra de la independencia y su epoca,* IV, p. 129.

59. Miot de Mélito, p. 150; Gaffarel, p. 129.

60. Miot de Mélito, *Ibid.*

61. *Correspondance,* No. 16918.

62. *Ibid.,* No. 17317.

63. Marshal Bessières.

64. *Correspondance,* No. 17446.

1809, Napoleon toyed with the idea of returning to the Peninsula and putting an end to the war there by capturing Portugal and driving Wellington into the sea. But then his marriage to Marie Louise the following year prevented him once more from crossing the Pyrenees. In his absence, his generals and his administrators continued to do as they pleased. In Andalucía, after the conquest of that province in early 1810, Marshal Soult, who was in charge of the southern army, apparently felt that he had acquired a ready-made kingdom and carried out only those orders of the King which he found suitable to his own position. As for the other occupied parts of Spain, "neither in Catalonia nor in Aragón were the decrees of the King obeyed any more than they would have been in Galicia . . . , where we had no troops," recalled Miot de Mélito.[65] Even in Madrid Joseph was not complete master in his own house. The military governor, General Belliard, who had been appointed by the Emperor, hardly took cognizance of the King's presence. The latter insistently asked for the recall of the governor but Napoleon kept him in Madrid in spite of his brother's appeals. Finally Joseph was successful, however, in persuading Napoleon to let him relieve Belliard of his command and replace him with a general in his own service.[66]

For this state of affairs Napoleon must shoulder a considerable share of the blame. After leaving Spain early in 1809 he had entrusted Joseph with the command of two army corps, but it was a purely nominal command. Old Marshal Jourdan, who played the role of chief of staff and military adviser to the King, was not liked by Napoleon and could therefore not contribute to reinforcing Joseph's jurisdiction in the military area. The generals and the French administrators in their respective provinces acted practically on their own authority and the result was chaos. "No measure dealing with domestic affairs, no financial plan could be carried out successfully, because the decisions of the French administrators blocked them. Above all it was necessary to pay and feed the French army, and with this pretext all taxes were siphoned off or consumed in advance. Ordering, regulating, taking, or destroying everything as they pleased in their provinces, these administrators not only did not

65. *Op. cit.*, p. 145.
66. *Ibid.*, p. 198; Artola, *Los afrancesados*, p. 181.

recognize the agents of the King, but even forbade all those under their orders to recognize them."[67]

The generals and the army killed all the hopes that Joseph might have entertained of bringing a measure of well-being to his Spanish subjects. The terribly heavy taxes levied by the military leaders for their own sake and for the sake of the army, and the consumption by the French army, living on the country, of all available resources, promptly reduced occupied Spain to economic misery and left Joseph penniless. The King's financial position was hopeless. Hence his endless pleas for money.

Spanish hostility to the *rey intruso*, which would have been strong in any case, was made even more unyielding by the behavior of French generals and troops, and specifically by French exactions, which to a large extent were behind Joseph's financial plight. As long as the basic hostility of the Spanish people to the French regime, and hence to Joseph's rule, remained strong, the King could not possibly establish anything approaching a stable administration. There were moments when it seemed to Joseph that he was making progress, but he never really achieved any lasting measure of popularity except among the *afrancesados*, many of whom served him at his court and in his administration. Unfortunately, the antagonism of the population often caused the *rey intruso* to adopt repressive measures, which in turn increased the hatred for him. Most Spaniards, even those who through personal contact had come to realize that he was not the Pepe Botellas and rey de copas depicted by Spanish caricatures but a man with considerable personal charm, rarely saw in him anything else but a tool in the unscrupulous hands of Napoleon. Consequently, opposition to him in the occupied territories, in the form of guerrilla activity, passive resistance, clandestine literature, and simply silent opposition, remained strong throughout his reign.

The correspondence of French ambassador La Forest and the memoirs of Miot de Mélito bear eloquent testimony to this inimical attitude on the part of the inhabitants of the capital. There were, of course, special occasions when amidst a select group of people Joseph could hear himself applauded and acclaimed, and there were moments, too, when some special order given by the King gained him

67. Miot de Mélito, p. 53.

the momentary goodwill of even his enemies. There were always enough *afrancesados* present at court functions and the theater, where the King could be assured of a minimum show of adhesion. On February 6, 1809, for instance, La Forest reported that the King had been acclaimed at the theater,[68] and on August 15, as Miot de Mélito recalled, acclamations greeted Joseph after a gala dinner for 200 persons.[69] Following the signing of the peace between France and Austria, while Joseph was planning to celebrate the event with public festivities, he was asked by Spanish general O'Farril and French general Merlin to pardon two deserters from one of the Spanish regiments formed earlier in the year. The two culprits had been condemned to run the gauntlet. At the last minute, when the ranks of soldiers were already drawn up and the punishment was about to begin, the news of their pardon arrived. As a result, according to La Forest, the cries of *Viva el rey* were louder and more general than they had ever been, and they reverberated from street to street.[70]

But aside from these occasions and aside from the visits of out-of-town delegations, forced by necessity to come to the capital and declare their loyalty to the regime, the hostility of the population of Madrid remained irreducible. On March 5, 1809, La Forest noted that "the attitude of Madrid is as absurd as ever."[71] On April 14, he reported that in spite of the vigilance of the government and the minister of police, posters were found every morning threatening all those Spanish officials who had taken the oath of loyalty to Joseph.[72] Miot de Mélito tells us how the population of Madrid was looking hopefully to the coming of Spanish and British troops when rumors were sweeping the capital that Joseph had been routed at Talavera: "An immense crowd moved toward the palace and the bridges of Segovia and Toledo to see [the Allies] arrive. Nevertheless there was no disorder, but the joy of the inhabitants was made manifest by much noise, and an extreme gaiety reigned everywhere."[73]

No matter how hard Joseph tried to gain the friendship of

68. *Correspondance*, ii, p. 46.
69. *Op. cit.*, pp. 66–67.
70. Dispatch of November 1, 1809, *Correspondance*, iii, p. 57.
71. *Ibid.*, ii, p. 109.
72. *Ibid.*, p. 187.
73. *Op. cit.*, p. 60.

madrileños he could not break through the impenetrable wall of enmity. Anxious to show them that he, too, was highly devout, he heard Mass regularly in his private chapel and at first lost no opportunity to make an appearance in the churches of the capital. But all his efforts were in vain. While Spaniards might be willing to admit that Joseph was animated to a certain extent by good intentions, all his acts could not erase the unpleasant reality that he was a foreign prince reigning in their capital against their will, and kept there by foreign bayonets.

On May 25, 1809, La Forest reported that the supporters of the Supreme Junta were constantly spreading false news about the situation of the French in the area of the capital.[74] A letter in French, in the Spanish national archives, dated August 15, 1809, speaks of Joseph's return to Madrid from Toledo and adds that "the people of Madrid as well as the monks behaved very badly in these days of crisis . . . They gave [the King] an almost chilly reception."[75] In September, recalls Mélito, "public opinion, still inflexible, rejected all that came from us, even the benefits."[76] In November, the terrible Spanish disaster of Ocaña[77] dampened considerably the optimism of *madrileños*. Until the first column of 16,000 prisoners entered the town on the twenty-second, most Spaniards had refused to believe the news of the French victory, but now they had to face the stark reality of the catastrophe. At first there was some gratitude among the population for the lenient treatment Joseph had ordered for the prisoners.[78] "But soon, hatred and hostility against the French got the upper hand, and neither the victory nor the moderation which [the French] used after the battle brought public opinion to the [French] side."[79] In vain Joseph appealed to *madrileños* to form a civic guard. By May, 1810, only 600 men had enlisted.[80]

74. *Op. cit.*, II, p. 261.
75. AHN, Estado, *legajo* 3100.
76. *Op. cit.*, p. 74.
77. See Chapter VIII.
78. After the prisoners left Madrid for France, however, they were treated abominably by their guards and many died on the road. See Chapter XVI.
79. Miot de Mélito, p. 78.
80. La Forest, III, p. 379. As a result, the decree of July 4, 1810 stipulated that all permanent residents of Madrid, except workingmen and domestics, were to serve in the Madrid militia, but it allowed substitutions or the

In La Forest's correspondence we read in the entry for August 9, 1810, that "insulting posters" suggested that Joseph abdicate. Two days earlier the King had allowed the opening of the convent church of San Cayetano. The priest, in the course of his sermon, had begun to praise the piety of the King. A voice had been raised in the audience to say that they had gone to church to hear the gospel and not adulation. Others had uttered their approval of this statement and the public had left the edifice. "The connivance of an *alcalde* prevented the culprits from being arrested."[81]

Mesonero Romanos remembered how his father had at first refused to read the *Diario* and the *Gaceta de Madrid* because they were official newspapers of the Napoleonic regime. Eventually his father's friends, however, had succeeded in introducing the forbidden French papers into the house, and the comments aroused by them among the menfolk made an indelible impression on the child's mind. While the women of the house were sewing and knitting around the *brasero*, the men would vent their impotent rage against what was printed in the official press. "If those bulletins said for instance: 'In such and such an action 500 Frenchmen were killed', immediately someone would exclaim: 'Surely more than that'. The bulletin would go on saying: 'and 5,000 Spaniards', and all would cry out: 'Of course, what else are they going to say?' Such and such a town had been occupied by the enemy. 'Impossible'. 'But look, even letters received from there say so', somebody would observe. 'The letters are wrong'. 'But the newspapers are printing it as an official announcement'. 'The newspapers are lying!' 'The French have smashed through the Despeñaperros pass'.[82] 'Ridiculous!' 'The French have entered Andújar, Córdoba, Sevilla. . . .'[83] Then [Mesonero's father] would stop reading and say with a mysterious and satisfied air: 'Don't

---

payment of a certain sum to avoid service (*Prontuario de las leyes y decretos del Rey Nuestro Señor Don José Napoleón I*, II, pp. 177–78). The previous year Joseph had ordered the establishment of urban militias throughout occupied Spain (*Ibid.*, I, pp. 279–84), repeating Napoleon's order of December 15, 1808, which had decreed the formation of "national guard" battalions in Spanish towns (*Correspondance*, No. 14569).

81. La Forest, IV, p. 76.
82. See Chapter VIII.
83. See Chapter VIII.

worry, all this is but a ruse of Lord Wellington. He will let them get farther and farther . . . .' "[84]

Shortly before Madrid was evacuated by Joseph in the summer of 1812 as a result of the battle of Salamanca,[85] La Forest reported that *madrileños,* though behaving cautiously, were dreaming about the arrival of the British and were anxiously awaiting them.[86] Faced with this uncompromising attitude on the part of the population of Madrid, Joseph, in the later years of his reign, appeared in public less and less frequently and isolated himself more and more from his subjects. But even at court poor Joseph was at times reminded of the hostile disposition of Spaniards toward his rule. On one occasion he came to realize that Spanish children entertained no fonder feelings for the French than their parents. The *corregidor* of Madrid, Don Dámaso de la Torre, decided one day to introduce to the King his son Carlitos, who was between seven and eight years of age. The proud father had the boy put on the uniform of the civic guard created by Joseph, and thus attired, brought him to the presence of the King. The latter, much pleased by the little man's aspect, stroked his head and asked him in his broken Italianate Spanish: *"E per qué tienes tú qüesta spada?"*[87] Answered the little boy unabashedly: *"Para matar franceses."*[88] His father, who at that moment would have liked to have the earth swallow him, stammered out his apology: "Pardon, Your Majesty, you know how children are, they repeat what they hear the servants and other people say . . . ," an explanation hardly calculated to erase the shock of the little angel's words.[89]

This unrelenting hostility was of course not limited to the walls of Madrid. The same feelings were in the hearts of most Spaniards living in French-occupied territory. At Alcalá de Henares, some seventeen miles east of the capital, an anonymous citizen of that town kept a diary throughout the war, and in it we glean much interesting information on the mood of its inhabitants in those trying times. The

84. *Op. cit.,* pp. 71–74.
85. See below.
86. Dispatch of July 26, 1812, *Op. cit.,* VI, p. 363.
87. "And why do you have this sword?"
88. "To kill Frenchmen."
89. Mesonero Romanos, *Memorias de un setentón,* p. 47.

alcalaíno[90] noted toward the end of March, 1810, that French authorities had posted an edict inviting the population to enroll in companies of 100 men each. This was necessary for the protection of the town against "bandits," i.e., guerrillas, the notice claimed. Only one man volunteered. He was a Spanish administrator appointed by the French.[91] In September, 1810, a great event was announced in Alcalá. His Majesty the King in person would visit the town on the eighteenth of the month. Streets were ordered swept and decked out. The inhabitants obeyed, but according to the Alcalaíno they did their worst. When Joseph entered the town, there were no *vivas* and no hats were taken off in his honor. That day the main church was presented by the King with a gift of a gold and diamond ring, "without any doubt," commented the diarist sarcastically, "as a reward for the 10 *arrobas*[92] [of the church treasure] he had ordered removed from the [temple]."[93]

But the main source of relentless enmity was the numerous bands of guerrilla fighters that had sprung up throughout occupied Spain in the early days of the war. They were the backbone of Spanish popular resistance to Napoleon, and Joseph was never allowed to forget about their activities. French couriers were constantly intercepted, and generals and administrators could never be sure that their mail reached its destination. Most roads were infested, and unless the French sent powerful military escorts along with mail carriers or civilian convoys, it was almost certain that many French lives would be lost or mail and other articles would fall into the hands of the guerrillas. These dauntless men reduced effective French control to the main roads and to the walls of the larger towns. An official wrote in August, 1809, from Burgos to the *afrancesado* minister of the interior in Madrid that the northern city was practically isolated by the guerrillas.[94]

90. Inhabitant of Alcalá.

91. "Libro de apuntes de un alcalaíno (1809–1814)," *Revue Hispanique*, Vol. xxxi, p. 174. Later however, the French forced the inhabitants into a civic guard organized by the *afrancesado* captain Don Antonio Viedma (*ibid.*, p. 179).

92. About 250 pounds.

93. "Libro de apuntes de un alcalaíno," *Op. cit.*, p. 177.

94. AHN, Estado, *legajo* 3100.

Most of the time Madrid found itself in a similar situation. The correspondence of La Forest abounds in remarks about guerrillas, whom he labeled "brigands" or "quadrilles."[95] On August, 14, 1809, he spoke of "brigands" who were infesting the country and had intercepted most of the couriers between Madrid and Segovia. He added that many smugglers, escaped prisoners, and deserters from the Spanish regiments that had been formed by the King after the battle of Uclés in January had joined the guerrillas.[96] On July 26, 1810, he noted that for the past six weeks attacks on French communications had been taking place with more frequency than ever before.[97] Even large convoys no longer kept the irregulars at bay. On August 23, 1810, the French ambassador reported the near loss of a convoy. As the latter had drawn within sight of Madrid, the officer commanding the military escort had thought it safe enough to take a road different from that followed by the convoy. "The officer did not know apparently," added La Forest sarcastically, "that in the woods of El Pardo and right up to the walls of the Casa de Campo there are enemy parties."[98] Almost to the day, a year later, La Forest wrote: "The 'quadrilles' and bands are present everywhere."[99]

On January 11, 1812, guerrillas frightened French authorities in Madrid out of their wits. At about 3:00 P.M. on that day, Colonel Choiseul was taking an afternoon ride with a servant along the promenade of Las Delicias, close to the walls of the capital. Suddenly, four horsemen wearing helments and red uniforms and appearing out of nowhere attacked the two riders. The Colonel was saved only through the speed of his horse, while his servant was seriously wounded. The four partisans were soon joined by twelve more, and the whole group then followed the avenue along the walls which led to Atocha Gate. Bullets whistled and a number of Frenchmen and *afrancesados* in uniform, walking along the promenade, fell to the ground, two of them dead. Meanwhile, *madrileños*, hearing that a force of Spaniards was wreaking havoc among the Frenchmen outside of Atocha, hurried hopefully to Las Delicias. But then a detach-

95. From Spanish *cuadrilla*, band of armed men.
96. La Forest, II, p. 363.
97. *Ibid.*, IV, p. 49.
98. *Ibid.*, p. 98.
99. *Ibid.*, V, p. 209.

ment of the garrison appeared and forced the intruders to withdraw. The incursion had ended, but La Forest and other French officials shuddered at the thought of what might have happened if a much larger band, which surely would have been received with open arms by the population, had attacked Atocha Gate.[1] By the summer of 1812, the guerrillas were acting as they pleased in the area of Madrid. On July 26, La Forest wrote that they were killing Frenchmen as near as Carabanchel and Chamartín.[2]

One of the few manifestations of loyalty, outside those displayed by Joseph's circle of *afrancesado* ministers and officials, such as Urquijo, Azanza, O'Farril, Cabarrús, and Mazarredo,[3] came from no other than Fernando VII. The young prince, a prisoner at Valençay, was spending his captivity in indolence. But worse than this, he did not hesitate to abase himself before Napoleon and Joseph to prove his devotion to them. In an abject letter, dated November 28, 1809, this unworthy object of Spain's affection begged Joseph to help him obtain Napoleon's approval for his marriage to a niece of the Emperor. He also asked to be granted membership in the royal order recently created by the *rey intruso*. The message could not end on a more sycophantic note: "I desire to prove to Your Majesty the sincerity of my feelings and my confidence in You. The devoted brother of Your Catholic Majesty, Fernando."[4]

[3]

It is indeed surprising that Joseph I, forced to "struggle at one and the same time against French and Allied generals, to stand up against the wishes of his brother and to have himself accepted by recalcitrant subjects, and this without resources, without money, almost without soldiers,"[5] made an attempt at reigning. Yet, the

1. Dispatch of January 12, 1812, *ibid.*, VI, pp. 15–19.
2. *Ibid.*, p. 363. On Spanish guerrillas see Chapter XV.
3. See Chapter XIII.
4. *Mémoires et correspondance politique et militaire du Roi Joseph*, VII, pp. 106–107.
5. Gaffarel, p. 127. The only troops under the King's own effective command were normally the royal regiments stationed in and near Madrid and composed mostly of Italian, German, and Spanish prisoners, all wearing the Spanish cockade.

attempt was made. Surrounded by Spanish and French ministers and courtiers, he planned ahead for the utopian times when Spain would be pacified and he would rule over a united and prosperous nation. Decree after decree, signed with the age-old, arrogant formula *Yo El Rey* (I The King), rolled off the royal presses, order after order went out from the capital. Due to the war and the impossible situation in which the King found himself most of the time, many edicts could never be enforced. Still, even so, historical evidence gives us a glimpse of the kind of Spain that might have been ruled by Joseph.

By the decree of February 6, 1809, the King established his cabinet, which included the ministries of State, Justice, Ecclesiastical Affairs, Foreign Affairs, Interior, Finance, War, Navy, the Indies, and Police,[6] and such *afrancesado* statesmen as Urquijo (State), Azanza (Indies), O'Farril (War), Cabarrús (Finance), and Mazarredo (Navy). The old Council of Castile, which had been abolished by Napoleon, was replaced with a Council of State of twenty-five members, selected from among persons who had shown their adhesion to the new order since Bayonne. Among the new councillors were the sinister Marquis de Caballero, minister of justice under Charles IV, Don Tomás de Morla, once the toast of Andalucía, and José Antonio Llorente, formerly secretary of the Inquisition, who centered in Joseph's regime his hopes for a more modern Spain.[7]

Subsequent decrees abolished seignorial rights, the *Voto de Santiago*,[98] the Mesta, interior customs, and all military and civil orders, except that of the Golden Fleece. A single order, the *Orden Real de España*, replaced them. Spaniards, contemptuous of the violet color of its decoration, called it the Order of the Eggplant (*La Orden de la Berenjena*).[10] From the first, Joseph had tried to force all civil servants to take an oath of loyalty. In October, 1808, they had been

6. *Prontuario de las leyes y decretos del Rey Nuestro Señor Don José Napoleón I*, I, pp. 83–94; AHN, Estado, *legajo* 3130.

7. *Prontuario*, I, pp. 171–77; Grandmaison, *L'Espagne et Napoléon*, II, p. 109.

8. See Chapter XI.

9. See Chapter I.

10. Mesonero Romanos. *op. cit.*, p. 79; Grandmaison, *op. cit.*, Vol. II, pp. 178–347.

given the choice of swearing fealty or losing their salaries or pensions. This measure had created a serious problem for patriotic Spaniards residing in the occupied areas and had forced many to take an oath repugnant to their conscience.[11] Those civil servants and clergymen who had been absent from their posts since November 1, 1808, were given by the decree of May 1, 1809, twenty days from the date of the edict to return, after which term they would face dismissal and confiscation of their property. The same decree warned that any secular or regular churchman who misled the people by spreading false news, or encouraged disobedience to and rebellion against the King's government would be arrested, taken to Madrid, and tried there by the special criminal junta which had been set up in the capital. Furthermore, in any town or village where a French soldier might be murdered, all monasteries and convents would be suppressed unless the murderer was arrested and the religious establishments proved that they had had no part in the crime.[12]

The decree of July 7, 1809 struck at owners of real estate who had left their place of residence without informing the intendant of the province, or who had moved to unoccupied areas of Spain. Their administrators or tenants would be entitled to keep the product of the rent or any payment due the landlord as an indemnity for the supplies requisitioned from them by French authorities.[13] After the battle of Talavera, when Spanish hopes for liberation had run high in Madrid and the hostility to the *rey intruso* had been most palpable, Joseph decided to strike a telling blow at some of Spain's most traditional institutions and at all those who had manifested their opposition in one way or another. Since the regular clergy was usually very active in fomenting rebellion against the "intrusive king," it was the first to suffer from the new toughness prevailing at the Court of Madrid. The decree of August 18, 1809 went one decisive step beyond Napoleon's decree of December, 1808.[14] It abolished all male religious orders and gave residents of monasteries

11. *Prontuario*, I, pp. 107–109; Artola, *Los afrancesados*, pp. 95–96.
12. *Prontuario*, I, pp. 168–71; AHN, Estado, *legajo* 3099.
13. *Prontuario*, I, pp. 236–38; AHN, Estado, *legajo* 2993/1.
14. See Chapter VII. Napoleon had already abolished the Inquisition (see Chapter VII).

fifteen days to leave their establishments and don the dress of the secular clergy. They were ordered to return to their place of birth or their legal residence, where they would receive a pension. Properties of the orders would be taken over by the State and sold to individuals.[15] On August 18, too, all the old councils, including the Council of the Indies, were eliminated, as well as the titles of the aristocracy, which was ordered to request a new concession under penalty of degradation. The measure attacked 119 grandees, 535 titles of Castile, and about 400,000 hidalgos.[16] All houses owned by persons who had taken refuge in the insurgent provinces were confiscated and ordered sold at once by the State. The previous month, all those who had sons serving with the insurgent armies had been ordered to give to Joseph's army one man in compensation or pay a sum of money according to a fixed rate calculated on the basis of three income brackets.[17]

The resentment these measures caused can well be imagined. The decree ordering the suppression of monasteries aroused particular hostility among the regular clergy and a large part of the population. Even the Cortes of Cádiz did not dare go quite that far in its efforts to diminish the influence of the Church. With a stroke of the pen Joseph practically eliminated an institution which had become almost an integral part of Spanish life. The great majority of Spanish monks and friars, above all friars, came from among the masses of the Spanish people and stood close to them in thought and feeling. Though frequently criticized by the secular clergy[18] and by the enlightened lay minority, they were still fairly popular, especially since they were playing such an important role in the national resistance against Napoleon. Joseph made the task of the Cortes of Cádiz easier, since the latter did not have to deal with an intact regular clergy, but with an organization that had been seriously, though only temporarily, hurt not only by the war itself, but also by

15. *Prontuario*, I, pp. 303–305; AHN, Estado, *legajo* 3099.

16. *Prontuario*, I, pp. 291–93; Grandmaison, II, p. 176. Exception was made by the decree of August 19 in the case of noblemen employed by the *intruso* government (*Prontuario*, I, pp. 306–307).

17. *Prontuario*, I, pp. 256–57, 289–90; Grandmaison, II, p. 177.

18. Cf. particularly the comments of the Spanish secular clergy on this question in Artola, *Los orígenes de la España contemporánea*, I, pp. 367–69.

the decrees of the *rey intruso*. But just as Joseph's decision brought hostility to his regime to paroxysmal fury among wide sectors of occupied Spain, so did the milder decree of the Cortes contribute to aligning the Church solidly against the liberals, thus constituting one of the main causes of the reformists' downfall.[19]

Many of Joseph's measures would no doubt have made Spain a better country to live in. He centralized and cut through the red tape of the chaotic Spanish administration. He eliminated laws which hampered the free circulation of merchandise and others that hindered the development of agriculture. He abolished hanging as a method of carrying out the death penalty and replaced it by the garrote. He created a commercial tribunal and a stock exchange in Madrid. Following the French pattern, Spain was divided into thirty-eight administrative units called *prefecturas* or *departamentos*. Public education was fostered by the creation of secondary schools in large towns, by the drawing up of a curriculum and of regulations for the admission of students, and by the establishment of a school for girls. The arts found a generous Maecenas in the "intrusive king." He decreed the foundation of a museum of painting in Madrid, to which he was ready to contribute canvases from his own palaces. At Granada he ordered the restoration of the Alhambra and the completion of the palace of Charles V. A new set of regulations for the stage was drawn up, and the busts of Lope, Calderón, Moreto, and Guillén de Castro were ordered brought to the Madrid theaters.[20]

The program of regeneration which had begun with the Constitution of Bayonne and continued through the difficult years of Joseph's rule was not very different from the reforms enacted by the liberals of Cádiz. Though Spanish reformists did not need the French example to become aware of the necessity for deep changes in Spain's political and social structure, they were constantly reminded that on the other side of the fence reforms were pushed by the intruder's

19. See Chapter XVIII.

20. *Prontuario*, I, pp. 371–72, 377–96, 415–16, 417–30, 459–61, 465–72; II, pp. 34–36, 56–132; AHN, Estado, *legajo* 2993/1; Mesonero Romanos, p. 75; Grandmaison, II, pp. 178–79, 342. Joseph subsidized the famous actor Isidoro Máiquez, who was called to Spain from France, where he had been residing since the *dos de mayo*, in which, according to Mesonero Romanos, he had taken an active part (*op. cit.*, p. 76).

regime. Though they hated the Napoleonic system, they could not ignore its efforts to effect basic changes, and the need for the Cortes to go forward with its work of political and social progress became consequently so much more pressing.

The external aspect of Madrid was perhaps the one element in Spain which benefited most from Joseph's reign. To grant the town more space, better views, and more squares he gave orders for the demolition of many blocks of obstructive buildings,[21] an activity which earned him the nickname of El rey plazuelas[22] from his sneering subjects.[23] A report to the King by the *corregidor* of Madrid, dated February 13, 1810, described what had been accomplished until then in the way of improvements for life in the capital. The document mentioned a cover built over the sewer of the Prado promenade, which emitted a foul odor in hot weather. The water supply to the city had been improved. The crosses that in the eyes of the *intruso* government had defaced squares and other spots had been placed in cemeteries and churches, "sheltered from any irreverence." To clear the Plaza Mayor and the streets leading into it from all excess market stands, two large squares, Santa Cruz and San Miguel, were being built in the vicinity. The report ended on the following note: "Señor, those interested in public welfare are happy to be living under a government which shows such liberal ideas in everything, and are looking forward to the innumerable benefits which the nation will derive from the reign of a sovereign who in the midst of the greatest difficulties devotes such generous attention to the comfort of the inhabitants of Madrid."[24]

The King did his best to bring a measure of gaiety to the normally dull life of the capital. In the times of Charles III and Charles IV amusements had been frowned upon, and Joseph, especially at the beginning of his reign, tried hard to divert *madrileños* with fiestas, the theater, and bullfights. Religious holidays were given new luster

21. For instance, the blocks occupying with the garden of La Priora the space on which stands today the Plaza de Oriente in front of the royal palace were torn down.

22. King Little Squares.

23. *Prontuario*, I, pp. 441–42; Mesonero Romanos, p. 81; Grandmaison, II, p. 343.

24. AHN, Estado, *legajo* 3113.

by the *intruso* government. During Holy Week in 1809, Madrid's religious brotherhoods paraded before the King, who, standing on the balcony of his palace and surrounded by his courtiers, knelt during each prayer uttered by the various delegations.[25] The celebration of Corpus Christi in June, 1810, was a most solemn and brilliant affair. The procession, which included the King and members of Joseph's government, began at noon and was seen by huge crowds of *madrileños*. In the evening, a gala ball in the palace, which began at 8:00 P.M. and ended at 12:30 A.M., marked the end of this most important Spanish holiday.[26]

The celebrations of Napoleon's saint's day (August 15), during the periods when the King was present in Madrid, and that of the ever-absent Queen Julie on May 22, 1810, were sparkling events, too. On August 15, 1809, after a day filled with official ceremonies, the King, having returned the same day from a victorious military campaign in the province of Toledo,[27] donned his costume as French Prince and sat down in the palace to a sumptuous meal attended by twenty-four guests, including the French ambassador, the diplomatic corps, French generals, and the ministers. In the royal armory of the palace, a table for two hundred persons had been set up for the officers of the King's guard and the French regiments. After supper, while fireworks were lighting the Madrid sky and a salvo of 100 rounds shook the town, His Catholic Majesty entered his carriage and proceeded to the opera through streets brightly lit by festive illuminations.[28] On May 22, 1810, celebrating his wife's saint's day, Joseph visited the Prado promenade, reviewed his troops, and returned to the palace through the Calle de Alcalá, the Puerta del Sol, and the Calle Mayor. Along the route the houses were decked out and a triumphal arch had been erected in front of the house of the governor of Madrid, General Belliard. At night there were illuminations and Madrid's three theaters[29] were filled, as entrance was free.[30] The

25. La Forest, dispatch of April 1, 1809, II, p. 163.
26. *Ibid.*, dispatch of June 22, 1810, III, p. 461.
27. See Chapter VIII.
28. La Forest, dispatch of August 16, 1809, II, pp. 367–68.
29. The Príncipe, the Cruz, and the recently reopened Caños del Peral.
30. La Forest, dispatch of May 24, 1810, II, pp. 401–403.

Carnival festivities of 1811 brought Joseph out of a long isolation, due to an exacerbation of his perennial difficulties,[31] and those of 1813, more lustrous than ever, were held shortly before he left the capital of Spain forever.[32]

Joseph was a great lover of dramatic art and missed no opportunity to attend the theater. Ambassador La Forest reported on February 2, 1809, that the King had reserved all the loge seats at the Caños del Peral and had distributed them to persons recently presented at court. He had been acclaimed at the theater, where he had entered his loge after torchbearers and heralds wearing old Spanish costumes had announced his arrival. His brilliantly decorated loge in the same building had the following words painted on its balcony: *Vive feliz, Señor, reyna y perdona*.[33]

On the King's saint's day in March, 1809, a curious little incident took place at the theater, which casts a somewhat amusing light on Joseph's exaggerated though understandable sensitivity to his position in Madrid. At the end of the performance "a cloud descended upon the stage and the actors gathered around a portrait of His Majesty, which they surrounded with garlands of flowers. Two French verses could be read [below the portrait]. The King had not been informed beforehand. He withdrew toward the rear of his loge and left shortly afterwards . . . The theater manager was put in jail."[34] What had aroused the ire of His Majesty? It was the slight he had sensed in the lines in French which had adorned his image: *C'est Lycurgue, Solon, c'est l'aîné des Césars*.[35] Being mentioned merely as the oldest brother of the Bonaparte clan had apparently made the King feel that the author had wittingly placed him in an inferior position vis-à-vis the Emperor.[36]

While the theater made the delight of the King, the Court, and the upper classes, bullfights attracted the masses of the people. "The holding of bullfights on Sundays until September has been decided

31. *Ibid.*, dispatch of February 26, 1811, IV, pp. 485–86.
32. See below.
33. Live happily, Sire, reign and forgive. *Op. cit.*, II, p. 35; Grandmaison, II, pp. 118–19.
34. La Forest, dispatch of March 20, 1809, II, p. 138.
35. He is Lycurgus, Solon, he is the oldest of the Caesar's family.
36. La Forest, *ibid.*

upon and has made the population of Madrid happy," wrote La
Forest on July 1, 1810. "There has been a bullfight this morning and
this afternoon. The King was not present, to the great regret of the
crowd."[37] How the ambassador was able to report that the mass of
aficionados had missed His Catholic Majesty is of course somewhat
of a mystery. On March 19, 1811, a special *corrida* was offered the
inhabitants to celebrate Joseph's saint's day, and La Forest noted that
it had attracted the usual throng.[38]

While these amusements, fiestas, and ceremonies undoubtedly lent
some passing glitter to life in Madrid and even called forth occasional
applause—applause produced by curiosity rather than genuine enthusiasm in most cases, however—the great majority of the population of
the capital did not forget that theirs was a city occupied by the
enemy.

As for life in Madrid, aside from the French ambassador's volumi-
nous reports on the happenings in the capital and the memoirs of
such eyewitnesses as Mesonero Romanos, the Madrid newspapers of
the years 1809–1813 furnish valuable information on the activities
taking place in the *villa coronada* in those extraordinary times. Let us
cast a hurried glance at the yellow, timeworn pages of the *Gaceta de
Madrid* of 1810—the high-water period of French domination in the
Peninsula—and capture some of the life that was and is no more. The
Gaceta of April 5, 1810, announced the appointments made on
March 18 for the new royal order instituted by Joseph. Three
clergymen, eighteen members of the military, two retired ship captains, and other individuals made up the list. In the *Gaceta* of May 11,
we read that the Teatro del Príncipe would present at 8:00 P.M. a
comedy in three acts entitled *La tía y la sobrina*[39] and the operetta *El
secreto*. In the issue of July 13, there appeared an installment of a
series of articles by the *afrancesado* J. Acedo,[40] filled with regalist
arguments. "The history of all the transgressions committed by the

37. *Ibid.*, IV, p. 6.
38. *Ibid.*, p. 540.
39. *The Aunt and the Niece.*
40. The title of the series is *Colección diplomática de varios papeles anti-
guos y modernos sobre dispensas matrimoniales y otros puntos de disciplina
eclesiástica española*. These and the following issues, from AHN, Estado, *legajo*
2993.

Popes and their supporters against the power of kings and of the efforts they have been making for nine centuries to establish their doctrine would be interminable" is a typical phrase from Acedo's pen.

On July 14, the Caños del Peral presented an opera in two acts, *La molinera* (*The Miller's Wife*), performed by an Italian company. On July 17, we read news from the French Empire and Spain, as well as from Russia, Sweden, Prussia, Hungary, and Italy. The supplement of the *Gaceta* of July 21 printed a list, commonly found in the newspapers of French-occupied Spain, enumerating properties taken over by the government from suppressed monasteries and from Spaniards who had sought refuge in free Spain, and put up for sale as *bienes nacionales*.[41] On the last page of almost every issue we find advertisements for books, many of which could be purchased in the bookstore of Quiroga on Calle Carretas. On July 28, a report from New York, dated May 15, spoke of disorder and confusion in the American government, while the last page announced the establishment of a "salon" on Calle de Fuencarral, where French books could be bought or read on the premises. The *Gaceta* of November 9 has an article in the *Variedades* section, dealing with the contagiousness of syphilis. By contrast, in the issue of November 16, *Variedades* offered an article entitled "Considerations on the Literary and Scientific Superiority of the Writers and Scholars of Antiquity."

What the newspapers did not print, of course, were the details of Joseph's private life or the immense difficulties which Joseph faced practically every day in his attempts to govern the country. Though he often tried hard to give himself fully to his work, his routine was generallly not too exacting. When he was not with the army he rose early, between 6:00 and 7:00 A.M., but audiences with his ministers, Marshal Jourdan, or French and Spanish generals began only at 10:00. Before this hour he would receive members of the royal household at 9:00 and have breakfast at 9:30. However, he would often spend many hours with his cabinet, which met on Mondays and Thursdays at 11:00 A.M. and could adjourn as late as 6:00. At 4:00, weather permitting, he went to the Casa de Campo, where he dined at the royal hunting lodge with Marshal Jourdan, Count Miot de

41. National property.

Mélito, and sometimes ladies of the court and officers of the royal household. After dinner he took a ride on horseback or in his carriage and then played a game of cards. Before retiring at night he sent off his mail to France.[42]

In his moments of indolence, caused by the sharp awareness of failure, he would let affairs of state go by the wayside, spending much of his time with intimate friends like O'Farril and Miot de Mélito. He would have his meals with his intimate circle and discuss with them French, Spanish, and Italian literature, political economy, and many other subjects. The gardens and woods of the Casa de Campo, which he had linked with the palace by a tunnel under the Manzanares, were his favorite refuge from the worries of his kingdom. There, forgetting the impossible task he had undertaken, he would relax in the company of his friends, which often included young women.[43]

Joseph's interest in the opposite sex was fully reciprocated. "He possessed to the highest degree the gift of being popular with women. In all the towns through which he passed he made conquests." Among the numerous Spanish ladies who bestowed their favors upon the "intrusive king," Countess Jarruco, a voluptuous *habanera*, niece of General O'Farril and widow of the governor of Havana, was perhaps the most intelligent and the most musically inclined.[44] One of the most attractive women and the one who became Joseph's favorite, was the Marquise de Montehermoso, wife of the complaisant Marquis de Montehermoso. She was highly talented, spoke excellent French and Italian, and wrote poetry in these languages. According to Abel Hugo, son of the general and brother of the famous poet Victor Hugo, who served in Joseph's page corps, she had "beautiful hair, the figure of a queen and the feet of a child."[45] She was very proud and took her role as official mistress quite seriously. Traveling throughout the occupied areas under cavalry escort she would insist that local governors acknowledge her

42. Grandmaison, II, p. 340; La Forest, II, p. 171; Hugo, III, p. 154.

43. Grandmaison, II, p. 342; La Forest, II, p. 244.

44. Grandmaison, II, p. 327. She trained the magnificent voice of her daughter Mercedes, whom the King married to French general Merlin.

45. "Souvenirs sur Joseph Napoléon," *Revue des Deux Mondes*, II, (1833), p. 116.

authority. Her husband was duly rewarded for his tact and understanding. He was appointed first chamberlain of the King, was made
a grandee, and awarded the royal order of Spain. After his death in
Paris in 1811, the *marquesa* married a French officer who had served
in Joseph's guard.[46]

[4]

There was a period in Joseph's reign when fortune seemed to smile
on him and he felt that success might not be beyond reach. These
were the euphoric months he spent in Andalucía in the early part of
1810. When it was thought in late 1809 that Napoleon would soon
return to the Peninsula to bring to an end the task he had left
unfinished, Joseph decided to avoid the unpleasant experience of
November–December, 1808, when he had been brushed aside by his
brother, and undertake a conquest of his own before the Emperor set
foot on Spanish soil once more. Andalucía was the objective and
results exceeded his fondest hopes. Spanish resistance in the southern
province, badly hurt by Ocaña,[47] collapsed. Joseph's campaign
turned out to be more a military parade than an expedition to subjugate a rebellious land. But it was more than a smashing victory.
Many people in the newly conquered areas seemed to show real enthusiasm for the "intrusive king" and many towns gave him a more
than cordial reception. This may seem strange when it is remembered
that Andalucía had for such a long time been the backbone of Spain's
resistance. But dissatisfaction with the administration of the Supreme
Junta, with its conduct of the war in general, and with the military
defeats Spain had suffered the previous year and had just suffered at
the passes of the Sierra Morena, had undermined to a certain extent
the morale of the southern province. The population felt, for a short
while at least, relief at seeing the war removed from its threshold,
and this feeling accounts for a great part for the apparent warmth
which greeted the King in many areas.

Much of the initial reaction, too, was caused by the excitement

46. *Ibid.*, pp. 327–29; Villa-Urrutia, pp. 24–28.
47. See Chapter VIII.

which any striking novelty may produce, as well as by simple curiosity and fear, as Miot de Mélito readily admitted when speaking of the
reception in Sevilla.[48] But soon resistance would rear its head in the
mountain fastnesses of the south, and with aid from impregnable
Cádiz would shatter the stability of French occupation. The easily
controlled Andalusian plains, however, where the large towns stand,
were to remain firmly in the hands of the French for more than two
years. After Joseph's departure for Madrid, the population of these
areas would remain passive under the foreign boot, resenting many
measures taken by the new rulers but without attempting to shake off
the yoke. Some sectors of the population, especially those wealthier
persons who had much to lose from continued warfare, collaborated
actively with the invaders and helped them keep order in a large part
of the province.

To Joseph, after all the disappointments suffered in Madrid, Andalucía was like a wonderful vacation. At Córdoba, amidst the applause
of the populace and cries of *Viva el Rey nuestro Señor*,[49] he was
accompanied by the cathedral chapter to the famous temple built by
the Moors.[50] "Spaniards," Joseph said in his proclamation drawn up
in Córdoba on January 27, "be reasonable and try to see in the
French soldiers friends ready to defend you. It is still time. Join my
cause and let a new era of happiness and glory begin for Spain on this
day."[51] The next day Joseph wrote to General Suchet: "The crossing
of the Sierra Morena, my dear Suchet, has been followed by successes
greater than I could hope for. All towns have sent me delegations and
since I have been here the inhabitants have given me more proofs of
adhesion than I ever received in the kingdom of Naples."[52] In Sevilla,
Joseph was received by large crowds of people who filled all streets
and squares along the route of the cortege, which stopped at the
Alcázar, the King's new residence. There he received the homage of
Sevilla's administrative authorities and businessmen as well as of
deputations from other Andalusian areas, who had hurried to Sevilla

48. *Op. cit.*, p. 101.
49. Long live the King our Lord.
50. Fée, p. 59.
51. *Gaceta del Gobierno de Granada*, February 9, 1810, AHN, Estado,
legajo 2993/1.
52. AHN, Estado, *legajo* 3003/2.

to pledge their loyalty to him. In the cathedral he was presented with the French eagles and flags captured at Bailén, which he sent back to France.[53]

Having decided to tour the newly conquered province, Joseph left Sevilla and traveled to Jerez, where, according to Miot de Mélito, he was again acclaimed.[54] On he went farther south until the royal retinue reached Puerto de Santa María and Buenavista Height, from which the *rey intruso* could contemplate the magnificent panorama of the Bay of Cádiz. From pretty Puerto de Santa María back to Jerez and thence to Arcos de la Frontera, where a Te Deum was sung. Through rough country the voyage continued to picturesque Ronda, standing on a high rock formation, at the foot of which the Guadiaro River flows through a narrow gorge. The 200-foot-high bridge spanning the latter and joining the two parts of the town was then and is still today one of the wonders of Spain.[55]

On March 4, Joseph entered Málaga, and the reception there "surpassed anything that could be expected from the most submissive and devoted people. The streets were strewn with flowers and embellished with tapestries. At the windows were women adorned with great refinement who waved their handkerchiefs. Shouts of *Viva el Rey* resounded everywhere in prolonged acclamations, and if Joseph Napoleon could ever believe he was truly sovereign of Spain, it was at this moment. He was given a ball, a bullfight; in short, nothing which affection, or in its place adulation, can invent to please, was neglected."[56]

On March 16, it was the turn of Granada. The enchanted town cleaned its streets and decked out its houses for the welcome. On the balconies stood the gentlemen, their heads bare, and the ladies, without their traditional mantillas. Joseph took up lodging in the palace of the chancellery. On March 19, Joseph's saint's day, a Te Deum was held in the cathedral by the archbishop, and on the same day the King received testimonies of loyalty from a number of deputations from nearby towns.[57]

53. Miot de Mélito, p. 103.
54. *Ibid.*, p. 110.
55. *Ibid.*, pp. 115–16.
56. *Ibid.*, p. 118.
57. Gallego y Burín, *Granada en la guerra de la independencia*, p. 76.

The return to Sevilla was made via Andújar, and on April 14, Joseph was once more in the southern capital. This time the reception was rather cool. Cádiz was still resisting in the south and all sorts of rumors were floating in the air about Napoleon's intentions with regard to Spain. Unfortunately these rumors were only too well founded. By the decree of February 8, 1810, Napoleon had for all practical purposes severed from the kingdom the territories to the north of the Ebro. Claiming that the French army in Spain was costing too much and that the Spanish administration was not extracting all the revenue it could, the Emperor had created four military governments, those of Catalonia, Aragón, Navarra, and Vizcaya. French generals commanding in each of these would be invested with full civil and military power. The revenue collected in the four governments would be earmarked for the army.[58]

Joseph found out about the decree in Ronda and was thunderstruck. The measure could not have come at a worse moment. Here he was in Andalucía, surrounded by signs that he might become a popular king, and now his brother, with one stroke of the pen undid all the goodwill he thought he had gained. For when Andalucía received the news, many who had received Joseph with open arms would turn away from him once more. Joseph was right. After the February decree the feeling of many who had seen the possibility of a hopeful future in the presence of the *rey intruso* cooled perceptibly. Soon their initial enthusiasm was gone, and while there were to be a good number of collaborators in Andalucía, the southern province was just another conquered territory.

Joseph, hiding at first the bad news from the Spanish people, made desperate efforts to make his brother revoke his fateful order. He paid no heed to Miot's advice to resign right then and there, but sent the trusted Azanza on a special mission to Paris to convince the Emperor of the necessity of changing his decision. Azanza left for France in April, carrying with him a strongly worded memorandum drawn up by Minister of State Urquijo, which considerably displeased the French foreign minister in Paris. This reaction augured badly for Azanza's mission.[59] Meanwhile, in Sevilla, Joseph tried hard to win back the friendship of his new subjects. He took part in all the

---

58. Miot de Mélito, p. 137; Artola, *Los afrancesados,* pp. 145, 256–58.
59. Miot de Mélito, pp. 139–40.

brilliant ceremonies of Holy Week, but to no avail. The ground lost through the February decree could not be recovered.[60] We should not, however, overestimate the effect of Napoleon's decision. Although it changed the attitude of many Andalusians, it did not affect radically the position of the southern province as a whole toward the French. Without the decree Joseph's honeymoon with Andalucía would have lasted longer, but sooner or later French domination would have become unbearable for the hardy folk of the mountainous areas. The Serranía de Ronda, the Alpujarras, and other regions whose geography favored guerrilla warfare would have risen under any circumstances. And then there was always Cádiz. The example of the Atlantic port and the material aid it could always furnish to resistance in the form of men and supplies would have made French rule secure only in the easily controlled plains. Thus, while the immediate effect of the February decrees was no doubt substantial, guerrilla warfare would have erupted in the long run no matter what Napoleon had done. As long as Cádiz stood, the flame of resistance would have remained alive regardless of how popular Joseph might have been in the large cities and the plains.

Dismemberment was not enough. Napoleon, bent on complete reorganization, formed the army of Portugal, which he placed under the command of Marshal Masséna and made for all practical purposes completely independent of Joseph's control. The French army in Andalucía was placed under the command of Marshal Soult, who became something of a viceroy of the south. The King's military authority was reduced to the troops which occupied the area of New Castile and parts of Old Castile. In theory Joseph would still be supreme commander of any army corps as soon as he was personally present in its area of operations. But in practice, since he could usually not leave Madrid, he could command directly only the contingents stationed close to the capital. On May 29, the February decree was supplemented by another, which added two more military governments to the four already created. Burgos on the one hand and Valladolid, Palencia, and Toro on the other constituted two additional territories administratively separated from the rest of Spain.[61]

60. *Ibid.*, p. 141.
61. *Ibid.*, pp. 148–49; Artola, *Los afrancesados*, pp. 147–48.

Joseph was back in Madrid in the middle of May. His last hope rested on the possible success of Azanza's mission. But Azanza got nowhere. Napoleon and his ministers would not go back on the decision taken earlier in the year. The Emperor was displeased with the constant drain the Spanish affair caused on French finances and was determined to make Spain pay for the upkeep of the French army south of the Pyrenees.

The failure of Azanza to change Napoleon's mind prompted Joseph to send to Paris the Marquis de Almenara.[62] In the fall, the King used other emissaries to soften Napoleon. Among them was Marius Clary, nephew of Joseph's wife. He was sent to France with a letter to Julie, in which her husband asked her to tell the Emperor that if no change in the King's position was forthcoming, he, Joseph, would definitely resign his post.[63] Napoleon was in an angry and uncompromising mood. To Joseph's pleas that he observe the Constitution of Bayonne, which in June and July, 1808, had been accepted as Spain's fundamental law, Napoleon replied with the thesis that the Constitution of Bayonne had not been accepted by Spain and that the presence of the King in Madrid was due solely to the strength of the French military machine.

In a communication to La Forest, dated November 7, 1810, the Emperor not only took a very clear stand on the Spanish question, but also painted a surprisingly candid picture of his brother's situation, admitting freely that the French efforts to win over Spain had failed. Since Napoleon tried to prove that Spain could only be ruled according to the law of conquest, he was bound to exaggerate somewhat the weakness of Joseph's position. But on the whole the picture was fairly accurate: "Andalusia and Seville . . . have been conquered by the French army," declared the Emperor. "But . . . no Spaniard has rallied to his king. No Spanish forces have fought against the insurrection, and 400,000 Frenchmen alone . . . have been forced to conquer all the provinces, all the strong points, all the towns, all the villages. Spain belongs to the Emperor by right of conquest. The King of Spain would be very little

62. This meant that Joseph would have three representatives in Paris: Azanza, Almenara, and the Duke of Frías, Spain's permanent ambassador.
63. Miot de Mélito, p. 156.

if he were not the brother of the Emperor and the general of his armies. He would be so little that a mere town of 4,000 souls would be stronger than all the supporters he may have in Spain. Even his guard is French. Not a single Spanish officer with a name has shed his blood for the King." And now came Napoleon's official position in the matter: "His Majesty is therefore no longer bound in the Spanish affair by the treaties of Bayonne. These treaties have not been ratified by the Spanish nation. His Majesty considers them as not being valid. He has, I believe, made enough mention of this when he proclaimed in Madrid that if the country did not submit, he would take the crown of Spain for himself." But, the message added, the Emperor was ready to make a last attempt at conciliation to ease his brother's task: Let Joseph open negotiations with the Cortes of Cádiz and let the latter recognize Joseph as king of Spain and the Constitution of Bayonne as the fundamental law of the land, and Napoleon would recognize the validity of such a treaty.[64]

This was essentially what the Marquis de Almenara, returning to Madrid on December 9, conveyed to Joseph: In case negotiations with the insurgents at Cádiz succeeded, France would guarantee the integrity of the Spanish territory and would recognize the Cortes of Cádiz as truly representative of the Spanish nation. If they failed, Napoleon would consider himself free of any engagements vis-à-vis Spain and Joseph could then convene another Cortes. But the territories beyond the Ebro could not be represented in this assembly. As Miot indicated in his memoirs, Napoleon did not expect such a contact between his brother and Cádiz to give any positive results. He would annex to France the lands to the north of the Ebro "with the intention of then leaving Spain to be fought over by two rival powers if the King succeeded in calling together his own Cortes."[65]

Joseph, realizing that a negotiation with Cádiz could only lead to failure[66] and fearing a permanent loss of Spain's northern provinces,

---

64. *Correspondance de Napoléon I*, No. 17111.

65. *Op. cit.*, pp. 162–63.

66. These negotiations did in effect take place, but the Regency rejected Joseph's offer (Toreno, p. 351). Several attempts were made during Joseph's reign to win over the Spanish patriots, but all these efforts met a similar fate (see Chapter VIII; see also, below).

became more discouraged than ever. Throughout the winter his financial situation kept worsening, and by March, 1811, he was again contemplating returning to France and retiring to his estate near Paris. "My presence here is today completely useless," he wrote to Napoleon on March 24.[67] Then, at the end of the month, he received news of the birth of his nephew. Napoleon, in an unusually friendly message dated March 20, informed him of the event which had occurred the same day, and asked him to be the child's godfather.[68] The Emperor did not mean that Joseph was to proceed to Paris to be present at the baptism, but the King, using this as a welcome pretext, decided that the time had come to go to France personally and talk the Spanish situation over face to face with Napoleon.

On March 30, Joseph congratulated his brother on the happy event and announced his coming journey. Napoleon remained silent, but Joseph ordered all necessary preparations made for the voyage. On April 23, the King, accompanied among others by General O'Farril, by the minister of state, the minister of foreign affairs, and Miot de Mélito, left Madrid. By the time Napoleon sent a message forbidding Joseph to leave Spain, the King had already crossed the Franco-Spanish border. On May 15, he was in Paris.[69]

Napoleon was not pleased to see his brother, but *faisant bonne mine à mauvais jeu*, he discussed Spain with him, and even agreed to make the baptism of the newborn heir the official reason of the King's visit. On June 9, the godfather of the *Roi de Rome* attended the ceremony dressed as a hereditary French prince in a gold-embroidered white costume.[70] All the worries and all the resentment he had accumulated for such a long time were pushed into the back of his mind for a short while, and the King of Spain spent some happy days, both in Paris and with his family at Mortefontaine.

There were sour notes, of course. The first meeting with Napoleon on May 16, which lasted six hours, is said to have been stormy. Some of the *afrancesados* in Joseph's retinue displeased the Emperor with their Spanish uniform and their red cockade and were on the point of

67. *Mémoires et correspondance*, VII, p. 493.
68. *Ibid.*, pp. 490–92.
69. Miot de Mélito, p. 185; Artola, *Los afrancesados*, pp. 177–80.
70. Miot de Mélito, p. 185.

being ejected from the imperial palace on orders of the Corsican. The latter is even reported to have admonished Joseph not to appear in his presence wearing the Spanish uniform and the red cockade.[71]

The immediate overall results of the voyage were, however, not unfavorable to the cause of the King of Spain. Joseph was promised 500,000 francs until July 1, and 1 million per month thereafter for the rest of the year. Half of this sum was earmarked for the army of the center, which was placed under the direct command of the King. The command of the army of the north would be given to a marshal who would meet with the approval of Joseph. Such a figure might be old Marshal Jourdan, who had been temporarily in disgrace with Napoleon. In the areas controlled by the armies of the north, of Aragón and Andalucía, justice and administration would be carried out in the name of the King, and in each army an official would collect one-fourth of the revenue for the royal treasury. All army marshals were to report to the King their military and political activities.[72]

On July 15, Joseph was back in Madrid. Miot reported that an arch of triumph had been erected in the vicinity of the capital to greet His Catholic Majesty. Many people were waiting for him and "numerous acclamations made this a happy day for the King."[73] But the days, the weeks, and the months that followed were far from happy. Nothing had really changed in the situation. The monthly subsidy was reduced to 500,000 francs. The army commanders paid no more attention to the King than before, and the latter's authority was, as before, restricted to the area around Madrid. An effort to gather a Cortes with representatives from the occupied regions never went beyond a timid start, and in September, the news that Napoleon was planning to annex Catalonia to France plunged Joseph into deep discouragement once more. "In this situation," he wrote his wife on Sep-

71. Villa-Urrutia, *El Rey José Napoleón*, p. 60. Since the insurgents wore the red cockade, the decree of August 18, 1809 had prohibited its use to all except military men and employees of the royal army and navy, and had stipulated that it could only be worn on three-cornered hats (*Prontuario*, I, pp. 301–302; AHN, Estado, *legajo* 3092).

72. Artola, *Los afrancesados*, p. 181; Miot de Mélito, p. 193; Grandmaison, II, p. 308.

73. *Op. cit.*, p. 200.

tember 24, "I must obtain a *decisive explanation* [74] from the Emperor. If I am to stay, the promises which have been made to me must be kept."[75]

Another calamity was added to Joseph's woes. During 1811, the scarcity of bread and the resultant rise in the price of this vital food had wrought increasing hardship on the population of Madrid. The causes of this scarcity were the endless requisitions of grain by French troops in the province of Toledo and the choking off of vital supply lines by guerrillas operating in the province of Cuenca and in La Mancha. By the end of the year the prices of other foods had risen in proportion, bread was practically inaccessible to the poor, and the capital was gripped by famine. The terrible hunger lasted well into 1812, and in spite of heroic efforts on the part of the King, about 20,000 persons died of the famine in Madrid. It was then that Joseph showed the most attractive side of his character. He earmarked half his personal income for the purchase of grain at any cost and had bread baked in the royal palace. It was then distributed among many poor by the King's servants, who were expressly forbidden to say where the bread came from. The King made a point of visiting the more stricken areas of the city, where people saw that he was neither one-eyed nor one-armed, nor drunk.[76]

"I am today reduced to Madrid," wrote Joseph to Napoleon on December 24, 1811, "I am surrounded by the most horrible misery."[77] On January 1, 1812, in a letter to the French ambassador in Madrid, the King complained bitterly that the Emperor's promises had not been kept and declared: "My presence here is no longer of any use. I say more, it is impossible. I must therefore wish to leave Madrid and Spain before the prolonged spectacle of public misery and its inevitable consequences eject me from here with violence."[78] At the beginning of 1812, Valencia fell, but the situation in the capital did not improve. Famine continued to take its toll. On March 23, another offer to abdicate went out to Napoleon. The Emperor, the message said, had indicated to Joseph that he would be permitted to leave

74. Italics in the text.

75. *Mémoires et correspondance*, VIII, pp. 92–93.

76. Mesonero Romanos, *Memorias de un setentón*, pp. 83–88; Miot de Mélito, p. 210; Abel Hugo, *op. cit.*, I, p. 284; Grandmaison, II, p. 313.

77. *Mémoires et correspondance*, VIII, p. 135.

78. *Ibid.*, pp. 272–73.

Spain if conditions did not improve. Well, they had not improved and it was time for the King to resign his post.[79]

But as far as Napoleon was concerned, this was certainly not the moment to consider his brother's offer. Other things were weighing heavily on his mind. The moment of decision was approaching. War with Russia had been in the cards for a long time, and the gigantic conflict was about to break out. Spain receded into the background, for once the colossus of the East had been smashed, all his problems in the Peninsula would be easily solved. This was the time to consolidate his rear and to hold Spain with what troops were still there. After many units had been withdrawn for service in the coming Russian campaign, there were still approximately 230,000 men south of the Pyrenees.[80] Napoleon was confident. This was sufficient for defensive operations directed at retaining the conquered provinces and keeping open communications with France. To provide some form of unified command for his forces in Spain and at the same time to placate his brother, more discouraged than ever by the incredible difficulties surrounding him and by the Emperor's quasi annexation of Catalonia in January, 1812,[81] Napoleon placed the command of all his armies in the Peninsula in the hands of the King. Marshal Jourdan, returning to his functions of *major général*, would be the chief of staff of the new supreme commander. A subsidy of 1 million francs per month during 1812, and 16 million francs from the 50-million contribution levied on Valencia, was promised.[82] In April, Napoleon suggested that Joseph call a Spanish national assembly which might even include deputies from the Cortes of Cádiz and from Catalonia, Navarra, and Guipúzcoa, though there would be no change of administration in these latter three areas. A constitution similar to that of Cádiz could be enacted, and then French troops would evacuate the Peninsula, since their presence would no longer be necessary.[83]

This proposal sounded too much like another one of Napoleon's

79. *Ibid.,* p. 335.
80. Grandmaison, III, p. 68.
81. Catalonia was divided into four departments on the French model, Ter, Montserrat, Bouches de l'Ebre, and Segre, and placed under the rule of two intendants.
82. Miot de Mélito, pp. 214, 223.
83. *Ibid.,* pp. 216–17.

empty gestures, but for a very short time Joseph regained his un-
steady confidence. Perhaps now that he had been put in the saddle,
with his brother far away in Russia, he could on his own reestablish
the situation in Spain. Perhaps he could defeat the enemy on the
battlefield and bring peace and unity to the country through a
convocation of the Cortes in which Spaniards of both sides would be
represented. Perhaps—but Joseph soon realized that he was contemplating a mirage. The 230,000 French soldiers still available had to
hold down a country infested with guerrillas, and the only way to
concentrate a sufficiently large force for offensive operations would
be through evacuation of an important province. But even then, with
an inadequate system of transport and magazines and with a countryside unable to feed a big army, a large-scale offensive would be an
exceedingly difficult, if not impossible, undertaking. The marshals,
accustomed to three years of independence, were as uncooperative as
ever. They still levied their own contributions and no money from
the outlying provinces reached the treasury. They refused to recognize the military authority of the King and of his chief of staff,
Marshal Jourdan. What was worse, they were so bent on personal
glory that they declined to help each other. Marshal Suchet, ruling in
Catalonia, Valencia, and Aragón, refused to lend Joseph troops to
cover Madrid, in order that the King might help Marshal Marmont
defend the north. Threatening to resign if Joseph insisted, he claimed
he was under orders from the Emperor to use his troops exclusively
for the defense of the east.[84] Marshal Soult in Andalucía declared he
saw no reason why he should send any troops under his command
north to aid Marmont. Instead, he proposed that Joseph join him in
Andalucía to turn the southern province into a French stronghold on
the Peninsula![85]

In the political field Joseph was no more successful than in the
administrative and military areas. In May, he made another effort to
gather a national congress under French auspices. Once more, after a

84. Suchet's fear of a possible Anglo-Sicilian landing on the east coast
explains to some extent his rebellious attitude (Oman, v, p. 500). An expeditionary force of 6,000 men landed at Alicante on August 9, 1812, to aid the
Spanish forces in that area (Toreno, p. 426).

85. Miot de Mélito, pp. 220-22; Grandmaison, III, pp. 68-73; Oman, v,
pp. 305-308.

flurry of activity, the attempt came to naught. The attitude of the military commanders, whose contempt for the authority of the monarch undermined his political position, was to a large extent to blame for the failure.[86] At the same time, new maneuvers aimed at establishing contact with the Cortes of Cádiz were undertaken. Though there were a number of individuals in Cádiz who favored negotiations with Joseph on the basis of the latter's proposals—recognition of the Napoleonic dynasty and acceptance by the King of a constitution patterned on the one enacted in Cádiz—the Cortes and the Regency were in no mood for meaningful discussions. This endeavor too, then, failed.[87]

Meanwhile, anti-French sentiment in the occupied areas was kept fiercely burning by British victories at Ciudad Rodrigo and Badajoz,[88] by the hopes Napoleon's new war in the east aroused in Spanish hearts, and especially by the activities of the guerrillas, which were now a real scourge in the French rear. "The ferocity of these bands," recalled Miot de Mélito, "the cruelties they perpetrated and the excesses of all kinds they committed, proved to what point exasperation and hatred against the French had risen. Almost the entire nation, whose hopes were being revived by our defeats and by the war against Russia, shared these feelings and showed them violently everywhere."[89]

The French army in Spain, torn by rivalry, ineffectually led by a monarch who was shown respect neither by his generals nor by his subjects, was to suffer in the summer of 1812 what was the forerunner of final and irrevocable defeat. Wellington, with his 60,000 men, was on paper much inferior to the combined forces of his enemies. But he was operating in friendly territory with troops in fine fighting trim and unencumbered by policing tasks. Thus, in June and July, he was able to concentrate the bulk of his Anglo-Portuguese-Spanish army for a showdown with Marshal Marmont. The latter, a dashing, boastful young commander, anxious to reap glory for himself, instead of waiting for reinforcements from the north and from Madrid,

86. Miot de Mélito, p. 225; Grandmaison, III, p. 74; Artola, *Los afrancesados*, pp. 210–15.
87. Toreno, pp. 408–409.
88. See Chapter IX.
89. *Op. cit.*, p. 225.

came to grips with the Allies on July 22 near Salamanca. The French army, numbering about 45,000, suffered one of the worst defeats of the war and retreated after suffering heavy losses. Joseph, who had left Madrid on July 21 to bring from 13,000 to 14,000 reinforcements to Marmont, was apprised of the defeat on the eve of what he had hoped would be the junction of the two armies. On August 2, he was back in the capital.[90]

He could not stay there, for the situation was too dangerous. It was decided that Madrid would be evacuated and that the government would move to Valencia to join with Suchet and with Soult's army of the south, which in turn would evacuate Andalucía. Thus, much of Spain was being given up by the Napoleonic armies in a stunning development which carried Wellington into the Spanish capital and plunged fleeing Joseph and his *afrancesados* into abysmal gloom.

The trek from Madrid to Valencia was a particularly harrowing affair, which has been described for posterity by a number of eyewitnesses. An immense convoy, made up of approximately 2,500 vehicles of every description and escorted by 20,000 troops including Spanish regiments in the service of Joseph, moved out of Madrid between August 10 and 12. Accompanying the King were thousands upon thousands of people: officials of the various ministries, lesser employees, French workmen, men, women, and children, in carriages, on horseback, on muleback, or on foot. About 10,000 of these refugees were *afrancesados*, collaborators, who were fleeing the wrath of their countrymen.

Day after day, under a blazing sky, enveloped in an enormous dust cloud, the convoy wound its way painfully through the bleak plains of La Mancha. Fortunately for the emigrants, the road was in fine condition. But water was scarce and the small number of wells available in the villages were soon dry because so many horses and beasts of burden in the convoy had to be watered. Everyone suffered from thirst, and there were cases of soldiers dying of it in front of their horrified comrades. The inhabitants of the villages fled at the approach of the convoy, taking with them their animals,

90. Grandmaison, III, pp. 103–106; Miot de Mélito, pp. 231–33.

destroying their ovens and mills, and sometimes poisoning their wells. What contributed to render the heat and thirst even more unbearable was the thick dust which penetrated into the best-protected carriages. It blinded civilians and soldiers, cavalry and infantry, made the tongue stick to the palate, and filtered into the lungs, causing a violent and painful cough. Most Spanish troops deserted, and many joined the guerrillas which followed the column and observed its flanks. Many Spanish government employees, too, unable to bear the privations of the retreat, deserted the French cause and returned to Madrid or hid in the villages on the way.

After seven days of this terrible march the immense convoy, plagued by incredibly hot days and uncomfortably chilly nights, by lack of water and food, crawled into Albacete. After another week the kingdom of Valencia was reached, and finally, on August 31, Joseph made his entrance into Valencia.[91] At about the same time, far away in eastern Europe, Napoleon was still moving on Moscow, which he was sure would soon be added to the long chain of Napoleonic conquests. But like his brother, the Emperor would be forced to undertake a retreat, and this retreat, too, marked the beginning of the end of a reign.

In Valencia, the authorities, prodded by the French occupation forces, gave the King a warm welcome. The city magistrates greeted the *rey intruso* at the gates of the city and handed him its keys. Representatives of the clergy accompanied him to the cathedral, where the usual Te Deum was sung. French eyewitnesses probably exaggerated the acclaim and applause with which Joseph was received, but there was in all probability a certain amount of genuine enthusiasm. Marshal Suchet, the conqueror and ruler of Valencia, though certainly not the model of justice and moderation which French writers, including Suchet himself, would like us to believe,[92]

91. Hugo, III, pp. 94–101; Miot de Mélito, pp. 236–40; *Mémoires et correspondance politique et militaire du Roi Joseph*, VIII, p. 222; La Forest, VII, pp. 8–9; Grandmaison, III, p. 303.

92. Cf. Suchet, *Memoirs of the War in Spain*, II, chap. XVIII; Hugo, III, pp. 105–107; Grandmaison, III, pp. 112–28.

was without question the most intelligent and successful military administrator representing France in the Peninsula. A highly gifted soldier, he also held title to some of the most impressive French victories in Spain. He had captured Lérida, Tortosa, Tarragona, and Valencia, and had defeated Spanish forces in the field on many occasions. For his victory at Valencia he had been rewarded by the Emperor with the title of Duke of Albufera.[93] Suchet was inflexible in exacting heavy contributions from the areas under his control, but he also saw to it that the principle of equality was observed in tax collection. He ruled with an iron hand, but rigid discipline was maintained in the ranks of the French occupation forces, and the inhabitants were generally not molested. Even Toreno admits that thanks to Suchet's efficient administration Valencia stood in marked contrast to other regions in the power of the enemy.[94] Nevertheless, even here there was much bitterness against the French because of the heavy taxes, and guerrilla bands were active in the countryside.[95]

Suchet showed Joseph the respect due to a monarch, even a monarch who had been forced to flee his capital, but Joseph knew he was a guest, a refugee in the domains of a powerful viceroy. There was of course no question of placing any part of the Valencian administration into the King's hand, and Joseph stayed a month and a half in Suchet's preserve, dreaming of a happier future. If only the necessary money could be raised to prop up his wandering government. If a truly unified command for all French armies in Spain could be established. If Soult's southern army and his own forces could join as soon as possible and march west quickly to reconquer Castile . . . .

For the last time Joseph's fortunes rose dramatically. On October 3, the long-awaited junction between his central army and Soult's troops, marching east from Andalucía, took place at Fuente de la Higuera, some fifty miles southwest of Valencia. Moving northwest along two parallel roads, through Cuenca and Albacete respectively,

---

93. Recalling the great lake near the city, called Albufera. He had been elevated to the rank of marshal by virtue of a decree of July, 1811.

94. *Op. cit.*, p. 475.

95. *Ibid.*, p. 401. On Suchet's administration, cf. Mercader Riba, *El Mariscal Suchet, "Virrey" de Aragón, Valencia y Cataluña* (Zaragoza, 1954).

the combined French forces comprising Joseph's and Soult's armies, more than 70,000 strong, then advanced on Castile.[96] Wellington, who in the meantime had laid siege to Burgos but had failed to eject the French strongly entrenched in the town's castle, gave orders to his troops in and around Madrid to evacuate the capital. On November 2, Joseph entered Madrid once more, but stayed only one day. The British were retreating all along the line and now was the time to score a smashing success which might restore the situation in Spain to what it had been in the best days of his reign. In hot pursuit of the British, Joseph's army crossed the Guadarrama range and entered Old Castile. At Peñaranda, a French army coming down from the north joined the central and southern armies and the combined force raced on and caught up with Wellington at Salamanca on November 13. The French had about 90,000 men and the British, Portuguese, and Spanish 70,000. Here was Joseph's chance. He was stronger than the enemy, and facing a foe who had retreated constantly, he felt victory within his grasp. But it was not to be. Joseph was not Napoleon and Wellington's luck held. Under cover of an all-day rainstorm he was able to withdraw once more and keep his army intact. While he escaped to Ciudad Rodrigo the French army occupied Castile, and Joseph, bitterly disappointed, returned to Madrid. On December 3 he was back in the Royal Palace.[97]

If the Russian campaign of 1812 marked the beginning of the end for Napoleon's central European empire, the disasters of the summer of 1812 in the Peninsula were the turning point in his fortunes south of the Pyrenees.[98] The question inevitably arises whether with a friendly Spain at his back, or at least an evacuated Spain, and 200,000 more men to hurl at Russia, he would have avoided the catastrophic retreat in the East. Perhaps yes, although in view of the staggering problems involved in the conquest of Russia, it is difficult to see how an additional 200,000 men could have effectively helped Napoleon.

96. Suchet, as before, remained in Valencia, in command of all French forces in the east.

97. Miot de Mélito, pp. 248–58; Oman, VI, pp. 111–42; Hugo, III, pp. 109–11; Grandmaison, III, pp. 307–308.

98. It must be kept in mind that though Joseph was able to drive Wellington back to the Portuguese border, all of Andalucía had been irretrievably lost.

But what is certain is that if all the forces in Spain had been free to fight elsewhere, their presence north of the Pyrenees would have meant the difference between victory and defeat in the year following Napoleon's Eastern disaster.

[5]

By the end of the year, the situation was as follows: The French controlled the Basque provinces, Navarra, Aragón, and Valencia, held Madrid, and were back in force in Old and New Castile. Asturias in the north had been reconquered in May but evacuated for the last time in June, because of the exigencies of the Salamanca campaign. In Biscay, Bilbao, given up in early September, was recaptured on December 31, but the port of Santander, farther west, which had been lost to a combined Anglo-Spanish amphibious operation in early August, was irretrievably gone. It was an important victory for the Allies, for "the Spanish 'Seventh Army' had at last a base behind it and a free communication with England for the stores and munitions it needed."[99] The biggest loss for Joseph was, of course, Andalucía. If he had crushed Wellington at Salamanca in November, perhaps the beautiful southern province might have been reconquered. But with Wellington refurbishing his forces for a new campaign, Andalucía was out of the question.

In the provinces held by the French, Spanish guerrilla activity had risen to such a crescendo that French rule was, to say the least, precarious. Soon it was to be even more shaky, for the disaster in Russia forced Napoleon to call substantial French forces north for the decisive campaign in central Europe that was foreshadowed for 1813. Consequently, Napoleon could not hope to keep all the Peninsular territory Joseph now controlled. The Emperor made up his mind quickly. In a communication to the French minister of war, Clarke, dated February 9, 1813, he gave orders for the King of Spain to establish his residence at Valladolid and hold Madrid and Valencia

99. Oman, v, p. 555.

with his left wing.¹ "It is indispensable for his head-quarters to be moved to Valladolid," he repeated in a message to Clarke on February 23. "[It is necessary] that he reestablish tranquillity in Navarra and Aragón; that he hold Madrid only with a flying corps. It is important to levy substantial contributions on Madrid and Toledo and to make them pay; to establish all [army] hospitals in Valladolid, Burgos, Vitoria, Tolosa, Pamplona; finally to occupy Salamanca and León and prepare siege equipment at Burgos in order to threaten Ciudad Rodrigo and arouse fear [among the Allies] of an invasion of Portugal."² These orders were reiterated again and again to Joseph and his marshals. The Emperor expected essentially three things from his forces in Spain: destruction of guerrilla bands, especially in the areas close to the border; securing of communications with France, and a constant readiness to take the offensive against the British.³

The last few months of Joseph's sojourn in Madrid were marked by an eerie carefree state, which was, however, merely the expression of an instinctive desire to hold at bay the deep worries caused by an unpromising future. "King Joseph ruled in Madrid," remembered Fée in his memoirs, "Marshal Soult ruled in Toledo, still surrounded by the signs of grandeur, and every general, in his command, tried to live as well as he could; all, seemingly, calm and confident, not seeing or not wishing to see the large clouds that were forming on the horizon. A terrible piece of news, that of the disaster of Moscow, robbed us of this sense of security, which actually was more apparent than real."⁴

But Joseph continued to live in a dream world. Realistic as he had been so many times in the past, when the situation had not been half as critical as now, he was unwilling in early 1813 to come to grips with the sad reality of the moment. More and more French troops left for France—12,000 in all—for the Emperor needed them desperately. Marshal Soult, too, was recalled, because Napoleon required the presence of his best generals. On March 2 the rapacious

1. *Correspondance*, No. 19561.
2. *Ibid.*, No. 19606.
3. Artola, *Los afrancesados*, p. 219.
4. *Op. cit.*, p. 210.

Soult passed through Madrid, followed by a large number of four-gons that carried the loot he had brought from Andalucía.[5]

In the meantime, Joseph obstinately persisted in believing or in making himself believe that he was still the legitimate ruler of Spain. An air of unreality issues from his decrees drawn up in 1813. "In our Palace of Madrid, on February 20, 1813," reads one of them, "Don Josef Napoleón by the Grace of God and the Constitution of the State . . . We have decreed and decree the following: Article 1: The Marquis de Almenara, our Minister of the Interior, is herewith placed in charge of the over-all administration of the provinces occupied by the army of the south."[6] As if to underline that he was still Spain's monarch, he came out of the isolation he sought so often, and showed himself to his subjects along the promenades, at the theater, and at bullfights. The carnival of 1813 was one of the gayest Madrid had ever known. On Shrove Tuesday a masked procession pranced merrily through the outskirts, displaying French military costumes from the remote times of Charlemagne to the recent, gaudy period of Louis XV.[7]

Finally, reluctantly, Joseph decided the time had come to say good-bye to his capital. On March 17, he departed from Madrid, leaving General Leval and 10,000 men behind to guard the Madrid area. With the baggage train went untold quantities of objects of art, paintings, tapestries, mirrors, anything of value that could be transported north. Most Spanish territory between the Tajo and the Duero had by this time been given up, and only Madrid, Toledo, and Aranjuez, now mere outposts in central Spain, were held a little longer.[8]

Joseph was gone, but his saint's day, on March 19, was still celebrated as though he were residing in the Royal Palace. On the eve of the holiday, cannons fired a hundred rounds to announce the event,

5. Miot de Mélito, p. 263; Oman, VI, p. 245. This included a number of paintings, two of them Murillos. Other masterpieces by Murillo and Zurbarán, which had been taken out of suppressed monasteries and sent to France by a French commission in Sevilla, were returned in 1815, but those carried away by Soult did not see Spain again (Toreno, p. 424).

6. AHN, Estado, *legajo* 3092.

7. Mesonero Romanos, pp. 107–109; Grandmaison, III, p. 313.

8. Miot de Mélito, p. 264; Grandmaison, III, p. 314.

and the same number were fired three times on the day itself. Gala dress and uniforms were worn by all authorities and there were illuminations and free bullfights. "But since then," reported La Forest on March 24, "Madrid has taken on a sad air. Public necessities absorb funds to such an extent that the city authorities have been forced to discontinue the lighting of the town, and under cover of darkness . . . murders, of which we have not heard for four years, are being committed once more."[9]

Then, on May 27 and May 28, came the last evacuation. Aranjuez and Madrid were given up—Toledo had already been evacuated. On May 27, General Hugo escorted with a regiment a convoy of 300 vehicles and the next day the last French left the capital. "There was great joy, but it was a calm joy. The population desired only two things, a lower price for bread and lower taxes."[10]

The dénouement of what Napoleon called *les affaires d'Espagne* was not far off. It was spring now and Wellington was ready. With a powerful Allied army the British commander lunged forward from the Portuguese border. Moving northeast, his forces, including 52,000 British, 29,000 Portuguese, and more than 20,000 Spanish troops, in razor-sharp fighting trim, captured Salamanca and Zamora at the end of May, and keeping up the speedy advance, followed the retreating French. Joseph could theoretically oppose 100,000 men to the Allies along the Duero and Tormes and in the north, but his forces were widely scattered and a considerable portion were fighting guerrillas in the northern mountains.[11] And so, after giving up the line of the Tormes, he evacuated Valladolid at the beginning of June. Thus the Duero, too, was abandoned. Nor could Burgos and Miranda on the Ebro, to the northeast, be held.

On June 21, Wellington caught up with Joseph at Vitoria, the capital of the Basque province of Alava. The Allies, between 75,000 and 80,000 strong, attacked an enemy composed of from 60,000 to 65,000 men. The French fought back bravely. But Wellington was not to be denied victory. The French gave way, and their retreat,

9. *Correspondance*, VII, p. 136.
10. Grandmaison, III, pp. 316–17.
11. Total French strength in the Peninsula was still over 200,000 (Oman, VI, p. 244).

made more difficult by a terrain crisscrossed by ditches and by the accompanying artillery and baggage train, soon turned into a rout. Having lost more than 8,000 men, Joseph sought refuge in French-held Pamplona, sixty miles to the east.[12] With him went the rest of his beaten army and thousands of *afrancesados*, who dared not fall into the hands of their compatriots.[13]

The immense convoy filled with loot, which had accompanied the King, had been lost on the plain of Vitoria, its contents scattered over a huge area, the prey of victorious Allied as well as retreating French soldiers.[14] "The road presented a most extraordinary sight—an apparently incalculable number of wagons, carriages, ammunition carts, and vehicles of all descriptions, most of which had been broken and whose less valuable contents were strewed in every direction: papers, maps, clothes, etc., completely covered the road. To give an idea of the immense quantity of wealth, and of the value and extent of the baggage of this annihilated army, it must be remembered that it consisted of the farewell plunder of the whole of Spain . . . All this pillage became the spoils of the vanquishers."[15]

"The battle was fiercely fought all day long," wrote Joseph to Julie from Irurzun on June 23, shortly before entering Pamplona.

12. Because it was feared that the enemy's progress on the French right flank would soon cut off or had already cut off retreat via the road to France leading out of Vitoria in a northeasterly direction, it was decided to retreat along the road leading east to Pamplona (Miot, p. 279).

13. Oman, VI, pp. 306, 313, 384–450; Weller, pp. 247–69; Bryant, *The Age of Elegance*, pp. 54–67.

14. Miot de Mélito, pp. 265–82; Hugo, III, pp. 138–40; Grandmaison, III, pp. 320–23; Madelin, *Histoire du Consulat et de l'Empire*, XIII, pp. 158–69. Another convoy, having left Vitoria by the northern road at 2 A.M. on June 21, reached the Franco-Spanish border safely.

15. Dallas, III, pp. 204–205. "The ground all round the town was littered with broken wagons of all kinds, boxes, cases, trunks and baggage, while masses of papers, maps, account books, and letters lay about as thick as snow. In their lust of plunder the soldiers had not only torn the cushions and seats of vehicles, and the enemy's palliasses, and strewn their contents abroad, but they had also pilfered all the wagons and boxes belonging to the civil and military accountancy departments of the army, and scattered the lists, letters and documents that had been accumulated for years. I saw huge and beautifully kept ledgers belonging to the Royal Treasury, wonderful maps, and expensively bound books from the Royal Field Library, trodden under foot and sodden with the rain that had fallen during the night" (Schaumann, *On the Road with Wellington*, p. 379).

"Our loss in dead and wounded is probably equal [to that of the enemy], but we lost all our baggage train and artillery through the poor condition of the roads. However, we saved all our horses . . . If the Emperor is back, tell him that after having established the armies on the border and gathered the forces in the north and in Aragón, I shall proceed to Mortefontaine, where I think I should have retired after the battle of Salamanca, as I then wrote you."[16]

Retirement was now the only course of action left open to the "intrusive king." On June 28, he was back in France, establishing his headquarters at Saint Jean de Luz. Napoleon, hearing of the disaster while he was fighting in Germany for the very existence of his empire, ordered his brother to Mortefontaine. On July 30, Joseph was on this property, close to Paris, which he had described so often as his sought-for haven in his letters from Madrid. Two days later he was joined by his wife.[17] The King had been enjoined by his brother not to leave Mortefontaine and show himself in Paris. But Joseph liked the theater too much to confine himself to the country when he was so close to Paris, and on several occasions he slipped into the French capital to enjoy a few plays.[18]

Joseph was officially still King of Spain, but it could now be only a question of time before all the Peninsula was evacuated. On July 12, Napoleon had appointed Marshal Soult his lieutenant general in command of his armies in Spain,[19] but Soult could only delay the inevitable invasion of France by the Allies. San Sebastián fell on August 31[20] and Pamplona on October 31. By the beginning of the latter month the Allied armies had already set foot in southwestern France. In eastern Spain Suchet had evacuated the city of Valencia in July, retreating slowly north. The same month, Zaragoza had to be given up and soon Suchet would be in possession only of Barcelona and a few strongpoints in Aragón, Catalonia, and Valencia.[21]

16. *Mémoires et correspondance*, IX, p. 309.
17. Miot de Mélito, p. 292.
18. *Ibid.*, p. 294.
19. *New Letters of Napoleon*, p. 310.
20. Its castle resisted until September 8.
21. Toreno, pp. 473–750. These strong points were Lérida, Mequinenza, Monzón, Figueras, Hostalrich, Barcelona, Tortosa, Peñíscola, and Sagunto (Suchet, *op. cit.*, III, p. 405).

Finally, the throne, too, had to be given up. In December, Napoleon, having lost the battle of Germany and facing invasion of French territory by Prussian, Russian, and Austrian armies, tried desperately to shore up his rear through some form of accommodation with Spain. Hoping to split Spain away from England, he signed the treaty of Valençay with Fernando, returning to this unworthy prince the Spanish crown. In a few months Fernando would go back to his land as king.[22] On January 7, 1814, Joseph tacitly abdicated, though his kingdom had formally ceased to exist the moment the treaty of Valençay had been signed. Napoleon, however, was ready to let him use the title of king. On January 10, the Emperor, preparing for his last campaign, wrote him as follows: "My brother, I have given orders for you to be addressed henceforth with the title of King Joseph and the Queen with that of Queen Julie, with the honors customarily reserved for French princes . . . I authorize you to don the uniform of my guard grenadiers, like the one I wear."[23] On January 24, Joseph was appointed lieutenant general of the emperor.

Just as the French troops that were still in Spain in 1813 might very well have turned the tide in central Europe, so now, in early 1814, the French soldiers who were fighting in the south to keep at bay British, Spaniards, and Portuguese might have saved Napoleon from ultimate disaster. But the hour of reckoning had come and Napoleon's empire crumbled about him. With the collapse of the edifice that his brother had built and with the evaporation of his royal and princely dreams, Joseph emigrated to Switzerland. He returned to Paris in March, 1815, to take part in the amazing 100-day epic which ended at Waterloo. After the final disintegration he left his family and sailed for America on an American ship. In New York he was soon recognized, excited much interest, and was given a fine reception. He would now be known as Count Survilliers,[24] and as Count Survilliers he spent some time in New York and Philadelphia.

Later, authorized to acquire property without being obliged to

22. See Chapter XVIII.

23. *Correspondance*, No. 21077.

24. This title had been given to him by Napoleon in July, 1813, when the Emperor had sent him to Mortefontaine. The name derived from a landed property near Mortefontaine which was another of Joseph's possessions (Miot de Mélito, p. 292).

become an American citizen, he bought land at Point Breeze, near Bordentown, New Jersey. With his money, his library, and his paintings, which had been sent to him, he now settled down to the life of a country squire in his fine property on the banks of the Delaware. He employed many men to work on his house, contributed to the improvement of roads and the building of several bridges in the surrounding area, and became very popular with the local inhabitants. His wife did not follow him to the United States, but he was joined in 1821 by his younger daughter Charlotte and in 1823 by his older daughter Zénaide and her husband.[25]

When not attending to his rustic interests, he was putting in order the papers which were to serve as a basis for his projected memoirs. In 1830, exciting events that had taken place in France sharpened once more his interest in world affairs. The Bourbon dynasty which had ruled France after Napoleon's downfall had been toppled by the July Revolution, and its last representative, Charles X, had been forced to make a hasty exit. Louis-Philippe of Orleans was the new king of France. Joseph promptly laid claim to the French throne on behalf of his nephew, the King of Rome, residing in Vienna. He even went so far as to send emissaries to the capital of the Austrian Empire to support the cause of Napoleon's son. In July, 1832, still hoping to restore the Napoleonic dynasty to the throne of France, Joseph Bonaparte left the New World, where he had spent so many pleasant years. When he arrived in London, he found out about the death of his nephew, L'Aiglon. As had happened so often in his life, his hopes had been dashed and now there was nothing left to do but look forward to an old age spent in retirement. In 1835 he crossed the ocean once more, but returned to England again the next year. He was not allowed to return to France, but in 1841 was granted permission to join his wife Julie in Florence, Italy, where the former queen of Spain had been living for many years. There Joseph died on July 28, 1844, at the age of seventy-six, to be followed to the grave shortly by his wife.[26]

25. Du Casse, *Mémoires et correspondance politique et militaire du Roi Joseph* (3d ed., 1856), I, pp. 16–20; Miot de Mélito, pp. 419–22; Nabonne, *Joseph Bonaparte, le roi philosophe*, chap. XIII and XIV.

26. Du Casse, *op. cit.*, p. 21; Miot de Mélito, p. 422; Nabonne, chap. XIV. With the headline "Bonaparte Family Entitled to Tract of Land in U. S.," the

His had been a long and interesting life. As the favorite brother of one of the greatest military and administrative geniuses of all time he was pushed to the forefront of history and reaped many benefits from his family tie with the great Corsican. All of the exalted positions he occupied during his lifetime he owed to Napoleon, and in the final analysis he was never more than a lesser star moving in the orbit of the Emperor's genius.

In Spain, Napoleon, having himself undertaken an impossible task, placed him in a situation which neither Joseph nor anybody else, including Napoleon, could have handled successfully. Joseph should really have resigned in the early days of his Spanish reign, when he grasped with great lucidity the futility of the undertaking. But he was vain and ambitious, and though he often offered to resign, he could not quite tear himself from royal splendor. "He should either not have reentered Madrid after the conquest of the capital in December, 1808," wrote Miot de Mélito, "or he should have decided to be merely the instrument of a military power. Joseph had adopted neither solution. He wanted to be king and exercise the power of royalty in all its extension. He wanted to create a national government and draw a strong dividing line between Frenchmen and Spaniards. But he had failed to take into account the fact that, since by these methods he did not gain the sympathy of the Spanish nation, he had nothing with which to oppose the Emperor, who could not possibly agree with this policy."[27]

Actually, Joseph had traits which, if his assumption of the throne had been surrounded by legitimacy, could have made him a fine sovereign, certainly a much better one than most representatives of Spanish royalty. His reforms were wise, and if applied would have

---

New York Herald Tribune, Paris edition of February 2, 1963, carried the following little news item from Bordentown, New Jersey: "A cranberry company has challenged members of the Bonaparte family to claim 24,000 square feet of vacant land here. Ocean Spray Cranberries Inc. has entered a civil suit seeking to foreclose any remaining Bonaparte interest in the land, which once belonged to Joseph Bonaparte, brother of Napoleon I. Joseph, King of Spain and Naples during Napoleon's reign, came to this rustic area after his brother abdicated in 1815. Ocean Spray operates a canning plant here and owns all the land adjoining the parcel in question. If no descendant of Joseph Bonaparte is found to claim the land, it will go to Ocean Spray."

27. Miot de Mélito, p. 183.

accomplished much for Spain. But there was always a fatal flaw in his reign. He had been imposed on the Spanish people by the force of French bayonets. No matter how magnificent a man and a ruler he might have been, this factor must perforce make him the object of hatred and contempt for the majority of the Spanish people. Thus, in spite of all his good intentions, this most important phase of his life was doomed to end in failure, and in dismal failure it did end.

XIII

THE COLLABORATORS

[1]

A NATION occupied over a long period of time by the armed forces of an enemy power will sooner or later produce a crop of individuals known in the terminology of our day as collaborators. In World War II, when both in Europe and Asia many lands experienced prolonged occupation by German and Japanese troops and administrative cadres, cooperation with the enemy, varying in degrees according to country and social group, became a feature of the great conflict. The term collaborator quickly acquired an emotional content capable of arousing an equally great or greater antagonistic reaction in pro-Allied circles than the enemy himself. The collaborators were traitors, but in the concept of collaboration what was emphasized was the contribution made by these men to the enemy cause rather than the purely negative aspect of the harm done to the fatherland. To a certain extent the more active collaborators, while as hateful as ordinary traitors who sell their country's military secrets or desert to the enemy, were considered even more dangerous, for they had fully accepted and were helping to propagate the nefarious ideology of the occupying power. Scorn and abuse were heaped upon the collaborators by the Allies and at the end of the war many of them were summarily executed or given the death sentence in courts of justice. Others were punished with heavy jail terms, and all were covered with indelible opprobrium.

The Spanish followers of Joseph Bonaparte who emerged after Napoleon's seizure of Spain suffered on the whole considerably less than the collaborators of the last war. Compared to the repression visited upon the Quislings of World War II, the punishment meted out to those who cooperated with the intrusive king was rather mild. But then the hatreds generated by the apocalyptic bestialities committed during World War II were much more intense than those loosened by the Napoleonic war in Spain, though for the times the latter was an exceedingly cruel conflict.

The Spanish collaborators of 1808–1813 are today commonly known as *afrancesados*[1] but this was not the term applied to them by their compatriots at the beginning of the war, though the word itself had been in use since the last third of the eighteenth century.[2] Until the great Spanish revolt against Napoleon the term *afrancesado* designated those Spaniards who imitated French manners, sprinkled their speech with gallicisms, and drank heavily from the fountain of French culture. At the beginning of the war, however, Spanish collaborators were not given the name *afrancesados* but rather that of *traidores* (traitors), *infidentes* (unfaithful ones, traitors) or *josefinos*. Later, in the case of Spaniards serving by choice or otherwise in the French army, the term *juramentados* (having taken the oath) made its appearance. A few years after the outbreak of war, and certainly by 1811, the expression *afrancesado* acquired a political content and was commonly used to designate sympathizers of Napoleon.[3] Without completely losing its original meaning of "culturally Frenchified" it became practically synonymous with collaborator and has been employed since then in the great majority of instances for this particular connotation.

Actually the word *afrancesado*, just like the word collaborator, stands for a variety of motives for cooperating with the enemy. There were *afrancesados* who had chosen the path of collaboration out of ideological motives and there were *afrancesados* who had supported the intrusive government because they believed that from a purely patriotic but also practical point of view Spain's national interests demanded this policy. There were *afrancesados* for personal

1. Frenchified.
2. Juretschke, *Vida, obra y pensamiento de Alberto Lista*, p. 233.
3. Juretschke, *Los afrancesados en la guerra de la independencia*, chap. IV; Méndez Bejarano, *Historia política de los afrancesados*, p. 169.

gain or advancement. Some became collaborators out of fear for themselves and their families, others simply because they were yearning for peace, and others still because they lacked the patriotic fervor or the energy to leave behind their livelihood in the occupied area and escape to free Spain, preferring to work with the conqueror.

To classify accurately the *afrancesados* of the War of Independence would be a next to impossible task, since in many instances two or more of the above-mentioned motives combined to incline Spaniards toward collaboration. Besides, in the case of quite a few known figures the motive cannot be determined in all exactness because of lack of documentary evidence. Thus, somebody who became an *afrancesado* from what he claimed were patriotic motives but which now seem to us mere opportunism might very well have been ideologically well disposed toward the Napoleonic system even before the national uprising. Moreover, there are instances in which the dividing line between collaboration and resistance cannot be clearly drawn. Well-known Spaniards who first sided with the patriots and later openly joined the French cause as their provinces were occupied by the enemy in the course of the conflict can easily be classified as *afrancesados*. But those Spaniards who first served Joseph and became patriots as the fortunes of war changed in favor of the cause of national resistance present a more difficult problem. Those who changed sides early in the conflict, after Bailén, in the summer of 1808, had much time left in which to serve their country and are for the most part considered patriots. But those who waited until the liberation of the national territory throughout 1812 and 1813 to show their patriotism must be adjudged at best opportunists and at worst collaborators. And then there were always Spaniards who remained in their homes and because of the nature of their activities could be said to collaborate passively. Others, also living in French-held Spain, did not in any way become involved in collaboration. They merely coexisted with the occupying force, while at the same time yearning for a patriotic victory. This was the case of the great majority of the Spanish people in the zones strongly held by the French and particularly in the larger towns. Finally there were those who seemed to be actively cooperating with the enemy but were really crypto-patriots playing a daring double role. But in this latter category there were doubtless also men who engaged in this dual activity as genuine double agents, insuring their future against all eventualities.

Without losing sight of the flaws inherent in any scheme of classification let us then separate the *afrancesados* into two main groups according to their mode of cooperating with the enemy: Active collaborators and passive collaborators. In the first group fall those who rendered positive, palpable service to the intrusive regime and were instrumental in helping to consolidate its hold on occupied Spain. Most of these collaborators found employment of some sort in the new administration. The second is made up of those who merely accepted the occupation as an accomplished fact and whose employment, usually an official or semiofficial position inherited from previous administrations and continued on the strength of an oath of loyalty to Joseph Bonaparte, brought them into repeated, and very often forced, contact with the invaders. Their posts involved at least some kind of cooperation, without at the same time their engaging in any overt or covert resistance activities. This latter category counted among its ranks the employees of the Spanish administrative bureaucracy who served Joseph's government as they had served that of Fernando VII and that of Charles IV. It also included those churchmen who, without actively preaching submission, did through their contact, social or otherwise, with the occupying authorities, contribute to keep the population from engaging in acts of resistance against the invaders.[4]

The great majority of collaborators was of course made up—as it was during the period of Axis occupation in Europe and Asia—by members of the second group. Compared to the passive collaborators, active collaborators were very few in numbers, but among them were many figures of imposing intellectual and administrative stature. Many *afrancesados* of this sector came from the intellectual and

4. It can readily be seen that in some cases it would be difficult if not impossible to separate this second category from those who simply coexisted with the French without involvement on any level with the occupying forces.

social elite of Spain and therefore constitute a group that deserves close study. It is they, the true *afrancesados*, who will engage much of our attention.

Most interesting among them and most worthy of study are the Spaniards who collaborated because they sincerely thought that political, social, economic, and cultural progress depended on close cooperation with Napoleonic France. They were reformists who yearned for a continuation of the enlightened despotism that had seen its golden age under Charles III. In the words of Miguel Artola, "the *afrancesados* are the spiritual children of Enlightenment and as such, their ideology finds a practical shape in Enlightened Despotism."[5] They wanted change in all spheres, but change promoted from above, whereby the authority of the monarch would remain unquestioned. They wanted reform but reform with order, without the tumult often attendant upon the democratic process. They remembered the more repulsive aspects of the French Revolution and rejected the system which had changed the structure of French society, though they admitted the necessity for many of the changes that had taken place in the neighboring country. And precisely because they were at one and the same time anxious for reforms and afraid of revolutionary excesses, they looked on Napoleon as the regenerator of Spain. They saw the decadence into which their fatherland had sunk and grasped at the hope that the French Emperor, the one figure capable of effecting lasting changes in Spain, would propel the Spanish nation into the nineteenth century. Some of these ideological *afrancesados* had been admirers of Napoleon for a long time. Dazzled by his military genius, by his administrative talents, and by the domestic peace and reforms he had brought to France, they wanted the Napoleonic system extended to Spain.

It is only fair to emphasize that among the active collaborators the truly ideological *afrancesados*, who saw the invasion of Spain by Napoleonic troops and the fall of the Bourbon dynasty at Bayonne as a boon for Spain, were very few in number. Even some of these felt this only after they had initially adopted a patriotic attitude. This was the case of Mariano Luis de Urquijo, who had served as prime

5. *Los afrancesados*, p. 38.

minister under Charles IV and who became Joseph Bonaparte's secretary of state,[6] and of Count Francisco Cabarrús, minister of finance of the *rey intruso*.[7] No such scruples, however, affected the poet José Marchena, who prior to 1808 had resided for many years in France.[8] Other ideological *afrancesados* were Juan Antonio Llorente, at one time secretary of the Inquisition and later director of Inquisitional archives under Joseph,[9] and Francisco Amorós, state counselor of the Bonapartist regime. In a tract written in Paris in 1814 and addressed to Fernando VII under the title of *Representación del consejero español Don Francisco Amorós a Su Majestad el Rey Don Fernando VII*, Amorós complained about the resurgence of reaction in Spain: ". . . the French did not fight in Spain only to support the king of a new dynasty," the ex-counselor wrote, "but to insure the triumph of enlightenment, of laws, of justice; and now it may already be seen that their undertaking was a generous one and that they do not have to be ashamed of the efforts they have made nor of the blood they have spilled, though the desired goal has not been reached and the banner of intolerance and fanaticism is waving once more over so many victims . . ."[10]

Even the clergy produced a number of active French sympathizers. In the free territories, of course, the great bulk of the Church stood solidly behind the war effort. In occupied Spain the Church either secretly encouraged resistance against the invader or tried to make the best of a bad situation by merely coexisting or passively collaborating with the French administration. Only the upper ranks of the clergy produced an appreciable number of active collaborators.[11] Clergymen who turned *afrancesados* for ideological reasons were naturally few. Those motivated by a deep yearning for enlightenment came mostly from the ranks of the progressive-minded or "Jansenist" priests who in the late eighteenth century had applauded regalism and reform from above. An example is found in the person

6. See below.
7. See below.
8. See Chapter XIV.
9. See below.
10. *Op. cit.*, p. 55.
11. See below.

of Josef González Aceijas, parish priest of Triana.[12] When Joseph entered Sevilla, Aceijas promptly chose the path of collaboration and plied his parishioners with sermons of a markedly *afrancesado* nature. Toward the end of March, 1810, a patriotic spy reported to the Regency at Cádiz that Aceijas had on one occasion spoken in the following terms of *el rey instruso:* "Happy days are these, when we see the end of a devastating war which was begun by error, sustained by egoism and lost by weakness. Happy days, in which we leave the darkness of ignorance for the light of reason. Happy days, in which Providence has given us a merciful, wise and just king." At this point it seems there was a commotion in the church, for many parishioners did not appreciate the tenor of the sermon and let the priest know their displeasure in no uncertain terms. The agent of the Regency reported that the tumult had reached such proportions that the *cura afrancesado*[13] was forced to seek refuge in the sacristy.[14]

Aceijas apparently rendered such important services to the occupying authorities that these appointed him "Apostolic Vicar of Extremadura." On January 10, 1811, in a written address to the clergy of this province, he stated: "The French army . . . has come to free you from the evils of anarchy. . . ."[15] Several months later, from Badajoz, he called for support for Joseph in another appeal to his colleagues in which he cleverly combined praise of the intruder king with emphasis on obedience and resignation, as demanded by the Church:

When has Religion, to which we attach such importance, urged us to kill? When has it taught us to reward good with evil, to fight force with force? . . . In these critical circumstances, if we want to harmonize our conduct with its maxims, [keep in mind that Religion] prescribes patience, exhorts us to be charitable, and recognizes the right of conquest as a legitimate right . . . We should thank Heaven for granting us a Sovereign who wants to be the servant of his people, who abhors luxury, loves work and aspires to no other glory than that of making our land safe for justice and abundance; who only wishes to encourage virtue and merit

---

12. A suburb of Sevilla, situated on the right bank of the Guadalquivir.
13. *Afrancesado* priest.
14. AHN, Estado, *legajo* 2994.
15. *Ibid., legajo* 3116.

with the corresponding rewards, and to eliminate vice and demerit through a punishment imposed by wise laws enacted by an enlightened[16] government.[17]

All active collaborators who did not cooperate merely for personal gain and advancement were of course partly motivated by ideological reasons. The importance of the ideological factor varied, however. As we have stated before, those who were pushed into the French camp primarily because of ideological motives were few. More numerous were those whose conduct was motivated as much, or more, by what they thought were patriotically practical considerations than by the ideological factor. They chose cooperation because cooperation with France seemed the only reasonable alternative to a suicidal war. Moreover they looked to history for a justification of their pro-French stand. The Franco-Spanish alliance had been the dominant reality of Spain's foreign policy during long periods of the eighteenth-century Bourbon dynasty. Now, when France was so tremendously more powerful under Napoleon, alliance with France—which at this stage could of course only mean complete subservience—was in their opinion the only possible course to follow. Also firmly anchored in the minds of some of these collaborators was the idea that England had been and still was Spain's main enemy and the principal threat to her colonies. The protection of Spain's overseas empire from British greed was in their eyes another powerful reason for unrestricted cooperation with Napoleonic France.

Collaborationist considerations of both an ideological and practical nature are clearly expressed in the anonymous *Dictamen que formará la posteridad sobre los asuntos de España, por un español imparcial,*[18] published in Madrid in 1808. After briefly painting a grim picture of the state of Spain before Bayonne, the author stated: "Our country is more beautiful than France, our coasts have more ports, our natives have as much innate intelligence and at least as much energy. But no longer was France ruled by degenerate princes, while

16. In the original the term used is *regenerador,* lit. regenerating.
17. AHN, Estado, *legajo* 2993/1.
18. *Ibid., legajo* 3004. *Judgment That Will Be Passed by Posterity on the Affairs of Spain, by an Impartial Spaniard.*

these were still reigning in Spain."[19] It was far better, then, to have a new dynasty while at the same time preserving the integrity of the national territory. "The present interest of Spain," wrote the "impartial Spaniard," "is to follow always the Great Man whom our Monarchs have chosen as their arbiter, just as he is the arbiter of all Europe, having imposed his will on destiny and victory, and whose army occupies all our [strategic] positions as well as the capital of our country."[20]

The last sentence is significant. The ideological motivation of *El español imparcial* was complemented by a realistic appraisal of the military situation of Spain vis-à-vis France. French troops were occupying in force great portions of Spain, including Madrid. It was sheer folly, then, to oppose the Emperor's designs. The welfare of the nation demanded submission. The provisional governing junta ruling in Madrid under Murat's heel placed heavy emphasis on French power in its proclamation of June 3, 1808, which was published and circulated by the timorous Council of Castile. After describing the advantages that would accrue to the nation from French occupation, it stressed the unpleasant fate which would inevitably befall a recalcitrant Spain: "Are you unaware of the multitude of French warriors in Spain? Do you not know that new armies are approaching our borders? The provinces which do not return immediately to [a posture of] obedience will be occupied by French troops and treated with all the rigor of military law . . . ."[21]

Typical of this propaganda is also the following appeal addressed in August, 1809, to the inhabitants of Palencia by Don Eugenio de Guzmán, the town's chief of police. "Does the most civilized nation in the world not back our rights and have our interest at heart?" asked the *comisario*. "Countrymen, enter France . . . and you will be amazed by her fine buildings, her roads, her canals, her industry, and her population . . . Fellow Spaniards, the French Nation does not persecute religion. It does fight superstition, fanaticism, barba-

19. *Ibid.*, p. 5.

20. *Ibid.*, p. 18. It is just possible that this tract was actually written by a French propagandist of the Napoleonic cause and then simply translated into Spanish, but in the absence of any concrete evidence in this direction, it must be accepted as the work of an *afrancesado*.

21. AHN, Estado, *legajo* 2982.

rism. It does fight hypocrisy, that hypocrisy which covers up the ugliest and most abominable vices, that hypocrisy which while feigning poverty lives in the midst of abundance, which . . . aspires to dominate the world . . . I can hear you accuse me of treason. But, inhabitants of Palencia, can you call traitor a man who loves you . . . ?"

Just in case praise of France and anticlericalism did not make enough of a dent in the patriotism of the *palentinos*,[22] the police commissioner ended his appeal on a more concrete and threatening note: "Could you . . . resist a power against whom 500,000 fighters in the North could accomplish nothing?[23] Do you want to see the most beautiful country in Europe devastated and transformed into a desert? . . . I hope *palentinos*, that . . . you will not ignore my counsel. Until now your town has been saved by your wisdom and prudence, and I hope that you will reject the perfidious and subversive advice of your enemies . . . Good and evil are on your thresholds. Follow with constancy the party of peace and tranquillity."[24]

This was also the position of Spaniards like Miguel José de Azanza and Gonzalo O'Farril, who served Joseph Bonaparte as minister of the Indies and of war respectively. Though not averse to seeing the Napoleonic reforms applied in Spain, but mainly imbued with the idea that Spain must preserve at all cost the French alliance, and overawed by Napoleon's military power, they joined the pro-French party for what they considered was purely a patriotically realistic appraisal of Spain's military capabilities and needs as a world power.

In a long treatise usually known as *Memoria justificativa*,[25] written in Paris in 1814, they explained the posture they had adopted throughout the war, presenting it as a course of action dictated solely by their love for their country and their wish to spare it the horrors of war. As members of the provisional governing junta they did their best to bring about a truce on May 2, 1808. When Charles IV and Fernando VII handed Spain's crown over to Napoleon and freed

22. Inhabitants of Palencia.
23. An allusion to the defeat of Austria in the War of 1809.
24. AHN, Estado, *legajo* 3112.
25. The full title is *Memoria de D. Miguel José de Azanza y D. Gonzalo O'Farril sobre los hechos que justifican su conducta política, desde marzo de 1808 hasta abril de 1814.*

Spaniards of their obligations to them, Azanza and O'Farril considered that since the Bourbon dynasty had transferred its patrimony to the head of another state, they were bound for the good of their fatherland to accept this decision and obey the new authority. Had Fernando given the necessary orders, they contended, the governing junta would have organized resistance to the French. But decrees calling for a firm stand had reached it too late, after it had received notification of the abdication and had been enjoined to give up its powers. The idea that it might be entirely legitimate for a people to rise against a foreign aggressive power against the official wishes of its sovereigns, one of whom at least had obviously been coerced into abdicating his rights, did not apparently present itself strongly to these honest but legal-minded men. If they had at all weighed the pros and cons of a national uprising, they had swiftly come to the conclusion that such an action was pure folly. "Has enough attention been given to all the risks inherent in such a decision, which threatened the nation with the loss of everything . . . ?" declared the two *afrancesado* statesmen. "And if any doubt remained in this respect, a brief look at the state of our armed strength in those days would dispel it."[26]

Charles and Fernando had abdicated and Spain was not militarily prepared to fight France. And so Azanza and O'Farril, sincerely believing that given these circumstances there was no other reasonable course left, joined Napoleon's brother and became his faithful servants. In their favor it must be said that while many Spaniards in high position, after having sworn allegiance to Joseph Bonaparte, deserted the "intrusive king" following the battle of Bailén, these two men did not and held firmly to the line of conduct they had laid down for themselves after the tragic events in Bayonne. They were undoubtedly right in pointing out that without Bailén the ranks of the collaborators would have swelled considerably. Had many well-known figures not taken an oath of allegiance to the new dynasty, only to change sides when the fortune of war seemed to smile on the cause of national resistance?

Indeed, some of the personages who after Bailén lent most important services to the patriotic cause could have been found in Joseph's

26. *Memorias de tiempos de Fernando VII*, I, in BAE, XCVII, p. 301.

camp before the fateful month of July, 1808. Don Pedro Cevallos, the first to publish a scathing report on Napoleon's machinations at Bayonne, had agreed to be Joseph's foreign minister. On June 8, 1808, Cevallos had written from Bayonne a letter to Don Eusebio Bardají, future minister of foreign affairs in the government of national resistance, in which he had spoken in glowing terms about Napoleon's brothers: "I have had the honor of being introduced to the king, who arrived yesterday from Naples," he had said, "and I have formed the opinion that his appearance, his kindness and the nobility of his heart, which is perceived at first sight, will be enough, without the need of armies, to calm his lands."[27] The list of grandees who at Bayonne had sworn loyalty to Joseph was headed by such names as Del Parque, Infantado, and Fernán Núñez. The first of these had traveled to Madrid sharing the same carriage with the new monarch in his newly-acquired capacity of captain of the royal guard. Later he was to lead Spanish troops in many engagements against French forces. Infantado, the chief of the Spanish forces of the center after the defeats of November and December, 1808, had been colonel in Joseph's guard. Fernán Núñez, later Spain's national government's ambassador in London, had accepted the post of *montero mayor*.[28] And then there had been the prince of Castelfranco, the dukes de Frías and de Híjar, the counts Orgaz, Santa Coloma, and Torre-Múzquiz, the marquis de Santa Cruz and the marquis de Catellanos, and many other Spanish aristocrats.

Had not José Colón, Manuel de Lardizábal, Ignacio Martínez de Villela, and Sebastián Torres, all members of the venerable Council of Castile, signed the Constitution of Bayonne? Had not the councils of State and the Indies sworn loyalty to Joseph, once the *rey intruso* had entered the capital in July, 1808? And what about Fernando and his retinue? Had they not been among the first to swear fealty to the new monarch and the new constitution?[29]

Yes, undoubtedly Azanza and O'Farril were right in insisting that Bailén had been more than a military battle, that it had been a turning point in the lives of many Spaniards who until then had either openly

27. Nellerto, *Memorias*, p. 91.
28. First game-beater.
29. Azanza and O'Farril, pp. 304–10; Nellerto, pp. 88–117.

stood for collaboration or had harbored collaborationist sentiments. "Many who considered the immense and organized power of France and our quasi impotence not only to resist but to improve our government, to enlighten ourselves by our own means," wrote García Pizarro, who as member of the Council of State had taken the oath to Joseph in July, 1808, "were saying: 'Let us accept this difficult situation and make the best of it.' At one time this idea seemed attractive to me, though I did not make up my mind. But when I found out about the resistance of a number of provinces . . . [I decided] that it was no longer a question of being cautious but of following the more honorable cause."[30]

Why were the collaborators of the first hour exonerated just because they changed sides after Bailén, asked Azanza and O'Farril. "If others took a view different from ours with respect to the battle of Bailén and the consequences it might have," wrote the two *josefinos*, "does this hide the fact that they had recognized, sworn loyalty to and served Joseph just as we had done . . ."[31] Only after Bailén, continued the authors a few pages later, did two parties really crystallize, those who anticipated victory for Spanish arms and those who still foresaw defeat for Spain. Following Bailén, the only factor that separated *afrancesados* and the rest of Spaniards was the opinion regarding the outcome of the war.[32] The only crime that could be imputed to the *afrancesados*, who had stayed at Joseph's side after Bailén and had thrown in their lot with the Napoleonic cause, was that of having guessed wrong. They had merely anticipated what had looked like the inevitable consequence of the uprising, complete annihilation of the patriotic forces. History did not bear out their forecasts. But was this really so reprehensible?

". . . in this critical situation only two choices seemed available," stated Azanza and O'Farril: "[Saving Spain's] independence and integrity, [accepting] a constitutional king supported by a powerful neighboring nation, the reform of all that which the nation considered already as abuses, and the guarantee of the most cherished rights of men gathered in society. Or on the other hand, the dream of . . .

30. *Op. cit.*, i, p. 107.
31. *Op. cit.*, p. 311.
32. *Ibid.*, pp. 313–14.

rescuing our monarch by the force of arms, [in which case] the immense sacrifices demanded by [the war] would not be justified by the aims fought for."[33]

Some people apply the criterion of the justice of a cause to judge the conduct of those who rejected war, they argued further. But if the principle of justice were always invoked without taking into consideration other factors, when the decision of war or peace had to be made, then all nations would be perpetually at war. "If sovereigns and nations fought all the wars that could be dictated by the purest patriotism and by the principle of justice, the world would never be at peace."[34]

In the eyes of Azanza and O'Farril Bailén did not matter. The overall strategic situation of Spain vis-à-vis France still looked bleak, if not hopeless, to them. Thus they continued to collaborate with the new dynasty. But, they claimed, even while collaborating they always placed Spain's national interests above all other considerations. Never had they been "instruments for the ills that were plaguing our countrymen."[35] As an example of their patriotic conduct during the war they pointed to the report they and other ministers of King Joseph[36] had drawn up for the monarch on August 2, 1808, at Buitrago, during the *intruso*'s first retreat from Madrid. In this document Joseph's ministers, with the imprint of Bailén still fresh on their minds, began by telling their sovereign that conquest of Spain was impossible. "We know our history and our land and all those invincible auxiliaries which we owe as much to our bad institutions as to nature itself: hunger, thirst, harsh and unhealthy seasons, and above all the national character, less adulterated perhaps than that of other peoples . . . Thus, Sire, Your Majesty would not be embarking on a conquest but centuries of war, the time the Romans were forced to devote to the same enterprise." Since conquest was out of the question, negotiations with the insurgents was the logical step to be taken. The patriot leaders, according to the *afrancesado* ministers, had only glory and the national welfare at heart. If they could be

33. *Ibid.*, p. 315.
34. *Ibid.*, p. 316.
35. *Ibid.*, p. 342.
36. The others were Mazarredo, Cabarrús, and Urquijo.

convinced that Joseph's party was the party which could guarantee Spain a prosperous future, they would swing the country over to the new dynasty's side. Uppermost in Spanish minds was the problem of the preservation of the Spanish overseas empire. This, however, could only be insured through peace with England. Consequently, notwithstanding Spain's ties with France, Joseph should think of Spanish interests first and strive for a separate peace with England. Other measures that would gain the sympathy of the nation would be the payment to Spain of the expenses incurred through the presence of the French army on Spanish soil; the annexation of Portugal; and—something demanded by many Spaniards—the assignment to the public treasury of the possessions of the Prince of the Peace.

These, then, were the proposals to put forward to the leaders of national resistance: peace with England, payment of the French army's expenses, annexation of Portugal, return to the nation of Godoy's ill-acquired fortune. There was no other reasonable alternative; ". . . the idea of drowning Spain in the blood of her inhabitants," the report ended, "will never be acceptable to [the ministers]."[37]

Azanza and O'Farril were right in their contention that they had tried to combine patriotism with subservience to a foreign power. While serving Joseph Bonaparte they had endeavored to protect what they considered Spain's national interests. This is confirmed by documentary evidence such as the aforementioned report and by the memoirs and correspondence of their contemporaries. But there was one basic flaw in their position. The postures they had attempted to harmonize could not possibly be reconciled. Collaboration with the foreign aggressor could not be fused with service to the nation. They had thrown in their lot with the regime which through wile and naked power had placed itself on the soil of the national territory and had deprived the nation of its dynasty, and whose acts of aggression had been heroically resisted in the spring and summer of 1808 by the immense majority of the Spanish people. They had cooperated with the invader, and in spite of all their good intentions, in spite of their

37. *Apud Mémoires et correspondance politique et militaire du roi Joseph,* IV, pp. 465–69; Azanza and O'Farril, pp. 322–23.

laudable attempts at salvaging a modicum of national independence, they had served a king imposed on Spain by foreign bayonets.

True, in April, 1808, the legitimate Spanish monarch, Fernando VII, had communicated to the junta governing in his stead in Madrid his desire to avoid by all means antagonizing the French. Only in a burst of defiance had he on May 5 signed the decrees taking the wraps off the nation's fists. But by the time these decrees reached Madrid news of his total surrender and his orders revoking the powers of the junta had arrived. Had Azanza and O'Farril, as well as the other members of the junta, therefore been justified in adopting a supremely cautious attitude throughout the dramatic days of Bayonne? Perhaps their reluctance to take any action while Fernando was still engaged in negotiations with the Emperor could find justification in the fact that the young monarch himself had directed his lieutenants to use caution in their relations with Murat and the French occupying forces and in the precarious situation of the King in Bayonne. But what about their attitude *after* Fernando's abdication? Could they still argue that certainly from a purely legalistic point of view they must follow in Fernando's footsteps, since he, the supreme head of the nation, had decided to submit? A report of Jovellanos dealing with the establishment of the Supreme Junta contains a few paragraphs which set down the moral imperative governing the actions of patriotic Spaniards in 1808 and furnishes a convincing answer to this question: "No people, whatever its constitution may be, has normally the right of insurrection. . . . But any people suddenly attacked by a foreign enemy . . . who realizes that those in authority are either bribed or terrorized, must naturally defend itself and therefore acquires an extraordinary and legitimate right of insurrection. The brave Spanish people made use of this right when it saw itself suddenly deprived of a king it adored and sold out to a perfidious foreigner by a monster unworthy of the name of Spaniard."[38]

Azanza and O'Farril's claim that it was only after Bailén that the two sides took shape and that following the battle *afrancesados* differed with their fellow-Spaniards only in their appraisal of the

38. Read Godoy. *Memoria en defensa de la Junta Central, op. cit.,* p. 584.

possibilities of Spain's national resistance is only partly admissible. The mass uprisings of May and June, 1808, were certainly the expression of the strongest of stands on the part of a very large part of the population. They had been prompted principally by the purest of all patriotic sentiments, anger at the aggression committed against the national dynasty and the national territory. These sentiments were still paramount in the ranks of the patriots after the victory in Andalucía. Although some Spaniards who had not chosen sides until Bailén joined the national resistance after the battle, any estimate on the insurgent side as to the prospects of successful resistance to Napoleon played on the whole a minor role in the struggle against the Emperor.[39] True, the governing organs of the *Ancien Régime* and many leading figures had at first accepted the *fait accompli* of Bayonne because they had seen no possibility of successfully opposing French might. A good number of these, like Cevallos, Infantado, Del Parque, and Fernán Núñez, transferred their allegiance again after Bailén. But while this switch was to a large extent opportunistic in nature and was prompted by a radical change in their appraisal of the military situation, the fact is that they did join the national cause while Azanza and O'Farril did not. One might, perhaps, admire the loyalty of these two men to Joseph Bonaparte, a loyalty which made them stand by him to the bitter end. But neither this nor the validity of some of the arguments adduced in their defense can obscure the fact that these men turned their backs on the cause of national independence and served the foreign aggressor.

[2]

More numerous than the ideologically motivated collaborators and the *afrancesados* siding with Joseph for what they considered primarily to be reasons of historical and patriotic necessity were

39. If the opinion as to the outcome of the war had been such an important factor, free Spain might very well have given up the fight after the disasters of December, 1808, and January, 1809. As we have seen earlier, free Spain fought on against great odds.

those who simply thought that a bad peace was preferable to a good war. Many of them were members of the upper clergy who cooperated openly with the enemy once his armed might had stamped out resistance in their dioceses. "The archbishops and bishops of Zaragoza, Santiago, Burgos, Valladolid, León, Salamanca, Palencia, Avila, Zamora, Madrid, Lugo, and Astorga not only recognized the new dynasty, but urged their flocks to follow the same course of docility. Few bishops left their posts. None became a martyr."[40] Particularly cooperative were the Bishop of Palencia, who invited General Lassalle to enter the city; the Bishop of Zaragoza, who received Marshal Lannes; and the Archbishop of Granada, who wrote to Joseph on February 21, 1810: "My heart, Sire, has been penetrated by the sweetest emotions on considering how different is today the aspect of my beloved congregation, happily united to its legitimate sovereign and following the path of happiness and duty . . . I beg Your Majesty to accept this solemn testimony of my deep veneration and of my submission to his royal person until I am granted the honor and the happiness to ratify in his august presence these sincere and respectful expressions of my loyalty and of the ardent will with which I wish to serve him."[41] The bishop who ruled the archbishopric of Sevilla in the absence of the prelate addressed on February 15, 1810, a letter to the clergy of his diocese containing the following passage: "And behold in the midst of this threatening war cloud the triumph of reason which indicated to your capital, Sevilla, that it must open its doors to a benevolent leader, to a victorious king, instead of defending them in vain against his soldiers who might have ravaged our fields and deprived us of our bread."[42]

Such was the collaboration of the higher ranks of the clergy in the occupied provinces that the Supreme Central Junta was forced to issue the decree of April 24, 1809, stipulating that all bishops who had openly sided with the enemy were unworthy of their exalted position and were declared traitors. Their incomes and properties were

40. Schepeler, II, p. 103. Schepeler overlooked the case of the Bishop of Coria (Extremadura), Don Juan Alvarez de Castro, an octogenarian, who was shot by marauders of the French army (Toreno, p. 211).

41. Gallego y Burín, *Granada en la guerra de la independencia*, p. 158.

42. AHN, Estado, *legajo* 2993/1.

to be seized wherever possible and they themselves would be handed over to the Tribunal of Public Safety.[43] After the French defeat the collaborationist clergymen claimed as one man that they had simply acted under duress. Few of them suffered for their conduct during the war.[44] Occasionally, but to a much lesser degree, the regular clergy, too, collaborated actively. Two examples were Fray José de la Consolación, who was instrumental in the surrender of Jaca in Aragón, and Padre García of Sevilla, who after the suppression of all regular orders, in accordance with the decree of 1809,[45] headed a unit of renegade Spanish gendarmes.[46]

After Zaragoza's incredible stand and after the destruction visited upon the town it was only to be expected that the desire for a lasting peace would turn at least some of the inhabitants to collaboration with the French occupant. If there was one city in Spain where the population really had a right to be sick of the war it was the capital of Aragón. The fact that Zaragoza placidly accepted French occupation and produced a number of *afrancesados* must simply be attributed to war weariness. In the *Gaceta Nacional de Zaragoza* of July 6, 1809, we read that festivities had been held the first few days of the month to celebrate General Suchet's victories. At the theater one of the actors, a certain Manuel Cruz, had recited some verse reeking with sycophancy: "Hail to the courageous commander,/To the brave general,/To the one who has chastised/The fury of insurrection./Hail to the merciful genius/Who dispenses to us/His heroic protection/And who has forgiven the guilty;/Hail to him who has restored/Peace to Aragón./Like Caesar/He came, attacked and conquered/And freed us from the /Inhuman rebel.[47]/Loyal public, since his hand/Keeps away fear/From our happy land/Show your gratitude/For such a favor/By saying:/Long live General Suchet,/Son of War."[48]

Where collaboration motivated by a powerful desire for peace was strongest was no doubt Andalucía. During the two and a half years

43. See Chapter VIII and below.
44. Schepeler, II, p. 104.
45. See Chapter XII.
46. Rodríguez Solís, *Los guerrilleros de 1808*, p. 455.
47. Read "the Spanish patriotic armies."
48. AHN, Estado, *legajo* 46, *carpeta* J, No. 274.

of French occupation (1810–1812), the plains and large towns of the southern province remained firmly in the hands of the occupant, and in these areas an appreciable number of Andalusians cooperated more or less actively with the occupation authorities. This collaboration often took the form of service in the civic militia brought into being by the decree of February 6, 1810 and patterned on the urban formations which Joseph had ordered established in 1809 in other areas of occupied Spain. In Córdoba, Jaén, Granada, and Sevilla one or more battalions of this force were set up to "watch over the interior calm of these towns." Membership was declared open to persons ranging from seventeen to fifty years in age, who were property owners or exercised a profession or trade.[49] This militia, later extended to other towns of these four Andalusian provinces, was complemented in August by the formation of brigades of *escopeteros* or riflemen slated to serve as escorts for couriers and travelers and to guard the countryside against the incursions of patriotic bands.[50] Doubtless not all members of the *guardia cívica* and the *brigadas de escopeteros* were true collaborators. Their service was frequently unwilling.[51] But even when they were forced into these formations, as they were "interested in the preservation of their own families, goods, and houses, they would often prevent the entry into their towns of any roving Spanish force which showed itself for a moment. For if they admitted any small band which went on its way immediately and could make no attempt to defend them on the reappearance of the enemy, they were liable to be executed as traitors by the French, and their town would be fined or perhaps sacked. Hence it was to their interest, so long as Soult continued to dominate all Andalusia, to keep the *guerrilleros* outside their walls."[52] There were enough men, however, who joined

49. *Ibid.*, *legajo* 2993/1; *Prontuario de las leyes ... del Rey ... Don José Napoleón I*, II, pp. 22–26; La Forest, III, pp. 252–53.

50. AHN, Estado, *legajo* 2993.

51. This seems to have been true especially in the case of the *brigadas de escopeteros*, formed at the order of Marshal Soult by the municipal councils. That service in the urban militias was also often unwilling is shown by Joseph's decree of July 4, 1810, dealing with the civic guard of Madrid (see Chapter XII, p. 511, n. 80).

52. Oman, V, p. 110.

these police formations out of their own volition and fought the guerrillas wholeheartedly to protect their tranquillity and their property.

Some *afrancesados* in Andalucía, rather than serving in French-sponsored armed formations to fend off guerrilla activity, actually formed partisan units to combat patriotic guerrillas actively. A case in point is that of a doctor in the town of Berja in the mountainous region of the Alpujarras southeast of Granada, who in 1810 or 1811 gathered some 100 men for the express purpose of hunting down patriotic rebels. The physician, known by the name of Martín de Llanos, began to crisscross the forbidding land of the Alpujarras, filling insurgent towns with terror and hatred. Shooting, hanging, sacking, and ransoming, he was incomparably more feared than the French troops patrolling the area. On September 7, 1811, the rebel town of Alcolea, north of Berja, felt the full wrath of Llanos and his French allies. The town was taken by force and sacked. Men, women, and children were killed, and the dead included two priests who had taken refuge in the church and had perished there.[53]

At the time of his antiguerrilla campaign Llanos was fifty-eight years old. He has been described as a tall, lean, swarthy, and very ugly man with a powerful voice. Before coming to Berja he had studied in Valencia and had begun to practice medicine in a town near the Mediterranean port. What made him turn so ferociously against his fellow-Spaniards? The Andalusian chronicler who tells his story does not illuminate us on this point. The fact seems to be, however, that the population of the Alpujarras trembled at the mere mention of his name.[54]

Happily for those elements in Andalucía who never gave up resisting the French, collaboration there took on but rarely this virulent form. Active *afrancesados* might serve in the civic militia or in the *brigadas de escopeteros,* or cooperate with the French in less militant fashion, such as taking up the pen for them in the newspapers. In Puerto de Santa María, for instance, across the bay from besieged Cádiz, the *Gaceta del Puerto de Santa María* started its

53. Del Moral, *Memorias de la guerra de la independencia,* RABM, XIX (1908), pp. 114–21.
54. *Ibid.,* p. 122.

collaborationist career on March 21, 1810, by printing an article which heaped ridicule on the ousted government of national resistance and praised King Joseph. According to the *Gaceta*, Spaniards had been fed nothing but lies under the rule of the Central Junta.

"When we were led to believe that the French were beyond the Pyrenees," exclaimed the author of the article, "they were entering, to our surprise, the gates of our towns, though preceded by those bands of ours, which like swarms of locusts were ruining everything in sight. We had also been led to believe that our enemies sacked churches and committed all sorts of excesses. But on seeing them enter in formation, perfectly dressed, their bands playing, we thought we were dreaming and were at a loss to understand why those who had been painted to us in such black colors were so good[55] and why those who were supposed to be fighting for our cause were so perverse . . . The first benefit we owe to the King our Lord, Don Josef I, is that of having been told the *Truth*[56] in all its purity . . . and having been allowed to speak the *Truth*. Let us therefore take advantage of such a great privilege, let us rise from the dismal lethargy in which we were submerged, let us speak the *Truth*, let us hear the *Truth* and let us avenge ourselves nobly of the odious *lie*, abjuring all its errors and abhorring it with all our hearts."[57]

In the Spanish National Archives there are a good number of letters written by Andalusian *afrancesados* and intercepted by guerrillas. These documents, more than newspapers published in the occupied zones, permit us to delve into the uneasy minds of these collaborators, most of them yearning for a peace which would allow them to enjoy the fruits of their work.[58] The guerrillas represented a

55. This is exactly the impression which Nazi troops made on many Frenchmen in 1940. The "correct" behavior of the invaders was favorably commented upon in a good number of French circles in the early days of the occupation.

56. Italics in text.

57. AHN, Estado, *legajo* 2993/1. It is, of course, often impossible to determine whether articles like this were actually written by collaborationist Spaniards or were simply translated from French originals and printed at the orders of French occupation authorities. In the absence of specific proof of this latter alternative, however, we must take these journalistic writings as the expression of authentic *afrancesado* sentiment.

58. At least some of the pro-French sentiments expressed in this correspondence can probably be accounted for by fear of French censorship. Some correspondents may indeed have been patriot sympathizers at heart. But even where the expression of collaborationist feelings is not sincere, the statements

constant threat to this longed-for tranquillity and they feared and detested them. One way in which the menace from the irregulars was made palpable was the unreliability of the mail service. No one knew whether a letter written to a friend or relative in another town or province would reach its destination. "Dear friend and master," wrote a certain Fernando de Osorno from Granada on August 1, 1810 to a Don Ignacio de Tejada, official in the ministry for ecclesiastical affairs, "either you do not receive my letters or your answers are lost. Within the past fifteen days I have written you three or four and it seems as if they had fallen into a well."[59]

"Dear Sir," wrote another man, from Arahal in Andalucía on May 9, 1810, "I am writing you for the fourth time and may God grant that I receive an answer." He went on to describe conditions in his area, lamenting what he called the "inopportune" resistance of Cádiz and complaining of the heavy charges placed on the towns by the presence of the huge French siege army. He censured the rebellion of the mountaineers of Ronda[60] against the "irresistible might of the French," and after stating that there was constant talk of the terrible retaliation visited upon the *serranos*[61] by the occupying forces he added: "We, the peace-loving inhabitants, are somewhat pleased with [this punishment], for we hope that these small number of people will [now] return to their senses and, seeing where their true interests lie, will submit to the government, so that we may enjoy some tranquillity."[62]

A man by the name of Ortega wrote from Málaga on May 15, 1810: "Dear Juan, I was very glad to receive your kind letter of the 5th inst. I am happy you and Mariquita are in good health. I am all right . . . María has been so worried since the last foray of the *serranos* that she trembles at the slightest noise. The troops who have

---

set down merely echoed those uttered by genuine *afrancesados* with whom the letter writers could not fail to come into contact in the course of daily business. These letters thus do enable us to catch a revealing glimpse of *afrancesado* attitudes in occupied Andalucía. The bulk of this correspondence, however, should be considered a genuine expression of pro-French sentiment.

59. *Ibid., legajo* 3119.
60. See chapters IX and XVI.
61. Mountaineers.
62. AHN, Estado, *legajo* 3119.

just arrived and are on their way to the mountains will, we hope, put an end to all this."[63]

The same basic feeling of aversion to any resistance against Napoleon's troops, but expressed in stronger and also more literary terms, can be found in a letter by a certain Pedro Vélez de Vera, written on May 26, 1810, from Sevilla to Antonio Guijarro, a priest in Estepona, on the Mediterranean coast west of Málaga. The author, possibly also a priest, had apparently arrived in Sevilla after a ten-day journey from another point in occupied Spain, perhaps from Madrid. He reported that in spite of all the talk of guerrillas infesting the roads, none had been seen by him during his trip. In flowery terms, typical of the epistolary style of the period, he flayed those who urged the continuation of war against France: "If God's infinite mercy does not lift the punishment of blindness and mad confidence in which these wretches[64] are submerged . . . all of us will become innocent victims or slaves, for it is to be feared that Napoleon, tired of so much foolhardiness, will give our King[65] another crown and divide this most beautiful kingdom among his generals, while sending more soldiers [to Spain] to destroy it."[66]

Mixed with this fear of more war, of more destruction, and with the yearning for peace, mixed, too, with motives of a more objective nature in the case of those who had become afrancesados out of conviction, there was no doubt also the conscious or at least subconscious desire for personal gain or advancement. Perhaps no active collaborator, not even the most convinced one, was entirely free from a more or less concealed drive for improving his own material position. Did Count de La Forest not report on September 15, 1809 that King Joseph had distributed considerable sums of money among some of his afrancesado ministers to indemnify them for the financial losses they had sustained during the retreat from Madrid in July, 1808? He mentioned among others Admiral Mazarredo and Azanza, who had received 300,000 reales each, O'Farril and Urquijo, who had been granted 200,000 each, Cabarrús, with 160,000, and Arribas, the

63. Ibid.
64. Read "the patriots."
65. Read "Joseph."
66. AHN, Estado, legajo 3078, carpeta P.

minister of police, with 120,000. Having lost much while in the service of the "intrusive king," these collaborators could of course be expected to look forward to some form of compensation. After all, they had run the risk of losing everything when they had accompanied Joseph north after Bailén and a claim to indemnification was perfectly legitimate within the structure of their collaborationist conduct. But La Forest also reported in the same dispatch that the *afrancesado* ministers showed some coolness in their comments on the indemnities they had just been awarded. "They expected considerable rewards," wrote the French ambassador. "They do not understand that the King doubtless wanted them to recoup their losses first and desired to keep his generosity in reserve for another occasion."[67] It seems, then, that at least some of these highly placed men were not satisfied with mere indemnification but were looking to actual pecuniary rewards.[68]

What was true in high places was also true in the lower echelons of the *afrancesado* world. Mesonero Romanos singled out as *afrancesados* motivated purely by egotistical reasons the Madrid police officials, the members of the *juntas criminales* or special courts set up by the Napoleonic regime, and of the military commissions, the *alcaldes de corte* or high magistrates of Madrid, and the *militares juramentados*[69] or soldiers who had taken the oath of loyalty to Joseph Bonaparte and served in his Spanish regiments.[70] In the majority of cases of active *afrancesados* the personal gain motive was an adjunct to other and, initially at least, more powerful factors which pushed them along the road of collaboration. It usually became stronger as the war went on, mainly because there seemed to be a possibility of recouping one's material losses incurred in those turbulent times or because it seemed natural to try to derive some

---

67. *Op. cit.,* II, p. 422.

68. To be entirely fair to Mazarredo, Azanza, O'Farril, Urquijo, and the others, it should be added that these indemnities were distributed in the form of special bonds which could only be used to buy property confiscated by Joseph's government. Moreover, O'Farril refused a special offer of 1 million reales which Joseph intended to allot to him from a special fund for rewards for conduct while in military service (*ibid.*).

69. From *juramentar,* to swear in.

70. *Op. cit.,* p. 78.

personal profit from the prevailing situation. The Spanish National Archives contain many petitions from collaborators to King Joseph, in which these persons often recite long lists of meritorious acts to gain favors from the monarch. Don Eustaquio María González Yebra, representing the royal treasury in the province of Zamora, began his petition to the King, dated February 21, 1810, with what we might call a *curriculum vitae*. He had studied literature, natural sciences, French, and Spanish in his younger days, and had served the monarchy for more than thirty-eight years in various responsible positions. On his way to Zamora to take up his new post he had been attacked by a band of "brigands,"[71] who had robbed him of all his money and baggage. He begged His Majesty to grant him the title of Knight of the Royal Order of Spain, instituted the previous year by the King.[72]

An ex-monk of the Benedictine Order reported on April 20, 1810, from Valladolid that he had left the province of Asturias, where he had been teaching theology in a private school, to join the French occupation forces in the town of Toro, between Valladolid and Zamora. From there he had written the minister of finance, revealing to him the location of caches in the province of Palencia where agents of the national army in Asturias were keeping huge sums of money to carry out the war against the French in the north. Now living in Valladolid, he was asking for a vacant canonship in the church of Zamora or of some other town.[73]

A certain Andrés Martín Pérez wrote from Palencia in August, 1810, to the minister of police in Madrid that he was tired of being a clergyman. It seems that in this holy profession he was never able to satisfy his appetite. Short on money and on the verge of starvation, he begged His Excellency the Minister to grant him a position in Madrid. He was willing to be a *cabo de policía*,[74] a *guarda de*

---

71. Read "guerrillas."

72. AHN, Estado, *legajo* 3068, *carpeta* G. "The only *afrancesado* who did not obtain the Royal Order of Spain in spite of having requested it directly from King Joseph in a letter written from Valençay on November 28, 1809, was the captive monarch Ferdinand." (Villa-Urrutia, *op. cit.*, p. 50). See Chapter XII.

73. *Ibid.*, *legajo* 3119.

74. Police corporal.

puertas,[75] anything provided he could eat. We detect something that might almost be termed a wry humor in the complaints of Andrés Martín Pérez. "I would like to shed my clerical garb[76] if this were possible," the hungry ecclesiastic exclaimed. "I would prefer anything to the choir and the breviaries."[77]

Don Francisco de Vargas in a petition written from Jerez in Andalucía on August 7, 1810, declared that he had protected the French nationals residing in Puerto de Santa María from the fury of the popular masses in May, 1808. He had loyally served the patriotic cause in the army of Castaños. After the battle of Tudela,[78] he had gone to Cádiz. There he had been jailed for fifteen days, presumably for having aroused the suspicion of the Cádiz authorities as a member of the army on which Spanish patriots had pinned all their hopes and which had suffered the terrible rout in the north. When Andalucía had fallen to the French, he had become chief of the civic militia of Jerez. He now begged the king to grant him a salary ample enough to support his wife and two daughters.[79]

From Pamplona, one Don Lorenzo de Villers, in command of the "Companies of Invalids" of the town, asked to be appointed subprefect[80] somewhere in occupied Spain.[81] From Pamplona, too, Captain Blas González addressed a letter to the minister of war recalling that he had sworn loyalty to Joseph after having been taken prisoner at Uclés[82] and expressing the wish to serve in one of the King's Spanish regiments. He was allowed to go to Madrid in June, 1810, and on the fifteenth he wrote to the minister: "Your Excellency may rest assured that under my most sacred word of honor I shall fulfill my obligations in whatever post to which I may be assigned and shall give my life for the glory of our sovereign and your Excellency."[83]

In France itself there were quite a few Spanish prisoners of war

75. A guard at the city gates.
76. In the text, *desclerizarme.*
77. AHN, Estado, *legajo* 3130.
78. See Chapter VII.
79. AHN, Estado, *legajo* 3119.
80. Second in command in the government of a *prefectura* or *departamento.* Joseph had divided Spain into thirty-eight *prefecturas* (see Chapter XII).
81. *Ibid.*
82. See Chapter VIII.
83. AHN, Estado, *legajo* 3068, *carpeta* G.

who indicated a desire to return to Spain and serve Joseph, often in the ranks of the King's Spanish military formations. Such a petition was filed by infantry captain Ramón Possé, who had been made a prisoner in Denmark at the time some Spanish contingents there had staged an escape on British ships.[84] Spaniards who joined Joseph's Spanish regiments were dubbed *militares juramentados*. But actually only a minority of these could be considered true collaborators who chose to serve Joseph for personal advancement or, in a very small number of cases, for objective reasons. Not a few of the prisoners who were kept in France merely looked upon the oath to the "intrusive king" as a means of returning to Spain, where they might be able to desert and join the forces of national resistance. Many took the oath and served in the King's regiments out of simple fear. Others were simply drafted, as were Spanish civilians, into service by the French. Before the war was over most of the *juramentados* deserted their units and went over to the insurgents. There remained only a hard core of officers and men, who out of fear of punishment at the hands of the patriots or out of conviction carried out to the letter the collaborationist obligations they had contracted and who stood by Napoleon's brother to the very end.

Afrancesados who joined Joseph's cause mainly for reasons of personal advancement are, of course, even more censurable than collaborators like Azanza and O'Farril. However, occasionally one comes across a Spaniard choosing the French side for personal motives which make his attitude understandable if not entirely excusable. A curious little anecdote told in the memoirs of one of the French soldiers of the first invasion force which occupied northern Spain in early 1808 shows that under certain circumstances a pro-French attitude could have some justification. The author of the memoirs related that during his stay in the town of Toro he and two colleagues paid a visit to a Franciscan monastery. A young friar, eighteen to twenty years of age, acted as their guide. During the tour of the establishment the monk showed them a cell in which there were assembled a number of instruments apparently designed to be used for penance in the form of corporal punishment, self-inflicted

---

84. *Ibid., legajo* 3078, *carpeta* P. See Chapter VII.

or otherwise. Presently, he asked them to help him lift a huge cross, six feet in length, which was lying on the floor. "We were surprised by its enormous weight," wrote the author. The young Franciscan then proceeded to uncover his shoulders, displaying a number of scars, then went up to the cross, pulled it down on his back, and dragged it to a few feet from where the Frenchmen stood. The latter helped him once more to place the cross upright. A little later the friar dragged a coffin to the middle of the cell, opened it, and disrobing, entered the casket and lay upon the skeleton of a Franciscan dressed in the garb of the Order. "We were dumbfounded," reported the author. "We prevailed upon him to leave his station and we were not a little surprised to see him, in spite of the rigorous cold . . . emerge from the coffin bathed in sweat. This condition was doubtless caused by the shock he felt on reflecting upon this image of our disintegration."

It seems that the young man was the younger of the two sons of a noble and wealthy family, who had been forced to enter monkhood so that his older brother might enjoy the entire family fortune. He expressed the hope that the French would effect great changes in Spain and would perhaps eliminate many monasteries and convents. The Frenchmen tried to impress upon him that the French army had come to northern Spain exclusively for operations against Portugal and that no action whatsoever was contemplated in Spain. But the young Franciscan was convinced that the arrival of the French army presaged great events. He offered to serve in the French ranks if the visitors could only help him leave his monastery. His pleas fell on deaf ears, however. The Frenchmen decided the whole scheme was out of the question since Spain was still France's ally.[85]

Here, then, was a potential *afrancesado*, who, when the French army later in the year shed its mask and became an occupying force, probably saw his wish come true.[86] Once out of the monastery he could be expected to have become a full-fledged collaborator. It would, however, be hard to condemn this young man, who perforce

85. Gille, *Mémoires d'un conscrit de 1808*, pp. 56–58.
86. Even if he had not been able to leave the monastery in 1808, he was certainly able to do so once the Napoleonic regime had suppressed all male regular orders (see Chapter XII).

looked upon the French soldiers as his only hope of liberation from an unwilling service in the Franciscan Order.

[3]

While the really active collaborators were few, passive *afrancesados* could be found in much greater numbers. Many were men who remained in what we might call today civil service positions under the French occupying authorities. "The excuse of such of these as afterwards thought it necessary to excuse their conduct was that being acquainted with the existing laws and customs of their fellow citizens, and partaking of the evils resulting from the intrusion of new ones, they were more likely to reconcile the old with the new state of things, and to render the burden less intolerable than a stranger and a foreigner, not to say a Frenchman."[87]

There was indeed a considerable number of men whose collaboration was to some extent mitigated by their charitable attitude toward their fellow Spaniards. There are examples of *afrancesados* who often acted as a sort of shield against French depredations and did their best to lessen the burden of occupation. Here a collaborator might prevail upon a French commander not to carry out reprisals against hostages, and there another might persuade French authorities to return to some Spanish owners some stolen or requisitioned property.[88]

A case in point is that of Don Joaquín de Uriarte y Landa. Sent by Joseph's government to Ronda—he claimed, against his will—to take charge of the administration of the town, he prevailed upon French general Maransin to put an end to the sack of nearby Algodonales, which had risen against French rule. Later he persuaded the same general to spare the lives of 121 inhabitants of the hamlet, who had been taken to Ronda to be shot there.[89]

87. Dallas, II, pp. 216–17.

88. Cf. Viñas Mey, "Nuevos datos para la historia de los afrancesados," *Bulletin Hispanique*, Vols. XXVI and XXVII; *Memorias del general Don Francisco Espoz y Mina*, I, BAE, CXLVI, p. 39.

89. *Manifiesto de D. Joaquín de Uriarte y Landa sobre su conducta política durante la dominación intrusa*, pp. 8–11.

There were churchmen who, while not going as far as collaborationist archbishops and bishops, maintained friendly relations with
the invader[90] and either discouraged resistance on the part of their
parishioners or at least did nothing to foster it. The Frenchman Fée
reported a conversation he had had with a canon in the town of
Zamora in early 1813, not long before Joseph met final defeat at
Vitoria. Some of the things the canon said shed some light on the
inner feelings of those liberal Spanish ecclesiastics who, while dis-
liking foreign occupation and not collaborating actively, could not
bring themselves to hate and oppose the French. "You are strange
people," he was quoted to have said. "I cannot hate you even when I
suffer from your presence, and if I feel obligated to harbor hatred for
you, I can only express it in the form of bad humor. A restoration
awaits us[91] and I fear it." And Fée added: "He realized that Spain was
going to escape us and he was sorry."[92] Perhaps Fée read into the
canon's soul a feeling of regret that really was not there. But it does
seem that this clergyman felt somewhat torn between what he must
have sensed to be his patriotic duty—to hate the foreign invader—
and a certain attraction to French ways. The tension and resultant
emotional paralysis produced by these conflicting feelings must have
kept him at the height of the French occupation in the area of passive
collaboration.

It can readily be seen how difficult it would be to separate clearly
passive collaborators from Spaniards merely coexisting with the
enemy. What was a Spaniard who was living in a town occupied by
the French and carried on a business that brought him into no
contact with the occupant involving collaboration of any kind, but
who did not engage in any acts, overt or covert, of resistance? It
would be unjust to classify him as an *afrancesado*, active or passive. It
could after all not be expected of all Spaniards, especially older
people, to prefer self-imposed exile in the free zone, with all the
resultant hardships, to staying in the enemy-occupied area. On the

90. These might take the form of making available their residence to
French officers and men even if their house was not requisitioned for billeting
purposes.

91. The restoration of Fernando VII and, probably in the eyes of the
canon, at least some features of the *Ancien Régime*.

92. *Op. cit.*, p. 238.

other hand, neither could men who simply coexisted with the occupation authorities be considered full-fledged, self-sacrificing patriots.

The picture is further complicated by the fact that many Spaniards living in the occupied zone, while pretending to collaborate actively or passively, were secretly aiding the insurgents. This was true of individuals as well as of town and village authorities. "Often a town was ostensibly held for King Joseph, but was privately supplying recruits, provisions, and money contributions to the national cause."[93]

And then, as in every war, there were those who somehow managed to win the confidence of both sides and played the role of go-betweens. A case in point is that of the canon Tomás Lapeña, a resident of Burgos, who was commissioned by King Joseph to establish contact with the Cádiz Regency and lay the groundwork for negotiations. To the Regency Lapeña claimed to have been told by Joseph at the time of the latter's passage through Burgos in July, 1811, that he was tired of the war and dissatisfied with his brother. Let another national assembly representing all of Spain be elected by all Spaniards and he would see to it that French troops evacuated the country, so that the Cortes could meet freely. The Regency was justly suspicious of the canon's mission, but it was also desirous to find out more about Joseph's intentions. It agreed in principle to have the canon meet somewhere between the front lines with two men appointed by Madrid for further contacts.[94] Lapeña was instructed to ascertain, without in any way engaging the Regency, how Joseph could possibly take French troops out of Spain, and to stress to the enemy representatives the indissolubility of the bond between patriotic Spain and England. On September 19, 1811, Lapeña wrote to O'Farril from Cádiz, announcing that the Regency had agreed to let him meet with two negotiators representing the Madrid government. He expressed the hope that O'Farril might be one of these two envoys. In early 1812 Lapeña made his way to the headquarters of General Abadía's army in Ponferrada, León. The general refused to

93. Oman, v, p. 110.

94. Joseph had suggested that two negotiators from the French side meet with two persons appointed by Cádiz.

let the canon proceed with his mission as the latter had not received permission from the new Regency, installed in January, 1812, to carry out negotiations in its name. Lapeña then moved on to Galicia, and in La Coruña, in May, he finally received word from the Regency to the effect that he could contact the *afrancesados*. By July, negotiators appointed by Madrid were ready to begin discussions with Cádiz representatives. But the French rout at Salamanca, in the same month, put an end to these maneuvers and nothing came of La Peña's mission.[95]

General Hugo, father of the celebrated poet, told a curious story in his memoirs, which is partly confirmed by the Spanish National Archives. While he was governor of the town of Avila in 1809, he engaged the services of an Augustinian friar, Fray Manuel Concha. For a while the latter acted as the general's secretary and then was charged with crossing the Spanish lines to deliver a message to Marshal Soult dealing with the battle of Talavera.[96] Concha set out on his journey and was captured by Spanish troops. Glibly he explained to his captors that he was about to hand over a most important French document to the Spanish commander-in-chief, General Cuesta. At Spanish headquarters, when presented with the message to Marshal Soult, Cuesta congratulated the friar, but not trusting him enough to let him recross the Spanish lines, he had him escorted to Sevilla, then the residence of the Supreme Central Junta. The members of the Suprema believed the story Concha told them and he later accompanied the government of national resistance to Cádiz. There he drew up a project to kill Napoleon, who at the time was expected to return to Spain to take command of the expedition against Wellington in Portugal. The project consisted in placing eighty barrels of powder on the rocks overlooking the road between Mondragón and Vergara, in the Basque provinces, and rolling them down on the Emperor's convoy. The Cádiz government liked the plan and commissioned Concha to carry it out.

The friar somehow made his way back to Hugo's headquarters and told his adventure to the amazed general. The latter then sent the collaborator to Paris, charging him with delivering a dispatch to the

95. AHN, Estado, *legajo* 2955; Toreno, pp. 351, 408–409.
96. See Chapter VIII.

Emperor, in which the project to assassinate him was outlined. Napoleon read the dispatch, but instead of rewarding Concha sent him to the dungeons of Vincennes. What was the reason for this action? Hugo declared he did not know. Perhaps the Emperor felt that this Spaniard, *afrancesado* or not, could not be completely trusted. Who, then, was Concha? Was he a real collaborator? Perhaps. And perhaps he was really fond of the French general and wanted to prove his loyalty to the French cause. But to a certain extent he was also a double agent, playing the French game while things were going smoothly, working with the Spanish side when there was no other way, and returning to the French when a reward seemed to be beckoning.[97]

Mysterious, too, in some aspects, is the case of Goya, the extraordinary artist and author of so many etchings, drawings, and paintings dealing with this crucial period in Spanish history. A number of writers have accused Goya of collaboration with the French,[98] claiming that his stay in Madrid under Joseph's rule, his contacts with personages of the *intruso*'s entourage, and his painting of at least one portrait of Joseph forcibly leads to this conclusion. Recently, however, there has been a tendency to exonerate Goya of the charges previously levelled against him. "Goya painted various portraits of the Frenchmen who came to Madrid with Joseph, but the belief that he was a painter to Joseph himself seems thoroughly doubtful."[99]

In the first two months of 1810, Goya, probably out of pressing financial need, did paint an *Allegory of the Town of Madrid* for the capital's municipal authorities, who were eager to please Joseph. The painting, now in the Madrid town hall, contains a medallion, which for a while held Joseph's face.[1] But Goya had to produce the portrait

97. Hugo, II, pp. 89–92, 134–40; AHN, Estado, *legajo* 41, *carpeta* c, No. 27.
98. The great French Hispanicist Morel-Fatio includes Goya in his list of *afrancesados*: "Don Francisco Amorós, marquis de Sotelo, fondateur de la gymnastique en France," *Bulletin Hispanique*, XXVI, p. 210.
99. Poore, Goya, p. 195.
1. Joseph's face was painted in and out according to the vicissitudes of war. Later, the word *Constitución* appeared on the shield on which the allegorical figure of Madrid leans. Today, the shield simply bears the words *Dos de Mayo*.

from a print lent him by a friend, and, besides, was never listed as the *intruso*'s official painter. In 1811, his name appeared on a list of 191 new recipients of the Royal Order of Spain instituted by Joseph, but he later claimed he never wore it. The fact that Goya remained in Madrid after Joseph evacuated the capital in August, 1812, and painted Wellington's portrait, speaks in his favor. If he had been severely compromised by too close an association with Joseph's court he would have fled to Valencia with the other *afrancesados* who ran for their lives in those stifling August days. After the war, Goya, then official painter of Ferdinand VII, was obliged to submit to a "purification" process, like all other employees of the royal household. The investigation of his attitude and activities during the occupation years began toward the end of 1814. A number of witnesses emphasized his patriotism and his refusal to hold any official position during the reign of the "intrusive king." As a result, Goya emerged from this test with flying colors and retained his position of "pintor de cámara," which he had held before the war.

Perhaps if Goya had been a lesser genius his reputation as a patriot would have come out more tarnished, perhaps not. The painter must be considered a borderline case in the history of collaboration during the Napoleonic war. His place is somewhere in that nebulous area stretching from passive collaboration through noninvolvement to the edges of patriotism. That he should be completely free from any suspicion cannot be seriously argued. After all, he did remain in Madrid, and though at one time, as one of the witnesses stated, he left the capital with the intention of escaping to free Spain, he refrained from doing so partly because of his children's entreaties but partly also because he was threatened with the loss of his property by Joseph's minister of police if he did not return. He did paint the portraits of Joseph and of a number of *afrancesados*, as well as that of the French general Nicolas Guye. His name did appear on a list of holders of the Royal Order of Spain. On the other hand, it may be argued that many other patriotic-minded Spaniards remained in Madrid when the French occupied the capital. Furthermore, Goya probably harbored deeply patriotic sentiments. In this respect Camón Aznar does the painter justice when he states: "Never have hatred of the invader, heroism leading to the most terrible deaths, the cruelty of war provoked by demented ambitions been sung as in the drawings, etchings, and paintings of Goya. They form the most glorious monument to a resistance which after all determined the fall of Napoleon."[2]

Still, sentiment is one thing and action another. In the case of Goya, from the point of view of patriotic resistance to Napoleon the latter certainly lagged behind the former. But not all men are capable of extreme self-sacrifice and heroism, and while all Spaniards could be expected to avoid collaborating with the enemy, not all Spaniards, especially those with family responsibilities, could be expected to grab a musket and take to the hills. If Goya had not been so well known he might not have become involved in his contacts with the *afrancesado* milieu. But his name as well as economic necessity pushed him into situations which he might very well have wished to avoid.[3]

The problem of collaboration growing out of the Spanish War of Independence had to be faced directly by countless Spaniards. But the conflicting pressures to which one was subjected in this respect would rise in direct proportion to the prominence of the position one occupied in the world of social strata or the world of the intelligentsia. The higher one's social or intellectual status the more difficult it was to opt for mere passive collaboration or mere coexistence. It was difficult if not impossible, for both internal and external motives, to adopt a neutral posture. It was to be expected, then, that the upper layer of Spanish society as well as Spain's foremost literary phalanx would be well represented in the ranks of fighting patriots as well as in those of active *afrancesados*. In the case of ministers of the *Ancien Régime*, titled aristocrats, and prelates who became involved in active collaboration, their attitude must be traced mainly to the fact that it was in their ranks, among the few to have the benefit of learning and education, that ideological motivation and other factors

2. *Goya en los años de la guerra de la independencia*, p. 20.
3. Cf. Pérez y González, *Un cuadro de historia;* Camón, *op. cit.;* Poore, *op. cit.* In 1963, a portrait purportedly painted by Goya and representing Joseph on horseback was discovered in Madrid and is now on exhibit in one of the Spanish capital's galleries. If the portrait should eventually be adjudged to be authentic, it would shed new light on Goya's activities during the war inasmuch as it would link him more closely to the *afrancesado* element.

beside self-interest and fear could be expected to act as powerful stimuli, but also to a certain extent to the fact that they were bound, through their position and/or reputation, to attract the attention of Napoleon and Joseph.

[4]

Until now, in discussing the question of collaboration in the War of Independence we have mainly examined motives and attitudes of the phenomenon as a whole. Let us now cast a glance—and it will have to be a hurried one, since space is lacking for more extensive delvings—at the individual personalities of some of the better-known *afrancesados*.[4] It has been said on occasion that the party of Joseph Bonaparte attracted the most gifted men, intellectually, administratively, and otherwise, available in the Spain of 1808–1812. While there were men of high caliber, even high moral character, if we overlook the area of patriotic duty, who chose collaboration, the foregoing statement is clearly an exaggeration. To quote Viñas Mey, "it is true . . . that there exists in the party of *afrancesados* a series of figures of high import in the history of our culture; but their total number within that of the Spanish intelligentsia of that time constitutes merely a minority . . ."[5]

We have discussed earlier Azanza and O'Farril in connection with their defense of their actions during the war. They were perhaps the most attractive men, morally speaking, of the group of *afrancesados* surrounding the "intrusive king." Both had served their country brilliantly before the fateful year 1808. Azanza, a Navarrese by birth, had fought against the British at Gibraltar and had held the positions of minister of war in 1793, viceroy of Mexico from 1796 to 1799, and minister of finance during the brief reign of Fernando VII in 1808. In Bayonne he had presided over the Spanish assembly, and under Joseph, who in 1811 made him Duke of Santa Fe, he became minister of the Indies. Forced to go into exile in France in 1813, he spent his

4. Foremost among these are a number of literary figures like Moratín and Meléndez Valdés. They will be discussed in the next chapter.
5. *Op. cit.*, xxvii, p. 97.

last years in penury and died in Bordeaux at the age of eighty. Azanza turned to collaboration from the start, and once he had chosen his course he did not deviate from it, like so many other Spaniards after Bailén. That he tried at all times to preserve the territorial integrity of Spain in spite of his functions as minister to Joseph is certain. French ambassador La Forest wrote in April, 1810: "He becomes seized with a sort of fanaticism as soon as his fatherland's independence and integrity are involved . . . He would prefer any solution to the cession of a few Spanish provinces."[6] Villa-Urrutia considers him a man of unblemished probity and a liberal *à l'anglaise*, opposed by temperament to any regime of force and violence.[7]

Gonzalo O'Farril, of Irish ancestry[8] and born in Havana in 1754, had gone to school in France but had fought in the Spanish army against the French Republic in 1793–1795. Spain's ambassador to Prussia in 1800–1805, he became minister of war in March, 1808,[9] a post he also held under Joseph. La Forest considered him in 1808 the most capable of all Spanish ministers.[10] He, Azanza, and Urquijo were perhaps the *afrancesado* officials least hated by the government of national resistance. His competence and basic honesty earned him the respect of his opponents. Included in the instructions which the Cádiz Regency handed to Tomás Lapeña[11] in 1811 was the suggestion to contact O'Farril and to inform him that in case he decided to change sides the national government might be willing to indemnify him for the financial losses he had incurred in the course of the war.[12]

These same instructions also mention the name of Mariano Luis de Urquijo, secretary of state of King Joseph. Lapeña was told to let

6. *Op. cit.*, III, p. 335.

7. *El Rey José Napoleón*, p. 33.

8. O'Farril's family had been established in Havana since 1717. In the previous century many Irish had come to Spain to escape Cromwell's persecution, and some of these immigrants later settled in the colonies. They gave the country many outstanding figures, especially in the military field.

9. It will be recalled that O'Farril was also a member of the junta left behind by Fernando in April (see chapters III and IV).

10. *Op. cit.*, I, p. 37.

11. See above.

12. AHN, Estado, *legajo* 2955.

him know that he was not as detested as some other *afrancesados*, that he was considered a moderate, and that the Regency understood that "only circumstances could have made Urquijo embrace the [cause of] Joseph."[13] This may have been a device to sound Urquijo out, but perhaps Cádiz underestimated the minister of state's loyalty to Joseph. The man who once had held the exalted position of prime minister[14] seemed to be one hundred percent loyal to the "intrusive king's" cause and much less inclined to a compromise peace with the patriots than some of his colleagues like Azanza and O'Farril. La Forest reported on April 4, 1809, that at a cabinet meeting Urquijo had opposed O'Farril's suggestions for an armistice while negotiations with Sevilla were attempted, and had declared that only the forward movement of French armies would guarantee a successful outcome of the demarches that had been undertaken.[15]

Urquijo, too, had rendered great services to his country before 1808. Protected by Floridablanca and Aranda, he had held several official positions. During his short term in office as prime minister in 1799–1800, he had fostered agriculture and industry, brought vaccination to Spain, sponsored Humboldt's scientific voyage to Spanish America, and had been a protector of the arts. In those days he had carried high the standards of reform. But he had made too many enemies. He could not resist the combined assault of the Inquisition, whose power he had sought to curb,[16] of Bonaparte, to whose demands he stood up with great courage, and of Godoy, who was waiting in the wings to return to his former position. Jailed by royal order first in Pamplona and later in his native Bilbao,[17] he was freed by Fernando VII after Aranjuez and did his best before Bayonne to persuade the young monarch to give up his trip to France. His collaboration with Joseph began early. In Bayonne he served as secretary of the Spanish assembly and shortly afterward he became

13. *Ibid.*

14. In 1799. It was the time when Godoy was temporarily out of favor at court. See Chapter I.

15. *Op. cit.*, II, p. 173. See Chapter VIII.

16. The Inquisition had persecuted him for a preface to a translation of Voltaire's tragedy *La Mort de César.*

17. He was born in 1768.

secretary of state. Of handsome appearance, he was magnanimous, loyal, and extremely outspoken. He was a man of great talent, but ambitious and terribly vain. Pizarro stated in his memoirs that "in the every-day routine of business he was immensely superior to all the talented men who had occupied posts in the ministries for many years."[18] His thirst for reform, and resentment of the Church, the bulk of which he knew had aligned itself with the insurgents in May–June, 1808, were no doubt the principal motives for his collaborationist posture in the summer of that year. But perhaps his vanity and his ambition also played a part in his decision to join Joseph Bonaparte. He accompanied Joseph to France, where he died in 1817.[19]

Very capable, also, was Francisco Cabarrús, Joseph's minister of finance, a Frenchman by birth, born in Bayonne in 1752, who had come to Spain as a young man. He had gone into business, had made a fortune and a name for himself as an outstanding financier. Charles III had made use of his talents, and in 1782 he had founded the Bank of San Carlos. Under Charles IV he had first been granted the title of count, then thrown into jail for the liberal ideas expressed in a treatise he had written on Charles III,[20] and subsequently released. Named ambassador to France in 1797, an appointment which was rejected by the French government, and exiled from the capital after the fall of Jovellanos, he had still been out of favor at the time of Fernando's assumption of the crown in 1808. The king gave him the post of minister of finance which he later also held under Joseph until his death in Sevilla in 1810.

In the chaotic financial situation in which Spain found herself during the war Cabarrús could work no miracles. Miot de Mélito spoke of him in the following terms: "He was a man of great intelligence, endowed with a great facility for business and indefatigable in his work. But he was criticized for lacking the

---

18. *Op. cit.*, i, p. 78.

19. He was buried in the Père Lachaise cemetery in Paris (cf. Villa-Urrutia, pp. 34–39).

20. Herr, p. 261. The official reason given was malversation of funds in the Bank of San Carlos.

necessary judgment and character to handle the nation's finances in difficult situations. Thoroughly acquainted with Spain's finances, which he would have probably managed skilfully under the *Ancien Régime,* he was incapable of directing them effectively in the chaos that followed the French conquest."[21]

Herr includes Cabarrús in the group of men—Campomanes and Jovellanos are the others—"who best typified the enlightened despotism of Carlos III," adding that "Cabarrús was especially noted for his enlightened point of view."[22] This reformist outlook clearly stands out in the financier's letters to his friend Jovellanos which were written toward the end of 1792 and the beginning of 1793, and were printed in Vitoria in 1808.[23] A fairly comprehensive program for reform, partly foreshadowing the course later taken both by Joseph's government and by the Cortes of Cádiz, the *Cartas* exalted reason and the public good as the fundamental factors which should always govern the form and functioning of political, social, and economic institutions. Cabarrús wrote eloquently in favor of personal freedom, of the separation of powers, of a limitation of aristocratic privileges, secularized education, a reduction in the expenses of the royal court, and the elimination of all obstacles to the free exchange of goods. "What I demand," stated Cabarrús in defining his basic credo, "is personal security, private property and freedom to express one's opinions."[24]

Cabarrús was the father of Madame Tallien, *née* Thérèse Cabarrús, who had played a role in the preparation of the 9th Thermidor and the overthrow of Robespierre. It was perhaps this tie with Thérèse, at the time the mistress of Barras, one of the French directors, which prompted the Directory to reject him as Spanish envoy to Paris, while giving as the official reason the fact that he had been born in France.[25] Pizarro described Cabarrús as "frank and noble" and in-

21. *Op. cit.,* III, p. 142.
22. *Op. cit.,* p. 261.
23. The complete title is *Cartas sobre los obstáculos que la naturaleza, la opinión y las leyes openen a la felicidad pública (Letters on the Obstacles Placed in the Path of Public Happiness by Nature, Public Opinion, and the Laws).*
24. *Op. cit.,* p. 71.
25. Villa-Urrutia, *Mujeres de antaño. Teresa Cabarrús,* p. 10.

cluded him in the number of those *afrancesados* who followed Joseph out of conviction.[26] Jovellanos, who before the war had been his intimate friend but broke with him in 1808,[27] spoke of him as an extraordinary man "in whom talents and extravagancy, the most noble qualities and the greatest defects coexisted."[28] Jovellanos had met Cabarrús at Zaragoza in the days of the city's rising against the French, and the Asturian scholar recalled that Cabarrús had been burning with patriotic resolve.[29] What had induced Cabarrús to collaborate? Jovellanos attributed his change of heart to fear or ambition, fear of displeasing the French, in the midst of whose armed forces he found himself when his appointment to the post of Joseph's minister of finance reached him at Burgos, and his ambition whetted by this same appointment; perhaps, too, a series of unpleasant incidents which forced Cabarrús to leave Zaragoza and put his life in danger after he left the town explain to some extent why the financier turned against the insurgents.[30] But if one remembers Cabarrús' connection with enlightened despotism; his advocacy of reforms that he probably later felt to be attainable only through a Napoleonic regime; his aversion, as a believer in reform from above, to popular upheavals; and perhaps, too, his French origin; ideological motivation must have played a prominent part in his decision to accept the cabinet post in Joseph's government, and most certainly in his later resolve to see things through at the side of Joseph when the latter's situation deteriorated in the summer of 1808.[31] He may very well have been genuinely enthusiastic at first with the patriotic movement

26. *Op. cit.*, I, p. 109.

27. In 1790, Jovellanos had tried without success to save Cabarrús from jail. See Chapter XIV.

28. *Memoria en defensa de la Junta Central, op. cit.*, p. 537.

29. *Ibid.*

30. In Zaragoza a district judge ordered the arrest of one of Cabarrús' servants. As a result the financier left the town (García Mercadal, *Palafox, Duque de Zaragoza*, p. 49). On passing through Tudela he was arrested and his belongings looted by the mob (Jovellanos, *Diarios, Obras*, IV, in BAE, LXXXVI, p. 158). Perhaps Cabarrús' French origin, perhaps also the fact that he had once been the friend of Godoy. caused this outbreak of popular suspicion.

31. This is clearly seen in a letter he addressed to Jovellanos at the end of August, 1808 (*Obras*, IV, in BAE, LXXXVI, pp. 341–42), when Joseph's armies had already been forced to evacuate a good deal of Spanish territory and when some first-hour collaborators had joined the national cause.

in the Spanish provinces, but this must have been a passing stage. Yet Jovellanos, in spite of his condemnation of Cabarrús' action, could not bring himself to damn this erstwhile friend completely: "The disfavor with which it is said he has always been looked upon by . . . Saint Cloud[32] and some ministers of Joseph proves perhaps that his heart had not been born to serve tyrants."[33]

Another intellectually outstanding *afrancesado* was Juan Antonio de Llorente, best known for his *Critical History of the Spanish Inquisition*, one of the earliest of its kind,[34] which appeared in Paris in four volumes in 1817 and 1818.[35] Llorente, born in 1756 in Rincón del Soto in northeastern Castile, where this province borders on Navarra, came from a noble but not wealthy family. Having lost his father very soon after his birth, and his mother at the age of ten, he was helped in his education by his uncle, a priest in the nearby town of Calahorra, and by a friend of this uncle, who eventually became dean of the cathedral of Tarazona. Young Llorente impressed everyone with his precocious intelligence and his application to his studies. He studied law at the University of Zaragoza and in 1780 received the degree of doctor in canon law. Having been ordained priest in 1779 by the bishop of Calahorra,[36] he was appointed three years later vicar general of Calahorra. He himself declared later in an autobiographical treatise that these were crucial years for his ideological formation. He apparently became the friend of an enlightened man of letters whose name Llorente did not reveal, and drank the heady wine of new ideas which were then spreading fast through Spain's

32. Read "Napoleon."

33. *Memoria en defensa de la Junta Central, op. cit.,* p. 538.

34. Earlier than Llorente's work, and in the opinion of Menéndez y Pelayo superior to the *Critical History*, is *La Inquisición sin máscara (The Inquisition Unmasked)*, by Antonio Puigblanch, which was published in Cádiz in 1811 and exercised a considerable influence on the liberals in the Cortes (Cf. *Historia de los heterodoxos españoles*, VII, pp. 94–95). I have been able to consult the edition published in Mexico in 1824. Rather than a critical history, *La Inquisición sin máscara* is an able disquisition against the Holy Office.

35. *Histoire critique de l'Inquisition d'Espagne depuis l'époque de son établissement par Ferdinand V jusqu'au règne de Ferdinand VII, tirée des pièces originales des archives du Conseil de la Suprême et de celles des tribunaux subalternes du Saint Office.*

36. By papal dispensation, in view of his youth.

intellectual minority. It was the period in which the young vicar abandoned "forever ultramontane principles of jurisprudence, scholasticism in the field of theology and the Peripatetics in the area of philosophy and the natural sciences.[37] He became more and more interested in poetry and the drama and letters in general and his whole *Weltanschauung* changed. ". . . I abandoned the books I had esteemed until then, I began to handle different ones and every day I became more aware of having studied on the basis of erroneous principles."[38] Here, then, was one of those enlightened priests who were part and parcel of the Spanish reformist movement at the turn of the century. He might perhaps have been in later years one of those liberal clergymen who played such a vital role in the Cortes of Cádiz. But a number of circumstances kept him away from that road. One of them was probably the close relationship he established in 1792 with a number of refugee priests from France, whose interpreter and confessor he was for a time and to whom he rendered services of all sorts. The tales of terror and persecution they brought from Revolutionary France must have banished from Llorente's mind any thought of democratic revolution he might have been entertaining.

Nonetheless he remained an admirer of the new philosophical spirit. One would not expect to find such a man connected in any way with the Spanish Inquisition. But this is exactly what happened. Llorente was acquainted with the then inquisitor general, D. Agustín Rubín de Cevallos, Bishop of Jaén, who apparently took a liking to him and in 1789 appointed him secretary of the Inquisition of Madrid. Sharing his time between Calahorra and the capital, he was introduced to Charles IV and Luisa, who granted him a canonship in Calahorra. In the former post he gained a first-hand look at the Inquisition's history, organization, and methods, and became revolted with the past and continuing cruelties of the Holy Office, albeit its activities were of a relatively moderate character in his day. His treatise on some of the methods of the Tribunal[39] caused him to lose the post of secretary at the time of the persecution unleashed

37. *Noticia biográfica*, p. 29.
38. *Ibid.*, p. 32.
39. *Discurso sobre el orden de procesar en los tribunales de Inquisición.*

against reformists and so-called Jansenists,[40] and in 1801 we find him once more in Calahorra. Four years later he was in Madrid again, commissioned by the court to write a history of the Basque provinces.[41] In 1806, the monarch rewarded him with the post of canon of the cathedral of Toledo, and the following year made him a member of the Royal Order of Spain, founded by Charles III.

Soon afterward Llorente's life, like so many other Spanish lives, took a fateful turn. But it was a turn which could really cause no surprise. The ex-secretary of the Holy Office desired reform, but not reform through popular revolutions. The violence of the uprising in the Spanish provinces must have recalled to his mind the harrowing stories told to him by the French refugee priests years before, confirming him in his desire for changes directed from above, as in the years of Spanish enlightened despotism. His experience with the Inquisition had convinced him of the necessity of a thoroughgoing reform of the Spanish Church. But in his eyes this reform could not come from the patriotic ranks, which fought under the traditionalist banner of "King, Fatherland, and Religion" and seemed to emphasize, at least at the beginning, the preservation of the status quo in the Church. Besides, even if it was true, as he indicates, that he declined to go to Bayonne when invited to do so by Murat,[42] he was in territory heavily occupied by French troops, and when a second invitation reached him, couched this time in no uncertain terms, he yielded and left for France.

Of all the attentions Joseph accorded Llorente,[43] who from then on wholeheartedly offered his services to the new order of things, the most important was doubtless that of entrusting to his care the archives of the Council of the Inquisition and of the Inquisitional tribunal of Madrid.[44] As a result, Llorente was able to write his

40. See Chapters X and XIV.

41. The work he wrote bears the title of *Noticia histórica de las provincias vascongadas*.

42. *Noticia biográfica*, p. 123.

43. These included the posts of councillor of state (1808), collector general of the property of suppressed monasteries (1809), and director general of property confiscated by the State and slated for sale (1809).

44. The King also ordered those persons in charge of the Inquisitional archives of Valladolid and other important towns to place at Llorente's disposal any material he might request.

history of the Inquisition. The work, though well documented, probably exaggerated the horror of the Holy Office and the number of its victims. It had considerable influence on the image Spain projected on nineteenth-century European thought and contributed to some extent to the growth of the *leyenda negra,* the "black legend," which, beginning with Padre Las Casas in the sixteenth century, emphasized Spanish religious fanaticism and cruelty toward believers in other religions as well as toward the Indians of Spanish America.[45]

In August, 1812, Llorente accompanied Joseph to Valencia, and in October he took up residence in Zaragoza. In July of the following year he emigrated to France and lived there until 1823, when he returned to Spain, to die in his homeland a few days after setting foot in Madrid. Fernando VII did not forgive him for his collaboration,[46] and his return to Spain was due to an amnesty granted in 1820 by the Spanish liberals, who at the time of his arrival in Madrid were still in power. But the liberals were not any more favorably inclined toward Llorente than Fernando. In their eyes he was still the man who had betrayed the national cause. In Llorente's favor it must be said that he was apparently a kind man, and his goodness of heart manifested itself particularly in the help he gave the French refugee priests in the 1790s and in his efforts on behalf of a number of Spaniards during the War of Independence. He claimed to have persuaded French Marshal Jourdan in August, 1808, to make restitution of more than 100 farm animals to the peasants of Logroño, and of more than 80 to those of Calahorra, and to have saved the lives of people condemned to death by the invader.[47] Some of these claims have been confirmed by documentary evidence.[48]

45. The *History of the Inquisition* was placed on the Index in 1817. Llorente is also the author of a history of the events in Spain in 1808, published in France in 1814 under the anagram of Nellerto with the title *Memorias para la historia de la revolución española.*

46. Llorente's property in Spain, which included an 8,000-volume library, was confiscated.

47. *Noticia biográfica,* p. 126.

48. Sarrailh, "D. Juan Antonio Llorente," *Bulletin Hispanique,* Vol xxv, p. 236. On Llorente cf. also Menéndez y Pelayo, *Historia de los heterodoxos españoles,* vii, pp. 12–24, and Juretschke, *Los afrancesados en la guerra de la independencia,* pp. 211–13.

Before we leave this gallery of better-known *afrancesados*, let us mention one of the more flamboyant personages that orbited around the Napoleonic star. This man was Colonel Francisco Amorós, a convinced collaborator, whose claim to fame rests, however, not so much on his activities in Spain as on his being the founder of calisthenics in France. Born in Valencia in 1770, he fought in the Spanish army in several campaigns and rose to the rank of colonel in 1807. Appointed secretary to King Charles IV in 1802 and later tutor of the Infante Francisco de Paula, he became a member of the Council of the Indies in 1808. On the recommendation of Godoy he was charged with numerous administrative tasks, including that of directing the Pestalozzian Institute in Madrid between 1806 and 1808 and establishing a botanical garden in the Andalusian town of San Lúcar de Barrameda. As a friend of Godoy he was naturally suspect to the aroused Spanish people after the fall of the Prince of the Peace, and his personal safety was threatened during the riots in Madrid following the events in Aranjuez. But he did not need this motivation of a personal sort to push him into the arms of Joseph Bonaparte. He was a wholehearted supporter of enlightened despotism and saw the Napoleonic regime as ideally fitted to rejuvenate Spain.[49]

Amorós served Joseph as military and political governor of the province of Santander (1808), councillor of state (1808), royal commissioner for Burgos, Guipúzcoa, Alava, and Vizcaya (1809), interim minister of police for Andalucía (1810), etc. Forced to emigrate to France after the final French defeats in Spain, he formed in Paris a school of calisthenics, in which military personnel as well as civilians trained assiduously in the art of developing supple bodies and strong muscles. The gymnasium of the Spanish colonel became an object of curiosity in the French capital, and the colonel's personality contributed in no small way to this fame. A fanatic on the subject of calisthenics, he advertised his school's excellence with unabashed showmanship, running contests and trumpeting the names of those students who had won prizes.[50] He fought endless battles to make his school a going concern, but the French Revolution of 1848

49. He was one of the signatories of the Constitution of Bayonne.
50. Morel-Fatio, "Don Francisco Amorós, marquis de Sotelo, fondateur de la gymnastique en France," *Bulletin Hispanique*, Vol. xxvii, p. 78.

led to the suppression of the gymnasium, and the same year the colonel died at the age of 78.

Amorós was a fiery man with a violent temper, who easily made enemies.[51] But unlike many *afrancesados*, who after the war made it appear that they had been forced to serve Joseph, the colonel had the courage of his convictions. In the *Representación* addressed by him in 1814 from exile to Fernando VII to protest against the expulsion of his wife from Madrid, he did not bow and scrape. "I have always known how to tell the truth to powerful men, as I am now telling it to you," he stated haughtily.[52] He did not ask for a pardon, as some were then doing. He was proud of having been a member of the Bayonne Assembly and of having held official positions under Joseph. "Far from repenting having followed this cause I am more and more pleased with my conduct," he underlined.[53] He was satisfied that he had chosen the only right course. After all, the Spanish monarchs themselves had ordered all Spaniards to obey the new regime, and Napoleon's power in 1808 had been so colossal that all other nations of the Continent had paid homage to him. Resistance by Spain alone had seemed out of the question. And most important, Joseph's government had been an enlightened one. It had brought to Spain justice and wise laws, which would have brought the reforms badly needed by the nation.[54] Yes, the colonel was a bird of a rare species, a truly unrepentant *afrancesado* who had no compunction about making a show of his collaborationist past.

[5]

In our century, World War II collaborators have fared very badly after their homelands were freed from the enemy. This came as no surprise in view of the bestialities committed by the invading forces

51. While in France he broke with his friend Domingo Badía y Leblich, another *afrancesado*, who had acquired fame through his adventurous travels in North Africa, Arabia, Syria, and Turkey (1803–1807), and became his bitter enemy.

52. *Op. cit.*, p. 35.

53. *Ibid.*, pp. 46–47.

54. *Ibid.*, pp. 47–55.

in the occupied territories. The Spanish War of Independence, too, was a cruel conflict abounding in atrocities, though in this respect it bears no comparison with World War II. Because of the bitterness with which the war was fought, the *afrancesados* received fairly harsh treatment from their countrymen.

Even at the high-water mark of the French occupation of Spain, the collaborators could feel safe only as long as they remained in areas heavily garrisoned by French troops. Woe to those who, venturing outside city limits, might fall into the hands of the ever-alert guerrillas. Alexander Dallas told the story of what happened to the wife of a wealthy *afrancesado* from Jerez, in Andalucía, who, "though not beautiful, was courted by all French officers of the garrison." One day she went on a ride with three French officers and had the misfortune of being captured by a band of patriots. Her companions were able to escape, but she remained a prisoner. Recognized by one of the guerrillas, a townsman of Jerez, she was tied to the trunk of a tree, "with her face to the tree, round which her arms were bound: a number of pieces of sharp prickly furze were then tied together in a bundle, with which one of the guerrillas without ceremony inflicted such chastisement upon the raging and blushing señora as is not unfrequently administered by a severe pedant to his idle or wicked scholars. Having continued this operation until they had rendered it highly inconvenient, if not impossible for the lady to make use of her horse, accompanying their more impressive arguments with a great variety of patriotic admonitions, they released her from the tree and politely offered to assist her to remount, which assistance she was however under the necessity of refusing, and taking her horse's bridle, she turned her steps toward Jerez, whilst the laughing *patriotas* galloped off in an opposite direction."[55] In this case the punishment was not as severe in the long run as the hair-shaving to which many female French collaborators were subjected at the end of World War II, but it certainly was more painful.

Male collaborators could, of course, expect to be meted out harsher punishment if they fell into patriotic hands. Don Carlos de las Muñecas, financial administrator of the province of La Mancha,

55. *Félix Alvárez, or Manners in Spain*, II, pp. 217–20.

reported to King Joseph on March 1, 1810 from Ciudad Real that when guerrillas had raided Ciudad Real the previous February the provincial treasury building had been surrounded by 400 "bandits" and Don Carlos had found himself in dire danger of losing his life. Taking with him 90,000 reales, he managed somehow to hide on a roof, where he was forced to remain for seven hours while the guerrillas were looking for him.[56]

The wife of an *afrancesado* wrote on June 1, 1810 from a town near Bilbao to her husband, then in Madrid, that life in the north was rather unpleasant. Guerrillas, whom she called *brigantes*,[57] were everywhere and French troops were nowhere present in sufficient numbers to protect the lives and property of the inhabitants.[58] One José Forcada wrote to his mother in Madrid from Guadalajara on July 16, 1810, that he had been attacked by 200 *brigantes* on horseback on the road between Alcalá de Henares and Guadalajara. Apparently he had managed to escape, but had been assaulted again, and wounded, close to Guadalajara. His wound must not have been a serious one, since in the same letter he also wrote that he did not wish to marry a certain Señorita de Falcó, as she was a very jealous young woman.[59]

Only the collaborators who were lucky enough to live in France while the war was still going on were relatively well off. One of those Spaniards addressed a letter to a friend of his in Valladolid from Paris on May 15, 1813, in which he painted life in the French capital in glowing terms. "This is a fine town, my friend," he wrote. "He who has a great deal of money and spends it somewhere else is a fool, for it seems to me impossible that there could exist another city in which comfort and pleasure are found to such a high degree. Unfortunately, as there are so many temptations and as it is very hard to resist them, money dissolves like smoke."[60]

The gentleman writing thus was soon to be joined in France by thousands of other collaborators, fleeing the wrath of their fellow

56. AHN, Estado, *legajo* 3113.
57. From French *brigand*.
58. AHN, Estado, *legajo* 3119.
59. *Ibid., legajo* 3069, *carpeta* F.
60. *Ibid., legajo* 3096.

Spaniards who had fought the Napoleonic regime throughout the war. This wrath made itself felt at an early stage of the conflict through punitive measures enacted by the government of national resistance. On the heels of the first withdrawal of Joseph from Madrid, in August, 1808, the property of a number of *afrancesados* was confiscated. In October, the newly-formed Supreme Central Junta set up a "Tribunal of Vigilance and Protection," which was charged with investigating all cases of collaboration.[61] After the December debacle, a "Tribunal of Public Safety," created in Sevilla in January, 1809, was entrusted with the fight against sedition and collaboration. Article X of the decree ordering the formation of this organism stated that the tribunal was to "take under its protection all those persons who behaved like good and loyal Spaniards, though by their residence in Bayonne or other places under French domination they may have become suspect in the eyes of the public, through some actions they could not avoid without endangering their lives; for it is one thing not to be a hero and quite another to be delinquent and criminal."[62] It seemed then that from the beginning the patriots realized that they would have to draw the line sooner or later between Spaniards who collaborated and those who were forced for one reason or another to coexist with the enemy.

On April 24, 1809, the property of all persons who had followed or were then following the French cause, especially twenty-seven of Joseph's ministers, was ordered seized, and on May 2 this decree was amplified to include twenty-six new individuals, for the most part councillors of state.[63] Though in the subsequent two years the territory held by the patriots shrank considerably, the problem of what to do with collaborators presented itself concretely in the form of men who were escaping from the occupied areas. Many of these were civil servants who had continued for a while in their posts under French domination. On June 30, 1811, an order of the Cortes stipulated that the cases of all these civil service employees would be

61. *Ibid., legajo* 29, *carpeta* A, No. 1.

62. *Ibid., carpeta* B, No. 19.

63. Artola, *Los afrancesados,* p. 233; Deleito y Piñuela, "La expatriación de los españoles afrancesados (1813–1820)," *Nuestro Tiempo* (June, 1921), p. 262; Méndez Bejarano, p. 26.

investigated by a special committee of the assembly, with the object of determining which ones could be given positions similar to those they had previously held, and which would lose their rank because of proven collaboration.[64]

It was in 1812, when the French suffered their first serious setbacks since Bailén, that the repression against collaborators really made itself felt. As much of the national territory, including Madrid, was liberated in the course of the summer, the collaborators, active or passive, who had remained in what was temporarily the free zone, and the families left behind by those who had fled to Valencia felt the heavy hand of retribution. As Artola points out, the repression was carried out on both the legal and the popular level.[65] The Cortes declared in August that Spanish officials appointed by Joseph, including judges and clergymen, were automatically considered as having forfeited their positions. However, the door for rehabilitation was left open to those who could prove that they had rendered services to the national cause. Shortly afterward, the decree of September 21, more rigorous than the previous one, made the employees of Joseph's administration ineligible to hold public office and deprived them of the right to vote. Later decrees, however, softened somewhat the government's stand on public officials who had served the "intrusive king."[66]

The persecutions launched against *afrancesados* in newly liberated towns were worse than the officially enacted repression. Denunciations caused many persons to land in jail, and as always happens in these cases, quite a number of innocent people shared the fate of genuine collaborators. By the end of August, Madrid jails were filled with all sorts of individuals accused or suspected of collaboration or of harboring sympathies for the French cause.[67] Death sentences involving collaborators were few, however. The *Diario de Madrid* reported on September 28, 1812, that a Don Francisco Navarro Sandoval had been caught disguised as a priest and bearing a message

64. AHN, Estado, *legajo* 3072, No. 1.
65. *Op. cit.*, p. 234.
66. CDF, CDXLV, pp. 459–61; Toreno, pp. 437–38; Méndez Bejarano, p. 334; Artola, p. 234.
67. Artola, pp. 235–36; Méndez Bejarano, p. 332; Deleito y Piñuela, p. 263.

from Marshal Soult to King Joseph. He had been condemned to die by the garrote on the morning of the twenty-eighth.[68]

Thousands of active *afrancesados* preferred exile to facing the hatred of their countrymen. On the orders of Napoleon, who did not want news of the Spanish debacle to spread throughout France, many settled in southwestern France or in towns along the Franco-Spanish border. It is not exactly known how many refugees crossed the frontier, but it seems that there may have been approximately 12,000 families involved.[69] Joseph did not forget his Spanish supporters in their hour of need. He asked his brother to grant financial help to the *afrancesados*,[70] and Napoleon, though fighting for his empire in central Europe, saw to it that the Spanish collaborators' needs were taken care of.[71]

In Spain, repression against those guilty of collaboration continued after the return of Fernando. The system of "purification," applied mainly with the object of depriving suspected public servants of their posts, went into effect in 1815. Many Spaniards now issued manifestos endeavoring to establish their innocence, and many were the "purification" proceedings to which individuals like Goya were forced to submit.[72] In 1818, a very restrictive amnesty was granted the *afrancesados* by the Spanish monarch and a few exiles were able to return to their native land. Two years later the liberal revolution granted a much more ample amnesty. However, returning *afrance-*

---

68. *Apud* Díaz Plaja, *El siglo XIX*, pp. 112–13. General Carlos de España, who was appointed governor of Madrid in August, 1812, was particularly cruel in his persecution of suspected collaborators (Toreno, p. 418).

69. Artola, p. 236; Deleito y Piñuela, p. 265. It is, of course, impossible to quote an accurate figure when it comes to passive collaborators, but in view of the extent of the spectrum pertaining to this type of cooperation, they were obviously in much greater number than active collaborators.

70. *Mémoires et correspondance*, IX, pp. 338, 388–89.

71. Artola, pp. 237–38. Among the exiles were Don Pablo Arribas, Joseph's notorious chief of police; counts Montarco, Teba, Guzmán, and Campo Alange; the Marquis de Caballero, the sinister figure behind the anti-Jansenist persecutions of 1800–1801; generals José Joaquín Martí and Juan Kindelán; the former inquisitor general Ramón José de Arce; the poets Juan Meléndez Valdés, Juan María Maury, and Norberto Pérez del Camino; the Arabist Juan Antonio Conde; the historian Antonio Cavanilles; and the jurist Manuel María Cambronero (Deleito y Piñuela, pp. 266–67).

72. Artola, p. 245.

sados were ineligible to recover their former privileges and honors or their former positions.[73]

Artola states that the *afrancesados* were too moderate in their ideological outlook to join either the liberals or the absolutists, who were in the saddle in 1814–1820 and again in 1823–1833.[74] However, it does seem that quite a few *afrancesados* did not fare badly at all under Fernando VII after he regained absolute power in 1823, and a number of former collaborators occupied important posts in the last ten years of his reign, while most of the prominent liberals lived in exile.[75] Suárez Verdeguer is even inclined to believe that it was the *afrancesados* who directed government policy behind the scenes toward 1830.[76]

For this and other reasons there is not much sense in trying to equate active *afrancesados* and Spanish liberals. A number of writers[77] have maintained that the liberals were really as foreign to the mass of the Spanish people as the collaborators, that their whole outlook was basically identical and that there was therefore no reason whatsoever for the liberals to join the patriotic side, which was basically traditionalist. Menéndez y Pelayo's comment on Quintana's attitude during the war is typical of this thinking: "He had the generous and blessed inconsistency to embrace the banner of old

73. *Ibid.,* pp. 247–48.

74. *Ibid.,* p. 249.

75. Some of the *afrancesados* who fared relatively well under Fernando were: The political writer Sebastián Miñano, who wrote propaganda material in favor of the absolutist king; the writer Gómez Hermosilla; and the poet-priest Félix José Reinoso, whose collaboration had limited itself to accepting from the French a canonship in the cathedral of Sevilla, but who in his *Examen de los delitos de infidelidad a la patria*, published first in 1815, strongly defended the principle of passive collaboration on the part of persons remaining in occupied territory, and especially on the part of civil servants, against the principle of all-out resistance to the foreign invader. In 1827, he became chief editor of the official *Gaceta;* the poet, literary theorist, and teacher Alberto Lista, director until 1825 of the Colegio de San Mateo in Madrid, who wrote pro-Fernandista propaganda between 1828 and 1833 (cf. Juretschke, *Vida, obra y pensamiento de Alberto Lista,* pp. 122, 130–149).

76. *Conservadores, innovadores y renovadores* . . . , pp. 27–30.

77. Especially Méndez Bejarano, *Historia política de los afrancesados.* Cf. also Menéndez y Pelayo, *Historia de los heterodoxos españoles,* VI and VII, and Villa-Urrutia, *Relaciones entre España e Inglaterra durante la guerra de la independencia,* III, pp. 494–97.

Spain and to adore for once all that which he had execrated and cursed."[78] In other words, since Spanish liberals saw eye to eye with the *afrancesados* on what was best for Spain, there was really no point for the former to choose resistance. Subservience to Napoleon was the only consistent course to take.

The treatment of former collaborators at the hands of absolutist Fernando VII between 1823 and 1833 should immediately caution us against the equation drawn up by authors attempting to show a close bond between the two groups. Actually, *afrancesados* and liberals were miles apart in their ideological outlook. True, both believed in social and economic reform, but *afrancesados*, suspicious of popular movements, believed in reform brought about by enlightened despotism or, lacking this, by an imperialist regime which in their eyes represented the ideal incarnation of this type of despotism. To a certain extent this is why they were able to accommodate themselves to the absolutism of Fernando VII in the last decade of his reign, though enlightenment was sadly missing from his rule. Liberals, on the other hand, wanted the necessary reforms brought about by the democratic process, not by a Napoleon or a Joseph, who were willing to allow a sham representation, but by a constitutional monarchy, in which all legislative power would reside in the national parliament. Between them and absolutism there was no possibility of compromise. Thus, when absolutism was enthroned in Spain, the liberals were completely out of the picture and many were jailed or forced to taste the bitter fruit of exile, both in 1814 and in 1823.

Yet, *afrancesados* and liberals were often linked by bonds of personal friendship and this friendship was occasionally not broken by the events of the war.[79] But this proves nothing, for personal

78. *Historia de los heterodoxos españoles*, VI, p. 330.
79. Lista and Quintana, for instance, saw each other frequently in Pamplona in 1818. Quintana was then imprisoned in the fortress of that town, and Lista had just returned from exile in France. Quintana the liberal and Lista the *afrancesado* had not seen each other since 1810. Blanco-White, who in 1810 fled Sevilla before the advancing French and later went to England, corresponded with both Lista and Reinoso, who had remained in the Andalusian city and had collaborated. Finally, Quintana did not hide his friendship for Meléndez Valdés, also an *afrancesado*, in the biography of the collaborationist poet which he wrote after the war (see next chapter).

friendship and ideological differences frequently coexist and simply progress along distinct paths.

The liberals' exaltation of the principles of national sovereignty, derived partly from Locke, Rousseau, and the French Revolution, their love of what they considered Spain's medieval tradition of political freedom and representation as well as their constant attempts to find a solution for Spain's problems in this past, were the ingredients which, combined with their basic pride of being Spaniards, exploded into their fiery patriotism of the war years. Far from being inconsistent, their attitude in 1808 was quite consistent with their whole outlook before the war. The *afrancesados*, who drank mainly from the fountain of eighteenth-century enlightened despotism, could easily justify to themselves that obedience to their own monarch's wishes, in this case subservience to Napoleon—in their eyes the perfect enlightened despot—was their first duty. Thus each group followed a course which had been largely determined long before the French invasion of Spain.

But even if we were to admit, in a purely hypothetical case, that liberals and *afrancesados* had identical points of view in every field, that they were both unconditional admirers of the Napoleonic system, could we really call inconsistent a group which in spite of this admiration of a foreign model, breaks with its own past and chooses resistance to what constitutes obvious aggression? *A la hora de la verdad*, at the moment of truth, as Spaniards would say, does the defense of one's homeland not rise far above one's ideology, and does one's sacred obligation to oppose any unprovoked invasion of one's motherland not constitute the basic, decisive criterion for judging one's actions in such a situation? In the end it was the liberals who chose the only course consistent with the principle of national dignity and self-defense, and the *afrancesados* who surrendered to armed force. *A la hora de la verdad* it was the liberals who fought against foreign aggression and the *afrancesados*, no matter how susceptible of rationalization their conduct may have been, who sided with the invader.

XIV

THE PEN'S MOMENT OF TRUTH

[1]

IN OUR endeavor to determine the nature and extent of the phenomenon of collaboration during the Spanish War of Independence we have come across many representatives of Spanish society. We have met ministers of the *Ancien Régime,* titled aristocrats, prelates, simple clergymen, and so on. There is one group which we have not mentioned yet, because we think that it deserves a special study in a chapter apart. This is a group of persons who because of their superior educational background; their acute awareness of the problems facing Man as well as of their own responsibilities as members of the nation's intellectual elite; their reputation acquired in their particular field of endeavor; and their influence on the thought of educated Spaniards, merit special interest on our part. These men were the writers of Spain, poets, playwrights, essayists, who in 1808 found themselves in the terrible maelstrom then engulfing the whole nation.

Some of Spain's most outstanding men of letters followed the Napoleonic banner and became tarnished with the stigma of collaboration. In spite of their great fame as literary figures this phase of their life inevitably detracted from their total reputation as men. Fortunately for Spain's literary kingdom, a good number of writers chose the opposite course and a few even played an active role in the highest organs of national resistance. Among all the tragedies caused by that bitter and cruel conflict not the least was the break which it frequently produced in the bonds that united many of the literati before the great upheaval. The literary community was rent in two, at least on the ideological level if not always in the area of personal friendship, and erstwhile bosom friends often found themselves on opposite sides, separated by the fire and smoke of war.

In at least one case, however, the gulf that opened between patriotic and *afrancesado* writers after 1808 existed already before the war. On the eve of the gigantic conflict which was to shatter the Spain of the *Ancien Régime*, there were in Madrid two well-known *tertulias* which attracted the literary talents of the capital. One was headed by Leandro Fernández de Moratín, the great playwright, the other by the poet Manuel José Quintana, whom we have already met at the beginning of this study. There were personal and ideological reasons for the chilliness between the two leaders. Quintana, though endowed with great qualities, was somewhat vain and resented Moratín's supercilious attitude toward his and his friends' poetry.[1] Conversely, Moratín was irritated by the criticism directed at some of his own literary production by Quintana.[2] Furthermore, while both groups desired reforms in the Spanish political and social structure, Moratín and his friends,[3] though also in favor of reforms, were moderates and abhorred revolutionary convulsions. Consequently, they were admirers of Napoleon and supporters of Godoy and did not hide their adulation of the Prince of the Peace. Quintana's *tertulia*

1. In his *Epístola a Andrés* (*Obras de D. Nicolás y D. Leandro Fernández de Moratín*, in BAE, II, 1944 ed., pp. 585-86), Moratín had poked fun at the poetic style of Quintana and his friends Meléndez Valdés and Cienfuegos.

2. *La mojigata*, Moratín's play presented in 1804, earned Quintana's praise on the whole, but a number of reservations, especially the one with regard to the main character of the play, could not fail to arouse Moratín's animosity. A friend of the playwright, the poet Juan Tineo, refuted Quintana's criticism in the latter's periodical *Variedades de Ciencias, Literature y Artes* (III, 1804, pp. 228-47, 295-305) and Moratín himself sent in a letter in which he stated, after denying that he had written the apology of the play: "I never answer criticisms of my work. I am always thankful for them, because, if they are well written . . . , I profit by them in my work and I keep quiet. If they are absurd they indirectly contribute to my celebrity. I laugh at them and at their authors and at the spirit that dictated them, and I also keep quiet" (*ibid.*, p. 306).

3. Some of these were Juan Antonio Melón, who had been appointed in 1805 chief of the Tribunal of Censorship, and the critics and poets Estala, Tineo, and Gómez Hermosilla.

on the other hand, and especially the leader himself, wanted far-reaching political reforms and considered Napoleon a traitor to French revolutionary ideals. Most members of the group were, of course, opposed to Godoy's dictatorship.

While Moratín, by 1807, had for all practical purposes come to the end of his dramatic production, Manuel José Quintana was reaching the plenitude of his career as bard, historian, and critic. But the power of circumstances was soon to make it impossible for him to devote much time to purely literary pursuits. The war would place immense demands upon his talents and he would be called upon to play an important role in the struggle for national independence. In 1807, Quintana was thirty-five years old, a tall, attractive young man, though austere in his appearance and demeanor. His wife María Antonia, whom he had married seven years before, was reputed to be one of the most beautiful women in Spain. The beauty of María Antonia actually caused the poet more grief than happiness. Research has unearthed evidence pointing to Señora de Quintana's infidelity. It was a harsh blow to Quintana's faith in his love and to his self-respect, but he bore his cross with the dignity which was part and parcel of his character.[4]

It was this dignity, coupled with his natural affability and an apparent modesty, hiding a considerable amount of self-esteem bordering on vanity, which, together with his great literary gifts, gained him the friendship of many of his contemporaries and explains the success of his *tertulia*. Quintana always lived modestly and shunned all kinds of ostentation. This was partly due to his disdain for luxury—he preferred to spend money on books rather than on furniture—but also to the fact that he came from a family without great economic means. Quintana's father had been an official of the Council of Military Orders in Madrid, where Manuel was born in 1772. The elder Quintana gave his son a good education—good for a time when the educational level of the country was dismally low—sending him first to a school in the capital and later to another

4. His wife died in 1820. It is said that she had been seduced during the War of Independence by Quintana's intimate friend Toribio Núñez, and that the poet never forgave her (Quintana, *Poesías*, ed. Alonso Cortés, pp. 9-10; Vila Selma, *El ideario de Manuel José Quintana*, pp. 13-14).

institution of learning in Córdoba, where he studied Latin. Later still, he studied rhetoric and philosophy in a seminar in Salamanca and civil and canon law at the historic city's university.

In Salamanca, then one of the channels through which European Enlightenment filtered into Spain, the young Quintana made friendships which were to have a profound and lasting influence on his ideological trajectory and on his literary production. He met among others Juan Meléndez Valdés and Nicasio Alvarez de Cienfuegos, who became intimate friends of the young student. For the former, Quintana formed an attachment which was to last many years. Even Meléndez' later collaboration with the French affected but passingly this profound feeling Quintana harbored for the man whom he considered his master.

At the time Quintana first met him, Meléndez was emerging as the greatest Spanish poet since the Golden Age, whose soft, slightly sensuous bucolic verse couched in impeccable style was applauded by most poets and critics of the neoclassic school, then setting the tone for Spanish letters. The young Quintana, a strong *aficionado* of poetry—one of his favorites was the sixteenth-century poet Herrera—sat at the feet of the lovable Batilo, as Meléndez Valdés was known to his friends,[5] and drank from what he considered the most exquisite poetic source in eighteenth-century Spain. "Glory to the great poet," he wrote in 1797 on the occasion of the publication of Meléndez' poems, "who has been destined/To arouse the Spanish genius from the slumber/And shameful oblivion/In which the sacred muses lie buried."[6]

But it was not so much the Batilo of the anacreontics and the eclogues who shaped the young law student's poetic expression as the Meléndez of philosophical, moral, and humanitarian themes. It was

5. It was the custom for poets of a certain literary group, in this case the so-called "School of Salamanca," which also included Fray Diego González (*Delio*) and Iglesias de la Casa (*Arcadio*), to be known by the name of a character in one of their poems. *Batilo* is a shepherd appearing in one of Meléndez Valdéz' most famous eclogues.

6. A free translation of the lines: "Gloria al grande escritor a quien fué dado/Romper el sueño y vergonzoso olvido/En que yace sumido/El ingenio español; donde confusas/Sin voz y sin aliento,/Se hunden y pierden las sagradas musas!" (*Obras de Quintana*, BAE, XIX, 1946 ed., p. 9).

from this aspect of Meléndez' poetry that Quintana was to draw much of his inspiration. The ode *El fanatismo* is an example of Meléndez' protest against the evils of this world. The poem, while furiously attacking religious fanaticism as a whole without mentioning the Spanish Church, contains obvious allusions to the Inquisition: "It [fanaticism] armed the hands of its ministers/With bloody daggers and fiery torches. They clamored/And the heedful people/Came running to the sound of their horrible voices./The unhappy monarchs, powerless/Before their horrible fury trembled/And oh, in the name of God the earth moaned/In the midst of unspeakable hatred and execrable war."[7] One is reminded of this passage when reading the following lines of Quintana's famous poem *A la invención de la imprenta* ("To the Invention of Printing"), published in 1802.[8] In them Quintana attacked the Papacy without naming it: "What is happening, tell me, to the filthy and ugly monster/Which the spirit of evil brought into the world, and which insolently/Dared to found its abominable throne/On the shattered Capitol/In order to devour the world with impunity."[9]

Nicasio Alvarez de Cienfuegos, another poet of Enlightenment, exercised on Quintana as strong an influence, or perhaps even stronger, than Meléndez. Cienfuegos lacked the exquisite form of Batilo, but his verse, in spite of its frequent bombastic quality, carries on occasion a fiery conviction and an emotion which make him a forerunner of Spain's nineteenth-century Romantics.[10] Philanthropism was a theme very much in the spirit of the latter part of the eighteenth century, but in his "Ode In Praise of a Carpenter Called Alfonso,"[11] Cienfuegos turned it into an ardent appeal for social justice: "Oh, afflicted/Hut of the poor! It is with you/That justice and reason found refuge/Ever since the first tyrant/Triumphed

---

7. *Poetas líricos del siglo XVIII*, II, BAE, LXIII (1952 ed.), p. 235.

8. It had to appear at that time in an auto-censored version to avoid difficulties with the Inquisition and the political authorities.

9. *Op. cit.*, p. 33.

10. Cf. for instance his *La rosa del desierto* and *La escuela del sepulcro*, *Poetas Líricos del siglo XVIII*, III, BAE, LXVII (1953 ed.), pp. 25–26 and pp. 29–31. Cf. Piñeyro, "Cienfuegos," *Bulletin Hispanique*, XI, pp. 31–54.

11. *En alabanza de un carpintero llamado Alfonso.*

over equality/While fiercely oppressing mankind."[12] Quintana, in spite of the relatively advanced political posture which he was to adopt in the course of his whole existence, would not be very interested in the problem of social equality. He did follow Cienfuegos and Meléndez, however, in their "ardent love for liberty and for progress and moral and Spartanlike austerity which Cienfuegos expressed artifically and bombastically in his verse . . . "[13] It was this type of poetic production in which Quintana was to excel some years later. It would stamp him as a poet, neoclassical in form, but using his craftsmanship to give expression to powerful emotions far from the sensibility which was the hallmark of the neoclassic compositions in eighteenth-century Europe. But his first book of poems, which saw the light in 1788, though perhaps preromantic in spirit,[14] was only a timid first step in his literary career.

Residing in the capital in the 1790s, he became a full-fledged lawyer in 1795 and in the same year received an official position on the Madrid Board of Trade. His post left him enough time to devote himself to his literary activities. In 1795 he composed his famous ode to the peace which had been signed between France and Spain,[15] and with this poem he established his reputation as a poet. His penchant for ideological themes, one of the characteristics of his poetry, now manifested itself in this ode in which he spoke about the disaster which war constituted for the nations forced to wage it.

Two years later Quintana wrote the ode "To Juan de Padilla,"[16] the leader of the *comuneros*, who in 1520–1521 had defied the central authority of Charles V and was a hero to those Spaniards for whom the word liberty had a magic ring and who thought they saw some of this liberty in the institutions of medieval Spain. The poem combined the themes of liberty, patriotism, and opposition to despotism in too

12. *Op. cit.*, p. 28.

13. Menéndez y Pelayo, *Quintana considerado como poeta lírico. Discursos de crítica literaria*, IV, p. 244.

14. Cf. Vila Selma, p. 9.

15. *Op. cit.*, pp. 8–9. In a letter to Lord Holland in 1823, Quintana apparently forgot what he had said about the peace in this ode and called it a "shameful peace" (*ibid.*, p. 534).

16. *Obras*, pp. 3–4.

strong a dose to be able to appear in print while an absolute monarch was sitting on the throne of Spain. "To Juan de Padilla" finally saw the light of day in October, 1808. Liberty also plays a key role in the ode "To the Invention of Printing," published in 1802 in mutilated form. "The great day arrived," exclaimed the poet in the tenth stanza, "when a divine mortal, shaking his head/Among universal supineness/With a powerful voice/Thundered out/To the whole world: 'Man is free!' " On the wings of Gutenberg's invention this declaration flew over mountains and seas, added the author, and thus was heard everywhere the valiant shout: "Man is free."[17]

Quintana's most powerful poem is without any doubt *El panteón del Escorial*,[18] written in 1805. In this superb piece, which Menéndez y Pelayo considered the only poem of Quintana with any genuine romantic elements,[19] the poet had the specters of the absolute kings of Spain's Austrian dynasty bewail the decadence of what had once been a glorious empire. Though Quintana could not hide his antipathy toward Charles V and Philip II, a certain grudging admiration for them is felt behind all the invectives against absolutism. This poem, too, had to await the year 1808 to make its appearance.

Poetry was not the only literary field which absorbed Quintana's creative energy. He must also be considered a historian, for in 1807 he published the first volume of his *Vidas de españoles célebres* (*Lives of Famous Spaniards*), of which the third and last came out in 1833; and a dramatist, for he wrote two plays, the *Duque de Viseo*[20] and the *Pelayo*.[21] The latter drama, which sings the epic of the first Spanish leader to successfully oppose the Moorish avalanche in the eighth century, ends with an amazingly prophetic stanza, fitting perfectly the events that soon were to burst upon the face of the Peninsula: "And if an insolent people some day/Endeavors to tie to its triumphal chariot/The nation which today we are setting free, may our grandchildren/Defend their independence with the same

17. *Ibid.*, p. 34. These lines did appear in the edition of 1802.
18. *Ibid.*, pp. 35–38.
19. *Discursos de crítica literaria*, IV, p. 251.
20. Presented in 1801.
21. Presented in 1805.

firmness/And may Spain have eternal glory and freedom/Through your heroic example."[22]

Finally, Quintana stands out as a literary critic of strong caliber, as is attested for instance by the essays written for his three-volume anthology of Castilian poets, published in 1807.[23] In the prologue dedicated to Meléndez Valdés, Quintana spoke of his debt to the former: "You began to love me since my childhood," he wrote, "you took an almost fatherly interest in my education, you gave me the first lessons of good taste and inspired me with this strong and sustained love for poetry which I have kept until now . . . ."[24]

On the eve of the War of Independence, Quintana looked forward to a quiet life devoted almost exclusively to literary activities. He had achieved fame through his poetic production and through his two plays as well as through his work as historian and literary critic. He was one of the great literary figures of the moment. He was famous enough to be made official theatrical censor in 1806, which shows that he had not fallen afoul of the authorities, i.e., of Godoy. Quintana was very much aware of the political situation through which the Spanish ship was then navigating and he had strong feelings about what he saw, but there was nothing he could do. Active opposition to the dictatorship of the Prince of the Peace was out of the question, especially for a man whose activities were limited to the intellectual field. And so Quintana, though lamenting Spain's low social and economic level and the corruption and favoritism in high places, would have continued his studious, retired way of life if the events of 1808 had not propelled him into the forefront of national resistance. "All my desires were directed toward spending my life in dedication to my studies and to solitude," he was to write years later about this period in his life, "cultivating books and friendships . . . composing a few tragedies . . . , and writing a good piece of history . . ."[25]

While Quintana never actively opposed the *Ancien Régime*, his

---

22. *Op. cit.*, p. 73.
23. *Poesías selectas castellanas, desde el tiempo de Juan de Mena hasta nuestros días. Recogidas y ordenadas por Don Manuel José Quintana.*
24. *Apud* Vila Selma, p. 18.
25. *Obras inéditas*, p. 168.

writings that appeared in print during the reign of Charles IV contained enough material indicating where the author stood on some fundamental issues. Bard of liberty in the poem to printing and in other verse, Quintana could not fail to arouse the suspicion of the most retrograde elements in high places. And of course his more outspoken verse, which was read in the circle of his friends and passed from hand to hand, helped keep alive the strong desire for reform among the enlightened intelligentsia. In 1806, Quintana was denounced to the Inquisition. The reason given was his ode to the Battle of Trafalgar, published the previous year.[26] It is difficult to understand what could have caused anybody to see anything subversive in this composition devoted to extolling Spanish heroism. The cause must have been, as Vila Selma points out, the oft-repeated praise of liberty found in his other works. At any rate, no action was taken by the Holy Office.[27]

Quintana's rival Moratín, though entertaining much more moderate political views, had aroused much greater anger among the ranks of ultramontane Spaniards. But this was perfectly natural, as Moratín, a successful playwright since the 1790s, had reached wider sections of such public opinion as there was in those days. His last two comedies in particular, *La mojigata* (*The Religious Hypocrite*, 1804) and *El sí de las niñas* (*Girls' Consent*, 1806) had given rise to furious outcries. Moratín, in his neoclassic style, following in the main the precepts laid down by French literary theorists in the seventeenth and eighteenth centuries but adapting it beautifully to the Spanish national genius, blasted in his plays the age-old family structure which reduced daughters to a condition bordering on slavery and turned them into hypocrites. In *La mojigata* the author, without forgetting caution, attacked the false devotion so often practiced by obedient daughters to please their parents, and took potshots at the institution of monasticism. Lines like the following, in which two girls discuss the pros and cons of life in a convent, were not calculated to endear Moratín to the hearts of the ultramontane: "Doña Clara: But don't you see that we are surrounded/

26. With the title *Oda a los marinos españoles en el combate del 21 de octubre*.

27. *Op. cit.*, p. 16.

By a thousand dangers in the world?/Doña Inés: Yes, I know. But do you think/That in the solitude of a cloister/A thousand dangers are not found?/Doña Clara: Practicing virtue . . . Doña Inés:/Practicing it, you will be happy/In any situation."[28]

Not counting the antagonism between Moratín and Quintana, basically a matter of personalities and only to a lesser extent of ideologies,[29] Moratín had made many real enemies among the ultra-conservatives, but also among those playwrights who composed the absurd dramas and melodramas still infesting the Spanish stage at the turn of the century, with their impossibly intricate plots and their ridiculous situations.[30] They saw in him a dangerous rival and resented the great success this neoclassicist was reaping with his plays. Some of these, like *El sí de las niñas*, are still highly readable today thanks to their essential simplicity and verisimilitude of plot, the vitality of their language—Moratín's Castilian is extraordinarily rich and pure, though he occasionally uses gallicisms—and their fine sense of humor. The partisans of the old style of playwriting joined forces with influential conservatives, shocked by some of his ideas which seemed to go against Spanish social traditions, and both groups did their utmost to jeopardize Moratín's career, even going so far as to denounce *El sí de las niñas* to the Inquisition.[31]

Fortunately for Moratín, his position was secure and for a good reason. The eighteenth century's greatest playwright[32] was the protégé of the Prince of the Peace. Though relations between the two never reached the intimate stage, they were quite cordial and Moratín wrote several poems to the favorite exuding adulation.[33]

28. *Obras*, BAE, II (1944 ed.), p. 399.

29. Both desired political and social reforms and both were neoclassicists and partisans of *buen gusto* in literary matters, though Quintana was criticized by Moratín for his frequent grandiloquence and the liberties which he took with the Spanish language.

30. Moratín had poked fun at those bombastic plays in his *La comedia nueva*, presented in 1792.

31. Cf. Moratín's prologue to *El sí de las niñas, op. cit.*, p. 418.

32. Chronological periods coincide but rarely with the phases of historical development, and the eighteenth century must really be considered as terminating with the end of the *Ancien Régime* and the outbreak of the War of Independence in 1808.

33. Thanks to Godoy Moratín was appointed in 1796 head of the government department of interpreters.

Godoy's protection was enough to save Moratín from the wrath of the conservatives, but the playwright had had enough. After *El sí de las niñas* he gave up writing for the stage.[34]

On the eve of the war Moratín was a man of middle stature, pale complexion, large and beautiful black eyes, thin straight nose, and brown hair parted in the middle.[35] An introvert, he was reserved, though he could be cordial, and had relatively few friends outside of his *contertulios*.[36] He was sickly and nervous, and though he was jovial at times, he was a pessimist at heart.[37] Perhaps the melancholy that seemed to emanate from him must be traced back to his childhood when, at the age of four, he was stricken with smallpox, which left scars. The disease seems to have left invisible scars as well, for an essential sadness never left him after it. The disappointment he suffered in his one great love was, of course, not calculated to make his disposition any happier. In 1807, his romance with the girl to whom he had given his heart was broken, and in September of the same year she married an army officer. Though he continued to love her and would later engage in correspondence with her, he lost all faith in women.[38] A frugal man with high moral standards, he would not hesitate to offer generous help to needy relatives or friends.[39] He was fluent in French, English, and Italian, and a great admirer of French culture. A true neoclassicist, he was not unreasonable in his literary posture and recognized that Lope de Vega was worthy of admiration in spite of what he called Lope's mistakes.[40]

Born in Madrid in 1760 of an old and noble family, he was the son of the well-known poet and playwright Nicolás Fernández de Moratín, himself a staunch supporter of French neoclassicism. After a trip to France in 1787–1788 as secretary to Cabarrús[41] — he had been recommended for this post by Jovellanos, who already knew him

34. His *La escuela de los maridos* and *El médico a palos*, performed in 1812 and 1814 respectively, were translations from Molière's *L'École des maris* and *Le Médecin malgré lui*.
35. Papell, *Moratín y su época*, p. 217.
36. Members of his *tertulia*.
37. *Ibid.*, p. 219.
38. *Ibid.*, p. 207.
39. *Ibid.*, pp. 22, 219–20.
40. *Ibid.*, p. 220.
41. On Cabarrús see Chapter XIII.

then—Leandro first gained the favor of Count Floridablanca and then of Godoy. In 1792, he set out on a much longer voyage, which took him to France, England,[42] and Italy, and ended only in December, 1796, when he returned to Spain through the Andalusian port of Algeciras. His stay in France was a short one. Two weeks after he arrived in Paris the attack on the Tuileries (August 10, 1792) took place. On the same day, while at home, he heard a furious noise outside, looked out of his window, and to his horror saw some heads being borne through the streets on pikes. On August 23, Moratín left revolution-torn Paris and started out for England.[43]

The awful experience in Paris had much to do with Moratín's aversion to the very idea of revolution. If we add to this the protection of Godoy, we can understand his respect for constituted authority. On the other hand, desiring reform—but in an orderly manner—he despised the conservative forces that impeded progress. For Moratín reforms were to be promoted from above, in the manner of enlightened despotism, which in his eyes was incarnated by Godoy. After the fall of the dictatorship and after the playwright found himself irremediably in the collaborationist camp, Joseph's regime seemed to him to hold out the promise of orderly progress.

Also destined to follow this course was Juan Meléndez Valdés, the mentor of Quintana. Born in 1754 of a noble family in Ribera del Fresno, a town of Extremadura, the poet had studied law at Salamanca and had taught Humanities and Grammar at the university between 1778 and 1789. In the course of his literary activities in the university town he had established a lasting friendship with Jovellanos, one of the giants of eighteenth-century Spanish Enlightenment, then residing in Sevilla. This relationship had begun by means of a correspondence in which the boundless admiration and affection of Meléndez for Jovellanos, as well as a charming modesty on the part of Meléndez,[44] shine forth on every page. In 1781, on a visit to Madrid, Meléndez met the great scholar for the first time in

42. His one-year sojourn in England helped him to master the English language sufficiently to produce the first translation of Hamlet into Spanish.

43. *Obras póstumas*, I, p. 39; III, pp. 244–48; BAE, II (1944 ed.) p. xxix; Papell, p. 133.

44. Cf. several of these letters in *Poetas líricos del siglo XVII*, II, in BAE, LXIII (1952 ed.), pp. 73–85.

person, and their friendship became even deeper from that moment on. But unfortunately for Meléndez, Jovellanos, after a spectacular rise to prominence in 1798, fell from power the same year, and, as was customary in the Spain of Charles IV, loss of one's ministerial post usually meant exile if not prison. Meléndez, too, became engulfed in the disgrace that had befallen Jovellanos. As a member of the enlightened Salamanca group and as a friend of Jovellanos he was bound to incur the wrath of the ultraconservatives who too often found a sympathetic listener in Charles IV.[45]

Meléndez had risen through successive magisterial posts in the country to that of *fiscal* or Crown solicitor of the important Sala de Alcaldes de Casa y Corte, the Madrid Justice Department of the Council of Castile. But now he was sent away to the Old Castilian town of Medina del Campo. Without much to do in the way of official duties he gave vivid proof of his generosity and his compassion by feeding and clothing poverty-stricken inmates of the hospital of Medina del Campo upon their discharge from this institution. In 1800, he was sent on half salary to Zamora, but two years later his full salary was reestablished and he settled once more in Salamanca, "whence so many motives of friendship and family ties,[46] so many tender and affectionate memories beckoned to him."[47] Quintana, who thus speaks of his friend's return to Salamanca, gives us the following description of Batilo: "Meléndez was taller than average, fair and blond, with fine features, strong limbs and a robust and healthy constitution. His expression was amiable and soft, his manners pleasant . . . he was tender and affectionate with his friends, attentive and courteous with everybody. Perhaps his character lacked some of that strength and fortitude which is capable of holding firmly to a position that has been chosen by reason. This was due to his excessive docility and his respect for the opinion of others."[48]

45. Godoy placed the blame for Meléndez' disgrace on the shoulders of José Antonio Caballero, who replaced Jovellanos as minister of grace and justice (*Memorias*, I, *op. cit.*, p. 259).

46. He had married in 1783 the daughter of one of the distinguished families of Salamanca, Doña María Andrea de Coca y Figueroa.

47. Quintana, *Noticia histórica y literaria de Meléndez, Obras*, in BAE, XIX (1946 ed.), pp. 109–118. He spent the next six years in and near Salamanca.

48. *Ibid.*, p. 120. Cf. Colford, *Juan Meléndez Valdés*, pp. 98–124. Demerson, "Meléndez Valdés, quelques documents inédits pour compléter sá biographie," *Bulletin Hispanique*, Vol. LV, No. 3–4 (1953), pp. 252–95.

Meléndez, like Moratín, suffered at the hands of the *Ancien Régime*. Though for a short time in the good graces of Godoy—he wrote a few poems dedicated to him—he never became a true protégé of the Prince of the Peace and was not as fortunate as Moratín, who escaped actual persecution. Even before he felt the heavy hand of absolutism on his shoulders he strongly condemned what he considered rotten in Spanish society. In *La despedida del anciano* (*The Farewell of the Old Man*), published for the first time in *El Censor* in 1787,[49] an old man on his way to exile exclaims: "Oh, would that merciful heaven/Not let the wrong done to me/Fall on you, blind fatherland!/You turn your wrath on good men;/And, a stepmother to your children,/You reward their virtues with opprobrium/And their enlightenment with shackles."[50] For Meléndez, the French regime would later seem to hold out the hope that Spain might some day be a country where enlightened men could live without fear. But as we shall see later, Meléndez was not strongly motivated by ideological conviction when he became an *afrancesado*. Rather than conviction it was the pressure of circumstances as well as his yearning for peace which pushed him into the arms of the invaders.

Meléndez, Moratín, and even Quintana had their difficulties with absolutism, but all the unpleasantness and persecution they had to suffer at the hands of Charles IV's government was mild in comparison with the calvary imposed on one of the greatest human beings ever produced by Spain, Gaspar Melchor de Jovellanos. Jovellanos was the incarnation of the spirit of Spanish Enlightenment. Combining an unquenchable intellectual curiosity with an extraordinary capacity for work, an encyclopedic and penetrating mind, and considerable literary talent, he devoted most of his life to promoting his country's progress. Statesman, economist, jurist, educationist, writer, poet, he was all these things, but most of all he was a patriotic Spaniard who wanted his country to shake off the weight of what he considered harmful in tradition and become a modern nation.

Different people have seen different facets of Jovellanos. Liberals

49. *Op. cit.*, Vol. VIII, *Discurso* 154, pp. 453–69.
50. Cf. *Poetas líricos del siglo XVIII*, II, in BAE, LXIII (1952 ed.), p. 255. It seems almost as if Meléndez were prophesying the fate that fourteen years later befell Jovellanos. See below.

have seen in him primarily the reformist and the opponent of the Inquisition. Conservatives have pointed to his opposition to revolutionary innovations, to his attachment for nobility, and above all to his unswerving Catholicism. A conservative like Menéndez y Pelayo stated flatly that the orthodoxy of Jovellanos was stainless, and went on to defend him against those who had attacked him as a revolutionary.[51] Actually, Jovellanos was all of these things. In many ways he was an innovator, in others he was a traditionalist. The greater part of his active life was spent during a time when great changes were sweeping over the Western World. At the onset of the American Revolution he was thirty-one years old, at the outbreak of the French Revolution, forty-five, and at the start of the Spanish War of Independence, sixty-four. It was the time when new ideas were finding their way into Spain and when the French Revolution left a lasting impact.

Jovellanos, receiving his intellectual formation during the enlightened despotism of Charles III and his ministers, possessed by a thirst for knowledge and a deep-rooted desire for progress, and acquiring in his readings a considerable baggage of foreign authors such as Montesquieu, Locke, Smith, and Rousseau, perforce absorbed many ideas which to staunch traditionalists sounded like heresy. In his famous *Informe sobre la ley agraria*[52] he did not hesitate to place the onus for Spain's agricultural backwardness on the practice of entailing landed estates and on the excessive accumulation of land in the hands of the Church. He demanded that the power of the Mesta[53] be curbed, that landholders be allowed to enclose their property to keep out the herds of sheep of this institution, and that individuals be allowed to acquire public land. It was a trumpet call for land reform in the spirit of the new economic doctrine of laissez-faire, which was to have a decisive influence on the legislators of the Cortes of Cádiz. In his two satires in verse to Arnesto,[54] he lashed

---

51. *Historia de los heterodoxos españoles*, VI, p. 343.

52. Published in 1795 under the title *Informe de la Sociedad Económica de esta Corte al real y supremo Consejo de Castilla, en el expediente de ley agraria.*

53. See Chapter I.

54. *El Censor*, Vol. VIII, (1787), *Discurso* 155, pp. 471–85; *Obras*, I, in BAE, XLVI (1951 ed.), pp. 32–36.

out against the many unworthy aristocrats who with their degenerate mores contributed to the decadence of the nation. In the area of education—one of Jovellanos' main fields of interest, considered by him as the indispensable prerequisite for socioeconomic progress —he proclaimed the necessity on the one hand of public education available to all, and on the other of the inclusion of natural sciences in any program of studies.[55] And in his short term as minister of grace and justice in 1798, he addressed a memorandum to Charles IV, in which he strongly suggested that Spanish bishops replace the Inquisition in the struggle against anti-Catholic subversion.[56]

On the other hand, his calls for reform were balanced by expressions of traditionalism. Though attacking the accumulation of landed property in the hands of the Church, he did not deny ecclesiastics the right to purchase such property but merely advocated they be forbidden to acquire new estates. Though lashing out against the corrupt nobles who abounded during his time, he indicated the necessity of retaining an aristocracy as an indispensable social group between the throne and the people. While preaching the inclusion of natural sciences in educational curricula he also recognized the need for humanities.[57] And though attacking the Inquisition, he gave more than ample proof of his religious orthodoxy. One needs only to read the last part of his *Tratado teórico-práctico de enseñanza*,[58] written incidentally while he was in exile in Mallorca, to grasp the profound religiousness which animated Jovellanos, or the following sentence on revelation uttered by him in his inaugural address at the opening of the Royal Asturian Institute in 1794: "Ah! Without revelation, without this divine light which descended from Heaven to illuminate and fortify our obscure, our weak reason, what would man have grasped of that which is beyond the boundaries of Nature?"[59]

---

55. Cf. for instance his *Memoria sobre educación pública o sea tratado teórico-práctico de enseñanza, ibid.*, pp. 230–67, and *Bases para la formación de un plan general de instrucción publica, ibid.*, pp. 268–76. Jovellanos attached a great importance to the study of foreign languages (*Memoria*, pp. 247–48).

56. Somoza, *Documentos para escribir la biografía de Jovellanos*, I, pp. 208–12.

57. Cf. *Memoria* and *Bases*.

58. *Op. cit.*, pp. 257–67.

59. *Obras*, I, in BAE, XLVI, p. 320.

Actually, when closely examined, Jovellanos' seemingly contradictory stands are not contradictory at all. Scorn for degenerate aristocrats did not preclude support for the institution of aristocracy. Unwillingness to let the Church acquire new land did not mean forced sale of land owned by the Church, and revulsion at the Inquisition did not preclude in any manner profound religious orthodoxy. In the words of Camacho y Perea, "Jovellanos was liberal in his ideas, reformist in his tendencies, a sincere believer in his Catholic faith, opposed to the predominance of the clergy in its relations with secular power, a lover of justice and therefore an enemy of all privileges, a defender of our traditions but wanting to achieve progress, prudent in his counsel and opposed to dangerous innovations."[60]

When meeting Jovellanos for the first time, some people carried away the impression that he was an exceedingly proud man with haughty manners. He may very well have given this impression when the pressure of business weighed particularly heavily on his shoulders. Lord Holland, who met him in Gijón in 1792 for the first time, had quite a different recollection of Jovellanos:

His conversation was equally delightful, clear, perspicuous, and natural, and though not divested of playfulness and pleasantry, elevated and instructive. There was too much benevolence both of countenance and manner to impose any unpleasant restraint on the company, and yet an unaffected simplicity and a certain dignity and purity both in language and sentiment, manifestly the offspring of an unblemished character and a philosophical mind, gave a tone of earnestness and propriety to conversation, such as is rarely preserved in the unrestricted dialogue of a southern society.[61]

Jovellanos was most generous, most loyal in his friendship, and so incapable of hypocrisy that he found it hard not to take at its face value anything said to him. He was a fairly tall, well-built man, with pleasant features and intense eyes, who was at all times most careful

60. *Estudio crítico de las doctrinas de Jovellanos en lo referente a las ciencias morales y políticas*, p. 164.

61. *Further Memoirs of the Whig Party, 1807–1821, with Some Miscellaneous Reminiscences*, p. 369.

about his appearance.[62] Even as a young man he "wore an austere and impeccable dark suit, which gave him a certain clerical air."[63]

He was born in 1744 in Gijón, in the northern province of Asturias. After studying at the universities of Oviedo, Avila, and Alcalá de Henares, he began his career as a judge in Sevilla, where he resided from 1768 to 1778. It was in Sevilla that he experienced true love for the first and last time in his life. It appears to have been an unhappy love affair, for reasons which are unknown.[64] His literary activities in this period of his life attracted the attention of the men of letters of Sevilla, especially his sentimental drama *El delincuente honrado* (*The Honorable Delinquent*). In Madrid, where he moved from the south, his scholarly and statesmanlike qualities came fully to the fore. As a member of a number of learned academies he wrote paper after paper on a wide range of subjects. His *Report on the Agrarian Law*, written during this period and completed in 1794, is considered one of the best examples of Spanish prose in the eighteenth century.[65]

In 1790, Jovellanos spent a few months in Salamanca,[66] and there Quintana was privileged to meet him and become his friend. The admiration of the young poet for the Asturian scholar grew in spite of the long period of time they lived without seeing each other. Of Jovellanos Quintana said many years later: "He had loved me very much ever since my young years and he had directed and encouraged my steps in the career of letters."[67] Few statements of Quintana express more intensely his admiration for Jovellanos than the one contained in the poem he composed on the occasion of the latter's

62. Ceán Bermúdez, *Memorias para la vida del Excmo. Señor D. Gaspar Melchor de Jovellanos y noticias analíticas de sus obras*, p. 12.

63. Papell, p. 47.

64. "A great and profound passion consumed his soul. His kindness, his nobility, his lack of mischievousness . . . his innocence in these battles ruined him; and seeking consolation in friendship, in letters and in the grave occupations of his post, he was able to attenuate, if not erase, the deep imprint of that immense love" (Somoza, *Las amarguras de Jovellanos*, p. 15).

65. Jovellanos also cultivated poetry with some success. His *epístola* entitled *Fabio a Anfriso* is a fine example of an early Romantic poem in Spanish literature (cf. *Obras*, I, pp. 41–42).

66. Ceán Bermúdez, pp. 43–44.

67. *Obras inéditas*, p. 181.

elevation to the post of minister of grace and justice in 1797: "Blessed be the moment/In which the reins of power are placed/In the hands of wisdom," he wrote then.[68] Their relationship was destined to reach its highest point eleven years later, when Spain was fighting for her life.

As a result of his intervention in 1790 on behalf of his friend Cabarrús, who was being accused of malversation of funds, Jovellanos was sent north, officially to draw up a report to the minister of the navy on the coal mines of Asturias. It amounted to a disguised exile. In the course of his forced residence in his native province he founded in Gijón the Instituto Asturiano, devoted to secondary education and in which mathematics and the sciences were well represented. At the same time he kept busy traveling throughout the north of Spain and studying the economic problems of that part of the country, keeping a detailed diary, and completing literary projects which he had begun earlier.

Appointed minister of grace and justice by Godoy[69] in 1797, he fell from power after eight months in office and was forced once more into exile. The exact reasons of this disgrace are somewhat shrouded in mystery, as are the motives of the infinitely worse persecution which was to befall him a few years later. Godoy, who had had to give up power five months earlier than Jovellanos, but had not lost his influence, must have resented the Asturian's criticism of his conduct and must have suspected him—perhaps rightly so—of having played a role in his fall from power.[70] The Queen, likewise, was offended by what Lord Holland called "his austerity" and "his refusal to promote her creatures."[71] But more important, his opposition to the Inquisition, clearly shown in his memorandum to

68. *Obras*, p. 24.

69. On the recommendation of Cabarrús, who had gained the favor of the Prince of the Peace.

70. Cf. Seco Serrano, *Estudio preliminar, Príncipe de la Paz, Memorias, 1,* in BAE, LXXXVIII (1956 ed.), p. liii. The Prince of the Peace laid the blame for Jovellanos' disgrace at the door of the man who replaced the latter, the Marquis de Caballero, a reactionary and an opportunist of the worst sort, quite capable of hurting Jovellanos (*Memorias,* I, in BAE, LXXXVIII, p. 259). On the other hand Lady Holland attested to the hatred of Godoy for Jovellanos (*Apud* Del Río, Jovellanos, *Obras escogidas,* I, p. xcviii).

71. *Ibid.,* p. lxxxi n.

Charles IV,[72] his recommendation of the "Jansenist" bishop of Osma, Antonio Tavira, to the bishopric of Salamanca with the suggestion that he reform the curriculum of the University, and his friendship with the Countess de Montijo, a prominent figure among the "Jansenists"[73] of the capital, all these factors must have played a role in his fall from favor. Angel Del Río in his excellent study of Jovellanos[74] unhesitatingly places the great scholar in the foremost rank of Spanish Jansenism, i.e., "the tendency . . . toward the emancipation of the national Church from the power of Rome; an ecclesiastic Hispanism which turned nostalgic eyes toward the purity of primitive Christianity, and a fervent desire to establish an austere moral discipline in the Church, removing it from the excessive participation in temporal matters . . . ."[75]

It was these sentiments which in early 1801 caused Jovellanos to be meted out a treatment which in spite of all the cruelties the world has witnessed in modern times, still makes us shudder today. The immediate pretext was that he had been praised in a translation of Rousseau's *Social Contract*, which had entered Spain clandestinely in 1800.[76] He was arrested and packed off to Mallorca, the largest of the Balearic Islands. There he remained confined, first in a monastery and later in the castle of Bellver, from 1801 until the abdication of Charles IV and the elevation to the throne of Fernando VII in 1808 freed him from prison.[77] During his long confinement he gave a meas-

72. See above.

73. See Chapter I.

74. *Obras escogidas,* I, *Clásicos castellanos,* Vol. CX.

75. *Op. cit.,* p. lxxx. Lord Holland thus characterized Jovellanos in this respect: "He was in creed, in character and political austerity a Jansenist and connected with many of that sect, which, in Spain as in other Roman Catholic countries, have always been found the least corruptible and most consistent party in the state (*Apud* Del Río, *op. cit.,* p. lxxxiv).

76. In this translation Urquijo too had been praised, while the Spanish government was criticized (cf. Artola, *Estudio preliminar, Obras de D. Gaspar Melchor de Jovellanos,* III, in BAE, LXXXV, pp. xxxv–xxxvii).

77. Godoy claimed that the minister of grace and justice, Caballero, had shown documents to Charles IV incriminating Jovellanos, and that he, Godoy, had been powerless to save the latter (*Memorias,* I, p. 343). It is difficult to believe that Godoy, who enjoyed such an extraordinary influence on the king, could do nothing in the course of the seven years of Jovellanos' confinement to help the Asturian scholar.

ure of the magnificent stoical resignation of which he was capable. Supporting the adverse fate which had been his lot with a constancy comparable only to that of Luis de León,[78] or Quevedo,[79] he devoted his time to productive thought, which resulted in some of his finest writings, such as the description of the Castle of Bellver. Those were years of great trial, but Jovellanos came through the ordeal an even greater writer and statesman, but especially an even greater man than when he had set out on his long exile.[80]

[2]

When the Spanish people rose in arms against Napoleon, Manuel José Quintana knew where he belonged. The poet of liberty, the humanitarian, the patriot who had written *Pelayo*, could take only one possible road, that of national resistance. It was not a question of choosing sides, it was a matter of putting into practice some of the things he had preached openly and others he had reserved for the intimate circle of his friends. On the eve of the nationwide revolt his patriotism was put to the test, but it was too incorruptible to waver even slightly. O'Farril, the minister of war of the junta left behind by Fernando, called on Quintana to join in the effort to keep Spain from plunging into a war which he indicated could only be tantamount to suicide. In other words the poet was invited to fill the position of a propagandist for appeasement. Quintana rejected the offer, remarking "that the moral instinct of the Spanish nation would be stronger than any political and military calculations; that . . . in view of Bonaparte's perfidious aggression the insurrection would sooner or later erupt and that destiny would decide the issue; that my talents and my studies . . . would then serve my fatherland in whatever capacity they could be useful . . ."[81]

78. The great ascetic and mystic poet, who was imprisoned by the Inquisition in 1572 and remained in jail until 1576.

79. One of the Golden Age's greatest writers, both in prose and poetry, who suffered jail in 1639 and was freed only four years later.

80. Cf. Ceán Bermúdez, pp. 81–93; Somoza, pp. 95–149; Del Río, pp. xcvi-ciii.

81. *Obras inéditas*, pp. 173–75.

A few days after this interview Quintana met his old friend the poet Cienfuegos, who had been approached with the same suggestion and who too had refused to write collaborationist propaganda. Quintana recalled Cienfuegos' words as they were about to part: "We did what we had to do and now let things take their course. After all, one can only die once."[82] Cienfuegos did not have long to live, but before he died he courageously defied the invader. The Madrid *Gaceta* published in May, 1808, an article reporting demonstrations in León in favor of the captive Fernando. As director of the newspaper, Cienfuegos was called before Murat and threatened with death. But the poet refused to apologize for allowing the article to appear. His life was spared, but in 1809, he was deported to France because of his known anti-French attitude and he died shortly after his arrival at Orthez.[83]

From the time the insurrection spread over the face of Spain, the pen of Quintana served the cause of patriotic resistance with single-minded energy. While the French were still in Madrid he composed two odes to free Spain and published them as soon as the enemy soldiers had evacuated the capital after Bailén.[84] The same summer, some of his earlier poems such as *A Juan de Padilla* and *A España después de la revolución de marzo* ("To Spain after the March Revolution")[85] appeared in print for the first time in a collection entitled *Poesías patrióticas*.[86] In the ode *A España después de la revolución de marzo*, one of his most moving patriotic compositions, Quintana prophesied the war against Napoleon. After recalling Spain's glorious past—he seemed to have forgotten for a moment, at least, his imprecations against the Habsburg dynasty and its conquests—he spoke of the tyrant of the world preparing shackles for Spain. But Spain, after a long decadence, had found herself and was ready to stand up to Napoleon and his host: "War, awful but now sublime word,/The only refuge from and holy shield

82. *Ibid.*, p. 176.
83. *Ibid.; Poetas líricos del siglo XVIII*, III, in BAE, LXVII (1953 ed.), pp. 1–7; Demerson, p. 292.
84. See Chapter IV.
85. Written in April, 1808, after the fall of Godoy the previous month.
86. *Obras inéditas*, p. 178.

against/The savage impetus/Of the ferocious Attila who oppresses the west!/War, Spaniards, war!"[87]

But for Quintana patriotism did not consist only in the struggle against a foreign aggressor but also in the struggle for a better Spain. And a better Spain meant a nation ruled by laws enacted by the people and not oppressed by tyranny. A shameful episode like the dictatorship of Godoy must never be allowed to occur again, and the causes which made a Godoy possible must be eliminated. Free institutions were needed, and free institutions united with patriotic self-sacrifice and an iron will to win would lead Spain to victory. These were some of the things the poet said, and said in ringing prose in the weekly *Semanario Patriótico,* which began to appear in September, 1808.[88]

Quintana and many, many other Spaniards from all walks of life wanted the Cortes to gather as soon as possible. This desire the poet expressed again and again to his friends on the Junta Central after the formation of this body. One of his friends on the Suprema was Jovellanos, and Jovellanos, according to Quintana, would confidentially say to his colleagues that the Junta Central, to end its days with honor, must die in the arms of the Cortes.[89]

Quintana sat down and wrote to his friends in Aranjuez. He suggested they speak openly and frankly to the nation, informing it of the true situation and of the dangers that still lay ahead. At the same time the rest of Europe should be informed by the Spanish people of the motives underlying their heroic stand. Quintana claimed later that he had not desired a propaganda job, since Jovellanos was the ideally suited person for the post. The idea, however, must have crossed his mind, and when he was called to Aranjuez and exhorted by Jovellanos and other members of the Suprema to put into practice what he had preached to them, he accepted.[90] From

---

87. *Obras*, pp. 38–39.
88. See Chapters VII, VIII, and X.
89. *Obras inéditas*, p. 181. Jovellanos had been released from his prison on Mallorca in the spring of 1808 and had been chosen in September to represent Asturias in the Junta Central. See below.
90. *Ibid.*, pp. 182–83.

now on the poet became the spokesman for the Junta Central, and the government was fortunate to acquire the services of such a formidable literary figure. Proclamation after proclamation rolled off the presses, all bearing the stamp of Quintana's eloquence and fiery patriotism.

While Quintana was thus occupied in the service of his country, his rival Moratín was residing in French-occupied Spain, working for the enemy. Actually, his future had been determined from the moment he had become a protégé of Godoy. When his protector fell he was bound to live through difficult times. In the fateful March days following the fall of the Prince of the Peace, riots swept through Madrid and threatened to engulf Moratín's residence on Calle de Fuencarral. The playwright was known to be a friend of the fallen favorite. After the revolution of March 19, he is reported to have declared—and this is very much to his credit—"I am not his [Godoy's] friend, nor his advisor, nor his servant. But everything I am I owe to him, and though the philosophy of receiving favors without being grateful for them is very much in vogue today . . . I have too much self-esteem to subscribe to such an infamy."[91]

The riots swirling around his house frightened Moratín out of his wits and, on the night of March 19, made him lock himself in the building. He had hated popular upheavals ever since he had witnessed that terrible scene from his window in Paris,[92] and he was now seeing outbursts that might have similar consequences. He escaped bodily harm this time, but he had been badly shaken. Later, when Madrid rose against the French on May 2, he stayed out of his house for several days and was glad to see order reestablished. When Joseph was proclaimed king of Spain, the natural thing for him to do was to accept a regime which seemed to guarantee order and security and which, besides, promised to push through necessary reforms. Thus Moratín became a collaborator, more through a craving for personal security and the force of circumstances than through any strong political conviction. He continued to fill the post of secretary of the department of interpreters, and when Joseph fled Madrid after

91. *Apud* Papell, p. 273.
92. See above.

Bailén, Moratín went north with the French army and established himself in Vitoria.[93]

While Moratín's defection to the enemy could not possibly shake Quintana's belief in humanity, that of Meléndez Valdés must have been a shattering blow to Manuel José. His dear Batilo, his teacher, his idol, on the side of the French! For the moment it was the end of a lifelong friendship. Later, when writing the biography of Meléndez, Quintana could look upon Meléndez' action with equanimity and come to the conclusion that Batilo had not chosen the path of collaboration but had been pushed into it by bad luck.

To a great extent this was true. The fact is, however, that following the *dos de mayo,* the poet, who had been allowed after the revolution of Aranjuez to reside once more in the capital, accepted to serve as magistrate under the French. In the latter part of May, he was commissioned by the Madrid authorities to go north to Asturias and calm tempers there. Meléndez, though reform-minded, had neither the all-consuming patriotism of a Quintana, nor his monolithic character. The persecution of which he had been a victim, had, if anything, made him more vacillating and more apt to be carried along by the power of circumstances than to dominate them. Thus, in the company of Count del Pinar he traveled north and found Asturias in an uproar. The people of Oviedo were in no mood to listen to moderation, and all their hatred for the French now concentrated on the emissaries from Madrid. They were insulted by the crowd that had gathered in front of their residence and for their safety had to be transferred to the town's fortress. On June 19, they were about to be sent on to Gijón, when an enraged mob broke into the fortress, seized them as well as three other prisoners, and led them to the Esplanade of San Francisco to be shot. Meléndez pleaded with the enraged mob, trying to reason with them, and even recited some patriotic verse he had composed before May 2.[94] But nothing he could say softened the heart of the would-be executioners and he was told to confess. He had the presence of mind to make his confession

93. *Vida, Obras póstumas,* I, p. 39; "Documentos referentes a D. Leandro Fernández de Moratín," RABM, Vol. II (1898), p. 221; Papell, p. 236; Entrambasaguas, *El Madrid de Moratín,* pp. 33–34.

94. *Alarma española, Poetas líricos del siglo XVIII,* II, in BAE, LXIII, p. 158.

last a while. After this act, however, he was tied to a tree and everything was ready for the execution. But then the opportune arrival of the town council and the religious communities, preceded by the Host, calmed the effervescence and saved the lives of the prisoners.[95]

After a trial, in the course of which Meléndez and Del Pinar were found not quilty, the two emissaries were allowed to return to Castile. Back in Madrid in the latter part of August—by this time the French had been gone for more than two weeks—Meléndez awaited the formation of the national government and then sought employment with the Central Junta. He felt the prospects for his obtaining a position were good, all the more since his friend Jovellanos was a member of the Suprema. Unfortunately, the renewed French offensive in the fall and the subsequent recapture of Madrid by Napoleon thwarted his hopes. He tried but was unable to leave Madrid. Later he was not strong enough to be able to refuse employment offered him by the government of Joseph. His weakness in face of pressure coupled with flattery, and perhaps also his wife, who was ambitious and dominated him to a considerable extent, played a role in his subsequent actions.[96] Accepting a number of official positions in the French regime, he became another *afrancesado*. As Quintana put it: "He accepted and thus became involved with a cause which was never the cause of his heart and his principles."[97]

While Moratín and Meléndez slid into collaboration, and while Quintana withstood successfully the pressure from the collaborationist war minister O'Farril, following the directives of his conscience and his principles, Jovellanos fought off far greater pressures to emerge once more as a model of patriotism and integrity. Freed from his prison in March, 1808, in poor physical condition, he spent some time in Mallorca and disembarked in Barcelona on May 20. His destination was the town of Jadraque, sixty-three miles northeast of

95. Demerson, *Don Juan Meléndez Valdés et son temps (1754–1817)*, pp. 261–77; *Noticia histórica . . . Obras de Quintana, op. cit.*, pp. 118–19; Colford, *Juan Meléndez Valdés*, pp. 126–27.

96. Demerson, *op. cit.*, p. 284; Papell, p. 264. Demerson points out that after two unsuccessful attempts to escape from Madrid Meléndez became too ill to leave the capital (*loc. cit.*).

97. *Noticia* . . . , p. 119. Cf. Colford, pp. 128–29.

Madrid and twenty-eight miles from Guadalajara, where his friend
Arias de Saavedra was awaiting him and where he hoped to repair his
broken health. On May 27, he arrived in Zaragoza, in the midst of the
feverish preparations for war following the uprising. The people,
who knew of his martyrdom, welcomed him enthusiastically and
many indicated vociferously their desire to retain him and use his
great talents and prestige for the national cause. General Palafox also
received Jovellanos with the greatest signs of admiration and respect
and tried to persuade him to stay on in the capital of Aragón. But
Jovellanos was too tired to plunge at once into political activities and
yearned for isolation and rest. He hoped he would find these in
Jadraque, where he took up residence on June 1.[98]

Alas, circumstances were not propitious for a well-deserved rest.
Hardly had he arrived in Jadraque than he began to receive messages
from Murat and highly placed *afrancesados*,[99] inviting him to join
them in Madrid. Jovellanos invoked his poor state of health, assuring
them that he would do everything in his power to serve the fatherland once he was cured.[1] On June 8, Azanza informed him from
Bayonne that Napoleon wanted him to go to Asturias and use his
influence in calming spirits in the northern province.[2] Jovellanos
on June 12 gave him essentially the same answer he had sent
to O'Farril and Mazarredo: He was too sick to undertake the voyage but would do so if the state of his health took a decisive turn
for the better. It would be a mistake to infer from the friendly and
placative tone of his letters and from his expressions of gratitude to
Napoleon[3] that he was actually vacillating between the two sides
now rapidly taking shape in the conflict. After seven years in prison
he was a tired old man and sincerely wanted to enjoy as long as
possible the pleasures of retirement. He simply did not wish to
become involved, not because of a true feeling of neutrality but
because he needed to recover from his long confinement and his
illness and get his bearings in a confusing situation. In this sense his

98. *Memoria en defense de la Junta Central, op. cit.*, p. 536; *Diarios, Obras,*
IV, in BAE, LXXXVI, pp. 147–157.
99. Piñuela, O'Farril, and Mazarredo.
1. Cf. this correspondence in *Obras*, IV, *op. cit.*, pp. 334–36.
2. *Ibid.*, pp. 336–37.
3. "I shall always conserve in my heart the confidence with which the
great Emperor honors me . . ." (*ibid.*, p. 338).

letters must be considered both as an effort to gain time and as the result of a natural desire to be most civil and sound as cooperative as possible to men whom, after all, he highly esteemed. If, during his brief stay in Zaragoza, he felt some discomfort at seeing the people in revolt,[4] after the first week in Jadraque his sympathy for the insurrection became stronger with each passing day and his cautiously diplomatic replies to the collaborationist officials were merely dictated by the demands of urbanity and the necessity of avoiding for the time being open commitment.[5]

As a matter of fact, we would not be far off the mark if in this same reply to Azanza we detected a note of pride in the revolt in Asturias: " . . . I know my countrymen [the Asturians] too well to expect that persuasion would have any influence on them. Those people are scattered throughout the countryside and are too numerous and fierce to be tamed with words."[6] But where Jovellanos' sympathy for the insurgents clearly stands out is in his letter of June 21 to Mazarredo: "No, my friend, it is necessary to face the facts," he wrote. "The Nation has generally taken a stand and it has taken a stand with a resolve which is as strong as the horror it felt upon seeing itself so cruelly deceived and scorned."[7] On July 16, when refusing the post of minister of the interior,[8] he did have some flattering things to say about Napoleon's brother,[9] but these again were merely diplomatic niceties without any substance.

4. Cf. *Diarios, op. cit.,* p. 153.

5. Artola, in his study of Jovellanos (*Estudio preliminar, op. cit.,* p. xli), writes that since Jadraque was free of French during his stay in the town, the consideration that his letters only aimed to gain time has no value. The fact that Jadraque was not occupied by the French means nothing, since the French army was capable of extraordinary mobility and could be expected to reach any point in Spain in a relatively short time. While it is true that Jovellanos was not the kind of man to be cowed by fear, his illness and general fatigue forcibly made him behave in a cautious manner. Therefore, though his sympathies undoubtedly lay with the insurgents, it would have been unwise to let this sympathy show in his correspondence.

6. *Obras,* IV, p. 337.

7. *Ibid.,* p. 339.

8. Joseph appointed him to this post on July 7 (*ibid.,* p. 341).

9. ". . . when Your Majesty, on occupying the throne of Spain tries to forge the happiness of my fatherland . . ." and ". . . receive the sincere expression of my gratitude together with the strongest desire to contribute . . . to the service of Your Majesty and to the good and happiness of the Nation" (*ibid.*).

Then, at the end of August and in September, came an exchange of letters with his friend Cabarrús. On August 29, Cabarrús announced to Jovellanos that in spite of insurgent victories in the south he would follow the French cause to the end, for in his eyes it was the only salvation for Spain. "This man [Joseph Bonaparte]," wrote the financier, "the most sensible, the most honorable and amiable man who has occupied a throne, whom you would love and esteem as I have if you dealt with him for a week, this man will be forced into the position of a conqueror, a prospect repugnant to his heart but which his security demands."[10]

The answer to this letter shows us a Jovellanos proud of Spain's resistance and victories and in no mood for compromise. It sounds like a trumpet call for the cause of independence. After reproaching his friend for his collaborationist attitude, he sets down with rare eloquence the war aims of fighting Spain: "Spain does not fight for the Bourbons nor for Fernando. She fights for her own rights, which are her original, sacred, imprescriptible rights, above, and independent of any family or dynasty. Spain fights for her religion, her Constitution,[11] her laws, her customs, her usages, in a word, for her freedom, which is the mortgage of so many and such sacred rights. Spain swore loyalty to Fernando de Borbón. Spain recognizes him and will recognize him for her king as long as he breathes. But if brute force holds him [captive], or if it deprives her of her prince, will she not be able to look for another [king] to govern her? And if she should fear that the ambition or weakness of a king should expose her to ills such as the ones she is suffering now, would she not be able to live without a king and govern herself?"[12]

Was Jovellanos hinting at the possibility of a republic if no suitable monarch could be found to replace Fernando? The idea must have crossed his mind as he was writing this paragraph. Yet Jovellanos was a confirmed monarchist, though favoring a monarchy tempered by some kind of constitution.[13] These last lines should therefore be considered only to a small extent as the vision of what was to him at

10. *Ibid.*
11. In this sense, the sum total of her traditional laws.
12. *Ibid.*, p. 343.
13. See below.

most a very remote possibility, but mainly as a bit of rhetoric dictated by the enthusiasm of the moment. Above all they are part of this powerful tribute to the Spanish nation, to her rights and to her righteous cause in her struggle for her freedom. Jovellanos now announced loudly and boldly his feelings in the terrible conflict which had just begun. He was totally committed to the cause of Spanish national resistance. None of the great literati of the turn of the century had suffered at the hands of despotism as much as Jovellanos. It would therefore not have been unnatural for him to have accumulated such hatred against the fallen regime that in spite of the Aranjuez revolution, anything connected with the Spanish government would have been distasteful to him. The French offered reforms, and some of the collaborationist ministers were men he knew and esteemed, and he was aware of their desire to see Spain rise from the morass in which she had been lying for such a long time. But the voice of patriotism was stronger than all these considerations. When the Spanish people rose against foreign aggression, Jovellanos only needed to regain his physical strength and his bearings to place himself resolutely on the side of national liberty. On September 17, he left Jadraque for Madrid and Aranjuez to represent Asturias in the Spanish national government.[14]

[3]

At the end of 1808, while Jovellanos and Quintana were devoting their time and their energies to the national cause, the enemy, lunging powerfully forward, was menacing once more the independence of Spain. By the beginning of December there could be no doubt. Napoleon could not be stopped and Madrid would fall once more into French hands. Quintana, true to his principles, remained in the capital till the end. On December 3, he slipped out of the city through Segovia Gate. Alone and on foot he covered the enormous distance to Avila, to proceed from there to Salamanca, then to Ciudad Rodrigo, south to Badajoz, and south again to Sevilla, where

14. *Memoria en defensa de la Junta Central, op. cit.,* p. 539.

he finally arrived on January 9, 1809. Finding himself without any employment, he gladly accepted the post of chief of the general secretariat of the Suprema offered to him by Martín de Garay, secretary of the Junta.[15] It was an official recognition of the great services he had hitherto rendered to the government and an invitation to continue his effective propagandistic activities on behalf of the struggle for national independence.[16]

As glad as he was to serve his country in the capacity of official propagandist, he would have no less liked to resume publication of *El Semanario Patriótico*, which had appeared in Madrid with so much success, and incidentally this was also the wish of the Junta. But he was much too occupied to plunge into the work of editing and writing for such an enterprise. Yet, though he himself was too busy, a few friends stepped forward and took charge of the project. Quintana had the satisfaction of seeing the *Semanario* appear in print once more in the spring of 1809. The editors were Isidoro Antillón, former professor of history and geography in Madrid,[17] Padre José Blanco y Crespo, a member of Quintana's Madrid *tertulia*,[18] and the poet Alberto Lista, now a fiery patriot, soon to be an *afrancesado*. Blanco, of Irish origin, occupies a unique position in the political and religious history of Spain as well as in the history of Spanish letters. Born a Spaniard and a Catholic, achieving great honors in the ecclesiastical career, a patriot in the first years of the War of Independence, he left Spain after the French conquest of Andalucía in 1810 and went to England, where he not only abjured Catholicism to embrace the Anglican faith, but turned into a bitter critic of Spain's institutions, her religion, and her policy with respect to her Spanish-American colonies. Torn by religious doubts, he abandoned Anglicanism to become a Unitarian. But even this liberal tendency within the Protestant community did not satisfy him, and he died in 1841 "in pure Deism," as Menéndez y Pelayo puts it.[19]

15. *Obras inéditas*, pp. 184–85.

16. Actually this position had already been offered to him while the Junta was still in Aranjuez, but Quintana had then refused it, accepting, however, that of unofficial propagandist. See above.

17. See Chapter VIII, p. 347.

18. See Chapter II.

19. *Historia de los heterodoxos españoles*, VII, p. 207.

Blanco was born in 1775 in Sevilla of an Irish-Spanish family — Irish on his father's side — which in the days of Fernando VI[20] had received the title of nobility and was engaged in commerce. The career of business was repugnant to young José and to his mother, and he chose the priesthood. While he studied divinity in the university he showed great literary talent, which was fostered by a fellow student, Don Manuel María de Arjona, at that time twenty-one years old and soon to be known as a poet of note.[21] Through his interest and talent in letters Blanco became a great friend of Alberto Lista and Félix Reinoso, who were to acquire considerable literary renown. The former, especially, was destined to become a key figure in the trajectory of Spanish literature in the nineteenth century. Together with Blanco and Arjona, and under the latter's leadership, they formed in 1793 an Academy of Letters, dedicated to resurrecting the poetic glory of the Sevilla of the Golden Age. Blanco's talents were such that the Academy could look upon him as one of its outstanding members.[22]

Shortly after José Blanco had become of age, his professional successes began to accumulate. He won the post of rector of the important College of Santa María de Jesús, then that of canon of the cathedral of Cádiz, and finally, at the age of twenty-six, he ascended in 1801 to the exalted position of magistral in the royal chapel of San Fernando in Sevilla. He had been fully ordained only the year before.[23] But Blanco had entered the clerical vocation in the age of Enlightenment, when it was fashionable in the Spanish intelligentsia to submit all faith to the piercing scrutiny of reason. Like so many other young intellectuals in Spanish universities, he became absorbed in the reading of books that were then considered subversive, and these books, as well as his own ratiocinations and the contact with friends similarly inclined, planted doubts in his mind which he would never be able to stifle. In the part entitled "A Few Facts Connected

20. 1746–1759.

21. During the war Arjona became an *afrancesado*.

22. *The Life of the Rev. Joseph Blanco-White, Written by Himself with Portions of His Correspondence*, ed. by John Hamilton Thom, I, pp. 1–23; Méndez Bejarano, *Vida y obras de D. José Ma Blanco y Crespo (Blanco-White)*, pp. 33–34.

23. *The Life* . . . I, pp. 65–105.

with the Formation of the Intellectual and Moral Character of a Spanish Clergyman," which form part of Blanco's *Letters from Spain* published in 1822 in London, the author tells us something of his rebellion against faith, which was to have such an influence on the trajectory of his life:

"I gave an exorbitant price for any French irreligious books," he wrote, "which the love of gain induced some Spanish booksellers to import at their peril. The intuitive knowledge of one another, which persecuted principles impart to such as cherish them in common, made me soon acquainted with several members of my own profession, deeply versed in the philosophical school of France. They possessed, and made no difficulty to lend me, all the anti-Christian works, which teemed from the French press. Where there is no liberty, there can be no discrimination. The ravenous appetite raised by a forced abstinence makes the mind gorge itself with all sorts of food. I suspect I have thus imbibed some false, and many crude notions from my French masters. But my circumstances preclude the calm and dispassionate examination which the subject deserves . . . Pretending studious retirement I have fitted up a small room, to which none but my confidential friends find admittance. There lie my *prohibited* books, in perfect concealment, in a well-contrived nook under a staircase. The *Breviary* alone, in its black binding, clasps, and gilt leaves, is kept upon the table, to check the doubts of any chance intruder."[24]

Blanco's disillusionment with the Church grew at a rapid pace, and his peace of mind was further disturbed by the fact that his two sisters had become nuns—one had died in the convent—and by the religious intolerance he was observing all around him. There came a time when he thought he could not bear his situation any longer. Being a priest and yet rebelling against the religion which he was preaching placed an intolerable strain upon the young man. He even contemplated emigrating to the United States, and only "the fear that such a step might occasion my parents' death, and the certainty that it would, at all events, make them wretched for the remainder of their life," caused him to stay on in Spain. The immorality he observed in many churchmen also upset him, but to this laxity he was eventually not to remain immune himself, for he was to carry on an

24. *Op. cit.*, 2d ed. (1825), pp. 117–18. The above-mentioned part (pp. 58–118) purports to be the manuscript drawn up by a Spanish clergyman and shown to the author in 1799. It obviously refers to Blanco's own experiences.

affair with a woman who bore him a son.[25] This was probably one of the reasons why, after having energetically served the patriotic cause with his pen,[26] he chose to leave Spain in early 1810 and took up residence in England. His desire to eliminate once and for all the danger of his illicit relations becoming known to his parents, the knowledge that in England he would be able to breathe the air of religious freedom, the apparently hopeless military situation in the Peninsula, and his own precarious pecuniary situation in Cádiz, where he had gone during the invasion of Andalucía by Joseph's armies, were all factors in his fateful decision to emigrate.[27]

He was to live thirty-one years in England, studying, writing, eternally searching for religious truth. He adopted the double name Blanco-White[28] and acquired such a mastery of the English language that he became well known through his writings in English.[29] His *Letters from Spain*, a brilliant account of life and customs in Spain, and especially in Andalucía, at the end of the eighteenth century, is a monument to the elegance and verve with which the author handled the language of his ancestors.[30] He joined the Church of England and

25. Méndez Bejarano, p. 64; Gallardo, *Noticia biográfica, Poetas líricos del siglo XVIII*, III, in BAE, LXVII (1953 ed.), p. 650; *The Life* . . . I, p. 132. Gallardo, one of his biographers, claimed that several children had been born. Méndez Bejarano states that he was unable, in spite of all his research, to find evidence of more than one. The son was raised in England and eventually joined the British army in India.

26. His work with the *Semanario* came to an end in August, 1809, when the paper suspended publication due to pressure from the Junta, which was irritated by criticism directed against it in the weekly and by what it considered an excess of radicalism on the part of the editors. Actually, at the beginning of his sojourn in Sevilla, his relations with the Suprema could not have been better. As official chaplain of the Suprema he had said the first Mass during the government's installation in its new capital.

27. *The Life* . . . I, pp. 143–165; Gallardo, *op. cit.*, p. 650. His mistress did not accompany him, but his child did (Méndez Bejarano, p. 64).

28. White had been the original name of the family when it settled in Spain. Blanco was its Spanish translation.

29. He also had a fine command of French and Italian.

30. Blanco is the author of a sonnet which is probably one of the outstanding poetic compositions of the English language. Its first stanza reads as follows: "Mysterious night! When our first parent knew/Thee, from report divine, and heard thy name,/Did he not tremble for this lovely frame,/This glorious canopy of light and blue?" Other writings of Blanco-White are *Inter-*

then left it, but he never found a satisfactory answer to his search for ultimate reality, and he died at Greenbank near Liverpool in 1841, practically without a religion.[31]

Soon after he arrived in England he began publishing a monthly paper, El Español, which shortly served to poison his relations with Spain and the Spaniards.[32] After espousing the liberal cause and approving of the measures of the Cortes in the first few numbers of the review, he began to attack the work of the Spanish national assembly, including its treatment of the Bishop of Orense and its uncompromising attitude toward the afrancesados,[33] and he took up the defense of the Spanish-American colonies in their struggle for independence. As early as July, 1810, he expressed the opinion that only under their own administration could the Spanish-American colonies emerge from the "indolent apathy in which they found themselves."[34] In August of the same year he wrote that independence did not mean separation, and as long as the colonies recognized Fernando as their sovereign, they were entitled to run their own affairs.[35] "The people of America have been for the past three hundred years in a state of complete slavery . . . ," exclaimed Blanco in December, 1810.[36] Needless to say, this more and more pronounced anti-Spanish stand was not calculated to gain him the sympathies of his fellow Spaniards. Vituperations against him in the

---

nal Evidences Against Roman Catholicism and Poor Man's Preservative Against Popery, as well as many articles in Spanish and English.

31. The Life . . . I, pp. 211–16; III, p. 310.

32. El Español was forbidden in Spain and the Spanish colonies by the decree of the Regency of November 15, 1810. Its last issue appeared in England in 1814. The British government eventually granted Blanco-White an annual pension of £250 for his efforts, through El Español, to promote a closer alliance between England and Spain (Méndez Bejarano, p. 95).

33. "The conduct of the Bishop of Orense seems to me so much in harmony with the purest principles of morality that he deserves under no circumstances the severe treatment which is being meted out to him (El Español, II, No. 9, p. 296). Cf. also Chapter XI, and his adverse comments on the harsh measures of the Cortes against collaborators in El Español of December 30, 1812 (CDF, CDXLV, pp. 564–67).

34. El Español, I, No. 4, p. 324.

35. Ibid., No. 5, pp. 369–77.

36. Ibid., II, No. 9, p. 336.

Cádiz press reached a level only comparable to his own increasing *anti-españolismo*.[37]

Yet Blanco-White did not turn his back on Spain completely; his interest in Spanish and Spanish-American affairs remained very much alive. At heart he continued to love his motherland, though he severely censured its institutions.[38] At times he felt a strong nostalgia for Spain and wrote Spanish poetry. In his last years he even began to write a novel which he never finished, entitled *Luisa de Bustamante, o La huérfana española en Inglaterra* (*The Spanish Orphan in England*), "filled with love for his *brethren* (as he liked to call Spanish Catholics) and hatred and scorn for the pruderie of the English upper class."[39]

A comparison with the exiled *afrancesados* comes to mind at once. For one thing, like the collaborators, Blanco criticized the Spain of national resistance. Moreover, from England he not only blasted the Cortes but engaged in correspondence with his friends Lista and Reinoso, who had remained in Sevilla and had collaborated with the French.[40] In a letter to his parents in Sevilla, written from London in

---

37. A further cause for friction between Blanco and Cádiz was the support he gave to the Duke of Alburquerque in his dispute with the Cádiz Junta (see Chapter IX). The manifesto issued by the Duke from London had been edited by Blanco (Méndez Bejarano, p. 95).

38. Cf. Méndez Bejarano, p. 569.

39. Menéndez y Pelayo, *Historia de los heterodoxos españoles*, VII, p. 208.

40. Alberto Lista, outstanding critic, poet, and teacher of a whole generation of Spanish writers during the reign of Fernando VII as well as in the 1830s and 1840s, lived in exile in France and returned to Spain in 1818. In the 1820s, at the head of the Colegio de San Mateo in Madrid, he began his work as intellectual guide to many gifted young men, who were to make a name for themselves in the field of Spanish letters. He continued in this role as director of studies of the Colegio de San Felipe Neri in Cádiz (1838–1843) and of the Colegio de San Diego in Sevilla (1844–1848). In Sevilla, of whose university he became dean and rector in 1845 and 1847 respectively, one of his students was the great poet Gustavo Adolfo Bécquer (cf. Juretschke, *Vida, obra y pensamiento de Alberto Lista*). Reinoso became notorious for the clever and somewhat captious defense he made of the policy of collaboration in his book *Examen de los delitos de infidelidad a la patria imputado a los españoles sometidos bajo la dominación francesa*, published in France in 1815 (cf. Díaz Cárdenas, *Biografía de Félix José Reinoso, Galería de españoles célebres*, Vol. VII, 1845; Cortines y Murube, "Noticias sobre un afrancesado," RABM, Tercera Época, Año XIII, Vol. XXI, 1909).

October, 1812, Blanco explained his position in the following terms: "Though I hate the French, I love the only true friends I have left . . . If some of them have made a mistake in joining the oppressors, I consider that they have done so on the false premise that resistance could only make things worse. How can I believe that those who have been models of manly conduct all their lives, could have become suddenly evil men?"[41] In 1831, when Lista spent some time in England, he paid a visit to his old friend Blanco in Oxford. Time had not blunted the friendship of the two men, who had continued to write to each other, and though the visit lasted only a few hours, they were no doubt among Blanco's happiest hours in England.[42]

Paradoxically—but at first sight only—Blanco's break with Spain was much deeper than that of the pro-French collaborators. While most *afrancesados* considered themselves true Spanish patriots and remained in the fold of the Catholic religion,[43] Blanco went from instinctive patriotism to denigration of Spain's religion, institutions, and approach to political problems. The religious factor played a paramont role in this trajectory. Blanco's anti-Catholicism was continually fed by the terrible constraint he felt as a priest, and once he had left his fatherland, his conversion was merely a matter of time. The change in faith—especially if we keep in mind that it was carried out by a clergyman—created a much deeper gulf between him and Spain than between most collaborators and their motherland, for it must necessarily lead to an exacerbation of his anti-Spanish feelings. Without any doubt, many Spaniards, contemporaries of his, if invited to choose between the renegade *afrancesados* and the apostate Blanco, would have chosen the former. In a sense it is surprising that with his ideological formation Blanco did not follow the road of collaboration with the French. He himself gives us an interesting insight into his attitude at the beginning of the War of Independence:

I am indeed ready to acknowledge that I never felt that kind of *patriotism*,[44] which makes men blind to the faults of their country, as well as

41. *Apud* Méndez Bejarano, p. 378. Cf. a letter from Reinoso to Blanco, *ibid.*, pp. 381-83.
42. Juretschke, p. 150.
43. Lista and Reinoso, for instance, were clergymen.
44. Italics in this passage are those used by Blanco.

to their own. Spain as a political body, miserably depressed by its government and Church, ceased to be an object of admiration to me at a very early period of my life. I never felt proud of being a Spaniard, for it was as a Spaniard that I found myself mentally degraded, doomed to bow before the meanest priest and layman, who might consign me any day to the prisons of the Inquisition . . . and yet . . . I had patriotism enough not to remain with the French party, supported as it was by the hitherto invincible armies of Napoleon, but made my way through dangers, and hardships, to the seat itself of bigotry, to Seville, where I had to resume my detested, and long-discontinued task of acting the hierophant before a blind, ignorant, deluded multitude! . . . I never for a moment doubted the *justice* of the Spanish cause, or justified the manner in which Napoleon endeavoured to bring about the change of the Spanish dynasty. I only questioned the *expediency* of a popular rising. But since that rising had actually taken place, I would have defended the cause of Spain against France at all risks.[45]

Thus spoke Blanco of his attitude during the crucial year 1808. He, probably more than most ideological *afrancesados*, realized Spain's backwardness in all fields and was ready to acknowledge the superiority of the French political and social structure. Yet, and this is fundamental, he saw the *justice* of the Spanish cause, while most *afrancesados* did not see it, and those who did were too afraid or too bent on personal profit to act in accordance with their innermost beliefs. Patriotism, though purely emotional and in conflict with an appreciation of the situation based on reason, was the dividing line which the war drew between those educated Spaniards who were ready to bow to what they saw as the inevitable or to what they believed was better than their national environment, and those who saw the glaring defects of the national fabric but for whom the just cause of the fatherland was still more sacred than all other considerations. Blanco, then, followed the dictates of his heart after the national uprising against Napoleon. But the conflict within him, caused by his feelings and his private life, was too great. In his eyes the Spanish cause was still as just as ever, but he, Padre Blanco, who had lost his religious faith, could not remain as a priest in Spain, any Spain, reformist, conservative, or collaborationist. It was not enemy France which he chose as a refuge from the pressures which were destroying him, but allied England, and on the soil of Spain's ally he

45. *The Life* . . . I, pp. 141–43.

continued to exalt the Spanish national cause in the first months of his sojourn there. But to all intents and purposes he had burned his bridges behind him, and his eventual conversion consummated his political and religious break with his motherland. Though his departure from his native country in the hour of its greatest peril is open to criticism, it must be recognized that his situation in Spain was an impossible one. Blanco-White is a tragically unique figure in the period when Spain's destinies were being shaped. At the same time, he is one of the many talented sons of Spain who left the Peninsula and made a distinguished name for themselves in other countries.

By the time the War of Independence ended, the friends of Blanco in Spain could probably be counted on the fingers of the hand, and there were few Spaniards of whom the expatriate was willing to say a kind word. One of those few was Jovellanos. "I respect the memory of Jovellanos," Blanco wrote, "he was a man of talent and of the highest honour." Yet his praise was not unmitigated: "But he was timid and full of prejudices of the most injurious kind considering the circumstances in which he had to act."[46] True, Jovellanos seemed often to lean more in the direction of conservatism than in that of reform. When it came to the question of the sovereignty of the nation, for instance, Jovellanos took a more conservative stand than his reformist colleagues and friends. "Sovereignty resides fully in the monarch," he stated flatly in a report to the Junta Central drawn up by him in May, 1809 on the question of the structure of the future Cortes, "and no part nor portion of it exists or can exist in any person or organism outside of it." But Jovellanos was by no means an absolutist, and though unwilling to recognize sovereignty outside of the king, he was disposed to grant that this royal sovereignty was by no means unlimited: "But the power of the sovereigns of Spain . . . is not absolute but limited by the laws . . . and the point where they draw the limit, there . . . the rights of the nation begin."[47]

Among these rights was the right to rebellion, but only in special cases. "No people, whatever its constitution may be, has normally the

46. *Ibid.*, p. 147.

47. *Memoria en defense de la Junta Central (Apéndices)*, *Obras*, I, in BAE, XLVI. (1951 ed.), p. 597.

right to insurrection," wrote Jovellanos in a report written also for the Suprema in October, 1808 . . . "But any people suddenly attacked by a foreign enemy . . . who realizes that those in authority are either bribed or terrorized . . . must naturally defend itself and therefore acquires an extraordinary and legitimate right of insurection."[48]

The necessity for gathering the Cortes was always recognized by Jovellanos. He had been one of the first to advocate such a move, shortly after the Suprema was established in Aranjuez, for he felt that the best guarantee of the Spanish nation against arbitrary power was its right to gather in Cortes, a right which "was born, as it were, with the institution of monarchy."[49] But here too, Blanco-White considered Jovellanos something of a reactionary: "He wished to restore the Cortes, but more like a piece of antiquity, in the full costume of the fifteenth century, than as an effectual depositary of power."[50] In this respect the expatriate really went too far, for while Jovellanos certainly wished to preserve Spain's traditional institutions, he realized that these would have to be considerably adapted to the needs of the nineteenth century if Spain was henceforth to govern herself at all effectively. This was his posture throughout his work with the Junta Central: Restoration with all the necessary improvements demanded by the times, but no dangerous innovations not suited to the character of the Spanish nation. The following paragraph from the report written in May, 1809, is typical of his thought in the matter of the need for a Spanish constitution: " . . . I hear much talk about drawing up a new constitution in the Cortes and even about putting it into practice, and this in my opinion would be very inadvisable and dangerous. Does Spain not have its constitution? Of course it has, because what else is a constitution but the sum total of fundamental laws which determine the rights of the Sovereign and of the subjects, and the appropriate means to protect both? And who can doubt that

48. *Ibid.*, p. 584. This passage has been quoted before in this study, but because of its importance as a fundamental argument against collaboration and as an illustration of Jovellanos' doctrinal stand on the right of the Spanish people to rise against Napoleon, it has been thought that its reappearance in the text is amply justified.

49. *Ibid.*, 598.

50. *Op. cit.*, p. 150.

Spain has these laws and knows them? Have any been attacked and destroyed by despotism? Let them be restored. Is there a need of any appropriate measure to insure the observance of all of them? Then let a provision be made for it. Our constitution will then be complete and will deserve to be envied by all people on earth who love justice, order, public tranquillity and true liberty, which cannot exist without them."[51]

Restoration of the traditional Cortes meant, of course, calling the assembly by *estamentos* or estates. It would be dangerous and unfair, thought Jovellanos, to suppress the historical privilege of the nobility and Church prelates to be called separately. For the sake of stability he wanted to see a two-chamber Cortes, similar to the English political structure which he greatly admired, and this desire found expression in the last decree of the Junta Central issued on January 29, 1810, providing precisely for a two-chamber congress.[52] "Nobody is more inclined than I to restore, strengthen and improve; nobody is more reluctant to alter and renovate," Jovellanos confided in a letter to his English friend Lord Holland in May, 1809. "I am very wary of political theories and more so of abstract ones. I believe that every nation has its character, that this is the result of its old institutions; . . . that different times do not precisely require other institutions but a modification of the old ones."[53]

That these old institutions must be reformed at all costs and that this must be a basic war aim of Spain, Jovellanos was the first to recognize, and not only in his writings connected with his exalted position of member of the Suprema and in his correspondence with Lord Holland, but also in one of the most eloquent and inspiring written utterances to come out of the Spanish War of Independence. To General Sebastiani, who in early 1809 invited him in a letter to

51. Obras, I, *op. cit.*, p. 599.

52. *Ibid.*, pp. 601–603, 605–606. This decree first appeared in print in the sixth number of *El Español* (September 30, 1810), published by Blanco-White (*op. cit.*, I, pp. 446–52). One of the members of the first Regency accused Quintana in 1811 of having hidden the document (*Manifiesto que presenta a la nación el consejero de estado D. Miguel de Lardizábal y Uribe, une de los cinco que compusieron el Supreme Consejo de Regencia de España e Indias, sobre su conducta política en la noche del 24 de setiembre de 1810*, p. 18). Quintana indignantly rejected this accusation in his *Memoria sobre el proceso y prisión de D. Manuel José Quintana en 1814* (*Obras inéditas*, p. 199).

53. *Obras*, IV, in BAE, LXXXVI, p. 377.

"abandon a party which only fights for the Inquisition . . . for the interest of a few Spanish grandees and for those of England," and join King Joseph, who would give Spain reforms in the framework of a constitutional monarchy, Jovellanos, at his inspired best, answered with the following immortal words:

General, I do not follow a party; I follow the holy and just cause of my fatherland . . . We are not fighting, as you pretend, for the Inquisition . . . nor for the interest of the grandees of Spain. We are fighting for the precious rights of our king, . . . our religion, our constitution and our independence . . . The desire and the aim to regenerate Spain and raise her to the level of splendor which she once enjoyed and which she shall from now on enjoy, is considered by us as one of our principal obligations. Perhaps not much time will go by before France and all Europe will recognize that the same nation which sustains with such courage and constancy the course of its king and its freedom . . . has also enough diligence, firmness of purpose and wisdom to correct the abuses which led her insensibly to the horrible fate which awaited her.

Though uncompromising and haughty in his manner, Jovellanos showed that he had not lost his capacity for irony. Shortly before the end of the letter we read the following sentence: "In brief, General, I shall be very willing to respect the humane and philosophic principles which, according to what you tell us, are professed by your king Joseph, when I see that by leaving our territory he recognizes that a nation which is at present being ravaged in his name by your soldiers is not the most appropriate theater for the application of these same principles."[54]

This was the period when Lady Holland saw Jovellanos in Sevilla. "The dispassionate and benevolent character of Jovellanos, considering all he has suffered, is very remarkable," she wrote in her journal. "There is such a mixture of dignity and mildness that it is impossible to avoid feeling the strongest inclination towards him of love and admiration. He views the active scene into which he is thrown with philosophical calmness, and should he see the cause he has espoused succeed he will enjoy the victory without triumphant exultation; and should it fail, he is prepared to fall without despondency or sinking into abject despair."[55]

54. *Memoria en defensa de la Junta Central, op. cit.,* pp. 590–91.
55. *The Spanish Journal of Elizabeth, Lady Holland,* p. 278.

It was a tragedy for Spain that Jovellanos was not present in the Cortes of Cádiz. Perhaps the only man capable of bridging the gulf that in the end separated traditionalists and reformists was the great Asturian. If his moderating voice had been heard in the national assembly it might have given rise to a powerful third party of moderate reformists who, though not giving Spain the progress demanded by the liberals, might have led the country along a path that could have avoided the fratricidal bitterness that finally destroyed the Cortes of 1814 and brought about the terrible reaction of Fernando VII. We are, of course, moving in the field of pure conjecture, but even if Jovellanos had never achieved all this, he might still have tempered the ardor of his liberal friends, perhaps prevailing on them to preserve part of the past and combine it with indispensable innovations. His scheme of setting up a two-chamber assembly, for instance, if adopted, might have given the Cortes more stability in the long run and eliminated the friction that rent the congress.

All this was not to be. When the Junta ceased to function, Jovellanos, deeply hurt by the invectives now hurled from all sides at the members of the former governing body, left the public life in which he had labored so selflessly in the service of his fatherland. On February 26, 1810, he boarded a boat for Asturias. Forced to remain in Muros de Noya, a Galician port, because his native Gijón was again in the hands of the French, he was molested by the Junta of La Coruña as a former member of the proscribed Suprema.[56] This action impelled him to write his *Memoria en defensa de la Junta Central*, an eloquent account of his own activities since his liberation from prison in Mallorca until the dissolution of the Junta Central, as well as a defense of that institution's actions during its term in office. It is at once a magnificent piece of writing, with Jovellanos at his best as master of Spanish prose, and an important document for students of the period.

When the French evacuated Asturias in July, 1811, he embarked for Gijón, where he was given a triumphant reception by the people of the port. In November the French returned, and Jovellanos was

56. *Memoria*, pp. 563–65.

forced once more to travel. He boarded a boat with the intention of reaching Cádiz, but a storm obliged him to seek refuge in the Asturian port of Vega. There, a sick old man, he died on November 29. His last words, as he was fighting death in his delirium, are reported to have been: "My nephew . . . Central Junta . . . France . . . Nation without a head . . . Woe is me!"[57] Spain had lost one of the ablest and most selfless men ever to have seen the light of day on her soil.

[4]

With Jovellanos gone, there was no great voice left that could preach harmony. Unoccupied Spain, split into two factions, was undergoing the polarization which was to bring such suffering to the nation. In the Cortes the great talents, oratorical and literary, were on the side of the liberals. Soon after the opening of the Cortes, Juan Nicasio Gallego, whose beautiful elegy *El dos de mayo*[58] had gained him lasting literary fame, became known as a defender of reform. Also in favor of change was the famous historian and critic Antonio Capmany, who in his *Centinela contra franceses* solemnly declared on the first page of the pamphlet: "Our precious liberty is threatened, the fatherland is in danger and requires defenders. Beginning today we are all soldiers, some with the sword and others with the pen."[59] Not yet in the Extraordinary Cortes of 1810 to defend principles dear to him, but soon to be elected to the Ordinary Cortes of 1813, was the twenty-two-year old Francisco Martínez de la Rosa. He would in later years play an important role in Spain's political

---

57. Somoza, *Amarguros de Jovellanos*, p. 216.

58. See Chapter IV.

59. *Op. cit.*, p. 1. Capmany had been a friend of long standing of Quintana. During the war years, however, their friendship turned to bitter enmity. Quintana attributed Capmany's change in attitude to envy and gave as the immediate cause of the Catalan's published attacks aginst him in 1811 the fact that he had not reviewed the *Centinela contra franceses* in the *Semanario Patriótico*, which had resumed publication in Cádiz under Quintana's direction (*Obras inéditas*, pp. 206–10). Capmany died in Cádiz in 1813 of yellow fever.

history[60] and would achieve the distinction of launching Romanticism on the Spanish stage with his drama *La conjuración de Venecia.*[61] Now, however, he was known only as a brilliant young man who had written two plays and an epic poem to the heroism of Zaragoza.[62] Three years younger than Martínez de la Rosa was another future celebrity, Angel de Saavedra, duque de Rivas, who was destined to write Spain's most Romantic drama.[63] He had bravely fought at Ontígola, the day before the disaster of Ocaña, and had suffered serious wounds. He was now working for the army's general staff and composing verse in his moments of leisure. Like Martínez he was an ardent liberal. And then there was Antonio Alcalá Galiano, another budding talent and another partisan of reform. Politics and literary criticism would later hoist him onto the stage of celebrity. To him we are greatly indebted for recording faithfully in his memoirs life in Spain in those turbulent years. Not in Cádiz in 1810, for he was a member of the Spanish legation in London, was the poet Juan Bautista Arriaza, author of the powerful *Profecía del Pirineo.*[64] He certainly did not share the liberal views of his colleagues in Cádiz, for he was a died-in-the-wool conservative. Most renowned, however, among this group of literati was Manuel José Quintana. Quintana was not elected to the national assembly, but appointed by the Regency to the post of chief of the Department of Interpreters, the same position Moratín had occupied in Madrid. His status left him with enough free time to devote himself to his studies and to pen the various proclamations of the executive branch of government.[65]

60. Among the high posts which he occupied during his political career were those of prime minister (1822, 1834–1835), ambassador in Paris (1844–1847), president of the Council of State (1858), and president of the Chamber of Deputies (1851 and 1860). He died in 1862.

61. First performed in 1834.

62. In 1812, two plays of Martínez de la Rosa were performed in Cádiz: The tragedy *La viuda de Padilla* (*The Widow of Padilla*), very much in keeping with the spirit of the time, and the anticonservative satire *Lo que puede un empleo* (*The Power of a Job*).

63. *Don Alvaro o la fuerza del sino* (*Don Alvaro, or The Power of Destiny,* first performed in 1835).

64. See Chapter IV.

65. *Obras inéditas,* pp. 196–98.

When the Cortes decreed freedom of the press, Quintana, appointed a member of the Supreme Censorship Junta,[66] took advantage of the new-won freedom to resurrect the *Semanario Patriótico*. The *Semanario* came out regularly until the proclamation of the Constitution in 1812 and then ceased publication as the editor considered that the liberal ideals expressed by the weekly had been fulfilled.[67]

Even before the Cortes had gathered, Quintana had taken a vigorous stand for reform in an article signed by him on September 14, 1810 in the Cádiz newspaper *El Observador*. In it Quintana the revolutionary emerged in full force. In a prose of extraordinary power, vibrating with patriotism, hatred for the invaders, and contempt for what he considered outworn in Spain's past, Quintana demanded a new type of national assembly untrammelled by tradition. He demanded freedom of the press and full and open discussion in order to bring about meaningful reforms. It was high-pressure propaganda, but sublime propaganda, and only a first-class poet could have written such sonorous, well-balanced, and richly metaphorical sentences. Today they may sound somewhat like empty oratory, but if we try to relive those extraordinary days, they will, for a fleeting moment at least, sound like a pealing of bells announcing the dawn of liberty: "Let the temple of the Fatherland open wide and in it let the august voice of freedom pronounce its divine oracles. With some of them let it strike down the tyrants, and with others let it erect the great edifice of national prosperity, in which the Spanish people must find the reward of the hard work and the sufferings to which it is now condemned by inexorable destiny."[68]

Sometimes, when reading passages like this of Quintana, one feels transported to the days of the French Revolution and the thundering speeches delivered on the floor of the Convention. The oratorical style of the French Revolution had of course a great influence on all propagandistic writings of the turn of the century and the early 1800s. Quintana himself was not free of it, nor could he escape the irresistible attraction which the dawn of that great event still exerted

---

66. See Chapter X.
67. *Ibid.*, pp. 201–203.
68. *El Observador*, No. 14, September 21, 1810, p. 221.

on many Spanish intellectuals. In the same article he recalled the original impact of the French Revolution: "When twenty years ago the voice of freedom was heard on the banks of the Seine, the heart of all good men fluttered with happiness at the sound of those inspiring echoes. How was it possible to shut out the wonderful feeling inspired by the banner of progress unfurled in the wind and sweeping away vice, abuses, errors of degraded humanity . . . ?" But then the Revolution degenerated into horrible persecution and massacres and ended up in the arms of a tyrant.[69] This, of course, was a theme often used by Spanish liberals of the early nineteenth century, and Quintana himself had dwelt upon it in a Madrid issue of the *Semanario Patriótico*.[70]

Quintana ended the article with the following rousing appeal:

These are, oh representatives of the people, the high commitments which you have undertaken, and these are the hopes which the political world is placing in the Spanish Cortes. Oh, may they not be illusory, fathers of our land! Frighten the enemy with the energy and the boldness of your decrees. Give hope to the nations of the world with the wisdom of your laws, and in the midst of the terrible storm in which we find ourselves, far from trembling at the lightning which is striking all around you, do hold high before Europe the torch of social progress.[71]

Like so many of his liberal friends, Quintana was to pay a high price for the reformist stand he had taken throughout the War of Independence. When he sensed in the spring of 1814 in Madrid that a terrible danger was threatening all those who had formed the liberal party in Cádiz, the idea of seeking safety in flight occurred to him. But flight was not his manner: "Persecution and adversity could sweep over me. But they would find me shielded behind truth, innocence and justice and my fate would be that of so many good men who perforce must suffer together with me."[72] Arrested on May 10, 1814, and thrown into jail, he was eventually sent to Pamplona in Navarra, where he spent six years in the town's citadel. Freed by the revolution of 1820 and taking an active part in the political life of the liberal triennium, he was exiled to Extremadura upon the fall of

69. *Ibid.*, pp. 225–26.
70. See Chapter X.
71. *Ibid.*, pp. 228–29.
72. *Obras inéditas*, p. 219.

the liberal regime in 1823. Five years later he was allowed to return to Madrid, and after the death of Fernando VII in 1833, he had the satisfaction of being one of the most admired and respected men in Spain. Several times a senator, he was for three years, in 1840–1843, the *ayo* or tutor of young Queen Isabel. The same queen, in 1855, placed upon the venerable head of the great writer and patriot the crown of poet laureate, an event which was both the final vindication and the culmination of his lifelong activities on behalf of his father-land. Two years later, in 1857, at the ripe old age of eighty-five, Manuel José Quintana died. In his last years, in spite of his renown,[73] he lived in penury, and it is said that he was obliged to borrow money to have the gala suit made with which he attended his own coronation.[74]

What, in the meantime, had happened to Quintana's rival Moratín, and to his erstwhile bosom friend Meléndez Valdés? The former, upon his return to Madrid in the wake of the Napoleonic armies, found his house on Calle de Fuencarral a shambles. It had been sacked, and his furniture, books, and papers had been badly damaged or burned. From now on his activity as a collaborator took a mark-edly active turn. In March, 1809, with the collaboration of a number of other *afrancesados*, he edited the *Imparcial o Gaceta Política y Literaria*. Depending mainly on French sources for its news, it praised the Emperor to high heaven and used the vilest terms when speaking of the insurgents. Its *leitmotif* was that only through accepting the authority of King Joseph, "the best of kings," could Spain achieve happiness.[75]

In 1811, Moratín was appointed chief librarian of the royal library and was granted the Royal Order. The same year, the playwright became a member of the recently created commission of theaters, charged with examining plays which were to be presented in the theaters of the capital. On March 12, 1812, his translation of Molière's

73. His really important poetic production came to an end for all practical purposes around 1830, and henceforward he wrote relatively little verse. He did bring out the second volume of his *Vidas de españoles célebres* in 1829, and the third in 1833. In 1823, he began to write his *Cartas a Lord Holland*, dealing with the political events of 1820–1823. They were published in 1852.

74. *Ibid.*, pp. vii, xiv–xxxiv, 219–234.

75. *Papell*, p. 244.

L'École des maris, an exquisite version of the original, made its debut on the stage of the Príncipe and was shown for several weeks. It was a great success, considering that in Joseph's last years in Madrid theaters did not attract much of the public.[76]

In Madrid Moratín frequently met Meléndez Valdés, also committed to the French cause and a member of Joseph's Consejo de Estado. The similar situation in which both now found themselves drew them together and made them forget earlier times when Leandro had criticized Batilo's poetry. The cause of the *afrancesados* may not have been that of Meléndez' heart and principles, as Quintana put it,[77] but he did not hesitate to write a most sycophantic ode to the *rey intruso*. The occasion was Joseph's promise to insure the future of a poor orphan. The poem appeared in the *Gaceta de Madrid* of May 3, 1810, and in it we read the following passage: "I saw you burn with the divine fire/That only burns in the breast/Soft with compassion and full of indulgence/ . . . I have loved you more and I swear/To love you more each day;/For my soul binds itself to yours/In mutual tenderness with love of the purest kind."[78]

Quintana, who later was able to forget Meléndez' collaborationist activities and only recall the sweet Batilo, his intimate friend and master whom he had loved so dearly, was no doubt thinking of him, but with quite different feelings, when in June, 1813, he wrote a blistering anti-*afrancesado* paragraph into the dedication to Cienfuegos of the second edition of his poems. In this dedication it was the Cienfuegos who had bravely opposed Napoleon's might and had died in France, who was called sweet friend and master. "From you," wrote Quintana, "I learned never to turn literature into an instrument of oppression and servitude." For the collaborators Quintana had only scorn: "Hypocrites of honor and patriotism, they have not been able to sustain themselves against the revolutionary avalanche which has torn away the masks with which they covered themselves and shown their abominable nudity. You knew many of them, you

76. *Ibid.*, p. 272.
77. See above.
78. *Apud* Méndez Bejarano, pp. 203–204. Meléndez Valdés wrote two odes to Joseph, the second on July 14, 1811, to welcome the King upon his return from Paris (cf. Demerson, *Don Juan Meléndez Valdés et son temps* [1754–1817], pp. 316–30).

loved them, you esteemed them."[79] Meléndez was doubtless at the back of Quintana's mind when he wrote these lines.

As numerous as Quintana's and Jovellanos' writings on the political situation were during the war, as few and scattered—outside of newspaper articles—were those of Moratín which dealt with the same topic. In a passage which he probably wrote in 1810 he declared: ". . . an extraordinary revolution is going to improve the existence of the monarchy by establishing it on the solid foundation of reason, of justice and of power . . . The throne whose security tried to establish itself on the nation's misery has fallen. The nation, deceived by its magistrates, its writers, its grandees, its military leaders, its prelates, has fought with its characteristic stubbornness against its own happiness."[80] This is how the *afrancesado* Moratín, still smarting from the threat of censorship that once had hovered over his plays, still remembering the howling mobs milling around his house after the fall of Godoy, saw the fight for independence: A struggle to continue living in misery under the mailed fist of absolutism and the Inquisition. Other collaborators, who had not undergone such harrowing experiences but were in need of rationalization, used the same arguments to justify their actions. Jovellanos in his letters to Cabarrús and to General Sebastiani gave a fitting answer to this line of attack.

Two years later, after he had fled to Valencia from Madrid in the great exodus of Joseph's court, Moratín wrote a poem in praise of Marshal Suchet, in which the French commander was described as a worthy representative of the master of the world—an obvious reference to Napoleon—and worthy of comparison with the Cid, a man in short who "protects you [the Turia, river of Valencia] while he threatens war."[81]

From Valencia he wrote to his friend Doña María Ortíz in Madrid on January 5, 1813: "I am well and fat"—he had been quite ill on his voyage from Madrid to Valencia—"I live in the Seminary of Nobles . . . where I have a magnificent room . . . Paquita, if you wanted to come here airborne on the back of an accommodating

79. *Obras*, pp. 1–2.
80. *Obras póstumas*, III, pp. 209–10.
81. *Obras*, BAE, II (1944 ed.), p. 591.

witch, you would see a big city, magnificent churches, a multitude of shops of all sorts, a square filled with people in the morning, with so much fruit, vegetables, raw and fried fish, baked pumpkins, radishes big as an arm, cheeses, sausages . . . The streets are full of people coming and going, always in a hurry . . . The countryside is full of farmhouses, with a multitude of irrigation ditches which water and fertilize it. [There are] many orange, lemon and palm trees, and a beautiful promenade similar to the Prado, which leads to the sea . . . "[82]

In Valencia, Moratín and his friends, including Meléndez Valdés, who, too, had come from Madrid,[83] would have their *tertulia* at the shop of the bookseller Salvador Faulí. Among the *contertulios* was a strange personage, one of the strangest figures ever to be propelled into the world of Spanish letters. His full name was Don José Marchena y Ruiz de Cueto, better known as the Abate (Abbé) Marchena. He was four feet eight inches in height and extraordinarily ugly. Persons who knew him said of him that he resembled a monkey. He was thin, stoop-shouldered, and bowlegged. His face was pockmarked and he had an unusually long nose. But he made up for these physical defects with his brilliant intelligence and his undeniable literary talents. Born in Utrera, Andalucía, in 1768, the son of a lawyer, he had taken minor orders. A rebel from the very beginning, toying with anticlericalism before he was twenty years old and using his marvellous command of Latin and French to devour all the books in these languages then considered subversive, he had studied in Sevilla, in the Reales Estudios de San Isidro in Madrid, in Salamanca, and probably in the Seminario de Vergara,[84] another hotbed of reformist thinking. In Salamanca he had met Meléndez Valdés, and the admiration which he conceived for the poet was to be a lasting one. His ideas, which he was not afraid to express both in oral and

82. *Obras póstumas*, II, pp. 200–201.

83. Among the indications that Meléndez Valdés accompanied Joseph to Valencia is a list, existing in the Archives of the Royal Palace, of government officials and employees who left for that city in August, 1812. Meléndez' name appears in the section entitled Consejo de Estado, made up of 33 names including Llorente (Archivo del Real Palacio, *Papeles reservados de Fernando VII*, x, ff. 2–10).

84. See Chapter II, p. 49.

written form—he was never known for his discretion—aroused the ire of the Inquisition, and to escape the clutches of the Holy Office he fled to Gibraltar, where he embarked for France in 1792.[85]

France was in the throes of the Revolution and Marchena threw himself into the turmoil with utmost enthusiasm. But some of the revolutionaries he met were much too radical in their thinking for this Spaniard. Though he would have been considered the incarnation of radicalism by any government or Inquisition official in his native Spain, he was by no means an extremist à la Marat,[86] Robespierre, and Saint-Just. Even his ideas for reforming Spain were of a rather moderate nature. In a letter to French minister Lebrun he suggested the importance of calling the Cortes, but of keeping in mind Spain's past institutions and its ardent Catholicism. "France," he wrote, "has doubtless the right to tell the Spanish people: 'You have a king who is my natural enemy. I shall make war on you until you have thrown him off his throne!' But [France] has no right to shape our nation according to its own image. Spain is the one who must give herself a constitution."[87] In his message to Spain, published by the revolutionary Club des Amis de la Constitution of Bayonne, which Marchena had joined upon his arrival in France in the spring of 1792, and distributed in Spain at the end of the same year, Marchena had attacked the Inquisition and demanded the immediate gathering of the Cortes, thus becoming actually the first Spaniard to raise his voice, though from a foreign land, for a meeting of the traditional national assembly.[88]

Marchena threw in his lot with the relatively moderate Girondist faction, and with the downfall of the latter he was thrown in jail by the triumphant Jacobins. It is said that when the Robespierre regime failed to send him to the guillotine—probably because he was a

85. Menéndez y Pelayo, "El Abate Marchena," *Estudios y discursos de crítica histórica y literaria,* IV, in *Obras completas,* IX, pp. 107–27; Herr, pp. 273–74; Bono Serrano, *Noticia biográfica, Poetas líricos del siglo XVIII,* III, in BAE, LXVII (1953 ed.), pp. 615–16.

86. At first a friend of Marat, he wrote in the latter's *Ami du Peuple,* but soon put an end to this activity.

87. *Apud* Menéndez y Pelayo, p. 137.

88. Herr, pp. 274–77. It was written in Spanish but the author pretended to be French. "It was, so far as is known, the first piece printed by the French in Spanish for readers" (*ibid.,* p. 275).

foreigner and of secondary importance—Marchena sent the Jacobin dictator the following message: "Tyrant, you have forgotten me. Either kill me or feed me, tyrant."[89] Saved by the turn events took on the 9th Thermidor, he later became a French citizen, served for a while on General Moreau's staff in the Army of the Rhine, and published many tracts on political and religious subjects.

After 1804, he became an imperialist, for he saw in the Empire the "last stage of the Revolution."[90] In 1808, he went to Spain as secretary of Murat and a few days after his arrival found himself in the jail of the Inquisition. Fortunately for him, Murat's grenadiers rescued him shortly from this unenviable situation. Before Bailén forced the French and their *afrancesado* friends to abandon the capital, he frequented the *tertulia* of Quintana, whom he had met years before in Salamanca.[91]

During Joseph's reign he was editor of the Madrid *Gaceta* and chief archivist of the Ministry of the Interior. Naturally he was decorated with the Royal Order for his services to the Josephist cause. In these years his literary talents manifested themselves brightly in his translation of Molière's *Tartuffe* and *L'École des femmes*, which were performed with great success in the theaters of Cruz and Príncipe in 1811 and 1812 respectively.[92]

This, then, was the background of the man who gathered with Moratín, Meléndez, and other *afrancesados* at the bookstore of Salvador Faulí in Valencia. He was a man of deep contradictions: A quarrelsome personage with a vitriolic tongue, he was courageous and intensely loyal in his friendships. He scandalized most of his collaborationist friends by his antireligious attitude. Yet, though a freethinker, he was capable of writing the moving *Oda a Cristo Crucificado*.[93] And one day, when Faulí went to see him to beg him not to come to his house any longer lest he frighten his daughter with his impious talk, imagine the bookseller's stupefaction when he found the Voltarian *abate* immersed in the *Guía de pecadores* (*Guide*

89. Menéndez y Pelayo, p. 152; Bono Serrano, p. 616.
90. Menéndez y Pelayo, p. 164.
91. *Ibid.*, p. 165.
92. *Ibid.*, pp. 172–73.
93. *Poetas líricos del siglo XVIII*, III, in BAE, LXVII, pp. 621–22.

of Sinners) of the great sixteenth-century ascetic prose writer Fray Luis de Granada. After explaining to Faulí that this book had been his companion in the worst moments of his life, even in the days of the Terror in Paris, he confessed: " . . . while I am reading it, it seems to me that I am a Christian as you and as the nuns and the missionaries who go to die for the Catholic faith in China or Japan. I cannot stop reading it, for I do not know in our language a more admirable book."[94]

Following the rout of Joseph Bonaparte, Marchena emigrated to France, where he passed through Nîmes and Montpellier to settle finally in Bordeaux. There he brought out in 1820 the two volumes of his *Lecciones de filosofía moral y elocuencia*, an anthology of some of Spain's greatest poets and prose writers, preceded by an introduction in which Marchena set down his opinions on literature, history, and religion. Allowed to return to Spain in 1820 after the outbreak of the liberal revolution, he was coolly received by the liberals, who remembered his pro-French attitude during the war. He died the next year in Madrid in the greatest indigence.[95] "Such was Marchena," exclaims Menéndez y Pelayo with his usual traditionalist vehemence, "*a repulsive scholar and a monstrosity full of talent*, propagandist of impiety with the zeal of a missionary and apostle, corruptor of a great part of Spanish youth over half a century, an intransigent and fanatic sectarian . . . ."[96]

Four years before Marchena died, Meléndez Valdés had passed away in Montpellier, France. After Joseph's final defeat at Vitoria he followed the withdrawing French armies across the border and lived in Toulouse, Nîmes, Alais, and Montpellier. He was a ruined man, for his house in Salamanca had been sacked by the French before they evacuated the town, and his precious library had been destroyed. It is reported that before he entered French territory he knelt and kissed the Spanish earth, saying: "I shall not tread on you again," while his tears were falling into the Bidassoa River.[97] He died

94. *Apud* Menéndez y Pelayo, p. 151.

95. On Marchena, cf. Menéndez y Pelayo, *op. cit.*, pp. 107–221; Herr, pp. 273–77; *Noticias biográficas, Poetas líricos* . . . *op. cit.*, pp. 615–21.

96. *Historia de los heterodoxos españoles*, VI, p. 473.

97. Quintana, *Obras*, BAE, XIX (1946 ed.), p. 119.

in 1817 in the arms of his wife, who had followed him into exile.[98]

As for Moratín, he left Valencia in July, 1813, for he knew that the end of French domination was a mere question of time. After a harrowing trip north he entered the picturesque promontory-fortress of Peñíscola, upwards of a hundred miles north of Valencia, which was still held by the French.[99] Spanish troops promptly laid siege to Peñíscola and for many months Moratín lived through the hell of bombardment, starvation, and disease. In May, 1814, the town fell, and the playwright returned to Valencia in June. General Elío, in command there, had him locked up in the citadel but later released him and allowed him to embark for France. But the ship ran into a storm and had to seek refuge in the port of Barcelona. There Moratín was allowed to reside for a number of years and there he presented on the stage his version of Molière's *Le Médecin malgré lui* (*El médico a palos*) on December 5, 1814. In 1817, feeling himself threatened by the Inquisition, he moved to France, where he lived in Montpellier and Paris. With the liberal revolution in 1820 he returned to Barcelona after a short stay in Bologna, Italy, but a yellow fever epidemic and political disorders drove him away once more, and by 1822 he was residing in Bordeaux in the house of his good friend Manuel Silvela, also an *afrancesado*.[1]

Silvela described the playwright's life in the great French port: "He would rise at eight or eight thirty, take two ounces of chocolate and a few glasses of water. He would read a newspaper and continue to read in his room until noon, if the weather was good and suitable for a walk, which lasted until one thirty. If the weather was bad, he would remain in his room until one and then come out into the living room where the ladies were, and there he would spend the time in pleasant conversation until two." Following the midday meal came the siesta, and after the siesta the conversation was resumed in the salon until it was time to go to the theater.[2]

Moratín's life came to an end in 1828 in Paris, where he had taken up residence in 1827, and he was buried in the Père Lachaise ceme-

98. *Ibid.*

99. The Spanish governor García Navarro had surrendered the fortress in January, 1812.

1. *Vida, Obras póstumas,* I, pp. 42–49; Papell, pp. 278–324.

2. *Vida, Obras póstumas,* I, p. 49.

tery.[3] On the pedestal of the monument erected to his memory the following words were inscribed:

AQUI YACE
DON LEANDRO FERNANDEZ DE MORATIN,
INSIGNE POETA COMICO Y LIRICO,
DELICIAS DEL TEATRO ESPAÑOL,
DE INOCENTES COSTUMBRES Y AMENISIMO INGENIO.
MURIO EL 21 DE JUNIO DE 1828.[4]

It seems to be Spain's fate that throughout her history many of her most talented sons must end their days in foreign lands and be buried on foreign soil. In the nineteenth century it was Cienfuegos, Blanco-White, Meléndez, Moratín, and many others, and today there are many more, as a result of the awful fratricidal war of 1936–1939, which robbed Spain of so many gifted men.

3. His body was later taken to Spain and now rests in a Madrid cemetary.
4. *Apud Vida, Obras,* in BAE, II (1944 ed.), p. xxxviii. Here lies/Don Leandro Fernández de Moratín,/Outstanding dramatic and lyric poet,/Delight of the Spanish stage,/Of simple habits and most entertaining talent./He died on June 21, 1828.

XV

THE BIG LITTLE WAR

[1]

THE War of Independence did not produce on the Spanish side great generals. A number of officers of the highest rank fought bravely during the war and some showed a good deal of military talent, but none could really be considered equal in their task to any one of the French marshals who led Napoleon's armies in the Peninsula. Nor did the conflict produce truly great political leaders. The coward Fernando, a captive in France, was out of the picture altogether, except as a myth acting powerfully on the patriotism of the mass of the Spanish people. The voice of the one man, Jovellanos, whose statesmanlike qualities would probably have earned him a place in the world of political greatness, was not heard in the Cortes of Cádiz. The men of the Cortes were for the most part ardent, selfless patriots, and some were endowed with unusual intellectual qualities. The assembly thus brought out the oratorical and political talents of an array of brilliant young men, whose performance in the national assembly was to be a stepping-stone on the road of their political career. But no towering giant of the caliber of a Mirabeau, a Danton, or a Robespierre stepped forward to stamp the congress with the mark of his personality.

The true giants, who on the Spanish side left an indelible imprint on the war years, must be sought elsewhere. They could be found in the years 1808–1813 in the craggy mountains, among the barren hills, in the forbidding gorges, in the thick forests, on the seemingly limitless rolling plains of the land of Spain. They were the leaders of those intrepid bands that almost from the very beginning made the war in Spain a nightmare for the Napoleonic armies. Swooping down from their mountainous hideouts, lurking behind trees in the woods, appearing out of nowhere, striking with deadly precision, vanishing as rapidly as they came into sight, they never let the invaders forget that the war was continuing, that Spain had not given up the fight.

It is not an exaggeration to say that these bands and the men who commanded them made history. They carried on the war against Napoleon when there were few regular Spanish forces left to continue the struggle, and through their perseverance and the damage they inflicted on the enemy, as well as the incalculable help they rendered Wellington's Anglo-Portuguese-Spanish forces, they must be given a large, perhaps decisive share of the credit for the Emperor's failure in the Peninsula. A tribute to their role in preserving Spanish independence is found in the fact that the term by which they became known has ramained in the military vocabulary of the nations whose armies fought in the Peninsula. This term is the word *guerrilla,* the diminutive of Spanish *guerra,* war, in other words, "little war." Ever since the War of Independence the word guerrilla has been widely used in English, for instance, in conjunction with the noun "warfare" (guerrilla warfare) to denote military action carried out by small, dispersed bands of irregulars, which take advantage of their mobility and of every feature of the terrain to harass the enemy.[1] It has also been used to designate a member of such a band. In French, on the other hand, the term is applied to both irregular warfare and to the bands carrying on such a war.[2]

1. The earliest use of *guerrilla* in the English language seems to have been made by Lord Wellington in a dispatch to British Secretary of War Castlereagh on August 8, 1809: "I have recommended to the Junta," wrote the British commander, "to set Romana, the Duque del Parque and the guerrillas to work towards Madrid" (*The Dispatches . . . ,* v, p. 9). In the same month Wellington wrote: ". . . wherever they can form a body of troops, or the guerrillas of the country can be put in motion, they should be employed upon the enemy's communications . . ." (*ibid.,* p. 12).

2. In French it is usually spelled *guérilla.* The *Nouveau Petit Larousse Illustré* (320th ed., 1945) gives the translation *guerre de partisans* and *troupe plus ou moins régulière pour faire cette guerre,* and illustrates with the sentence: *La guerre d'Espagne entreprise par Napoléon fut une perpétuelle guérilla.* The word is also used in German, either in conjunction with *Krieg,* viz. *Guerrillakrieg,* or alone, with the meaning of guerrilla band.

In modern Spanish *guerrilla* means a band of irregulars, but may also refer, in strictly regular-army terminology, to an open formation of troops, specifically a line of sharpshooters, and to a small unit of light infantry which uses its mobility to carry out surprise attacks.[3] These modern Spanish meanings seem to derive partly from eighteenth-century Spanish *guerrilla*, in the sense of "skirmish," and partly from French *petite guerre*, little war. A French military treatise with the title *La petite guerre*, dealing with the role of light infantry in war and published in 1756 by a certain Grandmaison, was translated into Spanish in 1780 as *La guerrilla* and became well known in Spanish military circles.[4] The translation of French *petite guerre* into *guerrilla*, combined with the influence exerted by the treatise, must have reactivated the literal meaning "little war" of Spanish *guerrilla*, which in itself was only one step removed from "skirmish," the eighteenth-century meaning of the term. Thus the confluence of "skirmish" on the one hand and *guerrilla* as a translation of *petite guerre*, as well as the influence of Grandmaison's treatise on the other, gave rise to the terms *guerrilla*, in the sense of small advance unit of a larger body of troops, used for scouting and skirmishing, and *partida de guerrilla* (lit. small-war band) or light infantry unit used for surprise attacks. Both were already in use at the

3. Guerrilla warfare is called *guerra de guerrillas* (lit. war of guerrilla bands). The member of a guerrilla band is a *guerrillero*. The word *guerrilla* had existed in the Spanish language long before the War of Independence. Corominas (*Diccionario crítico-etimológico de la lengua castellana*, II, article *guerra*) indicates that the word appeared in the early sixteenth century. Professor Rafael Lapesa was kind enough to point out to the author that the term is found in sixteenth- and seventeenth-century texts with the denotation of either internal war or punitive action carried out against internal rebels. The famous *Tesoro de la lengua castellana y española*, published in 1611 by Sebastián de Covarrubias (ed. of 1943 by Martín de Riquer) gives the following definition (p. 666): *Guerrilla—quando entre particulares ay pendencia y enemistad formada, pero éstas castigan los príncipes de las repúblicas severamente* (Guerrilla—when there is fighting and enmity between individuals, but this is severely punished by the princes of the lands). The various eighteenth-century editions of the *Dictionary of the Royal Spanish Academy* (cf. editions of 1734, 1780, 1783, and 1791) give the meaning *encuentro ligero de armas*, or skirmish, as well as "minor difference of opinion," and mention a card game by the name of *guerrilla*.

4. A second Spanish edition came out in 1794 and a third in 1819. All three are available at the Biblioteca Nacional of Madrid.

turn of the century in strictly regular-army terminology.[5] During the War of Independence *partida de guerrilla* was applied to the bands of irregulars which were to be the hallmark of the conflict, and soon *partida de guerrilla* evolved into simple *guerrilla*. The French, who used their own term *petite guerre* to designate the peculiar war they were forced to fight, eventually adopted the Spanish term to denote irregular warfare as well as the bands which caused them such harm.[6]

The war they called "little" was little in name only. In fact, by 1811 it was a gigantic conflagration engulfing practically all of Spain. There were guerrillas[7] everywhere, and everywhere they made life unbearable for the invader. Even before the war had ended, the deeds of many of these irregulars acquired a renown of epic proportions, and friends and foes alike spread news of their actions throughout the land. Not all irregulars were worthy patriots, and there were those

5. *Guerrilla*, in the strictly regular-army meaning of the term, appears, for instance, in Castaños' communiqué of the battle of Bailén (Gómez de Arteche, *Guerra de la independencia*, ii, pp. 692–96), issued on July 27, 1808, and in the diary of the *alcalde* of Otívar (Rivas Santiago, *El Alcalde de Otívar, héroe en la guerra de la independencia*, pp. 28, 30; see below, p. 694), as well as in *Apuntes de la vida y hechos militares del brigadier Don Juan Martín Díez El Empecinado* (p. 74), which appeared in 1814. The term *partida de guerrilla* in the sense of light-infantry unit is found, for instance, in Casamayor's *Diario de los sitios de Zaragoza* (pp. 52, 78), composed in 1808, and in Castaños' communiqué.

6. The theory according to which the modern denotation of the word *guerrilla* derives from French *petite guerre* (cf. Almirante, *Diccionario militar*, p. 692) is thus only partly correct. By the time the French treatise *La petite guerre* appeared in Spanish translation in 1780, the term *guerrilla* had existéd in the Spanish language for a long time. French *petite guerre* contributed to the emergence of the modern meaning of *guerrilla*, but cannot take exclusive credit for this development. Later, the influence of Spanish *guerrilla* with respect to the French language was more decisive than that of *petite guerre* with respect to Spanish, since French adopted *guérilla* as a new word in its vocabulary. It is interesting to note in this connection that O. Bloch's and W. von Wartburg's *Dictionnaire étymologique de la langue française* (3d ed., Paris, 1960) states that French *guérilla* was taken from Spanish *guerrilla*, without making any claim to a previous influence by French *petite guerre*.

7. *Guerrilla* in the most common Spanish meaning of "band of irregulars" appears in italics in this text, while guerrilla in the sense of member of such a band, standing alone or in conjunction with words such as "band" or "warfare," is not italicized.

who had taken to the hills for motives which were far from admirable, but by and large, and without forgetting the victors of Bailén and the defenders of Zaragoza, Gerona, and other towns, the guerrillas symbolize most concretely Spain's will to resist, and some of them have become truly legendary figures.

History has consistently shown that no large-scale guerrilla warfare is possible without wide popular support. The Spanish guerrillas could not have carried on their activities if they had not enjoyed, on the whole, the unflinching support of the majority of the population. Thus they were genuine representatives of the people of Spain, who through them served notice on the enemy that what he was facing was a war of national resistance. It was not the first time that the Spanish people had had recourse to these harassing tactics to fight an enemy. It was a warfare for which they have always seemed ideally suited, partly because of their traditional individualism and love of independence, and partly because their native land's topography lends itself perfectly to this type of military operation. The most important historical precedent for the guerrilla war of 1808–1813 was the long and ferocious resistance which the Iberians offered to the Roman legions in the days when Rome was carrying out its conquest of the Peninsula. Roman historians spoke of this endless resistance in their chronicles, and what they reported bears a striking similarity to what happened during the War of Independence. The armies of Rome, too, had to fight ceaselessly against an elusive enemy, always present, yet always slipping through their fingers, always ambushing straggling units, relentlessly swirling around their flanks, never giving the legionnaires a moment of rest. In the end, the power of Rome prevailed, but from the time the first soldiers of the Latin Republic penetrated into the Peninsula (218 B.C.) to the reign of Augustus, when the conquest of Hispania was completed, two hundred years had elapsed.[8]

8. Solano Costa, "Los guerrilleros," *La guerra de la independencia española y los sitios de Zaragoza*, pp. 404–405; Gómez de Arteche, "Juan Martín El Empecinado. La guerra de la independencia bajo su aspecto popular. Los guerrilleros," *La España del siglo XIX*, I, pp. 85–86. To a certain extent guerrilla warfare also took place in the Peninsula during the Morisco uprising against Philip II (1566–1569) and during the War of the Spanish Succession (1701–1714), but in extent and importance these manifestations of

Like the Romans, the French were not prepared for this "little war." In central Europe, after a few large-scale battles had been won, the war was over and the soldier could enjoy his rest among a submissive population. In Spain, winning battles meant nothing. With a few notable exceptions, smashing the regular Spanish armies proved easy. But the war continued in a different, more deadly, and certainly more enervating form—for the French, that is. After the regular Spanish armies had been routed in the fall and winter of 1808–1809, many soldiers simply took to the hills, and under the command of men endowed with the gifts of leadership and often no small military talents, kept up the fight through guerrilla warfare. Frequently these commanders were officers of the regular army who, after the defeat of the units in which they had served, decided to continue fighting on their own. The men who joined them were not merely dispersed soldiers but could also be civilian volunteers of all classes. But by and large, where the chief was an army officer, the band was organized along military lines and strict discipline was observed; and as the war progressed, these groups, whose numbers were swelling with streams of volunteers, operated more and more like small armies, cooperating with established military authorities. Of such a type were the bands of the regular army men Renovales, Villacampa, and Durán, who kept up the war in Aragón; Miláns del Bosch, Sarsfield, and Eroles, who harried the French in Catalonia, and especially Juan Díez Porlier, who gained great renown through his admirable feats of arms in the province of León, in Asturias, and in the area around Santander.[9]

The great military historian of the War of Independence, Gómez de Arteche, considers that strictly speaking these units should not be placed in the same category as the bands composed of civilians and dispersed soldiers or simply deserters, whose leaders, themselves civilians, wanted nothing to do with military organization and discipline.[10] Establishing such a clear-cut separation between two types of

---

irregular warfare cannot be compared to those of the War of Independence (cf. Solano Costa, *op. cit., Diccionario de historia de España*, I, pp. 1291–93).

9. After the war, in 1815, he led a revolt against Fernando VII in Galicia. The uprising was a failure and he was arrested and hanged (October, 1815).

10. *Op. cit.*, pp. 117–18.

guerrilla bands is possible in some cases but not in others. There were guerrillas who began to fight as civilians refractory to military organization, but eventually became for all practical purposes well-disciplined soldiers led by men who from civilian status had been promoted to high military rank by the national government on the strength of their performance. It is true, nevertheless, that when we think of the Spanish guerrillas of 1808–1813, we have in mind mainly those bands of men that arose in several areas of Spain, almost from the start of the conflict, under the leadership of fearless civilians, who, averse to military organization, settled accounts with Napoleon's armies in their own manner.

Who were these guerrillas and their leaders? A cross section of the whole Spanish nation, they included men from all walks of life. They were peasants, shepherds, students, smugglers, dispersed soldiers, or simply deserters who preferred to fight in groups untrammelled by military regulations and discipline to serving in the ranks of the remaining regular army units. There was an occasional nobleman and there were quite a few clergymen, but on the whole, the bulk of these groups was made up of the sons of the humblest classes, especially peasants. What drove them to take up the life of guerrilla fighters? At times it was pure patriotism, with others it was the desire to avenge a personal affront or injury suffered at the hands of the French, sometimes it was the wish to get away from military discipline and enjoy the relative freedom found in these fighting groups, and on other occasions it was the desire for personal gain to be derived from the booty collected in the course of guerrilla forays. At times two or more of these factors combined in the making of a guerrilla fighter.

Here a peasant took to the hills because he was outraged at the manner in which the French tried to make themselves masters of the country. There, the mayor of a *pueblo*, incensed at the exactions committed by the occupying troops, gathered some townsmen around him, fell upon the unsuspecting invaders, slaughtered them without giving quarter to anyone, and vanished into the countryside together with his companions. A priest, enraged by the contempt for religion exhibited by French troops, might decide that he would do more for religion by grabbing a rifle and killing the blasphemous foreigners than by preaching from the pulpit. A small landholder might see his plot of land trampled upon by French troops, his family insulted, perhaps his wife and daughters raped, and would then seek vengeance among the guerrillas. Or perhaps a smuggler or even a common criminal might feel that hauling in enemy booty constituted a more lucrative operation than mere smuggling or stealing. As we have stated before, not all guerrillas were selfless patriots or men burning with a desire for vengeance. As always happens, there were quite a few whose activities were often more censurable than worthy of admiration and whose presence in the Spanish countryside was as unwelcome to the Spanish population as that of the enemy. This last class of guerrillas was, however, often dealt with in summary fashion by patriotic bands, which were dedicated at all times to defending their countrymen from the foe as well as from degenerate irregulars.

While guerrilla activity began in earnest after the dispersion of the main Spanish armies in the fall of 1808 and the following winter, and greatly increased in 1810 to reach its peak in 1811 and 1812, the first bands sprang up practically from the moment when the Spanish nation took up arms against Napoleon. The famous guerrilla chieftain Juan Martín El Empecinado[11] is said to have been intercepting French couriers along the main north-south axis as early as April, 1808,[12] and we have seen how the Catalan *somatenes*, the Catalan population in arms fighting in guerrilla fashion, stopped the French at El Bruch in June of the same year.[13] By July, 1808, guerrilla bands were roaming the countryside of Castile, and during Joseph Bonaparte's short stay in Madrid this same month, irregulars threatened French communications with the capital. By the summer of 1809, "guerrillas were already crossing the whole Peninsula, [and] the communications of Madrid with France, with Navarra, [and] with La Mancha were cut."[14]

When the government of national resistance was formed in Sep-

11. See below.

12. *Apuntes de la vida y hechos militares del brigadier Don Juan Martín Díez El Empecinado por un admirador de ellos*, p. 6.

13. See Chapter IV.

14. Farias, *Memorias de soldados franceses durante la guerra de la independencia*, p. 344.

tember, 1808, it soon became aware of the immense benefit the struggle for independence could derive from these intrepid irregulars who kept up the spirit of resistance throughout occupied Spain. At the same time it tried to bring some order and organization to what many regular army men considered an anarchical way of fighting the war. The order issued on December 28, 1808, was expected to mold guerrilla warfare into a uniform and orderly pattern. It announced the creation of so-called *partidas* and *cuadrillas*[15] of 100 volunteers each, 50 of whom were to be mounted.[16] Each *partida* would have a chief with the title of *comandante* or major, and a second-in-command as well as 5 subalterns. Members of the band would earn from 6 to 10 *reales* per day and would be subject to the same military discipline as that followed in the regular army. Booty taken from the enemy would be divided among the irregulars in proportion to their pay, with the exception of weapons, munitions, stores, vehicles, and horses or mules, which would be taken over by the government, through the intendant or the commissioner[17]—against payment of an adequate sum of money. The task of the *partidas* was to prevent the enemy from requisitioning provisions in towns and villages and from otherwise molesting them, and to intercept convoys and continually harass the foe. Finally, the *partidas* would be considered as forming part of the regular army and would take orders from the generals commanding army units in the bands' areas of operations.[18]

15. *Partidas*, or *partidas de guerrilla* was the early name given by Spanish authorities to the guerrilla bands. *Partidas de guerrilla* was used as early as the spring of 1809. It appears in a report to the Junta Central dated May, 1809, about the activities of a *partida de guerrilla* led by a certain Don Toribio Bustamante in Extremadura (AHN, Estado, *legajo* 41, *carpeta* E, No. 148). As the war went on, *guerrilla*, denoting the band, came more and more into use. It is found for instance in a proclamation dated October 4, 1809 by the Spanish guerrilla leader Don Julián Sánchez (*Documentos pertenecientes a las observaciones sobre la historia de la guerra de España, que escribieron los señores Clarke, Southey, Londonderry y Napier*, II, pp. 105–106). The terms *partida* and *partida de guerrilla*, however, were employed throughout the war just as frequently, if not more so, than *guerrilla* alone.

16. Soldiers already serving in the armed forces were barred from serving in the *partidas*.

17. See Chapter VIII.

18. Díaz Plaja, *El siglo XIX*, pp. 73–76. The same *reglamento* stipulated that smugglers would be granted a pardon if they served in special formations, which would be called *cuadrillas* (*ibid.*).

The instructions to the Junta's commissioners, issued the next day, December 29, stressed the role as protectors of the countryside against French incursions, in which the Suprema had cast the *partidas*, and demanded to be informed of the names of irregulars who carried out particularly valiant deeds, so that they might be duly rewarded.[19] On January 23, 1809, the government repeated the regulation according to which booty, with the exception of weapons and horses, was the share of the members of the *partidas*.[20] And on April 17, in the famous decree covering so-called "privateering on land," similar regulations were outlined in eighteen articles. After lashing out at the inhumanity of Napoleon's soldiers, the government declared in Article I: "All the inhabitants of the provinces occupied by French troops who are capable of bearing arms are authorized to do so, even to the extent of using forbidden weapons, to attack and despoil . . . French soldiers, seize the provisions which are earmarked for them, and in short do them as much harm as possible . . . " Article XIII ordered the authorities of occupied towns and villages to furnish irregular detachments with all possible information on the strength and dispositions of the enemy and to deliver to them the necessary provisions against adequate payment. It was a call for a total war, in which the *partidas* would represent the population in arms. It was also another effort at regularizing the relationship between the guerrillas and the authorities. The importance which the Junta Central attached to the coordination of the efforts of regular and irregular units was once again underlined, for army generals were ordered to reward those band leaders who had particularly distinguished themselves.[21]

Throughout the war the government, whether Junta or Cádiz Regency, did everything in its power to maintain its authority over the guerrilla armies, to subordinate them to the armies in the field, and to give them regular military organization.[22] In this it was suc-

19. AHN, Estado, *legajo* 9, *carpeta* A, Nos. 1–4.
20. *Ibid., legajo* 9, *carpeta* B, Nos. 6–11.
21. *Ibid., carpeta* D.
22. The Regency, for instance, issued instructions on September 15, 1811, calling on the guerrillas (this document uses the expression *partidas de guerrilla*) to eliminate the *cuadrillas* of criminals which molested towns and villages; to collect taxes in occupied areas; to deliver these to the national government's intendant operating in these zones, and to pass on to the pro-

cessful only to a point. Many of these bands were refractory to any kind of authority and were wont to listen only to their leaders. Besides, the government was far away, especially in the years when it was protected by the ramparts of Cádiz at the southern end of the Peninsula, and orders from Junta or Regency often carried little weight. When Spain's military fortunes were at a low ebb, in 1810 and 1811, there were not many regular troops left on the national territory, and hence the guerrillas were usually the sole military authority in the districts in which they operated. Only *partidas* led by regular army officers like Díaz Porlier, or irregular *partidas* of a larger size like those of El Empecinado, Mina, or Julian Sánchez were more likely to be respectful of the national authority, cooperate with regular army units, and adopt the form and organization of a full-fledged army. In the case of the first category of guerrillas, this was due to the fact that their whole organization was closely patterned on the regular army, and in the case of the second, it was partly because their leaders were granted high rank in the national armed forces by virtue of their outstanding services, and partly also because their size itself demanded military organization.

It was naturally during 1809, when the government of national resistance was still in command of a large portion of the national territory and when Spain could still put sizable armies in the field, that the authority of the government over the bands of irregulars was greatest—though by no means at all times—and it was to be again, for obvious reasons, toward the end of the war. In May, 1809, for instance, Don Toribio Bustamante, chief of a *partida* apparently formed according to the pattern set in the Junta's regulations of December, 1808, dutifully reported that his sergeant Josef Serrano and eleven *guerrilleros* had routed a detachment of twenty-four French soldiers without losing a man.[23] In November of the same year the government decided to pay Fray José Pinilla, a Dominican turned guerrilla, a certain sum of money for the silver and the mules he had handed over to the authorities.[24] On December 31, 1809, the

vincial juntas the names of persons working for King Joseph (AHN, Estado, *legajo* 2972).

23. AHN, Estado, *legajo* 41, *carpeta* E, No. 148.
24. *Ibid.*, *carpeta* C, No. 58.

priest Don Juan de Tapia, proudly calling himself "the first insurgent of Old Castile," sent word to the Junta from Albacete in La Mancha that ever since he had left Andalucía with the official commission to organize new *partidas* and command them under the supreme orders of the Duke del Parque, he had been spreading throughout the areas he visited the spirit of insurrection against the enemy and of total adhesion and obedience to the national government.[25] In a proclamation to the citizens of Alcaraz in the province of Albacete, Tapia declared that he had been the first to raise guerrilla bands in Castile and that he intended to continue this type of warfare. "It is not enough to say 'I am a good Spaniard' to save Spain," said Tapia in the document, "but it is necessary to dispense with one's most cherished possessions." The aged and the rich must give up their comforts to enable the army and the *partidas* to fight, the *cura* (priest) continued, the young men must renounce all pleasures and enlist. He went on to ask the people of Alcaraz for hunting weapons and ended his appeal on the following note: "And if some of you wish to accompany me in such an honorable occupation, I am also ready to admit you as companions of arms, with the guarantee that the *Cura* Tapia will share equally with you in everything that may happen."[26]

Tapia deserved the best the government could give him. Not all guerrillas were like him, however. Even in 1809, while the Central Junta was still in power, there were quite a few cases of guerrillas who showed little disposition to accept the control of the regular army or that of the national government. In September, 1809, the captain-general of Old Castile, the Duke del Parque, complained to the Junta's minister of war about the lack of subordination to their leaders displayed by irregulars operating in his district. One Antonio Temprano, a friar, disobeying the orders of his superior, Don Josef Armengol, who had told him to hand in a captured mail bag to the Duke's headquarters, decided to take the booty to Sevilla, claiming that he was entitled to do with it as he pleased since the general did not pay a sufficiently high reward for such goods. Del Parque, also complaining that guerrillas were perpetrating all kinds of outrages in

25. *Ibid.*, No. 61.
26. *Ibid.*, No. 62.

Castilian towns and villages, demanded that the Suprema take steps to exercise a more rigid control over the *partidas* and *cuadrillas,* and specifically that it punish guerrillas who left their *partidas* without due authorization. In answer, the Junta stated that henceforth no booty would be accepted from any irregular if it did not come from the general under whom his band was supposed to serve, and that moreover such an individual would be punished. As to Fray Antonio Temprano, he was ordered to betake himself at once to the Duke's headquarters.[27]

A similar complaint was delivered to the Suprema in October from the Junta representing Navarra, to the effect that some irregulars in Navarra were subjecting villages to outrageous demands of provisions and money.[28] The Junta reiterated the stipulation that guerrilla bands could only be formed with its permission and would have to take orders from the general of the district's army.[29] In November, it was the turn of the province of Logroño, in northeastern Castile, to voice an official complaint about guerrillas, particularly against the *partida* chieftain Don Francisco Fernández de Castro, marquis of Barrio Lucio, a successful guerrilla leader, who was doing the French much harm but who apparently had also earned the antipathy of some of his countrymen.[30]

Where the power of the government was not sufficient to chastise undesirable guerrillas operating under the mask of patriotism, genuinely patriotic guerrilla leaders often took it upon themselves to eliminate the threats of these rogue *partidas.* Outstanding chiefs like Mina made sure that their districts remained free of criminal elements and did not hesitate to stamp out by force of arms any band that strayed off the path of honesty and patriotism. But it was natural that in a war of this type the Spanish territory could not be kept 100 percent clear of anarchical or criminal elements. Here and there certain guerrillas would attack French convoys, intercept French couriers, harass the flanks and rear of French armies, but would also engage in predatory activities against Spanish towns and villages.

27. *Ibid.,* No. 70.
28. *Ibid., carpeta* D, No. 78.
29. *Ibid., carpeta* E.
30. *Ibid.*

Documents preserved in the Bilbao archives show, for instance, that in January, 1810, two band leaders, Ochoa and Larracoechea, were executed by the *afrancesado* authorities on the testimony of a number of their countrymen, all of whom could not be suspected of testifying against these men simply for collaborationist motives. Ochoa and Larracoechea were accused of forced requisitions and robberies and were put to death by the garrote, while three of their accomplices were condemned to life imprisonment.[31]

Yes, there were undoubtedly rogue guerrillas preying on their countrymen almost as much as on their enemy. And even honest guerrillas were on occasion heavy-handed in gathering food and supplies in towns and hamlets. Yet the bad had to be accepted with the good, because the positive accomplishments of the irregulars, so far as national independence was concerned, overwhelmingly outweighed the negative aspects of the guerrilla war. What would have happened to Spanish resistance in Asturias, the Basque provinces, and Navarra, in Old and New Castile, in Aragón and Catalonia, and in Andalucía, after the disasters of 1809 and 1810, if it had not been for the guerrillas? Spanish regular forces in the few unoccupied provinces were in no condition to launch strong offensive actions, and the British in the summer and fall of the latter year were fighting for survival in Portugal. In those crucial months, when the Spanish government was forced to seek refuge in Cádiz and when Spain's armed might seemed shattered beyond repair, the guerrillas eloquently expressed the Spanish people's iron determination not to give up the struggle. By their ceaseless activity they tied down sizable French forces which might have been used to occupy Valencia at a much earlier date than that of its actual fall (January, 1812), or perhaps Murcia, or even Galicia, or which might have given Masséna's army the necessary punch to crash through Wellington's lines at Torres Vedras. Perhaps not as spectacular as the military operations which they caused to take place, but just as effective, was the moral expression created in the minds of friends and foes. For the

31. *Colección de documentos inéditos de la guerra de la independencia existentes en el archivo de la Excma. Diputación de Vizcaya*, pp. 75–94. The guerrilla leader Díaz Porlier had caught this band and had disarmed its members, but they had managed to escape.

Spaniard living in occupied territory who was not collaborating with the French in any way, the presence of at least one guerrilla band not far from his residence was a constant reassurance that there were Spaniards in the hills and woods who were fighting on. To the French these bands, "always beaten, never conquered . . . which when destroyed reformed at once," to quote a Gallic general who had fought in Spain,[32] were a constant reminder that the country had not been conquered. The morale of the occupying troops could not but be affected, and nowhere else in Europe, except of course in Russia during the retreat of 1812, was the Napoleonic soldier unhappier, even at the high-water mark of French conquest, than in Spain.

[2]

A strong ally of the Spanish *partidas* in the irregular warfare which they so successfully conducted against the army of occupation was the topography of Spain. The Iberian Peninsula is ideally suited for a war of ambushes, quick getaways, and constant harassment. Nobody has better described the intimate relationship between the guerrillas of the War of Independence and their land than the great novelist Benito Pérez Galdós.

"Imagine that the earth takes up arms to defend itself against invasion," he wrote in *Juan Martín El Empecinado*, "that the hills, the streams, the gorges, the grottos are death-dealing machines which come out to meet the regular troops, and go up, come down, roll, fall, crush, divide and shatter. Those mountains that were left behind and which now reappear; these winding ravines; those inaccessible peaks which fire bullets; those thousands of tiny rivers whose right bank has been conquered and which later turn and come up with countless people on the left bank; those heights, on whose slope the guerrilleros have been shattered and which later present another side where the guerrillas destroy the [enemy] army on the march. That and nothing more than that constitutes guerrilla warfare, that is to say, the country in arms, the territory, geography itself, taking up arms."[33]

32. *Mémoires du Général Baron Thiébault* (1792–1820), *Introduction et notes de Robert Lacour-Gayet* (Paris, 1962), p. 332.
33. *Op. cit.*, pp. 54–55.

This powerful ally, topography, would shelter the *partidas* after an incursion had been carried out and would permit them to rest between forays. It would enable them to disperse without being caught when coming upon a detachment superior in numbers, to regroup shortly after the action, and to prepare safely for the next attack. Naturally, the more mountainous the area of guerrilla operations, the more effective their activity, and it is significant that some of the greatest victories of the Spanish irregulars over French troops were gained in mountainous Navarra and Guipúzcoa.

The geographical factor, then, was of paramount importance in the success of the guerrillas. But geography must be complemented by the support of the population. If the hills and the woods meant shelter, the towns and villages meant food and clothing. Often, towns and villages also provided shelter. French troops passing through a hamlet could never be sure that those peaceful peasants and artisans, seemingly hard at work, were not actually *guerrilleros* who, when the enemy was gone, would pick up the weapons they had hidden in the houses.[34] There was never a guarantee that the young man they had come across at the entrance to the village, or that other one, enjoying his siesta at the foot of the fountain in the village square, was not a guerrilla spy. The French army was under continued observation and the *partidas* were always perfectly informed about the movements of the enemy. This information would enable them to be the eyes and the ears of whatever Spanish army headquarters was in command in the area. "To carry messages or news," wrote a French soldier in his memoirs, "they employed agile and vigorous young men, whom they placed near every inhabited place and in a suitable spot. There was always one of them at his post, eyes open and ears cocked, and as soon as he received a message he would dart across fields to hand it to a comrade. In this manner communications would reach the *corregidor* or the military authorities . . . These messengers never fell into our hands."[35] The young men who spied for their side were not always guerrillas themselves. They could be peasants living in towns or villages, or they might even be children who were only too thrilled to perform this service for the national

34. Farias, p. 311.
35. *Apud* Farias, p. 277.

cause. In some areas the whole population could be counted on by both guerrillas and regular troops to report faithfully the movements of the invader.

One of the most important services rendered by the guerrillas was the interception of enemy communications. It goes without saying that the *partidas* always knew when and where French couriers would carry their messages and ordinary mail, and unless a French courier was protected by a powerful escort his chances of ever carrying out his mission were slim indeed. Countless messages and pieces of correspondence fell into guerrilla hands during the war. Thanks to this ceaseless activity astride the French arteries of communications, Spanish archives are full of documents which were supposed to reach French or *afrancesado* hands but came into the possession of the fearless *partidas* and were turned over to patriotic civil or military authorities.

Another target of guerrilla activity was the constant French convoys that crisscrossed Spain. Woe to the convoy which did not carry a powerful complement of cavalry or infantry. If a strong *partida* was lying in wait for it somewhere along the road on which it must travel, it would never reach its destination. Some of the most spectacular successes obtained by the guerrillas against the occupying forces involved French convoys carrying military personnel and civilians. This was, of course, most likely to happen in the narrow defiles of which there are so many in Spain, and there were few French soldiers who, when entering such a passage, would not cast an anxious glance at the slopes overlooking both sides of the road.

Guerrillas would ordinarily not engage French detachments equal or superior in numbers, except when forced to do so, but they did not hesitate to fall upon regular army units inferior in size to the *partidas*, even though the enemy might be better armed. In the case of the powerful *partidas* of Mina and El Empecinado,[36] which at times comprised several thousand men respectively, pitched battles with French units approximately equal in numbers were a frequent occurrence. A relatively small *partida*, on the other hand, when apprised of the approach of a French detachment, which because of

36. See below.

its size it could not possibly hope to overwhelm even from ambush, would often concentrate on the enemy rearguard and inflict as much damage as possible before vanishing into the nearby woods or mountains.

What was the total number of guerrillas operating against the French? Many figures have been quoted, some highly exaggerated. For the year 1812, the high-water mark of guerrilla activity, Canga Argüelles placed it at 33,500.[37] Gómez de Arteche, on the other hand, mentioned 50,000.[38] Perhaps the true figure for this period of maximum guerrilla activity stood somewhere between 35,000 and 50,000. A small number indeed when we think of the damage inflicted on the French army, which in May, 1812, still counted more than 200,000 soldiers in the Peninsula. It is difficult to assess accurately French losses caused by guerrilla action, but they were undoubtedly heavy. Gómez de Arteche mentions that between January, 1809, and July, 1810, 24,000 men died in Madrid hospitals, while 8,000 of their military patients were crippled. In the fall of 1810, when the total success of the Napoleonic armies in the Peninsula still seemed a distinct possibility, French hospitals in Spain counted 43,050 sick or wounded, of whom some 220—and at times 285 and 430—died every day.[39] "The guerrillas," wrote French General Bigarré, "have caused more losses to the French armies than all the regular troops during the war in Spain. It has been proved that they murdered 100 of our men per day. Thus, during the period of five years they have killed more than 180,000 Frenchmen, without losing . . . more than 25,000."[40]

While the damage to the French army and its morale was considerable, the damage to King Joseph's authority was immense. This authority, already undermined by the chronic insubordination of French generals in the Peninsula, was further reduced by the ubiquitous *partidas*. Orders were intercepted, tax collection and requisitioning encountered obstacles at every step, and royal officials trying to carry out instructions in a given district lived in constant fear of

37. *Observaciones* . . . pp. 265–66.
38. *Op. cit.,* p. 125.
39. *Ibid.*
40. *Apud* Farias, p. 326.

the guerrillas. Not even in the area around the capital could royal authority be fully exercised, for here too the *partidas* made their presence felt.

French correspondence, reports, and memoirs bear eloquent testimony to the effectiveness of the guerrillas. As we have seen, French ambassador La Forest mentioned them frequently in his letters, usually referring to them as "brigands," or "quadrilles." On August 31, 1809, the ambassador reported: "The brigands are roaming around in numerous bands comprising between 50 and 150 men. It is said that there are no less than 6,000 scattered around us and to our rear."[41] A year later, on July 18, 1810, he wrote: "It is true that the *quadrilles* do much harm everywhere. [They] shrink the circumference of occupied towns and reduce the exercise of royal authority to very limited radii. It is an evil which demands a special treatment and which will not be destroyed until it is attacked everywhere by units set up for this sort of service."[42] La Forest's dispatch of July 26 spoke of a convoy which had been attacked between Burgos and Valladolid, and of mail lost between Mondragón and Villarreal in Guipúzcoa. It went on to describe in a few sentences the picture of a Spain whose principal towns were held by Napoleon's army but whose countryside was essentially controlled by the guerrillas: "The *quadrilles* appear everywhere in swarms and seem to show more boldness than heretofore. True, there exists no longer any Spanish army worthy of the name. But it is clear that the enemy, choosing the type of war which circumstances indicate to him, has scattered in all directions, while we occupy the main positions with masses of men . . . [their actions] deprive . . . the royal government of all resources and are contributing to its weakening. The evil has spread to such an extent that it demands the most serious attention."[43]

A month later the guerrillas were still very much on the ambassador's mind: "The *quadrilles* are causing enough difficulties! The insurrection has in its grip, through their actions, the wide areas where submission should be considered as having been achieved, and has

41. *Correspondance*, II, p. 398.
42. *Ibid.*, IV, p. 31.
43. *Ibid.*, p. 49.

almost isolated the capital."[44] On October 26, he reported the loss of a convoy at Illescas[45] as well as of its escort of eighty French soldiers.[46] "The *quadrilles* and bands are present everywhere," La Forest wrote on August 24, 1811,[47] and on October 18 he admitted ruefully: "[The guerrillas] have become so numerous and so well trained and their leaders are so intelligent . . . that they will be able . . . to hold . . . the whole countryside . . . This . . . is to be foreseen and requires special measures."[48]

The correspondence and reports of French generals merely confirm the French ambassador's dispatches. General Hugo, governor of the provinces of Avila, Soria, and Segovia, reported in April, 1810, that the "numerous bands of brigands which harass communications seem to have adopted the system of lying in wait with 300 to 400 men for the mail detachments, upon which they then fall." As a result the general was forced to set the minimum strength of French escorts at 60 men. Significantly, Hugo admitted that "the spirit of the Castilians is still coldly insurgent."[49] Let us keep in mind that this was the spring of 1810, when Andalucía had just been occupied by the French, and when Spanish fortunes seemed to have hit rock bottom.

The same type of reports poured into French headquarters from the north. General Thouvenot wrote to Marshal Soult from San Sebastián on May 10, 1810: "The road is full of prisoners coming from Astorga or Lérida,[50] but from the time they start out until they reach Bayonne, their number is considerably reduced by desertion and they simply swell the number of [guerrillas] who infest the roads. Those of Navarra especially are continually threatening the road from Irún to Mondragón."[51] From Madrid, the military governor, General Belliard, reported to King Joseph on April 10, 1810, on

44. Dispatch of August 23, 1810, *ibid.*, p. 98.
45. A town halfway between Madrid and Toledo.
46. *Ibid.*, p. 204.
47. *Ibid.*, v, p. 209.
48. *Ibid.*, p. 304.
49. AHN, Estado, *legajo* 3003/2.
50. Two towns that had recently been captured by the French. See Chapter IX.
51. *Ibid.*, *legajo* 3099.

the movements of guerrillas in the direction of Guadalajara,[52] and on July 25 he wrote to Marshal Berthier that 300 "brigands" had appeared on the fourth at the Guadarrama bridge between Navalcarnero and Móstoles.[53] Thus it went in the whole occupied Spanish territory, north, south, east, and west. The guerrillas absorbed the greater part of the French army's energy in constant small engagements, punitive expeditions, searches, and convoying. "The French armies could only obtain provisions and ammunition," recalled Rocca, "under convoy of very strong detachments, which were for ever harassed and frequently intercepted."[54]

As guerrilla activity increased in intensity the French feeling of frustration deepened up and down the ranks of the invading army. Frustration was accompanied by reprisals, which in turn precipitated counter-reprisals on the part of the *partidas*. For the French, the guerrillas were bandits who when caught were to be hanged from the nearest tree, and the guerrillas paid the French back in kind. This was to a great extent what gave the war in Spain its stamp of infernal cruelty. Only when faced with powerful bands like that of Mina in Navarra, which were capable of carrying out truly large-scale reprisals, did Napoleon's generals desist in the end from this type of extermination. The fury of the occupant did not limit itself to striking at the irregulars but was also directed at those who helped them. Suchet, governor-general of Aragón, issued on October 23, 1809, a decree which threatened to mete out stiff punishment to towns giving shelter to guerrillas. Article IV declared that the magistrates and clergy of those towns which did not arrest or inform French authorities of the presence within their walls of "smugglers or murderers" would be relieved of their duties and treated as criminals. Article V stipulated that those who accompanied, protected, or gave shelter to guerrillas would be treated as if they were members of the bands.[55] Similar decrees were published throughout

---

52. *Ibid., legajo* 3003/2. Guadalajara is approximately thirty-two miles east of Madrid.

53. *Ibid.,* Navalcarnero and Móstoles are twenty miles and eleven miles southwest of Madrid, respectively.

54. *Op. cit.,* p. 190.

55. AHN, Estado, *legajo* 3099.

the war, but far from cowing guerrillas and townspeople they merely served to fan the guerrilla war.

Napoleon was naturally not unaware of the harm the guerrillas were doing to his armies in the Peninsula. In a message to Marshal Berthier on November 20, 1811, the Emperor severely criticized the methods followed by his generals in dealing with the irregulars. "My cousin," he wrote, "write to Generals Dorsenne, Caffarelli and Thouvenot that the system employed in their districts is detestable; that immense forces are gathered in the villages against active bands of brigands, so that we are continually exposed to unpleasant surprises . . . ; that the main points should be occupied and flying columns should use them as starting points for the pursuit of the brigands; that if matters were handled in this way, many small disasters would be avoided; that this plan should be executed as soon as possible and active war made on the brigands; that the experience of the Vendée[56] has proved that the best method was to have many scattered mobile columns rather than stationary army corps."[57] In many instances Napoleon's generals had followed the very method that he prescribed in this dispatch and had sent out numerous flying columns to hunt down the indefatigable *partidas*. The three generals mentioned in the letter intensified their efforts in this direction, but always with the same meager result. The activities of the bands could not be kept down, and somehow they usually managed to evade the relentless pursuits launched against them. On March 29, 1812, shortly before he set out for the Russian campaign, a worried Napoleon complained to Berthier about the threat from the guerrillas operating in Spain's northern provinces. "Send me a report on the increase in the bands which, coming from Asturias and Galicia, inundate the rear of the army."[58]

Typical of the failure of the incessant French expeditions to catch Spanish guerrilla chieftains is the case of the one ordered by General Bigarré to capture the *guerrillero* El Abuelo (The Grandfather),

---

56. The long and bloody war French royalists conducted against the first French Republic in an extensive area of western France, including the department of Vendée.

57. *Correspondance*, No. 18276.

58. *Ibid.*, No. 18621.

whose band was harassing the French in the area east of Aranjuez. Having been informed that El Abuelo was staying in the town of Uclés, he surrounded Aranjuez with sentinels to prevent anybody from slipping out and warning the *guerrillero*. In the evening, 400 infantry and 25 cavalry left the former *real sitio*. In eight columns the French force stealthily advanced through a dark June night to arrive in Uclés at dawn. El Abuelo was sleeping and his wife was with him. Four of his men were mounting guard at the entrance to the house. As the enemy troops approached the building, the guerrillas fired their rifles and thus awakened their chief. El Abuelo promptly ran up to the grain loft, climbed down through a window, and managed to escape. The four *guerrilleros* were killed and General Bigarré took with him El Abuelo's wife. Later he returned her to her husband in exchange for a horse.[59]

The primary concern of the French was, of course, for their communications, and above all for the great artery Irún-Vitoria-Burgos-Valladolid-Segovia (or Aranda-Somosierra)-Madrid. Toward the end of 1809, Napoleon formed a special corps of French gendarmerie, 4,000 strong, entrusting to these troops the protection of the road from Bayonne to Madrid.[60] But even these picked units could not guarantee safety all along the road for small detachments traveling from the French border to the Spanish capital. Stronger and stronger convoys were therefore necessary for any sort of movement along this main north-south axis. One of these convoys, leaving France at the beginning of 1812, comprised a vanguard of 600 men, a flanking force of 600 more, and a rear guard 1,000 strong. In the middle traveled the fourgons and civilians, and officers who were not part of the escorting force. After passing through Irún on February 4, then Tolosa, Villarreal, and Mondragón, the convoy reached Vitoria, where the travelers rested for eight days. When it set out from Vitoria the expedition included 2,699 infantry, 25 Polish lancers, 30 dragoons, and 2 cannon. Before reaching the somber gorge of Pancorbo it met several convoys going to France, and shortly before entering the defile it was met by a special detachment of 600 men

59. Farias, pp. 351–52.
60. Oman, III, pp. 203–204; Grandmaison, III, pp. 251–52.

with two cannon sent forward to provide added protection during the passage of the Pancorbo. Eighteen days after leaving Irún the convoy arrived in Burgos, whence, after a rest of two days and with a reinforcement of an additional battalion and 50 lancers, it covered the distance to Valladolid in four days. Three days were spent in Valladolid, and on it went. Now the convoy had swollen to 3,000 infantry, 3 cannon, 60 lancers, and 50 dragoons, and comprised 62 vehicles carrying women, children, and supplies. At Santa María de Nieva another large convoy was met. It was taking north many generals, Marshal Victor, and a mistress of King Joseph. Then came Segovia, and finally, on March 11, thirty-seven days after leaving Bayonne, the convoy reached Madrid with a 4,000-man escort.[61]

The gendarmerie squadrons and other units permanently assigned to control arteries of communications such as the one mentioned above, as well as the garrisons of strategically situated hamlets throughout the occupied zone, would always have to make sure that their position was well fortified against guerrilla attack. If the spot where the detachment had to mount guard was in a village, then the French officer in command might choose for his garrison the church or monastery, or perhaps two or three isolated houses at the entrance of the hamlet. The troops turned the post immediately into a little fortress by palisading it and digging a ditch around it. All openings were eliminated except one door which was well defended. The walls were loopholed and one or several cannon were held in readiness. There were usually enough provisions and munitions to withstand a siege of two weeks.[62] If the garrison had to establish itself in the open countryside, the little fort that was erected presented essentially the same features. "The sentinels dared not remain without the fortified enclosures for fear of being carried off," recalled Rocca. "They therefore stationed themselves on a tower or on a wooden scaffolding built on the roof near the chimney to observe what passed in the surrounding country. The French soldiers thus shut up in their little fortresses frequently heard the gay sounds of the guitars of their enemies, who came to pass their nights in the

61. Farias, pp. 280–83.
62. *Ibid.*, p. 304; Grandmaison, III, p. 90.

neighboring villages, where they were always well received and feasted by the inhabitants."[63]

In spite of all the precautions, in spite of the convoys, the fortifications, the flying columns, the terrible reprisals, the guerrillas continued relentlessly to harass the foe. It must have always seemed to French soldiers and civilians forced to move about in occupied Spain that they were only seldom receiving full protection against the *partidas*. Many of them lost their lives during guerrilla attacks and many had close calls. When General Foy was carrying messages to Napoleon from Marshal Masséna in Portugal, his escort was attacked by guerrillas at Pancorbo. To escape the *guerrilleros* the general was forced to jump into a torrent. He hid behind a rock, submerged in water up to his waist, and remained in this uncomfortable position until French reinforcements rescued him. As he carried the dispatches on him, these could later be delivered to the Emperor. But the rest of Foy's belongings had fallen into the hands of the guerrillas.[64]

General Brun, aide-de-camp of Marshal Soult,[65] described in his memoirs his harrowing journey from Sevilla to the French border in May 1812, when he was ordered to deliver important messages to Napoleon, then in Germany. In La Mancha he was forced to travel slowly and under heavy escort, for the guerrillas there were very active. He arrived in Madrid, saw King Joseph, reported to him on the situation in Andalucía, and left the capital after having had supper at the Royal Palace. Close to Segovia, he and his 80-man German escort were attacked by a mounted *partida* of 400 men. Thirteen of his men were killed by the first discharge of the Spaniards, and the French detachment was able to escape total annihilation only by galloping off in the direction of the forest of San Ildefonso and then taking cover behind a walled enclosure used for corralling sheep. After three hours of sustaining a lively fusillade with the guerrillas, who were firing at the enclosure from behind rocks, Brun and his men were rescued by a French detachment coming from Segovia.

63. *Op. cit.*, p. 190.
64. Grandmaison, III, p. 190.
65. Brun then held the rank of major.

Brun was thus able to continue on his journey, but near Olmedo he was "surrounded by a cloud of guerrillas who, harassing my flanks and my rear-guard like Cossacks and Arabs, tried to confuse my escort. I had 200 or 300 men . . . and I kept them at a respectful distance." From Burgos to Vitoria the trip was uneventful, but at the pass of Arlabán he had a narrow escape. A strong guerrilla band was lying in wait for him and his detachment at the top of the pass, and when the four men of his escort who served as vanguard approached that spot, a volley of shots reverberated through the narrow valley and the four soldiers fell dead. Brun gave orders to his detachment to turn around and return as fast as possible to the entrance of the gorge, which they did with understandable alacrity. Fortunately for them the French had a fort with two cannon at the entrance to the valley. Thanks to these guns a party of 200 *guerrilleros,* which had moved to cut off the retreat of Brun and his men at that spot, was forced to give up its attempt. Without the fort and its cannon Brun would probably not have lived to write his memoirs. He finally arrived in France, "a country which during this voyage I had sometimes despaired of seeing again."[66]

General Brun's memoirs, full of interesting episodes of the war in Spain, also speak of the following curious incident involving the ubiquitous guerrillas and, of all people, the United States consul in Málaga. It seems that this gentleman, a Mr. Fitz Patrick, gave a fiesta in honor of Marshal Soult during the latter's stay in the Andalusian port in early 1810. He took the Marshal and his retinue to his country house, where his French guests were able to admire his fine cotton plantation. This show of friendship for the French commander was to cost him dearly, however. Several months later a guerrilla band, remembering his fiesta for Soult, attacked his property and ruined his cotton crop.[67]

It was in this southern Andalusian region that some of the bitterest guerrilla fighting of the war took place. It was a guerrilla war which at times took the form of a general insurrection.[68] The conflict

66. *Les Cahiers du général Brun,* pp. 129–33.

67. *Ibid.,* p. 117.

68. The uprising in Galicia in early 1809 was also more on the pattern of a general regional insurrection than on that of warfare by *partidas* (cf. Pardo

involved the *serranos* or mountaineers of the forbidding *serranía* (mountainous region) of Ronda, to the west of Málaga, and of the wild Alpujarras south of Granada. When the French thought they were in complete command of Andalucía they were suddenly faced with the uprising of the *serranos*. It began in early March, 1810, in the region of Ronda, one of the most picturesquely situated towns in Spain, standing on a rock and divided into two parts by a deep fissure bridged by a remarkable single-arch bridge over the river Guadiaro. The inhabitants of Ronda and the surrounding area counted many smugglers in their midst and were generally a tough sort of people, unwilling to accept the new authorities thrust upon them and not afraid of a fight. Jacob, who visited Ronda in January, 1810, shortly before the French occupation of Andalucía, spoke in the following terms of the men and women of Ronda:

The inhabitants of Ronda have peculiarities common to themselves and the other people in the mountainous districts, and obviously differ from the people on the plains. The dress both of the males and females varies as well in the color and shape of the garments as in the materials of which they are composed, and is peculiarly calculated for cold weather . . . The men are remarkably well formed, robust and active . . . There is an expression of sensibility in their women's countenances, and a peculiar grace in all their movements, which is extremely fascinating. On walking the streets the women wear veils, to cover their heads, as a substitute for caps and hats, neither of which are worn . . . The men wear . . . *montera* caps, made of black velvet or silk, abundantly adorned with tassels and fringe; and a short jacket with gold or silver buttons, and sometimes ornamented with embroidery . . . worn just sufficiently open to display a very highly-finished waistcoat. They wear leather or velvet breeches, with gaiters . . .[69]

The *serranos* quickly set up *partidas,* and soon the exploits of the guerrilla chieftains, especially those of Andrés Ortiz de Zárate, called El Pastor (The Shepherd), became known throughout the *serranía de Ronda.* The French, having occupied Ronda, but seeing their

---

de Andrade, *Los guerrilleros gallegos de 1809*). The same can be said of the Vendée war during the first French Republic and the uprising in 1809 of the Tyrolese mountaineers against the French and their puppet, Bavaria, to which Tyrol, formerly a part of Austria, was handed after the French-Austrian war of 1809.

69. *Op. cit.,* pp. 337–38.

convoys from Málaga to Ronda constantly attacked by numerous bands, did their utmost to eradicate this menace. Their flying columns crisscrossed the *serranía* and were forced to fight numerous fierce engagements with the mountaineers. Ronda itself, though occupied, was smoldering. Rocca recalled how laborers, sitting on rocks among olive groves, took potshots at French troops at the entrance to the town's suburbs. At night they would return to their houses in the town without the weapons, which they had hidden in farmhouses or in the fields. Rigorous searches yielded no results, and Rocca noted that only by killing all the inhabitants could the French have eliminated the threat from the *serranos*.[70] Though full of atrocities, the conflict did not present the features of mass exterminations so thoroughly practiced by Nazi occupying authorities in World War II. Napoleon was not Hitler, and mass extermination of civilians, a feature of our "civilized" twentieth century, was not his way.

A communiqué from Marshal Soult to the *Gaceta Extraordinaria de Sevilla* of May 7, 1810, indirectly rendered tribute to the fighting prowess of the brave *serranos*. It reported the destruction of the village of Algodonales, where the guerrilla leader Romero had entrenched himself with his *partida*. After a French column in the vicinity of Algodonales had been attacked by the band, the French surrounded the town and attacked the *partida*. All of the members of the band were killed, the last to fall being Romero himself. "Only ruins can now be seen where Algodonales once stood," continued the report. "This terrible example which should discourage the rest of the villages of the *serranía*, principally Grazalema,[71] which had previously suffered punishment [at French hands], has had little effect, since a strong band of inhabitants of Grazalema has tempted once more the fate of war. But it has been destroyed . . ."[72] In spite of these defeats the *serranos* did not lose heart. "Despite all the efforts of Soult's flying columns they could not be entirely dispersed, though they were hunted a hundred times from valley to valley. The

70. *Op. cit.*, p. 299.

71. A picturesque little town set high among the rocks of the *serranía de Ronda*.

72. AHN, Estado, *legajo* 2994.

power of Soult, the viceroy of Andalucía, stopped short at the foothills, though his dragoons kept the plains in subjection. Every time that Ronda and the other isolated garrisons in the mountains had to be revictualled, the convoy had to fight its way to its destination through swarms of serranos."[73]

The revolt of the *serranía de Ronda* had its counterpart in the rising of the Alpujarras, the inhospitable mountainous region between Granada and the Mediterranean. There a first-class guerrilla leader galvanized the inhabitants in the fight against the occupying army. He was a peasant named Juan Fernández Cañas, mayor of the village of Otívar. In May, 1810, he burned an order enjoining him to hand over to French authorities all the weapons in Otívar as well as a considerable sum of money. One day, shortly after this, when a requisitioning party made up of four Spanish soldiers in the service of the occupants, appeared in the village, the alcalde, an excellent shot, killed two of them and fled into the mountains. There he recruited men willing to accompany him and formed a *partida* of 100 men. Very soon the very mention of his name struck terror in the hearts of the invaders. The alcalde of Otívar attacked French posts again and again and with growing success. He took the castle of the town of Almuñécar on the Mediterranean, garrisoned by a French detachment, the latter having surrendered after the *guerrilleros* had set fire to their position. Juan Fernández went on to take Motril, on the sea, and then Padul, between Motril and Granada.

By now General Sebastiani, in command of Granada, had decided to put an end to the alcalde's activities. He attacked him with a large force on September 5 and routed the *partida*. The mayor, wounded fifteen times, escaped to the mountains, where he took refuge in a cave. There, joined by his wife and daughter, he waited for his wounds to heal, and six weeks later sallied forth at the head of 200 men to resume the struggle. The fierce guerrilla war flared up again. The alcalde fought both the French and the famous—or rather, infamous—*partida* of collaborators led by Martín de Llanos, the *afrancesado* doctor of Berja.[74] One day, as he was resting in a cave

73. Oman, III, p. 329.
74. See Chapter XIII.

with his family and some friends, the French came upon his hiding place and were already rejoicing at having finally caught this ferocious enemy. But somehow Juan Fernández managed to escape,[75] thus foiling the French once again. His wife and daughter, however, were taken to Granada as prisoners.[76] General Sebastiani then sent him emissaries to win him over to the French side. If the *guerrillero* gave up his resistance, he would be granted an important post in the French administration, the French commander promised. But Juan Fernández steadfastly rejected the general's overtures and continued to lead his guerrillas against the occupying forces. By this time the Regency in Cádiz had heard of the remarkable feats of the mayor of Otívar and the fearless chieftain was officially awarded the rank of colonel in the Spanish army. Juan Fernández fought on and had the satisfaction of seeing the enemy finally evacuate Andalucía. He died in 1815 as governor of Almuñécar.[77]

[3]

The alcalde of Otívar became famous for his gifts of leadership, his staying power, his extraordinary physical endurance, as well as his unflinching determination in the war against the French. These qualities placed him in the company of a number of guerrilla leaders who gained particular renown during the war years. We cannot examine the deeds of every one of those outstanding chieftains lest we give an excessive extension to this chapter. Let us therefore catch a glimpse of only a few other better-known *guerrilleros*.

Don Camilo Gómez was a rich peasant whose property lay be-

75. He escaped with his son and a friend.

76. They were set free seven months later.

77. Rivas Santiago, *El alcalde de Otívar, héroe en la guerra de la independencia;* Gómez de Arteche, *Nieblas de la historia patria,* 2d ed., "El alcalde de Otívar," pp. 104–50; Del Moral, "Memorias de la guerra de la independencia," RABM Tercera Época, Vol. XVIII, pp. 416–37; Vol. XXII, p. 284–301; Gallego y Burín, pp. 81–93. Rivas Santiago's and Gómez de Arteche's accounts of the actions of Juan Fernández are particularly valuable as they are based on the alcalde's war diary.

tween Talavera and Madrid. After his house was destroyed and his
wife and two daughters were raped by the French, he swore to
avenge himself. Setting up a guerrilla band, he became the scourge of
the French in the province of Toledo. Woe to any stragglers,
wounded, or sick who fell into his hands. Don Camilo knew no pity.
Equally cruel in his treatment of the enemy was Fray Lucas Rafael, a
Franciscan monk in a Castilian monastery. When he found out that
his father had been shot after refusing to take the oath to King
Joseph, he left his cell and became a guerrilla leader. At the end of
1809 he claimed to have killed with his own hands 600 Frenchmen
and captured merchandise and baggage worth 3 million reales, which
he stored in Ciudad Rodrigo.[78]

Juan Palarea, better known as El Médico, for he had been a
physician before becoming a *guerrillero*, was the terror of French
couriers and small detachments in wide areas of New Castile. It was
he who on January 11, 1812, carried out the bold raid under the very
walls of Madrid and gave the French authorities in the capital a bad
case of nerves. Though unrelenting in his war on the occupants, he
treated enemy prisoners better than many other chieftains. Colonel
Lejeune, aide-de-camp of Marshal Berthier, who was made a prisoner by the band of El Médico, has left us an interesting physical
description of the men who made up his *partida*. What he wrote
probably fitted many *guerrilleros* in the Peninsula:

Their hair was gathered at the back into a mass called a *catogan*, which
hung down on the nape of the neck. All of them, chiefs and men alike,
wore a coloured handkerchief knotted about the head, and hanging down
the back in a *négligé* manner. Above the handkerchief was worn a round
felt hat, with a high pointed crown, varying in colour from black and
russet-brown to grey, according to its state of decay, and decorated with a
few cock feathers and a twist of red cord. The chest and one shoulder,
black or red from constant exposure to the weather, were left bare. Some
of the men wore jackets like those of our hussars of different colours, and
others brown, black, or blue vests; but all had broad red silk or woolen
sashes, whilst many had belts over the sashes which could hold several
dozen cartridges, as I had good cause to remember. The short black velvet
or leather breeches were open at the knee, and the calves of the legs were
protected by leather gaiters coming down over Spanish sandals or big

78. Grandmaison, III, p. 222.

shoes with spurs on the heels. The men all shouted at the top of their voices, showing their pointed white teeth, which looked like those of angry wolves.[79]

One of the most famous chieftains was undoubtedly Don Julián Sánchez, from the province of Salamanca, a former soldier in the regiment of Mallorca. Don Julián was a well-to-do peasant who took up arms after seeing his sister raped and his relatives molested by enemy soldiers. He gathered a group of 100 lancers, took them to the Duque del Parque, who promptly gave him the rank of captain, and began a relentless guerrilla war against French couriers, detachments, and convoys. Soon the region between Salamanca and Ciudad Rodrigo was filled with the stories of the exploits of Don Julián and his ever-growing band of lancers.[80] General Marchand placed a price on his head in October, 1809, but Sánchez was never caught, though on one occasion 10,000 French soldiers under Salamanca's governor General Thiébault, almost destroyed his *partida*. He rendered invaluable service to Wellington when the British commander was fighting off Masséna's lunge into Portugal. Ceaselessly Don Julián's *guerrillas* swarmed around the rear guard of French detachments on the way to Torres Vedras, intercepted the enemy's couriers, harassed his convoys, and for all practical purposes cut the communications between the French army in Portugal and French forces in Spain. One of his most celebrated feats was the capture in February, 1811, of a convoy of 291 carts transporting 100,000 rations of biscuit and escorted by 160 Swiss (serving with the French) and 20 dragoons. While constantly harassing the French, Don Julián acted as a screen for Wellington's forces, which the enemy never managed to sweep away. As a result, during the long struggle along the Portuguese border French generals were generally in the dark about the true strength

79. *Memoirs of Baron Lejeune*, II, pp. 91–92. A German officer serving with Napoleon's army, who fell into the hands of the band of Francisquete, a guerrilla leader active in the area of La Mancha, described the chieftain as riding a horse with a red saddle and wearing a short blue jacket with red facings, a yellow-red sash, yellow pants, boots with silver spurs, a black peasant hat with a red ribbon, a long dragoon sword, and decorations taken from French prisoners (Holzing, p. 217).

80. The strength of his *partida* stood at about 1,500 men at the peak of its activities. (Canga Argüelles, *Observaciones*, I, pp. 265–66).

and the disposition of Wellington, while the latter was always perfectly informed about the strength and movements of his adversaries. Wellington thought highly of the man whose lancers had become the eyes and ears of Allied forces in the Peninsula. Gómez de Arteche called him the confidant and guide of the British commander. Wellington showed his esteem by presenting Sánchez with a "saber of honor" on behalf of the Regent of England and letting him cooperate in the military operations which led to the victories of Fuentes de Oñoro, Salamanca, and Vitoria.[81]

A German officer in the British army who was a luncheon host to Don Julián in August, 1811, described him as a "short, robust fellow with curly black hair." Upon hearing that a strong French reconnoitering party was near, Sánchez and his staff swung onto their horses "like lightning and vanished. His men looked magnificent, were splendidly mounted, and wore their national dress, to which they had added the huge bearskin caps of the French chasseurs of the Guard which they had taken from the enemy from time to time, or else picked up as spoil on the battlefield."[82]

The town of Ciudad Rodrigo erected a monument in 1960 to this valiant chieftain. On it is engraved part of the proud answer Julián Sánchez gave to General Marchand in October, 1809, who in a proclamation had ordered repressive measures against the population of the province because of the support they gave to the guerrillas: "This *guerrilla*[83] as well as the army will know how to defend to the last breath their religion, their legitimate and beloved king and the liberty of the fatherland."[84]

Much less attractive in his personality, though a more colorful figure, and even more feared by the French than Sánchez, was the famous priest Jerónimo Merino. During the war the French held the town of Burgos and the important points of this heart of Old Castile,

---

81. Gómez de Arteche, *Juan Martín el Empecinado* . . . pp. 114–17; Grandmaison, III, p. 219; Mesonero Romanos, *Memorias de un setentón*, pp. 123–24.

82. Schaumann, *On the Road with Wellington*, p. 325.

83. The word is used here without the accompanying *partida* and with the meaning of guerrilla band.

84. The complete answer in Canga Argüelles, *Documentos* . . . , II, pp. 105–106.

but Merino ruled a good part of the province of Burgos. The task of French couriers and soldiers on guard or traveling in small detachments was indeed not an enviable one. Everywhere, in the recesses of the barren earth of Old Castile, there might be lurking the men of the ferocious priest, whose very name sent a chill down the spine of French officers and men. But the occupants had only themselves to blame for having awakened the manhunter in Don Jerónimo. Born in the hamlet of Villoviado in 1769 of a family of peasants, he had become in 1796 the priest of this village set at the foot of the Sierra del Risco and exposed to the cold wind which often howled down from the mountains. A poor parish priest, he continued to take his sheep to the pasture grounds even after he had taken possession of his post. Once out in the hilly countryside, he liked to climb trees, and sitting in this high-perched position, to survey the ground below and his sheep through a looking glass. Merino, a simple man, led a frugal life, and his one great passion—at least as great as his religious devotion—was the hunt. His aim with a rifle was infallible.[85]

One day, in January, 1808, a French detachment passing through Villoviado demanded horses or mules to carry its supplies to the nearby town of Lerma, twenty-two miles south of Burgos. The *corregidor* shrugged his shoulders and said there were no pack animals in the village. The French, never short on initiative, decided that the inhabitants would be good substitutes for horses and proceeded to load them with military implements. Merino was granted the privilege of carrying the equipment of the regimental band. Loaded down with a large drum, a pair of cymbals, and a bugle, the priest, accompanied by the laughter of the soldiers, arrived at the main square of Lerma. There he stopped, dropped his load, turned to the French soldiers, and his eyes flashing fire, said: "You shall pay for this."[86]

Merino kept his word. The French paid with innumerable casualties the indignity inflicted on the clergyman. Shortly after this incident he left his house in Villoviado, took up position behind a large oak on the highway, and killed his first courier. Soon he was the chief

85. Ontañón, *El Cura Merino*, pp. 12–37; Gómez de Arteche, *op. cit.*, p. 110.
86. Ontañón, p. 53.

of a band of 300 men and the bane of French security in the province of Burgos. The French lost so many men and horses to his swiftly striking *partida* that they spared no efforts nor troops to destroy it. But all was in vain. Men, supplies, and correspondence continued to fall into the hands of the *Cura* Merino. He had spies everywhere, including in Burgos itself, who kept him informed of the slightest movement of the French units in the area. No French convoy went on its way without Don Jerónimo's knowing about it and weighing the chances of overpowering it. Recognized officially as commandant of his *guerrilla* in 1809 by the Junta Central, he kept in close touch with the local junta, which itself was a fugitive from the French. When this six-man organization was captured by the French in March, 1812, in the province of Segovia, and then taken all the way to Soria and hanged, Merino took terrible vengeance. He ordered his men to seize twenty French prisoners in his power for each executed member of the former junta, and he had them hanged. As a few more Frenchmen remained alive after this mass extermination, he had the cattle shed where they were held set on fire. The few who made an attempt to flee the flames were shot down. None escaped.[87]

Merino was a slightly built man of medium height and swarthy complexion. He had large and deep-set eyes, and his temples arched inward to such an extent that people who knew him often compared him to an old horse. His face usually bore a severe if not downright scowling expression. He was a man of few words, but his appearance as well as his hoarse voice and the brusqueness of his manners instilled respect and fear in his men, many of whom were not exactly model citizens. He neither smoked nor drank, and his frugality was proverbial. "He was the least interested and the least ambitious of men," wrote a man who harbored no sympathy for Merino.[88] He had few, if any, friends, was by nature very mistrustful, and could be exceedingly cruel. Whether he insulted and tormented his mother in such a manner that she died in grief, or had his brother murdered to prevent

87. *Ibid.*, pp. 54–152; Gómez de Arteche, pp. 110–11.
88. Malumbres, *Historia política del Cura Merino*, p. 15. On one occasion Merino is said to have distributed all the gold seized on a French convoy to his guerrillas, keeping for himself twelve pairs of silk stockings (*ibid.*).

him from taking over the leadership of the *guerrilla*, as was alleged by this same unsympathetic writer,[89] is open to question.

His guerrillas had the utmost veneration for this priest, who led them from one victory to another, indefatigable in his activity, inflexible in his determination to destroy the enemy. "He could hear better than a lynx," remembered his secretary, "he saw farther than an eagle, he ran faster than a buck, he jumped like a squirrel, he resisted hunger like a wolf, and evaded danger with more tricks than a fox . . . Upon returning from his raids he presented the same aspect as when he had left, without his face revealing any fatigue, without his eyelids indicating any lack of sleep."[90]

After the war ended and Fernando returned to Spain, the monarch made the *guerrillero* a full-fledged general and appointed him military governor of Burgos. Later he was given a canonship in Valencia, but, preferring the simple country life, he was back in Villoviado in 1820. A confirmed absolutist, he took to the hills during the short-lived liberal regime of 1820–1823 and fought the liberals with the same inflexibility and cruelty as he had fought the French. The return of Fernando to full power brought him back to his peaceful occupations, but in the 1830s he took up arms again for absolutism, this time on the side of the Carlists. With the defeat of the traditionalists in 1839, Merino went into exile to neighboring France, where he died in Alençon in 1844.[91]

The most noble figure among all the *guerrilleros* and second only to Francisco Espoz y Mina in fame and achievements was Don Juan Martín Díez, better known as El Empecinado.[92] He was certainly the most active guerrilla leader in Castile and acquired such fame during the war that in wide areas of Spain the word *empecinado* became synonymous with *guerrillero*. All reports that have come down to us about his deeds and his personality are in agreement on one point

---

89. *Ibid.*, pp. 4–5. The above account was published during the bitter and cruel Carlist War (1833–1839) by a constitutionalist sympathizer. Merino was then fighting on the Carlist side against the constitutionalist monarchy.

90. Marco, *El Cura Merino*, pp. 6–10; Gómez de Arteche, pp. 111–13.

91. Ontañón, pp. 161–238.

92. From the word *pecina*, slime, applied to the mud carried by the stream in the village where he was born.

above all, his humanity toward his own comrades-in-arms as well as to those enemies who fell into his hands. He was probably the most humane and generous guerrilla fighter produced by the war, incarnating to a supreme degree the virtues of the Castilian peasant, especially his sobriety, his honesty, and his respect for human life. That he was also a clever general was recognized by his adversary, General Hugo, who stated in his memoirs: "The *Empecinado* . . . handled his troops ably, possessed their full confidence, fought creditably in their midst, and added to many military qualities the most indefatigable activity."[93]

Juan Martín was a lean but powerfully built man of medium height and of swarthy complexion. Goya's painting of him conveys to us the extraordinary energy which animated this man. The lively eyes, the firm mouth topped by a long moustache, the strong chin, form a head which, crowned by a mass of black hair, is unforgettable in its proud bearing and in the willpower and essential nobility which one cannot help feeling when contemplating it. "He was slow and clumsy, but expressive, in his speech," says Pérez Galdós in *Juan Martín El Empecinado*, "and at every moment he showed that he had not studied in military or civil academies. He insisted on showing scorn for good manners, thinking that all those who were not models of primitive roughness were of a frivolous and effeminate character . . . His virtues and his benevolence were harsh like wild plants which contain healthful sap, but whose leaves are full of thorns."[94]

He was born into a family of fairly well-to-do peasants in the village of Castrillo de Duero (Old Castile), between Valladolid and Aranda de Duero, on September 2, 1775. Before he was sixteen years old he ran away from home to enlist in the army, but his parents brought him back, claiming, and justly so, that he was not of age to serve the king. During the war with the French Republic (1793–1795) he achieved a fine record in a cavalry regiment. After the war he married Doña Catalina de la Fuente and settled down in the village of Fuentecén, home of his wife, nine miles west of Aranda.

93. *Op. cit.*, II, p. 274.
94. *Op. cit.*, p. 52.

As early as the end of 1807, he was expressing to his neighbors his mistrust of the French, and in April, 1808, when Fernando VII passed through Aranda on his way north, Juan Martín, who happened to be in the town, is supposed to have remarked while he was in the crowd watching the royal cortege: "The French are infamous and Napoleon more than any of them. If Fernando enters France, he will not leave it until we bring him back."[95] At the end of the month he decided that it was time that somebody in the area took up arms against Napoleon, and in the company of two neighbors he began to attack French couriers on the main north-south highway. After the *dos de mayo* he increased his guerrilla activities by carrying out raids with a small band which comprised twelve men. But a regular army was being formed by Don Gregorio de la Cuesta, captain-general of Old Castile; and Juan Martín, after having delivered to the old general in Valladolid all the mail bags he had taken from the French, fought valiantly against the enemy in the disastrous battles of Cabezón and Medina de Río Seco.[96]

Following these defeats El Empecinado turned once more to guerrilla warfare. In August, 1808, when Joseph was withdrawing behind the Ebro, he achieved his first resounding feat of arms, the capture of a French convoy, in which traveled a lady, relative of Marshal Moncey. Juan Martín escorted her to his home and placed it at the lady's disposal—she happened to be pregnant—until she could be sent to the French-held zone.[97] As for the booty, he distributed it among his men, earmarking the bulk, however, for General Cuesta, to whom he handed it in Salamanca. As so frequently happens, his successes had aroused the jealousy of some neighbors, who in connivance with the local authorities succeeded in convincing Cuesta that El Empecinado had behaved unlawfully. The general ordered him jailed in Burgo de Osma, thirty-three miles southeast of Aranda. The citizens of Burgo knew better. They appealed to the general to ignore the calumnies spread against Juan Martín and to rescind his decision. Cuesta heeded this appeal and gave orders to release the valiant

95. *Apuntes de la vida y hechos militares del brigadier Don Juan Martín Díez, El Empecinado*, p. 6.

96. See Chapter IV.

97. She regained her freedom in the fall, when the French captured Aranda.

guerrillero. But partly because the French advance forced Cuesta to move out of Burgo in a hurry, and partly because the mayor had decided that by turning the prisoner over to the French he would spare the town a sack, El Empecinado was still in jail when the French were about to enter the town. With an energy born of desperation and helped by a few men, Juan Martín managed to escape from the jail and from Burgo just when the first enemy soldiers appeared in the streets.[98]

Juan Martín was too generous to harbor for a long time resentment against his countrymen who had persecuted him, and he devoted all his strength to fighting the common enemy. This time, among the friends and relatives joining his band were his three brothers, the youngest of whom was barely fifteen years old. Success now followed success. Couriers, convoys, detachments fell victim to his surprise attacks. His *partida* ranged far and wide in its relentless raids. He even appeared twice in the province of Salamanca. There he delivered important captured documents to Sir John Moore, who rewarded him with the sum of 18,000 reales[99] and left a large quantity of enemy prisoners in the fortress town of Ciudad Rodrigo. In April, 1809, the Junta Central, recognizing the great value of his services, granted him the rank of cavalry captain. The same year, during the Talavera campaign, he constantly harassed the flanks and rear of the French columns passing through the Baños pass fifty miles south of Salamanca to fall on Plasencia and catch Wellington's army in the rear.[1] Having accomplished his mission, he returned to Salamanca. Later, in the course of one of his forays in the area of Toro, he was wounded in an engagement with a party of French cavalry and returned to Castrillo to let his wounds heal and to see his mother and friends. His enemies, who had been responsible for his imprisonment in Burgo de Osma, went into hiding. El Empecinado had them sought out and insisted they be his guests at a meal in his house. To the neediest he gave some money and to all of them he "offered his most sincere friendship and took leave of them with the greatest humility."[2]

98. *Apuntes*, pp. 7–12.

99. El Empecinado used most of the money to buy horses for his *partida* (*ibid.*, p. 13).

1. See Chapters VIII and XVII.

2. *Apuntes*, p. 21; Gómez de Arteche, pp. 92–93.

His destination was the province of Guadalajara in New Castile, which from now on would be his main theater of operations and where he would gain undying renown as a guerrilla chieftain. Called there by the Junta of Guadalajara, which was constantly on the move to escape its French pursuers, El Empecinado entered the province in September, 1809, and soon the French garrisons of the towns of Guadalajara and Alcalá de Henares, and King Joseph in Madrid, were aware that they were no longer in safe command of the *mesetas* and deep valleys of Guadalajara. Not only was their hold on this region threatened, but their communications with the French-held areas of Aragón, where General Suchet's army was operating, were in grave jeopardy. But they also knew that the *guerrillero* who now lay in wait for their convoys and detachments was an unusual type of guerrilla leader. He scrupulously observed the laws of war and almost always treated French prisoners in exemplary fashion. As a result a very unusual thing happened in the struggle between the French army and El Empecinado. Although his men were often called brigands by the enemy, they were generally not harmed when taken prisoner.[3]

El Empecinado kept his men busy. His *guerrilla*, which by the middle of 1810 had grown to 1,000 men, was constantly harassing French garrisons and columns in the provinces of Madrid, Guadalajara, Soria, and Cuenca, and even in Aragón. Now his guerrillas were attacking Brihuega and Sigüenza; now they were crossing the Jarama and making the garrison of the capital nervous, and then they were suddenly falling upon an enemy column operating in the province of Soria, only to reappear with the speed of lightning in the province of Cuenca and protect its inhabitants from French foraging parties. In September, 1810, the Cádiz Regency informed him that it had promoted him to the rank of brigadier general, stating in the document containing the order that the government had taken this action "in view of his services and his modesty in not having asked for any reward."[4]

Earlier in the year the incessant raids and the growing power of Juan Martín had almost reduced the garrison of the town of Guadalajara to the status of prisoners. They were unable to send out

3. *Apuntes*, p. 26.
4. *Ibid.*, p. 34.

foraging columns or convoys for their couriers, and even their sentinels dared not leave the walls of the town unless they thought El Empecinado's men were not anywhere near Guadalajara. The French High Command sent one of its most skillful generals, Joseph Leopold Hugo, to exorcise the threat east of Madrid. Hugo was a veteran of the Vendée[5] and the conqueror of Fra Diavolo, who had for a time successfully defied French rule in the Abruzzi region of the kingdom of Naples. With his special force of 3,000 men and 12 guns the new governor of Guadalajara province was sure he could repeat in Spain what he had accomplished in Naples. But Hugo, though gaining a number of partial victories, was unable to destroy Juan Martín's band. While the French general would move from one town to the next, "from Sigüenza to Guadalajara or from Brihuega to Molina [in Aragón] in search of *El Empecinado*, the latter would be in Cuenca or would appear unexpectedly in the Casa de Campo [outside of Madrid] waiting to catch Joseph who was fond of going there."[6]

Hugo spared no efforts to rid the area under his command of El Empecinado, but he failed. He was open-minded enough to pay a fine compliment in his memoirs to Juan Martín, calling him "one of the most famous guerrilla fighters in Europe" and adding: "Surprising was the genius of this man, who far from being discouraged by reverses, seemed to derive new strength from them."[7] In these memoirs the French general reflected upon his experiences in Spain, and the peculiar form of war fought by the Spanish people elicited the following revealing comment:

It will be difficult to find in History a war, unless it be that of the Vendée, in which the people have had more sacrifices to make for the cause of a prince, and in which they have made them more unanimously and with more constancy than in the Spanish war. If the Juntas . . . ordered them to abandon their homes . . . they obeyed at once and whatever the season, which could often be very harsh, they fled into the woods and the mountains, without disposing most of the time of any means of feeding themselves. In its sublime devotion to its fatherland and to Fernando VII, the Junta [of Guadalajara] did not seek out palaces to hold its sessions. A cavern in the rocks, a poor hamlet in the woods, the ruins of some isolated

5. See p. 687, note 56.
6. Gómez de Arteche, p. 97.
7. *Op. cit.*, II, p. 162.

building in the mountains, became the seat of the administration, as soon as it was threatened by my movements or by my proximity.[8]

By the time the war ended, the small band with which El Empecinado had begun to fight had become an army of close to 5,000 men.[9] Feted by all of Spain, he could look back with satisfaction over the war years. He had not only worn down the French with his guerrilla tactics, but he had also on a number of occasions more than held his own against them in open battle. His action against the French garrison of Calatayud in Aragón in the fall of 1811 had been particularly brilliant. Aided by the guerrilla leader Durán, he had attacked the town, chased the garrison into a monastery, and forced it to surrender on October 4. Close to 800 prisoners had fallen into his hands.[10]

Yes, Hugo had tried hard to crush him. Once the French general had even endeavored to win him over to Napoleon's side. In December, 1810, he had sent a message to him, offering him and his men a post in Joseph's army. Juan Martín had proudly rejected the overture. "Keep in mind," he had written, "that even if one single soldier remained in my army, the war would not be finished. All of them, just like their chief, have sworn eternal war on Napoleon and the vile slaves who follow him. You may tell your king and all your companions that *El Empecinado* and his troops will die in defense of their fatherland, for they will never be able to join men . . . without honor, without faith nor religion of any kind . . ."[11]

There had been letters from other sources, and one that had aroused particular pride in Juan Martín's heart had been a message received in September 1812 at his headquarters in Cuenca. The princess of Brazil, sister of Fernando and infanta of Spain, Doña Carlota Joaquina de Borbón, had congratulated him on his exploits from her residence in Rio de Janeiro. "The important and heroic services with which you have defended in the present revolution the

8. *Ibid.*, p. 262.

9. *Apuntes*, p. 77. The figure of 10,000 given by Fernández Fernández (*Recuerdo histórico, El Empecinado*, p. 8) seems highly exaggerated.

10. Letter of El Empecinado to Antonio de Capetillo, October 18, 1811, AHN, Estado, *legajo* 3010; *Apuntes*, pp. 54-55.

11. *Apuntes*, p. 91.

rights of our beloved fatherland and those of my cherished brother, Fernando, to the throne, have elicited my special gratitude," she had written.[12]

Alas, the one person who should have been most grateful for these services, Fernando himself, the captive, cowardly Fernando, who had spent the war years comfortably in Talleyrand's chateau at Valençay while his people were bleeding to death in their struggle to bring him back to the throne, did not know the meaning of the word gratitude. After Fernando's return El Empecinado asked him to reestablish the Constitution of 1812, which the King had recently abolished. The Monarch, highly displeased, sent the guerrilla chieftain into exile to Valladolid. When the liberal revolution broke out in 1820, Juan Martín placed himself at the service of the new regime and fought the absolutist rebels with the same skill with which he had fought the French.[13] But absolutism triumphed in 1823 and the liberal general, who could have sought safety in Portugal, returned to Castile with guarantees that he would not be molested. Arrested in Olmos de Peñafiel, near Peñafiel, between Valladolid and Aranda de Duero, he was jailed in the town of Roa and kept in prison for two years in spite of his mother's pleas to the king. But Fernando was inexorable. After the long calvary, in the course of which he was often taken to the market place in a cage and exposed to the insults of the populace, he was taken out of jail one day in August, 1825 to be executed. At the foot of the gallows Juan Martín showed a last flash of rage and power. Somehow he managed to break his handcuffs and made a dash for freedom. But the soldiers lined up in the square of the town overpowered him and brought him back to the scaffold. He was duly hanged. Thus King Fernando rewarded him for his patriotic deeds during the war against Napoleon.[14]

Today, the memory of El Empecinado lingers on in some of the

12. CDF, CDXLV, pp. 516–17.

13. Merino, with whom El Empecinado had collaborated in the heroic days of 1808, was now an absolutist and the Civil War brought the two men to battle, but on opposite sides. Juan Martín and Merino fought an engagement in which the priest was routed.

14. Fernández Fernández, *Recuerdo histórico, El Empecinado*, pp. 15–19; *Memorias del Alcalde de Roa, Don Gregorio González Arranz*, ed. Sebastián Lazo, pp. 41–57.

places where he lived and fought. In Fuentecén, his one-time resi-dence, a typical *pueblo* of Old Castile, with its church, its fountain, its adobe houses, an old man might still remember stories of Juan Martín's first exploits.[15] Between Peñafiel and Fuentecén, on the highway leading from Valladolid to Aranda de Duero, there is a *caserío* or group of houses called El Empecinado. One of the build-ings is said to have been occupied at one time or another by the famous guerrilla leader. On the second story a stone tablet can be seen bearing the words El Empecinado.

[4]

We must now say something of the true genius of the guerrilla war in the Peninsula, the greatest guerrilla fighter of them all, the Navar-rese Don Francisco Espoz y Mina, better known simply as Mina. As a human being Mina was doubtless far less attractive than Juan Martín El Empecinado. Though moved by the highest patriotism and acting always with considerable honesty and disinterestedness, Mina could be inflexible to the point of cruelty. Fanatical in his desire to achieve a goal he had set himself, he would not shrink before measures which, though justified by the circumstances, are bound to cause revulsion in us. Though he did not engage in the systematic cruelty toward French prisoners of which some guerrilla chieftains were guilty, he would not hesitate to use terrible reprisals if the enemy had in his eyes brought these on himself. In him we find none of the softness that underlay the rough exterior of El Empecinado. Mina was a tough disciplinarian, though an extremely fair one, who all during the war commanded his forces as well as the population of Navarra with an iron fist. But this man, born a simple peasant, became a great leader of men and an excellent tactician. He had the respect and admiration of his subordinates, whose hardships he shared, and the complete support—in the measure that this was possible, of course—of the population of Navarra. Some of his exploits in the

15. The author had the fortune of meeting such an old man in Fuentecén in July, 1961, and hearing stories of El Empecinado's taking captured documents to Valladolid in the early days of the war, and of the hanging in Roa.

northern province as well as in the Basque provinces and in Aragón have rarely been equaled in modern guerrilla warfare. And he could boast of more victories in open battle with the enemy than any other Spanish guerrilla leader. The terror of the French, Mina was often called by friend and foe the "King of Navarra," and to a great extent he was.

"I was living in the midst of the deepest peace and the most perfect tranquility, when the revolts and convulsions of the fatherland at the beginning of the year 1808 snatched me from this happiness which I enjoyed." Thus Mina begins his memoirs.[16] He had been born, he further tells us, in the little town of Idocin, about thirteen miles southeast of Pamplona, Navarra's capital, the youngest son of Juan Esteban Espoz and María Teresa Ilundain. When he had reached the age of fifteen in 1796, his father had died and he had become the head of the family, which included two sisters and a brother.[17] Having worked on the property of his family ever since childhood, he was used to the hard life of a Spanish peasant, which in his case was made somewhat easier by the modest patrimony inherited from his father. Francisco's education was limited to knowing how to read and write, and the thought that one day he might be called upon to do great things for his country was far from his mind. But fate, or rather history, had disposed otherwise.[18]

Whenever his work left him some free time, he would go to Pamplona to see his brother Clemente and his sister Simona, and also his seventeen-year-old nephew Javier Mina, who was studying philosophy in the capital of Navarra. On February 9, 1808, Francisco happened to be in Pamplona. It was the day French troops under General D'Armagnac entered the town. The occupation of Navarra had begun.[19]

When the great rising took place throughout Spain, Francisco's nephew, Javier Mina, went to Zaragoza, where he fought valiantly in defense of the heroic town. After the surrender he escaped the occupying troops and returned to Navarra. Animated by an

16. *Memorias del General Don Francisco Espoz y Mina*, I, in BAE, CXLVI, p. 7.
17. His brother had become a priest.
18. *Ibid.*
19. *Ibid.*

unflinching patriotism and far from discouraged by the disaster in Aragón, the young Mina formed a guerrilla band and began to attack French convoys and isolated detachments. His uncle, meanwhile, had joined a battalion of regular troops organized by British commissioner Doyle and stationed in the Aragonese town of Jaca. When this fortress also fell into the hands of the enemy, Francisco, too, managed to avoid the fate of a prisoner of war and made his way back to neighboring Navarra, where he joined his nephew's *guerrilla*.[20] By early 1810 the French command in Navarra was sufficiently alarmed to launch an all-out offensive against Mina's 800 guerrillas. The new governor of the province, General Dufour, was lucky enough to catch young Mina on March 29 at the village of Labiana and take him prisoner. Javier owed it to the insistent pleas of Pamplona's patriots to Dufour that he was not simply hanged in Pamplona. He was, instead, sent to France and locked up in the fortress of Vincennes, outside of Paris.[21]

The war must go on, and so Francisco Espoz decided to continue in his nephew's footsteps. Taking over the command of the *partida*, he asked and received from the Junta of Aragón and Castile, then residing in the Mediterranean port of Peñíscola, the appointment of commander-in-chief of all *partidas* in Navarra. His next step was to bring under his authority the many guerrilla bands roaming the countryside of the northern province, some of which were composed of undesirable elements and were molesting the inhabitants as much as they were harassing the enemy. Except for two guerrilla chieftains,[22] he was soon successful in this enterprise, and within a short while had enough men to form three battalions of guerrilla fighters, constituting a force which for a while would be known as the *Corso*

20. *Ibid.,* pp. 10–11; Olóriz, *Navarra en la guerra de la independencia,* pp. 18–33.

21. *Memorias,* pp. 11–14; Olóriz, pp. 42–46. Freed by the fall of Napoleon in 1814, the younger Mina took part in his uncle's liberal plot in Pamplona in the fall of the same year. Following its failure, he emigrated to France and later to England, whence he traveled to the New World. Fighting against Spanish absolutist rule in Mexico, he was taken prisoner in 1817 by the royalist forces and shot (cf. Martín Luis Guzmán, *Mina el Mozo, héroe de Navarra*).

22. Echevarría and Hernández, who were both caught and shot later in the year by Mina's force.

terrestre de Navarra (Land Privateers of Navarra). Espoz now added to his name his nephew's surname, Mina, to avail himself of the latter's immense prestige, and was henceforth to be known as Espoz y Mina or simply Mina.[23]

The guerrilla war in Navarra now took on epic proportions. Mina, appointed colonel by the Cádiz Regency in September, 1810, had seen to it that his men were thoroughly disciplined and trained for their tasks. As a result his forces, to whom he now gave the title *División de Navarra*,[24] fell upon so many convoys and fought so many successful actions against the French that "in a short time he succeeded in winning the enthusiastic support of the inhabitants of that warlike province, who gave him all kinds of help, as well as the admiration of the Spanish government, which granted him all sorts of rewards."[25]

Mina was everywhere and nowhere. The rapidity with which he moved, the lightning speed with which he struck frequently kept his adversaries in a state of utter confusion. They might think he was operating near Pamplona and he would appear sixty miles farther west, wreaking havoc on an unsuspecting French convoy; or the French generals might be certain that he was about to launch a raid in central Navarra and he would attack French posts in upper Aragón. Shortly after he had taken command, in the summer of 1810, the French made an all-out effort to wipe out Mina's band. It was the time when Napoleon was hoping to throw the English into the sea and finish the war in the Peninsula. To achieve this object Masséna's army was moving into Portugal. At the same time, substantial French forces in the north were earmarked for a decisive campaign against the guerrillas. Navarra's new governor, General Reille, as well as his colleagues in Aragón, Burgos, Vitoria, and San Sebastián, coordinated their efforts to rid Navarra of Mina, and soon many flying columns comprising according to Mina, 30,000 men, were closing in from all sides on his 3,500 volunteers. Now began a series of epic marches and countermarches through the valleys and fastnesses of Navarra that has few equals in history. Hunted incessantly by the

23. *Memorias*, pp. 14–19.
24. *Ibid.*, p. 35.
25. Gómez de Arteche, p. 106.

enemy columns, Mina divided his forces, which had shrunk considerably as a result of the terrible hardships of these marches, into two segments, and both were finally able to cross the Ebro between Calhorra and Tudela and find a temporary haven in Castile.[26] Mina related this episode in the following words: "Always surrounded by innumerable columns, which hardly left us enough time to take a scanty amount of food and to repair with sleep our tired limbs; with the greater part of my volunteers practically without clothes, shoeless and in the greatest state of misery, it was extraordinary that we should be able to gather again one-half . . . of the number [of men] that were available when the tenacious and violent chase began."[27]

When Mina arrived in Castile he had the satisfaction of finding out that the thousands of French troops who had been chasing him for two whole months in Navarra had been destined to reinforce Masséna's army in Portugal. He had thus played a key role in delaying the arrival of these important reinforcements on the big battlefield in the west, where the fate of the British army under Wellington was hanging in the balance. Whether they were 30,000, as Mina claims, or considerably less, they might just have given the French forces in Portugal the necessary push to smash through the lines at Torres Vedras in October.[28]

The French had failed in their grandiose campaign to eradicate the guerrillas of Navarra, and by the end of the year Mina was once more in the northern province with more than 3,000 men under his command. On December 24, a French force of 1,500 infantry and 200 cavalry attacked the guerrillas near the town of Aibar, certain that these "brigands" were no match in open battle for Napoleon's vaunted soldiers. The enemy's confidence and pride cost him dearly. Half of the column was killed, wounded, or taken prisoner, while the casualties of the *División de Navarra* amounted to 180 men.[29]

One of Mina's most celebrated exploits took place in the spring of the following year. Another chase of epic proportions in early 1811

26. *Memorias,* pp. 29–33.
27. *Ibid.,* p. 34.
28. *Ibid.,* pp. 33–34. Actually Masséna began to receive reinforcements only in December. See Chapter IX.
29. *Ibid.,* p. 42.

placed Mina and his men in dire straits and even forced him to divide his army into small companies to escape the relentless pursuit of the enemy. But in May, when the French thought that Mina's men were still recovering from the hardships they had just undergone, they were actually marching westward to deliver a crushing blow to the invaders. Mina's magnificently organized information service—his spies were active everywhere, including Pamplona—had advised the guerrilla chieftain that Marshal Masséna, after his unsuccessful campaign in Portugal, was on his way back to France. On May 25, Mina's guerrillas, after two days and one night of forced marches, reached the pass of Arlabán, in the Basque region west of Navarra, and waited for the enemy convoy which had left Vitoria and was winding its way along the highway leading up to the pass. Let us now hear Mina's account of the action that followed: "Lying in wait at both sides of the pass, and in the greatest silence, we awaited the travelers. I ordered that nobody move until I gave the signal with a pistol shot, and that upon hearing it they were to attack according to my usual tactic, that is to say, with the bayonet, following a thick volley. The convoy arrived in front of our lines. The vanguard passed by, and as the middle section reached us I gave the signal. My men attacked, disorder gripped the convoy . . . , part of the escort fled, the other held its ground, the one which had fled returned to the fight, and the result was as horrible for the French as it was glorious for our division."[30] Of the 1,200 men of the escort, about 400 were able to return to Vitoria. The others were either dead, wounded, or prisoners. More than 1,000 English and Spanish prisoners were set free and an immense booty was taken. Fortunately for Marshal Masséna, he had not left Vitoria with the ill-fated convoy, for if he had, he would not have been able to report to Napoleon on the Portuguese campaign.[31]

The French were furious because of the loss of the convoy. Their hatred and fear of Mina had expressed itself from the start through the shooting of all Navarrese guerrillas falling into their hands and of all those who helped them, and through draconian measures of all sorts enforced throughout Navarra. Soon the war in the northern

30. *Ibid.*, p. 56.
31. *Ibid.*, pp. 56–57.

province reached a crescendo of atrocities which makes us shudder even today. On December 14, 1811, Mina, enraged by the refusal of the French to grant his men the status of prisoners of war when they had the misfortune to be caught, published a decree consisting of twenty-three articles, in which he declared war without quarter on all French soldiers and officers and even on the Emperor of the French; ordered the blockade of Pamplona; and stipulated that all French officers and men taken, with or without weapons in their hands, would be hanged and their bodies exposed on the roads. Severe punishment was to be meted out to those Navarrese who had moved from their own towns or villages to French-held places and who did not return to their homes within twenty days, and in general to all those who in whatever form collaborated with the enemy.[32]

Mina now carried out pitilessly the measures he had announced in the decree. He was perfectly able to do this because he had a large supply of prisoners in the remote Pyrenean valley of Roncal. For every Navarrese officer shot by the French [33] Mina shot four French officers. For every one of his soldiers executed by the enemy, twenty enemy soldiers fell under the bullets of a Navarrese firing squad.[34] After four French soldiers had been killed in the town of Estella, twenty-five miles southwest of Pamplona, French general Abbé had twenty hostages hanged at Pamplona. Mina's second-in-command, Gregorio Cruchaga, then ordered nine Frenchmen, including five officers, killed and mutilated, and their corpses hanged from trees with an insulting sign bearing his signature. Whereupon Abbé answered with the shooting of eighteen more hostages and eighteen of their relatives.[35] After several months of this butchery, the French had had enough and suggested a halt to the orgy of killing. Mina, too, was tired of the awful bloodletting and the atrocities gradually stopped.[36]

32. *Ibid.*, pp. 85–87.
33. Mina had introduced rank in his guerrilla army to put it on an equal footing with the French forces for the purpose of exchanging prisoners (Olóriz, pp. 154–158). The exchange of prisoners was systematized by both sides in the latter stages of the war (*Memorias*, p. 210).
34. Gómez de Arteche, p. 106.
35. Grandmaison, iii, p. 244.
36. *Memorias*, p. 100; Gómez de Arteche, p. 107.

In early 1812 Napoleon decided once more to launch an all-out offensive against the elusive guerrilla army of Navarra. General Suchet had just conquered Valencia.[37] This would enable some troops under his command to join in a concerted effort against Mina. At the same time, the Emperor, thinking of his coming campaign against Russia and therefore of the necessity of insuring at all costs Madrid's communications with France, considered it of utmost importance to eliminate the permanent threat to the French north-south routes posed by the guerrilla chieftain. This threat was once more made evident in January by the bloody defeat inflicted by Mina's battalions on General Abbé's column of more than 2,000 soldiers near Sangüesa. Mina's men behaved like veterans and drove the French back with irresistible fury. Six hundred French dead remained on the battlefield, and at least that many were wounded.[38]

Twenty-five thousand Frenchmen now closed in from all sides on the *División de Navarra*. Again Mina was hunted from peak to peak, from valley to valley, from village to village. But at the cost of heavy losses, marching and countermarching day and night through rain and snow, he proved himself entirely worthy of his recently-acquired title of general.[39] Again the French failed in their desperate effort to put an end to Mina's activities.[40]

When the French thought that Mina was licking his wounds in the fastnesses of Aragón, he struck again. The place was the same pass of Arlabán, which had seen the disaster of the great convoy the previous May. On the morning of April 9, 1812, the travelers and escort of another large convoy suddenly heard a terrible volley, and close to 3,000 guerrillas leaped forth from the thickets of green oaks overhanging the highway. Navarrese bayonets did their lethal work, and after a one-hour battle, what remained of the escort, made up of the seventh Polish regiment, fled, leaving behind 600 dead and 150 prisoners as well as 400 liberated Spanish prisoners who had been on their way to France.[41] Among the captives was Doña Carlota Azanza, wife

37. See Chapter IX.

38. *Memorias*, pp. 88–89; Olóriz, pp. 160–63.

39. The Regency had promoted him to the rank of general and Cruchaga to that of colonel in November, 1811 (*Memorias*, p. 82).

40. *Memorias*, pp. 101–105.

41. *Memorias*, p. 105. Mina reported that only five of his men had been killed and fifty wounded (*ibid.*).

of King Joseph's secretary, Deslandes, who was killed during the assault. Deslandes carried a number of letters from Joseph to Napoleon and one to his wife Julie, which Mina sent to the government of Cádiz. He sent five captured children back to Vitoria and had the several women prisoners taken in the battle, including Madame Deslandes, treated with the utmost courtesy. This gallant gesture caused the French to release his brother-in-law held a prisoner in Pamplona.[42]

Yes, in Navarra Mina ruled supreme. Even the French were forced to recognize this. As early as July 11, 1810, General Thouvenot had written to Marshal Soult from San Sebastián: "The brigands of Navarra multiply daily. They collect customs charges at the border; they force young men to enroll in their ranks; in short, they make the laws of Navarra."[43] Not only had Mina eluded the enemy's most frantic maneuvers, not only had he inflicted heavy losses on them in men and supplies, but he also governed the province as effectively as if he held sway in Pamplona.[44] "Everywhere uniforms were secretly made for his soldiers, and the highest mountains as well as almost impassable defiles were the seat of arms manufactories, munition dumps, and hospitals. His sick and at times his wounded were cared for in villages and hamlets, and quite a few in the very houses where those who had caused their wounds were lodging. Traitors were exceedingly rare."[45]

For the means to keep him equipped and supplied, Mina, reluctant to tax the population directly, relied mostly on booty captured from the enemy, on incomes siphoned off from former ecclesiastical prop-

42. *Ibid.*, pp. 105–107; Olóriz, pp. 181–184. Grandmaison (III, p. 242) speaks of a combined attack by the guerrillas of Mina and El Pastor. Neither Mina's memoirs nor Olóriz mention any cooperation between Mina and other guerrilla chiefs. The French historian places the number of French killed at 285 out of a total force of 1,800, an implausibly small number in view of the surprise attack. Furthermore, since Mina reported only 150 prisoners, this would mean either that the great majority of the escort was able to make a getaway, which is highly improbable, or that Mina lowered the figure for the prisoners, which would also be quite unusual.

43. *Gaceta de la Regencia*, August 28, 1810, AHN, Estado, *legajo* 3003/1.

44. Technically he had been since December, 1811, under the orders of General Gabriel de Mendizábal, commander of the Spanish Seventh Army (*Memorias*, p. 88).

45. Gómez de Arteche, p. 107.

erty, and especially on special customs units set up along the Franco-Spanish border. All French and Spanish merchants sending their goods across the frontier were placed before the choice of having these confiscated if found by the Navarrese guerrillas, or insuring their safe passage by paying a given sum to Mina's "customhouses." They did not like it, but they paid. The strangest part of the whole enterprise was that even the French customhouse at Irún made a deal with the chief of Navarra which insured all merchandise passing through the town by means of a monthly payment to his emissaries of 100 ounces in gold.[46]

The war went on and Mina collected more victories. By 1813 his men were no longer a ragged mass of partisans, but constituted a formidable division, 13,500 soldiers of all branches of the service, which was part of the Spanish Seventh Army. In August 1813 he had the satisfaction of forcing the surrender of the castle of Aljafería at Zaragoza and of seeing the French abandon the town in their general retreat which was to take them out of Aragón and soon afterward out of the remainder of French-held Spain.[47]

With the end of the war came the great disenchantment. Fernando VII was not the high-minded, forward-looking monarch Mina had imagined. Moreover, reasons of personal dissatisfaction combined with his disillusionment with the nature of the King and the regime installed by him. The troops that had been under Mina's command were placed under the order of Palafox, free again, and once more captain-general of Aragón. Mina, disgruntled, joined the liberal party and attempted an antiabsolutist coup at Pamplona, in September, 1814. It failed and Mina went into exile to neighboring France. In 1820, after the triumph of the liberal cause, he returned and as general-in-chief of the liberal army in Catalonia he fought successfully against the absolutists in the Civil War of 1822–1823. Again in exile following the victory of absolutism in 1823, he emigrated to England, whence he went to France in 1830. Back in Spain in 1834 after the death of Fernando VII, he was appointed general-in-chief of the Constitutional Army of the north, which was fighting desperately to put down the Carlist rebellion. He was far less successful

46. *Memorias*, p. 20.
47. *Ibid.*, pp. 160–163.

this time, mainly because he was already suffering from a stomach cancer. His failures to defeat the Carlists as well as his illness caused him to resign his post in April, 1835, but in October he was placed in command of the Constitutionalist Army in Catalonia. Following a number of victories Mina resigned again, but his resignation was not accepted by the government. He died in Barcelona on December 24, 1836, at the age of fifty-five.[48]

Ever since the date he had seen himself slighted by Fernando VII, Mina had been a convinced liberal. He had served the cause of liberalism well, though in his campaigns against the Carlists his cruelties had matched those of his adversaries. Unfortunately, the War of Independence and Fernando's reaction had spawned on the Spanish political scene an extremism and a combativity which have been Spain's bane ever since. Mina, great though he was in many respects, was not able to remain above the fratricidal melee. Nor did other guerrilla leaders stay out of the fray. Quite a few embraced liberalism. One of them was El Empecinado, and we have seen the tragic fate that befell him. Others were Porlier, who had valiantly fought in Asturias, Miláns del Bosch, the great Catalan guerrillero, and Francisco Abad Moreno, better known as Chaleco, who had distinguished himself in La Mancha, all of whom fought for constitutionalism.[49] Some remained loyal to the absolute monarchy. Merino fought for absolutism during the liberal triennium of 1820–1823 and the first Carlist War of 1833–1839. Zumalacárregui, who had distinguished himself in the *partida* of Jáureguy in the Basque region, became the able and feared general-in-chief of the Carlist forces. It has not been proven that officers with a guerrilla background who served in Fernando's army after the war and harbored liberal sympathies were more numerous than those with absolutist ideas, but this is more than

48. Artola, *Estudio preliminar, Memorias,* i, pp. xvi–xli; Quadrado, "Francisco Espoz y Mina," *Personajes célebres del siglo XIX,* ii, pp. 119–28. His wife, Doña María de Vega, countess Espoz y Mina, who published his memoirs, filled the post of *aya* or governess to young Queen Isabel II in 1841–1843.

49. Porlier was caught and executed (see above, p. 671, n.). Miláns succeeded in crossing the French border (1817). Abad Moreno was hanged (1827). (Cf. Vasco, *Don Francisco Abad Moreno [Chaleco] guerrillero de la independencia. Publicaciones del Congreso Historico Internacional de la guerra de la independencia y su época* (1807–1815), Zaragoza, 1909, Vol. ii, pp. 285–301).

likely since these men had risen to high rank, thanks to their deeds and not to their family background or wealth.[50]

The important fact to keep in mind, however, is that the guerrilla warfare that grew out of the epic struggle for independence is one of the several factors that deeply affected the political trajectory of nineteenth-century Spain. On the one hand the Spanish people acquired the habit of *echarse al monte*, of taking to the hills, a habit that was to become an ingrained national characteristic. Henceforward, a favorite reaction to an unwelcome political situation would be precisely this, *echarse al monte*. The antagonism between liberals and conservatives that emerged in wartime Spain and was exacerbated by Fernando VII's policies would be constantly taken out of the political arena to be settled by the force of arms. On the other hand, the War of Independence gave a simple peasant, a shepherd, or a laborer a chance to fight the enemy, untrammeled more often than not by military regulations, and to become a guerrilla leader through his own exploits. Eventually, if his actions justified it, he could even acquire officer's rank in the regular army. Because of his social background it could be expected that in the majority of cases he would not side with the old-school officers, many of whom came from noble families and supported the restoration of absolutism. Hence there was bound to be unrest among the newly-appointed officers. These would combine forces with officers with a regular army background who either held liberal ideas or felt the role they had played in the war was not being sufficiently appreciated by the King. Thus over the years a large proportion of the army would harbor increasingly liberal feelings. At the same time the importance the military element had acquired during the war would make itself felt in the increasingly weighty part the army would play in the life of the nation.

The army entered politics to stay. In the first two-thirds of the nineteenth century it would intervene by and large on the side of the liberals. Later it would become more and more conservative. The *caudillo* or military leader became a familiar figure on the national scene, and the *pronunciamiento* a common occurrence. These were some of the consequences, not only of the war itself and the conse-

50. Cf. Solano Costa, *El guerrillero y su trascendencia* (Zaragoza, 1959).

quent importance of the military element, but also of the peculiar form the war took in the areas nominally controlled by Napoleon's troops. To quote Galdós: "But the War of Independence, I repeat, was the great academy of *caudillaje* (bossism), because in it Spaniards became extremely well-trained in the art . . . of improvising armies and dominating a territory for more or less prolonged periods of time. They studied the science of insurrection, and for the things that seemed wonderful to us at the time we have had since then to pay with tears of blood."[51]

51. *Juan Martín El Empecinado*, p. 57.

XVI

THE FACES OF WAR

[1]

ALL WAR is hell, to amplify Sherman's famous remark, but it must be conceded that the war in Spain was one of the most infernal conflicts of modern times. Easily one of the most ferociously fought struggles of the nineteenth century, it was certainly the most terrible war of the Napoleonic period. The Russian campaign of 1812 exacted more casualties from the regular armies involved than did the Peninsular in any single year. But the Russian campaign was over in seven months, while the Peninsular War lasted six years. The atrocities of the War of Spanish Independence cannot, of course, compare in scope to the bestialities committed in our twentieth century, but to those who witnessed it it seemed that all the worst instincts of man had chosen the Iberian Peninsula to manifest themselves with a massive violence which dwarfed the conflicts waged in Europe in the previous century. The apocalyptic dimensions of the War of Independence derive mainly from the fact that it was a total war—the first truly total war of modern times—involving a whole nation and the greater part of its territory. There were many campaigns and many battles, but these alone could not have wrought the utter devastation which descended upon Spain during the years 1808–1814. It was the active and passive resistance of the majority of the Spanish people, expressing itself most dramatically in relentless guerrilla warfare, which gave the war its character. It was a conflict which spared neither age nor sex. Old men, women, children, as well as men of fighting age were its victims, and when they did not die from bullets or the bayonet, they perished through the slower agony of famine or disease.

The most graphic account of the innumerable and horrendous atrocities committed during the war is furnished by Goya's unforgettable series of etchings entitled "Los desastres de la guerra" ("The Disasters of War"). If one seeks to feel something of the atmosphere of those terrible years, one should turn to this gripping record of the horrors which accompanied Spain's struggle for national freedom. Man's inhumanity to man has nowhere been illustrated with more pitiless directness and at the same time with more anguish than in these remarkable plates. "The Disasters . . . constitute the most terrible document, because it is the truest which has remained to us, of the Spanish wars of independence, or for that matter of any war, past, present or future."[1]

It would be idle to try to determine exactly who began the incredible series of atrocities which turned the Peninsula into an inferno. Suffice it to say that Napoleon, by attempting to subjugate Spain in most treacherous fashion, sowed the seeds of a violence which, given the nature of the conflict, could only degenerate into wholesale savagery. The Spanish people, seeing their dignity trampled and their independence threatened, were bound to react with a hatred they would have displayed in no other type of war. The French and their satellites, not accustomed to having to subdue a whole population, were enraged by an attitude which was all the more unsettling as it was alien to their mentality and their experience in other lands. To feel the bitter hostility of townspeople and villagers, to have constantly the sensation that the enemy was everywhere and that one was in control solely of the ground trod upon, was a new and most unnerving experience,[2] which by itself frequently led to atrocities against civilians. But on top of this the ceaseless harassment by guerrillas, the constant killing of sentries, couriers, and whole detachments, and the frequent mutilation of corpses led to terrible reprisals which in turn could only result in more horrible counter-reprisals. Thus the war quickly acquired the bestial charac-

1. Faure, "Introduction to the Etchings," *The Disasters of War*, p. 43.
2. Except, perhaps, for those French soldiers who had fought against their own compatriots in the War of the Vendée.

ter illustrated so vividly in Goya's "Los desastres de la guerra."[3]

Spanish reports of atrocities committed by the enemy are found in abundance in most chronicles of the war written by Spaniards. During the war itself Spanish insurgent authorities protested often and loud against French excesses. In a manifesto addressed on March 20, 1809 by the Junta Central to French generals, the Spanish government berated the latter for the bad treatment accorded to Spanish prisoners. In the eyes of fighting Spain, the document claimed, all Spaniards capable of bearing arms were soldiers of the fatherland and had the right to be so considered by the French army, for this was a struggle of a whole nation against the yoke a foreigner was trying to impose on it. "Every member of this nation," the manifesto stated, "is consequently under the protection of the laws of war, and the general who does not respect them . . . is a bandit who arouses the wrath of heaven and the vengeance of men."[4]

In February, 1809, a survivor of the terrible sack of Uclés, which had taken place the previous month on the heels of the battle fought near that town, reported to the *Gaceta de Valencia* on the barbarities committed in the town by the victorious enemy troops.[5] The French were alleged to have gathered a number of regular and secular churchmen, loaded them with all the utensils they could lay their hands on, and made them climb to the top of the castle, where these utensils were burned in big bonfires. The bearers were then sent back to the town after having been beaten and stripped of their clothing. But worse was to follow. While the churches of Uclés were profaned, 69 persons, among them 12 clergymen and nuns, were murdered, and 300 women were raped.[6] The same month, the anonymous author of a chronicle dealing with events in Alcalá de Henares, wrote that in the town of Chinchón, some 23 miles south of Madrid, 100

3. "We were enraged by the part played in the war by the inhabitants, and we exacted vengeance according to the rules of war. Yet at heart we could feel only admiration for these men" (Holzing, *Unter Napoleon in Spanien*, p. 76).

4. Canga Argüelles, *Documentos* . . . , II, p. 107.

5. Uclés was not taken by assault. The French could therefore not argue that the sack was justified by the resistance of the town.

6. AHN, Estado, *legajo 46, carpeta* M, No. 308; Toreno, p. 162.

male inhabitants were executed after 2 or 3 French soldiers had been killed by the townspeople.[7]

In August, 1809, the Junta of Plasencia, after having escaped the advancing enemy, reported that the French were sending out foraging parties from Plasencia, stealing all the goods they encountered and devastating the countryside. Near the village of Serradilla eleven teamsters had been robbed and murdered, while a twelfth, left for dead, had somehow survived.[8] Plasencia itself was thoroughly sacked,[9] and thus joined the long list of towns reduced to shambles by the cruel war. Córdoba, Cuenca, Jaén, Bilbao, Coria, Lerma, Burgos, Salamanca. The roll of all the Spanish towns that were shattered by the invasion is a long one.[10] Let us single out a name not usually mentioned, that of Castro Urdiales, on the northern coast between Bilbao and Santander. Here, in May, 1813, a drunk *soldadesca* killed and raped in spite of efforts on the part of French officers to stop the atrocities. Townspeople were thrown out of their windows and were impaled on bayonets waiting for them in the streets. All women were raped without regard to age. The town was filled with corpses and everywhere naked women were fleeing from drunken soldiers.[11]

French officers often endeavored, as in Castro Urdiales, to prevent explosions of barbarism. Needless to say, they were too frequently unsuccessful, and in quite a number of instances they themselves contributed to make the war a butchery.[12] General Carrié, who was

7. "Libro de Apuntes de un Alcalaíno (1809–1814)," *Revue Hispanique*, xxxi (1914), p. 170.

8. Canga Argüelles, ii, p. 109.

9. Farias, *Memorias de soldados franceses durante la guerra de la independencia*, p. 195.

10. Let us note that Ciudad Rodrigo, Badajoz, and San Sebastián were also atrociously sacked, but by Wellington's men (see Chapter XVII).

11. *La Villa de Castro Urdiales en la Costa de Cantabria, saqueada, destruída y abrasada por los franceses el día 11 de mayo del año 1813*, pp. 4–6; Farias, p. 196.

12. Napoleon himself was not above committing acts of cruelty in Spain, as well as in other lands. The casual way in which he mentioned hanging insurgent Spaniards in a letter to Joseph is illuminating in this respect. On January 11, 1809, he wrote his brother from Valladolid: "Have a dozen individuals hanged in Madrid. There is no lack of rascals there. Without this nothing can be achieved (*Correspondance*, No. 14684). His cold-blooded

in command in the Old Castilian town of Palencia in early 1809, was one of these officers who thought that terror was a legitimate weapon. In a letter to Marshal Bessières dated February 3, 1809, he wrote that he had given orders to hang at Carrión half the Spanish prisoners taken in the north and to "keep the chiefs" for Palencia. "It would be indispensable," added the general, "to send immediately a hangman from Valladolid if the surplus should be executed here . . . ."[13] In a proclamation to the inhabitants of Palencia Carrié announced that a "band of brigands"[14] had murdered a number of Frenchmen and overpowered a convoy escorting British prisoners of war. At Galvana thirty-two of these guerrillas, including a captain, had been captured with their weapons. All had been hanged. The towns and villages of Paredes, San Ciprián, Carrión, and Galvana, which had received them on several occasions without warning French posts in the neighborhood, had been punished with a contribution of 20,000 francs and 200 oxen.[15]

One of the most cruel of French officers was General Dorsenne, in command of the Imperial Guard, with headquarters at Burgos. A man of great courage, who enjoyed the favor of Napoleon, he ruled Burgos with an iron fist. His ruthlessness made him one of the most feared and detested of all French generals in the Peninsula. Thiébault described him in his memoirs as "the man most indicated to create by himself more enemies for France than the entire Imperial Guard

---

reference to the deaths to be expected among Spanish prisoners of war in an order to the French war minister, dated March 6, 1809, is equally revealing: "Twelve thousand prisoners are arriving from Zaragoza. From 300 to 400 are dying every day. Thus it can be estimated that not more than six thousand will enter France. You will order a severe treatment for these men as well as measures to make them work . . . Most of them are fanatics who do not deserve any consideration (*Apud* Lecestre, "La Guerre de la Péninsule (1807–1813) d'après la correspondance inédite de Napoléon I°," *Revue des Questions Historiques*, Vol. LIX (1896), pp. 482–83).

13. Manuscript 1005 of Biblioteca Nacional, Madrid, *Registre de correspondance de M. le général Carrié sur la guerre d'Espagne, commencé le 31 janvier 1809 et fini le 24 avril de 1809.—Registre d'ordres au quartier général de Valladolid et à différents chefs militaires et d'une proclamation aux habitants de Palencia, 29 janvier 1809 à 22 avril 1809,* f. 8.

14. Read guerrillas.

15. *Ibid.,* f. 141.

could handle."[16] On a hill facing his house Dorsenne had had three huge gallows erected, from which there permanently hung the bodies of three alleged accomplices of guerrillas. Thébault recalled how one morning Dorsenne, on looking out of his window, saw only two corpses hanging from the sinister structures. Apparently the family of the third victim had taken down the body during the night to give him a decent burial. Instantly the general gave orders to choose a man from the Burgos jails and to make him take the place of the dead Spaniard who had disappeared. The order was carried out and Dorsenne had once more the satisfaction of seeing all three gallows fulfilling their function.[17]

Far from cowing the spirit of rebellion, measures like these only fanned the fire of resistance. Dorsenne's gallows were powerless against the guerrillas of the province, and the more Spaniards were hanged in Burgos, the more Frenchmen perished on the roads and in the woods. The rage of Dorsenne and his henchmen did not limit itself to hanging but spilled over into torture. One of the general's aides-de-camp was particularly apt at this grisly business. Spaniards arrested at his orders and whose answers did not satisfy him were tied by their thumbs, lifted from the ground and shaken until their arms were dislocated. "Old men and priests were thus exterminated. Those who survived were taken to the Burgos prisons, which was tantamount to a death sentence without a trial."[18]

These acts bring to mind Blayney's comment on the war in Spain: "Their wars, indeed, instead of being conducted on those principles of generosity, which the French in particular formerly prided themselves on, are wars of brigandage and extermination. That of Spain, in particular, presents a tissue of atrocities and wanton cruelties, that must render the name of a French soldier execrable to the latest posterity."[19]

Not all French *officiers*, however, were like the commander of the

16. *Mémoires du Général-Baron Thiébault*, 1792–1820 (ed. of 1962 by Lacour-Gayet), pp. 342–43.
17. *Ibid.*, pp. 344–45.
18. *Ibid.*, p. 344.
19. *Narrative of a Journey through Spain and France*, II, p. 96.

Imperial Guard and his ferocious aide-de-camp. General Hugo, father of France's great poet Victor Hugo, who for a while occupied the post of governor of the provinces of Avila, Segovia, and Soria, complained bitterly in a report drawn up in April, 1810, about excesses committed by the occupying *soldadesca*. "Some detachments of the 11th regiment of dragoons," he stated, " . . . treat the inhabitants like enemies, rob them and rape the women even in front of their husbands . . . If the troops do not abandon this system of laying everything waste, of spreading terror everywhere, they should give up the conquest of Spain."[20]

Like Hugo, there were many Frenchmen who, though devoted heart and soul to Napoleon, felt revulsion at the way the war was being conducted in the Peninsula. This feeling was reflected in many of the memoirs written after the war by soldiers of the occupying army. One such eyewitness, Fée, remembered how he had come across a column of Spanish prisoners taken at the battle of Ocaña.[21] "They were driven forward like a herd of cattle . . . They were treated harshly, and many among them, young and of a weak constitution, succumbed to fatigue. Those who could not walk were pitilessly shot down. 'It is the law of war' I was told. 'And the law of humanity?', I answered. These unfortunate men, who were escorted by Hanoverians, would have been treated with greater kindness by Frenchmen, though to tell the truth the war was already fought on both sides with a cruelty which the ferocity of the guerrillas soon brought to an extreme pitch."[22]

Fée should have added "as well as the ferocity of the invaders" if he had been able to divest himself of his basic prejudice. His hint that Frenchmen treated Spaniards better than soldiers of other nationalities serving in the Napoleonic army might seem at first a convenient device to place the blame of many atrocities on the shoulders of non-Frenchmen. Yet, though many acts of unspeakable cruelty were performed by Frenchmen, the testimony of eyewitnesses brings out the fact that in many instances Germans, Poles, Neapolitans, and other satellite troops, including renegade Spaniards, behaved worse

20. AHN, Estado, *legajo* 3003/2.
21. See Chapter VIII.
22. *Souvenirs de la guerre d'Espagne*, p. 26.

than French soldiers. Such an eyewitness was the Irish peer Lord Blayney, captured by the French in the course of an unsuccessful Allied raid on the Andalusian coast near Málaga in 1810.[23] This is what Blayney had to say on the subject: "I had indeed, many opportunities of observing, on our march, the superior liberality of the French officers and soldiers, to the Germans and Spaniards in the French service; both of the latter conducting themselves towards their prisoners with the most unmanly brutality, while the former treated the soldiers with humanity, and the officers with politeness and attention. Doubtless, these mercenary Germans and rebel Spaniards hope to recommend themselves to their French masters, by the ferocity of their behavior to their defenceless prisoners; no such effect, however, was produced, at least on the officers of our escort, who expressed a sovereign contempt both for the Germans and Spaniards, but more particularly for the former."[24]

Polish troops were among the finest fighting men ever to serve under Napoleon, but they were also among the most feared by the Spaniards, on account of their pitiless way of handling their enemies. Blayney reported that as he came across a dead Spaniard "with his brains knocked out, and covered with stabs," a Polish major observed: "The sentinel has done a fine job of killing him."[25] But it was the Germans who particularly attracted Blayney's attention with their heartlessness. Speaking of a German lieutenant in command of the Spanish town of Martos, Blayney wrote: "As we approached Martos this ruffian pointed out to me two poor wretches hanging on a tree, who had recently been executed by his order, observing with an infernal smile, 'that was the way to subdue Spain!' To which I could not help replying, 'that it would require a vast deal of rope and a great many hangmen to execute eleven millions of people, and that if one only remained, revenge would be his motto.' Clenching his fist, knitting his diabolical brows, and curling his bushy mustachios, he swore a terrible oath, that if it depended on him he would not leave one Spaniard in existence!"[26] If this amiable German officer had been

23. See Chapter IX.
24. *Narrative of a Forced Journey through Spain and France*, I, pp. 88–89.
25. *Ibid.*, pp. 166–67. In the original text: *La sentinelle l'a joliment tué.*
26. *Ibid.*, p. 143.

born 130 years later, his sanguinary nature would doubtless have had ample opportunity to express itself on a much larger scale.

To be entirely fair it should be underlined again that innumerable atrocities must be laid at the door of purely French soldiers and that orders too frequently issued by French commanders only added fuel to the raging fire of bestiality engulfing Spain. Speaking about a punitive expedition from the Andalusian town of Jaén to a village where some French soldiers had been murdered, Blayney noted that "it is a general order that the inhabitants of the place where such a crime is committed, are to be put to the sword, without exception of age or sex, and their habitations burned to the ground; nor is any enquiry ever made into the provocation that may have occasioned these excesses."[27]

Spaniards, too, dealt with their enemies in anything but a civilized manner, but at least Spain was the victim of an aggression and was fighting for a noble cause, its own independence and dignity. Still, accounts of Spanish treatment of French prisoners are often enough to make one's hair stand on end. An example of this is furnished by the account given by the German officer Holzing of the massacre which took place in the town of Arenas de San Pedro. This hamlet set in the Sierra de Gredos, about twenty-six miles northwest of Talavera de la Reina, was visited one day in February, 1809, by a detachment of twenty-five Westphalian dragoons sent there from Talavera by Marshal Victor in order to requisition food and wine for French headquarters. As the Germans sat down to eat they were overwhelmed by the infuriated population. One managed to escape. The others were taken up to a hill on which there stood a monastery. The men were about to line the prisoners up against a wall when a mob of enraged women broke through the cordon of their menfolk and threw themselves upon the prisoners with wild screams. The Germans were butchered in the most fiendish fashion. Arms and legs were broken, genitals were cut off, and hearts were ripped out.[28] A punitive expedition composed of two German and one Dutch regiment and some French dragoons, which set out from Talavera on February 24, exacted a terrible vengeance. A number of inhabitants

27. *Ibid.,* p. 146.
28. The story of the massacre was related to Holzing by a number of Spaniards later captured at Arenas.

of Arenas managed to escape into the mountains, but most of those who did not were given no quarter. Bullets and bayonets did their work with cold-blooded efficiency. "Sharpshooters," recalled Holzing, "amused themselves by running after the fleeing Spaniards and shooting them down like hares at a hunt. I have seen men burst out laughing when their victims fell into the grass."[29]

Needless to say, Arenas was sacked most thoroughly. Holzing has left us a vivid description of some of the scenes enacted in the town: "The marketplace seemed to have been converted into a carnival center. Some men had donned monks' attire, others ran around dressed in women's underwear, others still were making a hellish noise with some musical instruments. On the balcony of a house a drunk fellow was making a burlesque speech, while a comrade, facing him from another balcony and fully dressed as a priest, screamed some psalms at the mob, the text of which was anything but sacred."[30]

Unfortunately not all the doings were of a burlesque character. When a group of dragoons came upon three women, a mother with her two daughters, the mother was put to the sword and the daughters were raped and subsequently thrown into the flames of a burning house. In the marketplace other dragoons grabbed a woman carrying an infant. The latter's skull was crushed on the pavement, while the mother was raped. As she was finally released, she was immediately set upon by another band, but this time, insane with pain and grief, she was able to run into a burning house, which crashed down on her and became her fiery grave. Soon the flames engulfed the whole village and Arenas ceased to exist.[31]

One of the most terrible massacres occurred in the late spring of 1808 in the town of Manzanares, where Dupont's army had left a number of soldiers too ill to continue the march on Andalucía.[32] A member of Vedel's division, which was hurrying south in June to reinforce Dupont, passed through Manzanares and set down in his

29. *Unter Napoleon in Spanien*, p. 93.
30. *Ibid.*, p. 94.
31. *Ibid.*, pp. 95–96. Cf. another account of the sack of Arenas in Kircheisen, *Memoiren aus dem spanischen Freiheitskampfe, 1808–1811*, pp. 104–108. Arenas was, of course, rebuilt, and today it is a favorite summer vacation resort for many *madrileños*.
32. See Chapter V.

memoirs his impressions upon visiting the hospital of the town. As he entered the courtyard and the garden, he was thunderstruck by a most horrendous spectacle: There were about fifty corpses which had not yet been buried and which bore witness to the most frightful tortures. Some had been beaten to death, others had had their skulls split with axe blows. Others still had been plunged alive into cauldrons filled with boiling oil. For once, the French troops heeded the plea of the local authorities, who claimed that they had nothing to do with the killings and placed the blame on the shoulders of two peasant bands led by monks. No reprisals took place.[33]

Weeks later the same soldier witnessed some appalling scenes in the town of Jaén, which was attacked by troops of Vedel's division.[34] As French soldiers entered the town, one of their drummer boys, a child eight or nine years old, having gone forward too far while beating the charge, was caught by Spanish peasants. They were about to kill him when a Spanish officer appeared and ordered them to spare his life. Hardly had he left when the Spaniards grabbed the child again and pierced him with their bayonets. But the author of the memoirs did not hesitate to report a similar act of fiendish barbarism committed by a countryman of his: In a street of Jaén a Spanish woman, standing on the threshold of her house, pointed out to her five-year-old child a French soldier advancing at the head of a detachment. Making sure that no Spaniard saw her, she then quickly filled the apron of the child with victuals and told him to offer the food to the soldier. Whereupon the child ran toward the advancing Frenchman to fulfill his mother's wishes. The soldier stopped, took aim and fired. The child fell dead to the ground.[35]

The army of Dupont paid heavily, as we have seen earlier, for its acts during its short stay in Andalucía.[36] About 12,000 prisoners of Bailén wound up on the infamous pontoons in the bay of Cádiz, where 15 to 20 of them died every day of typhus. In the spring of 1809, under pressure from the population, who feared the spread of the epidemic, Spanish authorities began to take measures to rid the area of the prisoners. In May, more than 5,000 captives were shipped

33. *Mémoires d'un conscrit de 1808*, pp. 77–78.
34. See Chapter V.
35. *Ibid.*, pp. 88–90.
36. See Chapter V.

to the sinister Balearic isle of Cabrera, south of Mallorca. This number, augmented by most of the remaining men from the pontoons and other areas of free Spain, eventually rose to 16,000, of whom only about 1,000 officers and noncoms were lucky enough to be taken to England in 1810.[37] Those who remained went through hell to the bitter end, slowly starving to death, as food was brought from Mallorca only when the weather was good. At times the food situation was so bad that cases of cannibalism were reported. Finally, with the end of the war, the survivors were repatriated to Marseilles. Out of 16,000, 3,389 (not counting the 1,000 officers and noncoms) had returned.[38]

In other areas of free Spain, French prisoners often fared no better than in the bay of Cádiz or on Cabrera. In La Coruña, Galicia, for instance, thirty-three Frenchmen were arrested on July 31, 1808, and taken to a pontoon in the roadstead. Among them was an émigré priest who had sought refuge in Spain in 1792, a shoemaker, a baker, a watchmaker, a physician, a tailor, and two invalids who had served in the Spanish army for thirty-three and thirty-six years respectively.[39] All Frenchmen who had the bad luck of arriving in those troubled days at La Coruña on Spanish ships were also promptly transferred to the pontoon. Conditions on the hull were appalling, and a medical report of December, 1808, spoke of a "malignant fever" suffered by a number of prisoners.[40] Other French prisoners, held in a jail in La Coruña itself, were not much better off than their compatriots on the pontoon. The superintendent of the royal prison reported in September, 1808, to the Junta of Galicia that "I would be unfaithful to the most sacred duties of humanity if I failed to bring to the attention of Your Highness the situation of the unfortunate prisoners, who are forced to live without the privacy stipulated by the Laws of the Kingdom and without receiving any other ventilation than that of an air filled with noxious miasmas because of the large number of prisoners . . ."[41]

37. Husson, *Journal, Carnet de la Sabretache,* Deuxième Série (February, 1908), p. 170.
38. Lucas-Dubreton, *Napoléon devant l'Espagne,* pp. 480–85; Grandmaison, III, pp. 279–98.
39. AHN, Estado, *legajo 73, carpeta* C, No. 129.
40. *Ibid.,* No. 151.
41. *Ibid.,* No. 141.

The story of the prisoners, as in all conflicts, was a sad one. The starvation on Cabrera was a particularly black page in the history of the war. But many Spaniards also suffered and died from lack of nourishment. The years 1811 and 1812 were particularly bad—the progressive depopulation of the countryside, the constant movements of the warring armies and of the guerrillas, the poor harvests, and ceaseless requisitions brought about a terrible famine in many areas of Spain, notably Madrid and Sevilla. In the capital the poorer classes began to feel the pangs of hunger by September, 1811. By early 1812 people were dying in the streets by the hundreds. As an old man, Mesonero Romanos still shuddered in horror at the recollection of the terrible scenes he had witnessed as a child: " . . . this spectacle of despair and of anguish," he wrote in his memoirs, "the sight of an infinite number of human beings expiring in the middle of the streets and in the middle of the day; the lamentations of women and children at the side of the corpses of their fathers and brothers stretched out on the sidewalk, who were picked up twice a day by carts; that prolonged . . . and pitiful moan of agony coming from so many unfortunates, instilled in the few passers-by, equally starving, an unconquerable terror . . ."[42] Mesonero Romanos noted that French soldiers helped starving *madrileños* with alms. In some cases the latter proudly refused this aid, coming as it was from a hated enemy.[43]

The anonymous *alcalaíno*, on the other hand, in his own version of the situation in Madrid, underlined French unconcern for the starving. "I have seen many die . . . in the streets," he wrote, "while the French kept their stores full of wheat for their troops without thinking of alleviating this suffering."[44] This is, however, entirely compatible with what Mesonero Romanos indicated in his own memoirs. There were, no doubt, French soldiers who offered to help, and it is also known that King Joseph took a number of measures to remedy the situation.[45] But at the same time French authorities were determined to keep their soldiers fed. Thus the substantial aid that

42. *Memorias de un setentón*, p. 86.
43. *Ibid.*, p. 87.
44. *Op. cit.*, p. 191.
45. See Chapter XII.

could have flowed from their stores, which had been filled through endless requisitions, never reached the population in sufficient amounts to prevent the shameful scenes recorded by Mesonero Romanos and the *alcalaíno*. The pictures drawn by these two eyewitnesses of Madrid in the grip of starvation turns one's thoughts irresistibly to the plates of *Los desastres de la guerra* depicting scenes of the great famine. Goya in his own direct and stark manner conveyed to us the horror of those days as powerfully as did Mesonero Romanos and the *alcalaíno* with their pen. "From June 8th [1812] until the 26th," stated the *alcalaíno*, "during the time I spent in Madrid, I saw misfortunes and miseries which will be hard to believe for those who read about them. Thousands of persons lying on the streets and plazas, dying without finding anyone to help them or to give them a piece of bread to alleviate their suffering . . . Adults and old people from all walks of life, dropping dead . . . without finding aid. A large number of these had swollen legs, which pointed to a sure death, and a few days later . . . they died. In short, the unfortunates either die by the hundreds in the streets, like dogs, or are forced to leave Madrid . . . As a result this great capital is almost deserted, and within its walls there live only Frenchmen and *afrancesados,* thanks to the product of their robberies and to the lifeblood of the countryside, which they have completely ruined. In this first half year of 1812 more than 15,000 corpses, all victims of the famine, have been counted."[46]

Similar tragedies were taking place about the same time in other towns and villages of Spain. Commenting on the famine in Sevilla, Fée wrote: "We often saw unfortunate Spaniards, starving to death, receive the last rites on the steps of churches or on the pavement of the streets. Hardly would we start a meager meal, when our ears were struck by pitiful cries and words such as: 'I am dying; help me!' We saw men and women wandering through the streets, who seemed like living specters and whose sunken eyes looked at us with an expression that was at once an entreaty and a reproach."[47]

It was a terrible war, the most terrible French soldiers had ever

46. *Ibid.,* p. 210. The total number of the victims of the famine stood at about 20,000 (cf. Mesonero Romanos, *Memorias de un setentón,* p. 88).

47. *Op. cit.,* p. 134.

been called upon to fight, and they were well aware of it. A common saying among French troops in the Peninsula and one which appeared scribbled on many walls was: "Guerre d'Espagne . . . la mort du soldat, la ruine des officiers, la fortune des généraux (War in Spain . . . death for the soldier, ruin for officers, fortune for generals)."[48] Their awareness was also reflected in the memoirs they left and in the letters they sent to their relatives and friends in France. "They are fortunate to be able to leave this accursed Spain," wrote a French officer stationed in Chiclana to a friend in Sevilla, commenting on the departure for France of three officers of the same regiment. "I shall gladly seize the first opportunity I have of quitting this country."[49] "Dear mother," wrote a soldier from Andalucía to his mother in France on May 18, 1810, "I don't think that since the day I became a soldier I have ever been so badly off as now. For the past month and a half we have been in the mountains chasing brigands[50] . . . All these mountains have been pillaged in such a manner that there is not one soul that is not against us. We never find peasants in the villages here, so that we are the only inhabitants." Then follows a plea for some letters from home which would bring some comfort to those "deserts where one hears only about massacres."[51] "Dear brother and sister," we read in another one, "the war is still playing its game and we don't know when it will end . . . The peasants here are all brigands. Every day they murder some of our men. We burn their villages. But it is all in vain. They are incorrigible people."[52]

A soldier wrote to his father in May, 1810: "The unfortunate soldiers who are forced to remain in the rear are invariably butchered. It is absolutely impossible to move away from our camps or columns without running the same risks. As you see we are fighting in the most unpleasant country in the world." How different it was indeed in Spain, where death was everywhere, from Germany,

---

48. Parquin, *Souvenirs et campagnes d'un vieux soldat de l'Empire*, p. 241.
49. Intercepted and published in *La Centinela de la Patria*, July 17, 1810, AHN, Estado, *legajo* 3003/1.
50. Read "guerrillas."
51. AHN, Estado, *legajo* 3003/1.
52. *Ibid.*

where "we were at least safe everywhere, while here, from the youngest to the oldest, they are all our enemies."[53]

One of the most pathetic documents this writer has been able to find concerning the Spanish War of Independence is a letter in the Spanish National Archives, written in German, from Guebwiller in Alsace, France, and dated May 25, 1813. In it a young woman, writing a letter to her husband or sweetheart, a certain Monsieur Deck, whom she supposed to be at Toledo,[54] lamented the absence of letters from the man she loved. She had written him ten letters previous to this one and no answer had come back. "It is not enough that you have been torn away from me," she wrote, "but there are not even letters." To underline the depth of her feeling she had slipped into the envelope a lock of her brown hair wrapped in paper.[55] This lock, preserved for more than 150 years, gives the document a unique flavor. Here is a tiny but entirely real bit of the war that has come down to us; it gives us a chance to relive for a brief moment the anguish of a human being separated from her lover by distance and war. Was Monsieur Deck alive at the time the letter reached Spain? If he was, did he ever receive it, or was it lost in the general confusion of the last great French retreat? Does the hole in the envelope, which seems to have been made by a bullet, indicate that the missive fell into the hands of the guerrillas and that somebody involved in guarding the mail was killed? Or does it mean that Monsieur Deck actually received it but that it fell out of his pocket as he himself fell on the battlefield—perhaps Vitoria—struck down by a bullet? We shall never know the answer, but whatever its fate, it bears witness to one of the many personal tragedies brought about by the war.

[2]

In the midst of all the horror and bestiality that descended upon Spain there were some rays of light—not many, it is true, but enough nevertheless to sustain some faith in mankind. While the prisoners'

53. *Ibid.*
54. The address on the envelope is "General Delivery, Toledo."
55. AHN, Estado, *legajo* 3096.

lot was usually a harsh one on both sides of the fence, there were instances when generosity toward a foe reduced to helplessness took precedence over the much more common feeling of hatred and the thirst for vengeance. Those who benefited from such noble feelings were relatively few, but at least their experiences were welcome cases of civilization in what was otherwise a landscape of unrelieved barbarism.

The following story told by a French officer illustrates this occasional spark of humanity which saved some lives that would in the normal pattern of things have surely been sacrificed. A lieutenant, together with his servant, stopping at a *posada* on the road between Salamanca and Valladolid, was captured by a guerrilla band. The *partida* was led by an officer whose name the Frenchman recalled as being Aguillard, most probably a Frenchification of Spanish Aguilar. The French lieutenant, well aware of the fate that usually awaited Frenchmen who fell into guerrilla hands, threatened the Spaniards with the death of ten Spanish prisoners held in Salamanca if he and his servant were harmed. He must have been quite surprised when the guerrilla chieftain informed him that they would not be molested. The *guerrillero* then added: "*Hombre, demonio,* it is not the fate of our comrades in French hands which dictates our decision. They would know how to die, as all good Spaniards must, for God and Fatherland.[56] But if we were to kill you we would not deliver our country from its oppressors. We esteem your character and your resolution . . . Here are your weapons and let us be friends for a few minutes." They shook hands, the lieutenant and his servant shared the frugal meal of the guerrillas, and they parted on the most amicable terms.[57]

The lieutenant did not forget his captors' human behavior toward him, and from then on he did his best to treat Spanish prisoners decently. Once he freed a captured guerrilla after giving him an ounce of gold and a penciled note containing the following statement: "Officer Charles Parquin, of the 20th *Chasseurs,* who, taken

56. This unconcern for the fate of his countrymen who might be the objects of reprisals was probably genuine. Spanish guerrillas killed many French prisoners while perfectly aware that the French would wreak terrible vengeance on Spanish prisoners of war or Spanish civilians.

57. Parquin, pp. 263–64.

prisoner by lieutenant d'Aguillard (*sic*) and his guerrillas near Salamanca, owed his and his servant's life to their generosity, expresses to
them his gratitude on this August 10, 1811, in Extremadura, by
granting life and freedom to a Spaniard of the guerrilla band of *El
Médico*."[58] The Spaniard, who could not read, knelt in front of the
Frenchman, embraced his knees, and disappeared.[59]

Another officer who fought on the French side, Jean Michel
Rocca, recalled in his memoirs how, when lying wounded in a
Spanish home in Ronda, he was nursed by the owners of the house
and protected by them against a possible irruption of Andalusian
guerrillas into the town. While the *serranos* were attacking the
French garrison of Ronda and it was thought that the French might
succumb, this family prevailed upon two priests to place themselves
at the door of the house to defend it with their presence and thus
protect the life of the wounded Frenchman. Upstairs, the mother
remained with him and prayed, while the thunder of the battle
alternatively approached and receded into the distance. In the end
the attack was repulsed and Rocca was out of danger.[60]

We have seen that quite a number of clergymen fought in the
ranks of the Spanish regular and irregular armies. Some, especially
monks and friars, distinguished themselves by their ferocity against
French prisoners. But there were many others who gave friend and
foe an example of Christian charity and forgiveness. Lejeune, captured between Madrid and Toledo by El Médico's guerrillas, remembered that during his trek with the band a priest named Don Pablo
killed for the prisoner and his companions "the last fowl left to him
by the French." The next day, another priest, Don Mauricio, who
"was very well educated, and enjoyed a chat for once with civilised
people," insisted that Lejeune accept two or three of his shirts. For
the captive Frenchman this gift, coming as it was from a "naked man
on the crest of a mountain covered with snow," was more valuable
than "a lot of gold on a plain."[61]

As patriotic as their fellow religious were Spanish nuns, though

58. Juan Palarea (see Chapter XV).
59. Parquin, p. 274.
60. *Op. cit.*, p. 317.
61. *Memoirs of Baron Lejeune*, p. 96. The mountain referred to was
probably between Talavera de La Reina and the Sierra de Gredos, to which
El Médico's band first escorted their prisoners.

they could not express their feelings by taking up arms against the invaders. Yet their feelings did not preclude an occasional exercise of charity toward the enemies of their country. Of the nuns of Ronda Rocca wrote: "The nuns of the different convents of Ronda had doubled their prayers and penances from the time we had entered Andalusia. They passed the greater part of the nights in praying for the success of the Spanish cause, and during the day employed themselves in preparing medicines and comforts for wounded French."[62] These good nuns were probably under French orders to make bandages for wounded French soldiers. But there were ways of circumventing this type of orders. Apparently the nuns of Ronda placed the needs of helpless humanity on the same level as their patriotic duty.

During the French retreat in Andalucía in the summer of 1812, a group of marauding French soldiers entered a village which had been abandoned by its inhabitants at the approach of the enemy. The Frenchmen pillaged the houses and drank copious amounts of the wine they found in the cellars. All but one then rejoined their unit. The lone straggler woke up several hours later, surrounded by an enraged crowd of villagers who had returned upon ascertaining that the French had gone. The soldier was dragged to the village square. He was perfectly aware of what awaited him and asked for a confessor. The first reaction of the infuriated villagers was to refuse this request, but a peasant who found in the prisoner's pocket a small book illustrated with pious engravings convinced his friends that the Frenchman had as a Christian the right to die like one. A priest was called, and he began to listen to the soldier's confession. The latter, speaking in Spanish, begged the clergyman to save him. After all, did the thing he had done deserve death? He had been hungry and thirsty, and he had eaten and drunk. He had stolen nothing, as they had been able to ascertain upon searching him. Why punish him, he who was still so young and had a mother? The priest, profoundly moved, shook his hand and then turned around to speak to his parishioners: "He is a child of our church," he said, "a Christian like us. If you kill him you will never be able to go through this plaza

62. *Op. cit.*, p. 319.

without remembering that you have put a man to death here. You will not dare to amuse yourselves in this square any longer. You will always see before your eyes the pale face of this unfortunate. If on the other hand you spare his life, you will not cross it once without remembering your good deed. Your village will be all the more dear to us and God will reward you for having practiced the most difficult of all his precepts, the one which commands you to be kind even to your enemy." The words of the good priest were not lost on the villagers, and the laggard soldier was allowed to leave the village unharmed.[63]

Four years earlier, during the first French invasion of Andalucía, French General Chabert, before leaving Andújar for Córdoba,[64] had committed his wife and his sister-in-law as well as his most valuable possessions to the care of the alcalde of the town. The mayor gave him his word that he would guard to the best of his ability the persons and valuables left under his protection. After the French column had left Andújar, a band of insurgents appeared in the town in order to enlist in patriotic ranks all males capable of bearing arms. They immediately demanded that all French sick be delivered into their hands, doubtless with the aim of murdering them. The towns-people, however, refused to let them commit this outrage. Where-upon the irregulars asked for the two French ladies as well as for the valuables left behind by General Chabert. The alcalde resisted their demands and took refuge together with his charges in the town's jail. When the French army returned two weeks later the alcalde was able to deliver to Chabert the persons and the things entrusted to his care. "I have kept my word," he said, "I am placing in your hands the charge I had sworn to defend. I am leaving you in order to carry out the rest of my obligation. My countrymen have taken up arms for their independence. You can see them on those hills. That is where I belong. If I fall into your hands, remember what I have done for you." And the French narrator added: "Such was rather generally the Spanish character."[65]

Aside from the acts of generosity and charity which served to

63. Fée, pp. 161–62.
64. See Chapter V.
65. Chevillard, pp. 456–57.

humanize somewhat this terrible conflict, there were a number of instances of friendly coexistence. Much of this amicable contact took place naturally between Frenchmen and active or passive *afrancesados*.[66] Don Cayetano, a canon of the cathedral of Sevilla, was on very good terms with Blaze.[67] Another example was the wealthy host of Parquin, who took good care of this French officer when the latter lay wounded in his house situated in a village between Ciudad Rodrigo and Salamanca. This man, a passive collaborator with an attitude similar to that of the canon of Zamora,[68] one day opened his heart to his guest and told him: "Whatever ills the French have brought to Spain and whatever miseries they will bring us in the future, the harm they will have done us will never equal the benefit which will accrue to us from their action in destroying the Inquisition."[69]

But Frenchmen could occasionally, also, enjoy a more or less friendly coexistence with patriotic Spaniards who were the sworn enemies of Napoleon but into whose homes the power of the occupant had placed these unwelcome guests. Fée tells us about his experiences in a home in Chiclana, south of Cádiz, where he was billeted in 1810. His first contact was with the daughters of the household, both dressed as slovenly as possible in order to avoid any of the notorious "gallantries" for which the French army was famous. The two young ladies became quite frightened upon seeing the stranger enter the house, but as Fée spoke to them in a pleasant tone accompanied by much smiling they forgot their fears and became passably friendly. The older of the two sisters, María by name, "not exactly beautiful," except when she was singing songs calling the Spanish nation to arms, was an out-and-out patriot and hated the French. Somehow, however, she managed to get along with Monsieur Fée, especially since he was not a combatant but a medical officer, without at the same time ever losing an inch of her patriotism. The younger sister, Josepha, on the other hand, was a pretty girl who "did not know how to hate." Their mother, who "had a great

66. See Chapter XIII.
67. *Op. cit.*, p. 168.
68. See Chapter XIII.
69. Parquin, p. 261.

softness of manners," found that her guest resembled her son. Then there was the husband and father, Don Ambrosio Muñoz, who according to Fée "expressed his hatred of the foreigner with an energy and a frankness . . . which was completely new for me."[70]

Yet this did not prevent Don Ambrosio from organizing a little fiesta on the occasion of his lodger's birthday. A supper was served in the patio and the hosts as well as the guests were in fine spirits. Don Ambrosio presented the Frenchman with some Roman medals coined in the Gades (Cádiz) of antiquity, and a drawing representing the town of Chiclana. Even María, the older sister, was all smiles, forgetting for a few moments that Monsieur Fée was her enemy. After the meal the guests went up to the terrace and there, under the starry sky, María, at the request of her friends, sang one of the Spanish patriotic songs she was so fond of. It was a wonderful interlude in the war, but it was only that. It was one of those rare instants when friend and foe could soar above the hatred that was devouring the land. But the war went on and Fée was but rarely allowed to forget Spanish animosity. A Spaniard who had lost his sons in the war said to him one day: "Oh would that the strait of Gibraltar were filled with French blood and that I might drown in those bloody waves!" "He was grief-stricken," commented Fée, "I did not want to answer him."[71]

Friendly coexistence with the enemy, outside of the *afrancesados*, was normally a rather fleeting experience. Love, however, could be a fairly lasting feeling. Again we do not refer to the group of collaborators, among whom it was not uncommon for a girl to marry a French officer or a French employee of the French administration. Aside from these relationships there were instances of Spanish women who, though heart and soul on the patriotic side, did become romantically involved with soldiers or officers of the occupying army. One of the most interesting cases of this kind is described in the memoirs of Holzing, a German officer fighting in Napoleon's army. The account of the affair is spiced with many ultraromantic details and sounds somewhat implausible in spots. Yet there is no reason to believe that the whole thing was merely a figment of the

70. *Op. cit.*, pp. 67–69.
71. *Ibid.*, pp. 80, 89.

author's imagination, especially since all his other descriptions of the war in Spain seem truthful enough in the light of what we know.[72] According to Holzing his love was the daughter of a Spanish marquis whose son had been killed in Madrid on May 2, 1808, and who had refused to go to the Assembly of Notables in Bayonne. Her name was Rosa Vittoria[73] and she was a patriot, but she fell in love with this officer of the enemy army with a passion so characteristic of the daughters of Spain. At the same time she remained loyal in her heart to the cause of her country, and even tried, though unsuccessfully, to persuade her lover to desert to the Spanish side. A woman of contradictions, chaste at times, sensuous at others, she was according to the author a perennial "potential thunderstorm."[74] When Holzing was captured by the guerrillas of Francisquete in La Mancha, she somehow managed to follow him along the road taken by the guerrilla chieftain. In a *pueblo* on the way to Alicante—for it was to that eastern seaport that Holzing was being taken—as he was lying wounded on an ox-drawn cart with wooden wheels, which screeched its way through the town amidst the jeers of the populace, he saw Rosa on a balcony. With a quick gesture she threw her lover a shirt and a black overcoat in spite of the danger she ran by performing such a deed of charity for an enemy prisoner. Needless to say the people of the town did not approve of her act, but apparently she was known to be a completely trustworthy patriot, and no harm befell her.

And so, cared for by one of the guerrilla fighters, who had been given a generous sum of money by the Marquesa, Holzing arrived in Alicante after a harrowing eleven-day journey. His sweetheart appeared a few days later in the hospital to which he had been taken and saw to it that he was transferred from a pile of dirty straw to a whitewashed room with tiled flooring. After a few weeks in this hospital he was taken to another one. There Rosa came to him in

---

72. His account of the sack of Arenas, for instance, agrees with the description given of the same incident by Von Grolmann in Kircheisen's *Memoiren aus dem spanischen Freiheitskampfe, 1808–1811*, p. 108.

73. Holzing spelled it Vittoria. It is possible that this was her last name, although it is more probable that it was a misspelling of Rosa Victoria, a double Christian name.

74. *Unter Napoleon in Spanien*, pp. 219–29, 245–50, 266.

disguise and, the force of her patriotism somewhat weakened by her passion, pleaded with him to escape with her to Brazil. His wounds, however, prevented him from even giving the project a serious thought, for they became infected and kept him in bed with a high fever. As for Rosa, she had finally aroused the suspicion of the authorities through her relationship with the prisoner and was first placed under arrest and then exiled from Alicante.

Holzing, finally cured, was placed on a ship and taken to the Balearic Islands, first to Menorca and then to Mallorca. There he was sought out again by the Marquesa. Once more she asked him to go to Brazil with her. Holzing had strong feelings for Rosa, but he had left a sweetheart in Germany and he was not yet ready to set out on the adventure his Spanish lady friend suggested to him. From Mallorca the German officer was sent to the enchanting island of Ibiza, where he was joined for the last time by the Marquesa. He told her of his love for the German girl. Needless to say Rosa Victoria was deeply hurt. As they parted, however, Holzing realized that his passion for the Marquesa was stronger than his attachment to the girl back home. Alas, when he returned to Rosa's residence to ask her to marry him, he was informed that she was gone. He never saw her again. On June 1, 1814, he boarded an English ship to begin the long voyage home.

[3]

The town where circumstances forced coexistence with the enemy on the greatest number of Spaniards was, of course, Madrid. We have caught a glimpse of life in the capital of King Joseph Bonaparte through the eyes of a Spaniard, Mesonero Romanos, who in his old age remembered his childhood days in French-occupied Madrid. Let us now turn to a Frenchman who in his later years also recalled how as a nine-year old boy he had spent almost a year in Spain. This Frenchman was Victor Hugo, one of France's greatest poets and son of General Hugo, the relentless pursuer of Juan Martín El Empecinado. Young Victor set out for Madrid in the spring of 1811 in the company of his mother and his two brothers Abel and Eugène.[75] The family would finally have the satisfaction of seeing their husband and

75. Abel, the oldest, was eleven, and Eugène was ten.

father in the strange land where he was fighting to uphold the authority of the Emperor.

Madame Hugo and her three sons traveled in one of those immense convoys that were winding their way along the roads of Guipúzcoa and Castile. Their carriage was one of those huge old affairs "which appeared only in engravings" and which could carry large amounts of provisions of all sorts. Almost all the other vehicles in the convoy were more modern. They were all painted green, for green was the official color of the Empire, and the wheels were gilded, for gilt wheels were also one of the hallmarks of the *style empire*. A village along the road in the Basque region made an agreeable impression on Victor. Its name was Hernani and it had only one street, but this street was wide and beautiful. All the houses had sculptured coats-of-arms, most of them dating from the fifteenth century, which gave the hamlet a noble air. Later, when Victor Hugo wrote one of his famous Romantic dramas, he remembered the village in Guipúzcoa and gave the name Hernani to the play as well as to its hero.[76]

Guipúzcoa was pleasant enough, but then, close to the border of the province of Alava, came the pass of Arlabán, where a short while before Mina had performed one of his greatest feats. The mood of the convoy grew somber as the massacre of the other convoy was talked about in hushed tones. Further south, at the Pancorbo Gorge, there was real panic for a few minutes, when a group of men suddenly appeared on the heights overlooking the gloomy defile. But they turned out to be harmless muleteers, and the men who had hidden in their carriages trembling with fear, as well as the women who had covered their children with their bodies, could breathe easier. This time it had been a false alert.[77]

In Castile town after town, village after village had been reduced to heaps of ruins. But Victor and his brothers did not mind it, since they could play hide and seek all the better among the débris. Madame Hugo did not share their joy, for she did not relish having to spend the night practically in the open, but this is exactly what she was forced to do a few times, when the day's halt happened to be in a sacked town or village. Madame Hugo also bitterly complained

76. Hugo, *Victor Hugo, raconté par un témoin de sa vie.* I, pp. 137–47.
77. *Ibid.,* pp. 148–49.

about Spanish wine and olive oil, the former because it tasted of the *bota* (wineskin) in which it was kept, and the latter because of its rancid flavor. But what she most resented were the fleas and the bedbugs which seemed to take a sadistic pleasure in torturing her whenever there was a room in which she could spend the night.[78]

And what about the people they met along the way? "In the towns members of the convoy took up lodging with the inhabitants, when there were inhabitants," wrote Victor Hugo. But the reception accorded them was anything but cordial: "You stopped generally in front of a massive and strong house which looked like a fortress . . . You knocked, nobody [answered]). You knocked again, nothing. At the 10th blow of the knocker, and more often at the twentieth, a peep window opened and the face of a servant appeared, unsmiling lips pressed together, eyes icy." She then asked the travelers what they wanted, disappeared, reappeared, and opened the door. Inside, the atmosphere did not become warmer. "Even the furniture was hostile; the chairs received you badly and the walls told you: go away!" As for the hosts, they practically never saw them, for the Spaniards invariably retired with their children and their servants into the most removed part of the house. Only once did they see the owner of the house and his children. But then Madame Hugo made the mistake of asking him how much money he would accept for a silver vase which had caught her fancy. The answer came back haughty and icy like the wind of the sierras: His country was France's slave and he had behaved like a slave upon taking them into his home. But he was no merchant. Besides, he was surprised to see that Frenchmen showed such scruples in taking a pot when they showed so little in robbing whole towns.[79]

The Hugo family may not have seen many Spaniards on the way to Madrid, but needless to say there was no dearth of French soldiers. Some of these had been crippled in the war. As the soldiers of the escort laughed at the sight of some of the invalids, one of the latter quietly told them: "This is the way you will return," and another added: "If you return."[80]

78. *Ibid.,* pp. 156, 162–63.
79. *Ibid.,* pp. 158–62.
80. *Ibid.,* p. 164.

And then General Hugo's family arrived in Madrid. Their residence, where they awaited the return of the general, away on one of his many campaigns, was the sumptuous mansion of the Masserano family situated at the intersection of Calle del Alcalde and Calle de la Reina. While her sons shared a yellow room Madame Hugo installed herself in a blue room. She had entertained the hope that once in Madrid she would escape the ubiquitous fleas and bedbugs. But to her horror she discovered that the beds of the Masserano palace were the habitat of countless insects of the same breed. The unfortunate Frenchwoman then had recourse to a portable iron bed, the four posts of which were each placed in a pail of water. But alas, the fleas jumped up onto her from the floor, and the bedbugs fell upon her from the ceiling. Madame Hugo ran from her enemies into the servant quarters, but there, too, she was pitilessly devoured by the voracious bugs. She finally bowed to the inevitable and became accustomed to sleeping under these uncomfortable conditions.[81]

For the Hugo children life was at first full of games. At the beginning they played in the courtyard of the mansion, where a fountain attracted their attention for a while. But soon the sadness exuded by this yard, enclosed in its four walls, with its moldy pavement, drove them into the gallery of portraits, which became their favorite playground. It was made to order for games of hide-and-seek, with its pedestals, busts, and vases, and Victor Hugo became extremely fond of it. One could often find him sitting alone in some corner of the gallery, "looking silently at all those personages, in whom relived the dead centuries. The arrogance of the postures, the sumptuousness of the frames, the art mingled with pride of family and nationality, all this stirred the imagination of the future author of Hernani and deposited in it the germ of the scene of Don Ruy Gomes."[82]

Six weeks after their arrival in Madrid, General Hugo returned. But the children were not allowed to spend much time with their father. Abel was almost twelve and was being groomed for the Corps of Royal Pages.[83] The two younger boys, on the other hand, would

81. *Ibid.*, pp. 176–81.
82. *Ibid.*, pp. 185–86.
83. Abel Hugo left memoirs in which he described his experiences at the court of Joseph Bonaparte.

attend school. One day Madame Hugo had a carriage hitched up and after a short ride the vehicle stopped in front of a massive gate on Calle de Hortaleza. It was the school of San Antonio Abad. This secondary-level institution under the auspices of the Piarists or Escolapios, a religious order devoted to teaching, was to be the new home of Victor and Eugène.[84] Their first impression of the school, attended at the time by only twenty-four young scholars, was rather grim. Following their mother and a solemn-looking gentleman, the major-domo, they passed through interminable hallways with whitewashed walls where not a living soul seemed to reside. Finally they came out into a courtyard, where a door was opened by a cleric, dressed in a black robe and wearing a broad-brimmed hat. He was thin and pale and his sunken eyes betrayed no emotion whatsoever. The name of this man, who seemed more like an ivory statue than a human being, was Don Basilio. He would be one of their teachers and guardians. The other, whom they met later, was fat and jovial and his name was Don Manuel. Yet in spite of this joviality they soon found out that he was a hypocrite, who affected great friendliness in the presence of his students but later tattled on them to Don Basilio. The latter, on the other hand, eventually gained Victor's and Eugène's respect, for though severe he was honest and dependable.[85]

When Madame Hugo left her two boys at the school, they cried. But they soon became used to the rather Spartan regimen. The day began at 5:00 A.M., when a poor hunchbacked servant rapped three blows on each of the ten beds in the dormitory occupied by Victor and Eugène and the boys of their age group. Corcova (Hump) was the name the children gave the pathetic figure, and Victor later remembered him when he drew with masterful pen the picture of Quasimodo in *Notre Dame de Paris*. After Mass[86] came breakfast,

84. According to Victor Hugo the building was the Seminario de Nobles, which, before the war, had housed about 100 students (see Chapter II, p. 65). Recent research has proved, however, that the Seminario de Nobles was closed during Victor Hugo's stay in Madrid and that the institution was actually the school of San Antonio Abad (Simón Díaz, *Historia del Colegio Imperial de Madrid*, II, p. 219). The Piarists, in view of their special character, had apparently been allowed by Joseph's government to continue operating their school.

85. Hugo, *op. cit.*, pp. 189–92, 205–206.

86. The French boys were excused from serving Mass and were only required to hear it, as Madame Hugo had stated, falsely, that her sons were Protestant

which consisted of a cup of hot chocolate. The midday meal following the morning classes was more substantial and comprised two
dishes, one of them invariably the national *olla podrida*, a highly
seasoned combination of meat and vegetables cooked in a wide-
mouthed pot. The daily siesta, terminating at 3:00 P.M., would be
followed by a two-hour class period. Then there was an hour of
recreation to the munching of a piece of dry bread, and more
studying until 8:00. Supper consisted usually of a salad.[87]

These meals became more frugal as the food crisis of 1811–1812
deepened. In the winter the pupils, too, felt the pangs of hunger.
When they complained about the ridiculously small rations they
were receiving, Don Manuel made the sign of the cross on his fat
stomach and told them to do the same, for this would keep them fed.
He himself was becoming stouter and stouter, yet he did not con-
sume more food than his pupils, and the latter suspected him of eating
extra rations in his room.[88]

Madame Hugo brought Victor and Eugène extra food regularly,
but they were not able to enjoy it fully because they were forced to
share it with their companions. This, of course, gained them friends,
and it was just as well, for the majority of the boys in the school did
not hide their antipathy for the French regime and proclaimed
openly their wish to see Joseph ejected from Spain. Often heated
political arguments echoed forth in the age-old halls. Victor and
Eugène would ask by what right Fernando claimed a crown he had
given up by treaty, and the Spaniards would reply that the cession of
the crown had been obtained by sheer ruse. On one occasion words
gave way to action. It happened when an older student, Count
Belverana, took violent offense as Eugène poked fun at a seventeen-
year-old boy by the name of Lino, who had been taken prisoner at
Badajoz and had been confined to the school in view of his age.
Belverana, enraged by Eugène's attitude, grabbed a pair of scissors,

in order to spare them as much as possible participation in religious services.
They were also excused from confession and from taking communion. This
tolerance was of course due to the fact that Madrid was then French-occupied
and that the school needed every student it could possibly receive.

87. *Ibid.*, pp. 191–97.
88. *Ibid.*, p. 205.

rushed at the French boy, and struck out at him, inflicting a fairly deep gash in his cheek.[89]

Don Basilio, who, according to Victor Hugo, probably sympathized at heart with the Spanish boy, announced his decision to expel him from the school. But Eugène nobly came to the defense of his adversary and declared that he, too, would leave if Belverana was expelled. As Don Basilio seemed to be adamant, Eugène asked his mother to intervene, and she finally prevailed upon the priest to let the young offender stay. Victor harbored a deeper resentment against the Spanish boy and "avenged his brother in his own way by making one of the least attractive characters of his dramas [Gubetta of *Lucrèce Borgia*] a Count Belverana." Another butt of his literary scorn was a tall, ugly lad, with "kinky hair, hands like claws, uncombed, unwashed, lazy . . . and ridiculous." He became the Elespuru of *Cromwell.*[90]

But with most of the students the two brothers maintained fairly amicable relations. Victor remembered particularly the four brothers Benavente, the oldest of whom, Ramón, became his good friend. The four Spanish boys had not seen their mother for a whole year. One day, during a meal, the door of the immense dining hall opened and a woman of haughty aspect, wearing a dress of black satin, entered into the refectory. Ramón and his brothers rose and went toward her. She extended her hand to Ramón, who kissed it, and then to the other three boys by order of age, who did the same.[91]

On Thursdays and Sundays, Don Manuel and Don Basilio took the boys for a promenade in town or in the countryside. Thus "the Hugo children saw the outskirts of Madrid, which no Frenchman dared to visit. Excursions were dangerous, and recently a Frenchman who had gone a few hundred paces too far had been taken prisoner. But the [clergymen] did not have to worry about the guerrillas, [for the latter] knew their opinions."[92] Nor were the French boys in any danger, for if Don Basilio and Don Manuel had handed them over to one of the irregular bands roaming the outskirts of the capital, they

89. *Ibid.*, pp. 198–99, 206.
90. *Ibid.*, pp. 199–200.
91. *Ibid.*, p. 206.
92. *Ibid.*, p. 202.

themselves could hardly have returned to Madrid. And even if they had managed to clear themselves of any suspicion of complicity they would have lost two valuable boarders. In view of the small number of pupils studying at the school, this would have been a hard blow economically.[93]

Actually the two French boys were not to contribute to the upkeep of the school for as long a period of time as Don Basilio and Don Manuel would have liked. In early 1812, Madame Hugo had had enough of life in Madrid and packed her bags. Victor and Eugène accompanied their mother once more on a long and uncomfortable journey. Again it was a story of convoys, of sullen hostility, of fear. The most gruesome sight of their year in Spain, a sight which should have been recorded in Goya's *Desastres*, awaited them at the entrance of the town of Vitoria, capital of the Basque province of Alava. On a cross the authorities had nailed the limbs of a young guerrilla who had been cut into pieces. "They had taken . . . care to fashion a corpse out of these bits of flesh,"[94] wrote Victor, in whose mind this spectacle left an indelible imprint.

And thus Victor Hugo parted with the Spain of the War of Independence. He had spent less than a year in the capital of this strange and hostile country, but this short span of time was sufficient for Spain to make a lasting impression on him. These childhood impressions instilled an interest in and a love for the land south of the Pyrenees, which eventually found a most wonderful expression in his poetry and his dramas. In his writings Victor Hugo brought Spain to France, though it was a Spain distorted by the Romantic penchant for the flamboyant and the exotic. But the real Spain, the wartime Spain of 1811–1812, in which he himself had lived, had remained very clearly in his memory. His account of this episode in his life, published fifty years later, constitutes vivid proof of this.

93. *Ibid.*
94. *Ibid.*, p. 210.

XVII

ALBION IN SPAIN

[1]

It is time now to cast a glance at the third party involved in the extraordinary conflict in the Peninsula, England. South of the Pyrenees Napoleon was fighting against two powerful foes, the aroused Spanish people, represented throughout much of the war mainly by the indefatigable guerrillas, and the army of Wellington, made up of British, Portuguese, and later in the war, Spanish contingents, behind which stood Great Britain itself. Before 1808 Albion had for centuries been Spain's enemy, preying on her shipping and gnawing at the vulnerable spots in her colonial empire. To the Spanish mind the most galling reminder of British power was the rock of Gibraltar, which had been in the hands of England since 1704.[1] This, added to the wars waged since then against Britain at the side of France, the losses incurred in these conflicts, the disaster of Trafalgar in 1805 when Nelson had destroyed the combined Franco-Spanish fleet, and Great Britain's two lunges at Buenos Aires in 1806 and 1807,[2] had caused Spaniards to look upon England as the hereditary enemy.

Then the Napoleonic invasion of the Peninsula and the rising of Spain and Portugal burst upon Europe, and there was bound to be a

1. During the War of the Spanish Succession, 1701–1714, the British, backing the Archduke of Austria's claim to the Spanish throne with their armed might, seized the rock with the understanding it was to be handed to the Archduke when he became King of Spain. But when he was ultimately defeated and Philip V triumphed, England kept Gibraltar and resisted all Spanish attempts to recover it.

2. See Chapter II.

change. It was a unique opportunity for England, fighting for her life against Napoleon. Here at last was Great Britain's chance to acquire two new fighting allies on the continent, fronting on the Atlantic Ocean within easy reach of British naval power. Here was a chance to gain a firmer foothold on the mainland[3] and to break Napoleon's Continental blockade. His Majesty's Government did not pass up the opportunity. When the Asturian delegates arrived in London in June 1808,[4] there was no end to the expressions of friendship and admiration which official circles and the population showered on the visiting Spaniards. The enemy of yesterday became suddenly transformed into the heroic ally of the hour, an ally on whom the fondest hopes were pinned. On June 15 the Spanish patriots were promised all possible aid by Great Britain, and soon the first help was on the way in the form of equipment and money. Shortly troops sailed for the Peninsula. Arthur Wellesley, who had been chosen to lead an expedition against Spanish-held Venezuela and was awaiting final orders at Cork, Ireland, with 9,500 men, was instead dispatched to Portugal, where he arrived at the end of July.

A decisive foothold was thus gained on the European continent, and this foothold became eventually a Peninsular front, disturbing Napoleon's dreams of world domination. Spain was now allied to the French emperor's sworn enemy and the greatest maritime power in the world. The alliance was formalized in early 1809—it had been a fact for seven months—and in the end this coalition weighed heavily in the French Empire's final demise.

Few persons on either side of the Bay of Biscay could have foreseen in June, 1808, all the disappointments that were bound to arise within the newly-formed Anglo-Spanish alliance. At the beginning there was much enthusiasm. Patriotic Spaniards expected to see England swamp Spain with money and arms, thus allowing her to equip hundreds of thousands of her men and sweep the invaders out of the Peninsula. Men, they felt, were not needed, for there were enough men in Spain capable of shouldering weapons. But Spain's

3. There were British forces in Sicily and off the Swedish coast, but these troops could have no decisive effect on the course of events in Europe.
4. See Chapter IV.

confidence in her manpower, partly due to national pride, was not the only reason which caused Spanish authorities to look askance at any British offer to land men on Spanish territory. Though Spaniards were ready to welcome British aid with open arms, the memories of Gibraltar lingered on. Once British troops were allowed to disembark, say at Cádiz or La Coruña, they might just possibly decide to stay. Besides, it was not easy to accept the presence of troops who only the year before had attacked Spanish Buenos Aires. Neither the Junta of Sevilla nor the juntas of Galicia and Asturias were interested in seeing British soldiers land on their shores. Thus, thousands of British soldiers from Gibraltar, who could easily have disembarked in July, 1808 at Cádiz, were instead sent to Portugal[5] because of the reluctance of Spanish authorities to allow their allies to establish themselves in this vital position.[6]

But this did not mean that insurgent Spaniards were not ready to lionize those British representatives and agents who were sent to Spain in the early days of the war. Sir Arthur Wellesley, the future Lord Wellington, who landed at La Coruña on July 20, was given a most hearty welcome in the Galician port. He was impressed by the resolve of the population to win the war. The following day he wrote to Viscount Castlereagh, Secretary of War: "It is impossible to convey to you an idea of the sentiment which prevails here in favour

5. See Chapter VII.
6. Toreno, pp. 119–120; Villa-Urrutia, *Relaciones entre España y Inglaterra durante la guerra de la independencia. Apuntes para la historia diplomática de España de 1808 a 1814*, I, pp. 186, 328; Oman, II, p. 223; Bryant, *Years of Victory. 1802–1812*, p. 240. Wellington claimed in 1820 that he had offered to the Junta of Galicia on July 20, 1808, to disembark troops and that the Junta had refused his soldiers. Azcárate (*Wellington y España*, pp. 231–32) points to the fact that one of Wellington's two dispatches of July 21 to Castlereagh did not mention the offer, merely stating that the Junta had "not expressed any anxiety to receive the assistance of British troops" (*The Dispatches of Field Marshal, the Duke of Wellington, during his Various Campaigns in India, Denmark, Portugal, the Low Countries, and France, from 1799–1815*, compiled by Lieutenant-Colonel Gurwood, IV, p. 27) and that Wellington's instructions specifically stipulated that his mission was above all to free Portugal of the French (*ibid.*, pp. 8–10). Furthermore, in one of these dispatches Wellington wrote that the Junta of Galicia was ready to let British troops land at Vigo, farther south, if necessary (*ibid.*, p. 24).

of the Spanish cause . . . I understand that there is actually no French party in the country; and at all events I am convinced that no man now dares to show that he is a friend to the French."[7]

The British decision to free all Spanish prisoners taken during the late war and the arrival of British money and supplies caused British emissaries to be received all the more enthusiastically by their allies. The same day that Wellesley landed at La Coruña also saw the arrival of Charles Stuart, a British commissioner who brought 1 million duros for the Junta of Galicia.[8] The Spaniards thus saw complete evidence of British willingness to help and were immensely grateful. Other British agents who made their appearance in Spain in the summer of 1808 and were received with the most sincere expressions of welcome were Sir Thomas Dyer, Major Roche, and Captain Patrick, who arrived in Asturias on June 27,[9] and Sir Charles Stuart's secretary, Sir Charles Vaughan, who landed at La Coruña in early August,[10]

Stuart, termed by a British historian "one of the greatest British diplomatists of the early nineteenth century,"[11] landed in Spain with instructions from His Majesty's Government to keep British authorities informed of events in Spain, to serve as liaison man between the English government and the Spanish juntas, and to persuade the

7. *The Dispatches of Field Marshal, the Duke of Wellington,* IV, p. 26; Bryant, *Years of Victory, 1802–1812,* p. 239.

8. Stuart and Wellesley arrived on two different frigates (Villa-Urrutia, I, p. 185).

9. *Ibid.,* p. 146.

10. Vaughan, born in 1774, had studied at Oxford and had traveled widely throughout Europe and Asia. In Spain he accompanied Stuart to Madrid and Aranjuez, whence he went to Zaragoza in the company of Lieutenant Colonel Doyle (see Chapter VI). Leaving Doyle shortly before the battle of Tudela, he was the first to bring news of the disaster to Madrid and then to General Moore in Salamanca. After having covered in Spain 790 miles on horseback, he embarked at La Coruña with dispatches for Lord Castlereagh. He later joined Ambassador Henry Wellesley as secretary of the British Embassy in Spain. In 1820 he served under Sir Charles Stuart at the embassy in Paris, in 1823 he was appointed ambassador to Switzerland, and in 1825 to the United States. He died in 1845. Vaughan is the author of a narrative of the siege of Zaragoza and of a diary of his experiences in Spain. The latter, a part of his important private archives, is kept in Oxford's All Soul's College (Azcárate, "Memoria sobre los 'Vaughan Papers.' " BRAH, Vol. CXLI, October–December, 1957, pp. 723–26).

11. Petrie, *Great Britain and the War of Independence,* p. 9.

juntas to form a central government. At the end of August, Stuart attended the meeting in Lugo, Galicia, of the delegates of Galicia, León, and Castile, at which it was decided that each junta would appoint two deputies for the Central Junta, soon to gather at Aranjuez. The importance which Spaniards then attached to British collaboration was eloquently demonstrated when the president of the Lugo assembly asked Stuart to take part in the discussions. The British representative acceded to the request and thus set a precedent for the pattern that took shape during the war, when British envoys to successive Spanish governments played an active role in Spanish domestic politics, not always with the approval of Spanish authorities. It was necessary, Stuart argued, that a central government be established, which would convoke the Cortes and thus put an end to the revolutionary character of the national uprising.[12]

One of the most popular British agents—and not all British commissioners were popular in Spain—[13] was Thomas Dyer, who earned the sympathy and respect of the Asturians. Upon being awarded by the Spanish authorities the rank of lieutenant general he solemnly declared: "Worthy Asturians, my gratitude shall be eternal. The name of Asturias is engraved in my heart."[14] The main task of these British commissioners was, of course, to see to it that money and military equipment reached the Spaniards in ample quantities. It has been estimated that between June and the end of the year Great Britain sent the Spanish insurgents 200,000 muskets and more than 7 million duros, aside from much ammunition and clothing.[15]

The enthusiasm of the first hour necessarily lost some of its fire as the weeks and months dragged on and as the Allied cause fared badly. Spanish politicians were often annoyed at English criticism of the manner in which patriotic Spain conducted the war and at what seemed to them unwarranted British interference in Spanish internal affairs, England was quick to accuse her partner of not doing all its share in the common undertaking, and Spain resented British withdrawals from Spain. The suffering caused to the Spanish population

12. Villa-Urrutia, I, p. 193; Petrie, p. 10.
13. Especially unpopular was British Consul John Hunter, accredited to the Junta of Asturias (Villa-Urrutia, I, p. 149).
14. *Ibid.*, p. 147.
15. *Ibid.*, pp. 260–61; Petrie, p. 10.

on several occasions by misbehaving British troops also left their mark. It is difficult to gauge the influence the religious factor may have had, but in the more difficult moments of the alliance quite a few Spaniards no doubt turned their thoughts to the fact that many of the English soldiers were after all "heretics," and vice versa, Britons tended to look with suspicion at the "popishness" of their allies. But in spite of all the factors working against it, the alliance held firm and the mass of the Spanish people were able to keep within reasonable limits whatever aversion they felt toward their allies. And there were moments when the flame of friendship burned bright in Spanish hearts. In July, 1809, as the Honorable Frederick North, member of the House of Commons, passed through Valencia, the junta of the city expressed to him the gratitude of the inhabitants for the "nobility" with which the English had spilled their own blood on Spanish soil, prophesied that this conduct would render Anglo-Spanish friendship eternal, and pledged that the Valencians would teach their children to respect a nation whose men were sacrificing themselves to insure their independence.[16] The following year, Lord Blayney, captured during a poorly executed raid on the French-held Andalusian coast near Málaga and taken north by the French as a prisoner, was impressed with the generosity of the inhabitants of French-occupied Madrid toward British prisoners of war. He recalled "women of respectability conveying victuals and clothes" to him and his fellow countrymen.[17] In 1813, when the war was drawing to an end, the author of *Napoleón o el verdadero Don Quixote*, after noting the many unfriendly acts committed in the course of history by Great Britain against Spain, and observing that these could not easily be forgotten, appealed nevertheless for an ever closer alliance between the two nations, since only thus could both survive.[18]

As for the mass of the English people, whose contact with their Spanish allies was channelled almost exclusively through the experiences of their generals and their soldiers in the Peninsula, their early enthusiasm soon changed to disappointment. The high hopes pinned

16. Canga Argüelles, *Observaciones a la historia de la guerra de España que escribieron los señores Clarke, Southey, Londonderry y Napier*, I, pp. 16–17.
17. *Narrative of a Journey through Spain and France*, I, p. 267.
18. *Op. cit.*, VIII, pp. 7–8, 47 ff., 53.

in June, 1808, on the Anglo-Spanish alliance were not fulfilled. At
first, "Tories saw romantic visions of grave nobles and venerable
prelates mustering their tenants around the standards of national
independence; the Whigs of high-minded Spanish revolutionaries
succeeding where the French had failed and establishing an enlightened constitutional monarchy based on English precedent."[19] But by
early 1809, after the harrowing British retreat through Galicia,[20]
Britons held Spaniards partly to blame for the disaster. "The romantic dreams of Spanish valour and patriotism vanished in a night,"
writes Arthur Bryant. "The returned soldiers presented the Spaniards as heartless curmudgeons who had barred their doors and hidden their food and wine; as cravens who had fled from the battlefield,
leaving their would-be liberators surrounded. Nobody had a good
word to say for them or their beggarly country."[21]

It was a one-sided and an unfair story. British depredations during
the withdrawal to the sea, if mentioned by British soldiers, were
certainly not given the same prominence as alleged Spanish defects.
Moreover, the great sacrifices made by Spain during the summer of
1808 and the victories of Bailén, Valencia, and Zaragoza were simply
forgotten. Unfortunately subsequent events in the Peninsula, especially the Talavera Campaign,[22] as well as the revolt of the Spanish
American colonies, tended to accentuate the critical attitude with
which Spain and Spanish affairs were viewed from London. By the
end of the war and at the time of the Congress of Vienna,[23] with all
eyes focused on Napoleon's abdication, on the change of regime in
France, and on the European situation resulting from Bonaparte's

19. Bryant, p. 228.
20. See Chapter VII.
21. *Op. cit.*, pp. 295–96. Camden wrote in 1813: "In the summer and autumn
of 1808, it was almost the general wish of Great Britain to afford the people of
Spain every assistance in their power. The British cabinet was excited to lend
them all the aid in men and money that their situation and circumstances could
require. The experiment was tried, and the fate of Sir John Moore and his
brave army abundantly prove (*sic*) that the generality of the Spanish people
did not covet the interference of England to save them from what appeared
to us their much dreaded ruin" (*The History of the Present War in Spain and
Portugal from its Commencement to the Battle of Vittoria*, p. 220).
22. See Chapter VIII and below.
23. 1814–1815.

downfall, British interest shifted from the Peninsula to France and central Europe, and the erstwhile ally attracted British attention only through the continuing revolution in Spanish America. Spain, already held in relatively low esteem in England, sank even lower in British eyes. But for this the unspeakable Fernando VII must bear part of the blame, as we shall later see.[24]

In October, 1808, when no friction marred Anglo-Spanish harmony and when hopes were running high on both sides of the Bay of Biscay, His Majesty's Government appointed the Right Honorable John Hookham Frere to represent it as minister to the newly formed Junta Central. The choice was not a very fortunate one and was apparently due more to Frere's long-standing friendship with Foreign Secretary Canning than to the new envoy's statesmanlike qualities. Frere was, like so many of his prominent contemporaries, a diplomatist who prided himself on being also a man of letters. He had met Canning when both had studied at Eton, and had later continued his studies at Cambridge. A man with a profound feeling for literature, he was an ardent admirer of the classics of antiquity. During his sojourn in Madrid in 1802–1804 as head of the British legation he acquired a fine knowledge of the Spanish language and its literature and made many Spanish friends, including the Marquis de La Romana. According to Lord Holland he was a "man of a warm and generous disposition, of singular and original wit, and of great literary accomplishments, who was zealous in the cause of Spain."[25] Though he had had experience in public business as undersecretary for foreign affairs in 1799–1800 and as minister to Lisbon and Madrid, and though he knew Spain and the Spanish language well, it was, as we have stated above, not so much these factors as his friendship with Canning which pushed him into such a prominent position in 1808, at the age of thirty-nine. His mission was not to be a very successful one, on the whole. Lord Holland described him as a "bad man of business . . . He had no knowledge of men's characters, and even when he adopted their ideas and approved of their conduct, was

24. See below, and Chapter XVIII.
25. *Further Memoirs of the Whig Party, 1807–1821, with Some Miscellaneous Reminiscences,* p. 19.

neither communicative nor cordial in his official intercourse with them."[26]

But even a man with infinitely more diplomatic talent might very well have floundered in the difficult days that lay ahead. Napoleon was about to unleash his great offensive, which would carry him straight into Madrid, and the British troops which under the overall command of Sir John Moore were marching through Portugal toward the Spanish border[27] and moving southeast from La Coruña[28] would soon find themselves in grave danger. Frere saw how anxious the Spanish government of national resistance was for immediate aid from Moore's army and found himself in a difficult position. He ardently desired to see the Junta Central receive prompt help from its allies. But in his laudable endeavor to enlist all possible British support for the hard-pressed Spaniards the British envoy went too far. He urged Moore, then at Salamanca, to advance on New Castile at all costs in order to relieve the pressure on Madrid. But in this, Frere was far too willing to share the point of view of the more sanguine Spanish patriots who, filled with illusions even in the bleak period between the end of November and the first days of December, still saw a chance to defeat Napoleon. If Moore had followed his advice and had rushed to the aid of the capital, the British army would have been annihilated in central Spain by Napoleon's overwhelming superiority in numbers. Fortunately for Moore's army, it remained in the north, and though almost caught by Napoleon's speedy maneuver, it was able to escape—after a terrible retreat—through La Coruña.[29]

Later, in Sevilla, Frere continued to demonstrate his weakness as a diplomat. In early 1809, British transports were sent to Cádiz on the initiative of General Cradock in Lisbon, who, fearful that a rapid French advance southward would follow the collapse of the Spanish

26. *Ibid.*, p. 20.

27. See Chapter VII.

28. British troop transports bringing 12,000 men under General Baird appeared off La Coruña on October 13, but the suspicious Spaniards agreed to let them disembark only after the Supreme Junta in Madrid had been consulted. Thus, the total British force was ashore only on November 4 (Bryant, pp. 261–62).

29. Toreno, p. 154; Oman, I, pp. 506, 519–20; Maxwell, *Life of the Duke of Wellington*, I, pp. 423–24; Bryant, pp. 267–70. See Chapter VII.

armies in central Spain, hoped to be able to garrison with British troops the vital fortress of Cádiz. Frere, though well aware of Spanish touchiness on this point, rather undiplomatically tried to persuade the Central Junta to admit a few English battalions into the Atlantic port. The Spaniards refused and the British ships were forced to return to Portugal.[30] In July, the envoy was replaced by Marquess Wellesley, brother of the general. In spite of the suspicions he had aroused by his unwise stand on the question of British troops for Cádiz, the Central Junta was to a certain extent sorry to see Frere leave. It knew that this man, though no statesman, was a great friend of their country and had shown this when he had urged General Moore to think only of help to fighting Spain. Besides, it was during Frere's term as envoy that the solemn Anglo-Spanish alliance of January 14, 1809 had been concluded, pledging perpetual friendship between the two nations and Britain's continued cooperation with Spain in the common cause against Napoleon.[31]

The man who followed Frere in the post of minister of His Majesty's Government to the government of patriotic Spain had quite a different personality. Here was a man who came to Spain with an impressive record. The oldest of the five Wellesley brothers,[32] Richard Marquess Wellesley had acquired quite a reputation as a Latin scholar and as a statesman. He had gained celebrity as governor general of India through his administrative talents and his success in greatly extending the power of Great Britain in the subcontinent. And now he had been entrusted with this vital and sensitive post in the capital of Andalucía. A haughty and vain gentleman, Richard Wellesley was once described by the Prince of Wales as a "Spanish

---

30. Villa-Urrutia, I, pp. 330–38. Frere also became involved in an intrigue against Spanish General Cuesta, which had unpleasant repercussions. On the relations between the latter and Wellington, see below.

31. See Chapter VIII. Frere died in Malta in 1846, after having devoted most of the remainder of his life to the cultivation of letters: He was known as a poet and as a translator of passages from Spanish masterpieces such as the *Poema del Cid* and the works of Lope de Vega.

32. The others were, in the order of age, William (1763–1845), who became chief secretary for Ireland in 1809 and postmaster general in 1834; Arthur; Gerald, who became a clergyman; and Henry (1773–1847), who, appointed minister to Spain in 1809, remained at this post until 1822. He was later ambassador to Vienna (1823–1831) and to Paris (1841–1846).

grandee grafted on an Irish potato."[33] This arrogance was the result of his achievements in India and perhaps also of his success with the weaker sex. At the age of forty-nine, short of stature but of attractive features, Marquess Wellesley was apparently well liked by the ladies of his time, and he himself was quite a Don Juan.[34]

His landing in Cádiz on August 1, 1809[35] coincided with the arrival of news of the victory of Talavera, achieved by his brother Arthur in the last days of July. The people of Cádiz went wild with enthusiasm as the English envoy, stepping gingerly on a French flag laid out specially for him in lieu of a carpet, established contact with fighting Spain. "I was received at Cádiz with every demonstration of public honour and with the most cordial and enthusiastic expressions of veneration for his Majesty's person and respect for his government, of zealous attachment to the British alliance, and of affectionate gratitude for the benefits already derived by the Spanish nation from the generosity of his Majesty's councils, and from the persevering activity, valour and skill of his officers and troops," Wellesley wrote on August 11 to Foreign Secretary Canning.[36]

Alas, this honeymoon was not to last. Shortly after his arrival in Sevilla, the British minister began receiving complaints from his brother in the field to the effect that the Spanish government was doing nothing or next to nothing to keep the British army fed and supplied. If this state of affairs continued, he wrote, the British army would withdraw all the way to Portugal. With his customary energy the Marquess set about to right the situation. Letters dealing with the military situation now went back and forth between the British minister and Martín de Garay, the secretary of the Junta Central. On August 19, Wellesley requested of Garay that the Spanish commander-in-chief, General Cuesta, whom Sir Arthur despised,[37] be relieved of his command, and two days later Garay informed the

33. *Apud* Bryant, p. 358.
34. *Ibid.;* Villa-Urrutia, I, p. 388.
35. He was accompanied by his son Richard and his nephew William Pole, "two youngsters more inclined to seek adventures than to help the envoy in his diplomatic tasks" (Villa-Urrutia, II, p. 6).
36. *The Despatches and Correspondence of the Marquess Wellesley, K. G.,* ed. Montgomery Martin, p. 2; Villa-Urrutia, II, p. 11.
37. See below.

envoy that Cuesta had been "allowed" to take the baths in the kingdom of Granada.[38] The same day, August 21, Wellesley wrote Garay that Sir Arthur was still not being supplied with badly needed provisions and means of transportation, and that he had requested him to "give notice" to the Spanish government that he was about to withdraw the British army into Portugal.[39]

To the British minister's recriminations Garay would state that the Spanish government had done everything in its power to provide supplies for the English forces. " . . . from the very moment at which the approach to Spain of the English auxiliary army commanded by Sir Arthur Wellesley was made known to the Department of Finance," the Junta's secretary wrote on October 3, "it has not ceased to give and repeat the most conclusive and urgent instructions, in order that the English army might suffer no want in the towns which it passed or where it was cantoned: The constituted authorities being charged to treat it everywhere in the manner which so worthy and generous an ally merits."[40] These measures should have been sufficient, Garay pointed out, to keep the British army well supplied for the short time it was expected to stay in Extremadura. If after Talavera the Allied forces had continued their advance, they would have quickly reached the "lands of Toledo and the country of the Castiles, where, at the distance of four leagues from their position, they would [have met] with universal abundance, and the towns prepared to satisfy all the wants of the combined armies."[41] But then Sir Arthur had decided to retire into an area "where [the British army] was least to be expected, according to the plan of the campaign," and which was one of the most ravaged areas of Spain. Nevertheless, Garay claimed, the Junta had seen to it that the British forces received everything they needed. If not everything had come off as expected, it was perhaps because the methods of distribution were at fault. This remark, though it could of course also apply to the English army, was a sort of indirect admission of a communi-

38. *The Despatches and Correspondence* . . . , pp. 37–39.
39. *Ibid*, pp. 40–41.
40. *Ibid.*, p. 145.
41. *Ibid.*, pp. 145–46.

cation breakdown between the Spanish government and the local authorities, which, apparently, did not always carry out the orders of the Suprema.[42]

While Sir Arthur may have been partly justified in not pushing on after Talavera,[43] British withdrawal to the western part of Extremadura was certainly not calculated to keep the Anglo-Spanish alliance working smoothly. Tempers flared on both sides, and mutual recriminations flew back and forth. The continuous complaints of his brother concerning supplies and his disparaging comments on the fighting ability of Spanish troops, combined with the domestic difficulties through which the Suprema was passing,[44] convinced the Marquess that the Junta was not the right kind of government for fighting Spain. It was time for a change, the envoy thought, and this he indicated to his Spanish colleagues. Concentrating the strength of the executive power was essential, he felt. Only a strong executive "wisely constituted and deriving its authority and strength, not only from its more compact form, but from the support of the people and from the good-will of the nation," he wrote to Don Francisco de Saavedra, a member of the Junta, on November 8, "would afford the most certain protection against all projects of innovation or seditious mischief; as well as the most powerful security for the independence of the monarchy and for the general union and tranquillity of Spain."[45]

But if Wellesley was dissatisfied with the Junta he certainly was not eager to see it overthrown by force. As a man of order he hated revolutionary proceedings, and when he was approached in early September by the Duke of Infantado, head of an anti-Junta plot, who requested his support, he promptly revealed the plan to Garay and at the same time persuaded the members of the conspiracy to desist from their design. The plot was thus frustrated and a grateful Suprema offered the British minister the Order of the Golden Fleece. His Lordship declined, stating rather ungraciously that he "could not

42. *Ibid.*, pp. 146–47.
43. See below.
44. See Chapter VIII.
45. *The Despatches and Correspondence . . .* , pp. 181–82.

accept that high honour from an authority whose conduct towards the interests of Spain and the Alliance [he] could not approve."[46]

In November, 1809, the Marquess returned to England to take over the Foreign Office,[47] and for about three months the post of envoy to the Spanish government was filled by Bartholomew Frere, nephew of the former minister to the Junta. Frere continued the practice of his predecessor of intervening in the domestic affairs of patriotic Spain, and when King Joseph flooded Andalucía with French troops, the British representative put strong pressure on the Junta to form a regency as soon as possible. Later he intervened repeatedly with the Junta of Cádiz to have this organism recognize the newly-formed Regency.[48] On February 28, the new envoy, Henry Wellesley, the youngest of the Wellesley clan, who had been appointed minister to Spain in December, 1809, arrived in Cádiz. He was destined to remain at his post much longer than his two predecessors[49] and to play an even more important role in wartime Spain than Frere and Richard Wellesley.[50]

Henry was in Spain during the crucial years of the Cortes—he rose to the rank of full-fledged ambassador in 1811—and when Fernando returned in 1814, during the absolutist reaction of 1814–1820, and the liberal revolution of 1820. During the war years his influence on the Spanish Regency and the Cortes was substantial. The fact that his brother Arthur headed the British army in the Peninsula and from September, 1812 on was commander-in-chief of all allied forces, and that Richard was at the head of the Foreign Office until 1812, made his position an even stronger one. Pizarro, Spanish secretary of state

46. *Ibid.*, p. 160, n.

47. The Marquess held his position until January, 1812, when he resigned as foreign secretary. He later served as lieutenant general of Ireland (1821), lord steward (1830), and lord chamberlain (1835). Nine years after the death of his first wife in 1816, he remarried, his second wife being an American, Mary Anne Caton, widow of Robert Paterson, whose sister, Elizabeth Paterson, had been the first wife of Jerome Bonaparte. As Chastenet points out, the second Marquise Wellesley was thus related by marriage to both the victor and the loser at Waterloo (Chastenet, *Wellington*, p. 326 n.) The Marquess devoted his last years to the study of the classics and died in 1842 at the age of eighty-two.

48. Villa-Urrutia, II, pp. 47–56.

49. Twelve years, until 1822.

50. *Ibid.*, p. 64.

in 1812, described the ascendancy of His Majesty's ambassador in the following terms: "The British ambassador exerted a powerful influence on the Cortes and on [the Regency]. He behaved more like a Spanish potentate than as a foreign agent. He had a hand in the appointment to high and low offices and could promote and exclude whomever he wanted. His anger was a proscription for the person who incurred it. Thus the Regents visited him on the sly, flattered him fawningly, and feared him."[51] The picture drawn by Pizarro, who was no friend of the English, is probably exaggerated. Yet there can be no doubt that his prestige and power in Cádiz exceeded by far that normally enjoyed by diplomats accredited to an allied power.[52]

When the Cortes first began its sessions, Wellesley, like most Englishmen, placed high hopes on the work of the Spanish congress. His brother Richard, too, had wanted to see the Cortes gather as soon as possible. But few Englishmen were as vocal in their desire to have the national assembly gather as Lord Vassall Holland,[53] a friend of many members of Spain's intellectual elite, who after two earlier trips

51. *Op. cit.*, I, p. 147.

52. Cf., for instance Villanueva, *Mi viaje a las Cortes. Memorias de tiempos de Fernando VII*, II, in BAE, XCVIII, pp. 254-55, 284, 425, 431-33; Villa-Urrutia, II, pp. 300-301, 394. Wellesley's opposition to the candidacy to the Spanish crown of Fernando's sister Carlota Joaquina, princess of Brazil, probably contributed to the frustration of the intrigues which a number of members of the Spanish Cortes were carrying on on her behalf. Wellesley thought Carlota was too absolutist-minded and feared for the independence of Britain's traditional ally, Portugal, if she ascended the Spanish throne (*ibid.*, pp. 349-50). Of the third Regency elected in January, 1812, three members had been suggested by Wellesley (*ibid.*, p. 397). It was said by the middle of 1813 that the British ambassador had his own "party" in the Cortes, made up of thirty deputies (Villanueva, p. 432; cf. also Azcárate, "*Memorias sobre los 'Vaughan Papers,'*" pp. 730-34; Artola, *Los orígenes de la España contemporánea*, I, pp. 454-56).

53. Henry Richard Fox, Lord Holland, was born in 1773. In 1797, he married Elizabeth Vassall, who later accompanied her husband to Spain in 1803-1805 and 1809 and has left an interesting journal of the voyage. Lord Holland, a Whig, was for a short time a member of the Fox-Grenville cabinet in 1806. He had a fine knowledge of the Spanish language and of Spanish literature, and wrote a book on the life and works of Lope de Vega. In England he later extended his hospitality to José Blanco-White (see Chapter XIV), who spent a few years in his house. An ardent liberal, he hoped that the gathering of the Spanish Cortes would usher in a Spanish political renascence.

to the Peninsula[54] spent some time in wartime Spain in 1809. In Sevilla he and his beautiful wife entertained many outstanding personalities such as Jovellanos, Quintana, Capmany, Blanco, Garay, Saavedra, and many Spanish officers.[55] One of Holland's dearest friends was no doubt Jovellanos,[56] with whom he sustained a lively correspondence during the last three years of the latter's life. On May 5, 1809, the English liberal wrote from Cádiz to the great Spanish scholar, then a member of the Junta Central at Sevilla: "As for the Cortes, you know by now that they are my Hobby-horse[57] . . . The Cortes, adapted to the enlightenment of our century and, to a certain point, to the changes which time has wrought in the relations between cities and cities and provinces and provinces, and especially with an increase in their membership . . . seem to me to be all that is needed for the moment."[58] "For the love of God," begged the lord in his letter of May 21, "do not delay the announcement of the convocation of the Cortes, and if it is still possible, hasten their assembly."[59] The very next day Jovellanos was able to inform his friend that the gathering of the Cortes had just been decreed for the following year, "or before, if circumstances permit it." "Do not scold us," he added, "if urgent, the convocation will take place soon; if not, everything will be carefully thought out."[60] Three days later, Lord Holland gave vent to his joy at the good news: "But . . . the best news, the

54. In 1792–1793 and 1803–1805.

55. Villa-Urrutia, I, p. 416.

56. In 1805, Lord Holland had tried to interest Nelson in a project to free Jovellanos from his prison in Mallorca. Nelson, however, had turned the project down. In a letter to Holland written on September 13, 1805, from his property at Merton, England, where he lived the last months of his life with Lady Hamilton and his daughter, the illustrous sea captain wrote: "I have long deplored his [Jovellanos'] lot, would to God I could make that infernal Prince of Darkness change places with him, but it is very difficult in any way to try to be useful to him and would only hasten probably his death if it is known that an Englishman took an interest about him. Therefore we must look for the speedy downfall of the P.P. (*sic*) as the most likely mode of delivering Don Gaspar." *Cartas de Jovellanos y Lord Vassall Holland sobre la guerra de la independencia (1808–1811)*, ed. Somoza, pp. 88–89.

57. In English in the letter, which was, as all letters of Holland to Jovellanos, written in Spanish.

58. Jovellanos, *Obras*, IV, BAE, LXXXVI, p. 366.

59. *Ibid.*, p. 376.

60. *Ibid.*, p. 377.

greatest victory is yours, the *convocation of the Cortes*." Impatiently he asked many questions as to the form the national assembly would take: "What cities, what provinces, what districts shall vote? . . . How many deputies shall each province have? . . . How many chambers, one or two?"[61] One thing on which Holland insisted was the necessity for a large number of deputies, for as he put it in his letter of May 31: ". . . the matter of numbers is perhaps the main point, the *sine qua non* of a free government." Five hundred would not be an excessive quantity, especially in view of the fact that England had 658.[62] But Jovellanos was wary of such a scheme, for in his opinion, since the Spanish colonies would have to be represented in the congress, either the proportion of representation would have to be altered, which would present difficulties, or a really excessive amount of representatives would have to be admitted.[63]

Back in England, Holland informed his friend on August 31 that there was much disappointment in the British Isles concerning the situation in Spain, a disappointment he attributed to the lack of freedom of speech and of the press and to the delay in calling the Cortes.[64] The lord kept hammering at this theme in his subsequent letters: "Here people do not want to believe me when I assure them that the Cortes will be convoked," he wrote on September 8. "They all exclaim 'And why such slowness?'" "And meanwhile," he added, "what has been done in the realm of finance, of laws, or in the most important of all, freedom of the press? . . . Everybody inveighs here against the lack of liberty in Spain."[65] "Oh God," lamented Jovellanos' friend on November 1, 1809, "how much time . . . has been lost, and while Bonaparte has conquered Germany, you have not been able to settle the matter of the calling of the Cortes and establish freedom of the press."[66]

Finally, and unfortunately without Jovellanos, the Cortes met. Rather quickly Great Britain and her ambassador in Cádiz became

61. *Ibid.*, p. 380.
62. *Ibid.*, p. 388.
63. Letter of June 3, *ibid.*, p. 390.
64. *Ibid.*, p. 432.
65. *Ibid.*, p. 435.
66. *Ibid.*, p. 444.

disillusioned with the assembly and its work. If the Cortes emphasized the conduct of the war and reforms designed to improve
radically Spanish military and civilian organization, well and fine. But
if the politicians in Cádiz spent their time discussing a constitution
having in English eyes little relation to Spain's concrete needs, this
was of very little value for the alliance and therefore, as far as the
British were concerned, a pure waste of time. Camden's opinion,
expressed in 1813, summed up the feeling of many Englishmen: "The
Cortes met and deliberated upon state affairs in their way, but there is
no necessity to dwell long upon their proceedings during the year
1811: it is an ungrateful subject, and must weary and disgust every
real friend to the cause of Spain. As far as addresses to their countrymen, written with great force and eloquence, and pointing out the
duties and sacrifices required of them, in the most energetic and per-
suasive manner, could be of service, the Cortes performed their duty.
In all other respects, they either did nothing, or did what was manifestly injurious to their country."[67]

Actually, if the Cortes had abolished the Inquisition from the start
and had at the same time thrown wide the gates of Spanish American
trade to their allies and shown more flexibility with their rebellious
American colonies, England would have been much less critical of
the Spanish congress. The Inquisition was finally abolished in 1813,
but the issue of trade with Spanish America continued to poison
relations between Spain and England. The whole Spanish American
question, with the related matter of Anglo-South American commerce, were as a matter of fact the factors that probably aroused the
greatest ill feeling on both sides. It is common knowledge that the
eyes of Great Britain had been on the huge Spanish American empire
for centuries. English contraband and piracy, as well as attacks on the
Central and South American mainland, plagued Spanish American
possessions during the entire colonial period. We have seen how
England made two attempts, in 1806 and 1807, to seize Buenos Aires.
In the summer of 1808, thousands of troops were waiting in Cork to
sail for Venezuela in order to help the anti-Spanish revolution
planned by Francisco de Miranda, and if it had not been for the

67. *Op. cit.*, p. 335.

Spanish uprising Arthur Wellesley might have made a name of himself in South America rather than in the Peninsula.

But during the Spanish War of Independence Albion was much more interested in breaking the monopolistic trade barriers which the Spanish monarchy had erected around its colonial empire than in conquering new territories. Spanish authorities were well aware of British interest in free trade with Spanish America, but suspected from the beginning that if this should be granted, their ally would use commerce to break the links of the colonies with the mother country. In February, 1810, Jovellanos himself, though an admirer of the British form of government and an intimate friend of the Hollands, expressed his fears with regard to possible British encroachments in the New World in a letter to his friend Saavedra. "The English will want an independent America," he wrote, "but they will want it subjected to dangerous conditions. Besides, they will want some islands, and especially Havana and some coastal establishment in the Gulf of Mexico or in Caracas."[68]

When the overseas independence movements began in 1810, Spanish fears and suspicions toward British demands for free trade with the colonies increased proportionately. If the Spanish government had had its seat in another part of the Peninsula, this resentment might have been less virulent. But Cádiz happened to be the one place in free Spain most interested in maintaining the traditional monopoly, and neither the Regency nor the Cortes could remain indifferent to the tremendous pressures exerted by the Cádiz merchants to keep the ancient system intact.

That the British government was vitally interested in open trade with the Spanish American colonies cannot be denied. That it ardently desired to see those territories totally free from colonial shackles is open to question. But that it planned to use free trade as a wedge to insure Spanish American freedom was merely an intention read into His Majesty's Government's mind by an oversensitive Spain. The bitterness with which patriotic Spaniards viewed the British attitude toward the Spanish American revolution was

68. Artigas, "Los manuscritos de Jovellanos de la Biblioteca Menéndez y Pelayo," *Boletín de la Biblioteca Menéndez y Pelayo*, Año III (1921), p. 136.

reflected in a letter from Jovellanos to Holland, written in Gijón, Asturias, on August 17, 1811, a few months before the great scholar's death. Inveighing against Blanco-White, whose articles in *El Español* expressed his sympathies with the Spanish American cause,[69] and stating that the Creoles had revolted mainly because they were envious of the control exercised by the motherland, Jovellanos wrote that he did not attribute to the government of Great Britain the intention of provoking the separation of the colonies from Spain, but that he feared the "greed" of British merchants.[70]

True, most Britons probably looked favorably upon the prospect of Spanish American independence, especially since this would favor British trade, but governmental authorities, well aware of the importance of the Spanish alliance, did not extend a helping hand to the American insurgents.[71] As the terrible conflict in South America grew in intensity, however, many English citizens joined the rebels' ranks. The embarrassed British government could not convince the Regency and the Cortes, and especially the Cádiz merchants, that it did not stand in back of these volunteers and that it could not prevent individual Britons from joining the insurgent forces if they wanted to do so.[72]

His Majesty's Government was in a quandary. It was aware of the fact that many Englishmen felt a great sympathy for the rebels, and yet it wanted to do its utmost to avoid offending Britain's ally. It realized that in case some or all Spanish American colonies achieved independence it could not very well offend the English nation by giving up friendly relations with these territories. To find a way out of the dilemma, Great Britain formally proposed to its ally in May, 1811, that England take up the role of mediator in the conflict between the colonies and the motherland. As a means of insuring peace in the New World it was suggested that Great Britain be allowed to trade freely with Spanish America while negotiations were in progress. In the existing political climate the reaction of the

69. See Chapter XIV.

70. *Obras*, IV, in BAE, LXXXVI, pp. 477–78.

71. This was not the case, however, of British colonial authorities in the Americas, who more or less openly encouraged the Spanish American revolt (Villa-Urrutia, II, p. 383).

72. *Ibid.*, III, p. 136.

Cortes was bound not to be very favorable to this overture. However, a commission was formed and the project was extensively discussed in private sessions of the assembly. Finally, the Spanish government informed the Foreign Office that it accepted British mediation for the provinces of Río de la Plata, Venezuela, Santa Fe, and Cartagena; that during the negotiations, which would be allowed to last fifteen months, a general armistice would be in effect in the overseas territories, and that in the same period England would be permitted to trade freely with the dissident provinces. Unfortunately the Spanish government found it necessary to include a secret clause which provided for Great Britain's breaking off all contact with the colonies and helping Spain to subject them in case mediation efforts failed. The British ambassador strenuously objected to this article, and after much discussion Spain modified its stand somewhat, but then Britain demanded that New Spain (Mexico) be included in the mediation project. More acrimonious negotiations followed, in the course of which the strongly anti-British minister of state Pizarro resigned,[73] and eventually the whole scheme collapsed.[74]

As Villa-Urrutia noted, the mediation project never had a fighting chance, mainly because of Spanish suspicions of their ally's motives, but also because the Spanish government, still strongly filled with colonialist prejudices, would not consider the possibility of granting autonomy to its colonies.[75] If Spain and England had agreed on mediation, the Spanish American territories would probably have achieved autonomy and eventually full independence. But this was inevitable anyway, and Spain could have spared herself much blood, money, and effort if she had recognized this at an early date. Though some of Spain's suspicions of England's actions were justified, there was no foundation for the idea firmly anchored in the minds of some Spanish statesmen that the British government was primarily interested in severing the colonies from the motherland and in grabbing additional territories in the New World.[76] As for free trade, Britain

73. May, 1812.

74. Villanueva, pp. 199–200, 207, 256, 296, 319–20; Pizarro, I, pp. 150–53; Toreno, pp. 357–58; Becker, pp. 73–79; Villa-Urrutia, II, pp. 376–411.

75. *Op. cit.,* II, pp. 410–11.

76. Some of the British private traders, however, undoubtedly entertained such thoughts.

did not really need Spain's official permission to carry on unrestricted commerce with Spanish America, since British ships had been engaging in lucrative contraband trade with the colonies for a long time. The British government merely sought to legalize and expand something which in fact existed. In all fairness it should be added, however, that Great Britain might have used more discretion in her treatment of the ultrasensitive Spanish American matter. At times it seemed to the Spanish government, and rightly so, that its ally was exerting undue pressure on it in a matter which after all was primarily Spain's concern. Even Wellington, who could certainly not be accused of being unduly pro-Spanish, realized that England's policy could stand some correction. In a letter to his brother the ambassador, dated July 14, 1811, the general wrote: "My opinion has invariably been that, in all the concerns of Spain, Great Britain ought to take the liberal line of policy, and to lay aside, at least during the existing war, all considerations of mercantile profit . . . I am, and always have been, of opinion, that the notions of our merchants of the vast profits, to be made by an immediate direct intercourse with the Spanish colonies, were erroneous . . . The wild speculations of the colonies ought to have been checked; the authority of the mother country ought to have been countenanced; and the endeavours of our traders and captains of ships, to separate the colonies from Spain, ought to have been suppressed."[77]

While the question of the colonies was undoubtedly one of the greatest obstacles to a perfectly harmonious relationship between Great Britain and patriotic Spain, there were a number of other points of friction. One of them was the perennial question of British subsidies. While some British historians such as Napier and Southey have tended to exaggerate English material aid to Spain during the War of Independence, some Spanish historians—Gómez de Arteche and Canga Argüelles for instance—have gone to the other extreme, minimizing British help in money and equipment. It seems that the amount of money and material, while undoubtedly great,[78] was not as

77. *The Dispatches*, VIII, pp. 101–102.
78. Foreign Secretary Canning informed the Junta Central in November, 1808, that Great Britain had sent to Spain up to that date 160,000 rifles and would send 40,000 more to reach the 200,000 requested by the Spanish government. The juntas of Galicia, Asturias, and Sevilla had each received 1½ million duros, the Marquis de La Romana had been granted 225,000; Frere had brought

overwhelming in relation to the actual needs of fighting Spain as the British government was wont to believe.[79] On the other hand, there were good reasons why Britain did not continually shower Spain with subsidies. When Spain began to receive in 1809 large amounts of money from her American colonies, England felt that there was no necessity for subsidizing her ally as heavily as the previous year. Besides, as the burden of waging a continuous European war against Napoleon became heavier and heavier, the lack of specie made itself increasingly felt in Great Britain. The situation was so bad at one point, in 1809, that the English government was forced to request the Spanish authorities for silver in order to pay the British expeditionary forces in the Peninsula, offering in exchange drafts on the British Treasury.[80] After 1811, it became even more difficult for Great Britain to extend economic support to her ally, who now needed it desperately, since the Spanish American revolution had greatly affected the shipments of money from the colonies. The English harvest of 1811 was poor, the price of bread shot up, and the Continental blockade caused much unemployment with the resultant social disturbances. "Much suffering and misery were rife among the lower classes in England during the winter of 1811," wrote Lord Holland in his *Further Memoirs of the Whig Party*. "Trade was at its lowest ebb. The effects of Napoleon's decrees against English commerce and the orders in Council, issued by the Cabinet as a means of retaliation, fell heavily on the manufacturing districts."[81]

Thus, when in the winter of 1811–1812 Spain asked for a loan of £10 million and for a treaty of subsidies,[82] which would result, among other things, in keeping a Spanish army of 100,000 men completely dressed, armed, and equipped, there were bound to be

---

another million, and 2 million in silver bullion were on the way. This would constitute a total of 7,725,000 duros. The Junta had asked for 10 million (Villa-Urrutia, I, pp. 260–61).

79. Cf. Canga Argüelles, *Observaciones* . . . chap. XIV; Toreno, pp. 175–76; Gómez de Arteche, v, pp. 101–104, 446–50.

80. Villa-Urrutia, I, p. 309.

81. *Op. cit.*, p. 69.

82. Villanueva, p. 256. In exchange, the Spanish government offered Britain free trade with Spanish America for a period of three years (Villa-Urrutia, II, p. 395). In August, 1810, the then Spanish minister of state Bardaxí had asked without success for £4 million and then for £2 million.

raised eyebrows in the Foreign Office. England felt that the 1½ million duros it had given Spain in the past year and a half, as well as the help in arms and equipment for the Spanish army, was all it could afford in the prevailing circumstances. And so the Duke of Infantado, sent to London to negotiate the loan and the treaty of subsidies, returned empty-handed.[83]

Nevertheless, Great Britain continued to extend aid to Spain whenever possible. Ambassador Wellesley had at his disposal an annual sum of £1 million for the needs of Spanish armies operating in conjunction with Wellington's forces, for Spanish troops under the command of English generals, and for the Spanish government. In early 1812, Wellesley anticipated 1 million duros to the penniless Regency, and before the government moved back to Madrid it received another 300,000 to pay for the expense involved in the transfer of the seat of the Cortes to the capital.[84] And so with endless friction, now caused by the revolt in Spanish America, now by the problem of subsidies, now by Lord Wellington's clashes with the Spanish government,[85] and now by the ill feelings between the Spanish liberals and the English conservative government and its representatives in the Peninsula,[86] the two allies managed to walk together down the road to victory. Fortunately for the alliance there were enough military victories after 1811 to compensate for the bad moments, both political and military. After the war had ended, Great Britain and Spain signed a new treaty of alliance in July, 1814. But with the incredible Fernando on the throne, British public opinion shrank from too close an association with the absolutist regime of the Spanish monarch, and even the Tory ministers felt uncomfortable about being allied with a government which was viciously persecut-

---

83. *Ibid.*, p. 396.

84. *Ibid.*, p. 398, III, p. 197. "I believe that no regular subsidy was given to Spain till the year 1812, when a million was given, and clothing for 100,000 men . . ." Wellington, *The Dispatches*, x, p. 619.

85. See below.

86. The aversion felt by Spanish liberals toward Great Britain and Wellington was at times expressed in very outspoken terms by some of the liberal newspapers in Cádiz. Some of these articles precipitated real diplomatic crises (Villa-Urrutia, III, pp. 168–69). What anti-British sentiment there was in Spain was, however, much stronger in Cádiz than in the country as a whole (*ibid.*, p. 212; cf. also *Napoleón o el verdadero Don Quixote, loc. cit.*).

ing many of those who had fought for independence. And Spain's policy with regard to her colonies was not calculated to render her less unpopular with the English public. As a result, the English alliance brought little profit to Spain. Ten years after the treaty's signature, Spanish American independence, with the exception of Cuba and Puerto Rico, was a fact; England and the United States had effectively blocked the threat of French intervention in the New World on the side of Spain to crush the Spanish American insurgents; and His Majesty's Government quickly recognized the newly formed republics in the Western Hemisphere.[87]

[2]

The most popular Englishman in Spain during the War of Independence was without a doubt Lord Wellington. What suspicion and aversion there was toward the British allies—some of it provoked by Wellington's attitude toward Spanish authorities and by his strategy—was time and again swept away by the great victories of the English general. After Talavera,[88] after the capture of Ciudad Rodrigo and Badajoz, and after Salamanca and Vitoria, Wellington was the toast of the mass of patriotic Spaniards. If his retreats in 1809, 1811, and 1812 had caused resentment, his brilliant feats of arms fully restored Spanish confidence in him. Few Spaniards, if any, questioned his military ability. In the summer of 1813 his relations with the Spanish liberal party in the Cortes soured considerably, however. Yet this friction, too, was in the end completely overshadowed by the extraordinary prestige he had acquired throughout Spain as the magnificent commander who had led Allied troops in the Peninsula to victory over the French armies.

England was indeed fortunate to have a man of such caliber south of the Pyrenees. His country owed him much. Another military leader might have chosen evacuation in the dark days of 1810, when

87. The United States had recognized the independence of most Spanish American republics by 1824.

88. Before his retreat to the Spanish-Portuguese border.

it seemed that nothing could stem the French juggernaut rolling through Portugal toward Lisbon. But Wellington's foresight, which had stealthily erected the lines of Torres Vedras, saved the day, the British expeditionary force was spared the fate of Moore's army at La Coruña,[89] and Napoleon's hopes of seeing his troops enter Lisbon once more and throwing the British into the sea had been irremediably frustrated. The British army was in the Peninsula to stay. Between the Anglo-Portuguese forces and the Spanish guerrilla and regular forces, Napoleon's host in Spain was eventually crushed.

Great Britain realized what a great asset it had in Wellington and showed its gratitude by amply rewarding her hero.[90] In 1808, Wellesley was a lieutenant general and had already a brilliant military record behind him, including some important victories. But since these had been achieved in faraway India during his sojourn there between 1797 and 1805, his return to England had not been accompanied by any triumphal reception by his people, who cared more for what was happening on their doorstep in continental Europe than in the remote subcontinent. Elected in 1806 to the English Parliament as M.P. for Rye, he had become the following year chief secretary for Ireland. In 1808, he was chosen by Secretary of War Lord Castlereagh to head the expedition to the Peninsula, but because of matters of seniority he was forced to serve in his first Peninsular campaign under the orders of two senior officers. Having beaten the French at Roliça and Vimiero, in Portugal, he was back in England after the Cintra Convention.[91] In London, a court of inquiry absolved him and

89. See Chapter VII.

90. Granted in 1809 the titles of Baron Douro of Oporto and Viscount Wellington of Talavera, he was three years later made successively earl, with an annuity of £2,000, and marquis with an award of £100,000. The Order of the Garter followed in 1813, with the title of Duke of Wellington in 1814 and £300,000. The Portuguese and Spanish governments, too, heaped distinctions on the general: Portugal made him Count of Vimiero and Duke of Vitoria and gave him the Grand Cross of the Order of the Tower and Sword, while Spain created for him the title of Duke of Ciudad Rodrigo, which brought him into the ranks of Spanish grandees, and granted him the Order of the Golden Fleece, "which he seems to have prized above all others" (Wellesley, *The Man Wellington, Through the Eyes of Those Who Knew Him*, p. 260. Cf. also pp. 180, 228, 229, 259, 266, 313).

91. See Chapter VII.

his two superiors of any wrongdoing in connection with the controversial agreement.[92]

In April, 1809, Wellesley was back in Portugal, this time as commander-in-chief of the British expeditionary forces. Before his arrival the British government, considerably shaken by the disastrous end of Sir John Moore's expedition, had hesitated to mount another full-fledged operation in Portugal. A memorandum from Arthur Wellesley to Castlereagh in March, 1809, had greatly contributed to make up the British minister's mind. The report illustrated Wellesley's remarkable grasp of the overall needs of the British and Portuguese armies in the Peninsula and turned out to be prophetic in its estimate of the military situation. "I have always been of opinion," Wellesley stated, "that Portugal might be defended, whatever might be the result of the contest in Spain; and that, in the mean time, the measures adopted for the defence of Portugal would be highly useful to the Spaniards in their contest with the French."[93] Wellesley advocated that the Portuguese forces be placed under the command of English officers, emphasizing that the "staff of the army, the commissariat in particular, must be British."[94] His most remarkable statement of the whole memorandum is the following: "My opinion was, that even if Spain should have been conquered, the French would not have been able to overrun Portugal with a smaller force than 100,000 men; and that, as long as the contest should continue in Spain, . . . [the Anglo-Portuguese army], if it could be put in a state of activity, would be highly useful to the Spaniards, and might eventually have decided the contest."[95] The accuracy of Wellesley's estimate was shown in the following year, when Masséna's 65,000 failed to capture Lisbon.

92. *Ibid.*, pp. 116–57; Maxwell, *Life of the Duke of Wellington*, i, chaps. xx–xxiv.

93. *Apud* Maxwell, i, p. 505.

94. This idea was in fact adopted. General Beresford was made commander-in-chief of Portuguese forces, which were "taken into English pay, placed under English officers, organized on the same system, subjected to the same regulations, and in every respect made, for the time being, an integral portion of the British army" (*ibid.*, p. 508).

95. *Ibid.*, p. 505.

This capacity for perceiving with remarkable lucidity the possibilities, military as well as political, of a given situation, and his caution, which could, however, never be equated with pusillanimity, combined with a readiness to strike swiftly whenever the opportunity seemed to present itself, were some of the qualities which made Wellington one of the greatest British field commanders in history. Not endowed with the extraordinary military genius of Napoleon, whose handling of battlefield intricacies often bordered on the miraculous, he was nevertheless a great strategist as well as a great tactician. His uncanny ability to anticipate the enemy's movement and to accurately gauge the enemy's and his own capabilities beat his opponents time and again. His energy during a campaign was proverbial. Getting along on little rest, writing out orders and dispatches day and night, capable of riding over huge distances without stopping, he kept himself informed of every administrative and military detail and seemed to be everywhere at once, at the head, at the rear, and in the center of his columns. His soldiers felt, and rightly so, that the mere presence of Lord Wellington in their midst was worth to them thousands of reinforcements.

On the battlefield he was superb. Cool and collected under the most terrible fire, he was at the same time taut as a spring, ready to take advantage of the slightest mistake of his opponent and uncoil in lightning and deadly fashion. At Salamanca, in July, 1812, Wellington had for days been waiting for Marshal Marmont to make a false move, and for days the two armies had marched along parallel routes. On the afternoon of the twenty-second, having concealed the mass of his troops behind rises in the terrain, he watched patiently but with an eagle eye the maneuvering of the enemy, about a mile away. As the French left wing, trying to envelop his own right wing, moved away dangerously from the main body of the French troops, thus creating a gap in the French line, Wellington saw his chance and struck. The result was the utter defeat of the French army.[96]

96. Wellington is said to have been sitting on a hillside, eating his meal, when he was apprised of the French movement. He sprang up and grabbed the telescope. Muttering something to the effect that Marmont was making a dire mistake, he mounted his horse and ordered the attack (Maxwell, II, pp. 504; Oman, I, p. 434, n. 1). Perhaps he simply said "That will do," as other sources have reported (Bryant, *The Age of Elegance*, p. 32).

One of the factors in the victory at Salamanca[97] was the disposition of Wellington's troops. The mass of his forces was hidden from the enemy. It was Wellington's favorite tactic whenever he gave battle. As the French would come on in their massed columns preceded by clouds of light infantry—a mode of attack which gave such amazing results against the armies of other nations—the British commander would await them, with his troops forming ordinarily two lines well concealed behind a natural obstacle such as a rise or dip in the ground. Slowing down the enemy *tirailleurs* (skirmishers) with his own light infantry, he would let the latter return to their lines, and when the French columns were practically on top of him, order his concealed lines to emerge and decimate the enemy columns with well-directed musket fire.[98] The results were often disastrous for the French. Napoleon became painfully aware of this at Waterloo.

Paradoxically, Wellington's soldiers, though respecting him and admiring him, felt no particular personal attachment to their commander. The adulation of which Napoleon was the object on the part of his troops was missing in the relationship between Wellington and his army. The fact that he was a tough disciplinarian who firmly believed in flogging and the gallows does not really explain this. Strict discipline is not sufficient to detract from the affection soldiers feel for their general. To a certain extent it was his seemingly cold and stern manner of dealing with his subordinates. This was often interpreted as contempt and arrogance, but could very possibly have been superimposed by sheer willpower on a warm but exceedingly shy nature.[99] In part it was also his authoritarianism, which made him frown on any independent action carried out without his own specific orders, and often provoked in him tremendous outbursts of temper against his officers. This temper can perhaps be traced to his Anglo-Irish ancestry—he was born in Ireland of a family which had originally come from England—or perhaps simply to his constant but often unsuccessful struggle to keep his basic sensi-

97. The Spaniards call it the battle of the Arapiles, because of the two knolls, the Arapiles, which rise from the undulating plain where the encounter took place.

98. Oman, I, pp. 114–16.

99. Cf. for instance Davies, *Wellington and his Army*, chap. I.

tivity under control. His temper was often responsible for unjust reprimands directed against the behavior of his officers and troops, and the frequent injustice and lack of discrimination of this criticism made many soldiers, especially officers, detest him most cordially as a person. He had few real friends in his life, but perhaps, as Muriel Wellesley puts it, "there never lived a soul who craved more for affection than this man who has been denied the capacity for even feeling it."[1]

It has been said that Wellington cared for his soldiers only insofar as they represented a tool which would give him victory.[2] This was perhaps true, but at the same time it must be admitted that he always saw to it that his men's material discomfort was reduced to a minimum.[3] He certainly was not as wasteful of his soldiers' lives as Napoleon. Could Wellington's caution in this respect be attributed solely to his realization that he had only a limited number of troops at his disposal? Perhaps, but the fact is that he could state in later life that the six years he was in the Peninsula had cost him no more than 36,000 casualties.[4] Whatever else may be said about his personality, he was "unsparing of himself and careless of praise or blame."[5] His integrity was of the highest order and he was always willing to fight all the way for what he thought was right.[6]

In 1811, halfway through the Peninsular Campaign, Lord Wellington, then forty-two years old, "was . . . in the prime of life, a well-made man, 5 feet 10 inches in height, lean and muscular, with broad shoulders and well-developed chest . . . and a strong virile face, with pronounced nose, and aquiline features, surmounted by a crop of crisp dark hair which showed a decided inclination to curl."[7] His dress was usually unpretentious, and he was as unconcerned about the attire of his subordinates as he was about his own. More often

---

1. *Op. cit.*, p. 6; cf. also Davies, *loc. cit.*

2. Oman, II, p. 302.

3. Cf. for instance his letters to Marshal Soult and General Kellerman after Talavera, asking them to care for the wounded he had been forced to leave behind (*The Dispatches*, v, pp. 15–16).

4. Davies, p. 17.

5. Oman, II, p. 310.

6. *Ibid.*

7. Wellesley, pp. 212–13.

than not he would be seen in a blue coat, a short cape, and a small cocked hat. At times he would appear in civilian clothes, wearing gray trousers and a round hat. He was most frugal in his everyday life. In contrast with other English officers, especially those who had served in India and had acquired habits of luxury—his brother Richard, for example—he managed with only one manservant, whose principal duty was to clean his boots.[8] He required little sleep or food. "No commander-in-chief ever travelled with less baggage or more Spartan fare."[9] His pastimes behind the battle lines were limited almost exclusively to hunting—he neither drank nor gambled—and to feminine companionship. His fondness for women may have been exaggerated,[10] but though married and the father of two children,[11] he kept a mistress in the Peninsula[12] and later in France was not insensitive to feminine charms.[13]

It was not surprising, in view of Wellington's character, of which cool, calculating efficiency was one of the main traits, that the British commander did not get along too well with his Spanish colleagues, both in the political and the military hierarchy. His relations with the Junta Central were decidedly unfriendly. In the summer of 1809, during the Talavera Campaign, his dispatches revealed his continuous, seething dissatisfaction with the alleged lack of cooperation on the part of the Spanish civilian and military establishment. His complaints about the supply situation were endless. His troops did no doubt suffer privations on the way from Plasencia to Talavera, at Talavera itself, and during their retreat through Extremadura, but he also exaggerated the lack of food and supplies.[14] Besides, the Spanish army itself had little to live on in barren Extremadura, and "Cuesta's troops were living from hand to mouth on supplies sent from Andalucía."[15] And the fact that he did not receive the transport the Central

8. Villa-Urrutia, I, p. 395.
9. Oman, II, p. 295.
10. Cf. Davies, pp. 6–8.
11. In 1806, he had married Catherine Pakenham, who gave him two children, in 1807 and 1808, respectively.
12. Bryant, *Years of Victory*, p. 356.
13. Chastenet, *Wellington*, p. 179.
14. Cf. Azcárate, *Wellington y España*, pp. 74–76.
15. Oman, II, p. 485.

Junta had promised him could not be attributed solely to Spanish inefficiency and certainly not to unwillingness to help. There just were not enough carts nor draft animals, either for his troops or for the Spanish forces.[16]

But Wellington did not see it this way. Inefficiency or some more sinister explanation must be behind the Spaniards' failure to deliver supplies to his army. Even before the battle of Talavera (July 27–28) he began to threaten withdrawal from Spain. On July 16, he sounded this ominous note in a letter to Spanish general O'Donojú from Plasencia, in which he complained specifically about the lack of transport: "All countries in which an army is acting are obliged to supply these means; and if the people of Spain are unable or unwilling to supply what the army requires, I am afraid that they must do without its services."[17] On July 24, he wrote to Frere in Sevilla: "I certainly lament the necessity which obliges me to halt at present, and will oblige me to withdraw from Spain, if it should continue. There is no man that does not acknowledge, even General Cuesta himself acknowledges, the justice and propriety of my conduct in halting now, or in eventually withdrawing." The British commander now gave full vent to his wrath or perhaps to his Irish temper: "And I can only say, that I have never seen an army so ill-treated in any country, or considering that depends upon its operations, one which deserved good treatment so much."[18] Wellesley further contended in this letter that the French soldiers, in contrast with the British, were well fed. This, however, seems highly improbable, since Marshal Victor himself had written to King Joseph from the same area on June 25 that his army was on the verge of starvation.[19] On July 31, following the great battle, he sat down and wrote a letter to Frere which is probably as ferociously anti-Spanish as any ever penned by him: ". . . It is not a difficult matter for a gentleman in the situation of Don M. de Garay[20] to sit down in his cabinet and write his lines of the glory which would result from driving the French through the

16. Villa-Urrutia, II, p. 21.
17. *The Dispatches*, IV, p. 487.
18. *Ibid.*, p. 496.
19. *Apud* Villa-Urrutia, II, p. 21.
20. Martín de Garay, the secretary of the Junta Central.

Pyrenees; and I believe there is no man in Spain who has risked so much, or who has sacrificed so much, to effect that object as I have. But I wish that Don M. de Garay, or the gentlemen of the Junta, before they blame me for not doing more, or impute to me before-hand the probable consequences of the blunders, or the indiscretion of others, would either come or send here somebody to satisfy the wants of our half-starved army . . . ; at this moment there are nearly 4,000 wounded soldiers dying in the hospital in this town from want of common assistance and necessaries, which any other country in the world would have given even its enemies . . ."[21]

After the victory at Talavera he blamed his inactivity and subse-quent withdrawal westward and across the Tajo[22] on a number of factors, including the poor supply situation. Granted that the Spanish authorities, central or local—especially the latter—did not do every-thing in their power, the British army was in an area ravaged by the previous passage of the French, Spanish, and British armies, where the Spanish forces fared little better.[23] Besides, if the Allied army had advanced in pursuit of the retreating French, it would have come into far more fertile territory, where many of the supply deficiencies would have been remedied. The British commander furthermore attributed his backward movement to the threat of Marshal Soult's army coming down from Salamanca upon his rear.[24] While it is true that this maneuver by the French marshal was sufficient ground for

21. *The Dispatches*, iv, pp. 518-19. That not all Englishmen felt like Wellington is shown in a dispatch from a Spanish official in Lisbon to Garay, dated October 26, 1809. The Spaniard reported that Brigadier Robert Wilson had assured him before leaving for England that in Spain he had always found good faith, friendship, and limitless hospitality, adding that the opinion that Spaniards were not courageous and could not fight was absurd (Canga Argüelles, *Documentos* . . . , ii, pp. 128-30).

22. The British army left Talavera on August 2 and crossed the Tajo two days later at Puente del Arzobispo.

23. Wellington himself stated in a dispatch of August 8 from Deleytosa to his brother: "This part of Spain is but thinly inhabited, and but ill cultivated in proportion to its extent and its fertility, and it is nearly exhausted." (*The Dispatches*, v, p. 10).

24. Spanish troops were supposed to have occupied in force the pass of Baños controlling the road from Salamanca through Béjar to Plasencia. But this was not done and the French army went through the pass unopposed (*The Dispatches*, iv, pp. 522, 529).

retreat once it had become known at Allied headquarters, Wellesley, as a modern Spanish historian points out, was apprised of the enemy movement on July 30, and his advance against the French withdrawing toward Madrid should have begun on the twenty-ninth or at dawn on the thirtieth.[25] Wellesley also mentioned the fatigue of his troops. Yet, if the French army, after having been bloodied in fruitless attacks, could begin to move in the night of July 28 to 29, why could the Allied army not do the same?[26]

It seems, then, that the supply situation, Soult's advance, the fatigue of his troops, as well as the attitude of General Cuesta, his colleague in the Talavera Campaign, and the battlefield performance of the Spanish troops[27] constituted for Wellesley—Lord Wellington after Talavera—a series of convenient justifications for his retreat. But there were probably other reasons, perhaps more compelling than the supply crisis, for his failure to advance immediately after the French had been repulsed and before he learned of Soult's move upon his rear. After all, his main objective in the Talavera Campaign had been the removal of the French threat to Portugal either by achieving the destruction of Marshal Victor's forces between the Tajo and the Guadiana or by hurling the French army eastward. The victory of Talavera had achieved this aim, and instructions from his superiors in England did not really give him latitude to undertake an advance toward the Spanish capital.[28] Besides, as we have stated earlier,[29] the French army had not really suffered a decisive defeat at Talavera and its morale could not be presumed to be broken. On the contrary, news of Napoleon's victory over Austria could be expected to boost it considerably. Yet Wel-

25. Azcárate, *Wellington y España*, p. 72.

26. *Ibid.*

27. See below.

28. *Ibid.*, pp. 39, 44, 79. That the idea of retreating had crossed Wellesley's mind even before Talavera is shown by his threats, before the battle, to withdraw (see above). According to Canga Argüelles (*Documentos . . .* , II, p. 10), British minister Frere had announced three days before the battle of Talavera that Wellesley intended to withdraw since his objectives in the campaign had been achieved. Though Frere had not mentioned it, one of these objectives was the elimination of the French threat to Portugal. Even before the battle this menace seemed, perhaps, to have been removed.

29. See Chapter VIII.

lington's use of the matter of supplies and of Soult's offensive, and of other reasons, to justify his conduct, and his failure to mention his other motives does not change the fact that in the light of the overall strategic situation his retreat was necessary. If he and the Spanish army after him had not withdrawn and crossed the Tajo, Allied forces might very well have been entrapped between Soult's army to the west and Victor's troops to the east. At best he might have had to parry an extremely dangerous attack on his rear.

To justify his withdrawal Wellington also adduced the "impracticability—as he put it—of the Spanish general, Gregorio de la Cuesta,[30] sixty-eight years old, and the low fighting ability of the Spanish troops involved in the campaign. True, the Spanish general had not spoken a word to the British commander during their meeting at Miravete Pass on July 10, since he refused to speak French and Wellington spoke no Spanish at the time.[31] Yet Cuesta had received Wellington well and had been, in Wellington's own words, "very attentive" to him.[32] On the other hand Cuesta had not fully agreed to his colleague's plan of operations, opposing the latter's suggestion for a strong Spanish diversion toward Avila to the north.[33] Cooperation between the two men was anything but harmonious thereafter. But Cuesta's rather negative attitude must be attributed partly, at least, to the deep suspicion the Spanish general harbored toward Wellington. Cuesta suspected Wellington of being a party to the intrigue then being fostered by Frere in Sevilla with the object of reducing his own authority and giving another general, the Duke of Alburquerque, very popular with British headquarters, an independent command. Thus, by fractioning Spanish military leadership, the way would be open for eventually placing supreme leadership of all Allied troops in Wellington's hands. The latter did not, of course, openly countenance the intrigue against the old gentleman, though he was aware of it, but neither did he disavow it, and he certainly would not have objected to Cuesta's being relieved of his command.

30. "I find General Cuesta more and more impracticable every day." Wellesley to Frere, Talavera de la Reina, July 24, 1809 (*The Dispatches*, IV, p. 498).

31. General O'Donojú acted as interpreter.

32. *The Dispatches*, IV, p. 478.

33. *Ibid.*, p. 477.

Cuesta sensed this and hence the lack of harmony between the two generals, which is reflected in Wellington's correspondence between the conference at Miravete and Cuesta's resignation.[34]

As for the Spanish troops, the Talavera Campaign was the first operation which afforded Wellington a close glance at his allies' equipment, training, and battlefield performance. He was rather unfavorably impressed by what he saw at Cuesta's headquarters seventeen days before Talavera and later during the battle itself.[35] Between the Talavera Campaign and the end of the war he rarely had a kind word for the fighting ability of the Spanish soldier. His scorn for his allies in uniform often led him to make undiscriminating, sweeping, and unjustifiably scathing statements on the quality of Spanish troops, who, after all, were more often than not merely armed peasants and could not be expected to have the military training of experienced soldiers. To be sure, on the evening of July 27, about 2,000 Spanish troops facing the French at Talavera, possibly shaken by their own fire or by a French cavalry attack, broke and ran to the rear. This was regrettable but certainly involved but a small part of the Spanish army, more than 30,000 strong. Yet Wellington wrote to his brother the Marquess on August 24: "In the

34. *The Dispatches*, IV, pp. 476–535, V, pp. 1–38; Azcárate, pp. 49–54; Oman, II, pp. 463–82. Wellington charged that Cuesta's departure from Talavera on August 3 was not justified by the military situation, and accused the Spanish general of abandoning the British wounded in the English field hospital at Talavera. Oman points out that if Cuesta had stayed any longer in Talavera, his retreat across the Tajo at Puente del Arzobispo might very well have been cut off by Marshal Soult's forces (*op. cit.*, II, p. 579). With respect to the wounded, Cuesta did not place enough transport at the disposal of the British officer in charge of the hospital. But the lack of vehicles was general and was felt by the Spaniards too. Of the 4,000 wounded, 2,000 made their way to Trujillo, 1,500 were left behind and were taken prisoner by the French, and 500 died or fell into French hands during their attempt to rejoin their units (*The Dispatches*, V, p. 8; Oman, II, p. 581). Cuesta had a stroke in the night of August 12–13. The Spanish government accepted his resignation on August 14 and he was replaced by General Eguía.

35. Oman, II, pp. 471–72. Lord Londonderry, who saw the Spanish troops at Miravete, described them as "remarkably fine men" and wrote that "it would not have been easy to find a stouter or more hardy looking body of soldiers in any European service." Their equipment, training, and discipline was according to this eyewitness below standard: "Speaking of them in the aggregate they were little better than bold peasantry, armed partially like soldiers, but completely unacquainted with a soldier's duty . . ." (*apud* Oman, *ibid.*).

battle of Talavera, in which the Spanish army, with very trifling exceptions, was not engaged, whole corps threw away their arms, and ran off in my presence."[36] He did not see fit to report that on the whole Spaniards had fought well during the battle.[37] In the same letter Wellington stated: "I have found upon inquiry and from experience the instances of the misbehaviour of the Spanish troops to be so numerous and those of their good behaviour so few that I must conclude that they are troops by no means to be depended upon."[38] And the next day to Castlereagh: "It is impossible to calculate upon any operation with these troops. It is said that sometimes they behave well; though I acknowledge I have never seen them behave otherwise than ill . . . Nothing can be worse than the officers of the Spanish army."[39] And again on the subject of Spanish officers to Marshal Beresford, on September 24 from Badajoz:[40] "There never was anything like the madness, the imprudence, and the presumption of the Spanish officers, in the way they risk their corps, knowing that the national vanity will prevent them from withdrawing them from a situation of danger, and that, if attacked, they must be totally destroyed."[41]

Though Wellington had returned to Portugal, English and Spanish armies continued to collaborate whenever possible during 1810 and 1811,[42] and in some instances Spanish troops fought valiantly, notably

---

36. *The Dispatches*, v, p. 81.

37. Oman, ii, p. 555; Azcárate, p. 67. Oman writes about Talavera: "The Spaniards had little to do upon July 28, but what little they had to do was well done." Surprisingly enough, this is what Wellington reported on July 29 in his official dispatch to Castlereagh and in a letter to his brother in Sevilla. This letter, mentioned by Azcárate, has apparently never been published. Neither the dispatch nor the letter mention the panic of the 2,000 Spanish troops (*op. cit.*, p. 68).

38. *The Dispatches*, *loc. cit.*

39. *Ibid.*, p. 85.

40. Wellington remained at Badajoz from September 3 until December 27 (except for his visits to Lisbon and Andalucía), with his army of 25,000 cantoned along the Guadiana River near the Portuguese border. At the end of December the British moved back into Portugal (Oman, ii, p. 607; Maxwell, ii, pp. 125–29).

41. *The Dispatches*, v, p. 176.

42. Spain sent 8,000 men to help defend Lisbon in the fall of 1810 (see Chapter IX). In March, 1811, both Spanish and British troops took part in the expedition to Algeciras and the subsequent battle of Chiclana (see Chapter

at the battle of Albuera in May, 1811. Yet Wellington always found grounds upon which to criticize Spanish behavior on the battlefield. At Albuera, where Wellington was not present[43] — one of the reasons for the terrible casualties suffered by the British — the Spaniards had withstood French attacks with admirable firmness, but had not maneuvered properly and had failed to give adequate support to their allies. On May 22, from Elvas, across the Portuguese border from Badajoz, the Duke, at his sarcastic best, wrote to his brother Henry the ambassador: "The Spanish troops, I understand, behaved admirably," adding immediately: "They stood still like stocks, both parties at times firing on them, but they were quite immovable, and this is the great cause of all our losses . . . These Spaniards can do nothing but stand still, and we consider ourselves fortunate if they do not run away."[44]

To Earl Bathurst he wrote in October, 1812, from Villa Toro: "I am sorry that I cannot say that the Spanish troops are at all improved in their discipline, their equipment, their organization, or their military spirit." However, the Duke of Ciudad Rodrigo, who had but recently been appointed commander-in-chief of all Spanish armies,[45] went on to say that Spanish soldiers serving together with British units, presumably under overall British command, would perform creditably: "I entertain but little doubt that in the same field with our troops they will behave well."[46] In other words the essential fighting quality of the Spanish soldier was here recognized — a rare and significant admission indeed on the part of the Duke. On December 4, 1812, he wrote to the Spanish minister of war: "I am concerned to

IX), and of course Wellington's army could always count on the help of the Spanish guerrillas, notably those of Julián Sánchez.

43. The commanders were Beresford and the Spaniards Castaños and Blake.

44. *The Dispatches*, VII, p. 568. Albuera was in the words of Oman "the most bloody of all fights of the Peninsular War in proportion to numbers engaged" (*op. cit.*, IV, p. 393). British casualties were 4,200 men out of a total force of 10,000. The 10,000 Portuguese lost 389 men, the Spaniards 1,368 out of 14,000, and the French suffered 7,000 casualties out of 24,000 (Weller, *Wellington in the Peninsula*, pp. 183–85; Oman, IV, pp. 373–403).

45. By the decree of the Cortes of September 22, 1812, which was published only after the official approval of the Prince-Regent of England, obtained on October 26 (Villa-Urrutia, III, p. 150).

46. *The Dispatches*, IX, p. 470.

have to inform you that the discipline of the Spanish armies is in the very lowest state; and their efficiency is, consequently, much deteriorated."[47]

It was Wellington's *leitmotif* throughout the war; yet, as we have just seen, the Duke's basic fairness and courtesy occasionally triumphed over his scorn. Schepeler told the story of how English officers dining with Lord Wellington one day made a number of disparaging comments about Spanish soldiers. Spanish General Zayas, who was present, answered: "Gentlemen, these same soldiers . . . were the defenders of El Ferrol, Tenerife and Buenos Aires."[48] Whereupon Wellington is supposed to have added: "Gentlemen, you have earned this lesson."[49]

When Spanish troops repelled a strong French attack in August, 1813, against their position at San Marcial, close to the Franco-Spanish border, Wellington praised his allies and referred in his official dispatch to the Spanish minister of war to the "most gallant style of the Spanish troops whose conduct was equal to that of any troops that I have ever seen engaged."[50] And after final victory had been achieved in the Peninsula and southern France, when the Allied commander was ready to sail for England, he included the following phrase in his official resignation sent on June 13, 1814 from Bordeaux to King Fernando VII—no doubt, with a touch of diplomatic nicety: "I shall always be happy to testify to the military virtues of the Spanish soldier."[51]

47. *Ibid.*, p. 596.
48. Where Spanish troops had successfully resisted English attacks in previous wars.
49. *Op. cit.*, I, pp. 151–52.
50. *The Dispatches*, XI, p. 67.
51. *Ibid.*, XII, p. 58. In French in the original: *et je me trouverai toujours heureux de donner mon témoignage aux vertus militaires des soldats espagnols.* The sincerity of this parting compliment is of course open to question. If Spanish regulars inspired no admiration in him, he did, however, have a rather high regard for the guerrillas. We have seen his attitude toward Julián Sánchez (see Chapter XV). On May 13, 1812, the British general informed Don Miguel Pereyra Forjaz that the guerrillas were very active throughout Spain and had recently carried out many successful actions against the enemy (*apud* Toreno, p. 404 n.). Muriel Wellesley notes that during his term as Allied commander-in-chief Wellington did his best to have Spanish troops well clothed and fed. According to F. S. Larpent, the advocate-general of the British forces, Wellington was quite popular with the Spanish rank and file (Wellesley, p. 284).

Actually Spaniards could not harbor too much resentment toward Wellington in this touchy matter involving national pride, since the British general often spoke about his own soldiers in most depreciatory terms, though he had the highest regard for their fighting qualities. "I have long been of opinion," he wrote John Villiers from Coimbra, Portugal, on May 30, 1809, "that a British army could bear neither success nor failure . . . They have plundered the country most terribly, which has given me the greatest concern."[52] The same day he wrote to Castlereagh: "The army behave terribly ill. They are a rabble who cannot bear success any more than Sir John Moore's army could bear failure . . ."[53] And shortly before the battle of Salamanca, to the Earl of Liverpool: "The outrages committed by the British soldiers belonging to this army have become so enormous, and they have produced an effect upon the minds of the people of the country so injurious to the cause and likely to be so dangerous to the army itself, that I request your Lordship's early attention to the subject."[54] "We have in the service the scum of the earth as common soldiers," he complained to Earl Bathurst shortly after the battle of Vitoria . . . As to the non-commissioned officers, as I have repeatedly stated, they are as bad as the men . . ."[55]

Wellington had indeed good reasons for thus qualifying his own soldiers. The methods of recruitment used in the British army frequently brought highly undesirable elements into the ranks. Unfortunately many men enlisted for drink, and drunkenness was consequently the scourge of Wellington's army throughout the Peninsular War.[56] Even before he had become chief of the British forces in the Peninsula, English troops had made themselves known for their unjustifiable behavior toward the inhabitants of León and Galicia. During the withdrawal to La Coruña in December, 1808 and January, 1809, many outrages were committed by the retreating English troops. Of the sack of Villafranca, Commissary General Schaumann wrote: "In the end Villafranca was literally plundered, and the

52. *The Dispatches*, IV, p. 343.
53. *Ibid.*, p. 352.
54. *Ibid.*, IX, p. 227.
55. *Ibid.*, X, p. 496.
56. Davies, pp. 19–20.

drunkenness that prevailed among the troops led to the most shameful incidents."[57]

In January, 1812, Wellington scored a major victory when his troops took Ciudad Rodrigo by storm. The successful assault, which cost his army upward of 1,000 casualties, was followed by the sack of the town. Only few inhabitants were killed, but the excesses committed by the victorious soldiers were incredible. "After all resistance had ceased, the usual scene of riot, plunder, and confusion . . . occurred. Every house was entered and despoiled; the spirit stores were forced open; the soldiery got desperately excited; and in the madness of their intoxication, committed many acts of silly and wanton violence."[58]

The worst plundering took place in April of the same year after the fall of the fortress town of Badajoz to Anglo-Portuguese troops. The French garrison had resisted valiantly and inflicted huge losses on the attacking forces.[59] Following the assault the victors gave themselves over to an orgy of raping, killing, and plundering, the like of which was seen only on few occasions in the Peninsular War. True, military custom in the early nineteenth century dictated that a garrison resisting to the last was not entitled to any consideration,[60] and furthermore "there was a close connexion in the minds of all soldiers . . . between the idea that an over-obstinate garrison had forfeited quarter, and the idea that the town they had defended was liable to sack."[61]

The French had applied this unwritten law in the hours following

57. *Op. cit.*, p. 113. Cf. also Oman I, pp. 546–78.

58. Maxwell, II, p. 440. Cf. also Bryant, *Years of Victory*, p. 465.

59. The final assault cost the Anglo-Portuguese attacking forces 2,200 men (Oman, v, p. 250). It is said that when Wellington was informed about the high number of casualties in his ranks he was grief-stricken (Napier, *History of the War in the Peninsula and in the South of France from the Year 1807 to the Year 1814*, IV, p. 123.

60. Napoleon had decreed that a fortress should stand at least one assault before surrendering. This ordinance was severely criticized by many Englishmen, as it was bound to result in more obstinate and even desperate French defenses of towns and heavier losses among the attacking forces (Napier, v, p. 269).

61. Oman, v, p. 260.

the storming of Tarragona in 1811, when many defending soldiers and many civilians lost their lives after the victorious forces had irrupted into the town. But Tarragona's inhabitants were not France's allies, and though there was no excuse for the horrors visited upon the population of the Catalan port, from the French point of view it was an enemy town. Yet even in those days the garrisons of towns like Tarragona that had been taken by assault were not necessarily put to the sword, partly for humanitarian reasons and partly because of the fear of reprisals. And the British army in the Peninsula did not liquidate French garrisons whose fortresses had been stormed. For example, Badajoz was a Spanish fortress occupied by French forces. It might have been expected that the attacking troops would vent their fury upon the garrison, but certainly not on the Spanish population; yet the reverse happened. While the French were relatively well treated and while there were even cases of fraternization between British and French troops,[62] the town itself was subjected for two days and two nights to the most horrible sack.

Napier, who certainly cannot be accused of pro-Spanish partiality, described the destruction of Badajoz in the following terms:

Now commenced that wild and desperate wickedness which tarnished the lustre of the soldier's heroism. All indeed were not alike, hundreds risked and many lost their lives in straining to stop the violence, but madness generally prevailed, and as the worst men were leaders here all the dreadful passions of human nature were displayed. Shameless rapacity, brutal intemperance, savage lust, cruelty and murder, shrieks and piteous lamentations, groans, shouts, imprecations, the hissing of fires bursting from the houses, the crashing of doors and windows, and the reports of muskets used in violence, resounded for two days and nights in the streets of Badajos (*sic*). On the third, when the city was sacked, when the soldiers were exhausted by their own excesses, the tumult rather subsided than was quelled.[63]

Wellington was either unwilling or unable to stop the crimes that were being committed under his nose in Badajoz. Perhaps he was too crushed by the terrible losses suffered by his army to bestir himself to vigorous action. Be that as it may, on April 7, at the end of the day,

62. Villa-Urrutia, II, p. 483.
63. *Op. cit.,* IV, p. 122.

when the raping, plundering, and killing had been continuing for fifteen to eighteen hours, the Duke of Ciudad Rodrigo issued a rather odd-sounding order: "It is now full time that the plunder of Badajoz should cease, an officer and six steady non-commissioned officers will be sent from each regiment, British and Portuguese, of the 3rd, 4th, 5th and Light Division into the town at 5:00 A.M. tomorrow morning, to bring away any men still straggling there."[64]

Fortunately for Anglo-Spanish relations the sack of Badajoz came at a time when Spain was desperately waiting for a victory to offset the disaster of Valencia.[65] Ciudad Rodrigo's fall the previous January, though a great success, did not have the importance of the key fortress of Badajoz, which for the French constituted a precious link between their northern and southern armies. And not only did the sack of Badajoz cause very little protest on the Spanish side, but the Cortes sent their thanks to the British army and the Regency granted Wellington the Cross of San Fernando.[66]

By August, 1812, after the victory of Salamanca, whatever rancor had remained over Badajoz was forgotten. Wellington's popularity with Spaniards now reached its high-water mark,[67] and the Duke of Ciudad Rodrigo, taking possession of Madrid, had the satisfaction of being given a hero's welcome. This was not a Spanish town that had to be taken by force and then, like Ciudad Rodrigo and Badajoz, had to suffer rape, plunder, and murder. This was the capital of Spain, which the enemy had abandoned and which was opening its arms to its allies. "It is impossible to describe the joy manifested by the inhabitants of Madrid upon our arrival," wrote Wellington to Earl Bathurst on August 13, one day after setting foot in Madrid.[68] "Every-

64. *Supplementary Dispatches*, VII, p. 311, *apud* Oman, v, p. 261.
65. See Chapter IX.
66. Toreno, p. 405.
67. It was the time when Spanish poems, like the following, were composed in his honor: "May fame's trumpet/Spread the news/From East to West/That nothing in the world/Can stop him . . . Generous Albion/Has with a wise hand/Laid the groundwork for your triumphs/Against the tyrant . . . /May Spain inscribe/Your memory in marble/ . . . May your friendship, Lord Wellington/Be eternal,/As all loyal Spain wishes it . . . /Eternal glory to the invicible Duke/And to our ally, the English nation (CDF, Vol. CMV, pp. 84–85).
68. *The Dispatches*, IX, p. 350.

body was shouting Velintón, Belintón, Vellíston," wrote Mesonero Romanos, recalling the memorable days preceding the Duke's entrance into Madrid.[69] Once in the capital Wellington was solemnly received at the city hall, where he went upstairs to the balcony and answered the crowds' enthusiastic applause with "all the courtesy compatible with English severity."[70] The welcome given the British soldiers by the inhabitants of Madrid could be compared only to that granted Fernando VII when he arrived from Aranjuez in March, 1808. "I never before witnessed such a scene," remembered Private Wheeler. "At the distance of five miles from the gates we were met by the inhabitants, each had brought out something, viz, laurel, flowers, bread, wine, grapes, lemonade . . . , tobacco, sweetmeats, etc. The road represented a moving forest, from the great multitude of people carrying boughs . . . Thus we moved slowly on, amidst the sweet voices of thousands of the most bewitching and interesting little devils I had ever seen . . . But as we approached the city the crowd increased, the people were mad with joy . . . Wellington was at the head of the column. When we entered the city the shouting increased tenfold, every bell that had a clapper was set ringing, the windows were ornamented with rich drapery embroidered with gold and silver, such as is only used on great festivals when the Host is carried. The whole of the windows and tops of the houses were crowded with Spanish beauty, waving white handkerchiefs. The people endeavoured to drag us into their houses. Suffice it to say that we were several hours going to the convent where we were to be quartered, that under ordinary circumstances might have been walked in fifteen minutes."[71]

Alas, the occupation of Madrid did not mean final victory. More than a year and a half of fighting lay ahead, and in that interval another Spanish town felt the full wrath of victory-drunk Anglo-Portuguese soldiery. On August 31, 1813, it was the turn of San Sebastián, in the north, close to the French border. Anglo-Portuguese troops took the town by assault after overcoming last-

69. *Memorias de un setentón*, p. 95.
70. *Ibid.*, p. 97.
71. *The Letters of Private Wheeler, 1809–1828*, pp. 90–91.

ditch resistance on the part of the French garrison. Here too, rape, murder, and plunder raged through the captured town for hours and a terrible fire completed the work of destruction. And again, French soldiers were treated kindly by the victors while the Spanish inhabitants suffered. "The storms of Badajoz and Rodrigo were followed by the worst excesses; yet they fell infinitely short of those committed after San Sebastián was carried by assault," wrote Maxwell.[72] And Napier: "At Rodrigo intoxication and plunder had been the principal object; at Badajos (*sic*) lust and murder were joined to rapine and drunkenness; but at San Sebastián, the direst, the most revolting cruelty was added to the catalogue of crimes . . ."[73] The origin of the fire which reduced San Sebastián to smoldering ruins is unclear. While the British blamed it on the French, the Spaniards blamed it on the British and some quarters in Cádiz even claimed that the destruction of the port had been ordered in high British spheres to eliminate San Sebastián's commercial importance. The British, and Wellington in the first place, indignantly rejected these charges,[74] but were forced to admit that their troops had once more behaved atrociously.[75]

Badajoz had been bad enough, but it had happened the previous year, when Napoleon had not yet been defeated in Russia and when Allied victory in the Peninsula was by no means assured. There had been little unfavorable reaction in free Spain to the atrocities committed in the fortress on the Guadiana. But San Sebastián fell at a time when final victory seemed to be just around the corner and a number of Spaniards were no longer willing to tolerate such excesses. Consequently the protests in the Cádiz press, especially the liberal newspa-

72. *Op. cit.*, III, p. 227.
73. *Op. cit.*, V, p. 278.
74. In Villa-Urrutia's opinion, the blame must be laid at the Allies' door, but it was not ordered by the British government or military chiefs. It was simply a case of a fire breaking out in the general disorder accompanying the sack of the town (*op. cit.*, III, pp. 181–82).
75. Canga Argüelles, *Documentos* . . . II, pp. 171–74; Toreno, p. 479; Wellesley, *The Man Wellington*, pp. 280–83. ". . . In regard to the plunder of the town by the soldiers," wrote Wellington to his brother Henry on October 9, 1813, "I am the last man who will deny it, because I know that it is true." (*The Dispatches*, XI, p. 173).

pers, mounted throughout the month of September, 1813, and Wellington, stung by the vociferous criticism, complained bitterly to his brother about the Cádiz newspapers.[76]

It was a bad year for Wellington's relations with the Spanish government, but then, just like his country's collaboration with Spain, his own dealings with the Spanish authorities had been beset with difficulties from an early stage. We have seen the friction between him and the Junta Central. The fall of this organism and the establishment of the Regency and the Cortes in Cádiz coincided with his withdrawal into Portugal and his further retreat in the summer of 1810 before the power of the French offensive. Cádiz was fighting for its life and so was Wellington's army. Relations between the English general and the Spanish government consequently ceased to be a problem for the time being, since there was little communication between them. This state of affairs continued well into 1812, when Wellington was once more firmly established on Spanish soil and when the extraordinary prestige which he had acquired through his victories was to earn him shortly the post of commander-in-chief of the Allied armies in the Peninsula. During the years which Wellington spent in Portugal and along the Spanish-Portuguese frontier, he kept himself well informed, however, on the political situation in Cádiz, and he was well aware of the momentous changes that were taking place on the Spanish political scene.

Wellington never had a high opinion of the Spanish national assembly. As early as September 22, 1809, he had written to his brother Richard, then minister in Sevilla: "I acknowledge that I have a great dislike to a new popular assembly . . . I declare that if I were in Bonaparte's situation, I should leave the English and the Cortes to settle Spain in the best manner they could; and I should entertain very little doubt but that in a very short space of time Spain must fall into the hands of France."[77] To Wellington's ultraconservative political views the reforms enacted in the Cortes were anathema. Besides, he was primarily interested in measures tending to strengthen Spain's military effort, and in his opinion the new govern-

76. Villa-Urrutia, III, pp. 170, 195; cf. Wellington, *The Dispatches*, XI, pp. 171–233.

77. *The Dispatches*, V, p. 170.

ment was not working in this direction. "What can be done for this lost nation?" he exclaimed in a letter to Henry Wellesley from Madrid, on August 23, 1812.[78]

For the Constitution of Cádiz he had little regard, though he had it faithfully proclaimed in the towns—including Madrid—which his troops won back from the French. In a long letter to Don Andrés Angel de la Vega Infanzón, a member of the Cortes representing Asturias and one of his unconditional admirers,[79] written from his winter quarters at Freneda, Portugal, on January 20, 1813, he proceeded to lecture his friend on the flaws he saw in the Spanish form of government. Among other things the Duke of Ciudad Rodrigo suggested that the Cortes repeal Article 110 of the Constitution, which prevented deputies from being reelected, as well as the entire seventh chapter, which set up the Council of State. "But the greatest objection which I have to the whole system established by the Constitution," wrote Wellington, "is that in a country in which almost all property consists in land, and there are the largest landed proprietors which exist in Europe, no measures should have been adopted, and no barriers should have been provided, to guard landed property from the encroachments, injustice, and violence to which it is at all times liable, but particularly in the progress of revolutions." The solution in the eyes of the Duke was the establishment of an "assembly of the great landed proprietors," patterned on the British House of Lords, "having concurrent powers of legislation with the Cortes." Wellington also suggested that the Regency be concentrated in the hands of one person, preferably "of the blood royal," assisted by a Council of Regency consisting of five persons who should be members of the Cortes. In this manner there would be a

78. *Ibid.*, IX, p. 369. Though Wellington had a low opinion of almost everything Spanish, it is interesting to note that one of his closest personal friends—and he had very few of them during his life—was a Spaniard. This man was General Miguel Ricardo de Alava, who served as Wellington's aide-de-camp during the Peninsular War and in 1815 at the battle of Waterloo. When the restoration of absolutism in 1823 forced Alava to emigrate to England, Wellington accorded him a gracious and generous hospitality (cf. Azcárate, pp. 268–74).

79. It is possible that Vega Infanzón, who had accompanied Toreno to London in June, 1808, was acting as an agent of the British embassy in Cádiz (Azcárate, p. 135).

connection between the executive and the legislative branches of government, which was lacking in the prevailing political structure. In some of his suggestions Wellington showed a keen understanding and profound knowledge of political theory, though his preoccupation with the protection of landed property sounds to us unreasonably conservative. His remarks on the necessity of a closer connection between the executive and the legislative, of the possibility of reelection of deputies, and of a second chamber were quite wise. A higher chamber had also been advocated by Jovellanos and might have in the end saved the Cortes. "I have written to you in English," concluded Wellington, "because I write in this language with more ease; but if you should answer me, write in Spanish, which I can read perfectly."[80]

Wellington's appointment as commander-in-chief of Allied forces in the Peninsula in the fall of 1812 should have inaugurated an era of happy collaboration between the general and the Cortes, especially since the Spanish government had dealt firmly with General Ballesteros, who had rebelled against this measure, by exiling him to Ceuta in Africa. But unfortunately the opposite happened. Causes for friction were numerous: First of all, the extent of the Duke's authority, which he of course wanted as ample as possible, while Spanish authorities were bound to resist some of his demands.[81] During his visit to Cádiz in December, 1812, though he was extremely well received,[82] this difficulty was not completely ironed out and continued to plague Anglo-Spanish cooperation practically until the end of the campaign. Then there was the matter of the *jefes políticos* (political chiefs) of the provinces, whom Wellington wanted to be subordinated to the generals in command of the corresponding military regions, a request which the Cortes denied.[83] Nor did Wellington agree with the Spanish government's policy toward the *afrancesados*. In a letter to Spanish Minister of War O'Donojú, written on

---

80. *The Dispatches*, x, p. 66. This letter, pp. 61–66. This was true but his written Spanish was apparently well below his level of comprehension (cf. Azcárate, pp. 273–74).

81. One of these was that his recommendations should determine the amount of money earmarked for military necessities (*ibid.*, p. 138).

82. See Chapter IX.

83. *Ibid.*, p. 139.

June 11, 1813, he urged the Cortes to "grant a general amnesty, with certain exceptions."[84] There was also the question of the liberal press in Cádiz, which in early 1813 began to attack British policy in the Peninsula and thus aroused the ire of the British ambassador and his illustrious brother the general.[85] This campaign reached its climax after the sack of San Sebastián and continued into the fall of 1813. Even before the polemic over San Sebastián, on August 30, Wellington, stung by the action of the Regency in removing two Spanish generals from their command without consulting him,[86] had announced his resignation as commander-in-chief. The question was brought before the Cortes, but on November 29 the assembly, by a unanimous vote, expressed its desire to see Wellington continue in his position.[87]

By this time most liberals, who at first had welcomed Wellington's appointment,[88] had become decidedly disgruntled over the attitude of the commander-in-chief, and it was the *serviles* who now supported him.[89] The feeling between the liberals and the British general was mutual. On June 29, 1813, Wellington indicated his contempt for the political structure of Spain in a letter to Earl Bathurst: "We and the powers of Europe are interested in the success of the war in the Peninsula; but the creatures (*sic*) who govern at Cádiz appear to feel no such interest. All that they care about really is to hear the praise of their foolish Constitution. There is not one of them who does not feel that it cannot be put in practice; but their vanity is interested to force it down people's throats." Wellington, as an ultraconservative, could not possibly grasp the true meaning of the revolution of Cádiz. But it cannot be denied that he was also a supreme realist and that some of his observations on the Spanish reforms were not devoid of common sense. He undoubtedly despised the Spanish Inquisition—his Anglo-

84. *The Dispatches*, x, p. 431.
85. Villa-Urrutia, III, pp. 168–69.
86. Azcárate, pp. 142–44. The generals were Castaños and his nephew Girón, both highly inimical toward the liberal majority in the Cortes (*ibid.*).
87. Villa-Urrutia, III, p. 197; Azcárate, p. 144.
88. Among the supporters of Wellington's appointment to this post were such outstanding liberals as Toreno, Argüelles, Calatrava, and Mejía (Villa-Urrutia, III, p. 148).
89. Azcárate, p. 144.

Irish Protestant background could only reinforce his natural aversion as an Englishman toward this institution. Consequently, what he had to say about the Spanish Holy Office in this same letter cannot be dismissed as the ravings of a fanatical reactionary: "I apprized them, when at Cádiz, of the danger of hurrying on that measure[90] . . . But they were determined to persevere, although they knew that the abolition of the Inquisition was disagreeable to the clergy, and to the great body of the people."[91] Wellington may have been right. The Cortes did perhaps proceed too hastily in eliminating the Inquisition. At any rate, as we pointed out earlier,[92] tackling both the Church and the absolute monarchy at one and the same time was a task to which the Cortes was not equal.

On July 8, 1813, Wellington wrote to Lieutenant General Bentinck: "Neither government nor Cortes appear to me to care much about the foreign war. The former are a mere instrument and creature of the latter. All that these care about is the praise of their stupid Constitution, and how to carry on the war against the Bishops and priests . . . "[93] Four days later, in a communication to Earl Bathurst, Wellington, while advising the British government against intervening for the time being in the internal affairs of Spain, "at least directly"—on the side of the conservatives, of course—expressed the hope that the "violence and democratic principles [of the liberals] will induce some of the provinces to declare against them." Then Britain might "come forward, particularly if its support or its opinions should be asked for." In case such a situation did not develop, His Majesty's Government should simply wait with patience "for the termination of all this folly, till a regular government shall be established in Spain."[94]

When the "folly" ended, that is, when Fernando VII smashed the structure of reform erected at Cádiz, Wellington paid one last visit to Madrid on May 24, 1814. The story has generally been until recently that the Duke went to Spain primarily to prevent civil strife and that

90. The abolition of the Inquisition.
91. *The Dispatches*, x, p. 474.
92. See Chapter XI.
93. *Ibid.*, p. 516.
94. *Ibid.*, 524-25.

he cautioned Fernando against reactionary excesses.[95] Even liberal historians like Toreno have sustained this thesis.[96] Azcárate has recently advanced the opinion, however, that Wellington was primarily interested in achieving an alliance between Spain and England involving far-reaching political and commercial cooperation. This alliance was designed to give Great Britain a share of the trade with Spanish America in return for British support for Spain's policy with respect to her colonies.[97] Wellington, we are told, was only marginally interested in bringing his moderating influence to bear on the Spanish monarch's reactionary fury.[98] The Spanish historian has also pointed out that on his way to the Spanish capital the Allied commander-in-chief exerted great pressure on the chiefs of two Spanish armies which might very well have defied the king and backed the Constitution, and secured their submission to Fernando. Wellington may thus have prevented civil war, but in the process he made it easy for the king to wreak vengeance on the liberals.[99]

The Duke, no doubt, did urge moderation on the Spanish court,[1]

95. Villa-Urrutia, III, p. 198; Gleig, *The Life of the Duke of Wellington,* pp. 210–11; Guedalla, *The Duke,* p. 251; Wellesley, p. 314. "I propose to go to Madrid in order to try whether I cannot prevail upon all parties to be more moderate, and to adopt a constitution more likely to be practicable and to contribute to the peace and happiness of the nation" (Wellington to the Earl of Liverpool, Paris, May 9, 1814, *The Dispatches,* XII, p. 4). And on May 25, he ended a letter to Sir Charles Stuart from Madrid with the words: "I have accomplished my object in coming here; that is, I think there will certainly be no civil war at present; and I propose to set out on my return on the 5th of June" (*ibid.,* p. 28).

96. *Op. cit.,* p. 525.

97. A new treaty of alliance was actually signed in July, but Spanish American trade was not opened to Great Britain.

98. *Op. cit.,* pp. 223–28. Cf. Wellington, *The Dispatches,* XII, pp. 28, 37–45. Wellington did consider Fernando's repressive measures "highly impolitic" (letter to Charles Stuart, May 25, 1814, *The Dispatches,* XII, p. 27).

99. Cf. Wellington's letters to the Duke of San Carlos and to Castlereagh on May 21, 1814, *ibid.,* pp. 25–26.

1. As Azcárate has underlined (*op. cit.,* pp. 226–27), the space taken up by Spanish internal affairs in Wellington's memorandum to Fernando of June 1, 1814 (*The Dispatches,* XII, pp. 40–75) constitutes only a small part of the document when compared to that devoted to the other aspects of his negotiations. However, his report, also of June 1, to Castlereagh, now foreign secretary (*ibid.,* pp. 37–40), starts off with the matter of the political persecutions. According to the general, the Duke of San Carlos, the new secretary of state,

but his démarche did not stop the wave of persecutions which was engulfing Spain. After he left Madrid on June 5, Spanish jails continued to be filled with hapless men whose sole crime had been the endeavor to build a new Spain.[2]

When Wellington left Spain he carried with him the conviction that his Anglo-Portuguese troops had had the lion's share in the final Allied victory. He had indicated this time after time in his correspondence during the war: The British-Portuguese forces had to rely on themselves since little help could be expected from the inefficient Spaniards. The theme was taken up by a number of British historians, who thus tended to consider British military contribution to final victory a decisive factor in the struggle in Spain and Portugal, belittling Spanish achievements. Conversely Spanish historians have naturally emphasized Spain's role, often to the point of minimizing British help. As time affords a clearer perspective, each side has become more willing to recognize that neither ally could have been dispensed with if final victory were to be attained. Gone are the days when a British historian would assert: "When an English force took the field, the Spaniards ceased to act as principals in the contest carried on in the heart of their country, and involving their existence as an independent nation . . . Copious supplies from England and the valour of the Anglo-Portuguese troops supported the war, and it was the gigantic vigour with which the Duke of Wellington resisted the fierceness of France, and sustained the weakness of three inefficient cabinets that delivered the Peninsula."[3]

Most English students of this period will today recognize that Spanish resistance was as vital to the Allied triumph in the Peninsula as Wellington's victories. True, Spanish regular armies operating

---

had promised him that the "decree for calling the Cortes should appear forthwith; secondly, that all the prisoners should be released on St. Ferdinand's day, the 30th May, excepting such as it was determined to bring to trial, who should be *fairly* tried, without loss of time; thirdly, that the king was determined to carry into execution all he had promised in his decree of the 4th of May . . ." The Duke of Ciudad Rodrigo was forced to admit that these promises had not been kept. He further stated that he had told San Carlos that Fernando could not count on English support unless he changed his methods (*ibid.*, p. 38).

2. Wellington formed a favorable opinion of the King, though not of his ministers (letter to Stuart, *loc. cit.*).

3. Napier, I, pp. xvii–xviii.

independently were usually routed, but, not counting Zaragoza and Gerona, quite a few Spanish fortress towns fought well. Ciudad Rodrigo's stand in 1810 was of particular importance to the Anglo-Portuguese force, for it held up Masséna's army six precious weeks, which gave Wellington time to prepare for the coming onslaught on Portugal.[4] But aside from Spanish fortress cities and Spain's regular armies, which, though regularly beaten, so often regrouped to fight another day, the great contribution on the Spanish side was the resistance of the Spanish people as a whole. If it had not been for this relentless hostility, which manifested itself in ceaseless guerrilla activity and passive opposition, Wellington could not possibly have triumphed. The British army never had more than 60,000 men in the Peninsula, and the Anglo-Portuguese forces never had more than 81,000. In 1813, before the battle of Vitoria, when Wellington could count on this latter force, the French had still more than 200,000 soldiers in Spain.[5] Why were the French marshals unable to take advantage of their overwhelming superiority in numbers? Simply because they had to hold down the huge areas they occupied with a sufficient quantity of forces to fight the ever-present guerrillas and to discourage any full-scale explosion by a hostile population. If Spain had been a friendly nation or a nation suffering the presence of foreign troops with a resignation devoid of any potential for resistance, the French could very well have left skeleton garrisons behind and concentrated the necessary number of men to crush Wellington's much smaller force. During the winter of 1808–1809, Napoleon, his army not yet tied down by the garrisoning of huge territories in central and southern Spain, was able to hurl 80,000 soldiers against Moore, forcing him into a disastrous retreat.[6] But as the war progressed the picture changed. Concentrating, say, 100,000 men in the Peninsula meant giving up territory to insurrection, and until late in the war the French were not ready to make this sacrifice. If in the summer of 1810, the thousands upon thousands of French troops

4. See Chapter IX.
5. Weller, p. 248.
6. If Soult at La Coruña had had even half of the total French force which originally began the pursuit, he would have overwhelmed Moore's 15,000 and the British would not have been able to extricate their expeditionary force through evacuation.

fighting the guerrillas in Navarra, the Basque provinces, and other areas had been free to join Masséna's march on Portugal, they might have tipped the balance decisively in favor of Masséna and might have been sufficient to smash through Torres Vedras. But Mina and other guerrilla leaders gave the French no peace and tied down troops urgently needed elsewhere. It was more or less the same story throughout most of the war. The French were prisoners of the occupied areas. True, at times it was rivalry and jealousy among French marshals which prevented effective coordination of efforts and concentration of large masses of men for a given operation. But by and large this was not the main reason for French inability to deal Wellington a concentrated blow. French commanders knew that if they withdrew the majority of their troops from a given territory to fight elsewhere in the Peninsula, this region would be lost to the guerrillas and the population behind them. The prospect of withdrawing and concentrating for a difficult campaign to eliminate the British, and of then having to reestablish through more bitter fighting their control over the abandoned territories, was more than even the intrepid Napoleonic marshals could stomach. This is essentially what spared Great Britain another painful evacuation after 1809.

In the fall of 1812, King Joseph was finally able to concentrate 100,000 men against Wellington and chase him right back to the Portuguese border. That the British commander was not overwhelmed was due as much to French caution and to dismal weather as to his great military talent, and also due to the fact that he was now leading a veteran Allied army of respectable size—70,000 men—which had tasted victory the preceding summer. King Joseph had not succeeded in smashing Wellington, but he had scored an impressive success. In the process however, and this is most significant, he had had to give up irrevocably all of Andalucía.

Now let us just suppose that Napoleon had crushed the British army in the summer and fall of 1810 and had pushed it into the sea. Would this have enabled him to subject all Spain? Perhaps, but let us keep in mind that it took the Roman Empire two centuries to subjugate the Iberian Peninsula. And, looking back at recent history, let us not forget that France was unable in seven years of atrocious warfare to stamp out the Algerian guerrillas, in spite of her 400,000 troops and her ultramodern weapons. To this it could be objected that the Algerian guerrillas received help from neighboring Tunisia and Morocco. But then, what would have prevented Spanish guerrillas from receiving aid from British ships cruising along the long Spanish coastline, as in fact happened during the war?[7] And, if Britain had fallen or had made a peace which would have abandoned fighting Spain to its enemies, what then? But let us not waste time on hypothetical situations. We don't really know what would have happened if England had been decisively defeated. Let us pay homage to Wellington's immense military talent and recognize the tremendous impact of his victories. But let us also give fighting Spain her due. The Englishman William Jacob, who had been traveling throughout Andalucía in 1809 and early 1810, did precisely this in most eloquent terms in February, 1811, when Masséna's legions were still deep in Portugal:

I am far from undervaluing the assistance we have afforded to the cause of Spain; an army of forty thousand British troops, under such a general as now, for the honour of England, commands in Portugal, must be esteemed a most powerful and beneficial assistance . . . But if the hopes of Spain had been destroyed by the dispersion of her armies; if the capture of her cities and her towns had subdued the spirit of the country; if the severe sufferings of the peasantry had reduced them to apply for mercy to the victors; would this small number of British warriors, with all their discipline, and all their courage, have been able to withstand the numerous, the overwhelming forces, which France had destined to combat them? Could British arms, deprived of that powerful aid which operates without éclat, which in the obscurity of local patriotism acquires no fame beyond its own district, but which creates distrust and terror in the enemy have made that firm stand which has lately been displayed? Are not we, is not Europe, then indebted to the persevering habits, to the patriotic feelings, to the everlasting hatred of France which animates the people of Spain? Does not the only hope of civilized man depend, in a great degree, on that resistance to France, of which Spain has exhibited the most persevering, if not the most brilliant, examples? And if Spain be conquered; if she be so conquered as to yield no resistance to the

7. Especially the guerrillas fighting in the areas of Santander and the Basque provinces, in the north of Spain.

oppressor (for I should not consider the expulsion of the British army, the dispersion of her own regular troops, and the capture of all her strong towns, as a conquest), what prospect remains to the continent but the lengthened continuance of that gloomy despotism, which threatens to bury in darkness all that has elevated the character of man.[8]

8. *Travels in the South of Spain,* pp. 397–98.

XVIII

AN END AND A BEGINNING

[1]

As THE year 1814 dawned on Spain, few Spaniards could doubt that the end of the war was in sight. The French were still holding parts of Catalonia and a few fortresses in the kingdom of Valencia. But the end was in sight. Napoleon was being threatened by Allied invading forces from the east as well as from the south, where Wellington's Anglo-Portuguese-Spanish army was making steady progress. It was merely a question of time before the last invaders would be driven from the national soil and before Fernando would return from France. Spaniards, though following the war news with great interest and proud that Spanish troops were now advancing through south-western France under Wellington, showed as much, if not greater, interest in domestic affairs.

For in this area, too, war was raging. It was a war which had begun in Cádiz and had spread throughout free Spain. It was a bitter conflict, though waged for the time being only with words. The Cortes had opened its sessions in the capital on January 15 in the ramshackle building of the old theater Los Caños del Peral. Conservatives were in the majority,[1] but they lacked the cohesion and the

1. It will be recalled that the elections for the ordinary Cortes the previous year had given conservative elements the majority. As many of the newly elected deputies had not gone to Cádiz, where a yellow fever epidemic had broken out, their places had been taken by members of the outgoing extraordinary Cortes. Through this device the liberals had been able to maintain their advantage as long as the Cortes had remained in the Isle of León (see Chapter XI).

leadership to assert themselves decisively. The liberals, who could still come up with the more effective parliamentary leadership, made full use of their cohesion and their intellectual superiority to make up for their numerical inferiority.[2] Throughout the early part of the year tension steadily increased within as well as without the Congress. In the Cortes, on February 3, Don Juan López Reina, conservative deputy for Sevilla, enraged the liberals but apparently also shocked a good number of moderate conservatives, when he calmly declared: "When his Majesty, Don Fernando VII was born, he was born with a right to absolute sovereignty over the Spanish nation. When, through the abdication of Charles IV he obtained the crown, he acquired the right to wield the power of absolute monarch and lord . . ." Shouts from all sides interrupted the conservative speaker but he calmly proceeded to make his point: "When Don Fernando VII . . . occupies the throne once more, it is indispensable that he exercise absolute sovereignty from the moment he sets foot on the border . . . " This was too much for the Cortes, whose predecessors had done away with absolutism—on paper at least—when they had adopted, two years before, the Constitution of Cádiz. López Reina was not allowed to continue and was expelled from the hall. Ultra-conservatives, now numerically stronger, tried to let the matter rest there, but the liberals were able to have the whole matter referred first to a special commission and then to the Tribunal of the Cortes. However, since López Reina went into hiding and since the Cortes did not have long to live, the affair simply died out.[3]

Outside of the assembly, while liberal and conservative newspapers were hurling invectives at each other and were warning their respective supporters to be ready to use force in the struggle against the opposition,[4] conservatives were plotting to bring about a change in the prevailing form of government. In a number of large cities such as Madrid, Sevilla, and Córdoba, leaders of the *serviles*, including

2. According to British Ambassador Wellesley, writing to Castlereagh on February 25, 1814, the *serviles* had a two-to-one superiority (*apud* Baumgarten, I, p. 583). The task of the liberals was made easier by the fact that no crucial reform was voted on during the 1814 session (Toreno, p. 513).

3. Toreno, p. 504.

4. Artola, *Los orígenes de la España contemporánea*, I, pp. 618–20. Particularly militant on the conservative side was the newspaper *La Atalaya de la Mancha*, published by a Hieronymite monk, Padre Agustín Castro.

generals such as O'Donnell, at the time on leave in Córdoba, decided that their first aim must be to get rid of the Regency. The three-man executive, composed of Cardinal Luis de Borbón, Don Pedro Agar, and Don Gabriel Císcar, was too liberal for them. If only some conservatives like General Castaños and Don Miguel de Lardizábal[5] could form a council of regency presided over by a person closely related to Fernando VII, such as Princess Carlota Joaquina of Brazil, the liberal regime would suffer a damaging blow from which it might not recover.[6] But the liberals were not asleep. They were not unaware of the machinations of their adversaries and took measures to block the plans of the *serviles*. To prevent a coup d'état they had seen to it that General Villacampa, a confirmed liberal, was appointed to the post of military governor of Madrid. Villacampa's vigilance soon brought about the arrest of a number of persons trying to promote antireformist disorders in the capital.[7]

But the *serviles* were indefatigable. All means were considered legitimate if they brought about the downfall of the liberal regime. An impostor by the name of Jean Barteau was paid by certain antireformist elements in the southern towns of Granada and Baza to pose as a French general and accuse a number of liberals, including Agustín Argüelles, of plotting with Napoleon and his agents. Assuming the fictitious title of General Audinot, the impostor declared that Spanish liberals were contemplating installing in Spain an Iberian republic sponsored by the French government. While the *serviles* were rubbing their hands, *liberales* were indignantly rejecting the charges of the "French general." In the Cortes Argüelles offered to submit to an investigation to confound the calumniator. The matter was turned over to the judicial authorities, and fortunately for the *liberales*, Audinot finally confessed the whole scheme, thus saving them from even more vicious persecution at the hands of Fernando, who by then had returned to Spain.[8]

While the liberals could hold their own in the Cortes in what were

5. Both had been members of the first Regency. The latter was the author of the pamphlet which in 1811 bitterly attacked the Cortes (see Chapter XI).

6. Toreno, p. 503; Baumgarten, II, p. 10.

7. Toreno, p. 505.

8. *Ibid.*, p. 513. *La Atalaya de la Mancha* alleged in April and May that the Cortes had drawn up a secret constitution. The newspaper even went so far as to publish it (Artola, I, p. 620).

merely acrimonious debates, throughout the country they were dealing with powerful forces which, in the end, could not be stopped
with oratory or parliamentary knowhow. But these forces, to win
the day, still needed the support of the King. If the King should
accept the Constitution and the reforms enacted in Cádiz, the conservatives might still lose. But if he should not, things were bound to
change.

In the meantime, Fernando had prepared to return to his kingdom,
after having signed in December, 1813, the Treaty of Valençay, by
which Napoleon made peace with Spain, recognized his prisoner as
king of Spain, and undertook to evacuate all French troops remaining
south of the Pyrenees, while stipulating that British troops would
also leave Spanish territory. But Fernando had sent the Duke of San
Carlos, who had also spent the war years in France,[9] to Madrid, to
apprise the Spanish Regency of the treaty and to find out what the
regents' reaction would be. After San Carlos had left Valençay,
Fernando had called on General Palafox, the heroic defender of
Zaragoza, finally freed from his French prison. Palafox was to carry
copies, signed by Fernando, of the treaty and of other documents
given earlier to San Carlos, as well as new letters to the Regency, in
case something happened to the Duke and the papers could not be
delivered. Then Palafox, too, left for Spain. San Carlos arrived in
Madrid on January 4, 1814, and soon after, went into conferences
with the regents. For the latter the matter was relatively simple.
Fernando had signed a treaty while on enemy territory. The decree
of January, 1811[10] had been issued to cover just such a
contingency—an act of the King while held captive would not be
recognized by the Spanish nation. San Carlos and Palafox were so
informed and were handed answers to Fernando's messages. The
Duke went back to Valençay with a letter[11] and a copy of the decree
of 1811.

Palafox, given a hero's welcome wherever he went, left Madrid for

9. He had been one of the members of Fernando's retinue at the time of
the trip to Bayonne (see Chapter III). First residing in Paris, he was later exiled to Lons-le-Saunier.

10. See Chapter IX.

11. This letter abstained from commenting upon the treaty (cf. Toreno,
p. 500).

Zaragoza at the end of January, preparing to join the King in Catalonia, where Fernando was expected to arrive shortly.[12]

The Cortes had been alarmed by the whole affair of the Treaty of Valençay. It was obviously a last-minute maneuver on the part of Napoleon to extricate himself from Spain, and thus bring home the troops sorely needed for the defense of Paris, while at the same time sowing discord between England and Spain. The treaty would not be ratified by the nation,[13] but what if Napoleon let Fernando go back to Spain regardless of the attitude of the Cortes and the Regency? What action should the government take to allay any doubts Great Britain might entertain about the loyalty of Spain to the alliance? How should the monarch be received if and when he crossed the border? On this matter *liberales* were still able to make the Cortes follow their lead, and on February 2 a decree was passed by a large majority, which stipulated among other things that the King would not be considered free and therefore would not be obeyed until he took the oath to the Constitution prescribed by Article 173 of the Charter; that upon his arrival at the border he would be handed a copy of this decree and a letter from the Regency informing him of the state of the nation, of its "heroic sacrifices," and of the measures taken by the Cortes to insure final independence and the liberty of the monarch; that no armed forces of the enemy nor any foreigner, not even a servant, nor any *afrancesado* would be allowed to cross the frontier with the King; that the King's itinerary from the border to the capital would be mapped out by the Regency; that the president of the Regency, who would hand the sovereign a copy of the Constitution, would accompany him on his voyage to the capital, and that only after having sworn allegiance to the Constitution in Madrid would he be recognized as Spain's legitimate sovereign.[14]

Even Toreno admitted that some of the provisions of this decree

12. Toreno, pp. 496–501; García Mercadal, *Palafox, Duque de Zaragoza,* pp. 145–53.

13. Particularly unacceptable for Spain, aside from the article covering the evacuation of Spanish territory by both English and French troops, was a provision of the treaty dealing with *afrancesados.* The treaty stipulated that they would regain their possessions as well as their social positions, and would thus enjoy their prewar status.

14. *Apud* Toreno, pp. 501–502.

were rather unnecessarily harsh. It might have been wiser not to encumber the return voyage of the King with such petty prescripts and not to delay so much the recovery of his sovereignty.[15] Particularly superfluous was the stipulation that the Regency would map out the sovereign's itinerary. This would have annoyed a man of much higher caliber than Fernando, and Fernando could only see in this a further attempt to strip him of his God-given rights.

The liberals, as well as a number of moderates on the conservative side, who often cast their votes with their liberal colleagues, being unaware of the true character of Fernando and of his intentions, proceeded on the assumption that the authority of the Cortes could not possibly be questioned. Neither Fernando nor anybody else would dare to disobey rules laid down by the national assembly. Absolutism had been eliminated once and for all and the clock could never be turned back. A letter written by Fernando to the Regency from Valençay on March 10 seemed to confirm the impression that Fernando was bound to accept the new order of things. It ended with the following words: "The reestablishment of the Cortes of which the Regency has appraised me as well as anything done during my absence that is beneficial to the kingdom, will receive my approval as being in accord with my Royal intentions."[16]

While this was no doubt sweet music to liberal ears, the political struggle at home, which continued unabated, was certainly disquieting, for their opponents, relentlessly whipping up antireformist sentiments, were giving them no peace. After Fernando had finally set foot on free Spanish soil on March 24,[17] conservative hopes soared. Everywhere he went he was received triumphantly. The allegiance of the masses of the people to their beloved Fernando could not be denied. Now was the time to show the monarch that within the Cortes, too, there were those who were opposed to the work of reform pushed through in Cádiz by the liberals. Following his arrival in Valencia,[18] Fernando was handed by conservative deputy Mozo de

15. *Ibid.*, pp. 502–503.

16. *Apud* Toreno, p. 511.

17. See below.

18. Valencia was on the official itinerary mapped out by the Regency. See below.

Rosales a long manifesto, which bore the signature of sixty-nine deputies.

This famous manifesto[19] became known as the *Manifiesto de los persas* (Manifesto of the Persians), for it began with the following words: "Sir, it was a custom among the old Persians to spend five days in anarchy after the passing of their King in order that the experience of murders, thefts, and other misfortunes should oblige them to be more faithful to his successor. To be faithful to your Majesty, Spain did not need such a test during the six years of your captivity. Among the Spaniards who are happy to see your Majesty restored to the throne of your ancestors are those who have signed this reverent exposition in their quality of representatives of Spain; but in the absence of your Majesty the system prevailing at the time this "captivity" began has been changed and as we find ourselves at the head of the nation in a Congress which decrees the opposite of what we feel and of what our Provinces desire, we believe it is our duty to state our wishes and the circumstances which stifle them, with the concision which six complicated years of revolution permit."

Whereupon followed a summary of the events between the departure of the King for France, and the gathering of the Cortes. The majority of the assembly's deputies were labeled unrepresentative of the provinces, since they "had attended the Congress without special or general powers from them." The procedure of electing substitute deputies hailing from certain provinces and who had happened to be in Cádiz at the time of the convocation was of course attacked. So were the many measures enacted in the Cortes, and especially the Constitution of 1812 to which the King was urged not to swear allegiance.[20] "Absolute monarchy . . . is a work of reason and intelligence," declared the conservative deputies. "It is subordinate to divine law, to justice and to the fundamental law of the State. It was established by right of conquest or by the voluntary submission of the first men who elected their Kings." However, absolute monarchy

19. The author might have been Mozo de Rosales (Suárez Verdeguer, *La crisis política del antiguo régimen*, p. 91).

20. Under particularly severe attack came the proclamation of national sovereignty, the establishment of a unicameral congress, the enactment of freedom of the press, and the abolition of the Inquisition.

could not be equated with arbitrary monarchy. In an absolute monarchy the king could not dispose of the lives of his subjects, for governing the relationship of prince and people were certain norms of behavior which were renewed through the oath taken by each king upon ascending the throne. Man was no less free in absolute monarchy than in a republic, and a tyrannical republic was more to be feared than a tyrannical monarchy. Besides, the king who saw his power limited by the privileges of the people would do his utmost to break the bonds that hampered him, and violence was then to be expected. And then, before concluding this long exposition, the absolutist deputies asked the sovereign to declare null and void the Constitution and the decrees of the Cortes of Cádiz, and to gather a new assembly according to traditional procedure.[21] The new Cortes should then undo all the evils caused by the ministerial despotism under which Spain had suffered before the war and make the necessary improvements in Spain's body of traditional law. It should insure among other things a fair administration of justice, an equitable system of taxation, and freedom and security for the individual. The *persas* asked for the punishment of those who "attacked the integrity of Spain" and called the attention of the monarch to the importance of annulling the Constitution "because we consider the fundamental laws that it contains to be of an incalculable and transcendental danger, which requires the gathering of Spanish Cortes convoked in freedom and in accordance with all the traditional laws."[22]

"The *Manifiesto de los persas* is for the royalists what the Constitution of 1812 was for the liberals," comments Suárez Verdeguer.[23] But the doctrines which it contained were not really new. As Artola points out, this is basically the ideology of the Spanish seventeenth

21. That is, by *brazos* or estates.
22. *Manifiesto que al Señor Don Fernando VII hacen en 12 de abril del año de 1814 los que subscriben como diputados en las actuales Cortes ordinarias de su opinión acerca de la soberana autoridad, ilegitimidad con que se ha eludido la antigua constitución española, mérito de ésta, nulidad de la nueva, y de cuantas disposiciones dieron las llamadas Cortes generales y extraordinarias de Cádiz, violenta opinión con que los legítimos representantes de la nación están en Madrid impedidos de manifestar y sostener su voto, defender los derechos del monarca, y el bien de su patria, indicando el remedio que creen oportuno.*
23. *La crisis política del antiguo régimen*, p. 89.

century, somewhat tinged with more modern thought probably derived from such political writers as Martínez Marina.[24] We might add that to a certain extent some of the pronouncements of the *manifiesto* were in harmony with the thoughts of Jovellanos. Jovellanos, too, preferred reforming Spain's traditional legislation to enacting a brand-new constitution and he, too, had recommended that the Cortes be called on the traditional pattern. We do not know exactly what Jovellanos would have said about the Cádiz Constitution, since he died before it was published, but we can surmise what his opinion would have been in the light of his political writings and of his comments on the work of the Cortes. On December 5, 1810, he wrote a letter to Lord Holland in which he strongly criticized the measures enacted until then in the Cortes. He opposed the one-chamber system and lamented the lack of effective power in the executive branch of the government. He criticized the manner in which the doctrine of national sovereignty had been included in the official oath of allegiance to the Cortes. Jovellanos admitted that the theory of national sovereignty was accepted by political writers, but he questioned its appropriateness for the Spanish people before they had had a chance to understand it and gauge the consequences of its practical application.[25]

Most of this we also find in the *Manifiesto de los persas*. But we must keep in mind that the *persas* above all defended absolutism—something which Jovellanos, the admirer of English constitutionalism, decidedly had not done—and urged the voiding of all the reforms enacted in Cádiz, which Jovellanos would never have recommended. They did offer to temper absolutism with a national representation inspired in the political structure of the Middle Ages and with guarantees of individual freedom and of an equitable administration. But if the signers of the manifesto really tried to "improve the concrete Spain in which they lived and which had a specific history and specific characteristics" rather than "endeavor to regenerate the nation," to quote Suárez Verdeguer,[26] they, the party of the

24. *Op. cit.*, I, p. 623. See Chapter XI.
25. *Obras*, IV, in BAE, LXXXVI, p. 473.
26. *Conservadores, innovadores y renovadores en las postrimerías del Antiguo Régimen*, p. 35.

King, the party that was soon to emerge victorious from the struggle, certainly did nothing after Fernando's reassumption of absolute power to convince the monarch to bring about these improvements. Needless to say, the renovation the conservative deputies proposed was never given a chance by the very sovereign to whom this petition was addressed.[27] Admitting that the *persas* were to a certain extent sincere in their proposals, it also appears, however, that the constructive part of the manifesto was an attempt at reassuring those segments of the population, not necessarily in the camp of the liberals, who could be expected to be disturbed by this appeal to do away with the Cortes and annul its work. After all, as members of a constitutional assembly with a reformist background, to whom they were supposed to be loyal and to whose basic charter they had taken an oath of allegiance, they could not very well advocate its elimination without making at the same time some proposals which would render their action palatable to the country at large and redeem them in the eyes of history.

The *persas* must be considered essentially the continuators of the ultraconservative deputies in the Cortes of Cádiz, who had voted against most of the fundamental reforms enacted between 1810 and 1813.[28] Now much more powerful numerically than their predecessors, they represented ultraconservative forces throughout the country. The latter had become stronger with each passing day since the start of the clash between the liberals and the Church and were increasingly drawing into their camp the moderate conservatives. Throughout the country, even more actually than in the Cortes, there were now two increasingly extremist movements facing each other.

To the liberals, of course, the manifesto could have only one meaning, open declaration of war against all that the Cortes had achieved, an avowed intention to turn the clock back. It was a trumpet call for revolt appealing to the King and to absolutist

27. Suárez' explanation that the royalists had confidence in the word of the King to call the Cortes and showed, therefore, no signs of impatience in the period 1814–1820 (*ibid.*, p. 101) is not very convincing.

28. It is difficult, if not impossible, to look upon the *persas*, in the manner of Suárez Verdeguer, as a distinctly reformist group within the conservative party, opposed to another group, the true conservatives or out-and-out absolutists with no taste for any reform whatsoever.

sentiment throughout the nation. And yet liberals, though well aware of the maneuvering of their enemies, would not believe that there might be any danger from the King himself. There had been some disquieting signs, though. From Gerona Fernando had sent a letter to the Regency couched in ambiguous language. Then Fernando had not obeyed the directions of the Regency to proceed to Valencia along the Mediterranean coast and had passed through Zaragoza.[29] The news from Valencia was not good. There was considerable activity which seemed designed to push the King along a reactionary path. Two letters from the Cortes to the monarch had remained unanswered.[30] But the liberals, optimists to the very last, feverishly prepared with the other deputies of the Cortes for the day when the King would set foot in the capital and would take the oath to the Constitution.[31]

To this effect workmen were frantically rushing to completion the new hall of sessions of the Cortes in the Augustinian Monastery of María de Aragón, where the congress was to have its home beginning May 2.[32] But not only working men were doing their utmost to have the new assembly room ready by this date, which had been proclaimed a national holiday and which would be the occasion for solemn activities. Men, women, and children from all walks of life offered their help in the task of erecting the new Hall of the Cortes, and persons from well-to-do classes paid the wages of those laboring in the old monastery. Finally the work was completed, and on the façade between the statues representing Religion, Fatherland, and Liberty an elegant marble tablet could be seen with the gold-lettered words, "The power to enact the laws resides in the Cortes together with the King." It was Article 15 of the Constitution of Cádiz. The Constitution of Cádiz which still ruled but which was living through its last days.[33]

On May 2 the citizens of Madrid were wakened by gun fire and

29. See below.
30. Toreno, pp. 512, 518, 520.
31. *Ibid.*, p. 520.
32. On March 1, the Cortes had begun its annual three-month session for the year 1814, as prescribed by the Constitution. It was the second year of the term. According to the Constitution deputies were to be elected every two years.
33. Mesonero Romanos, *Memorias de un setentón*, pp. 137–38.

the tolling of church bells. It was the signal for the commencement of the day's ceremonies. *Madrileños* of all ages and classes rushed to the Prado Promenade, where at a spot dubbed Campo de la Lealtad (Field of Loyalty) Mass was held on an improvised altar, on which stood a huge urn containing the exhumed remains of patriots shot in that place on May 2, 1808. Other masses of people walked to the park of Monteleón, scene of the heroic stand by a handful of patriots six years before. There a solemn procession started off, made up principally of a body of artillery men with their guns and a magnificently decorated coach drawn by eight horses, which bore two urns with the remains of Daoiz and Velarde, the best remembered heroes of the *dos de mayo*.[34] Preceded by flags, military trophies, and bands playing funeral marches, the cortege passed through the streets of the city on its way to the new palace of the Cortes, where the deputies awaited the procession in order to join it. The solemn march continued to the city hall, and augmented by the municipal authorities, it wound its way to the Prado. Now a second carriage carrying the funeral urn from the Prado joined the imposing cortege, and through the Carrera de San Jerónimo, the Puerta del Sol, the Calle de Carretas, the Calle de Atocha, and the broad Calle de Toledo, the procession marched to the Church of San Isidro. There the three urns were placed on a sumptuous catafalque, illuminated by 100 wax tapers. Now followed a final, most reverential funeral service, which ended at five o'clock in the afternoon. The end of this memorable day's rites was announced by round after round of cannon fire.[35]

"On May 2nd, 1814 all inhabitants of Madrid without exception shared the same feelings," wrote Mesonero Romanos.[36] Little did *madrileños* foresee then that this show of unity which allowed *liberales* and *serviles* to forget briefly about their disputes, would shortly be shattered by brute force. Few, if any, could imagine that many of the political leaders then surrounded by an aura of prestige would soon wind up behind bars. "Who could even suspect," exclaimed Mesonero Romanos, still horrified at the thought of events long past,

34. Shortly before May 2, 1814 the remains of the two soldiers had been exhumed for this occasion.
35. Mesonero Romanos, pp. 128–42.
36. *Ibid.*, p. 143.

"that those illustrious men, that those proven patriots who today were seen by us on the pedestal of their glory, would, a few days later, find themselves in irons in filthy dungeons, exiled to Africa, or escaping abroad, fleeing perhaps from the gallows which their persecutors were preparing for them."[37]

[2]

If the liberals had known Fernando VII a little better they would not have been so confident about the future of the Constitutional regime. Though they must have suspected that he was not entirely the unblemished hero that so many Spaniards imagined him to be,[38] they had not fathomed the crooked soul of this young man. From the point of view of patriotic duty Fernando's conduct during his captivity at Talleyrand's Castle of Valençay had certainly been anything but exemplary. For Fernando's prime concern had always been, and would always be, his personal safety. Nothing else mattered. His country might be bleeding to death and his countrymen might be sacrificing their lives by the thousands for their Fernando, El Deseado, the desired one, but the desired one had had no thoughts except those involving his own personal situation. Always a coward, frightened by Napoleon, afraid the Emperor might one day deal with him as he had dealt with the Duke of Enghien, he had been ready to humble himself before the warlord as many times as was necessary. He had basely congratulated Joseph Bonaparte upon the latter's taking possession of the Spanish crown; he had written cringing letters to Napoleon, congratulating the Emperor upon his victory against Austria in 1809,[39] and on his marriage to the Archduchess

37. *Ibid.*, p. 144.

38. The French newspaper *Le Moniteur* had inserted during the war a number of submissive letters to Napoleon written by Fernando. Many Spaniards convinced themselves that these were forgeries. However, to annul the effects of any marriage between Fernando and a princess of the Bonaparte family—in 1810 this was rumored as a distinct possibility—the Cortes had passed the decree of January 1, 1811. More recently the Treaty of Valençay had aroused suspicions in Spain, though most Spaniards wanted to see in this a Napoleonic maneuver foisted upon the captive king.

39. It was said that he had gone so far as to congratulate Joseph Bonaparte on the occasion of the Battle of Ocaña (Talleyrand, *Mémoires*, II, p. 70).

Marie Louise, requesting the hand of a princess of the Imperial family and asking Napoleon to make him his adoptive son. He had even gone so far as to denounce to the French authorities a man who had offered to arrange for his escape from Valençay.[40]

Nor did this long sojourn of Fernando at Valençay offer much interest in other respects. Talleyrand, the owner of the new home of Fernando, his brother Carlos, and his uncle Antonio,[41] summarized the life of the Spanish princes with the following words "All that one could say about them during those five years, is that they lived."[42] Living, in the case of this uninspiring trio, was little more than vegetating. Talleyrand tells us of his efforts to have his Spanish hosts read some of the books in his library, and he confesses his failure to entice the princes to devote some time to intellectual pursuits. When he realized that he could not rouse their interests through the subject matter of the books, he tried to focus their attention on purely external aspects, such as the beauty of some editions or of a number of engravings, and even the simple illustrations to be found in many volumes. But to no avail. "Don Antonio, their uncle, who feared the effects of the greater part of the books which make up a good Library, would quickly come upon a reason to make them return to their apartments."[43]

This is not to say that the princes never looked at a book during their stay at Valençay. If not the imbecile Don Antonio, at least Fernando and his brother did some reading and even some translating from French into Spanish. But most of their time was spent in promenades, in coach or on horseback through the park of the castle, in games such as billiards and lottery, and especially in prayer. While the activities of Fernando and Carlos certainly presented no particular interest, the pastimes of their uncle could only be described as those of a stupid old man. The addle-brained Antonio would spend

40. During the war a number of schemes were tried—all of them unsuccessful—to rescue Fernando from his prison. On Fernando's life in Valençay cf. the excellent study by Manuel Izquierdo Hernández, *Antecedentes y comienzos del reinado de Fernando VII*, pp. 529-632.

41. And their staff of attendants and servants.

42. *Mémoires*, ii, p. 68.

43. *Ibid.*, p. 65.

much of his time, not counting the intervals taken up by religious exercises, walking through the park, embroidering, or tearing illustrations deemed indecent by his underdeveloped mentality, out of the magnificent books of Talleyrand's library. As for feminine companionship, there were enough opportunities for the princes to enjoy it during their captivity. But those gentlemen withstood in stalwart fashion the temptations of the flesh, thinking, on occasion with good reason, that these were just traps set by their jailers to place even their most secret thoughts within reach of the Emperor. Especially in the early days, when Talleyrand was in Valençay, repeated attempts were made to seduce the princes. After all, Napoleon had hinted broadly in this direction in his famous letter to Talleyrand.[44] But the resistance of Fernando and his relatives to these enticements could not be overcome.[45]

An interesting question is whether Fernando was aware of what went on in Spain while he was spending his days in nonchalant fashion in Valençay. It seems that this must be answered in the affirmative. Not only was Fernando fairly well informed of the political and military situation in the Peninsula, but he also most probably received a copy of the Constitution of Cádiz. His source of Information? Izquierdo Hernández points to the physician of Fernando, Doctor Francisco Vulliez and his family, as well as to the widow of the Marquis de Guadalcázar, a Frenchwoman who had met her husband at Valençay and had followed him to Madrid when he had been expelled from the castle on French orders in 1809. Vulliez' family was in Spain in 1808, but in 1809 one of his sons was able to join his father in France and in early 1811 one of his daughters arrived in Valençay. Almost at the same time the widowed Marquise de Guadalcázar reached the castle. These two women were, of course, able to tell the princes much of what was happening in their homeland. Furthermore, Dr. Vulliez, a skilled physician, had become very popular in the neighborhood and it is to be presumed that his

---

44. See Chapter III, p. 119.

45. Izquierdo Hernández, pp. 556, 562, 600, 633–34; Talleyrand, op. cit., pp. 63–64; Memorias del Marqués de Ayerbe, Memorias de tiempos de Fernando VII, I, in BAE, XCVII, pp. 231–32.

French friends told him much of what they knew. It also must have been from the Doctor that Fernando was able to secure a copy of the Constitution.[46]

It was only natural that the Constitution should arouse suspicions and anger in Fernando's mind. A monarch of a much higher human and intellectual caliber, but reared in the spirit of absolutism, would have no doubt felt displeasure upon reading its text. But Fernando, with his deplorable upbringing, his suspicious, cowardly character, and his memories of the struggle for the throne, when he had feared to see the crown snatched from his hands by Godoy, was bound, from the very moment that he laid his eyes on the Constitution, to receive it most bitterly. The refusal of the Regency to ratify the Treaty of Valençay, though perfectly justified, and the decree of February 2,[47] with its rather humiliating "don'ts" and its statement to the effect that the Regency would map out the King's itinerary from the time he crossed the border to the moment he entered the Hall of the Cortes in Madrid, could only deepen Fernando's hostility.

But Fernando was a coward and at the same time a master of dissimulation. He did not indicate his displeasure to the Cortes, he did not protest against the more annoying provisions of the decree of February 2. He acted as he had always acted. He decided to shroud himself in a veil of ambiguity and say or do nothing concrete until he had seen for himself what possibilities there were of destroying the constitutional edifice that had been erected against what to him were his unalienable rights. And so, after sending off on March 10, 1814, an innocuous message to the Regency which could even be interpreted as a sympathetic nod to reform, Fernando ended slightly less than six years of captivity when he left Valençay on March 13, accompanied by Carlos and Antonio. On March 22 he set foot on Spanish soil, at the eastern end of the Franco-Spanish border. Two days later, passing through the French lines,[48] he crossed the Fluviá River, which separated the French and Spanish armies. He was solemnly received by General Francisco de Copons, commander of the Spanish forces

46. *Op. cit.*, pp. 620–26, 680.

47. See above.

48. It must be kept in mind that Suchet's French forces still occupied part of Catalonia, including Barcelona.

in the area, who later handed him a copy of the decree of February 2 and a letter from the Regency, as well as various documents.[49]

Almost immediately Fernando realized that at least in Catalonia, among the masses of the people, his prestige was as high as ever. Everywhere he went he was greeted with utmost enthusiasm by his subjects, who had finally been granted their long-standing wish to see El Deseado once more in their midst. He had suspected even in Valençay that his popularity had not waned, but now he was given in Catalonia concrete proof of the absolute loyalty of the masses. This popular devotion gave him considerable confidence, but it was still much too early to arrive at a definite conclusion, since there were other factors to consider and since he was seeing so far only a small part of Spanish territory.

On March 24, from Gerona, he wrote to the Regency: "I have arrived here in good health, thank God, and General Copons has just handed me the letter of the Regency as well as the enclosed documents. I shall give these my attention, and I assure the Regency that nothing is so important to me as giving it proof of my satisfaction and my desire to do everything in my power which will benefit my subjects. It is a great consolation to me to find myself already in my territory in the midst of a nation and an army which have displayed towards me a constant and generous loyalty."[50] These were ambiguous words and they were meant to be, for Fernando was still careful not to show his hand. On March 28 the King, his brother and uncle, left Gerona with the intention of traveling to Valencia as the Regency had stipulated in accordance with the decree of February 2.

On April 2, they arrived in the town of Reus, ten miles northwest of the port of Tarragona. There Fernando was met by General Palafox, who had brought with him a message from the provincial deputation[51] of Aragón, requesting that he visit Zaragoza. Palafox, too, urged him to pay a visit to the town which had done so much to uphold the rights of its monarch five years before. Fernando saw that

49. Toreno, pp. 511–512; Izquierdo Hernandez, p. 715.

50. *Apud* Toreno, p. 512.

51. A body created by the Constitution of Cádiz for the government of each province.

this was a chance to assert his independence from the constitutional government. The Regency had stated that he must go directly to Valencia, but the citizens of Zaragoza now asked him to spend some time with them, and why should he refuse their petition? Disobeying the Regency, then, Fernando traveled to Zaragoza, where he arrived on April 6.[52]

If Fernando needed any further proof of his immense popularity, this proof was given to him in Zaragoza. At the sight of their king and of heroic Palafox, the Zaragozans burst into an enthusiasm which even the liberal Toreno termed "indescribable."[53] For five days the King remained in the town. Needless to say, he visited its monuments, including the famous basilica of El Pilar, and inspected the glorious ruins, mute yet eloquent testimony to the terrible struggle that had been waged in his name.[54]

The voyage continued southward on the eleventh, and on the night of the same date, at Daroca, Fernando held a meeting with his retinue. Present, aside from the monarch and his brother Carlos, were the dukes of San Carlos, Osuna, and Frías, General Palafox, and Count Montijo the arch-plotter. The meeting was to map out the strategy to be followed by the King with respect to the constitutional government and concretely with respect to the Constitution. Fernando had more or less decided what he wanted, or rather did not want, to do, but he was anxious to hear the opinion of his advisers. Of all the persons present, it seems that only Palafox thought that the King should take an unconditional oath to the Constitution. While the Duke of Frías was of the opinion that the monarch ought to swear allegiance, he also declared that Fernando should reserve the right to introduce modifications. Osuna was undecided. As for the others, they all expressed the opinion that Fernando should definitely not take the oath. Nothing was decided officially, but at the suggestion of San Carlos, Fernando sent Montijo to the capital to spy on the liberals and stir up the lower classes against the Cortes.[55]

52. Toreno, p. 518.
53. Ibid.
54. García Mercadal, pp. 157–63.
55. Historia de la vida y reinado de Fernando VII, Rey de España, II, pp. 17–18; Toreno, p. 519; García Mercadal, p. 165.

On it went to Teruel and thence to Segorbe, where Fernando arrived on the fifteenth. Another meeting was held here, without the Count of Montijo, but on the other hand with some members of the King's entourage who had not taken part in the previous council. Among these were the Infante Don Antonio, who had gone on to Valencia from Reus and who had now joined his nephews in Segorbe, and the Duke of Infantado and Don Pedro Gómez Labrador, both of whom had arrived from Madrid.[56] The latter was to be Spain's delegate at the Congress of Vienna.[57] While Palafox and Frías maintained the position they had taken at Daroca,[58] Don Carlos spoke vehemently against the oath. The Duke of Infantado then declared: "There are only three ways: to swear, not to swear, or to swear with reservations. As for not swearing, I share to a great extent the fears of the Duke of Frías . . . " The Duke seemed to support the idea of an oath with certain restrictions. The one who spoke most violently against swearing allegiance to the Constitution was Don Pedro Gómez Labrador, who declared that it was time to show the liberals who was the master.[59]

The voyage to Valencia continued on the next day. Near the town of Puzol, about ten miles northeast of Valencia, a historic meeting took place. Fernando and his retinue came upon the president of the Regency, the Cardinal de Borbón, who had gone from Madrid to Valencia to receive the monarch. Both men emerged from their carriages and stood on the road waiting for the other to approach. Finally, it was the Cardinal who went over to the King. Fernando

56. Escoiquiz, who had also returned from France, was in Valencia plotting against the Constitution.

57. He had gone to Bayonne with Fernando and had spent some years in captivity in France. Managing to escape, he reached Cádiz in the summer of 1812 when the French had raised the siege of the port (on his life cf. Villa-Urrutia, *España en el Congreso de Viena*).

58. In spite of his opposition to the idea of a coup d'état, Palafox was confirmed in his post of captain-general of Aragón by Fernando VII. In 1834 he was made duke of Zaragoza and later became commander of the Royal Provincial Guard, senator for Huesca, and head of the National War Invalids Institution. During the Carlist war of 1833–1839 he sided with the Queen Regent and the constitutionalists. He died in 1847 (cf. García Mercadal, *op. cit.*).

59. Toreno p. 519; *Historia de la vida y reinado de Fernando VII Rey de España*, II, p. 19; García Mercadal, p. 166; Izquierdo Hernández, p. 730.

extended his hand for the usual hand-kissing act. The Cardinal hesitated. Was it proper for him, the president of the Constitutional Regency, to kiss the hand of a constitutional king, and a king who had not as yet taken the oath to the Constitution and could not therefore be legally recognized as such? After a few seconds Fernando, his face red with anger, pushed his hand into the face of the Cardinal and said "Kiss," and the president of the Regency obeyed. It was a symbolic victory for El Deseado.[60]

The same afternoon Fernando entered Valencia, acclaimed by thousands upon thousands of people. If he had any doubts as to the course of action which he was already considering, these were finally dispelled in the great Mediterranean port. Here absolutist feeling had been whipped up by a number of ultraconservative personalities who had flocked to the city. The groundwork for a coup had been laid by the Infante Antonio and his entourage, by Escoiquiz, and by men like Juan Pérez Villamil and Miguel de Lardizábal, both former regents.[61] Soon a number of newspapers appeared in Valencia spreading absolutist propaganda and stirring up the inhabitants. But the key figure in the support for absolutism was the captain-general of Valencia, Don Francisco Javier Elío, a dyed-in-the-wool traditionalist who hated the constitutional government, particularly because he had been the object of criticism in the Cortes and in the liberal press for his conduct of military operations. On April 17,[62] as Fernando was walking back to his palace surrounded by his entourage, and as he passed in front of a regiment in formation, General Elío, who was present, grabbed a flag and made a speech. It ended with the words: "The blood which remains in all Spanish soldiers will be spilled to preserve for you the Throne with the plenitude of the rights which nature granted you."[63]

This act has been called Spain's first *pronunciamiento* in the nine-

60. Toreno, p. 519; Izquierdo Hernández, p. 731.

61. See Chapters X and XI.

62. The previous afternoon Fernando had been handed a copy of the Constitution of 1812 by Cardinal de Borbón. The King is said to have received the document quite graciously (Izquierdo Hernández, p. 732).

63. *Historia de la vida y reinado de Fernando VII, Rey de España*, II, p. 25; Izquierdo Hernández, p. 732.

teenth century,[64] and rightly so, for it was the first time a military commander "pronounced" against a legally constituted government, thus rebelling against its authority. Elío thus set a precedent which was unfortunately followed too often in Spain throughout the last century and down to our day. Both in Spain and in Spanish America the *pronunciamiento* has too frequently seemed the normal way of effecting a change in government. Elío's action and the *Manifiesto de los persas*, as well as the absolutist frenzy now reigning in Valencia and the extraordinary enthusiasm which had greeted him everywhere in the course of his trip, convinced the monarch. He could now strike with impunity at the Cortes. The masses seemed to be with him and so did the Church and the nobility. The troops in the Valencia area could be counted upon, and even in the Cortes there was a strong group who favored a return to absolutism, as the *Manifiesto de los persas* proved.

On May 2 the people of Valencia smashed the tablet bearing the words *Plaza de la Constitución*, the name that had been given to the former *Plaza de la Virgen de los Desamparados*, and put another in its place with the words *Real Plaza de Fernando VII*. This action was to be repeated in many towns of Spain within the next few days and weeks. Almost all the squares formally known as *Plaza Mayor* had been renamed *Plaza de la Constitución*. Now, in a very short time, they would be known once more as *Plaza Mayor* except in those cases when they would be graced with the name of Fernando VII.[65]

Fernando's mind was made up. On May 4 he sat down with Don Pedro Gómez Labrador and Don Juan Pérez Villamil, and with their help drew up a decree which bears this date but was published only on May 11 in the Spanish capital. A long and rambling document, the decree began by reviewing Spanish affairs since the abdication of Charles IV at Aranjuez and the subsequent events at Bayonne. It had the effrontery to state that the King during his long captivity had "always kept in his memory" the love and loyalty of his people. It

64. Cf. Soldevila, *Historia de España*, vi, pp. 367–68; Ballesteros y Beretta, *Historia de España y su influencia en la historia universal*, vii, p. 144.

65. Izquierdo Hernández, p. 734.

mentioned Fernando's decree of May 5, 1808,[66] which had convoked the Cortes for the purpose of raising subsidies to wage war, without of course mentioning the decree of May 6 which had revoked the powers of the Provisional Junta in Madrid and had urged submission. Recalling that the Cortes of Cádiz had gathered in a manner never followed in Spanish history and claiming that their reforms were passed by a small seditious clique amidst "shouts and threats from those sitting in the galleries," Fernando accused the assembly of robbing him of his sovereignty and of enacting a Constitution derived from the "revolutionary and democratic principles" of the French Constitution of 1791. The Constitution of Cádiz, according to Fernando, converted the monarch into a mere delegate of the nation, though the term "king" had been kept to "hallucinate and seduce unsuspecting [citizens] and the Nation."

"I abhor and detest Despotism," the decree read. The enlightenment and culture of the European nations did not allow it any longer, and neither had Spanish kings ever been despots, nor did Spanish laws authorize despotism. True there had been abuses, but the new Cortes which was to gather as soon as "order had been established," would enact laws guaranteeing individual freedom and security and establishing freedom of the press "within those limits prescribed to all by . . . sovereign and independent reason." The laws passed by the new congress would prove that the King was not a tyrant but a "Father of his Subjects."

And now came the really significant part of the decree: "I declare that it is my royal will not only not to take the oath to the said Constitution, nor to any Decree of the general and extraordinary Cortes or of the Ordinary Cortes now in session, i.e. those which undermine the rights and prerogatives of my Sovereignty established by the Constitution[67] and the laws by which the Nation has lived for a long time, but to declare that Constitution and those Decrees nil and of no value or effect, now or ever, as if such acts had never taken place . . ." It was very simple. The Cortes of Cádiz was relegated to the realm of the imaginary. It just had not existed. Everything had been a bad dream and it was now time to awaken to reality. And

66. See Chapter IV.
67. Read "the body of traditional Spanish law."

to top it all, anybody bold enough to advocate in any way obedience to the Constitution or to the decrees of the Cortes was herewith declared guilty of the crime of lese majesty and as such punishable by death. The judicial mechanism set up by the Cortes in provinces and towns would continue until the new Cortes decided what part of this mechanism was to be discarded and what part would be kept. As for the Cortes then in session, it was to be suspended forthwith. Its archives were to be deposited in the Madrid city hall, while its library would be incorporated into the Royal Library. Finally, all persons arrested for infraction of the Cádiz Constitution were to be set free at once.[68]

That was that. One stroke of the pen ended a momentous revolution, or at least it seemed to do so. A new Cortes was promised and changes were indicated more or less along the lines laid down in the *Manifiesto de los persas,* but the immediate task at hand was the destruction of liberal power. This was quickly accomplished. On May 4, the ultrareactionary General Francisco Eguía was appointed captain-general of New Castile and governor of Madrid, and given instructions to publish the King's decree and carry out its provisions upon arriving in Madrid. General Elío was designated to accompany the King, his brother, and his uncle to Madrid at the head of an army division. On May 5 Fernando left Valencia for Madrid. In the towns and villages along the way the scenes he had witnessed during his voyage through the eastern part of the country were reenacted; enthusiastic crowds everywhere, *vivas* to the King and imprecations against the Cortes. In many towns the tablets with the words *Plaza de la Constitución* were torn from the Plazas Mayores and smashed to pieces. It is doubtful whether Fernando's conscience bothered him at the sight of such transports.[69]

While Fernando was still on his way and was refusing to see a delegation from the Cortes, which had gone out to meet him in La Mancha, dramatic events took place in Madrid. During the night of May 10–11, General Eguía, who had arrived in the capital, went to

68. *Apud* Toreno, pp. 522–23.

69. *Ibid.,* p. 521. Padre Vélez quoted newspapers of 1814 to show that in most towns such as Jerez and Sevilla demonstrations resulting in the smashing of tablets bearing the sign *Constitución* had taken place in the month of April (*Apología del altar y del trono,* II, pp. 282–84).

see the president of the Cortes, Don Antonio Joaquín Pérez, and announced to him His Majesty's decision to dissolve the Cortes. The president was only too willing to obey, since he was among the signers of the *Manifiesto de los persas*. The same night, and according to the instructions of Fernando, Eguía and his henchmen, backed up by a considerable number of troops, arrested all the important liberal deputies of the Cortes as well as a number of known reformists. Among those carted off to jail were Argüelles, Calatrava, Muñoz Torero, and Manuel José Quintana. One of the few who escaped was Toreno, who was able to flee abroad. The arrests continued on the following days and spread to the provinces, whence were brought to the Madrid prisons other liberal deputies such as Juan Nicasio Gallego. Soon the jails of Spain were filled with liberals or presumed liberals, while crowds surged through the streets acclaiming the return of absolutism.[70]

In Madrid, too, the mobs went on a rampage. Perhaps 200 or 300 among them had been recruited by the Count of Montijo, an old hand at this sort of game. Shortly after 10:00 A.M. on May 11, when the decree of May 4 was posted in Madrid, members of the lower classes and soldiers burst into the Plaza Mayor and tore down the sign reading *Plaza de la Constitución*. They then marched on the Palace of the Congress, dragging the tablet through the streets and shouting "Long Live Fernando VII," "Long Live Religion," "Down with the Cortes," and "Long Live the Inquisition." At the Cortes all objects in the hall of sessions, including several statues, were smashed, and the word *Constitución*, which had been inscribed with letters of gold in a prominent spot, was erased. All buildings bearing the sign *Nacional* were stoned. A portrait of Fernando was carried through the city and passersby who did not seem to approve of the demonstrations were molested in the streets.

Thus passed May 11, 1814, a black day in Spanish history.[71]

Two days later, for the second time in his life, Fernando made his entrance into his capital as king. There were triumphal arches, troops lined up along the royal route, and a sumptuous cortege. This time it

70. *Ibid.*, pp. 521-22.

71. Izquierdo Hernández, p. 771; Mesonero Romanos, pp. 149-53; Toreno, p. 522.

was not the unanimous enthusiasm which had prevailed in March, 1808, that greeted him, but the majority of people who witnessed this march through the city were probably expressing genuine joy at seeing El Deseado. The most vociferous in their enthusiasm were the *chisperos* of the Barquillo and Maravillas districts, and the *manolas* of Lavapiés.[72]

The coup d'état ushered in by the *pronunciamiento* of Elío in Valencia had succeeded with remarkable ease. Everywhere the edifice the liberals had built crumbled and everywhere the reformists were subjected to pitiless persecution. The liberal leaders were tried, but their judges were hard put to impute real and tangible crimes to them. But this was no obstacle for Fernando. In December, 1815, he himself decreed what punishment should be meted out to the reformists. Toreno, who had escaped, was condemned to death in absentia; Quintana was sent to the Fortress of Pamplona; Argüelles, Martínez de la Rosa, and others were sent to the Spanish possessions in Morocco. As for the promise to call the Cortes contained in the decree of May 4, it was conveniently forgotten. From 1814 to 1820 Spain was to live years of counterrevolutionary terror and black reaction, without any protest from those who supposedly wanted to "renovate" the country and had signed the *Manifiesto de los persas*. The clock was turned back. The Inquisition was reestablished and so were the old councils that had existed prior to the outbreak of the war. Freedom of the press was abolished. The landlords recovered their feudal privileges, the regular clergy recovered its monasteries, convents, and other properties, and provincial and municipal governments were returned to the old authorities.

[3]

The question must now be asked why the liberal regime crumbled like a house of cards, practically without resistance. Was liberal sentiment really limited only to a few reform-minded and professional men, as their opponents charged? Were the Spanish people so overwhelmingly absolutist, traditionalist, and suspicious of reforms

72. Mesonero Romanos, pp. 155–57.

that they would approve wholeheartedly a return to age-old privileges and institutions?

We would much prefer to state that this was definitely not so and that the Spanish people were merely robbed of their rightful gains by a combination of force and duplicity, and that absolutism returned in all its absurd pageantry against a background of sullen popular opposition. But unfortunately we cannot say this, for it would be flying in the face of facts.

In the first place, throughout the war the liberals, though growing in strength, remained a minority in Spain. In Cádiz they gained the upper hand by a favorable combination of circumstances and their intellectual caliber, as well as through the ineptitude of their opponents. But they did not leave a sufficiently deep mark in the minds of the popular masses. Yes, there had been much propaganda in favor of the Constitution and reforms, and homage was paid to the Constitution in as many towns and villages as possible. But this was often done as a consequence of the reoccupation of French-held areas and appeared too frequently as a by-product of military victory.[73]

For the Spanish peasant, the artisan, and other lower class elements, all of whom constituted the backbone of the population, the Constitution had little concrete meaning and was often unknown altogether. The masses were still superstitious and easily influenced and led by the Church, and if they were told by priests and friars—out of sight of army officers, *jefes políticos*, and government employees sent by the Cádiz regime—that the Constitution and the reforms were evil, they believed this. They believed it especially if it was explained to them that the liberals had curtailed the powers of the King, their idolized King. Among the masses the prestige of the King had not suffered during the war. On the contrary, if this was at all possible, it had grown. And since the government of national resistance always referred to the King with the greatest devotion, and since all decrees were rendered in his name, the people had no reason whatsoever to lose their extraordinary faith in what they felt to be the symbol of

73. Padre Vélez no doubt exaggerated when he wrote that in the towns of La Mancha and Castile bayonets rammed the Constitution down the throats of the people (*Apología del altar y del trono*, II, p. 126), but military force doubtless lent much prestige to the charter.

their salvation. To the Spanish peasant the terms absolutism, liberalism, and despotism did not mean much.

The Spanish masses were also profoundly religious, and though they doubtless disapproved of many unworthy priests and friars, and possibly considered that there were far too many monasteries and convents in Spain, their attachment to the Church was not to be shaken. Therefore when they were told by disgruntled clergymen that the abolition of the Inquisition, the closing of many monasteries and convents, and the use of Church properties for the prosecution of the war was the work of devilish revolutionaries taking their cue from France, they believed this also. The unsophisticated Spanish masses could not be won over to the new political doctrines except through a long and thorough indoctrination. But for this the liberals simply did not have time. A centuries-old *Weltanschauung* could hardly be changed within the very short span of a few years, especially when education for the lower classes had been almost totally lacking.

There was really only one way in which the broad masses of the Spanish people could perhaps have been decisively won over in the short time available before the return of Fernando. A social and economic reform pushed through regardless of opposition might have counterbalanced adhesion to king and Church. Before the war the Spanish people were no doubt dissatisfied with their social and economic condition. The wretched existence on land which more often than not they could not consider their own, the harshness of the landlords, the ceaseless tributes to nobles and Church, the *quintas* which forced them into military service, the poverty, could not possibly elicit any enthusiasm. There was no doubt resentment at these conditions and at times the people revolted against them.[74] Perhaps the uprising of May–June, 1808 throughout Spain could be ascribed in part to a grudge against the rich and powerful. It will be recalled that when so many of these failed to do their duty, they were either killed or forced to side with the insurrection. Perhaps the social and economic factor played more of a role in the Spanish uprising than has been suspected until now. If the Cortes had placed social and economic considerations above other factors and if it had

74. See Chapter I.

centered its reformist effort on social and economic improvements which would have benefited the lower classes as well as the emerging middle class, then perhaps those lower classes would have followed its lead.

The Cortes did attack a number of problems in this field, but its reforms did not go far enough, or were not specifically designed to help the poor, or were carried out only lukewarmly, or simply sabotaged by the local authorities. The elimination of the *señoríos* was one of the most notable achievements and one which should have pleased the peasants most. It did no doubt elicit a favorable response among the rural masses living on the land of the *señores*, but when it was seen that the government was unable in many instances to carry out the reform because of the resistance of the *señores*, or because of sabotage on the part of local officials and even on the part of the courts, the peasants were bound to lose confidence in the Cortes.[75] Besides, as landowning *señores* in almost all cases remained in possession of their land and many feudal privileges merely turned into rent to be paid by the tenant, the benefits to be derived from the measure were too often unclear.

Of course it must be kept in mind that the liberals, representing essentially the progressive-minded middle class and championing individual freedom and laissez-faire, could not be expected to be ready to go as far as expropriation, for this would have meant an attack on private property, which to liberal minds was one of the sacred rights of man. When they did declare themselves ready to distribute land among those who did not own any, it was at the expense of lands belonging to towns and villages. The decree of January, 1813 on the sale and distribution of communal lands, though providing for distribution of small plots to soldiers and to landless peasants, in the end benefited the rich, who merely became wealthier through the purchase of landed property. Nor did the elimination of the guilds in June, 1813 prove of particular benefit to city artisans. On the contrary, the security afforded by the guild system, in spite of all its difficulties, soon gave way to nineteenth-century industrial exploitation. At the time the decree was passed artisans no doubt saw some advantages in the measure, but it could hardly result in wide-

75. Cf. Artola, I, pp. 473–79.

spread enthusiasm for the liberal cause. In all fairness it must be emphasized again that with more time at their disposal the Cortes would perhaps have been able to accomplish much more in the social-economic field as well as in the political area.

No, the reforms of the Cortes of Cádiz had not linked the masses of the Spanish people to the liberal cause. Their mood concerning the Cortes at the time of Fernando's return may, with notable exceptions, be presumed to have been ranging from indifferent to hostile. On this mass it was of course easy for the actively disgruntled elements to play successfully. Who were these elements? Mostly those whose political, social, or economic positions had been damaged by the Cortes, among them the old cumbersome institutions wielding both administrative and judicial power. The Council of Castile and other councils such as the Council of the Indies and the military orders had been eliminated at Cádiz, and their members were for the most part highly dissatisfied with this state of affairs. In place of the Council of Castile in Madrid, once the topmost judicial as well as administrative authority in the country, there was a supreme court. The old *audiencias* in the provinces had had their administrative powers taken away from them and were reduced to the state of courts of justice. The same discontent was to be found at the local level where executive and judicial functions had finally been separated. The old *corregidores* and *alcaldes mayores* could, of course, be counted on to fan antiliberal feelings in the provincial towns.

The landholding aristocrats became, of course, opponents of the Cortes after the decree of August, 1811 had stripped them of their feudal privileges. So did many employees in the pay of *señores* previously holding jurisdictional privileges, who had managed their masters' affairs in the towns and villages under their jurisdiction. As to the functionaries who had served Joseph Bonaparte, it is not easy to determine exactly which way they leaned, nor could any generalization be made. They were aware that a number of reforms enacted in Cádiz were similar to measures taken by Joseph's government, and at least some of them probably did not reject the Cádiz regime. On the other hand Argüelles' assertion that those men were in the conservative camp[76] must also be given serious consideration.

76. *Exámen histórico de la reforma constitucional*, II, p. 259.

Angered by the rather harsh anticollaborationist attitude of the liberal Cortes of Cádiz, as a result of which a good number of them lost their positions, the majority of those men must have preferred a return to a less militant nationalism and patriotism, for which an absolutist triumph seemed to hold out more hope.

Now it may be true that some passive collaborators became constitutionalists to make the government forget their previous conduct, but this certainly did not include all of them, as Padre Vélez asserted.[77] Besides, even if we admit this claim of a more or less forced conversion to liberalism on the part of a number of passive collaborators, as soon as they saw that the wind was blowing in another direction, they must perforce turn against the reformists both to avenge themselves and to curry favor with what looked to be the future order of things. The constitutionalism of those persons who had gone over to liberalism under duress was at best only a sham constitutionalism.

And then there was the Church. At first the Church had welcomed reforms, but when the reform movement began to affect directly its interests it became an implacable enemy of the Cortes. Naturally there were exceptions in the clergy. Jansenist priests and those secular ecclesiastics who resented the influence of the religious orders were inclined to accept many, if not all, of the reforms enacted in Cádiz. But the great majority of the Church was by 1814 well in the camp of absolutism.

While the old governmental authorities and the old bureaucracy, the landowners, and the church were lined up solidly against the liberals, there could be some question as to the attitude of the regular army. After all, army commanders had seen to it that in most liberated areas the Constitution was proclaimed in the reoccupied territories. Many subaltern officers were reform-minded, especially those who, like the guerrilla chieftains, had won their rank through their courage and talent. As for the rank and file, coming mostly from the uneducated lower classes, they were not as a whole politically minded. However, as can be gathered from the abortive liberal revolts which broke out in army circles after the restoration of absolutism, blind loyalty to the king and his commands was still very

77. *Apología*, II, pp. 239–40.

much an integral part of the soldiers' outlook and was apparently not
sufficiently taken into account by liberal officers like Espoz y Mina
and Porlier, who were not followed by their men.

While many of the subaltern officers had been won over to the
new ideology, the top of the pyramid, except liberal-minded guerrilla chiefs such as Espoz y Mina, Villacampa, Porlier, and El Empecinado, was for the most part conservative and ready to follow the
king's orders, whatever those might be. Many of them had held high
rank under the absolute monarchy, and a return to the old order of
things was no calamity to their way of thinking. Besides, a number of
key figures had axes to grind against the Cortes. One of them was
Castaños, who had been removed from his post in 1813 because of his
inimicable attitude toward the constitutional government; another
one also ousted from his command was Girón, Castaños' nephew. A
third one, and the most important, Elío, a dyed-in-the-wool conservative, had been criticized in Cádiz for his unsuccessful military
operations. Even where a general harbored neither personal resentment against the Cortes, nor inimicable feelings toward reforms,
loyalty to the king superseded, more often than not, all other considerations. This was the case of General Francisco Copons, who received Fernando in Catalonia. He certainly did not encourage the
monarch to abolish the Constitution, but neither did he try to stop
what he could see was in the offing.[78] As for the generals of the third
and fourth Spanish armies in France, in which sentiment for the
Constitution was said to be strong, we have seen how Wellington
succeeded in keeping them from turning against absolutism.[79]

Finally, the centralist spirit of the Cortes had alienated a good
proportion of the population of some regions which still clung to
their local *fueros* or privileges. Navarra and the Basque provinces, for
instance, were not at all attracted by a centralizing, uniformity-bent
liberal state, in which time-honored administrations, customs, and
privileges peculiar to these provinces would disappear and give way
to the one and supreme law and administrative structure of the
land.[80]

78. Cf. Izquierdo Hernández, pp. 718–25.
79. See Chapter XVII.
80. Olóriz, *Navarra en la guerra de la independencia*, pp. 286–99.

Faced with the combined hostility of the old institutions and the old bureaucracy, the landowners, the nobility, the Church, and a large proportion of the inhabitants of the regions which had enjoyed special *fueros*, and not backed by the army or the masses of the Spanish people, whom could the liberals count on? A minority of the population of course: the progressive-minded middle class of the large cities, principally that of Cádiz; the intellectuals; members of the professions; some liberal clergymen; a number of subaltern officers, especially among the ex-guerrilla forces, which were now part of the regular army; as well as some of their chiefs. But this was about all the support the liberals really had in 1814. And it was obviously not enough. The masses, still completely loyal to the King, were led back into the fold of absolutism by the clever propaganda of the leading absolutist sectors, and the liberals tasted the bitterness of humiliating defeat. Wellington's letter to Charles Stuart of May 25, 1814, unfortunately depicted the real state of affairs: "You will have heard," he wrote, "of the extraordinary occurrences here, though not probably with surprise. Nothing can be more popular than the King and his measures, as far as they have gone to the overthrow of the Constitution. The imprisonment of the *Liberales* is thought by some, I believe with justice, unnecessary, and it is certainly highly impolitic; but it is liked by the people at large."[81]

The absolutist reaction achieved practically nothing positive for Spain. Abroad, the prestige of the country, which should have stood at an all-time high after the extraordinary resistance it had offered to Napoleon, sank to a new low. The persecution of the liberals and the inept diplomacy of Fernando's regime combined to rob Spain of the influence she should have exercised at the monumental Congress of Vienna (1814–1815), and of the benefits she should have derived thereof. All that Fernando had to show for, after the termination of the Congress, was the Duchy of Lucca in Italy for the son of his sister María Luisa, former queen of Etruria, and his right to succeed in the patrimony of Parma to Archduchess Marie Louise, ex-empress of France, after her death.[82]

In Spain itself the task of reconstruction would have taxed the intelligence and energy of men of immensely greater caliber than

81. *The Dispatches*, XII, p. 27.
82. Cf. Villa-Urrutia, *España en el Congreso de Viena*.

that of Fernando and his camarilla. For all practical purposes the country's economy was in ruin. The war had wrought terrible ravages in many regions. Agriculture was in a state of neglect, industry and trade were at a standstill, and finances were a shambles. But all of Fernando's energies went into destroying to the last vestige the work of reform that had been accomplished in his absence. Yet in spite of his ukase of May 4 and the subsequent terror, the imprint that liberalism had left on the country's consciousness could not be eradicated. There were enough people left who yearned for reform and were ready to answer Fernando's absolutist repression with force if necessary. Plans were hatched and revolts were staged at regular intervals throughout the first absolutist period, from 1814 to 1820. The continuing revolution in Spanish America placed an additional drain on Spain's already sorely strained resources and also served to fan discontent among the soldiers sent to fight the Spanish American rebels.

This dissatisfaction among soldiers and officers, many of whom had been won for liberalism by the coordinated activities of the Spanish Masonic lodges[83] working for the liberal cause, combined with residual liberal influence in a number of large cities, burst into revolution in 1820. Fernando, realizing that he could not stop the movement, accepted the Constitution of 1812. Reform was again the order of the day.

But the new constitutional regime lasted only three years. In 1823, backed by French troops which invaded Spain, absolutism was given another lease on life. Again Fernando, who had learned nothing, launched an atrocious counterrevolutionary terror. His death in 1833 brought to an end what has been known as the *ominosa década*, the abominable decade, of Spanish history. Fernando's demise was the signal for the outbreak of a bloody civil war, the first Carlist War (1833–1839), in which liberals and moderates supported Fernando's daughter Isabel[84] against the ultramontane Carlists led by Fernando's

83. In this period Spanish Masonic lodges, especially the one functioning in Cádiz, were instrumental in keeping discontent against the government at a high pitch among the middle classes, intellectuals, and officers (cf. Zabala, *España bajo los Borbones*, pp. 284–87).

84. In 1830 Fernando published the law reestablishing the traditional Spanish order of succession, which allowed females to reign in the absence of male heirs. In 1713 Philip V had established the Salic Law in Spain, which barred

brother Carlos. The defeat of the Carlists insured victory for the liberal bourgeoisie.

Thirty years after the proclamation of the Constitution of Cádiz liberalism in all spheres, political, economic, and social, waging a hard, uphill struggle since 1810, had finally remained in command of the battlefield and its principles had triumphed. *Señorios*, which had been eliminated in 1811, reestablished in 1814, and eliminated again during the second Constitutional period of 1820–1823, only to be brought back by absolutism in 1823, were finally disposed of in 1837. In the Cortes of 1810–1814 a number of liberals had wanted to put an end to *mayorazgos* or entailed estates, but the movement for abolition had not been strong enough. The Cortes of 1820 suppressed *mayorazgos*. Fernando annulled the reform, but *mayorazgos* were swept out once and for all in 1841.

The Inquisition had been abolished in 1813, brought back in 1814, abolished again in 1820, reestablished in 1823, and eliminated for good in 1834. The disamortization of Church property, actually begun by Godoy and continued by the Cortes of 1810–1814 and the Cortes of 1820, was given a decisive impulse in 1836, when male religious orders, with few exceptions, were banned and their property was confiscated.[85]

Constitutional monarchy, national representation, ministerial responsibility, separation between judicial and administrative functions, equality before the law and in matters of taxation, simplification in the fields of provincial and governmental machinery, administrative and judicial centralization and uniformity, and laissez-faire in the economic realm were the main principles to which liberalism had given concrete form and by which Spain was to be governed henceforth. It took a generation before Spain accepted them, but once they were in the saddle they stayed there for a hundred years. Some of them rule Spain even today.

females from the throne, but in 1789 the Cortes had asked for the reestablishment of the traditional order of succession, and this had been adopted by Charles IV, who, however, had not published the law.

85. Ecclesiastical property was then sold to individuals. This sale, which continued for about four decades, gave rise to a new and wealthy middle class.

CONCLUSION AND EPILOGUE

[1]

THE Spanish War of Independence stands in history as one of the fiercest, most admirable efforts made by any nation in defense of its national freedom. Except for the decisive Russian Campaign of 1812 it was this conflict which contributed more to undermine the Napoleonic Empire than anything else that happened on the European continent between the years 1808 and 1814. By tying up a considerable portion of the Emperor's best troops—even in 1813 Napoleon had more than 200,000 men in the Peninsula—and by allowing Britain to open up its only effective front on the Continent, Spain became the cancer which ate away relentlessly the foundations of Bonaparte's imposing structure. From 1808 on, Napoleon was never given a rest south of the Pyrenees. Now it was the Spanish field army at Bailén which struck a blow at France's might that was heard around Europe; now it was Zaragoza and Gerona, which stood off assault after assault of Napoleon's most feared shock troops; now it was the ever-present guerrillas who limited French domination in Spain literally to the ground held at a given moment. By their incessant harassing action they facilitated Wellington's task and made a shambles of Joseph Bonaparte's reign.

It has been justly noted that Napoleon was the principal architect of the nationalism that was to dominate modern Europe. In the case of Spain it could be said that Spain was the first and most striking example of the power of a European nationalism directly released by

Napoleon's greed for conquest. In Spain the supreme warlord sought to effect a change of dynasty through fraud and trickery and was faced by an upsurge of national indignation such as the world has but rarely seen. The forces that shot out of the Pandora box opened by the Corsican in Bayonne were to haunt him for the rest of his career. The Spanish war was a people's war in the true sense of the term, and it inspired other enslaved European nations, which followed Spain's example and rose to shake off the oppressor's yoke.

Unfortunately the War of Independence, which should have brought Spain substantial gains and the undying respect of Europe, had in the field of foreign relations no beneficial consequences for the nation that had contributed so much to the common victory. Victorious but materially ruined, and—what was much worse—ruled by a Fernando VII, it was pushed to the sidelines while the powers decided the fate of Europe. Only when absolutism was threatened in Spain in 1823 did Europe turn its attention to Spain, and then only to give Fernando the possibility once more to rule his subjects according to his whims. By 1824 the Spanish American colonies were lost with the exception of Cuba and Puerto Rico, and Spain was beginning to be regarded more as an object of curiosity than as a world power. By the time Fernando died (1833) European interest in Spain had revived, but it was more the interest of the literati and artists than that of the statesmen. Thanks to the guerrillas and the heroism displayed during the war by the Spanish people, to the many stories brought back by soldiers who had fought in the Peninsula, to such perceptive and articulate visitors as Lord and Lady Holland, John Hookham Frere, William Jacob, and Byron, to the presence in England and France of many Spanish émigrés between 1814 and 1833, and thanks, too, to Goya's paintings and etchings, Spain and everything Spanish became one of the ingredients that went into European Romanticism. The European Romantics adopted Spain and through their own exotic prism gave the world a distorted view of the Spanish nation, often emphasizing the picturesque and superficial without seeking out the essential elements that makes Spaniards what they are. It is a view which even today still conditions the reactions of many non-Spaniards to the land of Velázquez and Goya.

[2]

Spanish historians have often emphasized that aside from being a war for national independence, the events of 1808–1814 must also be considered as a revolution. The title of Toreno's account of the conflict is in this respect significant. For him it was a *Historia del levantamiento, guerra y revolución de España*. And no doubt a revolution it was, a revolution which shaped much of the Spain we know today.

It is axiomatic in the study of history that revolutionary events do not occur without deep underlying causes. An evolutionary process must reach a stage of development after which any extraordinary event may set the revolution in motion. Such a process had been going on in Spain since the middle of the eighteenth century.

It was then that the assimilation by the Spanish intellectual elite of Western European philosophic rationalism leading to a critical and scientific attitude toward the essential problems of man in his world encouraged the growth of an enlightened minority, both within and without the government, that began to pry Spain loose from its age-old manner of being. This minority was willing to cooperate with the despotism of the throne, for it considered that only unrestricted power from above could push through the reforms it deemed essential. It was the age of enlightened despotism. Then the French Revolution burst upon Western Europe, and as a result, this intellectual elite developed what might be called a latent split: those who, frightened by the cataclysm in France, clung more and more to the purely despotic aspect of enlightened despotism, and those who, drawn to some of the ideas underlying the French Revolution, though repelled by its bloody excesses, were looking forward to the day when those principles might triumph in Spain. Among the former were quite a few future *afrancesados* and among the latter a good number of future liberals.[1]

1. Classification is always dangerous, and a clear-cut division of this type is never foolproof. There were, of course, those to whom this criterion could not be applied, but on the whole this view seems to me the most correct way

When speaking of the dawn of the nineteenth century one cannot as yet speak of a true political polarization. The ingredients were there, but neither reformists nor traditionalists constituted an organized political force. The traditionalist offensive of 1800–1801, when Jovellanos felt the heavy hand of the ultramontane, did not constitute a struggle between two cohesive groups. It was a punitive expedition of the absolute monarchy, egged on by ultraconservative elements, against individualists suspected of politico-religious heresy. Afterward, the difference between the conservative majority and the reformist minority was overshadowed in most cases by the common, ever-growing opposition to Godoy, which fostered the spread of the desire for reforms to a much wider sector of the population.

Thus, by 1808, the yearning for reforms in the Spanish political, economic, and social structure was not limited to the enlightened minority. Many other persons of some importance in the Spanish monarchy desired changes. The immense majority of the population from the grandee to the lowliest peasant wanted an end to the despotism of Godoy. Almost everyone, unaware of the true character of the Prince of the Asturias, Fernando, dreamed of the day when the young prince would succeed his imbecile father on the throne, sweep away the influence of the Queen and the Prince of the Peace, and correct the many things that were wrong in Spain.

Then, in March, 1808, came the riot of Aranjuez which, though organized by highly placed supporters of Fernando, brought into play the popular element and thereby acquired a revolutionary character. For the first time in Spanish history since the advent of absolutism, a king and his *privado* had been overthrown by a palace coup, backed by soldiers and common people and enjoying the overwhelming support of Spanish popular opinion. Tradition had thus been shattered, and if Fernando, who had been elevated to the throne through revolutionary means, had been allowed to reign uninterruptedly, Spanish history would have developed along different lines. It is idle to speculate on what would have happened, but it seems possible that absolutism might in the end have yielded through an evolutionary process to a regime more in consonance with modern

of interpreting the evolution of eighteenth-century Spanish Enlightenment (cf. Artola, *Los afrancesados*).

times, especially if men like Jovellanos and Urquijo had been permitted to remain as ministers at the side of the young king.[2]

But this did not happen. War broke out, a war which was to bring about the momentous revolution of Cádiz. Napoleon, making one of the greatest errors in his career, tore the crown from the head of the Spanish Bourbons and thereby gained the undying hatred of the Spanish people. The latter revolted against the French invaders in one of the greatest mass uprisings in history, which shook the Spanish *Ancien Régime* to its foundations. The mass of the Spanish people was the great factor in the insurrection and forced the creation of revolutionary juntas which sprang up throughout the country. These constituted in turn a revolutionary central organism, the Junta Suprema, which ruled Spain until January, 1810. The nationwide revolt and relentless war waged by the Spanish people against Joseph Bonaparte and his regime gave the reformist minority a unique chance to present its program to the nation. Reforms became the order of the day, reforms to win the war and to effect far-reaching changes in the political structure of the country, which, it was hoped, would never again allow it to be converted into an easy prey for a foreign aggressor.

As yet there was no true political division in free Spain, since the majority desired reforms and demanded the gathering of the national Cortes to bring about the much-needed changes. But though most Spaniards desired reforms—and the Constitution of Bayonne and the decrees of Joseph Bonaparte served to a certain extent to spur this feeling on the insurgent side—only the intellectual and professional minority had a more or less clear idea of what it wanted.

When, as a result of military defeat, the national Cortes were forced to meet in Cádiz, this group pushed through truly revolutionary reforms, and as a result the latent political division that had developed under the surface since the late eighteenth century emerged clearly for the first time. It was in Cádiz that took place the polarization of political outlooks which has affected Spanish history

2. It should be kept in mind, however, that the few measures of a domestic nature which Fernando took in the short-lived first stage of his reign did not particularly point in the direction of reform. It will be recalled, for instance, that he suspended the sale of Church property (see Chapter III).

down to our day and has caused Spaniards to gravitate around political extremes. This split between the irreconcilable views on what kind of Spain Spaniards should live in, reinforced by the Spanish disinclination to compromise,[3] signalled the beginning of a civil war which, with intervals and with considerable shifts in the original components of the two antagonistic parties, culminated in the terrible conflict of 1936–1939 and may again one day tear Spain apart.

By the end of 1813, *liberales*, the reformist faction, and *serviles*, the conservatives of all shades, were lining up ominously their respective forces throughout liberated Spain. The Conservatives were more powerful quantity-wise and could count on the eventual support of a popular mass in which liberalism had not made a sufficient dent. The reformist minority had grown in strength, but it was still a minority and had not yet won over the broad masses of the people. In this initial test of strength it was bound to succumb.

Fernando, who should have remained above the political struggle and acted as a mediator, took the side of absolutism and did his best to stamp out liberalism. In this he failed, for reformism was now on the march, and though crushed in 1814 and again in 1823, the liberal bourgeosie stood off the ultratraditionalist or Carlist bid for power in the bloody civil war of 1833–1839, and in the end was able to consolidate the work of reform begun in Cádiz in 1810.

The key instrument in this process of consolidation was the army. The military establishment had been from the start a favorite target for liberal propaganda. It was the army which had been the corner-stone of the success of the liberal revolution of 1820, and it was the army which in the end crushed the hopes of Carlism, first in 1833–1839, then in 1845–1849, and later in 1872–1876, and which brought about the downfall of Isabel II in 1868. For the greater part of the nineteenth century the military establishment remained, with notable exceptions, in the camp of liberalism. Down to our day it has remained one of the primary factors in Spanish political life. The

3. With all due caution with regard to generalizing about so-called national characteristics, it is only realistic to consider the existence of a residuum of national traits, produced of course by a number of factors which cannot always be encompassed by historical investigation.

peculiar nature of the War of Independence determined that military power and at the same time the individualism and lack of discipline which had been given free rein by guerrilla warfare would henceforth dominate the historical development of the nation. *Pronunciamientos* have made and unmade governments, and in spite of the present lull, brought about by the bloodiest *pronunciamiento* of all, there is no guarantee that this endemic national disease will not continue to ravage the face of Spain in the future.

While the army supported liberalism for many years, its officer corps, drawn mainly from an increasingly conservative nobility and middle class, was bound to make it a traditionalist force with time. And this is what it is today. Much of the erstwhile liberal middle class, too, eventually turned into a conservative element. Enriched by the acquisition of Church property, by industrialization and commerce, and becoming more and more allied—often through matrimony—with the frequently impoverished landowning aristocracy, the upper bourgeoisie found itself fighting a no-quarter battle to preserve the status quo against demands of an ever-growing urban and rural proletariat, often supported by professionals, intellectuals, and reform-minded sectors of the lower middle class.

As new social forces and new political doctrines entered the stage, what had originally been reformist was bound to become conservative. Only the Spanish Church remained in the position it had taken at the end of the War of Independence. In 1812–1813 it joined one of the two political groups emerging in the Cortes and evolved from what had been one of the foundations of the State into the ally of the conservatives. For the past 150 years it has allied itself fairly consistently with the conservative elements in the nation. The anticlericalism created among liberals by its support of Fernando VII and its continued alliance with the forces that could guarantee it best against liberal assaults on its position has continued to be a hallmark of a large sector of Spanish intellectuals and professionals.

The urban and rural proletariat, which had supported absolutism in 1814 and 1823, seeing the Church solidly in the camp of the forces maintaining the status quo, assimilated this anticlericalism and has often given concrete proof of it in a most violent and bloody manner.

Thus, except for the Church,[4] the original two groups forged by the War of Independence have undergone considerable changes. But while changing social and economic conditions have brought about considerable shifts in the original political positions,[5] the fundamental abyss between what we call today the Right and the Left, has remained as wide as ever. The great political polarization between extreme points of view to which the War of Independence gave birth has been the fundamental law of Spanish politics during the past 150 years. No, the abyss has not been bridged, for the spirit of compromise, absent at Cádiz, under Fernando VII, and in the civil wars of the nineteenth century[6] has again been notably lacking in our twentieth century. The end of the great rift is unfortunately not yet in sight.[7]

4. There are signs that partly under the influence of the new attitudes prevailing today in the Vatican some sectors of the Church, principally among the younger clergy, are ready to move in a more liberal direction in political as well as in social and economic questions.

5. Catalan and Basque demands for regional autonomy have further complicated this picture in the present century.

6. The period between 1876 and 1917 was marked by relative political stability, though Spanish anarchism made itself felt with increasing virulence through direct action, especially in Catalonia, in the first decade of this century.

7. The civil war of 1936–1939 has been followed by a long period of peace —twenty-five years as of today (1964)—but this has been achieved by a military dictatorship and not by a compromise between the two contending forces. When this dictatorship ends, the old antagonisms can be expected to flare up once more.

BIBLIOGRAPHY

Abrantès, Laure St. Martin Permon, duchess of, *Mémoires*, 10 vols. (Paris, n.d.).

Alcaide Ibieca, Agustín, *Historia de los sitios que pusieron a Zaragoza en los años de 1808 y 1809 las tropas de Napoleón*, 3 vols. (Madrid, 1830–1831).

Alcalá Galiano, Antonio, *Memorias*, 2 vols. (Madrid, 1886).

——, *Recuerdos de un anciano* (Madrid, 1878).

Alcalaíno, "Libro de apuntes de un . . . (*1809–1814*)," RH, XXXI (1914), pp. 169–258.

Almirante, José, *Diccionario Militar* (Madrid, 1869).

Alvarado, Francisco, *Cartas críticas*, 3 vols. (Madrid, 1824–1825).

Alvarez de Cienfuegos, *Poesías, Poetas líricos del siglo XVIII*, III, in BAE, LXVII (Madrid, 1953).

Amado Lóriga, Santiago, "Palafox, general y caudillo," *La guerra de la independencia española y los sitios de Zaragoza* (Zaragoza, 1958).

Amador de los Ríos, Rodrigo, "Episodios históricos de la guerra de la independencia," *Revista de España*, CVIII (1886).

——, "Los 'del Montón.' El Dos de Mayo de 1808," *La España Moderna* (October, 1908), pp. 56–94.

Amador y Carrandi, Florencio, *La Universidad de Salamanca en la guerra de la independencia* (Salamanca, 1916).

Amorós, Francisco, *Representación del consejero español Don Francisco Amorós, a S.M. el Rey Don Fernando VII* (Paris, 1814).

Antón del Olmet, Fernando, *Aclaración histórica. El arma de infantería en el levantamiento del 2 de mayo de 1808* (Madrid, 1908).

Apuntes de la vida y hechos militares del brigadier Don Juan Martín Díez El Empecinado, por un admirador de ellos (Madrid, 1814).

Arango, Rafael de, *El dos de mayo de 1808* (Madrid, 1837).

Archivo del Real Palacio (Madrid), *Papeles reservados de Fernando VII*: 9, 10, 97, 102, 104.

Archivo Histórico Nacional (Madrid), section Estado:
Letters from Godoy to Queen Luisa, 2821
Correspondence of *afrancesados*, 3068, 3069, 3070, 3073, 3078, 3096, 3119
Papeles de la Junta Central, 2, 6, 9, 10, 12/2, 13, 20, 22, 29, 38, 39, 41, 46, 50, 51, 52, 60, 62, 65, 70, 73.

Various materials on the War of Independence, 149, 2849, 2955, 2962, 2972, 2982, 2993/1, 2993/2, 2994, 2995, 3003/1, 3003/2, 3004, 3010, 3059, 3072, 3082/1, 3082/2, 3092, 3099, 3100, 3104, 3105, 3110, 3111, 3112, 3113, 3116, 3130, 3146.

Argüelles, Agustín, *Examen histórico de la reforma constitucional*, 2 vols. (London, 1835).

Arriaza, Juan Bautista, *Poesías, Poetas líricos del siglo XVIII*, III, in BAE, LXVII (Madrid, 1953).

Artigas, Miguel, "Avisos amistosos de Jovellanos a Saavedra," in "Los manuscritos de Jovellanos de la Biblioteca Menéndez y Pelayo," *Boletín de la Biblioteca Menéndez y Pelayo* (1921), pp. 118–52.

Artola, Miguel, *Los afrancesados* (Madrid, 1953).

——, "La guerra de guerrillas," *Revista de Occidente*, Segunda Epoca, No. 10, (January, 1964).

——, *Los orígenes de la España contemporánea*, 2 vols. (Madrid, 1959).

Arzadún, Juan, *Los guerrilleros en la guerra de la independencia* (Madrid, 1910).

——, *Daoiz y Velarde* (Madrid, 1908).

Aunós Pérez, Eduardo, *Itinerario histórico de la España contemporánea (1808–1936)* (Barcelona, 1940).

Aviso importante y urgente a la nación española. Juicio imparcial de sus cortes, in CDF, CDLXIII (La Coruña, 1811; Madrid, 1815).

Ayerbe, Marquis of, *Memorias sobre la estancia de Fernando VII en Valençay y el principio de la guerra de la independencia, Memorias de tiempos de Fernando VII*, I, in BAE, XCVII (Madrid, 1957).

Azanza, Miguel José, and O'Farril, Gonzalo, *Memoria sobre los hechos que justifican su conducta política, desde marzo de 1808 hasta abril de 1814, Memorias de tiempos de Fernando VII*, I, in BAE, XCVII (Madrid, 1957).

Azcárate, Pablo de, "Memoria sobre los 'Vaughan Papers,'" BRAH, CXLI (October–December, 1957), pp. 721–44.

——, *Wellington y España* (Madrid, 1960).

Bainville, Jacques, *Napoléon* (Paris, 1931).

Ballesteros y Beretta, Antonio, *Historia de España y su influencia en la historia universal*, VII (Barcelona, 1934).

Baumgarten, Hermann, *Geschichte Spaniens vom Ausbruch der französischen Revolution bis auf unsere Tage*, 2 vols. (Leipzig, 1865).

Becker, Jerónimo, *Acción de la diplomacia española durante la guerra de la independencia (1808–1814), Publicaciones del Congreso Histórico Internacional de la guerra de la independencia y su época (1807–1815)* (Zaragoza, 1909).

Bedoya, Juan Manuel, *Retrato histórico de D. Pedro de Quevedo y Quintano, Obispo de Orense* (Madrid, 1835).

Belda Carreras, José, "Estudio histórico-crítico del sitio de Cádiz de 1810 a

1812," RABM, Tercera Época, XXVIII (January–June, 1913), pp. 241–64, 291–310.

Belda Carreras, José, and De Labra, Rafael, *Las Cortes de Cádiz en el Oratorio de San Felipe* (Madrid, 1912).

Belmas, J., *Journaux des sièges faits ou soutenus par les français dans la Péninsule, de 1807 à 1814*, 5 vols. (Paris, 1836–1837).

Beltrán y Rózpide, Ricardo, *Isidoro de Antillón, geógrafo, historiador y político* (Madrid, 1903).

Benavides Moro, Nicolás, and Yagüe Laurel, José, *El Capitán General D. Joaquín Blake y Joyes, Regente del Reino, fundador del cuerpo de Estado Mayor* (Madrid, 1960).

Bermejo, Ildefonso Antonio, *Historia anecdótica y secreta de la corte de Carlos IV*, 2 vols. (Madrid, n.d.).

Blanco y Crespo (Blanco-White), José María, *Letters from Spain*, 2d ed. (London, 1825).

———, *The Life of the Rev. Joseph Blanco-White, Written by Himself with Portions of His Correspondence*, ed. by John Hamilton Thom, 3 vols. (London, 1845).

———, *Poesías, Poetas líricos del siglo XVIII*, III, in BAE, LXVII (Madrid, 1953).

Blayney, Lord, *Narrative of a Forced Journey Through Spain and France*, 2 vols. (London, 1814).

Blaze, Sebastián, *Memorias de un boticario* (Buenos Aires, n.d.).

Bonaparte, Joseph, *Mémoires et correspondance politique et militaire du Roi Joseph*, ed. A. Du Casse, 2d ed., 10 vols. (Paris, 1854); 3d ed. (Paris, 1856).

Bourgoing, Jean François, *Modern State of Spain*, tr. from Paris ed. of 1807 of *Tableau de l'Espagne moderne*, 4 vols. (London, 1808).

Boussagol, Gabriel, *Angel de Saavedra, Duc de Rivas* (Toulouse, Paris, 1926).

Brun, Louis, *Les cahiers du général Brun, Baron de Villeret, Pair de France, 1773–1845*, ed. Louis de Saint-Pierre (Paris, 1953).

Bryant, Arthur, *The Age of Elegance, 1812–1822* (London, 1950).

———, *Years of Victory, 1802–1812* (London, 1944).

Cabarrús, Francisco, Count, *Cartas sobre los obstáculos que la naturaleza, la opinión, y las leyes oponen a la felicidad pública* (Vitoria, 1808).

Calvo Serer, Rafael, "España y la caída de Napoleón," *Historia de España, Arbor* (Madrid, 1953).

Calzada Rodríguez, Luciano de la, *La evolución institucional. Las Cortes de Cádiz: Precedentes y consecuencias* (Zaragoza, 1959).

———, "La ideología política de la guerra de la independencia," *La guerra de la independencia española y los sitios de Zaragoza* (Zaragoza, 1958).

Camacho y Perea, Angel María, *Estudio crítico de las doctrinas de Jove-*

llanos en lo referente a las ciencias morales y políticas (Madrid, 1913).

Cambronero, Carlos, "La cruz de Madrid," *La España Moderna,* XII (1908), pp. 5–22.

Camden, Theophilus, *The History of the Present War in Spain and Portugal from Its Commencement to the Battle of Vittoria* (London, 1813).

Camón Aznar, José, *Goya en los años de la guerra de la independencia* (Zaragoza, 1959).

Canella Secades, Fermín, *Memorias astudianas del año ocho* (Oviedo, 1908).

Canga Argüelles, José, *Diccionario de hacienda,* 5 vols. (London, 1826–1827).

———, *Documentos pertenecientes a las observaciones sobre la historia de la guerra de España, que escribieron los señores Clarke, Southey, Londonderry y Napier, publicadas en Londres el año de 1829 por Don José Canga Argüelles,* 2 vols. (Madrid, 1835–1836).

———, *Observaciones a la historia de la guerra de España que escribieron los señores Clarke, Southey, Londonderry y Napier,* 3 vols. (London, 1829–1830).

Capmany, Antonio de, *Centinela contra franceses* (Sevilla, 1810).

Casamayor, *Diario de . . . los sitios de Zaragoza,* ed. José Valenzuela la Rosa (Zaragoza, 1908).

Casariego, J. E., *Jovellanos o el equilibrio* (Madrid, 1943).

Cascales y Muñoz, José, *Rasgos de nuestra epopeya* (Madrid, 1918).

Castel, Jorge, *La Junta Central Suprema y Gubernativa de España e Indias. Su creación, organización y funcionamiento* (Madrid, 1950).

Castro, Adolfo de, *Cádiz en la guerra de la independencia* (Cádiz, 1862).

Castro Urdiales, La villa de, en la costa de Cantabria, saqueada, destruida y abrasada por los franceses el día 11 de mayo del año 1813 (Madrid, 1815).

Cevallos, Pedro, *Exposición de los hechos y maquinaciones que han preparado la usurpación de la corona de España y los medios que el emperador de los franceses ha puesto en obra para realizarla, Memorias de tiempos de Fernando VII,* I, in BAE, XCVII (Madrid, 1957).

Chastenet, Jacques, *Godoy, Master of Spain, 1792–1808* (London, 1953).

———, *Wellington* (Paris, 1945).

Chevillard, Jean-Baptiste, "Souvenirs d'Espagne (1808)," *Revue de Paris,* IV (1906), pp. 449–74, 766–75.

Clerc, Lt. Col., *Guerre d'Espagne. Capitulation de Baylen. Causes et conséquences* (Paris, 1903).

Colección de los decretos y órdenes que han expedido las Cortes Generales y Extraordinarias . . . , 4 vols. (Cádiz, 1811–1813), in CDF, LXXVII, LXXVIII, LXXIX, LXXX.

Colección de documentos inéditos de la guerra de la independencia exis-

tentes en el archivo de la Excma. Diputación de Vizcaya (Bilbao, 1959).

Colección de papeles interesantes sobre las circunstancias presentes (Madrid, 1808).

Colección Documental del Fraile, in the library of the Servicio Histórico Militar in Madrid (more than 1,000 volumes of pamphlets, proclamations, periodicals, newspapers, and books of the eighteenth and early nineteenth centuries gathered by the Capuchin monk Fray Joaquín de Sevilla): VIII, XVIII, XXVII, LXII, LXVII, LXVIII, LXIX, LXXIV, LXXVI, LXXVII, LXXVIII, LXXIX, LXXX, LXXXIX, CXXIII, CXXVI, CXXXIII, CCXXVII, CCLIX, CDXXXV, CDXLV, CDLXIII, DCCLXII, DCCLXXXVIII, DCCCLXIV, CMV.

Colford, William, *Juan Meléndez Valdés* (New York, 1942).

Coloma, Luis, *Retratos de Antaño*, 3d ed., 2 vols. (Madrid, 1914).

Comellas, José Luis, "Las Cortes de Cádiz y la Constitución de 1812," REP, CXXVI (November–December, 1962), pp. 69–110.

Constant, *Mémoires de . . . , Premier valet de chambre de l'Empereur, sur la vie privée de Napoléon, sa famille et sa cour*, IV (Paris, 1830).

Constitución política de la Monarquía Española (Constitution of 1812), CDF, DCCLXII, pp. 149–70.

Corona, Carlos, "Carácter de las relaciones hispano-francesas en el reinado de Carlos IV," *La guerra de la independencia española y los sitios de Zaragoza* (Zaragoza, 1958).

——, *Las ideas políticas en el reinado de Carlos IV* (Madrid, 1954).

——, *Precedentes ideológicos de la guerra de la independencia* (Zaragoza, 1959).

——, *Revolución y reacción en el reinado de Carlos IV* (Madrid, 1957).

Cortines y Murube, F., "Noticias sobre un afrancesado," RABM, Tercera Epoca, XXI (1909).

Dallas, Alexander, *Felix Alvarez or Manners in Spain, Containing Descriptive Accounts of Some of the Prominent Events of the Late Peninsular War, and Authentic Anecdotes Illustrative of the Spanish Character*, 3 vols. (London, 1818).

De Laborde, Alexandre, *Itinéraire descriptif de l'Espagne*, 5 vols. (Paris, 1808).

Deleito y Piñuela, José, "La expatriación de los españoles afrancesados (1813–1820)," *Nuestro Tiempo* (June–July, 1921), pp. 257–73.

Del Moral, Juan Gabriel, "Memorias de la guerra de la independencia," RABM, XVIII (1908), pp. 416–37; XXII (1910), pp. 284–301.

Del Río, Angel, *Historia de la literatura española*, 2 vols. (New York, 1948).

Demerson, Georges, "Meléndez Valdés. Quelques documents inédits pour compléter sa biographie," BH, LV (1953), No. 3–4, pp. 252–95.

——, *Don Juan Meléndez Valdés et son temps (1754–1817)* (Paris, 1962).

Demostración de la lealtad española. Colección de proclamas, bandos, órdenes, discursos, estados de ejército, y relaciones de batallas publicadas por las Juntas de Gobierno, o por algunos particulares en las actuales circunstancias, 7 vols. (Madrid, Cádiz, 1808–1809).

De Pradt, M., *Mémoires historiques sur la révolution d'Espagne* (Paris, 1816).

Desdevises du Dézert, G., "Le Conseil de Castille en 1808," RH, XVII (1907), pp. 66–378.

———, *La Constitution de Bayonne, Publicaciones del Congreso Histórico Internacional de la guerra de la independencia y su época (1807–1815)*, II (Zaragoza, 1909).

———, *L'Espagne de l'Ancien Régime. Les institutions* (Paris, 1899).

———, *L'Espagne de l'Ancien Régime. La société* (Paris, 1897).

Diario de las discusiones y actas de las Cortes, 23 vols. (Cádiz, 1811–1813), Vols. I, VI, VII, VIII, XIV, XVI in CDF, LXII, LXVII, LXVIII, LXIX, LXXIV, LXXVI, respectively.

Díaz-Plaja, Fernando, *La historia de España en sus documentos. El siglo XIX* (Madrid, 1954).

———, *La vida española en el siglo XVIII* (Barcelona, 1946).

Diccionario razonado manual para inteligencia de ciertos escritores que por equivocación han nacido en España (Cádiz, 1811).

Discusión del proyecto de decreto sobre el Tribunal de la Inquisición (Cádiz, 1813).

Domínguez Ortiz, Antonio, *La sociedad española en el siglo XVIII* (Madrid, 1955).

Entrambasaguas, Joaquín de, *El Madrid de Moratín* (Madrid, 1960).

Escoiquiz, Juan de, *Idea sencilla de las razones que motivaron el viaje del Rey Don Fernando VII a Bayona en el mes de abril de 1808, Memorias de tiempos de Fernando VII,* I, in BAE, XCVII (Madrid, 1957).

———, *Memorias, Memorias de tiempos de Fernando VII,* I, in BAE, XCVII (Madrid, 1957).

España en el año de 1808. Colección de todos los papeles patrióticos publicados en los meses de agosto, septiembre, octubre y noviembre de dicho año, assembled by Manuel Sayz Gómez del Campo, 23 vols. (Madrid, 1814).

España y el Español a presencia de sus Cortes en 1810 (Valencia, 1810).

Espoz y Mina, Francisco, *Memorias del general Don Francisco Espoz y Mina,* I, in BAE, CXLVI (Madrid, 1962).

Farias, *Memorias de la guerra de la independencia, escritas por soldados franceses* (Madrid, 1920).

Fée, A. L. A., *Souvenirs de la guerre d'Espagne* (Paris, 1856).

Fernández Almagro, Melchor, "Del Antiguo Régimen a las Cortes de Cádiz," REP, CXVI (November–December, 1962), pp. 9–28.

————, *Orígenes del régimen constitucional en España* (Barcelona, Buenos Aires, 1928).

Fernández de Moratín, Leandro, *Obras*, BAE, II (Madrid, 1944).

————, *Obras póstumas*, 3 vols. (Madrid, 1867–1868).

Fernández Fernández, León, *Recuerdo histórico. El Empecinado* (Madrid, 1905).

Fernández-Largo, Jacinto, *Introducción al estudio del filósofo rancio* (Madrid, 1959).

Fernández Martín, Manuel, *Derecho parlamentario español*, 3 vols. (Madrid, 1885–1900).

Fernández y González, Modesto, *La hacienda de nuestros abuelos* (Madrid, 1874).

Fernsworth, Lawrence, *Spain's Struggle for Freedom* (Boston, 1957).

Foy, Maximilien, *Histoire de la guerre de la Péninsule sous Napoléon*, 4 vols. (Paris, 1827).

Fuentes Cervera, Eduardo de, "La organización de nuestro ejército en la guerra de la independencia," *La guerra de la independencia española y los sitios de Zaragoza* (Zaragoza, 1958).

Fugier, André, *Napoléon et l'Espagne (1799–1808)*, 2 vols. (Paris, 1930).

Gaffarel, Raymond, *Règne de Joseph Bonaparte de 1810 à 1812. Les difficultés gouvernementales*, Publicaciones del Congreso Histórico Internacional de la guerra de la independencia y su época (1807–1815), IV (Zaragoza, 1910).

Gallardo, Bartolomé José, *Diccionario crítico-burlesco del que se titula "Diccionario razonado manual para inteligencia de ciertos escritores que por equivocación han nacido en España,"* (Cádiz, 1812).

Gallardo y de Font, Jerónimo, *Proceso de D. Bartolomé José Gallardo y Blanco por su Diccionario crítico-burlesco (1812–1813)*, Publicaciones del Congreso Histórico Internacional de la guerra de la independencia y su época (1807–1815), III (Zaragoza, 1910).

Gallego, Juan Nicasio, *Poesías, Poetas líricos del siglo XVIII*, III, in BAE, LXVII (Madrid, 1953).

Gallego y Burín, *Granada en la guerra de la independencia* (Granada, 1923).

García Guijarro, Luis, *La guerra de la independencia y el guerrillero Romeu* (Madrid, 1908).

García Mercadal, J., *Palafox, Duque de Zaragoza (1775–1847)* (Madrid, 1948).

García Prado, Justiniano, *Historia del alzamiento, guerra y revolución de Asturias (1808–1814)* (Oviedo, 1953).

García Rámila, Ismael, "España ante la invasión francesa," BRAH, XCIV (1929), pp. 498–616.

858]   BIBLIOGRAPHY

García Rodríguez, José, *Guerra de la independencia*, 2 vols. (Barcelona, 1945).

Garnier, Jean-Paul, *Murat, roi de Naples* (Paris, 1959).

Gascón, Domingo, *La provincia de Teruel en la guerra de la independencia* (Madrid, 1908).

Geoffroy de Grandmaison, Charles Alexandre, *L'Ambassade française en Espagne pendant la révolution (1789–1804)* (Paris, 1892).

———, "Les débuts de Joseph Bonaparte à Madrid (janvier–avril 1809)," RQH, LXXXIII (1908), pp. 543–74.

———, *L'Espagne et Napoléon*, 3 vols. (Paris, 1908–1931).

———, "Saragosse et l'Empereur," *Le Correspondant* (April–June, 1901).

———, "Savary en Espagne," RQH, XXIII (1900), pp. 188–213.

Gille, Philippe, *Mémoires d'un conscrit de 1808* (Paris, 1892).

Godoy, Manuel, *Memorias*, 2 vols. with a preliminary study by Carlos Seco Serrano, BAE, LXXXVIII and LXXXIX (Madrid, 1956).

Gómez Centurión, José, "Causas del destierro de Jovellanos," BRAH, LXIV (1914), pp. 227–31.

Gómez de Arteche, José, *Guerra de la independencia. Historia militar de España de 1808 a 1814*, 14 vols. (Madrid, 1868–1903).

———, "Juan Martín El Empecinado. La guerra de la independencia bajo su aspecto popular. Los guerrilleros." *La España del siglo XIX, Colección de conferencias históricas celebradas durante los cursos de 1885–1886 y 1886–1887*, 3 vols., I, Ateneo Científico, Literario y Artístico (Madrid, 1886).

———, *Nieblas de la historia patria*, 2d ed. (Barcelona, 1888).

———, *Reinado de Carlos IV*, 3 vols., *Historia general de España*, XVI–XVIII (Madrid, 1893).

Gómez Imaz, Manuel, *Los garrochistas en Bailén* (Sevilla, 1908).

———, *Sevilla en 1808* (Sevilla, 1908).

González Arranz, Gregorio, *Memorias del alcalde de Roa, Don Gregorio . . .* , ed. Sebastián Lazo (Madrid, 1935).

Goodspeed, D. J., *The British Campaigns in the Peninsula, 1808–1814* (Ottawa, 1958).

Goya, *The Disasters of War*, with an essay on the artist's life and works by Xavier de Salas and an introduction to the etchings by Elie Faure (Garden City, N. Y., 1956).

Grandmaison, see Geoffroy de Grandmaison.

Grasset, André, *La guerre d'Espagne (1807–1813)*, 3 vols. (Paris, 1914–1932).

Guzmán, Martín Luis, *Mina el Mozo, héroe de Navarra* (Madrid, Barcelona, 1932).

Hazard, Paul, *El pensamiento europeo en el siglo XVIII* (Madrid, 1958).

Herr, Richard, *The Eighteenth-Century Revolution in Spain* (Princeton, 1958).

Historia de la guerra de España contra Napoleón Bonaparte, escrita y publicada de orden de S.M. (Madrid, 1818).

Historia de la vida y reinado de Fernando VII, Rey de España, 3 vols. (Madrid, 1842).

Holland, Elizabeth, *The Spanish Journal of Elizabeth, Lady Holland* (London, 1910).

Holland, Henry Richard Vassall, Lord . . . , *Further Memoirs of the Whig Party (1807–1821), With Some Miscellaneous Reminiscences* (London, 1905).

Holzing, Karl Franz von, *Unter Napoleon in Spanien* (Berlin, 1937).

Hugo, Abel, "Souvenirs sur Joseph Napoléon," *Revue des Deux Mondes,* I (1833), pp. 260–84, II (1833), pp. 113–42.

Hugo, Joseph Léopold, *Mémoires,* 3 vols. (Paris, 1823).

Hugo, Victor, *Victor Hugo, raconté par un témoin de sa vie,* 2 vols. (Paris, 1863).

Hume, Martin, *Modern Spain* (London, 1923).

Husson, Adjutant-Major, *Journal de campagne que j'ai faite en Espagne et des malheurs que j'ai éprouvés pendant ma captivité dans les années 1808, 1809 et 1810, jusqu'à mon arrivée en Angleterre, le 29 septembre 1810, Carnet de la Sabretache,* Deuxième Série (February, 1908).

Instrucción pastoral de los ilustrísimos señores obispos de Lérida, Tortosa, Barcelona, Urgel, Teruel, y Pamplona al clero y pueblo de sus diócesis (Mallorca, 1813; Santiago, 1814).

Instrucción sobre las facultades de los señores Comisarios de la Junta Suprema Gubernativa del Reyno, en las provincias, CDF, DCCLXXXVIII, pp. 241–42.

Izquierdo Hernández, Manuel, *Antecedentes y comienzos del reinado de Fernando VII* (Madrid, 1963).

——, "Informes sobre España (diciembre de 1807–marzo de 1808) del gentilhombre Claudio Felipe, Conde de Tournon-Simiane al Emperador Napoleón I," BRAH, CXXXVII (October–December, 1955), pp. 315–57.

Jackson, George, *The Diaries and Letters of Sir George . . . ,* 2 vols. (London, 1872).

Jacob, William, *Travels in the South of Spain in Letters Written* A.D. *1809 and 1810* (London, 1811).

Jiménez de Gregorio, Fernando, *La convocación a Cortes Constituyentes en 1810. Estado de la opinión española en punto a la reforma constitucional* (Madrid, 1955).

Jovellanos, Gaspar Melchor de, *Cartas de Jovellanos y Lord Vassall Holland sobre la guerra de la independencia (1808–1811),* ed. Julio Somoza, 2 vols. (Madrid, 1911).

——, *Manuscritos inéditos, raros, o dispersos,* ed. Julio Somoza (Madrid, 1913).

——, *Obras,* I, in BAE, XLVI (Madrid, 1951).

——, *Obras,* III, in BAE, LXXXV (Madrid, 1956).

——, *Obras,* IV, in BAE, LXXXVI (Madrid, 1956).

——, *Obras escoguidas,* ed. Angel del Río, 3 vols., *Clásicos Castellanos,* CX, CXI, CXXIX (Madrid, 1955).

Junta de Iconografía Nacional, *Guerra de la independencia. Retratos* (Madrid, 1908).

Juretschke, Hans, "Concepto de Cortes a comienzos de la guerra de la independencia, carácter y actualización," *Revista de la Universidad de Madrid,* IV, No. 15 (1955).

——, "El coronel von Schepeler. Carácter y valor informativo de su obra," REP, CXXVI (November–December, 1962), pp. 229–48.

——, *Los afrancesados en la guerra de la independencia* (Madrid, 1962).

——, *Vida, obra y pensamiento de Alberto Lista* (Madrid, 1951).

Kalendario manual y guía de forasteros (Madrid, 1807).

Kircheisen, Friedrich M., *Memoiren aus dem spanischen Freiheitskampfe 1808–1811* (Hamburg, 1908).

Konetzke, Richard, *La guerra de la independencia y el despertar del nacionalismo europeo* (Zaragoza, 1959).

Labra, Rafael María de, *Muñoz Torrero y las Cortes de Cádiz, La España del siglo* XIX, I (Madrid, 1886).

La Forest, Count, *Correspondance du Comte de La Forest,* ed. Geoffroy de Grandmaison, 7 vols. (Paris, 1905).

Lafuente, Modesto, *Historia general de España,* 30 vols. (Madrid, 1850–1867).

Lagüens, Gerardo, *Relaciones internacionales de España durante la guerra de la independencia,* (Zaragoza, 1959).

Lardizábal y Uribe, Miguel, *Manifiesto que presenta a la nación el Consejero de Estado D. Miguel de Lardizábal y Uribe, uno de los cinco que compusieron el supremo consejo de Regencia de España e Indias sobre su conducta política en la noche del 24 de setiembre de 1810* (Alicante, 1811).

Las Cases, Count, *Mémorial de Sainte-Hélène,* IV (Paris, 1824).

Lea, Henry Charles, *A History of the Inquisition of Spain,* 4 vols. (New York, 1906–1907).

Le Brun, Carlos, *Retratos políticos de la revolución de España* (Philadelphia, 1826).

Lecestre, Léon, "La guerre de la Péninsule (1807–1813) d'après la correspondance inédite de Napoléon I," RQH, LIX (1896), pp. 442–90.

Lejeune, Baron, *Memoirs of Baron Lejeune,* 2 vols. (London, 1897).

Lema, Salvador Bermúdez de Castro, Marquis of, *Antecedentes políticos y diplomáticos de los sucesos de 1808* (Madrid, 1912).

Livermore, Harold, *A History of Spain* (London, Liverpool, 1958).

Llorens Castillo, Vicente, *Liberales y románticos. Una emigración española en Inglaterra* (Mexico City, 1954).

Llorente, Juan Antonio, *Memorias para la historia de la revolución española, con documentos justificativos, compilados por Juan Nellerto* (Paris, 1814).

——, *Noticia biográfica o memorias para la historia de su vida* (Paris, 1818).

——, *Historia Critica de la Inquisición de Espana*, 5 vols. (Madrid, 1822).

Lucas-Dubreton, J., *Napoléon devant l'Espagne. Ce qu'a vu Goya* (Paris, 1946).

Madariaga, Salvador de, *Spain* (New York, 1958).

Madelin, Louis, *Histoire du Consulat et de l'Empire*, VII (*L'Affaire d'Espagne* (Paris, 1945).

Madol, Hans Roger, *Godoy* (Berlin, 1932).

Malumbres, Ignacio, *Historia política del Cura Merino* (Zaragoza, 1836).

Manifiesto de D. Joaquín de Uriarte y Landa sobre su conducta política durante la dominación intrusa (Sevilla, 1816).

Manifiesto imparcial y exacto de lo más importante ocurrido en Aranjuez, Madrid y Bayona desde 17 de marzo hasta 15 de mayo de 1808, sobre la caída del Príncipe de la Paz, y sobre el fin de la amistad y alianza de los franceses con los españoles (Madrid, 1808).

Manifiesto que al Señor Don Fernando VII hacen en 12 de abril del año de 1814 los que subscriben como diputados en las actuales Cortes ordinarias . . . (Manifiesto de los Persas) (Aranjuez, 1814).

Maravall, José Antonio, "El pensamiento político en España a comienzos del siglo XIX: Martínez Marina," REP, LXXXI (May–June, 1955), pp. 29–82.

Marbot, Baron, *Mémoires*, 3 vols. (Paris, 1946–1951).

Marchena, José, *Poesías, Poetas líricos del siglo XVIII*, III, in BAE, LXVII (Madrid, 1953).

Martínez Cachero, Luis Alfonso, *Alvaro Flórez Estrada. Su vida, su obra política y sus ideas económicas* (Oviedo, 1961).

Martínez Colomer, Vicente, *Sucesos de Valencia desde el día 23 de mayo hasta el 28 de junio del año 1808* (Valencia, 1810).

Martínez Kleiser, Luis, *Del siglo de los chisperos* (Madrid, 1925).

Martínez Marina, Francisco, *Discurso sobre el origen de la monarquía y sobre la naturaleza del gobierno español*, ed. José Antonio Maravall (Madrid, 1957).

Mateos y Sotos, Rafael, *La provincia de Albacete en la guerra de la independencia* (Albacete, 1910).

Maxwell, W. H., *Life of the Duke of Wellington*, 6th ed., 3 vols. (London, n.d.).

Meléndez Valdés, Juan, *Poesías, Poetas líricos del siglo XVIII*, II, in BAE, LXIII (Madrid, 1952).

Mélito, Count Miot de, *Mémoires*, 3 vols. (Paris, 1858).

Méndez Bejarano, Mario, *Vida y obras de D. José Blanco y Crespo (Blanco-White)* (Madrid, 1920).

———, *Historia política de los afrancesados* (Madrid, 1912).

Menéndez y Pelayo, Marcelino, *Estudios y discursos de crítica histórica y literaria*, IV, in *Obras completas*, IX (Santander, 1942).

———, *Historia de los heterodoxos españoles*, VI (Madrid, 1930); VII (Madrid, 1932).

———, "D. Manuel José Quintana. La poesía lírica al principiar el siglo XIX," *La España del siglo XIX*, III (Madrid, 1887).

Mercader Riba, Juan, *Barcelona durante la ocupación francesa, 1808–1814* (Madrid, 1949).

———, *El Mariscal Suchet, "Virrey" de Aragón, Valencia y Cataluña* (Zaragoza, 1954).

———, *La organización administrativa francesa en España* (Zaragoza, 1959).

Mesonero Romanos, Ramón de, *El antiguo Madrid* (Madrid, 1861).

———, *Memorias de un setentón* (Madrid, 1881).

Molins, Elías de, "Evacuación de Madrid por los franceses en 1808," RABM (July–August, 1908), pp. 136–39.

Montholon, Count, *History of the Captivity of Napoleon at St. Helena*, 2 vols. (London, 1846).

Mor de Fuentes, José, *Bosquejillo de la vida y escritos de . . . , Memorias de tiempos de Fernando VII*, I, in BAE, XCVII (Madrid, 1957).

Moreau de Jonnès, Alexandre, *Statistique de l'Espagne* (Paris, 1834).

Morel-Fatio, A., "Don Francisco Amorós, Marquis de Sotelo, fondateur de la gymnastique en France," *Bulletin Hispanique*, XXVI (1924); XXVII (1925).

———, "Une lettre de Palafox," BH, XX (1918), pp. 43–50.

Moret y Prendergast, Segismundo, "La sociedad española al principiar el siglo XIX," *La España del siglo XIX*, I (Madrid, 1886).

Mozas Mesa, Manuel, *Bailén. Estudio político y militar de la gloriosa jornada* (Madrid, 1940).

———, *Castaños* (Madrid, 1947).

Muñoz Maldonado, José, *Historia política y militar de la guerra de la independencia de España contra Napoleón Bonaparte desde 1808 a 1814*, 3 vols. (Madrid, 1833).

Murat, Prince, *Lettres et documents pour servir à l'histoire de Joachim Murat (1767–1815)*, V (Paris, 1911); VI (1912).

Muriel, Andrés, *Historia de Carlos IV*, 6 vols., in *Memorial Histórico Español*, XXIX–XXXIV (Madrid, 1893–1894).

Nabonne, Bernard, *Joseph Bonaparte, le roi philosophe* (Paris, 1949).

Napier, W. F. P., *History of the War in the Peninsula and in the South of France from the Year 1807 to the Year 1814*, 6 vols. (London, 1890–1892).

Napoléon I, *The Confidential Correspondence of Napoleon Bonaparte with his Brother Joseph*, 2 vols. (London, 1856).

——, *Correspondance de . . .* , 32 vols. (Paris, 1857–1870).

——, *Correspondance inédite de . . .* , ed. Ernest Picard and Louis Tuetey, 2 vols. (Paris, 1912).

——, *Lettres inédites de . . .* , ed. Léon Lecestre, 2 vols. (Paris, 1897).

——, *New Letters of Napoleon*, ed. Mary Loyd (New York, 1897).

Napoleon o El Verdadero D. Quixote de la Europa, o sean comentarios crítico-patriótico-burlescos a varios decretos de Napoleon y su hermano José, distribuidos en dos partes y cincuenta capítulos, y escritos por un español amante de su patria . . . , 8 vols. (Madrid, 1813).

Napoleón rabiando, quasi comedia del día . . . por D. Timoteo De Paz y Del Rey (Madrid, 1808).

Olóriz, Hermilio de, *Navarra en la guerra de la independencia. Biografía del guerrillero D. Francisco Espoz (Espoz y Mina) y noticia de la abolición y restablecimiento del régimen foral* (Pamplona, 1910).

Oman, Charles, *A History of the Peninsular War*, 7 vols. (Oxford, 1902–1930).

——, *Diary of Charles Vaughan in Spain, 1808. Publicaciones del Congreso Histórico Internacional de la guerra de la independencia y su época (1807–1815)* (Zaragoza, 1909).

Ontañón, Eduardo de, *El Cura Merino. Su vida en folletín* (Madrid, 1933).

Orense, Obispo de, *Respuesta dada a la Junta de Gobierno por el Obispo de Orense, Don Pedro Quevedo y Quintano, con motivo de haber sido nombrado diputado para la Junta de Bayona*, CDF, XXVII, pp. 224–25.

Pabón, Jesús, *Las ideas y el sistema napoleónicos* (Madrid, 1944).

Palacio Atard, Vicente, "El despotismo ilustrado español," *Historia de España, Arbor* (Madrid, 1953).

——, *Fin de la sociedad española del antiguo régimen* (Madrid, 1952).

Pano y Ruata, Mariano de, *La Condesa de Bureta y el Regente*, 2 vols. (Zaragoza, 1908–1947).

Papell, Antonio, *Moratín y su época* (Palma de Mallorca, 1958).

Paradas Agüera, E., *Las comunidades religiosas en la guerra de la independencia* (Sevilla, 1908).

Pardo de Andrade, M., *Los guerrilleros gallegos de 1809* (La Coruña, 1892).

Parquin, Commandant, *Souvenirs et campagnes d'un vieux soldat de l'Empire* (Paris, Nancy, 1892).

Pastor Díaz, Nicomedes, and Cárdenas, Francisco de, *Galería de españoles célebres contemporáneos*, 9 vols. (Madrid, 1841–1846).

Paulin-Ruelle, Captain, *Les Souvenirs du Général Baron Paulin* (Paris, 1895).

Pereyra, Carlos, *Cartas confidenciales de la Reina María Luisa y de Don Manuel Godoy* (Madrid, n.d.).

Pérez-Chao Fernández, Juan, "La artillería en la guerra de la independencia. Primero y segundo sitios de Zaragoza," *La guerra de la independencia española y los sitios de Zaragoza* (Zaragoza, 1958).

Pérez de Guzmán y Gallo, Juan, *El dos de mayo de 1808 en Madrid* (Madrid, 1908).

———, "El reinado de Carlos IV en las conferencias del Ateneo," *La España Moderna* (September, 1908), pp. 5–30.

———, "Estudios sobre Moratín. La primera representación de 'El sí de las niñas,'" *La España Moderna* (December, 1902), pp. 103–37.

———, *La historia inédita. Estudios de la vida, reinado, proscripción y muerte de Carlos IV y María Luisa de Borbón, reyes de España* (Madrid, 1909).

———, "Reparaciones a la vida e historia de Carlos IV y María Luisa. La primera calumnia," RABM, Tercera Epoca, x (January–June, 1904), pp. 243–68.

Pérez Galdós, Benito, *Bailén* (Madrid, 1943).

———, *Cádiz* (Madrid, 1916).

———, *El equipaje del rey José* (Madrid, 1946).

———, *Gerona* (Madrid, 1916).

———, *Juan Martín El Empecinado* (Madrid, 1950).

———, *Napoleón en Chamartín* (Madrid, 1948).

Pérez-Prendes, José Manuel, and Muñoz de Arracó, "Cortes de Castilla y Cortes de Cádiz," REP, CXXVI (November–December, 1962), pp. 321–429.

Pérez Villanueva, Joaquín, *Planteamiento ideológico inicial de la guerra de la independencia* (Valladolid, 1960).

Pérez y González, Felipe, *Un cuadro de historia. Alegoría de la villa de Madrid, por Goya. ¿Goya fue afrancesado?* (Madrid, 1910).

Petrie, Charles, *Great Britain and the War of Independence* (Zaragoza, 1959).

———, *The Spanish Royal House* (London, 1958).

Piñeyro, Enrique, "Cienfuegos," BH, XI (1909), pp. 31–54.

Pitollet, Camille, "Napoléon à Valladolid en 1809," RABM, Tercera Epoca, XXIX (July–December, 1913), pp. 328–52.

Pizarro, José García de León y, *Memorias*, 2 vols. (Madrid, 1953).

Poore, Charles, *Goya* (New York, London, 1939).

Priego López, Juan, *Guerra de la independencia* (*1808–1814*) (Madrid, 1947).

Prieto Llovera, Patricio, *El Grande de España, Capitán General Castaños, Primer Duque de Bailén y Primer Marqués de Portugalete* (Madrid, 1958).

Prontuario de las leyes y decretos del Rey Nuestro Señor Don José Napoleón I, 3 vols. (Madrid, 1810–1812).

Puigblanch, Antonio, *La Inquisición sin máscara, o disertación en que se prueban hasta la evidencia los vicios de este tribunal y la necesidad de que se suprima* (Mexico, 1824).

Quadrado, José María, *Personajes célebres del siglo XIX*, ed. Pablo Beltrán de Heredia, 2 vols. (Madrid, 1944).

Quintana, Manuel José, *Obras completas*, BAE, XIX (Madrid, 1946).

——, *Obras inéditas* (Madrid, 1872).

——, *Poesías, Poetas líricos del siglo XVIII*, III, in BAE, LXVII (Madrid, 1953).

——, *Poesías*, ed. Narciso Alonso Cortés, *Clásicos Castellanos*, LXXVIII (Madrid, 1958).

Registre de correspondance de Mr. le Général Carrié sur la guerre d'Espagne, commencé le 31 janvier, 1809, et fini le 24 avril de 1809; registre d'ordres au quartier général de Valladolid et à différents chefs militaires, et d'une proclamation aux habitants de Palencia, 29 janvier, 1809 à 22 avril, 1809. Manuscript No. 1005, Biblioteca Nacional, Madrid.

Rehfues, J. F., *L'Espagne en 1808* (Paris, Strasbourg, 1811).

Reinoso, Félix José, *Examen de los delitos de infidelidad a la Patria imputados a los españoles sometidos bajo la dominación francesa*, 2d ed. (Bordeaux, 1818).

Revista de Occidente, *Diccionario de historia de España* (Madrid, 1952).

Rico, Juan, *Memorias históricas sobre la revolución de Valencia* (Cádiz, 1811).

Rivas Santiago, Natalio, *Anecdotario histórico contemporáneo* (Madrid, 1944).

——, *El alcalde de Otívar, héroe en la guerra de la independencia* (Madrid, 1940).

Rocca, M. de, *Memoirs of the War of the French in Spain* (London, 1815).

Rodríguez Aranda, "La recepción y el influjo de las ideas políticas de John Locke en España," REP, LXXVI (July–August, 1954).

Rodríguez Casado, Vicente, "La 'revolución burguesa' del XVIII español," *Historia de España, Arbor* (Madrid, 1953).

Rodríguez Solís, E., *El primer guerrillero* (Madrid, 1898).

——, *Los guerrilleros de 1808* (Madrid, n.d.).

866]   BIBLIOGRAPHY

Roederer, P. L., Count, *Journal du Comte* . . . , ed. Maurice Vitrac
(Paris, 1909).

Rognat, Baron, *Relation des sièges de Saragosse et de Tortose par les
français, dans la dernière guerre d'Espagne* (Paris, 1814).

Rovigo, Duke of, *Mémoires du Duc de Rovigo, pour servir à l'histoire
de l'Empereur Napoléon*, iii, iv (Paris, 1828).

Ruméu de Armas, Antonio, *El bando de los alcaldes de Móstoles. Nueva
aportación documental* (Toledo, 1940).

Salcedo Ruiz, Angel, *La época de Goya* (Madrid, 1924).

Sánchez Agesta, Luis, *Historia del constitucionalismo español* (Madrid,
1955).

——, "Introducción al pensamiento español del Despotismo Ilustrado,"
Historia de España, Arbor (Madrid, 1953).

San Miguel, Evaristo, *De la guerra civil de España* (Madrid, 1836).

Santiago Gadea, Augusto de, *El intendente del primer sitio de Zaragoza Calbo de Rozas* (Madrid, 1909).

Sarrailh, Jean, "D. Juan Antonio Llorente," BH, xxv (1923), pp. 226–36.

——, *L'Espagne éclairée de la seconde moitié du 18e siècle* (Paris,
1954).

Schaumann, August, *On the Road with Wellington,* ed. Anthony Lu-
dovici (London, 1924).

Schepeler, Colonel Berthold von, *Geschichte der Revolution Spaniens
und Portugals,* 3 vols. (Berlin, 1826–1827).

Schraudenbach, Ludwig, *Psyche und Organisation des Volkskrieges*
(Berlin, 1926).

Ségur, Philippe, Count, *Histoire et mémoires,* iii (Paris, 1873).

Serrano Montalvo, Antonio, *Algunos aspectos íntimos y familiares del
general Palafox* (Zaragoza, 1957).

——, "El pueblo en la guerra de la independencia: La resistencia en las
ciudades," *La guerra de la independencia española y los sitios de
Zaragoza* (Zaragoza, 1958).

——, "La vida municipal zaragozana en el otoño de 1808," *Jerónimo
Zurita, Cuadernos de Historia,* iii (Zaragoza, 1954), pp. 123–52.

Sevilla Andrés, Diego, "La Constitución de 1812, obra de transición,"
REP, cxxvi (November–December, 1962), pp. 113–39.

Simón Díaz, José, *Historia del Colegio Imperial de Madrid,* 2 vols. (Madrid, 1952–1959).

Sociedad Militar de Excursiones, *Sitios de Zaragoza y Gerona y Ac-
ciones del Bruch* (Madrid, 1911).

Solano Costa, Fernando, *El guerrillero y su transcendencia* (Zaragoza,
1959).

——, "Influencia de la guerra de la independencia en el pueblo español," *Jerónimo Zurita, Cuadernos de Historia, III* (Zaragoza,
1954), pp. 103–21.

———, "La resistencia popular en la guerra de la independencia: el guerrillero," *La guerra de la independencia española y los sitios de Zaragoza* (Zaragoza, 1958).

Solar y Taboada, Antonio, and Rújula y de Ochotorena, José de, *Godoy, Príncipe de la Paz* (Badajoz, 1944).

Somoza, Julio, *Amarguras de Jovellanos* (Gijón, 1889).

———, *Documentos para escribir la biografía de Jovellanos*, 2 vols. (Madrid, 1911).

Soldevila, Fernando, *Historia de España*, VI (Barcelona, 1957).

Solís, Ramón, *El Cádiz de las Cortes* (Madrid, 1958).

Stille, Arthur, *Dépêches suédoises de Cadix en 1808, Publicaciones del Congreso Histórico Internacional de la guerra de la independencia y su época (1807–1815)*, II (Zaragoza, 1909).

Suárez Verdeguer, Federico, *Conservadores, innovadores y renovadores en las postrimerías del Antiguo Régimen* (Pamplona, 1955).

———, "Génesis del liberalismo político español," *Historia de España, Arbor* (Madrid, 1953).

———, *La crisis política del Antiguo Régimen en España (1800–1840)* (Madrid, 1958).

———, *Las tendencias políticas durante la guerra de la independencia* (Zaragoza, 1959).

———, "Planteamiento ideológico del siglo XIX español," *Historia de España, Arbor* (Madrid, 1953).

———, "Sobre las raíces de las reformas de las Cortes de Cádiz," REP, CXXVI (November–December, 1962), pp. 31–64.

Talleyrand Périgord, Charles Maurice, Duke of, *Mémoires*, ed. Paul-Louis and Jean-Paul Couchoud, 2 vols. (Paris, 1957).

Taxonera, Luciano de, *Godoy, Príncipe de la Paz y de Bassano* (Barcelona, 1946).

Thiébault, Paul, *Mémoires du Général-Baron Thiébault, 1792–1820*, ed. Robert Lacour-Gayet (Paris, 1962).

Thiers, Adolphe, *Histoire du Consulat et de l'Empire*, VIII, IX (Paris, 1849).

Toreno, José María Queipo de J lano, Count, *Historia del levantamiento, guerra y revolución de España*, BAE, LXIV (Madrid, 1953).

Tratchevsky, A., "L'Espagne à l'époque de la révolution française," *Revue Historique*, XXXI (1886), pp. 1–55.

Vasco, Eusebio, *D. Francisco Abad Moreno (Chaleco), guerrillero de la independencia, Publicaciones del Congreso Histórico Internacional de la guerra de la independencia y su época (1807–1815)*, II (Zaragoza, 1909).

Vélez, Rafael de, *Apología del altar y del trono*, 3 vols. (Madrid, 1818–1825).

———, *Preservativo contra la irreligión* (Madrid, 1813).

Vila Selma, José, *Ideario de Manuel José Quintana* (Madrid, 1961).

Villanueva, Joaquín Lorenzo, *Mi viaje a las Cortes, Memorias de tiempos de Fernando VII*, II, in BAE, XCVIII (Madrid, 1957).

Villa-Urrutia, Wenceslao Ramírez, Marquis of, *El Rey José Napoleón* (Madrid, 1927).

———, *España en el Congreso de Viena*, 2d ed. (Madrid, 1928).

———, *Fernando VII, rey constitucional* (Madrid, 1922).

———, *Mujeres de Antaño. Teresa Cabarrús* (Madrid, 1927).

———, *La reina María Luisa, esposa de Carlos IV* (Madrid, 1927).

———, *Relaciones entre España e Inglaterra durante la guerra de la independencia. Apuntes para la historia diplomática de España de 1808 a 1814*, 3 vols. (Madrid, 1911-1914).

———, *Talleyrand*, 2d ed. (Madrid, 1943).

Viñas Mey, Carmelo, "Nuevos datos para la historia de los afrancesados," BH, XXVI (1924); XXVII (1925).

Wellesley, Marquess, *The Despatches and Correspondence of the Marquess Wellesley, K. G.*, ed. Montgomery Martin (London, 1838).

Wellington, *The Dispatches of Field Marshal the Duke of Wellington During His Various Campaigns in India, Denmark, Portugal, Spain, the Low Countries, and France, from 1779 to 1815*, ed. Lt. Col. Gurwood, 12 vols. (London, 1834-1838).

Wheeler, William, *The Letters of Private Wheeler, 1809-1828*, ed. Capt. B. H. Liddell Hart (London, 1951).

Zabala y Lera, Pío, *España bajo los Borbones*, 5th ed. (Barcelona, 1955).

INDEX